A TREASURY OF THE FAMILIAR

THE MACMILLAN COMPANY
NEW YORK · BOSTON · CHICAGO
DALLAS · ATLANTA · SAN FRANCISCO

MACMILLAN AND CO., LIMITED
LONDON · BOMBAY · CALCUTTA
MADRAS · MELBOURNE

**THE MACMILLAN COMPANY
OF CANADA, LIMITED**
TORONTO

A TREASURY

OF THE FAMILIAR

EDITED BY

Ralph L. Woods

WITH A FOREWORD BY

JOHN KIERAN

THE MACMILLAN COMPANY

NEW YORK · 1943

Copyright, 1942, by
RALPH L. WOODS

PEOPLES BOOK CLUB PRINTING

ABOUT THE APPEARANCE OF BOOKS IN WARTIME

A recent ruling by the War Production Board has cur-
tailed the use of paper by book publishers in 1943.

In line with this ruling and in order to conserve materials and manpower, we are co-operating by:

1. Using lighter-weight paper which reduces the
bulk of this book.

2. Printing books with smaller margins.

Slimmer and smaller books will save paper and
materials. We are sure that readers will understand the
publishers' desire to co-operate as fully as possible with
the objectives of the War Production Board and our
government.

TO MY DAUGHTER
PATRICIA JOAN WOODS

And the music's not immortal;
but the world has made it sweet.

—ALFRED NOYES, *The Barrel-Organ*

FOREWORD

Upon first peering at the material that Ralph L. Woods poured into this *Treasury of the Familiar*, there came to mind two lines from "Le Juge de Charenton," one of the glorious and hilarious songs of Pierre-Jean Béranger, to wit:

> Et patati, et patata,
> Il a mis de tout dans ce discours-là.

The author had "put everything into it," indeed! And not a little of everything, but a great deal of everything. That so much and such varied poetry and prose, ancient and modern, light and heavy, of high and low degree, could or under any circumstances would be gathered within the confines of one printed volume appeared astonishing—almost appalling—at first sight. Even upon longer and cooler meditation, it remains somewhat baffling. Why was it done? How was it accomplished? And how long, O Catiline, did it take?

Since a deep study of police methods as exhibited in detective story fiction leads to the conclusion that it is bad strategy in puzzling cases to grill the real culprit first, especially if he is a hardened hand at the game (Ralph L. Woods was known to be the author of *America Reborn* and *Pilgrim Places in North America,* previously published), this second-chop Sherlock Holmes went another way about unraveling the mystery. There was apprehended for questioning a material witness, a collateral accessory before the fact, one David Woods, brother of Ralph L. Woods.

Realizing that the massive literary "corpus delicti" was about to be exposed in plain view for all to see—embalmed for posterity—printed and bound with his brother's name on it, David of the Woods family freely confessed all that he knew. He said that Ralph was an omnivorous reader from childhood days in St. Louis, Missouri. When the youthful and ready reader came across things that he liked very much, he cut them out and pasted them in a scrapbook. His clippings were of prose and poetry, public documents and private pleas, writings cosmical and comical, philosophy and fable—in fact, anything that he found and liked for any reason under the sun.

He filled one scrapbook. He filled another. He filled a series of scrapbooks. Why was he doing it? Because it amused him. Why didn't he sort them out in some fashion and offer them for publication? That, Ralph admitted, was an idea. And this is it in book form. It took him three years to weigh and consider, select and arrange, and finally deliver to the publishers the astounding collection of rhyme and reason, Scripture and satire, fun and philosophy, fact and fiction, that the reader now has in hand.

Here we have, within the same volume, George Washington's Farewell Address upon his retirement from the Presidency and that barroom ballad, "The Man on the Flying Trapeze." We have the solemn Declaration of Independence and Dorothy Parker's tidbits of social satire in verse. We have selections from Plato and a convivial chorus entitled "No More Booze." We have John Keats' "Ode to a Nightingale" and, by way of infinite contrast, "Father, Dear Father, Come Home with Me Now." We have Charles Lamb's "Dissertation on Roast Pig" and Robert W. Service's "The Cremation of Sam McGee." We have sections of the Bible, copiously quoted, and excerpts from the speeches and writings of Tom Paine and Colonel Robert G. Ingersoll, who were not noted as evangelists. We have "For A' That and A' That" by Robert Burns with its opening line "Is there for honest poverty" and, to cap that in another quarter, we have "The Man Who Broke the Bank at Monte Carlo." We have "The Lady of Shalott" and "Casey Jones"—not by the same author! We have the beautiful sermon of St. Francis of Assisi to the birds and the root-toot-shooting rhyme of "Frankie and Johnny." We have stately Thomas Jefferson's inaugural address and an opus entitled "When Father Carves the Duck." We have Shakespeare, Ella Wheeler Wilcox, Aesop, and Anonymous.

A final warning. When not in use, this volume should be kept in a cool dry place, well away from draperies, loose papers, and other inflammable material. It is apparent that the contents are an exciting mixture, possibly explosive.

John Kieran

A TREASURY OF THE FAMILIAR

THE WAY OF THE WORLD

Ella Wheeler Wilcox

Laugh, and the world laughs with you,
Weep, and you weep alone,
For the brave old earth must borrow its mirth—
But has trouble enough of its own.
Sing and the hills will answer,
Sigh, it is lost on the air;
The echoes rebound to a joyful sound
And shrink from voicing care.

Rejoice, and men will seek you,
Grieve, and they turn and go;
They want full measure of your pleasure,
But they do not want your woe.
Be glad, and your friends are many,
Be sad, and you lose them all;
There are *none* to decline your nectared wine,
But *alone* you must drink life's gall.

Feast, and your halls are crowded,
Fast, and the world goes by.
Forget and forgive—it helps you to live,
But no man can help you to die;
There's room in the halls of pleasure
For a long and lordly train,
But one by one, we must all march on
Through the narrow isle of pain.

THESE ARE THE TIMES THAT TRY MEN'S SOULS

Thomas Paine

These are the times that try men's souls. The summer soldier
and the sunshine patriot will, in this crisis, shrink from the service
of their country; but he that stands it *now*, deserves the love and

1

thanks of man and woman. Tyranny, like hell, is not easily conquered; yet we have this consolation with us, that the harder the
conflict, the more glorious the triumph. What we obtain too
cheap, we esteem too lightly; it is dearness only that gives everything its value. Heaven knows how to put a proper price upon its
goods; and it would be strange, indeed, if so celestial an article as
FREEDOM should not be highly rated. Britain, with an army to
enforce her tyranny, has declared that she has a right (*not only to*
TAX) but "to bind *us in* ALL CASES WHATSOEVER," and if being
bound in that manner, is not slavery, then is there not such a thing
as slavery upon earth. Even the expression is impious; for so
unlimited a power can belong only to God.

Whether the independence of the continent was declared too
soon, or delayed too long, I will not now enter into as an argument;
my own simple opinion is, that had it been eight months earlier,
it would have been much better. We did not make a proper use
of last winter, neither could we, while we were in a dependent
state. However, the fault, if it were one, was all our own; we
have none to blame but ourselves. But no great deal is lost yet.
All that Howe has been doing for this month past, is rather a
ravage than a conquest, which the spirit of the Jerseys, a year ago,
would have quickly repulsed, and which time and a little resolution will soon recover.

I have as little superstition in me as any man living, but my
secret opinion has ever been, and still is, that God Almighty will
not give up a people to military destruction, or leave them un-
supported to perish, who have so earnestly and so repeatedly
sought to avoid the calamities of war, by every decent method
which wisdom could invent. Neither have I so much of the infidel
in me, as to suppose that He has relinquished the government of
the world, and given us up to the care of devils; and as I do not,
I cannot see on what grounds the king of Britain can look up to
heaven for help against us; a common murderer, a highwayman,
or a housebreaker, has as good a pretence as he.

(From The American Crisis)

THE TREE OF LIBERTY

The tree of liberty only grows when watered by the blood of
tyrants.

(From Bertrand Barère's speech in the
Convention Nationale, 1792)

2

'TIS THE LAST ROSE OF SUMMER

Thomas Moore

'Tis the last rose of Summer,
Left blooming alone;
All her lovely companions
Are faded and gone;
No flower of her kindred,
No rosebud is nigh,
To reflect back her blushes,
Or give sigh for sigh!

I'll not leave thee, thou lone one,
To pine on the stem;
Since the lovely are sleeping,
Go sleep thou with them.
Thus kindly I scatter
Thy leaves o'er the bed
Where thy mates of the garden
Lie scentless and dead.

So soon may I follow,
When friendships decay,
And from Love's shining circle
The gems drop away!
When true hearts lie withered,
And fond ones are flown,
Oh! who would inhabit
This bleak world alone?

ANTONY'S ORATION OVER CÆSAR'S BODY

William Shakespeare

Ant.   Friends, Romans, countrymen, lend me your ears;
I come to bury Cæsar, not to praise him.
The evil that men do lives after them;
The good is oft interred with their bones;
So let it be with Cæsar. The noble Brutus
Hath told you Cæsar was ambitious:
If it were so, it was a grievous fault,

3

And grievously hath Cæsar answer'd it.
Here, under leave of Brutus and the rest—
For Brutus is an honourable man;
So are they all, all honourable men—
Come I to speak in Cæsar's funeral.
He was my friend, faithful and just to me:
But Brutus says he was ambitious;
And Brutus is an honourable man.
He hath brought many captives home to Rome,
Whose ransoms did the general coffers fill:
Did this in Cæsar seem ambitious?
When that the poor have cried, Cæsar hath wept:
Ambition should be made of sterner stuff:
Yet Brutus says he was ambitious;
And Brutus is an honourable man.
You all did see that on the Lupercal
I thrice presented him a kingly crown,
Which he did thrice refuse: was this ambition?
Yet Brutus says he was ambitious;
And, sure, he is an honourable man.
I speak not to disprove what Brutus spoke,
But here I am to speak what I do know.
You all did love him once, not without cause:
What cause withholds you then, to mourn for him?
O judgement! thou art fled to brutish beasts,
And men have lost their reason. Bear with me,
My heart is in the coffin there with Cæsar,
And I must pause till it come back to me.
   First Cit.   Methinks there is much reason in his sayings.
   Sec. Cit.   If thou consider rightly of the matter,
Cæsar has had great wrong.
   Third Cit.   Has he, masters?
I fear there will a worse come in his place.
   Fourth Cit.   Mark'd ye his words? He would not take the crown;
Therefore 'tis certain he was not ambitious.
   First Cit.   If it be found so, some will dear abide it.
   Sec. Cit.   Poor soul! his eyes are red as fire with weeping.
   Third Cit.   There's not a nobler man in Rome than Antony.
   Fourth Cit.   Now mark him, he begins again to speak.
   Ant.   But yesterday the word of Cæsar might
Have stood against the world; now lies he there,
And none so poor to do him reverence.
O masters, if I were disposed to stir

Your hearts and minds to mutiny and rage,
I should do Brutus wrong, and Cassius wrong,
Who, you all know, are honourable men:
I will not do them wrong; I rather choose
To wrong the dead, to wrong myself and you,
Than I will wrong such honourable men.
But here's a parchment with the seal of Cæsar;
I found it in his closet, 'tis his will:
Let but the commons hear this testament—
Which, pardon me, I do not mean to read—
And they would go and kiss dead Cæsar's wounds
And dip their napkins in his sacred blood,
Yea, beg a hair of him for memory,
And, dying, mention it within their wills,
Bequeathing it as a rich legacy
Unto their issue.

    Fourth Cit.   We'll hear the will: read it, Mark Antony.
    All.   The will, the will! we will hear Cæsar's will.
    Ant.   Have patience, gentle friends, I must not read it;
It is not meet you know how Cæsar loved you.
You are not wood, you are not stones, but men;
And, being men, hearing the will of Cæsar,
It will inflame you, it will make you mad:
'Tis good you know not that you are his heirs;
For, if you should, O, what would come of it!
    Fourth Cit.   Read the will; we'll hear it, Antony;
You shall read us the will, Cæsar's will.
    Ant.   Will you be patient? will you stay awhile?
I have o'ershot myself to tell you of it:
I fear I wrong the honourable men
Whose daggers have stabb'd Cæsar; I do fear it.
    Fourth Cit.   They were traitors: honourable men!
    All.   The will! the testament!
    Sec. Cit.   They were villains, murderers: the will! read **the will.**
    Ant.   You will compel me, then, to read the will?
Then make a ring about the corpse of Cæsar,
And let me show you him that made the will.
Shall I descend? and will you give me leave?
    Several Cit.   Come down.
    Sec. Cit.   Descend.
    Third Cit.   You shall have leave.

                              [*Antony comes down.*
    Fourth Cit.   A ring; stand round.

First Cit.   Stand from the hearse, stand from the body.
Sec. Cit.   Room for Antony, most noble Antony.
Ant.   Nay, press not so upon me; stand far off.
Several Cit.   Stand back; room; bear back.
Ant.   If you have tears, prepare to shed them now.
You all do know this mantle: I remember
The first time ever Cæsar put it on;
'Twas on a summer's evening, in his tent,
That day he overcame the Nervii:
Look, in this place ran Cassius' dagger through:
See what a rent the envious Casca made:
Through this the well-beloved Brutus stabb'd;
And as he pluck'd his cursed steel away,
Mark how the blood of Cæsar follow'd it,
As rushing out of doors, to be resolved
If Brutus so unkindly knock'd, or no;
For Brutus, as you know, was Cæsar's angel:
Judge, O you gods, how dearly Cæsar loved him!
This was the most unkindest cut of all;
For when the noble Cæsar saw him stab,
Ingratitude, more strong than traitors' arms,
Quite vanquish'd him: then burst his mighty heart;
And, in his mantle muffling up his face,
Even at the base of Pompey's statua,
Which all the while ran blood, great Cæsar fell.
O, what a fall was there, my countrymen!
Then I, and you, and all of us fell down,
Whilst bloody treason flourish'd over us.
O, now you weep; and, I perceive, you feel
The dint of pity: these are gracious drops.
Kind souls, what, weep you when you but behold
Our Cæsar's vesture wounded? Look you here,
Here is himself, marr'd, as you see, with traitors.
First Cit.   O piteous spectacle!
Sec. Cit.   O noble Cæsar!
Third Cit.   O woful day!
Fourth Cit.   O traitors, villains!
First Cit.   O most bloody sight!
Sec. Cit.   We will be revenged.
All.   Revenge! About! Seek! Burn! Fire! Kill! Slay! Let not a
  traitor live!
Ant.   Stay, countrymen.
First Cit.   Peace there! hear the noble Antony.

Sec. Cit. We'll hear him, we'll follow him, we'll die with him.

Ant. Good friends, sweet friends, let me not stir you up
To such a sudden flood of mutiny.
They that have done this deed are honourable:
What private griefs they have, alas, I know not,
That made them do it: they are wise and honourable,
And will, no doubt, with reasons answer you.
I come not, friends, to steal away your hearts:
I am no orator, as Brutus is;
But, as you know me all, a plain blunt man,
That love my friend; and that they know full well
That gave me public leave to speak of him:
For I have neither wit, nor words, nor worth,
Action, nor utterance, nor the power of speech,
To stir men's blood: I only speak right on;
I tell you that which you yourselves do know;
Show you sweet Cæsar's wounds, poor poor dumb mouths,
And bid them speak for me: but were I Brutus,
And Brutus Antony, there were an Antony
Would ruffle up your spirits and put a tongue
In every wound of Cæsar that should move
The stones of Rome to rise and mutiny.

All. We'll mutiny.

First Cit. We'll burn the house of Brutus.

Third Cit. Away, then! come, seek the conspirators.

Ant. Yet hear me, countrymen; yet hear me speak.

All. Peace, ho! Hear Antony. Most noble Antony!

Ant. Why, friends, you go to do you know not what:
Wherein hath Cæsar thus deserved your loves?
Alas, you know not: I must tell you, then:
You have forgot the will I told you of.

All. Most true. The will! Let's stay and hear the will.

Ant. Here is the will, and under Cæsar's seal.
To every Roman citizen he gives,
To every several man, seventy five drachmas.

Sec. Cit. Most noble Cæsar! We'll revenge his death.

Third Cit. O royal Cæsar!

Ant. Hear me with patience.

All. Peace, ho!

Ant. Moreover, he hath left you all his walks,
His private arbours and new-planted orchards,
On this side Tiber; he hath left them you,
And to your heirs for ever, common pleasures,

7

To walk abroad, and recreate yourselves.
Here was a Cæsar! when comes such another?
 First Cit. Never, never. Come, away, away!
We'll burn his body in the holy place,
And with the brands fire the traitors' houses.
Take up the body.
 Sec. Cit. Go fetch fire.
 Third Cit. Pluck down benches.
 Fourth Cit. Pluck down forms, windows, anything.
       [*Exeunt Citizens with the body.*
 Ant. Now let it work. Mischief, thou art afoot,
Take thou what course thou wilt!
        (From Julius Cæsar)

THE BLIND MEN AND THE ELEPHANT

John G. Saxe

It was six men of Indostan
To learning much inclined,
Who went to see the elephant
(Though all of them were blind),
That each by observation
Might satisfy his mind.

The first approached the elephant,
And, happening to fall
Against his broad and sturdy side,
At once began to bawl,
"God bless me! but the elephant
Is very like a wall!"

The second feeling of the tusk
Cried: "Ho! what have we here
So very round and smooth and sharp?
To me 'tis mighty clear
This wonder of an elephant
Is very like a spear!"

The third approached the animal,
And, happening to take
The squirming trunk within his hands,

Thus boldly up and spake:
"I see," quoth he, "the elephant,
Is very like a snake!"

The fourth reached out his eager hand,
And felt about the knee;
"What most this wondrous beast is like
Is mighty plain," quoth he;
" 'Tis clear enough the elephant
Is very like a tree."

The fifth, who chanced to touch the ear,
Said: "E'en the blindest man
Can tell what this resembles most.
Deny the fact who can,
This marvel of an elephant
Is very like a fan!"

The sixth no sooner had begun
About the beast to grope,
Than, seizing on the swinging tail
That fell within his scope,
"I see," quoth he, "the elephant
Is very like a rope!"

And so these men of Indostan
Disputed loud and long,
Each in his own opinion
Exceeding stiff and strong,
Though each was partly in the right,
And all were in the wrong!

So, oft in theologic wars
The disputants, I ween,
Rail on in utter ignorance
Of what each other mean,
And prate about an elephant
Not one of them has seen!

* * *

This is the final test of a gentleman: his respect for those who
can be of no possible service to him.
—William Lyon Phelps

LINCOLN'S FAREWELL

MY FRIENDS:

No one not in my position can appreciate the sadness I feel at this parting. To this people I owe all that I am. Here I have lived more than a quarter of a century; here my children were born, and here one of them lies buried. I know not how soon I shall see you again. A duty devolved upon me which is, perhaps, greater than that which has devolved upon any other man since the days of Washington. He never could have succeeded except for the aid of Divine Providence, upon which he at all times relied. I feel that I cannot succeed without the same Divine Aid which sustained him; and in the same Almighty Being I place my reliance for support; and I hope you, my friends, will all pray that I may receive that Divine Assistance, without which I cannot succeed, but with which success is certain. Again I bid you all an affectionate farewell.

THE CREATION

Holy Bible, Genesis 1, 2:1–3

1

1 In the beginning God created the heaven and the earth.

2 And the earth was without form, and void; and darkness was upon the face of the deep. And the Spirit of God moved upon the face of the waters.

3 And God said, Let there be light: and there was light.

4 And God saw the light, that it was good: and God divided the light from the darkness.

5 And God called the light Day, and the darkness he called Night. And the evening and the morning were the first day.

6 And God said, Let there be a firmament in the midst of the waters, and let it divide the waters from the waters.

7 And God made the firmament, and divided the waters which were under the firmament from the waters which were above the firmament: and it was so.

8 And God called the firmament Heaven. And the evening and the morning were the second day.

9 And God said, Let the waters under the heaven be gathered together unto one place, and let the dry land appear: and it was so.

10 And God called the dry land Earth; and the gathering together of the waters called he Seas: and God saw that it was good.

11 And God said, Let the earth bring forth grass, the herb yielding seed, and the fruit tree yielding fruit after his kind, whose seed is in itself, upon the earth: and it was so.

12 And the earth brought forth grass, and herb yielding seed after his kind, and the tree yielding fruit, whose seed was in itself, after his kind: and God saw that it was good.

13 And the evening and the morning were the third day.

14 And God said, Let there be lights in the firmament of the heaven to divide the day from the night; and let them be for signs, and for seasons, and for days, and years:

15 And let them be for lights in the firmament of the heaven to give light upon the earth: and it was so.

16 And God made two great lights; the greater light to rule the day, and the lesser light to rule the night: he made the stars also.

17 And God set them in the firmament of the heaven to give light upon the earth,

18 And to rule over the day and over the night, and to divide the light from the darkness: and God saw that it was good.

19 And the evening and the morning were the fourth day.

20 And God said, Let the waters bring forth abundantly the moving creature that hath life, and fowl that may fly above the earth in the open firmament of heaven.

21 And God created great whales, and every living creature that moveth, which the waters brought forth abundantly, after their kind, and every winged fowl after his kind: and God saw that it was good.

22 And God blessed them, saying, Be fruitful, and multiply, and fill the waters in the seas, and let fowl multiply in the .earth.

23 And the evening and the morning were the fifth day.

24 And God said, Let the earth bring forth the living creature after his kind, cattle, and creeping thing, and beast of the earth after his kind: and it was so.

25 And God made the beast of the earth after his kind, and cattle after their kind, and every thing that creepeth upon the earth after his kind: and God saw that it was good.

26 And God said, Let us make man in our image, after our likeness: and let them have dominion over the fish of the sea, and

over the fowl of the air, and over the cattle, and over all the earth, and over every creeping thing that creepeth upon the earth.

27 So God created man in his own image, in the image of God created he him; male and female created he them.

28 And God blessed them, and God said unto them, Be fruitful, and multiply, and replenish the earth, and subdue it: and have dominion over the fish of the sea, and over the fowl of the air, and over every living thing that moveth upon the earth.

29 And God said, Behold, I have given you every herb bearing seed, which is upon the face of all the earth, and every tree, in the which is the fruit of a tree yielding seed; to you it shall be for meat.

30 And to every beast of the earth, and to every fowl of the air, and to every thing that creepeth upon the earth, wherein there is life, I have given every green herb for meat: and it was so.

31 And God saw every thing that he had made, and, behold, it was very good. And the evening and the morning were the sixth day.

2

1 Thus the heavens and the earth were finished, and all the host of them.

2 And on the seventh day God ended his work which he had made; and he rested on the seventh day from all his work which he had made.

3 And God blessed the seventh day, and sanctified it: because that in it he had rested from all his work which God created and made.

LEAD, KINDLY LIGHT

John Henry Newman

Lead, kindly Light, amid the encircling gloom,
Lead Thou me on!
The night is dark, and I am far from home—
Lead Thou me on!
Keep Thou my feet; I do not ask to see
The distant scene,—one step enough for me.

I was not ever thus, nor prayed that Thou
Shouldst lead me on.

I loved to choose and see my path; but now
Lead Thou me on!
I loved the garish day, and, spite of fears,
Pride ruled my will: Remember not past years.

So long Thy power has blest me, sure it still
Will lead me on
O'er moor and fen, o'er crag and torrent, till
The night is gone;
And with the morn those angel faces smile
Which I have loved long since, and lost awhile!

SORROWS OF WERTHER

William Makepeace Thackeray

Werther had a love for Charlotte
  Such as words could never utter;
Would you know how first he met her?
  She was cutting bread and butter.

Charlotte was a married lady,
  And a moral man was Werther,
And for all the wealth of Indies
  Would do nothing for to hurt her.

So he sighed and pined and ogled,
  And his passion boiled and bubbled,
Till he blew his silly brains out,
  And no more by it was troubled.

Charlotte, having seen his body
  Borne before her on a shutter,
Like a well-conducted person,
  Went on cutting bread and butter.

NO TRUER WORD

Walter Savage Landor

No truer word, save God's, was ever spoken,
Than that the largest heart is soonest broken.

ON READING AND WRITING

Francis Bacon

Crafty men condemn studies; simple men admire them; and wise men use them: for they teach not their own use: but that is a wisdom without them, and above them, won by observation. Read not to contradict and confute; nor to believe and take for granted; nor to find talk and discourse; but to weigh and consider.

Some books are to be tasted, others to be swallowed, and some few to be chewed and digested; that is, some books are to be read only in parts; others to be read, but not curiously; and some few to be read wholly, and with diligence and attention. Some books also may be read by deputy, and extracts made of them by others; but that would be only in the less important arguments, and the meaner sort of books; else distilled books are like common distilled waters, flashy things. Reading maketh a full man, conference a ready man, and writing an exact man. And therefore if a man write little, he had need have a great memory; if he confer little, he had need have a present wit; and if he read little, he had need have much cunning, to seem to know that he doth not.

(From the Essays)

PLAIN LANGUAGE FROM TRUTHFUL JAMES

TABLE MOUNTAIN, 1870

Bret Harte

Which I wish to remark,
And my language is plain,
That for ways that are dark
And for tricks that are vain,
The heathen Chinee is peculiar,
Which the same I would rise to explain.

Ah Sin was his name;
And I shall not deny,
In regard to the same,
What that name might imply;
But his smile it was pensive and childlike,
As I frequent remarked to Bill Nye.

It was August the third,
And quite soft was the skies;
Which it might be inferred
That Ah Sin was likewise;
Yet he played it that day upon **William**
And me in a way I despise.

Which we had a small game,
And Ah Sin took a hand:
It was Euchre. The same
He did not understand;
But he smiled as he sat by the table,
With the smile that was childlike and bland.

Yet the cards they were stocked
In a way that I grieve,
And my feelings were shocked
At the state of Nye's sleeve,
Which was stuffed full of aces and bowers,
And the same with intent to deceive.

But the hands that were played
By that heathen Chinee,
And the points that he made,
Were quite frightful to see—
Till at last he put down a right bower,
Which the same Nye had dealt unto me.

Then I looked up at Nye,
And he gazed upon me;
And he rose with a sigh,
And said, "Can this be?
We are ruined by Chinese cheap labor"—
And he went for that heathen Chinee.

In the scene that ensued
I did not take a hand,
But the floor it was strewed
Like the leaves on the strand
With the cards that Ah Sin had been hiding,
In the game "he did not understand."

In his sleeves, which were long,
He had twenty-four packs—

Which was coming it strong,
Yet I state but the facts;
And we found on his nails, which were taper,
What is frequent in tapers—that's wax.

Which is why I remark,
And my language is plain,
That for ways that are dark,
And for tricks that are vain,
The heathen Chinee is peculiar—
Which the same I am free to maintain.

WHERE THERE'S A WILL THERE'S A WAY

Eliza Cook

We have faith in old proverbs full surely,
  For Wisdom has traced what they tell,
And Truth may be drawn up as purely
  From them, as it may from "a well."
Let us question the thinkers and doers,
  And hear what they honestly say;
And you'll find they believe, like bold wooers,
  In "Where there's a will there's a way."

The hills have been high for man's mounting,
  The woods have been dense for his axe,
The stars have been thick for his counting,
  The sands have been wide for his tracks,
The sea has been deep for his diving,
  The poles have been broad for his sway,
But bravely he's proved in his striving,
  That "Where there's a will there's a way."

Have ye vices that ask a destroyer?
  Or passions that need your control?
Let Reason become your employer,
  And your body be ruled by your soul.
Fight on, though ye bleed in the trial,
  Resist with all strength that ye may;
Ye may conquer Sin's host by denial;
  For "Where there's a will there's a way."

Have ye Poverty's pinching to cope with?
  Does Suffering weigh down your might?
Only call up a spirit to hope with,
  And dawn may come out of the night.
Oh! much may be done by defying
  The ghosts of Despair and Dismay;
And much may be gained by relying
  On "Where there's a will there's a way."

Should ye see, afar off, that worth winning,
  Set out on the journey with trust;
And ne'er heed if your path at beginning
  Should be among brambles and dust.
Though it is but by footsteps ye do it,
  And hardships may hinder and stay;
Walk with faith, and be sure you'll get through it;
  For "Where's there's a will there's a way."

ARABIAN PROVERB

He who knows not and knows not that he knows not,
  He is a fool—shun him;

He who knows not and knows he knows not,
  He is simple—teach him;

He who knows and knows not he knows,
  He is asleep—wake him;

He who knows and knows he knows,
  He is wise; follow him.

TRUTH, THE INVINCIBLE

William Cullen Bryant

Truth crushed to earth shall rise again,—
  The eternal years of God are hers;
But Error, wounded, writhes with pain,
  And dies among his worshippers.

WHEN THE HOUNDS OF SPRING

Algernon Charles Swinburne

When the hounds of spring are on winter's traces,
   The mother of months in meadow or plain
Fills the shadows and windy places
   With lisp of leaves and ripple of rain;
And the brown bright nightingale amorous
Is half assuaged for Itylus,
For the Thracian ships and the foreign faces;
   The tongueless vigil, and all the pain.

Come with bows bent and with emptying of quivers,
   Maiden most perfect, lady of light,
With a noise of winds and many rivers,
   With a clamor of waters, and with might;
Bind on thy sandals, O thou most fleet,
Over the splendor and speed of thy feet;
For the faint east quickens, the wan west shivers,
   Round the feet of the day and the feet of the night.

Where shall we find her, how shall we sing to her,
   Fold our hands round her knees, and cling?
O that man's heart were as fire and could spring to her,
   Fire, or the strength of the streams that spring!
For the stars and the winds are unto her
As raiment, as songs of the harp-player;
For the risen stars and the fallen cling to her,
   And the southwest-wind and the west-wind sing.

For winter's rains and ruins are over,
   And all the season of snows and sins;
The days dividing lover and lover,
   The light that loses, the night that wins;
And time remember'd is grief forgotten,
And frosts are slain and flowers begotten,
And in green underwood and cover
   Blossom by blossom the spring begins.

The full streams feed on flower of rushes,
   Ripe grasses trammel a travelling foot,
The faint fresh flame of the young year flushes
   From leaf to flower and flower to fruit;

And fruit and leaf are as gold and fire,
And the oat is heard above the lyre,
And the hooféd heel of a satyr crushes
    The chestnut-husk at the chestnut-root.

And Pan by noon and Bacchus by night,
    Fleeter of foot than the fleet-foot kid,
Follows with dancing and fills with delight
    The Mænad and the Bassarid;
And soft as lips that laugh and hide
The laughing leaves of the trees divide,
And screen from seeing and leave in sight
    The god pursuing, the maiden hid.

The ivy falls with the Bacchanal's hair
    Over her eyebrows hiding her eyes;
The wild vine slipping down leaves bare
    Her bright breast shortening into sighs;
The wild vine slips with the weight of its leaves,
But the berried ivy catches and cleaves
To the limbs that glitter, the feet that scare
    The wolf that follows, the fawn that flies.
              (First Chorus of Atalanta in Calydon)

* * *

When it shall be found that much is omitted, let it not be forgotten that much likewise is performed.
(From Samuel Johnson's Preface to his English Dictionary)

THE WRECK OF THE HESPERUS

Henry Wadsworth Longfellow

It was the schooner Hesperus,
    That sailed the wintry sea;
And the skipper had taken his little daughter,
    To bear him company.

Blue were her eyes as the fairy flax,
    Her cheeks like the dawn of day,
And her bosom white as the hawthorn buds
    That ope in the month of May.

The skipper he stood beside the helm,
His pipe was in his mouth,
And he watched how the veering flaw did blow
The smoke now West, now South.

Then up and spake an old Sailor,
Had sailed to the Spanish Main,
"I pray thee, put into yonder port,
For I fear a hurricane.

"Last night, the moon had a golden ring,
And to-night no moon we see!"
The skipper, he blew a whiff from his pipe,
And a scornful laugh laughed he.

Colder and louder blew the wind,
A gale from the Northeast;
The snow fell hissing in the brine,
And the billows frothed like yeast.

Down came the storm, and smote amain
The vessel in its strength;
She shuddered and paused, like a frighted steed,
Then leaped her cable's length.

"Come hither! come hither! my little daughter,
And do not tremble so;
For I can weather the roughest gale
That ever wind did blow."

He wrapped her warm in his seaman's coat
Against the stinging blast;
He cut a rope from a broken spar,
And bound her to the mast.

"O father! I hear the church-bells ring,
Oh say, what may it be?"
" 'Tis a fog-bell on a rock-bound coast!"
And he steered for the open sea.

"O father! I hear the sound of guns,
Oh say, what may it be?"
"Some ship in distress, that cannot live
In such an angry sea!"

"O father! I see a gleaming light,
Oh say, what may it be?"
But the father answered never a word,—
A frozen corpse was he.

Lashed to the helm, all stiff and stark,
With his face turned to the skies,
The lantern gleamed through the gleaming snow
On his fixed and glassy eyes.

Then the maiden clasped her hands and prayed
That saved she might be;
And she thought of Christ, who stilled the waves
On the Lake of Galilee.

And fast through the midnight dark and drear,
Through the whistling sleet and snow,
Like a sheeted ghost, the vessel swept
Towards the reef of Norman's Woe.

And ever the fitful gusts between
A sound came from the land;
It was the sound of the trampling surf,
On the rocks and the hard sea-sand.

The breakers were right beneath her bows,
She drifted a dreary wreck,
And a whooping billow swept the crew
Like icicles from her deck.

She struck where the white and fleecy waves
Looked soft as carded wool,
But the cruel rocks, they gored her side
Like the horns of an angry bull.

Her rattling shrouds, all sheathed in ice,
With the masts went by the board;
Like a vessel of glass, she stove and sank,
Ho! Ho! the breakers roared!

At daybreak, on the bleak sea-beach,
A fisherman stood aghast,
To see the form of a maiden fair,
Lashed close to a drifting mast!

The salt sea was frozen on her breast,
The salt tears in her eyes;
And he saw her hair, like the brown sea-weed,
On the billows fall and rise.

Such was the wreck of the Hesperus,
In the midnight and the snow!
Christ save us all from a death like this,
On the reef of Norman's Woe!

THE TEN COMMANDMENTS

Holy Bible, Exodus 20:1–17

1 And God spake all these words, saying,

2 I am the Lord thy God, which have brought thee out of the land of Egypt, out of the house of bondage.

3 Thou shalt have no other gods before me.

4 Thou shalt not make unto thee any graven image, or any likeness of any thing that is in heaven above, or that is in the earth beneath, or that is in the water under the earth:

5 Thou shalt not bow down thyself to them, nor serve them: for I the Lord thy God am a jealous God, visiting the iniquity of the fathers upon the children unto the third and fourth generation of them that hate me;

6 And shewing mercy unto thousands of them that love me, and keep my commandments.

7 Thou shalt not take the name of the Lord thy God in vain; for the Lord will not hold him guiltless that taketh his name in vain.

8 Remember the sabbath day, to keep it holy.

9 Six days shalt thou labour, and do all thy work:

10 But the seventh day is the sabbath of the Lord thy God: in it thou shalt not do any work, thou, nor thy son, nor thy daughter, thy manservant, nor thy maidservant, nor thy cattle, nor thy stranger that is within thy gates:

11 For in six days the Lord made heaven and earth, the sea, and all that in them is, and rested the seventh day: wherefore the Lord blessed the sabbath day, and hallowed it.

12 Honour thy father and thy mother: that thy days may be long upon the land which the Lord thy God giveth thee.

13 Thou shalt not kill.

14 Thou shalt not commit adultery.

15 Thou shalt not steal.

16 Thou shalt not bear false witness against thy neighbour.

17 Thou shalt not covet thy neighbour's house, thou shalt not covet thy neighbour's wife, nor his manservant, nor his maid-servant, nor his ox, nor his ass, nor any thing that is thy neighbour's.

I'LL TAKE YOU HOME AGAIN, KATHLEEN

Thomas P. Westendorf

I'll take you home again, Kathleen,
Across the ocean wild and wide,
To where your heart has ever been,
Since first you were my bonny bride.
The roses all have left your cheek,
I've watched them fade away and die;
Your voice is sad when e'er you speak,
And tears bedim your loving eyes.

Chorus:

Oh! I will take you back, Kathleen,
To where your heart will feel no pain;
And when the fields are fresh and green,
I'll take you to your home again.

I know you love me, Kathleen, dear,
Your heart was ever fond and true;
I always feel when you are near,
That life holds nothing dear but you.
The smiles that once you gave to me,
I scarcely ever see them now,
Though many, many times I see
A darkening shadow on your brow. (*Chorus.*)

To that dear home beyond the sea,
My Kathleen shall again return,
And when thy old friends welcome thee,
Thy loving heart will cease to yearn.
Where laughs the little silver stream,
Besides your mother's humble cot,
And brightest rays of sunshine gleam,
There all your grief will be forgot. (*Chorus.*)

23

LITTLE BROWN JUG

Anonymous

My wife and I live all alone
In a little brown hut we call our own,
She loves gin and I love rum,
Tell you what, don't we have fun?

Chorus:
    Ha, ha, ha, 'tis you and me,
    Little brown jug don't I love thee?
    Ha, ha, ha, 'tis you and me,
    Little brown jug, don't I love thee?

If I had a cow that gave such milk
I'd dress her in the finest silk,
Feed her on the choicest hay,
And milk her forty times a day. (*Chorus.*)

'Tis you that makes my friends my foes,
'Tis you that makes me wear old clothes,
But seeing you are so near my nose,
Tip her up and down she goes. (*Chorus.*)

When I go toiling on my farm,
Take little brown jug under my arm,
Set it under some shady tree,
Little brown jug, don't I love thee? (*Chorus.*)

Then came the landlord tripping in,
Round top hat and peaked chin,
In his hand he carried a cup,
Says I, "Old Fellow, give us a sup." (*Chorus.*)

If all the folks of Adam's race,
Were put together in one place,
Then I'd prepare to drop a tear
Before I'd part with you, my dear. (*Chorus.*)

* * *

That which is everybody's business is nobody's business.
    —Izaak Walton

THE BALCONY SCENE

William Shakespeare

Enter ROMEO

Rom.   He jests at scars that never felt a wound.

> [*Juliet appears above at a window.*

But, soft! what light through yonder window breaks?
It is the east, and Juliet is the sun.
Arise, fair sun, and kill the envious moon,
Who is already sick and pale with grief,
That thou her maid art far more fair than she:
Be not her maid, since she is envious;
Her vestal livery is but sick and green
And none but fools do wear it; cast it off.
It is my lady, O, it is my love!
O, that she knew she were!
She speaks, yet she says nothing: what of that?
Her eye discourses; I will answer it.
I am too bold, 'tis not to me she speaks:
Two of the fairest stars in all the heaven,
Having some business, do entreat her eyes
To twinkle in their spheres till they return.
What if her eyes were there, they in her head?
The brightness of her cheek would shame those stars,
As daylight doth a lamp; her eyes in heaven
Would through the airy region stream so bright
That birds would sing and think it were not night.
See, how she leans her cheek upon her hand!
O, that I were a glove upon that hand,
That I might touch that cheek!

Jul.   Ay me!

Rom.   She speaks:
O, speak again, bright angel! for thou art
As glorious to this night, being o'er my head,
As is a winged messenger of heaven
Unto the white-upturned wondering eyes
Of mortals that fall back to gaze on him
When he bestrides the lazy-pacing clouds
And sails upon the bosom of the air.

Jul.   O Romeo, Romeo! wherefore art thou Romeo?
Deny thy father and refuse thy name;
Or, if thou wilt not, be but sworn my love,

And I'll no longer be a Capulet.

    Rom. [*Aside*] Shall I hear more, or shall I speak at this?

    Jul. 'Tis but thy name that is my enemy;
Thou art thyself, though not a Montague.
What's Montague? it is nor hand, nor foot,
Nor arm, nor face, nor any other part
Belonging to a man. O, be some other name!
What's in a name? that which we call a rose
By any other name would smell as sweet;
So Romeo would, were he not Romeo call'd,
Retain that dear perfection which he owes
Without that title. Romeo, doff thy name,
And for that name which is no part of thee
Take all myself.

    Rom.   I take thee at thy word:
Call me but love, and I'll be new baptized;
Henceforth I never will be Romeo.

    Jul. What man art thou that thus bescreen'd in night
So stumblest on my counsel?

    Rom.   By a name
I know not how to tell thee who I am:
My name, dear saint, is hateful to myself,
Because it is an enemy to thee;
Had I it written, I would tear the word.

    Jul. My ears have not yet drunk a hundred words
Of that tongue's utterance, yet I know the sound:
Art thou not Romeo and a Montague?

    Rom. Neither, fair saint, if either thee dislike.

    Jul. How camest thou hither, tell me, and wherefore?
The orchard walls are high and hard to climb,
And the place death, considering who thou art,
If any of my kinsmen find thee here.

    Rom. With love's light wings did I o'erperch these walls;
For stony limits cannot hold love out,
And what love can do that dares love attempt;
Therefore thy kinsmen are no let to me.

    Jul. If they do see thee, they will murder thee.

    Rom. Alack, there lies more peril in thine eye
Than twenty of their swords: look thou but sweet,
And I am proof against their enmity.

    Jul. I would not for the world they saw thee here.

    Rom. I have night's cloak to hide me from their sight;
And but thou love me, let them find me here:

My life were better ended by their hate,
Than death prorogued, wanting of thy love.

Jul. By whose direction found'st thou out this place?

Rom. By love, who first did prompt me to inquire;
He lent me counsel and I lent him eyes.
I am no pilot; yet, wert thou as far
As that vast shore wash'd with the farthest sea,
I would adventure for such merchandise.

Jul. Thou know'st the mask of night is on my face,
Else would a maiden blush bepaint my cheek
For that which thou hast heard me speak to-night.
Fain would I dwell on form, fain, fain deny
What I have spoke: but farewell compliment!
Dost thou love me? I know thou wilt say 'Ay,'
And I will take thy word: yet, if thou swear'st,
Thou mayst prove false; at lovers' perjuries,
They say, Jove laughs. O gentle Romeo,
If thou dost love, pronounce it faithfully:
Or if thou think'st I am too quickly won,
I'll frown and be perverse and say thee nay,
So thou wilt woo; but else, not for the world.
In truth, fair Montague, I am too fond,
And therefore thou mayst think my haviour light:
But trust me, gentleman, I'll prove more true
Than those that have more cunning to be strange.
I should have been more strange, I must confess,
But that thou overheard'st, ere I was ware,
My true love's passion: therefore pardon me,
And not impute this yielding to light love,
Which the dark night hath so discovered.

Rom. Lady, by yonder blessed moon I swear
That tips with silver all these fruit-tree tops—

Jul. O, swear not by the moon, the inconstant moon,
That monthly changes in her circled orb,
Lest that thy love prove likewise variable.

Rom. What shall I swear by?

Jul.   Do not swear at all;
Or, if thou wilt, swear by thy gracious self,
Which is the god of my idolatry,
And I'll believe thee.

Rom.   If my heart's dear love—

Jul. Well, do not swear: although I joy in thee,
I have no joy of this contract to-night:

It is too rash, too unadvised, too sudden;
Too like the lightning, which doth cease to be
Ere one can say 'It lightens.' Sweet, good night!
This bud of love, by summer's ripening breath,
May prove a beauteous flower when next we meet.
Good night, good night! as sweet repose and rest
Come to thy heart as that within my breast!
 Rom. O, wilt thou leave me so unsatisfied?
 Jul. What satisfaction canst thou have to-night?
 Rom. The exchange of thy love's faithful vow for mine.
 Jul. I gave thee mine before thou didst request it:
And yet I would it were to give again.
 Rom. Wouldst thou withdraw it? for what purpose, love?
 Jul. But to be frank, and give it thee again.
And yet I wish but for the thing I have:
My bounty is as boundless as the sea,
My love as deep; the more I give to thee,
The more I have, for both are infinite.

          [Nurse calls within.
I hear some noise within; dear love, adieu!
Anon, good nurse! Sweet Montague, be true.
Stay but a little, I will come again.

             [Exit, above.

 Rom. O blessed, blessed night! I am afeard,
Being in night, all this is but a dream,
Too flattering-sweet to be substantial.

      Re-enter Juliet, *above*
 Jul. Three words, dear Romeo, and good night indeed.
If that thy bent of love be honourable,
Thy purpose marriage, send me word to-morrow,
By one that I'll procure to come to thee,
Where and what time thou will perform the rite;
And all my fortunes at thy foot I'll lay
And follow thee my lord throughout the world.
 Nurse. [*Within*] Madam!
 Jul. I come, anon.—But if thou mean'st not well,
I do beseech thee—
Nurse. [*Within*] Madam!
 Jul.   By and by, I come:—
To cease thy suit, and leave me to my grief:
To-morrow will I send.

Rom.   So thrive my soul—
Jul.   A thousand times good night!

                                                      [*Exit, above.*
Rom.   A thousand times the worse, to want thy light.
Love goes toward love, as schoolboys from their books,
But love from love, toward school with heavy looks.

                                                      [*Retiring.*
                    Re-enter JULIET, *above*

Jul.   Hist! Romeo, hist! O, for a falconer's voice,
To lure this tassel-gentle back again!
Bondage is hoarse, and may not speak aloud;
Else would I tear the cave where Echo lies,
And make her airy tongue more hoarse than mine,
With repetition of my Romeo's name.
Rom.   It is my soul that calls upon my name:
How silver-sweet sound lovers' tongues by night,
Like softest music to attending ears!
Jul.   Romeo!
Rom.   My dear?
Jul.   At what o'clock to-morrow
Shall I send to thee?
Rom.   At the hour of nine.
Jul.   I will not fail: 'tis twenty years till then.
I have forgot why I did call thee back.
Rom.   Let me stand here till thou remember it.
Jul.   I shall forget, to have thee still stand there,
Remembering how I love thy company.
Rom.   And I'll still stay, to have thee still forget,
Forgetting any other home but this.
Jul.   'Tis almost morning; I would have thee gone:
And yet no further than a wanton's bird;
Who lets it hop a little from her hand,
Like a poor prisoner in his twisted gyves,
And with a silk thread plucks it back again,
So loving-jealous of his liberty.
Rom.   I would I were thy bird.
Jul.   Sweet, so would I:
Yet I should kill thee with much cherishing.
Good night, good night! parting is such sweet sorrow,
That I shall say good night till it be morrow.

                                                      [*Exit above.*
Rom.   Sleep dwell upon thine eyes, peace in thy breast!
Would I were sleep and peace, so sweet to rest!

Hence will I to my ghostly father's cell,
His help to crave, and my dear hap to tell.

[Exit.

(From Romeo and Juliet)

TIME, YOU OLD GIPSY MAN

Ralph Hodgson

Time, you old gipsy man,
  Will you not stay,
Put up your caravan
  Just for one day?

All things I'll give you
Will you be my guest,
Bells for your jennet
Of silver the best,
Goldsmiths shall beat you
A great golden ring,
Peacocks shall bow to you,
Little boys sing.
Oh, and sweet girls will
Festoon you with may,
Time, you old gipsy,
Why hasten away?

Last week in Babylon,
Last night in Rome,
Morning, and in the crush
Under Paul's dome;
Under Paul's dial
You tighten your rein—
Only a moment,
And off once again;
Off to some city
Now blind in the womb,
Off to another
Ere that's in the tomb.

Time, you old gipsy man,
  Will you not stay,
Put up your caravan
  Just for one day?

SOCRATES, ON HIS CONDEMNATION TO DEATH

For the sake of no long space of time, O Athenians, you will incur the character and reproach at the hands of those who wish to defame the city, of having put that wise man, Socrates, to death. For those who wish to defame you will assert that I am wise, though I am not. If, then, you had waited for a short time, this would have happened of its own accord; for observe my age, that it is far advanced in life, and near death. But I say this not to you all, but to those only who have condemned me to die. And I say this too to the same persons. Perhaps you think, O Athenians, that I have been convicted through the want of arguments, by which I might have persuaded you, had I thought it right to do and say anything so that I might escape punishment. Far otherwise: I have been convicted through want indeed, yet not of arguments, but of audacity and impudence, and of the inclination to say such things to you as would have been most agreeable for you to hear, had I lamented and bewailed and done and said many other things unworthy of me, as I affirm, but such as you are accustomed to hear from others.

But neither did I then think that I ought, for the sake of avoiding danger, to do anything unworthy of a freeman, nor do I now repent of having so defended myself; but I should much rather choose to die having so defended myself than to live in that way. For neither in a trial nor in battle is it right that I or any one else should employ every possible means whereby he may avoid death; for in battle it is frequently evident that a man might escape death by laying down his arms and throwing himself on the mercy of his pursuers. And there are many other devices in every danger, by which to avoid death, if a man dares to do and say everything.

But this is not difficult, O Athenians, to escape death, but it is much more difficult to avoid depravity, for it runs swifter than death. And now I, being slow and aged, am overtaken by the slower of the two; but my accusers, being strong and active, have been overtaken by the swifter, wickedness. And now I depart, condemned by you to death; but they condemned by truth, as guilty of iniquity and injustice: and I abide my sentence and so do they. These things, perhaps, ought so to be, and I think that they are for the best.

In the next place, I desire to predict to you who have condemned me, what will be your fate: for I am now in that condition in which men most frequently prophesy, namely, when they are about to die. I say then to you, O Athenians, who have condemned me to death, that immediately after my death a punishment will overtake you, far more severe, by Jupiter, than that which you have inflicted on me. For you have done this thinking you should be freed from the necessity of giving an account of your life. The very contrary however, as I affirm, will happen to you. Your accusers will be more numerous, whom I have now restrained, though you did not perceive it; and they will be more severe, inasmuch as they are younger and you will be more indignant. For, if you think that by putting men to death you will restrain any one from upbraiding you because you do not live well, you are much mistaken; for this method of escape is neither possible nor honorable, but that other is most honorable and most easy, not to put a check upon others, but for a man to take heed to himself, how he may be most perfect. Having predicted thus much to those of you who have condemned me, I take my leave of you.

But with you who have voted for my acquittal, I would gladly hold converse on what has now taken place, while the magistrates are busy and I am not yet carried to the place where I must die. Stay with me then, so long, O Athenians, for nothing hinders our conversing with each other, whilst we are permitted to do so; for I wish to make known to you, as being my friends, the meaning of that which has just now befallen me. To me then, O my judges, —and in calling you judges I call you rightly,—a strange thing has happened. For the wonted prophetic voice of my guardian deity, on every former occasion, even in the most trifling affairs, opposed me, if I was about to do anything wrong; but now, that has befallen me which ye yourselves behold, and which any one would think and which is supposed to be the extremity of evil, yet neither when I departed from home in the morning did the warning of the god oppose me, nor when I came up here to the place of trial, nor in my address when I was about to say anything; yet on other occasions it has frequently restrained me in the midst of speaking. But now it has never throughout this proceeding opposed me, either in what I did or said. What then do I suppose to be the cause of this? I will tell you: what has befallen me appears to be a blessing; and it is impossible that we think rightly who suppose that death is an evil. A great proof of this to me is the fact that it is impossible but that the accustomed signal should have opposed me, unless I had been about to meet with some good.

Moreover, we may hence conclude that there is great hope that death is a blessing. For to die is one of two things: for either the dead may be annihilated and have no sensation of anything whatever; or, as it is said, there is a certain change and passage of the soul from one place to another. And if it is a privation of all sensation, as it were, a sleep in which the sleeper has no dream, death would be a wonderful gain. For I think that if anyone, having selected a night in which he slept so soundly as not to have had a dream, and having compared this night with all the other nights and days of his life, should be required on consideration to say how many days and nights he had passed better and more pleasantly than this night throughout his life, I think that not only a private person, but even a great king himself would find them easy to number in comparison with other days and nights. If, therefore, death is a thing of this kind, I say it is a gain; for thus all futurity appears to be nothing more than one night.

But if, on the other hand, death is a removal from hence to another place, and what is said be true, that all the dead are there, what greater blessing can there be than this, my judges? For if, on arriving at Hades, released from these who pretend to be judges, one shall find those who are true judges, and who are said to judge there, Minos and Rhadamanthus, Æacus and Triptolemus, and such others of the demigods as were just during their own life, would this be a sad removal? At what price would you not estimate a conference with Orpheus and Musæus, Hesiod and Homer? I indeed should be willing to die often, if this be true. For to me the sojourn there would be admirable, when I should meet with Palamedes, and Ajax, son of Telamon, and any other of the ancients who has died by an unjust sentence. The comparing my sufferings with theirs would, I think, be no unpleasing occupation.

But the greatest pleasure would be to spend my time in questioning and examining the people there as I have done those here, and discovering who among them is wise, and who fancies himself to be so but is not. At what price, my judges, would not any one estimate the opportunity of questioning him who led that mighty army against Troy, or Ulysses, or Sisyphus, or ten thousand others, whom one might mention, both men and women? with whom to converse and associate, and to question them, would be an inconceivable happiness. Surely for that the judges there do not condemn to death; for in other respects those who live there are more happy than those that are here, and are henceforth immortal, if at least what is said be true.

You, therefore, O my judges, ought to entertain good hopes with respect to death, and to meditate on this one truth, that to a good man nothing is evil, neither while living nor when dead, nor are his concerns neglected by the gods. And what has befallen me is not the effect of chance; but this is clear to me, that now to die, and be freed from my cares, is better for me. On this account the warning in no way turned me aside; and I bear no resentment toward those who condemned me, or against my accusers, although they did not condemn and accuse me with this intention, but thinking to injure me: in this they deserve to be blamed.

Thus much, however, I beg of them. Punish my sons, when they grow up, O judges, paining them as I have pained you, if they appear to you to care for riches or anything else before virtue, and if they think themselves to be something when they are nothing, reproach them as I have done you, for not attending to what they ought, and for conceiving themselves to be something when they are worth nothing. If ye do this, both I and my sons shall have met with just treatment at your hands.

But it is now time to depart,—for me to die, for you to live. But which of us is going to a better state is unknown to every one but God.

(From Plato's Apology)

GOD, GIVE US MEN!

Josiah Gilbert Holland

God, give us Men! A time like this demands
Strong minds, great hearts, true faith and ready hands;
    Men whom the lust of office does not kill;
Men whom the spoils of office cannot buy;
    Men who possess opinions and a will;
Men who have honor; men who will not lie;
Men who can stand before a demagogue
    And damn his treacherous flatteries without winking!
Tall men, sun-crowned, who live above the fog
    In public duty and in private thinking;
For while the rabble, with their thumb-worn creeds,
Their large professions and their little deeds,
Mingle in selfish strife, lo! Freedom weeps,
Wrong rules the land and waiting Justice sleeps.

LINCOLN REVIEWS A BOOK

For those who like this kind of a book, this is the kind of a book they will like.

THE LORD GAVE . . .

Holy Bible, Job 1:20–21

20 Then Job arose, and rent his mantle, and shaved his head, and fell down upon the ground, and worshipped.

21 And said, Naked came I out of my mother's womb, and naked shall I return thither: the Lord gave, and the Lord hath taken away; blessed be the name of the Lord.

PREAMBLE TO THE CONSTITUTION

We, the People of the United States, in order to form a more perfect union, establish justice, insure domestic tranquility, provide for the common defense, promote the general welfare, and secure the blessings of liberty to ourselves and our posterity, do ordain and establish this Constitution for the United States of America.

BARBARA ALLEN

Anonymous

In scarlet town, where I was born,
    There was a fair maid dwellin',
Made every youth cry *Well-a-way!*
    Her name was Barbara Allen.

All in the merry month of May
    When green buds they were swellin',
Young Jemmy Grove on his death-bed lay,
    For love of Barbara Allen.

He sent his man in to her then,
    To the town where she was dwellin',
"O haste and come to my master dear,
    If your name be Barbara Allen."

So slowly, slowly rase she up,
    And slowly she came nigh him,
And when she drew the curtain by—
    "Young man, I think you're dyin'."

"O it's I'm sick and very very sick,
    And it's all for Barbara Allen."
"O the better for me ye'se never be,
    Tho' your heart's blood were a-spillin'!

"O dinna ye mind young man," says she,
    "When the red wine ye were fillin',
That ye made the healths go round and round,
    And slighted Barbara Allen?"

He turn'd his face unto the wall,
    And death was with him dealin':
"Adieu, adieu, my dear friends all,
    And be kind to Barbara Allen!"

As she was walking o'er the fields,
    She heard the dead-bell knellin';
And every jow the dead-bell gave
    Cried "Woe to Barbara Allen."

"O mother, mother, make my bed,
    O make it saft and narrow:
My love has died for me today,
    I'll die for him to-morrow.

"Farewell," she said, "ye virgins all,
    And shun the fault I fell in:
Henceforth take warning by the fall
    Of cruel Barbara Allen."

THE BEAUTIFUL SNOW

John Whittaker Watson

Oh! the snow, the beautiful snow,
Filling the sky and the earth below!
Over the housetops, over the street,
Over the heads of the people you meet:
            Dancing,
                Flirting,
                    Skimming along.
Beautiful snow! it can do nothing wrong.

Flying to kiss a fair lady's cheek,
Clinging to lips in a frolicsome freak,
Beautiful snow from the heavens above,
Pure as an angel, gentle as love!

Oh! the snow, the beautiful snow!
How the flakes gather and laugh as they go
Whirling about in their maddening fun!
It plays in its glee with everyone,
        Chasing,
           Laughing,
              Hurrying by;
It lights on the face and it sparkles the eye,
And even the dogs, with a bark and a bound,
Snap at the crystals that eddy around.
The town is alive and its heart in a glow,
To welcome the coming of beautiful snow!

How the wild crowd goes swaying along!
Hailing each other with humor and song!
How the gay sledges, like meteors, flash by,
Bright for a moment, then lost to the eye;
        Ringing,
           Singing,
              Dashing they go—
Over the crust of the beautiful snow—
Snow so pure when it falls from the sky,
To be trampled in mud by the crowd rushing by,
To be trampled and tracked by the thousands of feet,
Till it blends with the horrible filth in the street.

Once I was pure as the snow—but I fell!
Fell, like the snowflakes, from heaven—to hell;
Fell, to be trampled as the filth of the street;
Fell, to be scoffed, to be spit on and beat;
        Pleading,
           Cursing,
              Dreading to die,
Selling my soul to whoever would buy,
Dealing in shame for a morsel of bread,
Hating the living and fearing the dead.
Merciful God! have I fallen so low?
And yet I was once like this beautiful snow!

Once I was fair as the beautiful snow,
With an eye like its crystals, a heart like its glow;
Once I was loved for my innocent grace,
Flattered and sought for the charms of my face!
Father,
Mother,
Sisters, all,
God and myself, I have lost by my fall.
The veriest wretch that goes shivering by
Will take a wide sweep lest I wander too nigh;
For all that is on or about me, I know,
There is nothing that's pure but the beautiful snow.

How strange it should be that this beautiful snow
Should fall on a sinner with nowhere to go!
How strange it would be, when the night comes again,
If the snow and the ice struck my desperate brain!
Fainting,
Freezing,
Dying alone;
Too wicked for prayer, too weak for my moan
To be heard in the streets of the crazy town,
Gone mad in the joy of the snow coming down;
To lie and to die in my terrible woe,
With a bed and a shroud of the beautiful snow.

THE FOX AND THE GRAPES

A Fox, very hungry, chanced to come into a vineyard, where there hung branches of charming ripe grapes; but nailed up to a trellis so high, that he leaped till he quite tired himself, without being able to reach one of them. At last—"Let who will take them!" says he, "they are but green and sour; so I will even let them alone."

(From Aesop's Fables)

AN HONEST MAN

A wit's a feather and a chief a rod;
An honest man's the noblest work of God.
(From Pope's Essay on Man)

THE DAY IS DONE

Henry Wadsworth Longfellow

The day is done, and the darkness
Falls from the wings of Night,
As a feather is wafted downward
From an eagle in his flight.

I see the lights of the village
Gleam through the rain and the mist,
And a feeling of sadness comes o'er me
That my soul cannot resist:

A feeling of sadness and longing,
That is not akin to pain,
And resembles sorrow only
As the mist resembles the rain.

Come, read to me some poem,
Some simple and heartfelt lay,
That shall soothe this restless feeling,
And banish the thoughts of the day.

Not from the grand old masters,
Not from the bards sublime,
Whose distant footsteps echo
Through the corridors of Time.

For, like strains of martial music,
Their mighty thoughts suggest
Life's endless toil and endeavor;
And tonight I long for rest.

Read from some humbler poet,
Whose songs gushed from his heart,
As showers from the clouds of summer,
Or tears from the eyelids start:

Who, through long days of labor,
And nights devoid of ease,
Still heard in his soul the music
Of wonderful melodies.

Such songs have power to quiet
The restless pulse of care,
And come like the benediction
That follows after prayer.

Then read from the treasured volume
The poem of thy choice,
And lend to the rhyme of the poet
The beauty of thy voice.

And the night shall be filled with music,
And the cares, that infest the day,
Shall fold their tents, like Arabs,
And as silently steal away.

LUCY

William Wordsworth

She dwelt among the untrodden ways
  Beside the springs of Dove;
A maid whom there were none to praise,
  And very few to love.

A violet by a mossy stone
  Half hidden from the eye!
Fair as a star, when only one
  Is shining in the sky.

She lived unknown, and few could know
  When Lucy ceased to be;
But she is in her grave, and O,
  The difference to me!

BLOW, THOU WINTER WIND

William Shakespeare

Blow, blow, thou winter wind,
Thou art not so unkind
  As man's ingratitude;
Thy tooth is not so keen,
Because thou art not seen,
  Although thy breath be rude.

Heigh-ho! sing, heigh-ho! unto the green holly:
Most friendship is feigning, most loving mere folly:
　　Then, heigh-ho, the holly!
　　This life is most jolly.

　Freeze, freeze, thou bitter sky,
　That dost not bite so nigh
　　As benefits forgot:
　Though thou the waters warp,
　Thy sting is not so sharp
　　As friend remember'd not.
　　　　　　　(Song from As You Like It)

ABOU BEN ADHEM

James Henry Leigh Hunt

Abou Ben Adhem (may his tribe increase!)
Awoke one night from a deep dream of peace,
And saw, within the moonlight in his room,
Making it rich, and like a lily in bloom,
An Angel writing in a book of gold:
Exceeding peace had made Ben Adhem bold,
And to the Presence in the room he said,
"What writest thou?" The Vision raised its head,
And with a look made of all sweet accord
Answered, "The names of those who love the Lord."
"And is mine one?" said Abou. "Nay, not so,"
Replied the Angel. Abou spoke more low,
But cheerily still; and said, "I pray thee, then,
Write me as one that loves his fellow men."

The Angel wrote, and vanished. The next night
It came again with a great wakening light,
And showed the names whom love of God had blessed,
And lo! Ben Adhem's name led all the rest!

AS THE TWIG IS BENT

'Tis education forms the common mind;
Just as the twig is bent, the tree's inclined.
　　　　　　　(From Pope's Moral Essays)

THE GODLY AND THE UNGODLY

Holy Bible, Psalm 1

1 Blessed is the man that walketh not in the counsel of the ungodly, nor standeth in the way of sinners, nor sitteth in the seat of the scornful.

2 But his delight is in the law of the Lord; and in his law doth he meditate day and night.

3 And he shall be like a tree planted by the rivers of water, that bringeth forth his fruit in his season; his leaf also shall not wither; and whatsoever he doeth shall prosper.

4 The ungodly are not so: but are like the chaff which the wind driveth away.

5 Therefore the ungodly shall not stand in the judgment, nor sinners in the congregation of the righteous.

6 For the Lord knoweth the way of the righteous: but the way of the ungodly shall perish.

ELEGY WRITTEN IN A COUNTRY CHURCH-YARD

Thomas Gray

The curfew tolls the knell of parting day,
The lowing herd winds slowly o'er the lea,
The ploughman homeward plods his weary way,
And leaves the world to darkness and to me.

Now fades the glimmering landscape on the sight,
And all the air a solemn stillness holds,
Save where the beetle wheels his droning flight,
And drowsy tinklings lull the distant folds;

Save that from yonder ivy-mantled tower
The moping owl does to the moon complain
Of such as, wandering near her secret bower,
Molest her ancient solitary reign.

Beneath those rugged elms, that yew-tree's shade,
Where heaves the turf in many a mouldering heap,
Each in his narrow cell for ever laid,
The rude forefathers of the hamlet sleep.

The breezy call of incense-breathing morn,
The swallow twittering from the straw-built shed,
The cock's shrill clarion, or the echoing horn,
No more shall rouse them from their lowly bed.

For them no more the blazing hearth shall burn,
Or busy housewife ply her evening care;
No children run to lisp their sire's return,
Or climb his knees the envied kiss to share.

Oft did the harvest to their sickle yield,
Their furrow oft the stubborn glebe has broke;
How jocund did they drive their team afield!
How bowed the woods beneath their sturdy stroke!

Let not ambition mock their useful toil,
Their homely joys, and destiny obscure;
Nor grandeur hear with a disdainful smile
The short and simple annals of the poor.

The boasts of heraldry, the pomp of power,
And all that beauty, all that wealth e'er gave,
Awaits alike th' inevitable hour:—
The paths of glory lead but to the grave.

Nor you, ye proud, impute to these the fault,
If memory o'er their tomb no trophies raise,
Where through the long-drawn aisle and fretted vault
The pealing anthem swells the note of praise.

Can storied urn or animated bust
Back to its mansion call the fleeting breath?
Can honor's voice provoke the silent dust,
Or flattery soothe the dull, cold ear of Death?

Perhaps in this neglected spot is laid
Some heart once pregnant with celestial fire;
Hands, that the rod of empire might have swayed,
Or waked to ecstacy the living lyre;

But knowledge to their eyes her ample page,
Rich with the spoils of time, did ne'er unroll;
Chill penury repressed their noble rage,
And froze the genial current of the soul.

Full many a gem of purest ray serene
The dark unfathomed caves of ocean bear;
Full many a flower is born to blush unseen,
And waste its sweetness on the desert air.

Some village Hampden, that with dauntless breast
The little tyrant of his fields withstood;
Some mute inglorious Milton here may rest,
Some Cromwell, guiltless of his country's blood.

Th' applause of listening senates to command,
The threats of pain and ruin to despise,
To scatter plenty o'er a smiling land,
And read their history in a nation's eyes,

Their lot forbade; nor circumscribed alone
Their growing virtues, but their crimes confined;
Forbade to wade through slaughter to a throne,
And shut the gates of mercy on mankind;

The struggling pangs of conscious truth to hide,
To quench the blushes of ingenuous shame,
Or heap the shrine of luxury and pride
With incense kindled at the Muse's flame.

Far from the madding crowd's ignoble strife,
Their sober wishes never learned to stray;
Along the cool sequestered vale of life
They kept the noiseless tenor of their way.

Yet e'en these bones from insult to protect
Some frail memorial still erected nigh,
With uncouth rhymes and shapeless sculpture decked,
Implores the passing tribute of a sigh.

Their name, their years, spelt by th' unlettered Muse,
The place of fame and elegy supply;
And many a holy text around she strews,
That teach the rustic moralist to die.

For who, to dumb forgetfulness a prey,
This pleasing anxious being e'er resigned,
Left the warm precincts of the cheerful day,
Nor cast one longing, lingering look behind?

On some fond breast the parting soul relies,
Some pious drops the closing eye requires;
E'en from the tomb the voice of Nature cries,
E'en in our ashes live their wonted fires.

For thee, who, mindful of th' unhonored dead,
Dost in these lines their artless tale relate;
If chance, by lonely contemplation led,
Some kindred spirit shall inquire thy fate,—

Haply some hoary-headed swain may say:
"Oft have we seen him, at the peep of dawn,
Brushing with hasty steps the dews away,
To meet the sun upon the upland lawn.

"There at the foot of yonder nodding beech
That wreathes its old fantastic roots so high,
His listless length at noontide would he stretch,
And pore upon the brook that babbles by.

"Hard by yon wood, now smiling as in scorn,
Muttering his wayward fancies, he would rove;
Now drooping, woeful-wan, like one forlorn,
Or craz'd with care, or cross'd in hopeless love.

"One morn I missed him on the customed hill,
Along the heath, and near his favorite tree;
Another came, nor yet beside the rill,
Nor up the lawn, nor at the wood was he;

"The next, with dirges due, in sad array
Slow through the church-way path we saw him borne;—
Approach and read (for thou canst read) the lay
Graved on the stone beneath yon aged thorn."

THE EPITAPH

Here rests his head upon the lap of earth
A youth, to fortune and to fame unknown;
Fair science frowned not on his humble birth
And melancholy marked him for her own.

Large was his bounty, and his soul sincere;
Heaven did a recompense as largely send:
He gave to misery all he had, a tear;
He gained from heaven ('twas all he wished) a friend

No farther seek his merits to disclose,
Or draw his frailties from their dread abode,
(There they alike in trembling hope repose,)
The bosom of his Father and his God.

BATTLE-HYMN OF THE REPUBLIC

Julia Ward Howe

Mine eyes have seen the glory of the coming of the Lord:
He is trampling out the vintage where the grapes of wrath are
  stored;
He hath loosed the fateful lightning of his terrible swift sword.
    His truth is marching on.

I have seen him in the watch-fires of a hundred circling camps;
They have builded him an altar in the evening dews and damps;
I can read his righteous sentence by the dim and flaring lamps.
    His day is marching on.

I have read a fiery gospel, writ in burnished rows of steel:
"As ye deal with my contemners, so with you my grace shall deal;
Let the Hero, born of woman, crush the serpent with his heel,
    Since God is marching on."

He has sounded forth the trumpet that shall never call retreat;
He is sifting out the hearts of men before his judgment-seat:
O, be swift, my soul, to answer him! be jubilant my feet!
    Our God is marching on.

In the beauty of the lilies Christ was born across the sea,
With a glory in his bosom that transfigures you and me;
As he died to make men holy, let us die to make men free,
    While God is marching on.

THE HIPPOCRATIC OATH

I swear by Apollo Physician, by *Asclepius*, by Health, by Heal-
All, and by all the gods and goddesses, that, according to my ability and judgment, I will keep this oath and stipulation; to reckon
him who taught me this art equally dear to me as my parents, and
share my substance with him and relieve his necessities if re-

quired. To regard his offspring as on the same footing with my own brothers and to teach them this art if they should wish to learn it, without fee or stipulation; and that by precept, lecture and every other mode of instruction I will impart a knowledge of the art to my own sons and to those of my teachers and to disciples bound by a stipulation and oath, according to the law of medicine, but to none others.

I will follow that method of treatment which, according to my ability and judgment, I consider for the benefit of my patients, and abstain from whatever is deleterious and mischievous. I will give no deadly medicine to anyone if asked, nor suggest any such counsel. Furthermore, I will not give to a woman an instrument to produce an abortion.

With Purity and with Holiness I will pass my life and practice my art. I will not cut a person who is suffering with a stone, but will leave this to be done by practitioners of this work. Into whatever houses I enter I will go into them for the benefit of the sick and will abstain from every voluntary act of mischief and corruption; and further from the seduction of females or males, bond or free.

Whatever, in connection with my professional practice, or not in connection with it, I may see or hear in the lives of men which ought not to be spoken abroad, I will not divulge, as reckoning that all such should be kept secret.

While I continue to keep this oath unviolated, may it be granted to me to enjoy life and the practice of the art, respected by all men, at all times, but should I trespass and violate this oath, may the reverse be my lot.

THE CROOKED FOOTPATH

Oliver Wendell Holmes

Ah, here it is! the sliding rail
    That marks the old remembered spot—
The gap that struck our schoolboy trail—
    The crooked path across the lot.

It left the road by school and church,
    A penciled shadow, nothing more,
That parted from the silver birch
    And ended at the farmhouse door.

47

No line or compass traced its plan,
  With frequent bends to left or right.
In aimless, wayward curves it ran,
  But always kept the door in sight.

The gabled porch, with woodbine green—
  The broken millstone at the mill—
Though many a rood might stretch between,
  The truant child could see them still.

No rocks across the pathway lie,
  No fallen trunk is o'er it thrown,
And yet it winds, we know not why,
  And turns as if for tree or stone.

Perhaps some lover trod the way
  With shaking knees and leaping heart—
And so it often runs astray
  With sinuous sweep or sudden start.

Or one, perchance, with clouded brain,
  From some unholy banquet reeled—
And since our devious steps maintain
  His track across the trodden field.

Nay, deem not thus—no earth-born will
  Could ever trace a faultless line;
Our truest steps are human still—
  To walk unswerving were divine!

Truants from love, we dream of wrath—
  Oh, rather let us trust the more!
Through all the wanderings of the path,
  We still can see our Father's door!

VANZETTI TO JUDGE THAYER

If it had not been for these things, I might have live out my life, talking at street corners to scorning men. I might have die, unmarked, unknown, a failure. Now we are not a failure. This is our career and our triumph. Never in our full life can we hope to do such work for tolerance, for joostice, for man's onderstanding

48

of man, as now we do by an accident. Our words—our lives—our pains—nothing! The taking of our lives—lives of a good shoemaker and a poor fish peddler—all! That last moment belong to us—that agony is our triumph!

THE CONQUERED BANNER

Abram Joseph Ryan

Furl that Banner, for 'tis weary;
Round its staff 'tis drooping dreary;
Furl it, fold it, it is best;
For there's not a man to wave it,
And there's not a sword to save it,
And there's no one left to lave it
In the blood which heroes gave it;
And its foes now scorn and brave it;
Furl it, hide it—let it rest!

Take that Banner down! 'tis tattered;
Broken is its staff and shattered;
And the valiant hosts are scattered
Over whom it floated high.
Oh! 'tis hard for us to fold it;
Hard to think there's none to hold it;
Hard that those who once unrolled it
Now must furl it with a sigh.

Furl that Banner! furl it sadly!
Once ten thousand hailed it gladly,
And ten thousand wildly, madly,
Swore it should forever wave;
Swore that foeman's sword should never
Hearts like theirs entwined dissever,
Till that flag should float forever
O'er their freedom or their grave.

Furl it; for the hands that grasped it,
And the hearts that fondly clasped it,
Cold and dead are lying low;
And that Banner—it is trailing!
While around it sounds the wailing
Of its people in their woe.

49

For, though conquered, they adore it!
Love the cold, dead hands that bore it!
Weep for those who fell before it!
Pardon those who trailed and tore it!
But, oh! wildly they deplore it,
Now who furl and fold it so.

Furl that Banner! True, 'tis gory,
Yet 'tis wreathed around with glory,
And 'twill live in song and story,
Though its folds are in the dust:
For its fame on brightest pages,
Penned by poets and by sages,
Shall go sounding down the ages—
Furl its folds though now we must.

Furl that Banner, softly, slowly!
Treat it gently—it is holy—
For it droops above the dead.
Touch it not—unfold it never,
Let it droop there, furled forever,
For its peoples' hopes are dead!

O MY LUVE'S LIKE A RED, RED ROSE

Robert Burns

O my Luve's like a red, red rose
  That's newly sprung in June:
O my Luve's like the melodie
  That's sweetly played in tune.

As fair art thou, my bonnie lass,
  So deep in luve am I;
And I will luve thee still, my dear,
  Till a' the seas gang dry:

Till a' the seas gang dry, my dear,
  And the rocks melt wi' the sun;
I will luve thee still, my dear,
  While the sands o' life shall run.

And fare thee weel, my only Luve!
And fare thee weel awhile!
And I will come again, my Luve,
Tho' it were ten thousand mile.

FAITHLESS NELLY GRAY

A PATHETIC BALLAD

Thomas Hood

Ben Battle was a soldier bold,
And used to war's alarms;
But a cannon-ball took off his legs,
So he laid down his arms.

Now as they bore him off the field,
Said he, "Let others shoot;
For here I leave my second leg,
And the Forty-second Foot."

The army-surgeons made him limbs:
Said he, "They're only pegs;
But there's as wooden members quite,
As represent my legs."

Now Ben he loved a pretty maid,—
Her name was Nelly Gray;
So he went to pay her his devours,
When he devoured his pay.

But when he called on Nelly Gray,
She made him quite a scoff;
And when she saw his wooden legs,
Began to take them off.

"O Nelly Gray! O Nelly Gray!
Is this your love so warm?
The love that loves a scarlet coat
Should be more uniform."

Said she, "I loved a soldier once,
For he was blithe and brave;
But I will never have a man
With both legs in the grave.

"Before you had those timber toes
  Your love I did allow;
But then, you know, you stand upon
  Another footing now."

"O Nelly Gray! O Nelly Gray!
  For all your jeering speeches,
At duty's call I left my legs
  In Badajos's breaches."

"Why, then," said she, "you've lost the feet
  Of legs in war's alarms,
And now you cannot wear your shoes
  Upon your feats of arms!"

"O false and fickle Nelly Gray!
  I know why you refuse:
Though I've no feet, some other man
  Is standing in my shoes.

"I wish I ne'er had seen your face;
  But, now, a long farewell!
For you will be my death;—alas!
  You will not be my Nell!"

Now when he went from Nelly Gray
  His heart so heavy got,
And life was such a burden grown,
  It made him take a knot.

So round his melancholy neck
  A rope he did intwine,
And, for his second time in life,
  Enlisted in the Line.

One end he tied around a beam,
  And then removed his pegs;
And, as his legs were off,—of course
  He soon was off his legs.

And there he hung till he was dead
  As any nail in town;
For, though distress had cut him up,
  It could not cut him down.

A dozen men sat on his corpse,
　　To find out why he died;—
And they buried Ben in four cross-roads
　　With a stake in his inside.

INCIDENT OF THE FRENCH CAMP

Robert Browning

You know, we French stormed Ratisbon;
　　A mile or so away,
On a little mound, Napoleon
　　Stood on our storming-day;
With neck out-thrust, you fancy how,
　　Legs wide, arms locked behind,
As if to balance the prone brow,
　　Oppressive with its mind.

Just as perhaps he mused, "My plans
　　That soar, to earth may fall,
Let once my army-leader Lannes
　　Waver at yonder wall,"—
Out 'twixt the battery-smokes there flew
　　A rider, bound on bound
Full-galloping; nor bridle drew
　　Until he reached the mound.

Then off there flung in smiling joy,
　　And held himself erect
By just his horse's mane, a boy:
　　You hardly could suspect—
(So tight he kept his lips compressed,
　　Scarce any blood came through)
You looked twice ere you saw his breast
　　Was all but shot in two.

"Well," cried he, "Emperor, by God's grace
　　We've got you Ratisbon!
The marshal's in the market-place,
　　And you'll be there anon
To see your flag-bird flap his vans
　　Where I, to heart's desire,
Perched him!" The chief's eye flashed; his plans
　　Soared up again like fire.

The chief's eye flashed; but presently
  Softened itself, as sheathes
A film the mother-eagle's eye
  When her bruised eaglet breathes;
"You're wounded!" "Nay," his soldier's pride
  Touched to the quick, he said:
"I'm killed, sire!" And his chief beside;
  Smiling the boy fell dead.

HARK, HARK! THE LARK

William Shakespeare

Hark, hark! the lark at heaven's gate sings,
  And Phœbus 'gins arise,
His steeds to water at those springs
  On chaliced flowers that lies;
And winking Mary-buds begin
  To ope their golden eyes:
With every thing that pretty is,
  My lady sweet, arise:
    Arise, arise.

(From Cymbeline)

THE CONCORD HYMN

Ralph Waldo Emerson

By the rude bridge that arched the flood,
Their flag to April's breeze unfurled,
Here once the embattled farmers stood,
And fired the shot heard round the world.

The foe long since in silence slept;
Alike the conqueror silent sleeps;
And Time the ruined bridge has swept
Down the dark stream which seaward creeps.

On this green bank, by this soft stream,
We set today a votive stone;
That memory may their deed redeem,
When, like our sires, our sons are gone.

Spirit, that made those spirits dare
To die, and leave their children free,
Bid Time and Nature gently spare
The shaft we raise to them and thee.

FROM GREENLAND'S ICY MOUNTAINS

Bishop Reginald Heber

From Greenland's icy mountains,
From India's coral strand;
Where Afric's sunny fountains
Roll down their golden sand:
From many ancient rivers,
From many a palmy plain,
They call us to deliver
Their land from error's chain.

What tho' the spicy breezes
Blow soft o'er Ceylon's isle;
Though every prospect pleases,
And only man is vile?
In vain with lavish kindness
The gifts of God are strown;
The heathen in his blindness
Bows down to wood and stone.

Shall we, whose souls are lighted
With wisdom from on high,
Shall we to men benighted
The lamp of life deny?
Salvation! O Salvation!
The joyful sound proclaim,
Till earth's remotest nation
Has learned Messiah's name.

Waft, waft, ye winds, His story,
And you, ye waters, roll,
Till, like a sea of glory,
It spreads from pole to pole:
Till o'er our ransomed nature
The Lamb for sinners slain,
Redeemer, King, Creator,
In bliss returns to reign.

THE HEAVENS DECLARE THE GLORY OF GOD

Holy Bible, Psalm 19

1 The heavens declare the glory of God; and the firmament sheweth his handywork.

2 Day unto day uttereth speech, and night unto night sheweth knowledge.

3 There is no speech nor language, where their voice is not heard.

4 Their line is gone out through all the earth, and their words to the end of the world. In them hath he set a tabernacle for the sun,

5 Which is as a bridegroom coming out of his chamber, and rejoiceth as a strong man to run a race.

6 His going forth is from the end of the heaven, and his circuit unto the ends of it: and there is nothing hid from the heat thereof.

7 The law of the Lord is perfect, converting the soul: the testimony of the Lord is sure, making wise the simple.

8 The statutes of the Lord are right, rejoicing the heart: the commandment of the Lord is pure, enlightening the eyes.

9 The fear of the Lord is clean, enduring for ever: the judgments of the Lord are true and righteous altogether.

10 More to be desired are they than gold, yea, than much fine gold: sweeter also than honey and the honeycomb.

11 Moreover by them is thy servant warned: and in keeping of them there is great reward.

12 Who can understand his errors? cleanse thou me from secret faults.

13 Keep back thy servant also from presumptuous sins; let them not have dominion over me: then shall I be upright, and I shall be innocent from the great transgression.

14 Let the words of my mouth, and the meditation of my heart, be acceptable in thy sight, O Lord, my strength, and my redeemer.

FAREWELL ADDRESS (September 19, 1796)

George Washington

FRIENDS AND FELLOW-CITIZENS:

The period for a new election of a citizen, to administer the executive government of the United States, being not far distant, and the time actually arrived, when your thoughts must be employed in designating the person who is to be clothed with that important trust, it appears to me proper, especially as it may conduce to a more distinct expression of the public voice, that I should now apprise you of the resolution I have formed, to decline being considered among the number of those out of whom a choice is to be made.

I beg you, at the same time, to do me the justice to be assured, that this resolution has not been taken without a strict regard to all the considerations appertaining to the relation which binds a dutiful citizen to his country; and that, in withdrawing the tender of service, which silence in my situation might imply, I am influenced by no diminution of zeal for your future interest; no deficiency of grateful respect for your past kindness; but am supported by a full conviction that the step is compatible with both. . . .

Interwoven as is the love of liberty with every ligament of your hearts, no recommendation of mine is necessary to fortify or confirm the attachment.

The unity of government, which constitutes you one people, is also now dear to you. It is justly so; for it is a main pillar in the edifice of your real independence, the support of your tranquillity at home, your peace abroad; of your safety; of your prosperity; of that very liberty which you so highly prize. But as it is easy to foresee, that, from different causes and from different quarters, much pains will be taken, many artifices employed, to weaken in your minds the conviction of this truth; as this is the point in your political fortress against which the batteries of internal and external enemies will be most constantly and actively (though often covertly and insidiously) directed, it is of infinite moment, that you should properly estimate the immense value of your national Union to your collective and individual happiness; that you should cherish a cordial, habitual, and immovable attachment to it; accustoming yourselves to think and speak of it as of the palladium of your political safety and prosperity; watching for its preservation with jealous anxiety; discountenancing whatever may suggest even a suspicion, that it can in any event be abandoned; and indignantly frowning upon the first dawning of every attempt to alienate any portion of our country from the rest, or to enfeeble the sacred ties which now link together the various parts.

For this you have every inducement of sympathy and interest. Citizens, by birth or choice, of a common country, that country has a right to concentrate your affections. The name of AMERICAN, which belongs to you, in your national capacity, must always exalt the just pride of patriotism more than any appellation derived from local discriminations. With slight shades of difference, you have the same religion, manners, habits, and political principles. You have in common cause fought and triumphed together; the independence and liberty you possess are the work of joint counsels and joint efforts, of common dangers, sufferings, and successes. . . .

To the efficacy and permanency of your union, a government for the whole is indispensable. No alliances, however strict, between the parts can be an adequate substitute; they must inevitably experience the infractions and interruptions which all alliances in all times have experienced. Sensible of this momentous truth, you have improved upon your first essay, by the adoption of a constitution of government better calculated than your former for an intimate union, and for the efficacious management of your common concerns. This government, the offspring of your own choice, uninfluenced and unawed, adopted upon full investigation and mature deliberation, completely free in its principles, in the distribution of its powers, uniting security with energy, and containing within itself a provision for its own amendment, has a just claim to your confidence and your support. Respect for its authority, compliance with its laws, acquiescence in its measures, are duties enjoined by the fundamental maxims of true liberty. The basis of our political systems is the right of the people to make and to alter their constitutions of government. But the constitution which at any time exists, till changed by an explicit and authentic act of the whole people, is sacredly obligatory upon all. The very idea of the power and the right of the people to establish government presupposes the duty of every individual to obey the established government. . . .

Towards the preservation of your government, and the permanency of your present happy state, it is requisite, not only that you steadily discountenance irregular oppositions to its acknowledged authority, but also that you resist with care the spirit of innovation upon its principles, however specious the pretexts. One method of assault may be to effect, in the forms of constitution, alterations, which will impair the energy of the system, and thus to undermine what cannot be directly overthrown. In all the changes to which you may be invited, remember that time and habit are at least as necessary to fix the true character of governments as of other human institutions; that experience is the surest standard by which to test the real tendency of the existing constitution of a country; that facility in changes, upon the credit of mere hypothesis and opinion, exposes to perpetual change, from the endless variety of hypothesis and opinion; and remember, especially, that, for the efficient management of your common interests, in a country so extensive as ours, a government of as much vigor as is consistent with the perfect security of liberty is indispensable. Liberty itself will find in such a government, with powers properly distributed and adjusted, its surest guardian. It is, indeed, little else than a name, where the government is too feeble to withstand the enterprises of faction, to confine each member of the society within the limits prescribed by the laws, and to maintain all in the secure and tranquil enjoyment of the rights of person and property.

I have already intimated to you the danger of parties in the State, with particular reference to the founding of them on geographical discrimination. Let me now take a more comprehensive view, and warn you in the most solemn manner against the baneful effects of the spirit of party, generally.

This spirit, unfortunately, is inseparable from our nature, having its root in the strongest passions of the human mind. It exists under different shapes in all governments, more or less stifled, controlled, or repressed; but in those of the popular form it is seen in its greatest rankness, and is truly their worst enemy.

The alternate domination of one faction over another, sharpened by the spirit of revenge, natural to party dissension, which in different ages and countries has perpetrated the most horrid enormities, is itself a frightful despotism. But this leads at length to a more formal and permanent despotism. The disorders and miseries which result, gradually incline the minds of men to seek security and repose in the absolute power of an individual; and sooner or later the chief of some prevailing faction, more able or more fortunate than his competitors, turns this disposition to the purposes of his own elevation, on the ruins of public liberty. . . .

There is an opinion, that parties in free countries are useful checks upon the administration of the government, and serve to keep alive the spirit of liberty. This within certain limits is probably true, and in governments of a monarchial cast, patriotism may look with indulgence, if not with favor, upon the spirit of party. But in those of the popular character, in governments purely elective, it is a spirit not to be encouraged. From their natural tendency, it is certain there will always be enough of that spirit for every salutary purpose. And there being constant danger of excess, the effort ought to be, by force of public opinion to mitigate and assuage it. A fire not to be quenched, it demands a uniform vigilance to prevent its bursting into a flame, lest, instead of warming, it should consume. . . .

Of all the dispositions and habits which lead to political prosperity, religion and morality are indispensable supports. In vain would that man claim the tribute of patriotism, who should labor to subvert these great pillars of human happiness, these firmest props of the duties of men and citizens. The mere politician, equally with the pious man, ought to respect and to cherish them. A volume could not trace all their connections with private and public felicity. Let it simply be asked, Where is the security for property, for reputation, for life, if the sense of religious obligation desert the oaths, which are the instruments of investigation in courts of justice? And let us with caution indulge the supposition, that morality can be maintained without religion. Whatever may be conceded to the influence of refined education on minds of peculiar structure, reason and experience both forbid us to expect, that national morality can prevail in exclusion of religious principle.

It is substantially true that virtue or morality is a necessary spring of popular government. The rule, indeed, extends with more or less force to every species of free government. Who, that is a sincere friend to it, can look with indifference upon attempts to shake the foundation of the fabric?

Promote, then, as an object of primary importance, institutions for the general diffusion of knowledge. In proportion as the structure of a government gives force to public opinion, it is essential that public opinion should be enlightened.

As a very important source of strength and security, cherish public credit. One method of preserving it is, to use it as sparingly as possible; avoiding occasions of expense by cultivating peace, but remembering also that timely disbursements to prepare for danger frequently prevent much greater disbursements to repel it; avoiding likewise the accumulation of debt, not only by shunning occasions of expense, but by vigorous exertion in time of peace to discharge the debts, which unavoidable wars may have occasioned, not ungenerously throwing upon posterity the burden which we ourselves ought to bear. The execution of these maxims belongs to your representatives, but it is necessary that public opinion should cooperate. To facilitate to them the performance of their duty, it is essential that you should practically bear in mind, that towards the payment of debts there must be revenue; that to have revenue there must be taxes; that no taxes can be devised which are not more or less inconvenient and unpleasant; that the intrinsic embarrassment, inseparable from the selection of the proper objects (which is always a choice of difficulties), ought to be a decisive motive for a candid construction of the conduct of the government in making it, and for a spirit of acquiescence in the measures for obtaining revenue which the public exigencies may at any time dictate.

Observe good faith and justice towards all nations; cultivate peace and harmony with all. Religion and morality enjoin this conduct; and can it be, that good policy does not equally enjoin it? It will be worthy of a free, enlightened, and, at no distant period, a great nation, to give to mankind the magnanimous and too novel example of a people always guided by an exalted justice and benevolence. Who can doubt, that, in the course of time and things, the fruits of such a plan would richly repay any temporary advantages, which might be lost by a steady adherence to it? Can it be, that Providence has not connected the permanent felicity of a nation with its virtue? The experiment, at least, is recommended by every sentiment which ennobles human nature. Alas! is it rendered impossible by its vices?

In the execution of such a plan, nothing is more essential than that permanent, inveterate antipathies against particular nations, and passionate attachments for others, should be excluded; and that, in place of them, just and amicable feelings towards all should be cultivated. . . .

Against the insidious wiles of foreign influence (I conjure you to believe me, fellow-citizens), the jealousy of a free people ought to be constantly awake, since history and experience prove that foreign influence is one of the most baneful foes of republican government. But that jealousy, to be useful, must be impartial; else it becomes the instrument of the very influence to be avoided, instead of a defence against it. Excessive partiality for one foreign nation, and the excessive dislike of another, cause those whom they actuate to see danger only on one side, and serve to veil and even second the arts of influence on the other. Real patriots, who may resist the intrigues of the favorite, are liable to become suspected and odious; while its tools and dupes usurp the applause and confidence of the people, to surrender their interests.

The great rule of conduct for us, in regard to foreign nations, is, in extending our commercial relations, to have with them as little political connection as possible. So far as we have already formed engagements, let them be fulfilled with perfect good faith. Here let us stop. . . .

Harmony, liberal intercourse with all nations, are recommended by policy, humanity, and interest. But even our commercial policy should hold an equal and impartial hand; neither seeking nor granting exclusive favors or preferences; consulting the natural course of things; diffusing and diversifying by gentle means the streams of commerce, but forcing nothing; establishing, with powers so disposed, in order to give trade a stable course, to define the rights of our merchants, and to enable the government to support them, conventional rules of intercourse, the best that present circumstances and mutual opinion will permit, but temporary, and liable to be from time to time abandoned or varied, as experience and circumstances shall dictate; constantly keeping in view, that it is folly in one nation to look for disinterested favors from another; that it must pay with a portion of its independence for whatever it may accept under that character; that, by such acceptance, it may place itself in the condition of having given equivalents for nominal favors, and yet of being reproached with ingratitude for not giving more. There can be no greater error than to expect or calculate upon real favors from nation to nation. It is an illusion, which experience must cure, which a just pride ought to discard.

In offering to you, my countrymen, these counsels of an old and affectionate friend, I dare not hope they will make the strong and lasting impression I could wish; that they will control the usual current of the passions, or prevent our nation from running the course which has hitherto marked the destiny of nations. But, if I may even flatter myself, that they may be productive of some partial benefit, some occasional good; that they may now and then recur to moderate the fury of party spirit, to warn against the mischiefs of foreign intrigue, to guard against the impostures of pretended patriotism; this hope will be a full recompense for the solicitude for your welfare, by which they have been dictated.

How far in the discharge of my official duties, I have been guided by the principles which have been delineated, the public records and other evidences of my conduct must witness to you and to the world. To myself, the assurance of my own conscience is, that I have at least believed myself to be guided by them. . . .

Though, in reviewing the incidents of my administration, I am unconscious of intentional error, I am nevertheless too sensible of my defects not to think it probable that I may have committed many errors. Whatever they may be, I fervently beseech the Almighty to avert or mitigate the evils to which they may tend. I shall also carry with me the hope that my country will never cease to view them with indulgence; and that, after forty-five years of my life dedicated to its service with an upright zeal, the faults of incompetent abilities will be consigned to oblivion, as myself must soon be to the mansions of rest.

Relying on its kindness in this as in other things, and actuated by that fervent love towards it, which is so natural to a man who views in it the native soil of himself and his progenitors for several generations, I anticipate with pleasing expectation that retreat, in which I promise myself to realize, without alloy, the sweet enjoyment of partaking, in the midst of my fellow-citizens, the benign influence of good laws under a free government, the ever favorite object of my heart, and the happy reward, as I trust, of our mutual cares, labors, and dangers.

LIFE'S MIRROR

Madeline S. Bridges *

There are loyal hearts, there are spirits brave,
There are souls that are pure and true;
Then give to the world the best you have,
And the best will come back to you.

Give love, and love to your life will flow,
A strength in your utmost need;
Have faith, and a score of hearts will show
Their faith in your work and deed.

Give truth, and your gift will be paid in kind,
And honor will honor meet;
And the smile which is sweet will surely find
A smile that is just as sweet.

Give sorrow and pity to those who mourn;
You will gather in flowers again
The scattered seeds from your thought outborne,
Though the sowing seemed but vain.

For life is the mirror of king and slave,
'Tis just what we are and do;
Then give to the world the best you have
And the best will come back to you.

* That is, Mary Ainge De Vere.

63

"SAIL ON, O SHIP OF STATE!"

Henry Wadsworth Longfellow

Thou, too, sail on, O Ship of State!
Sail on, O Union, strong and great!
Humanity with all its fears,
With all its hopes of future years,
Is hanging breathless on thy fate!
We know what Master laid thy keel,
What Workmen wrought thy ribs of steel,
Who made each mast, and sail, and rope,
What anvils rang, what hammers beat,
In what a forge and what a heat
Were shaped the anchors of thy hope!
Fear not each sudden sound and shock,
'Tis of the wave and not the rock;
'Tis but the flapping of the sail,
And not a rent made by the gale!
In spite of rock and tempest's roar,
In spite of false lights on the shore,
Sail on, nor fear to breast the sea!
Our hearts, our hopes, are all with thee,
Our hearts, our hopes, our prayers, our tears,
Our faith, triumphant o'er our fears,
Are all with thee,—are all with thee!

(From The Building of the Ship)

NO MORE BOOZE

Anonymous

There was a little man and he had a little can,
And he used to rush the growler;
He went to the saloon on a Sunday afternoon,
And you ought to hear the bartender holler:

Chorus:
　　No more booze, no more booze,
　　No more booze on Sunday;
　　No more booze, no more booze,
　　Got to get your can filled Monday.

She's the only girl I love,
With a face like a horse and buggy.
Leaning up against the lake,
O fireman! save my child!

The chambermaid came to my door,
"Get up, you lazy sinner,
We need those sheets for table-cloths
And it's almost time for dinner."

Chorus: No more booze, etc.

A VISIT FROM ST. NICHOLAS

Clement C. Moore

'Twas the night before Christmas, when all through the
    house
Not a creature was stirring, not even a mouse;
The stockings were hung by the chimney with care,
In hopes that St. Nicholas soon would be there;
The children were nestled all snug in their beds,
While visions of sugar-plums danced in their heads;
And mamma in her kerchief, and I in my cap,
Had just settled our brains for a long winter's nap,—
When out on the lawn there arose such a clatter,
I sprang from my bed to see what was the matter.
Away to the window I flew like a flash,
Tore open the shutters and threw up the sash.
The moon on the breast of the new-fallen snow
Gave a lustre of midday to objects below;
When, what to my wondering eyes should appear,
But a miniature sleigh and eight tiny reindeer,
With a little old driver, so lively and quick
I knew in a moment it must be St. Nick.
More rapid than eagles his coursers they came,
And he whistled and shouted, and called them by name:
"Now, Dasher! now, Dancer! now, Prancer and Vixen!
On, Comet! on, Cupid! on, Donder and Blitzen!
To the top of the porch, to the top of the wall!
Now dash away, dash away, dash away all!"
As dry leaves that before the wild hurricane fly,
When they meet with an obstacle, mount to the sky,

So up to the house-top the coursers they flew,
With the sleigh full of toys,—and St. Nicholas too.
And then in a twinkling I heard on the roof
The prancing and pawing of each little hoof.
As I drew in my head, and was turning around,
Down the chimney St. Nicholas came with a bound.
He was dressed all in fur from his head to his foot,
And his clothes were all tarnished with ashes and soot;
A bundle of toys he had flung on his back,
And he looked like a pedler just opening his pack.
His eyes how they twinkled! his dimples how merry!
His cheeks were like roses, his nose like a cherry;
His droll little mouth was drawn up like a bow,
And the beard on his chin was as white as the snow.
The stump of a pipe he held tight in his teeth,
And the smoke it encircled his head like a wreath.
He had a broad face and a little round belly
That shook, when he laughed, like a bowl full of jelly.
He was chubby and plump,—a right jolly old elf,
And I laughed, when I saw him, in spite of myself.
A wink of his eye and a twist of his head
Soon gave me to know I had nothing to dread.
He spoke not a word, but went straight to his work,
And filled all the stockings; then turned with a jerk,
And laying his finger aside of his nose,
And giving a nod, up the chimney he rose.
He sprang to his sleigh, to his team gave a whistle,
And away they all flew like the down of a thistle;
But I heard him exclaim, ere he drove out of sight,
"Happy Christmas to all, and to all a good-night!"

THE GLOVE AND THE LIONS

James Henry Leigh Hunt

King Francis was a hearty king, and loved a royal sport,
And one day, as his lions fought, sat looking on the court.
The nobles filled the benches, with the ladies in their pride,
And 'mongst them sat the Count de Lorge, with one for whom he
sighed:
And truly 'twas a gallant thing to see that crowning show,
Valor and love, and a king above, and the royal beasts below.

Ramped and roared the lions, with horrid laughing jaws;
They bit, they glared, gave blows like beams, a wind went with
their paws;
With wallowing might and stifled roar they rolled on one another,
Till all the pit with sand and mane was in a thunderous smother;
The bloody foam above the bars came whisking through the air;
Said Francis then, "Faith, gentlemen, we're better here than there."

De Lorge's love o'erheard the King, a beauteous lively dame,
With smiling lips and sharp bright eyes, which always seemed the
same;
She thought, The Count my lover is brave as brave can be;
He surely would do wondrous things to show his love of me;
King, ladies, lovers, all look on; the occasion is divine;
I'll drop my glove, to prove his love; great glory will be mine.

She dropped her glove, to prove his love, then looked at him and
smiled;
He bowed, and in a moment leaped among the lions wild:
The leap was quick, return was quick, he has regained his place,
Then threw the glove, but not with love, right in the lady's face.
"By Heaven," said Francis, "rightly done!" and he rose from
where he sat;
"No love," quoth he, "but vanity, sets love a task like that."

LAMENT FOR IMOGEN

William Shakespeare

Fear no more the heat o' the sun,
    Nor the furious winter's rages;
Thou thy worldly task hast done,
    Home art gone, and ta'en thy wages:
Golden lads and girls all must,
As chimney-sweepers, come to dust.

Fear no more the frown o' the great;
    Thou art past the tyrant's stroke;
Care no more to clothe and eat;
    To thee the reed is as the oak:
The sceptre, learning, physic, must
All follow this, and come to dust.

Fear no more the lightning-flash,
   Nor the all-dreaded thunder-stone;
Fear not slander, censure rash;
   Thou hast finish'd joy and moan:
All lovers young, all lovers must
Consign to thee, and come to dust.

No exorciser harm thee!
Nor no witchcraft charm thee!
Ghost unlaid forbear thee!
Nothing ill come near thee!
Quiet consummation have;
And renowned be thy grave!
            (From Cymbeline)

INTREAT ME NOT TO LEAVE THEE

Holy Bible, Ruth 1:16–17

16 And Ruth said, Intreat me not to leave thee, or to return from following after thee: for whither thou goest, I will go; and where thou lodgest, I will lodge: thy people shall be my people, and thy God my God:

17 Where thou diest, will I die, and there will I be buried: the Lord do so to me, and more also, if ought but death part thee and me.

THE DEATH OF SOCRATES

(Socrates, an Athenian philosopher, was condemned to death by the authorities because of alleged impiety and innovation. His friends came to his prison to offer him an easy escape through the bribery of the officials. But the seventy-year-old leader of the revolting party refused, telling them "Be of good cheer, and say that you are burying my body only." In one of the great passages of the world's literature Plato tells the rest of the story.)

You, Simmias and Cebes, and all other men, will depart at some time or other. Me already, as the tragic poet would say, the voice of fate calls. Soon I must drink the poison; and I think that I had better repair to the bath first, in order that the women may not have the trouble of washing my body after I am dead.

When he had done speaking Crito said: And have you any commands for us, Socrates—anything to say about your children, or any other matter in which we can serve you?

Nothing particular, he said: only, as I have always told you, I would have you look to yourselves; that is a service which you may always be doing to me and mine as well as to yourselves. And you need not make professions; for if you take no thought for yourselves and walk not according to the precepts which I have given you, not now for the first time, the warmth of your professions will be of no avail.

We will do our best, said Crito. But in what way would you have us bury you?

In any way that you like; only you must get hold of me, and take care that I do not walk away from you. Then he turned to us, and added with a smile:—I cannot make Crito believe that I am the same Socrates who has been talking and conducting the argument; he fancies that I am the other Socrates whom he will soon see, a dead body—and he asks, How shall he bury me? And though I have spoken many words in the endeavour to show that when I have drunk the poison I shall leave you and go to the joys of the blessed,—these words of mine, with which I have comforted you and myself, have had, as I perceive, no effect upon Crito. And therefore I want you to be surety for me now, as he was surety for me at the trial. But let the promise be of another sort; for he was my surety to the Judges that I would remain, but you must be my surety to him that I shall not remain, but go away and depart; and then he will suffer less at my death, and not be grieved when he sees my body being burned or buried. I would not have him sorrow at my hard lot, or say at the burial, Thus we lay out Socrates, or, Thus we follow him to the grave or bury him; for false words are not only evil in themselves, but they infect the soul with evil. Be of good cheer, then, my dear Crito, and say that you are burying my body only, and do with that as is usual, and as you think best.

When he had spoken these words he arose and went into the bath-chamber with Crito, who bade us wait; and we waited, talking and thinking of . . . the greatness of our sorrow; he was like a father of whom we were being bereaved, and we were about to pass the rest of our lives as orphans. . . . Now the hour of sunset was near, for a good deal of time had passed while he was within. When he came out, he sat down with us again . . . but not much was said. Soon the jailer . . . entered and stood by him, saying: To you, Socrates, who I know to be the noblest and gentlest and best of all who ever came to this place, I will not impute the angry feelings of other men, who rage and swear at me when, in obedi-ence to the authorities, I bid them drink the poison—indeed I am sure that you will not be angry with me; for others, as you are aware, and not I, are the guilty cause. And so fare you well, and try to bear lightly what must needs be; you know my errand. Then bursting into tears he turned away and went out.

Socrates looked at him and said: I return your good wishes and will do as you bid. Then turning to us, he said, How charming the man is; since I have been in prison he has always been coming to see me, and now see how generously he sorrows for me. But we must do as he says, Crito; let the cup be brought, if the poison is prepared; if not, let the attendant prepare some.

Yet, said Crito, the sun is still upon the hilltops, and many a one has taken the draught late; and after the announcement has been made to him he has eaten and drunk, and indulged in sensual de-lights; do not hasten then, there is still time.

Socrates said: Yes, Crito, and they of whom you speak are right in doing thus, for they think that they will gain by the delay; but I am right in not doing thus, for I do not think that I should gain anything by drinking the poison a little later; I should be sparing and saving a life which is already gone; I could only laugh at my-self for this. Please then do as I say, and not to refuse me.

Crito, when he heard this, made a sign to the servant; and the servant went in, and remained for some time, and then returned with the jailer carrying the cup of poison. Socrates said, You, my good friend, who are experienced in these matters, shall give me directions how I am to proceed. The man answered: You have only to walk about until your legs are heavy, and then to lie down, and the poison will act. At the same time he handed the cup to Soc-rates, who in the easiest and gentlest manner, without the least fear or change of color or feature, looking at the man with all his eyes, as his manner was, took the cup and said: What do you say about making a libation out of this cup to any god? May I or not? The man answered: We only prepare, Socrates, just so much as we deem enough. I understand, he said; yet I may and must pray to the gods to prosper my journey from this to that of the other world—may this then, which is my prayer, be granted to me. Then, holding the cup to his lips, quite readily and cheerfully he drank the poison.

And hitherto most of us had been able to control our sorrow; but now when we saw him drinking, and saw too that he had finished the draught, we could no longer forbear, and in spite of myself my own tears were flowing fast; so that I covered my face and wept over myself; for certainly I was not weeping over him, but at the thought of my own calamity in having lost such a companion. Nor was I the first, for Crito, when he found himself unable to restrain his tears, had got up and moved away, and I followed; and at that moment Apollodorus, who had been weeping all the time, broke out into a loud cry which made cowards of us all. Socrates alone retained his calmness: What is this strange outcry? he said. I sent away the women mainly in order that they might not offend in this way, for I have heard that a man should die in peace. Be quiet, then, and have patience. When we heard that, we were ashamed, and restrained our tears; and he walked about until, as he said, his legs began to fail, and then he lay on his back, according to the directions, and the man who gave him the poison now and then looked at his feet and legs; and after a while he pressed his foot hard and asked him if he could feel; and he said No; and then his leg, and so upwards and upwards, and showed us that he was cold and stiff. And then Socrates felt them himself, and said, When the poison reaches the heart, that will be the end. He was beginning to grow cold about the groin, when he uncovered his face (for he had covered himself up) and said,—they were his last words,—Crito, I owe a cock to Asclepius; will you remember to pay the debt? The debt shall be paid, said Crito; is there anything else? There was no answer to this question; but in a minute or two a movement was heard, and the attendant uncovered him; his eyes were set, and Crito closed his eyes and mouth.

Such was the end of our friend, whom I may truly call the wisest, the justest, and best of all the men whom I have ever known.

(From Plato's Phaedo, transl. Benjamin Jowett)

AMERICA THE BEAUTIFUL

Katharine Lee Bates

O beautiful for spacious skies,
For amber waves of grain,
For purple mountain majesties
Above the fruited plain!

America! America!
God shed His grace on thee
And crown thy good with brotherhood
From sea to shining sea!

O beautiful for pilgrim feet,
Whose stern, impassioned stress
A thoroughfare for freedom beat
Across the wilderness!
America! America!
God mend thine every flaw,
Confirm thy soul in self-control,
Thy liberty in law!

O beautiful for heroes proved
In liberating strife,
Who more than self their country loved,
And mercy more than life!
America! America!
May God thy gold refine
Till all success be nobleness
And every gain divine!

O beautiful for patriot dream
That sees beyond the years
Thine alabaster cities gleam
Undimmed by human tears!
America! America!
God shed His grace on thee
And crown thy good with brotherhood
From sea to shining sea!

THE LORD IS MY SHEPHERD

Holy Bible, Psalm 23

1 The Lord is my shepherd; I shall not want.

2 He maketh me to lie down in green pastures; he leadeth me beside the still waters.

3 He restoreth my soul; he leadeth me in the paths of righteousness for his name's sake.

4 Yea, though I walk through the valley of the shadow of death,

I will fear no evil; for thou art with me; thy rod and thy staff they comfort me.

5 Thou preparest a table before me in the presence of mine enemies: thou anointest my head with oil; my cup runneth over.

6 Surely goodness and mercy shall follow me all the days of my life; and I will dwell in the house of the LORD for ever.

THE BIVOUAC OF THE DEAD

Theodore O'Hara

The muffled drum's sad roll has beat
    The soldier's last tattoo!
No more on life's parade shall meet
    The brave and fallen few.
On Fame's eternal camping ground
    Their silent tents are spread,
And glory guards with solemn round
    The bivouac of the dead.

No rumor of the foe's advance
    Now swells upon the wind,
Nor troubled thought of midnight haunts,
    Of loved ones left behind;
No vision of the morrow's strife
    The warrior's dreams alarms,
No braying horn or screaming fife
    At dawn to call to arms.

Their shivered swords are red with rust,
    Their plumèd heads are bowed,
Their haughty banner, trailed in dust,
    Is now their martial shroud—
And plenteous funeral tears have washed
    The red stains from each brow,
And the proud forms by battle gashed
    Are free from anguish now.

The neighing troop, the flashing blade,
    The bugle's stirring blast,
The charge,—the dreadful cannonade,
    The din and shout, are passed;

Nor war's wild notes, nor glory's peal
  Shall thrill with fierce delight
Those breasts that nevermore shall feel
  The rapture of the fight.

Like the fierce Northern hurricane
  That sweeps the great plateau,
Flushed with the triumph yet to gain,
  Come down the serried foe,
Who heard the thunder of the fray
  Break o'er the field beneath,
Knew the watchword of the day
  Was "Victory or death!"

Rest on, embalmed and sainted dead,
  Dear is the blood you gave—
No impious footstep here shall tread
  The herbage of your grave.
Nor shall your glory be forgot
  While Fame her record keeps,
Or honor points the hallowed spot
  Where valor proudly sleeps.

Yon marble minstrel's voiceless stone
  In deathless song shall tell,
When many a vanquished year hath flown,
  The story how you fell.
Nor wreck nor change, nor winter's blight,
  Nor time's remorseless doom,
Can dim one ray of holy light
  That gilds your glorious tomb.

LITTLE ANNIE ROONEY

Michael Nolan

A winning way, a pleasant smile,
Dress'd so neat but quite in style,
Merry chaff your time to while,
Has little Annie Rooney;

Ev'ry ev'ning, rain or shine,
I make a call twixt eight and nine,
On her who shortly will be mine,
Little Annie Rooney.

Chorus:
> She's my sweetheart, I'm her beau,
> She's my Annie, I'm her Joe,
> Soon we'll marry, never to part,
> Little Annie Rooney is my sweetheart.

The parlor's small but neat and clean,
And set with taste so seldom seen,
And you can bet the household queen
Is little Annie Rooney!
The fire burns cheerfully and bright,
As a family circle round, each night
We form and every one's delight
Is little Annie Rooney. (*Chorus.*)

We've been engaged close on a year,
The happy time is drawing near,
I'll wed the one I love so dear,
Little Annie Rooney!
My friends declare I am in jest,
Until the time comes will not rest,
But one who knows its value best,
Is little Annie Rooney. (*Chorus.*)

When married we'll so happy be,
I love her and she loves me,
Happier wife you'll never see,
Than Little Annie Rooney.
In a little cozy home,
No more from her I'll care to roam;
She'll greet you all when-e'er you come,
My Little Annie Rooney. (*Chorus.*)

* * *

Was this the face that launched a thousand ships
And burnt the topless towers of Ilium?
Sweet Helen, make me immortal with a kiss.
(From Marlowe's Tragedy of Dr. Faustus)

BANNOCKBURN

Robert Burns

Scots, wha hae wi' Wallace bled,
Scots, wham Bruce has aften led,
Welcome to your gory bed,
    Or to victorie!

Now's the day, and now's the hour;
See the front o' battle lour;
See approach proud Edward's power—
    Chains and slaverie!

Wha will be a traitor knave?
Wha can fill a coward's grave?
Wha sae base as be a slave?
    Let him turn and flee!

Wha, for Scotland's King and Law,
Freedom's sword will strongly draw,
Free-man stand, or Free-man fa',
    Let him follow me!

By Oppression's woes and pains!
By your sons in servile chains!
We will drain our dearest veins,
    But they shall be free!

Lay the proud Usurpers low!
Tyrants fall in every foe!
Liberty's in every blow!—
    Let us do or die!

A LITTLE LEARNING IS A DANGEROUS THING

Alexander Pope

A *little learning* is a dangerous thing;
Drink deep, or taste not the Pierian spring:
There shallow draughts intoxicate the brain,
And drinking largely sobers us again.

76

Fired at first sight with what the muse imparts,
In fearless youth we tempt the heights of arts,
While from the bounded level of our mind,
Short views we take, nor see the lengths behind;
But more advanced, behold with strange surprise
New distant scenes of endless science rise!
So pleased at first the towering Alps we try,
Mount o'er the vales and seem to tread the sky,
The eternal snows appear already pass'd,
And the first clouds and mountains seem the last:
But, those attain'd, we tremble to survey
The growing labours of the lengthen'd way,
The increasing prospect tires our wandering eyes,
Hills peep o'er hills, and Alps on Alp arise!

(From An Essay on Criticism)

THERE WAS A LITTLE GIRL

Anonymous

There was a little girl,
And she had a little curl
Right in the middle of her forehead.
When she was good
She was very, very good,
And when she was bad she was horrid.

One day she went upstairs,
When her parents, unawares,
In the kitchen were occupied with meals
And she stood upon her head
In her little trundle-bed,
And then began hooraying with her heels.

Her mother heard the noise,
And she thought it was the boys
A-playing at a combat in the attic;
But when she climbed the stair,
And found Jemima there,
She took and she did spank her most emphatic.

(Sometimes attributed to
Henry Wadsworth Longfellow)

HOME-THOUGHTS, FROM ABROAD

Robert Browning

Oh, to be in England
  Now that April's there,
And whoever wakes in England
  Sees, some morning, unaware,
That the lowest boughs and the brush-wood sheaf
Round the elm-tree bole are in tiny leaf,
While the chaffinch sings on the orchard bough
In England—now!

And after April, when May follows,
And the whitethroat builds, and all the swallows!
Hark, where my blossomed pear-tree in the hedge
  Leans to the field and scatters on the clover
Blossoms and dewdrops—at the bent spray's edge—
  That's the wise thrush; he sings each song twice over,
Lest you should think he never could recapture
The first fine careless rapture!
And though the fields look rough with hoary dew,
All will be gay when noontide wakes anew
The buttercups, the little children's dower
—Far brighter than this gaudy melon-flower!

FAREWELL TO THE OLD GUARD

Napoleon Bonaparte

  Soldiers of my Old Guard: I bid you farewell. For twenty years
I have constantly accompanied you on the road to honor and glory.
In these latter times, as in the days of our prosperity, you have
invariably been models of courage and fidelity. With men such as
you our cause could not be lost; but the war would have been
interminable; it would have been civil war, and that would have
entailed deeper misfortunes on France.
  I have sacrificed all my interests to those of the country.
  I go, but you, my friends, will continue to serve France. Her
happiness was my only thought. It will still be the object of my
wishes. Do not regret my fate; if I have consented to survive, it is to

78

serve your glory. I intend to write the history of the great achieve-
ments we have performed together. Adieu, my friends. Would I
could press you all to my heart.

I WILL LIFT UP MINE EYES UNTO THE HILLS

Holy Bible, Psalm 121

1 I will lift up mine eyes unto the hills, from whence cometh
my help.

2 My help cometh from the Lord, which made heaven and
earth.

3 He will not suffer thy foot to be moved: he that keepeth thee
will not slumber.

4 Behold, he that keepeth Israel shall neither slumber nor sleep.

5 The Lord is thy keeper: the Lord is thy shade upon thy right
hand.

6 The sun shall not smite thee by day, nor the moon by night.

7 The Lord shall preserve thee from all evil: he shall preserve
thy soul.

8 The Lord shall preserve thy going out and thy coming in from
this time forth, and even for evermore.

THE CHARACTER OF A HAPPY LIFE

Sir Henry Wotton

How happy is he born or taught
    That serveth not another's will;
Whose armor is his honest thought
    And simple truth his utmost skill!

Whose passions not his masters are,
    Whose soul is still prepared for death,
Untied unto the world by care
    Of public fame or private breath;

Who envies none that chance doth raise
    Nor vice; hath ever understood
How deepest wounds are given by praise;
    Nor rules of state, but rules of good:

Who hath his life from rumors freed,
   Whose conscience is his strong retreat;
Whose state can neither flatterers feed,
   Nor ruin make oppressors great;

Who God doth late and early pray
   More of His grace than gifts to lend;
And entertains the harmless day
   With a religious book or friend;

—This man is freed from servile bonds
   Of hope to rise, or fear to fall;
Lord of himself, though not of lands;
   And having nothing, yet hath all.

THE WALRUS AND THE CARPENTER

Lewis Carroll

The sun was shining on the sea,
   Shining with all his might:
He did his very best to make
   The billows smooth and bright—
And this was odd, because it was
   The middle of the night.

The moon was shining sulkily,
   Because she thought the sun
Had got no business to be there
   After the day was done—
"It's very rude of him," she said,
   "To come and spoil the fun!"

The sea was wet as wet could be,
   The sands were dry as dry,
You could not see a cloud, because
   No cloud was in the sky:
No birds were flying overhead—
   There were no birds to fly.

The Walrus and the Carpenter
   Were walking close at hand:

They wept like anything to see
    Such quantities of sand:
"If this were only cleared away,"
    They said, "it would be grand!"

"If seven maids with seven mops
    Swept it for half a year,
Do you suppose," the Walrus said,
    "That they could get it clear?"
"I doubt it," said the Carpenter,
    And shed a bitter tear.

"O Oysters, come and walk with us!"
    The Walrus did beseech.
"A pleasant walk, a pleasant talk,
    Along the briny beach:
We cannot do with more than four,
    To give a hand to each."

The eldest Oyster looked at him,
    But never a word he said:
The eldest Oyster winked his eye,
    And shook his heavy head—
Meaning to say he did not choose
    To leave the oyster-bed.

But four young Oysters hurried up,
    All eager for the treat:
Their coats were brushed, their faces washed,
    Their shoes were clean and neat—
And this was odd, because, you know,
    They hadn't any feet.

Four other Oysters followed them,
    And yet another four;
And thick and fast they came at last,
    And more, and more, and more—
All hopping through the frothy waves,
    And scrambling to the shore.

The Walrus and the Carpenter
    Walked on a mile or so,

And then they rested on a rock
  Conveniently low:
And all the little Oysters stood
  And waited in a row.

"The time has come," the Walrus said,
  "To talk of many things:
Of shoes—and ships—and sealing wax—
  Of cabbages—and kings—
And why the sea is boiling hot—
  And whether pigs have wings."

"But wait a bit," the Oysters cried,
  "Before we have our chat;
For some of us are out of breath,
  And all of us are fat!"
"No hurry!" said the Carpenter,
  They thanked him much for that.

"A loaf of bread," the Walrus said,
  "Is what we chiefly need:
Pepper and vinegar besides
  Are very good indeed—
Now, if you're ready, Oysters dear,
  We can begin to feed."

"But not on us!" the Oysters cried,
  Turning a little blue.
"After such kindness, that would be
  A dismal thing to do!"
"The night is fine," the Walrus said,
  "Do you admire the view?

"It was so kind of you to come!
  And you are very nice!"
The Carpenter said nothing but
  "Cut us another slice.
I wish you were not quite so deaf—
  I've had to ask you twice!"

"It seems a shame," the Walrus said,
  "To play them such a trick.

After we've brought them out so far,
    And made them trot so quick!"
The Carpenter said nothing but
    "The butter's spread too thick!"

"I weep for you," the Walrus said:
    "I deeply sympathize."
With sobs and tears he sorted out
    Those of the largest size,
Holding his pocket-handkerchief
    Before his streaming eyes.

"O Oysters," said the Carpenter,
    "You've had a pleasant run!
Shall we be trotting home again?"
    But answer came there none—
And this was scarcely odd, because
    They'd eaten every one.

THE MOUNTAINS IN LABOR

The Mountains were said to be in labor, and uttered most dreadful groans. People came together far and near to see what birth would be produced; and, after they waited a considerable time in expectation, out crept a Mouse.

(From Aesop's Fables)

THE THREE FISHERS

Charles Kingsley

Three fishers went sailing out into the west—
    Out into the west as the sun went down;
Each thought of the woman who loved him the best,
    And the children stood watching them out of the town;
For men must work, and women must weep;
And there's little to earn, and many to keep,
    Though the harbor bar be moaning.

Three wives sat up in the lighthouse tower,
    And trimmed the lamps as the sun went down;

83

And they looked at the squall, and they looked at the shower,
    And the rack it came rolling up, ragged and brown;
But men must work, and women must weep,
Though storms be sudden, and waters deep,
    And the harbor bar is moaning.

Three corpses lay out on the shining sands
    In the morning gleam as the tide went down,
And the women are watching and wringing their hands,
    For those who will never come back to the town;
For men must work, and women must weep,—
And the sooner it's over, the sooner to sleep,—
    And good by to the bar and its moaning.

SONG FOR A LITTLE HOUSE

Christopher Morley

I'm glad our house is a little house,
    Not too tall nor too wide:
I'm glad the hovering butterflies
    Feel free to come inside.

Our little house is a friendly house,
    It is not shy or vain;
It gossips with the talking trees,
    And makes friends with the rain.

And quick leaves cast a shimmer of green
    Against our whited walls,
And in the phlox, the courteous bees
    Are paying duty calls.

SONG OF THE CHATTAHOOCHEE

Sidney Lanier

Out of the hills of Habersham,
    Down the valleys of Hall,
I hurry amain to reach the plain,
Run the rapid and leap the fall,
Split at the rock and together again,

Accept my bed, or narrow or wide,
And flee from folly on every side
With a lover's pain to attain the plain
    Far from the hills of Habersham,
    Far from the valleys of Hall.

All down the hills of Habersham,
    All through the valley of Hall,
The rushes cried *Abide, abide,*
The willful waterweeds held me thrall,
The laving laurel turned my tide,
The ferns and the fondling grass said *Stay,*
The dewberry dipped for to work delay,
And the little reeds sighed *Abide, abide,*
    Here in the hills of Habersham,
    Here in the valleys of Hall.

High o'er the hills of Habersham,
    Veiling the valleys of Hall,
The hickory told me manifold
Fair tales of shade, the poplar tall
Wrought me her shadowy self to hold,
The chestnut, the oak, the walnut, the pine,
Overleaning, with flickering meaning and sign,
Said, *Pass not, so cold, these manifold*
    Deep shades of the hills of Habersham,
    These glades in the valleys of Hall.

And oft in the hills of Habersham,
    And oft in the valleys of Hall,
The white quartz shone, and the smooth brook-stone
Did bar me of passage with friendly brawl,
And many a luminous jewel lone
—Crystals clear or a-cloud with mist,
Ruby, garnet, and amethyst—
Made lures with the lights of streaming stone
    In the clefts of the hills of Habersham,
    In the beds of the valleys of Hall.

But oh, not the hills of Habersham,
    And oh, not the valleys of Hall
Avail: I am fain for to water the plain.
Downward the voices of Duty call—
Downward, to toil and be mixed with the main,

The dry fields burn, and the mills are to turn,
And a myriad flowers mortally yearn,
And the lordly main from beyond the plain
    Calls o'er the hills of Habersham,
    Calls through the valleys of Hall.

THE FLAG GOES BY

Henry Holcomb Bennett

    Hats off!
Along the street there comes
A blare of bugles, a ruffle of drums,
A flash of color beneath the sky:
    Hats off!
The flag is passing by!

Blue and crimson and white it shines,
Over the steel-tipped, ordered lines.
    Hats off!
The colors before us fly;
But more than the flag is passing by:

Sea-fights and land-fights, grim and great,
Fought to make and to save the State;
Weary marches and sinking ships;
Cheers of victory on dying lips;

Days of plenty and years of peace;
March of a strong land's swift increase;
Equal justice, right and law,
Stately honor and reverend awe;

Sign of a nation great and strong
To ward her people from foreign wrong;
Pride and glory and honor,—all
Live in the colors to stand or fall.

    Hats off!
Along the street there comes
A blare of bugles, a ruffle of drums;
And loyal hearts are beating high:
    Hats off!
The flag is passing by!

THE SANDS OF DEE

Charles Kingsley

"O Mary, go and call the cattle home,
    And call the cattle home,
    And call the cattle home,
    Across the sands of Dee!"
The western wind was wild and dank with foam,
    And all alone went she.

The western tide crept up along the sand,
    And o'er and o'er the sand,
    And round and round the sand,
    As far as eye could see.
The rolling mist came down and hid the land:
    And never home came she.

"Oh! is it weed, or fish, or floating hair—
    A tress of golden hair,
    A drowned maiden's hair
    Above the nets at sea?
Was never salmon yet that shone so fair
    Among the stakes on Dee."

They rowed her in across the rolling foam,
    The cruel, crawling foam,
    The cruel, hungry foam,
    To her grave beside the sea:
But still the boatmen hear her call the cattle home
    Across the sands of Dee.

RETRIBUTION

Henry Wadsworth Longfellow

Though the mills of God grind slowly,
Yet they grind exceeding small;
Though with patience he stands waiting,
With exactness grinds he all.

CORONATION DAY SERMON

Cardinal Mercier

Jerusalem was made an habitation of strangers;
Her festival days were turned into mourning.
I Maccabees 1:40–41

BELOVED BRETHREN: We ought to have met together here to celebrate the 86th anniversary of our national independence.

To-day, in fourteen years' time, our restored cathedrals and our
rebuilt churches will be thrown widely open; the crowds will
surge in; our King Albert, standing on his throne, will bow his
unconquered head before the King of Kings; the Queen and the
Royal Princes will surround him; we shall hear again the joyous
peals of our bells, and throughout the whole country, under the
vaulted arches of our churches, the Belgians, hand in hand, will
renew their vows to their God, their Sovereign, and their liberty,
while the bishops and the priests, interpreters of the soul of
the nation, will intone a triumphant Te Deum in a common
transport of joyous thanksgiving.

To-day the hymn of joy dies on our lips.

The Jewish people in captivity at Babylon, sitting in tears on
the banks of the Euphrates, watched the waters of the river flow
by. Their dumb harps were hung on the willows by the bank.
Who amongst them would have the courage to sing the song of
Jehovah in a strange land? "O Jerusalem," cried the Psalmist, "if
ever I forget thee, let my right hand wither, let my tongue cleave
to the roof of my mouth if I do not remember thee; if thou art
no longer the beginning of my joys."

The Psalm ends in imprecations: but we do not allow ourselves
to repeat them: we are not of the Old Testament, tolerating the
laws of retaliation: "An eye for an eye, and a tooth for a tooth."
Our lips, purified by the fire of Christian charity, utter no words
of hate. To hate is to make it one's object to do harm to others
and to delight in so doing. Whatever may be our sufferings, we
must not wish to show hatred towards those who have inflicted
them. Our national unity is joined with a feeling of universal
brotherhood. But even this feeling of universal brotherhood is
dominated by our respect for the unconditional justice, without
which no relationship is possible, either between individuals or
between nations.

And that is why, with St. Thomas Aquinas, the most authoritative teacher of Christian Theology, we proclaim that public retribution is commendable.

Crimes, violation of justice, outrage on the public peace whether enacted by an individual or by a group must be repressed. Men's minds are stirred up, tortured, uneasy, as long as the guilty one is not put back in his place, as the strong, healthy, colloquial expression has it. To put men and things back in their places is to reëstablish order, readjust the balance and restore peace on a just basis.

Public retribution in this sense may distress the affected sentimentality of a weak nature; all the same, it is, says St. Thomas, the expression and the decree of the highest, the purest form of charity, and of the zeal which is its flame. It does not make a target of suffering, but a weapon wherewith to avenge outraged justice.

How can one love order without hating disorder; intelligently wish for peace without expelling that which is destroying it; love a brother, that is to say wish him well, without desiring that willingly, or by force, his will shall bend before the unalterable edicts of justice and truth?

It is from these heights that one must view the war in order to understand the greatness of its extent.

Once more, perhaps, you will find yourself face to face with effeminate natures for whom the war means nothing beyond explosions of mines, bursting of shells, massacres of men, spilling of blood, piling up of corpses. You will meet politicians of narrow vision who see no further stake in a battle beyond the interest of one day, the taking of so much ground, of a stretch of country, or of a province.

But no! If, in spite of its horrors, war, I mean a just war, has so much austere beauty, it is because war brings out the disinterested enthusiasm of a whole people, which gives, or is prepared to give, its most precious possession, even life itself for the defense and the vindication of things which cannot be weighed, which cannot be calculated, but which can never be swallowed up: Justice, Honor, Peace, Liberty!

Do you not feel that, in these two years, the war, the ardent unflagging interest which you give to it, purifies you, separates your higher nature from the dross, draws you away to uplift you towards something nobler and better than yourselves?

You are rising towards the ideals of justice and honor. They support you and draw you upwards.

And, because this ideal, if it is not a vain abstraction, which evaporates like the phantasies of a dream, must have its foundation in a living subject, I am never tired of maintaining this truth, which holds us all under its yoke. God reveals Himself as the Master, the Director of events, and of our wills, the holy Master of the universal conscience.

Ah, if we could clasp in our arms our heroes who are fighting for us over there, or are awaiting anxiously in the trenches their turn to go under fire; if we could take them by surprise, and feel the beating of their hearts, would not each one of them say to us: I am doing my duty, I am sacrificing myself on the altar of justice?

And you, wives and mothers, tell us in your turn of the beauty of these tragic years; wives, whose every thought goes, sad, but resigned, towards the absent one, bringing him your hopes, your long expectation, your prayers. Mothers, whose divided existence is consumed in unceasing anguish, you have given your sons, and you will not take them back; we stand breathless with unceasing admiration before you.

The head of one of our noblest families wrote to me: "Our son in the 7th Line Regiment has fallen; my wife and I are broken-hearted, and yet, if it had to be, we would give him again."

One of the curates of the capital has been condemned to twelve years penal servitude. I was allowed to go into his cell to embrace and to bless him. "I have three brothers at the front," he said, "and I think I am here chiefly because I helped the youngest, he is only seventeen—to rejoin the elder ones; one of my sisters is in a neighbouring cell, but, thank God, my mother is not left alone; indeed she has sent us a message to say so; she does not weep."

Is it not true that our mothers make us think of the mother of the Maccabees?

What lessons of moral greatness there are to be learnt here around us, and in exile and in the prisons, and in the concentration camps, in Holland and in Germany!

Do we think enough of what those brave men must be suffering, who since the beginning of the war, from the morrow of the defense of Liège and Namur, or the retreat from Antwerp, saw their military career shattered, and now chafe and fret under their inability to bear arms; these guardians of our rights, and of our communal liberties, whose valor has reduced them to inaction?

It needs courage to throw oneself forward, but it needs no less to hold oneself back. Sometimes it is more noble to suffer in silence than to act.

And what of these two years of calm submission by the Belgian people before the inevitable; this unshakable tenacity, which moved a humble woman, before whom the possibilities of an approaching conclusion of peace were being discussed, to say: "Oh, as for us, we must not worry; we can go on waiting." How beautiful is all this, and how full of instruction for the generations to come.

This is what you must look at, my brothers, the greatness of the nation in her sacrifice; our universal and enduring brotherhood in anguish and in mourning, and in the same unconquerable hope; this is what you must look at to appraise your Belgian fatherland at its true value.

Now the first exponents of this moral greatness are our soldiers. Until that day when they return to us, and when grateful Belgium acclaims the living, and places a halo of glory about the memory of her dead, let us build up for them in our hearts a permanent monument of sacred gratitude.

Let us pray for those who are no more. Let us exclude no one from our commiseration; the blood of Christ was shed for all. Some of them are atoning in Purgatory for the last remnants of their human weakness. It is for you to hasten their entry into Paradise. Succor the poor in distress, both the poor who are known to you and those who are ashamed to beg. Give of your abundance to those who are in need of the necessities of life. Be present at the Mass, which is celebrated every week in your parish churches for our dead soldiers; take your children with you, encourage them to communicate, and communicate with them.

Let us also pray for those who are still holding the firing line on the field of battle. Remember that, even at this moment, while I am speaking to you, some of them are in the agony of death. The prospect of eternity stretches out before them. Let us think of them, let us mortify ourselves for them, resign ourselves to God for them, and obtain for them a holy death.

"Our soldiers are our masters," wrote a French Academician yesterday; "they are our leaders, our teachers, our judges, our supporters, our true friends; let us be worthy of them, let us imitate them, so that we may not do less than our duty; they are always ready to do more than their own."

The hour of deliverance approaches, but it has not yet struck. Let us be patient. Let us not suffer our courage to waver. Let us surrender to Divine Providence the work of making perfect our national probation.

Young women, young girls, let me ask if you are thinking seriously enough about the gravity of this present time? I entreat you not to turn aside from the mourning of your country. There are attitudes, there are ways of behaving which are an insult to grief.

For your modesty is at all times a virtue and a halo of glory; but to-day it is in addition a patriotic duty.

You, also, must think of the privations and of the endurance of our soldiers.

Let us all try to adopt the great principle of austerity in our lives.

"How much," continues the patriot whom I have just quoted, "how much ought we, in the relatively easy conditions and the less exposed districts, which are ours, and which do not deserve the name of fire zones, to endeavor to reduce and simplify our needs, and like the soldiers, though in our own sphere, to show more concentrated energy. Let us not allow ourselves a moment's distraction or relaxation. Let us devote every minute in our lives to the magnificent cause for which our brothers are so devoutly sacrificing theirs.

"And, just as our heroes at the front show us a wonderful and consoling spectacle of indissoluble unity, of a brotherhood in arms which nothing can destroy, even so, in our ranks, less compact and well-disciplined though they may be, we shall earnestly strive to maintain the same patriotic sense of union. We will respect the truce imposed on our quarrels by the one great Cause which alone ought to use and absorb all our powers of attack and combat; and if there are any godless or unfortunate people, who fail to understand the urgency and the beauty of this national precept, and insist, in spite of all, on keeping alive and fomenting the passions which divide us when other matters are concerned, we will turn aside our heads, and continue without answering them, to remain faithful to the pact of fellowship, of friendship, of loyal and true confidence which we have concluded with them, even in spite of themselves, under the great inspiration of the war."

The approaching date of the first centenary of our independence ought to find us stronger, more intrepid, more united than ever. Let us prepare ourselves for it with work, with patience and in true brotherhood.

When, in 1930, we recall the dark years of 1915–1916, they will appear to us as the brightest, the most majestic and, if, from to-day we resolve that they shall be so, the happiest and the most fruitful in our national history. *Per crucem ad lucem*—from the sacrifice flashes forth the light!

DE PROFUNDIS

Holy Bible, Psalm 130

1 Out of the depths have I cried unto thee, O Lord.

2 Lord, hear my voice: let thine ears be attentive to the voice of my supplications.

3 If thou, Lord, shouldest mark iniquities, O Lord, who shall stand?

4 But there is forgiveness with thee, that thou mayest be feared.

5 I wait for the Lord, my soul doth wait, and in his word do I hope.

6 My soul waiteth for the Lord more than they that watch for the morning; I say, more than they that watch for the morning.

7 Let Israel hope in the Lord: for with the Lord there is mercy, and with him is plenteous redemption.

8 And he shall redeem Israel from all his iniquities.

WHO IS SILVIA?

William Shakespeare

Who is Silvia? what is she,
   That all our swains commend her?
Holy, fair, and wise is she;
   The heaven such grace did lend her,
That she might admired be.

Is she kind as she is fair?
   For beauty lives with kindness.
Love doth to her eyes repair,
   To help him of his blindness,
And, being helped, inhabits there.

Then to Silvia let us sing,
   That Silvia is excelling;
She excels each mortal thing
   Upon the dull earth dwelling:
To her let us garlands bring.
   (From Two Gentlemen of Verona)

STAND TO YOUR GLASSES *

Anonymous

We meet 'neath the sounding rafter,
    And the walls around are bare;
As they shout back our peals of laughter
    It seems that the dead are there.
Then stand to your glasses, steady!
    We drink in our comrades' eyes:
One cup to the dead already—
    Hurrah for the next that dies!

Not here are the goblets glowing,
    Not here is the vintage sweet;
'Tis cold as our hearts are growing,
    And dark as the doom we meet.
But stand to your glasses, steady!
    And soon shall our pulses rise:
A cup to the dead already—
    Hurrah for the next that dies!

There's many a hand that's shaking,
    And many a cheek that's sunk;
But soon, though our hearts are breaking,
    They'll burn with the wine we've drunk.
Then stand to your glasses, steady!
    'Tis here the revival lies:
Quaff a cup to the dead already—
    Hurrah for the next that dies!

Time was when we laughed at others;
    We thought we were wiser then;
Ha! Ha! Let them think of their mothers,
    Who hope to see them again.
No! stand to your glasses, steady!
    The thoughtless here is the wise:
One cup to the dead already—
    Hurrah for the next that dies!

Not a sigh for the lot that darkles,
    Not a tear for the friends that sink;

---

* Supposed to have been written in India at the time of the plague; attributed
to both Alfred Domett and Bartholomew Dowling.

94

We'll fall, midst the wine-cup's sparkles,
   As mute as the wine we drink.
Come, stand to your glasses, steady!
   'Tis this that the respite buys:
A cup to the dead already—
   Hurrah for the next that dies!

There's a mist on the glass congealing,
   'Tis the hurricane's sultry breath;
And thus does the warmth of feeling
   Turn ice in the grasp of Death.
But stand to your glasses, steady!
   For a moment the vapor flies:
Quaff a cup to the dead already—
   Hurrah for the next that dies!

Who dreads to the dust returning?
   Who shrinks from the sable shore,
Where the high and haughty yearning
   Of the soul can sting no more?
No, stand to your glasses, steady!
   The world is a world of lies:
A cup to the dead already—
   And hurrah for the next that dies!

Cut off from the land that bore us,
   Betrayed by the land we find,
When the brightest have gone before us,
   And the dullest are most behind—
Stand, stand to your glasses, steady!
   'Tis all we have left to prize:
One cup to the dead already—
   Hurrah for the next that dies!

THE MAN AND HIS GOOSE

A certain Man had a Goose, which laid him a golden egg every
day. But, not contented with this, which rather increased than
abated his avarice, he was resolved to kill the Goose, and cut up
her belly, that so he might come at the inexhaustible treasure
which he fancied she had within her. He did so; and, to his great
sorrow and disappointment, found nothing.

(From Aesop's Fables)

A WISE OLD OWL

Edward Hersey Richards

A wise old owl sat on an oak,
The more he saw the less he spoke;
The less he spoke the more he heard;
Why aren't we like that wise old bird?

AFTER VISITING THE TOMB OF NAPOLEON

Robert G. Ingersoll

A little while ago I stood by the grave of Napoleon, a magnificent tomb of gilt and gold, fit almost for a dead deity, and gazed
upon the sarcophagus of black Egyptian marble where rests at last
the ashes of the restless man. I leaned over the balustrade and
thought about the career of the greatest soldier of the modern
world. I saw him walking upon the banks of the Seine contemplat-
ing suicide; I saw him at Toulon; I saw him putting down the
mob in the streets of Paris; I saw him at the head of the army of
Italy; I saw him crossing the bridge at Lodi with the tricolor in
his hand; I saw him in Egypt in the shadows of the pyramids; I
saw him conquer the Alps and mingle the eagle of France with
the eagles of the crags. I saw him at Marengo, at Ulm and Auster-
litz. I saw him in Russia, where the infantry of the snow and the
cavalry of the wild blast scattered his legions like Winter's withered leaves. I saw him at Leipsic in defeat and disaster, driven by
a million bayonets back upon Paris, clutched like a wild beast,
banished to Elba. I saw him escape and retake an Empire by the
force of his genius. I saw him upon the frightful field of Waterloo,
when chance and fate combined to wreck the fortunes of their
former King. And I saw him at St. Helena, with his hands crossed
behind him, gazing out upon the sad and solemn sea. I thought
of the orphans and widows he had made; of the tears that had
been shed for his glory and of the only woman who had ever loved
him pushed from his heart by the cold hand of ambition. And I
said I would rather have been a French peasant and worn wooden
shoes. I would rather have lived in a hut with a vine growing
over the door and the grapes growing purple in the kisses of the
Autumn sun. I would rather have been that poor peasant with my
loving wife by my side, knitting as the day died out of the sky,
with my children upon my knee and their arms about me. I would

rather have been that man and gone down to the tongueless silence of the dreamless dust than to have been that imperial impersonation of force and murder known as Napoleon the Great. And so I would ten thousand times.

INVICTUS

William Ernest Henley

Out of the night that covers me,
Black as the Pit from pole to pole,
I thank whatever gods may be
For my unconquerable soul.

In the fell clutch of circumstance
I have not winced nor cried aloud.
Under the bludgeonings of chance
My head is bloody, but unbowed.

Beyond this place of wrath and tears
Looms but the horror of the shade,
And yet the menace of the years
Finds and shall find me unafraid.

It matters not how strait the gate,
How charged with punishments the scroll,
I am the master of my fate;
I am the captain of my soul.

GUNGA DIN

Rudyard Kipling

You may talk o' gin and beer
When you're quartered safe out 'ere,
An' you're sent to penny-fights an' Aldershot it;
But when it comes to slaughter
You will do your work on water,
An' you'll lick the bloomin' boots of 'im that's got it.
Now in Injia's sunny clime,
Where I used to spend my time
A-servin' 'Er Majesty the Queen,
Of all them blackfaced crew

97

The finest man I knew
Was our regimental bhisti, Gunga Din.
     He was "Din! Din! Din!
  "You limpin' lump o' brick-dust, Gunga Din!
    "Hi! slippery *hitherao*!
    "Water, get it! *Panee lao*!
  "You squidgy-nosed old idol, Gunga Din."

The uniform 'e wore
Was nothin' much before,
An' rather less than 'arf o' that be'ind,
For a piece o' twisty rag
An' a goatskin water-bag
Was all the field-equipment 'e could find.
When the sweatin' troop-train lay
In a sidin' through the day,
Where the 'eat would make your bloomin' eyebrows crawl.
We shouted "Harry By!"
Till our throats were bricky-dry,
Then we wopped 'im 'cause 'e couldn't serve us all.
     It was "Din! Din! Din!
  "You 'eathen, where the mischief 'ave you been?
    "You put some *juldee* in it
    "Or I'll *marrow* you this minute
  "If you don't fill up my helmet, Gunga Din!"

'E would dot an' carry one
Till the longest day was done;
An' 'e didn't seem to know the use o' fear.
If we charged or broke or cut,
You could bet your bloomin' nut,
E'd be waitin' fifty paces right flank rear.
With 'is mussick on 'is back,
'E would skip with our attack,
An' watch us till the bugles made "Retire"
An' for all 'is dirty 'ide
'E was white, clear white, inside
When 'e went to tend the wounded under fire!
     It was "Din! Din! Din!"
  With the bullets kickin' dust-spots on the green
    When the cartridges ran out,
    You could hear the front-ranks shout,
  "Hi! ammunition-mules an' Gunga Din!"

I shan't forgit the night
When I dropped be'ind the fight
With a bullet where my belt-plate should 'a' been.
I was chokin' mad with thirst,
An' the man that spied me first
Was our good old grinnin', gruntin' Gunga Din.
'E lifted up my 'ead,
An' he plugged me where I bled,
An' 'e guv me 'arf-a-pint of water green:
It was crawlin' and it stunk,
But of all the drinks I've drunk,
I'm gratefullest to one from Gunga Din.
    It was "Din! Din! Din!
  " 'Ere's a beggar with a bullet through 'is spleen;
    " 'E's chawin' up the ground,
    "An' 'e's kickin' all around:
    "For Gawd's sake git the water, Gunga Din!"

'E carried me away
To where a dooli lay,
An' a bullet come an' drilled the beggar clean.
'E put me safe inside,
An' just before he died,
"I 'ope you liked your drink," sez Gunga Din.
So I'll meet 'im later on
At the place where 'e is gone—
Where it's always double drill and no canteen;
'E'll be squattin' on the coals
Givin' drinks to poor damned souls,
An' I'll get a swig in hell from Gunga Din!
    Yes, Din! Din! Din!
  You Lazarushian-leather Gunga Din!
    Though I've belted you and flayed you,
    By the livin' Gawd that made you,
  You're a better man than I am, Gunga Din!

THE FOURTH ESTATE

Thomas Carlyle

Burke said there were three estates in Parliament, but in the reporters' gallery yonder there sat a Fourth Estate more important far than them all.

99

MARY WHITE

William Allen White

The Associated Press reports carrying the news of Mary White's death declared that it came as the result of a fall from a horse. How she would have hooted at that! She never fell from a horse in her life. Horses have fallen on her and with her—"I'm always trying to hold 'em in my lap," she used to say. But she was proud of few things, and one was that she could ride anything that had four legs and hair. Her death resulted not from a fall, but from a blow on the head which fractured her skull, and the blow came from the limb of an overhanging tree on the parking.

The last hour of her life was typical of its happiness. She came home from a day's work at school, topped off by a hard grind with the copy on the High School Annual, and felt that a ride would refresh her. She climbed into her khakis, chattering to her mother about the work she was doing, and hurried to get her horse and be out on the dirt roads for the country air and the radiant green fields of the spring. As she rode through the town on an easy gallop she kept waving at passers-by. She knew everyone in town. For a decade the little figure with the long pigtail and the red hair ribbon has been familiar on the streets of Emporia, and she got in the way of speaking to those who nodded at her. She passed the Kerrs, walking the horse, in front of the Normal Library, and waved at them; passed another friend a few hundred feet further on, and waved at her. The horse was walking and as she turned into North Merchant street she took off her cowboy hat, and the horse swung into a lope. She passed the Tripletts and waved her cowboy hat at them, still moving gaily north on Merchant street. A Gazette carrier passed—a High School boy friend—and she waved at him, but with her bridle hand; the horse veered quickly, plunged into the parking where the low-hanging limb faced her, and, while she still looked back waving, the blow came. But she did not fall from the horse; she slipped off, dazed a bit, staggered and fell in a faint. She never quite recovered consciousness.

But she did not fall from the horse, neither was she riding fast. A year or so ago she used to go like the wind. But that habit was broken, and she used the horse to get into the open to get fresh, hard exercise, and to work off a certain surplus energy that welled up in her and needed a physical outlet. That need had been in her heart for years. It was back of the impulse that kept the dauntless, little brown-clad figure on the streets and country roads of this community and built into a strong, muscular body what had been a frail and sickly frame during the first years of her life. But the riding gave her more than a body. It released a gay and hardy soul. She was the happiest thing in the world. And she was happy because she was enlarging her horizon. She came to know all sorts and conditions of men; Charley O'Brien, the traffic cop, was one of her best friends. W. L. Holtz, the Latin teacher, was another. Tom O'Connor, farmer-politician, and Rev. J. H. J. Rice, preacher and police judge, and Frank Beach, music master, were her special friends, and all the girls, black and white, above the track and below the track, in Pepville and Stringtown, were among her acquaintances. And she brought home riotous stories of her adventures. She loved to rollick; persiflage was her natural expression at home. Her humor was a continual bubble of joy. She seemed to think in the hyperbole and metaphor. She was mischievous without malice, as full of faults as an old shoe. No angel was Mary White, but an easy girl to live with, for she never nursed a grouch five minutes in her life.

With all her eagerness for the out-of-doors, she loved books. On her table when she left her room were a book by Conrad, one by Galsworthy, "Creative Chemistry" by E. E. Slossen, and a Kipling book. She read Mark Twain, Dickens and Kipling before she was 10—all of their writings. Wells and Arnold Bennett particularly amused and diverted her. She was entered as a student in Wellesley in 1922; was assistant editor of the High School Annual this year, and in line for election to the editorship of the Annual next year. She was a member of the executive committee of the High School Y. W. C. A.

Within the last two years she had begun to be moved by an ambition to draw. She began as most children do by scribbling in her school books, funny pictures. She bought cartoon magazines and took a course—rather casually, naturally, for she was, after all, a child, with no strong purposes—and this year she tasted the first fruits of success by having her pictures accepted by the High School Annual. But the thrill of delight she got when Mr. Ecord, of the Normal Annual, asked her to do the cartooning for that book this spring, was too beautiful for words. She fell to her work with all her enthusiastic heart. Her drawings were accepted, and her pride—always repressed by a lively sense of the ridiculousness of the figure she was cutting—was a really gorgeous thing to see. No successful artist ever drank a deeper draught of satisfaction than she took from the little fame her work was getting among her schoolfellows. In her glory, she almost forgot her horse—but never her car.

For she used the car as a jitney bus. It was her social life. She never had a "party" in all her nearly seventeen years—wouldn't have one; but she never drove a block in the car in her life that she didn't begin to fill the car with pick-ups! Everybody rode with Mary White—white and black, old and young, rich and poor, men and women. She liked nothing better than to fill the car full of long-legged High School boys and an occasional girl, and parade the town. She never had a "date," nor went to a dance, except once with her brother, Bill, and the "boy proposition" didn't interest her—yet. But young people—great, spring-breaking, varnish-cracking, fender-bending, door-sagging carloads of "kids"—gave her great pleasure. Her zests were keen. But the most fun she ever had in her life was acting as chairman of the committee that got up the big turkey dinner for the poor folks at the county home; scores of pies, gallons of slaw; jam, cakes, preserves, oranges and a wilderness of turkey were loaded in the car and taken to the county home. And, being of a practical turn of mind, she risked her own Christmas dinner by staying to see that the poor folks actually got it all. Not that she was a cynic; she just disliked to tempt folks. While there she found a blind colored uncle, very old, who could do nothing but make rag rugs, and she rustled up from her school friends rags enough to keep him busy for a season. The last engagement she tried to make was to take the guests at the county home out for a car ride. And the last endeavor of her life was to try to get a rest room for colored girls in the High School. She found one girl reading in the toilet, because there was no better place for a colored girl to loaf, and it inflamed her sense of injustice and she became a nagging harpy to those who she thought could remedy the evil. The poor she had always with her, and was glad of it. She hungered and thirsted for righteousness; and was the most impious creature in the world. She joined the Congregational Church without consulting her parents; not particularly for her soul's good. She never had a thrill of piety in her life, and would have hooted at a "testimony." But even as a little child she felt the church was an agency for helping people to more of life's abundance, and she wanted to help. She never wanted help for herself. Clothes meant little to her. It was a fight to get a new rig on her; but eventually a harder fight to get it off. She never wore a jewel and had no ring but her High School class ring, and never asked for anything but a wrist watch. She refused to have her hair up; though she was nearly 17. "Mother," she protested, "you don't know how much I get by with, in my braided pigtails that I could not, with my hair up." Above every other passion of her life was her passion not to grow up, to be a child. The tom-boy in her, which was big, seemed to loath to be put away forever in skirts. She was a Peter Pan, who refused to grow up.

Her funeral yesterday at the Congregational Church was as she would have wished it; no singing, no flowers save the big bunch of red roses from her Brother Bill's Harvard classmen—Heavens, how proud that would have made her! and the red roses from the Gazette force—in vases at her head and feet. A short prayer, Paul's beautiful essay on "Love" from the Thirteenth Chapter of First Corinthians, some remarks about her democratic spirit by her friend, John H. J. Rice, pastor and police judge, which she would have deprecated if she could, a prayer sent down for her by her friend, Carl Nau, and opening the service the slow, poignant movement from Beethoven's Moonlight Sonata, which she loved, and closing the service a cutting from the joyously melancholy first movement of Tschaikowski's Pathetic Symphony, which she liked to hear in certain moods on the phonograph; then the Lord's Prayer by her friends in the High School.

That was all.

For her pallbearers only her friends were chosen; her Latin teacher, W. L. Holtz; her High School principal, Rice Brown; her doctor, Frank Foncannon; her friend, W. W. Finney; her pal at the Gazette office, Walter Hughes; and her brother Bill. It would have made her smile to know that her friend, Charley O'Brien, the traffic cop, had been transferred from Sixth and Commercial to the corner near the church to direct her friends who came to bid her goodbye.

A rift in the clouds in a gray day threw a shaft of sunlight upon her coffin as her nervous, energetic little body sank to its last sleep. But the soul of her, the glowing, gorgeous, fervent soul of her, surely was flaming in eager joy upon some other dawn.

RECESSIONAL

Isaac Watts

O God, our Help in ages past,
Our Hope for years to come,
Our Shelter from the stormy blast,
And our Eternal Home!

Before the hills in order stood,
Or earth received her frame,
From everlasting Thou art God,
To endless years the same.

A thousand ages in Thy sight,
Are like an evening gone;
Short as the watch that ends the night
Before the rising sun.

Time, like an ever-rolling stream,
Bears all its sons away;
They fly, forgotten, as a dream
Dies at the opening day.

O God, our Help in ages past,
Our Hope for years to come,
Be Thou our Guard while life shall last,
And our Eternal Home.

TRY, TRY AGAIN

Anonymous

'Tis a lesson you should heed,
    Try, try again;
If at first you don't succeed,
    Try, try again;
Then your courage should appear,
For, if you will persevere,
You will conquer, never fear;
    Try, try again.

Once or twice though you should fail,
    Try, try again;
If you would at last prevail,
    Try, try again;
If we strive, 'tis no disgrace
Though we do not win the race;
What should you do in the case?
    Try, try again.

Time will bring you your reward,
    Try, try again.
All that other folks can do,
Why, with patience, should not you?
Only keep this rule in view;
    Try, try again.

HAPPY IS THE MAN THAT FINDETH WISDOM

Holy Bible, Proverbs 3:11–18

11 My son, despise not the chastening of the Lord; neither be weary of his correction:

12 For whom the Lord loveth he correcteth; even as a father the son in whom he delighteth.

13 Happy is the man that findeth wisdom, and the man that getteth understanding.

14 For the merchandise of it is better than the merchandise of silver, and the gain thereof than fine gold.

15 She is more precious than rubies: and all the things thou canst desire are not to be compared unto her.

16 Length of days is in her right hand; and in her left hand riches and honour.

17 Her ways are ways of pleasantness, and all her paths are peace.

18 She is a tree of life to them that lay hold upon her: and happy is everyone that retaineth her.

LORD ULLIN'S DAUGHTER

Thomas Campbell

A Chieftain, to the Highlands bound,
    Cries, "Boatman, do not tarry!
And I'll give thee a silver pound
    To row us o'er the ferry!"—

"Now who be ye, would cross Lochgyle,
    This dark and stormy water?"
"O, I'm the chief of Ulva's isle,
    And this, Lord Ullin's daughter.—

105

"And fast before her father's men
  Three days we've fled together,
For should he find us in the glen,
  My blood would stain the heather.

"His horsemen hard behind us ride;
  Should they our steps discover,
Then who will cheer my bonny bride
  When they have slain her lover?"—

Out spoke the hardy Highland wight,—
  "I'll go, my chief—I'm ready:—
It is not for your silver bright;
  But for your winsome lady:

"And by my word! the bonny bird
  In danger shall not tarry;
So, though the waves are raging white,
  I'll row you o'er the ferry."—

By this the storm grew loud apace,
  The water-wraith was shrieking;
And in the scowl of heaven each face
  Grew dark as they were speaking.

But still as wilder blew the wind,
  And as the night grew drearer,
Adown the glen rode armèd men,
  Their trampling sounded nearer.—

"O haste thee, haste!" the lady cries,
  "Though tempests round us gather;
I'll meet the raging of the skies,
  But not an angry father."—

The boat has left a stormy land,
  A stormy sea before her,—
When, O! too strong for human hand,
  The tempest gather'd o'er her.

And still they row'd amidst the roar
  Of waters fast prevailing:
Lord Ullin reach'd that fatal shore,—
  His wrath was changed to wailing.

For, sore dismay'd through storm and shade,
   His child he did discover:—
One lovely hand she stretch'd for aid,
   And one was round her lover.

"Come back! come back!" he cried in grief
   "Across this stormy water:
And I'll forgive your Highland chief,
   My daughter!—O my daughter!"

'Twas vain: the loud waves lash'd the shore,
   Return or aid preventing:
The waters wild went o'er his child,
   And he was left lamenting.

JENNY KISS'D ME

James Henry Leigh Hunt

Jenny kissed me when we met,
Jumping from the chair she sat in.
Time, you thief! who love to get
Sweets into your list, put that in.
Say I'm weary, say I'm sad;
Say that health and wealth have missed me;
Say I'm growing old, but add—
Jenny kissed me.

SOMEBODY'S MOTHER

Mary Dow Brine

The woman was old and ragged and gray
And bent with the chill of the Winter's day.

The street was wet with a recent snow
And the woman's feet were aged and slow.

She stood at the crossing and waited long,
Alone, uncared for, amid the throng

Of human beings who passed her by
Nor heeded the glance of her anxious eye.

Down the street, with laughter and shout,
Glad in the freedom of "school let out,"

Came the boys like a flock of sheep,
Hailing the snow piled white and deep.

Past the woman so old and gray
Hastened the children on their way.

Nor offered a helping hand to her—
So meek, so timid, afraid to stir

Lest the carriage wheels or the horses' feet
Should crowd her down in the slippery street.

At last came one of the merry troop,
The gayest laddie of all the group;

He paused beside her and whispered low,
"I'll help you cross, if you wish to go."

Her aged hand on his strong young arm
She placed, and so, without hurt or harm,

He guided the trembling feet along,
Proud that his own were firm and strong,

Then back again to his friends he went,
His young heart happy and well content.

"She's somebody's mother, boys, you know,
For all she's aged and poor and slow.

"And I hope some fellow will lend a hand
To help my mother, you understand,

"If ever she's poor and old and gray,
When her own dear boy is far away."

And "somebody's mother" bowed low her head
In her home that night, and the prayer she said

Was "God be kind to the noble boy,
Who is somebody's son, and pride and joy!"

CHARACTER OF THE HAPPY WARRIOR

William Wordsworth

Who is the happy Warrior? Who is he
That every man in arms should wish to be?
—It is the generous Spirit, who, when brought
Among the tasks of real life, hath wrought
Upon the plan that pleased his boyish thought:
Whose high endeavours are an inward light
That makes the path before him always bright:
Who, with a natural instinct to discern
What knowledge can perform, is diligent to learn·
Abides by this resolve, and stops not there,
But makes his moral being his prime care;
Who, doomed to go in company with Pain,
And Fear, and Bloodshed, miserable train!
Turns his necessity to glorious gain;
In face of these doth exercise a power
Which is our human nature's highest dower;
Controls them and subdues, transmutes, bereaves
Of their bad influence, and their good receives:
By objects, which might force the soul to abate
Her feeling, rendered more compassionate;
Is placable—because occasions rise
So often that demand such sacrifice;
More skilful in self-knowledge, even more pure,
As tempted more; more able to endure,
As more exposed to suffering and distress;
Thence, also, more alive to tenderness.
—'Tis he whose law is reason; who depends
Upon that law as on the best of friends;
Whence, in a stage where men are tempted still
To evil for a guard against worse ill,
And what in quality or act is best
Doth seldom on a right foundation rest,
He labours good on good to fix, and owes
To virtue every triumph that he knows:
—Who, if he rises to station of command,
Rises by open means; and there will stand
On honourable terms, or else retire,
And in himself possess his own desire;
Who comprehends his trust, and to the same

Keeps faithful with a singleness of aim;
And therefore does not stoop, nor lie in wait
For wealth, or honours, or for worldly state;
Whom they must follow, on whose head must fall,
Like showers of manna, if they come at all:
Whose power shed round him in the common strife,
Or mild concerns of ordinary life,   •
A constant influence, a peculiar grace;
But who, if he be called upon to face
Some awful moment to which Heaven has joined
Great issues, good or bad for human kind,
Is happy as a Lover; and attired
With sudden brightness, like a Man inspired;
And through the heat of conflict, keeps the law
In calmness made, and sees what he foresaw;
Or if an unexpected call succeed,
Come when it will, is equal to the need:
—He who, though thus endued as with a sense
And faculty for storm and turbulence,
Is yet a Soul whose master-bias leans
To homefelt pleasures and to gentle scenes;
Sweet images! which, wheresoe'er he be,
Are at his heart; and such fidelity
It is his darling passion to approve;
More brave for this, that he hath much to love:—
'Tis finally, the Man, who, lifted high,
Conspicuous object in a Nation's eye,
Or left unthought-of in obscurity,—
Who, with a toward or untoward lot,
Prosperous or adverse, to his wish or not—
Plays in the many games of life, that one
Where what he most doth value must be won:
Whom neither shape of danger can dismay,
Nor thought of tender happiness betray;
Who, not content that former worth stand fast,
Looks forward, persevering to the last,
From well to better, daily self-surpast:
Who, whether praise of him must walk the earth
For ever, and to noble deeds give birth,
Or he must fall, to sleep without his fame,
And leave a dead unprofitable name—
Finds comfort in himself and in his cause;
And, while the mortal mist is gathering, draws

His breath in confidence of Heaven's applause:
This is the happy Warrior; this is He
That every Man in arms should wish to be.

IS THERE FOR HONEST POVERTY?

Robert Burns

Is there for honest poverty
  Wha hangs his head, and a' that?
The coward slave, we pass him by;
  We dare be poor for a' that.
For a' that, and a' that,
  Our toil's obscure, and a' that;
The rank is but the guinea's stamp,—
  The man's the gowd for a' that.

What though on hamely fare we dine,
  Wear hoddin gray, and a' that?
Gie fools their silks, and knaves their wine,—
  A man's a man for a' that.
For a' that, and a' that,
  Their tinsel show, and a' that;
The honest man, though e'er sae poor,
  Is king o' men for a' that.

Ye see yon birkie ca'd a lord,
  Wha struts, and stares, and a' that,—
Though hundreds worship at his word,
  He's but a coof for a' that;
For a' that, and a' that,
  His riband, star, and a' that;
The man of independent mind,
  He looks and laughs at a' that.

A prince can mak a belted knight,
  A marquis, duke, and a' that;
But an honest man's aboon his might,—
  Guid Faith, he maunna fa' that!
For a' that, and a' that;
  Their dignities, and a' that,
The pith o' sense, and pride o' worth,
  Are higher ranks than a' that.

Then let us pray that come it may,—
  As come it will for a' that,—
That sense and worth, o'er a' the earth,
  May bear the gree, and a' that.
For a' that, and a' that,
  It's coming yet, for a' that,—
When man to man, the warld o'er,
  Shall brothers be for a' that!

O! SUSANNA

Stephen Foster

I came from Alabama
Wid my banjo on my knee;
I'm gwine to Louisiana,
My true love for to see.
It rained all night the day I left,
The weather it was dry,
The sun so hot I froze to death;
Susanna, don't you cry for me.

Chorus:

  O! Susanna, O don't you cry for me;
  I've come from Alabama
  Wid my banjo on my knee.

I jumped aboard de telegraph
And trabbled down the ribber,
De 'lectric fluid magnified
And killed five hundred nigger;
De bullgine bust, de horse run off,
I really thought I'd die;
I shut my eyes to hold my breath;
Susanna, don't you cry. (*Chorus.*)

I had a dream de odder night
When ebery t'ing was still;
I thought I saw Susanna
A-coming down the hill;

The buckwheat cake was in her mouth,
The tear was in her eye;
Says I, "I'm coming from the South,
Susanna, don't you cry." (*Chorus.*)

I soon will be in New Orleans,
And den I'll look all round,
And when I find Susanna
I will fall upon the ground;
And if I do not find her
Dis darkie'll surely die,
And when I'm dead and buried,
Susanna, don't you cry. (*Chorus.*)

GOD BLESS US EVERY ONE

Charles Dickens

Then up rose Mrs. Cratchit, Cratchit's wife, dressed out but poorly in a twice-turned gown, but brave in ribbons, which are cheap, and make a goodly show for six pence; and she laid the cloth, assisted by Belinda Cratchit, second of her daughters, also brave in ribbons; while Master Peter Cratchit plunged a fork into the saucepan of potatoes, and getting the corners of his monstrous shirtcollar (Bob's private property, conferred upon his son and heir in honor of the day) into his mouth, rejoiced to find himself so gallantly attired, and yearned to show his linen in the fashionable Parks.

And now two smaller Cratchits, boy and girl, came tearing in screaming that outside the baker's they had smelled the goose, and known it for their own; and basking in luxurious thoughts of sage and onion, these young Cratchits danced about the table, and exalted Master Peter Cratchit to the skies, while he (not proud, although his collars nearly choked him) blew the fire, until the slow potatoes, bubbling up, knocked loudly at the saucepanlid to be let out and peeled.

"What has ever got your precious father, then?" said Mrs. Cratchit. "And your brother, Tiny Tim? And Martha warn't as late last Christmas Day by half an hour!"

"Here's Martha, mother," said a girl, appearing as she spoke.

"Here's Martha, mother!" cried the two young Cratchits.

"Hurrah! There's such a goose, Martha!"

"Why, bless your heart alive, my dear, how late you are!" said Mrs. Cratchit, kissing her a dozen times, and taking off her shawl and bonnet for her with officious zeal.

"We'd a deal of work to finish up last night," replied the girl, "and had to clear away this morning, mother!"

"Well! Never mind so long as you are come," said Mrs. Cratchit. "Sit ye down before the fire, my dear, and have a warm, Lord bless ye!"

"No, no! There's father coming," cried the two young Cratchits, who were everywhere at once. "Hide, Martha, hide!"

So Martha hid herself, and in came little Bob, the father, with at least three feet of comforter, exclusive of the fringe, hanging down before him, and his threadbare clothes darned up and brushed to look seasonable, and Tiny Tim upon his shoulders. Alas for Tiny Tim, he bore a little crutch, and had his limbs supported by an iron frame!

"Why, where's our Martha?" cried Bob Cratchit, looking around.

"Not coming," said Mrs. Cratchit.

"Not coming!" said Bob, with a sudden declension in his high spirits; for he had been Tim's blood-horse all the way from church and had come home rampant. "Not coming upon Christmas Day!"

Martha didn't like to see him disappointed, if it were only in joke; so she came out prematurely from behind the closet door, and ran into his arms, while the two young Cratchits hustled Tiny Tim, and bore him off into the washhouse, that he might hear the pudding singing in the copper.

"And how did little Tim behave?" asked Mrs. Cratchit, when she had rallied Bob on his credulity, and Bob had hugged his daughter to his heart's content.

"As good as gold," said Bob, "and better. Somehow he gets thoughtful, sitting by himself so much, and thinks the strangest things you ever heard. He told me, coming home, that he hoped the people saw him in the church, because he was a cripple, and it might be pleasant to them to remember upon Christmas Day who made lame beggars walk and blind men see."

Bob's voice was tremulous when he told them this, and trembled more when he said that Tiny Tim was growing strong and hearty.

*　　*　　*

His active little crutch was heard upon the floor, and back came Tiny Tim before another word was spoken, escorted by his brother and sister to his stool beside the fire; and while Bob, turning up his cuffs—as if, poor fellow, they were capable of being made more shabby—compounded some hot mixture in a jug with gin and lemons, and stirred it round and round, and put it on the hob to simmer, Master Peter and the two ubiquitous young Cratchits went to fetch the goose, with which they soon returned in high procession.

Such a bustle ensued that you might have thought a goose the rarest of all birds; a feathered phenomenon, to which a black swan was a matter of course—and in truth, it was something very like it in that house.

Mrs. Cratchit made the gravy (ready beforehand in a little sauce-pan) hissing hot; Master Peter mashed the potatoes with incredible vigor; Miss Belinda sweetened up the applesauce; Martha dusted the hot plates; Bob took Tiny Tim beside him in a tiny corner at the table; the two young Cratchits set chairs for everyone, not forgetting themselves, and, mounting guard upon their posts, crammed spoons into their mouths, lest they should shriek for goose before their turn came to be helped.

At last the dishes were set on, and grace was said. It was succeeded by a breathless pause, as Mrs. Cratchit, looking slowly all along the carving-knife, prepared to plunge it in the breast; but when she did, and when the long-expected gush of stuffing issued forth, one murmur of delight arose all round the board, and even Tiny Tim, excited by the two young Cratchits, beat on the table with the handle of his knife and feebly cried Hurrah!

There never was such a goose. Bob said he didn't believe there ever was such a goose cooked. Its tenderness and flavor, size and cheapness, were the themes of universal admiration. Eked out by applesauce and mashed potatoes, it was a sufficient dinner for the whole family; indeed, as Mrs. Cratchit said with great delight (surveying one small atom of a bone upon the dish), they hadn't ate it all at last! Yet every one had enough, and the youngest Cratchits, in particular, were steeped in sage and onion to the eyebrows! But now, the plates being changed by Miss Belinda, Mrs. Cratchit left the room alone—too nervous to bear witnesses to take the pudding up, and bring it in.

Suppose it should not be done enough! Suppose it should break in turning out! Suppose somebody should have got over the wall of the back-yard and stolen it, while they were merry with the goose—a supposition at which the two young Cratchits became livid! All sorts of horrors were supposed.

Hallo! A great deal of steam! the pudding was out of the copper. A smell like a washing-day! That was the cloth. A smell like an eating-house and a pastry-cook's next door to each other, with a laundress's next door to that! That was the pudding!

In a half a minute Mrs. Cratchit entered—flushed, but smiling proudly—with the pudding, like a speckled cannonball, so hard and firm, blazing in half of half-a-quartern of ignited brandy, and bedight with Christmas holly stuck into the top.

Oh, a wonderful pudding! Bob Cratchit said, and calmly, too, that he regarded it as the greatest success achieved by Mrs. Cratchit since their marriage. Mrs. Cratchit said that, now the weight was off her mind, she would confess she had her doubts about the quantity of flour. Everybody had something to say about it, but nobody said or thought it was at all a small pudding for a large family. It would have been flat heresy to do so. Any Cratchit would have blushed to hint at such a thing.

At last the dinner was all done, the cloth was cleared, the hearth swept, and the fire made up. The compound in the jug being tasted, and considered perfect, apples and oranges were put upon the table, and a shovelful of chestnuts on the fire. Then all the Cratchit family drew round the hearth in what Bob Cratchit called a circle, meaning half a one; and at Bob Cratchit's elbow stood the family display of glass. Two tumblers and a custard-cup without a handle. These held the hot stuff from the jug, however, as well as golden goblets would have done; and Bob served it out with beaming looks, while the chestnuts on the fire sputtered and cracked noisily. Then Bob proposed:

"A Merry Christmas to us all, my dears. God bless us!"

Which all the family re-echoed.

"God bless us every one!" said Tiny Tim, the last of all.

(From A Christmas Carol)

THE VIOLET

Jane Taylor

Down in a green and shady bed
    A modest violet grew;
Its stalk was bent, it hung its head,
    As if to hide from view.

And yet it was a lovely flower,
  Its color bright and fair;
It might have graced a rosy bower,
  Instead of hiding there.

Yet there it was content to bloom,
  In modest tints arrayed;
And there diffused a sweet perfume,
  Within the silent shade.

Then let me to the valley go,
  This pretty flower to see,
That I may also learn to grow
  In sweet humility.

WHERE DID YOU GET THAT HAT?

Joseph J. Sullivan

Now how I came to get this hat 'tis very strange and funny;
Grandfather died and left to me his property and money.
And when the will it was read out, they told me straight and flat:
If I would have his money, I must always wear this hat!

Chorus:
  Where did you get that hat? Where did you get that tile?
  Isn't it a nobby one, and just the proper style?
  I should like to have one just the same as that!
  Where'er I go they shout! "Hello! Where did you get that
    hat?"

If I go to the op'ra house, in the op'ra season,
There's someone sure to shout at me, without the slightest reason,
If I go to a "chowder club", to have a jolly spree;
There's someone in the party, who is sure to shout at me: (*Chorus.*)

At twenty-one I thought I would to my sweetheart be married,
The people in the neighborhood had said too long we'd tarried,
So off to church we went right quick, determined to get wed,
I had not long been in there, when the parson to me said: (*Chorus.*)

A THING OF BEAUTY IS A JOY FOREVER

John Keats

A thing of beauty is a joy forever:
Its loveliness increases; it will never
Pass into nothingness; but still will keep
A bower quiet for us, and a sleep
Full of sweet dreams, and health, and quiet breathing.
Therefore, on every morrow, are we wreathing
A flowery band to bind us to the earth,
Spite of despondence, of the human dearth
Of noble natures, of the gloomy days,
Of all the unhealthy and o'er-darken'd ways
Made for our searching: yes, in spite of all,
Some shape of beauty moves away the pall
From our dark spirits. Such the sun, the moon,
Trees old and young, sprouting a shady boon
For simple sheep; and such are daffodils
With the green world they live in and clear rills
That for themselves a cooling covert make
'Gainst the hot season; the mid-forest brake,
Rich with a sprinkling of fair musk-rose blooms:
And such too is the grandeur of the dooms
We have imagined for the mighty dead;
All lovely tales that we have heard or read:
An endless fountain of immortal drink,
Pouring unto us from the heaven's brink.

Nor do we merely feel these essences
For one short hour; no, even as the trees
That whisper round a temple become soon
Dear as the temple's self, so does the moon,
The passion poesy, glories infinite,
Haunt us till they become a cheering light
Unto our souls, and bound to us so fast,
That, whether there be shine, or gloom o'ercast,
They always must be with us, or we die.

(From Endymion)

* * *

You can't make a silk purse out of a sow's ear.
—Jonathan Swift

CROWDED WAYS OF LIFE

[Written in reply to THE HOUSE BY THE SIDE OF THE
   ROAD, by Sam Walter Foss.]

'Tis only a half truth the poet has sung
   of the "house by the side of the way."
Our Master had neither a house nor a home,
   But He walked with the crowd day by day.
And I think, when I read of the poet's desire,
   That a house by the road would be good;
But service is found in its tenderest form
   When we walk with the crowd in the road.

So I say, Let me walk with the men in the road,
   Let me seek out the burdens that crush,
Let me speak a kind word of good cheer to the weak
   Who are falling behind in the rush.
There are wounds to be healed, there are breaks
                              we must mend,
   There's a cup of cold water to give;
And the man in the road by the side of his friend
   Is the man who has learned to live.

Then tell me no more of the house by the road;
   There is only one place I can live--
It's there with the men who are toiling along,
   Who are needing the cheer I can give.
It is pleasant to live in the house by the way
And be a friend, as the poet has said;
But the Master is bidding us: "Bear ye their load,
   For your rest waiteth yonder ahead."

I could not remain in the house by the road
    And watch as the toilers go on,
Their faces beclouded with pain and with sin,
    So burdened their strength nearly gone.
I'll go to their side, I'll speak in good cheer,
    I'll help them to carry their load;
And I'll smile at the man in the house by the way,
As I walk with the crowd in the road.

Out there in the road that goes by the house,
    Where the poet is singing his song,
I'll walk and I'll work 'midst the heat of the day,
    And I'll help falling brothers along --
Too busy to live in the house by the way,
    Too happy for such an abode.
And my heart sings its praise to the Master of all,
    Who is helping me serve in the road.

                    Walter S. Gresham.

AFTER DUNKIRK

Winston Churchill

We shall not flag nor fail. We shall go on to the end. We shall fight in France and on the seas and oceans; we shall fight with growing confidence and growing strength in the air.

We shall defend our island whatever the cost may be; we shall fight on beaches, landing grounds, in fields, in streets and on the hills. We shall never surrender and even if, which I do not for the moment believe, this island or a large part of it were subjugated and starving, then our empire beyond the seas, armed and guarded by the British Fleet, will carry on the struggle until in God's good time the New World, with all its power and might, sets forth to the liberation and rescue of the Old.

(From the speech of June 4, 1940)

THE HOUSE BY THE SIDE OF THE ROAD

Sam Walter Foss

There are hermit souls that live withdrawn
In the place of their self-content;
There are souls like stars, that dwell apart,
In a fellowless firmament;
There are pioneer souls that blaze their paths
Where highways never ran—
But let me live by the side of the road
And be a friend to man.

Let me live in a house by the side of the road,
Where the race of men go by—
The men who are good and the men who are bad,
As good and as bad as I.
I would not sit in the scorner's seat,
Or hurl the cynic's ban—
Let me live in a house by the side of the road
And be a friend to man.

I see from my house by the side of the road,
By the side of the highway of life,

119

The men who press with the ardor of hope,
The men who are faint with the strife.
But I turn not away from their smiles nor their tears,
Both parts of an infinite plan—
Let me live in a house by the side of the road
And be a friend to man.

I know there are brook-gladdened meadows ahead,
And mountains of wearisome height;
That the road passes on through the long afternoon
And stretches away to the night.
But still I rejoice when the travelers rejoice,
And weep with the strangers that moan,
Nor live in my house by the side of the road
Like a man who dwells alone.

Let me live in my house by the side of the road,
It's here the race of men go by—
They are good, they are bad, they are weak, they are strong,
Wise, foolish—so am I;
Then why should I sit in the scorner's seat,
Or hurl the cynic's ban?
Let me live in my house by the side of the road
And be a friend to man.

YOUNG AND OLD

Charles Kingsley

When all the world is young, lad,
  And all the trees are green;
And every goose a swan, lad,
  And every lass a queen;
Then hey for boot and horse, lad,
  And round the world away;
Young blood must have its course, lad,
  And every dog his day.

When all the world is old, lad,
  And all the trees are brown;
And all the sport is stale, lad,
  And all the wheels run down:

120

Creep home, and take your place there,
    The spent and maimed among:
God grant you find one face there
    You loved when all was young.

THE TEMPEST

James T. Fields

We were crowded in the cabin,
    Not a soul would dare to sleep,—
It was midnight on the waters
    And a storm was on the deep.

'Tis a fearful thing in winter
    To be shattered by the blast,
And to hear the rattling trumpet
    Thunder, "Cut away the mast!"

So we shuddered there in silence,—
    For the stoutest held his breath,
While the hungry sea was roaring,
    And the breakers talked with Death.

As thus we sat in darkness,
    Each one busy in his prayers,
"We are lost!" the captain shouted
    As he staggered down the stairs.

But his little daughter whispered,
    As she took his icy hand,
"Isn't God upon the ocean
    Just the same as on the land?"

Then we kissed the little maiden,
    And we spoke in better cheer,
And we anchored safe in harbor
    When the morn was shining clear.

* * *

They have learned nothing, and forgotten nothing.
    —Talleyrand (referring to the Bourbons)

SPARTACUS TO THE GLADIATORS AT CAPUA

E. Kellogg

Ye call me chief; and ye do well to call him chief who, for twelve long years, has met upon the arena every shape of man or beast the broad Empire of Rome could furnish, and who never yet lowered his arm. If there be one among you who can say that ever, in public fight or private brawl, my actions did belie my tongue, let him stand forth and say it. If there be three in all your company dare face me on the bloody sands, let them come on. And yet I was not always thus—a hired butcher, a savage chief of still more savage men!

My ancestors came from old Sparta, and settled among the vine-clad rocks and citron groves of Cyrasella. My early life ran quiet as the brooks by which I sported; and when, at noon, I gathered the sheep beneath the shade, and played upon the shepherd's flute, there was a friend, the son of a neighbor, to join me in the pastime. We led our flocks in the same pasture, and partook together our rustic meal.

One evening, after the sheep were folded, and we were all seated beneath the myrtle which shaded our cottage, my grandsire, an old man, was telling of Marathon and Leuctra; and how, in ancient times, a little band of Spartans, in a defile of the mountains, had withstood a whole army. I did not then know what war was; but my cheeks burned, I knew not why, and I clasped the knees of that venerable man until my mother, parting the hair from off my forehead, kissed my throbbing temples, and bade me go to rest, and think no more of those old tales and savage wars. That very night the Romans landed on our coast. I saw the breast that had nourished me trampled by the hoof of the war-horse; the bleeding body of my father flung amid the blazing rafters of our dwelling!

Today I killed a man in the arena; and when I broke his helmet-clasps, behold! he was my friend. He knew me, smiled faintly, gasped, and died—the same sweet smile upon his lips that I had marked when, in adventurous boyhood, we scaled the lofty cliff to pluck the first ripe grapes and bear them home in childish triumph! I told the pretor that the dead man had been my friend, generous and brave; and I begged him that I might bear away the body, to burn it on the funeral pile, and mourn over its ashes. Ay! upon my knees, amid the dust and blood of the arena, I begged that poor boon, while all the assembled maids and matrons, and the holy virgins they call Vestals, and the rabble shouted in derision, deeming it rare sport, forsooth, to see Rome's fiercest gladiator turn pale and tremble at sight of that piece of bleeding clay! And the pretor drew back as if I were pollution, and sternly said—"Let the carrion rot; there are no noble men but Romans!" And so, fellow-gladiators, must you, and so must I, die like dogs.

O Rome! Rome! thou hast been a tender nurse to me. Ay! thou hast given to that poor, gentle, timid shepherd-lad, who never knew a harsher tone than a flute-note, muscles of iron and a heart of flint; taught him to drive the sword through a plaited mail and links of rugged brass, and warm it in the marrow of his foe:—to gaze into the glaring eye-balls of the fierce Numidian lion even as a boy upon a laughing girl! And he shall pay thee back, until the yellow Tiber is red as frothing wine, and in its deepest ooze thy life-blood lies curdled.

Ye stand here now like giants, as ye are! The strength of brass is in your toughtened sinews; but tomorrow some Roman Adonis, breathing sweet perfume from his curly locks, shall with his lily fingers pat your red brawn, and bet his sesterces upon your blood. Hark! hear ye yon lion roaring in his den? 'Tis three days since he tasted flesh; but tomorrow he shall break his fast upon yours— and a dainty meal for him ye will be!

If ye are beasts, then stand here like fat oxen, waiting for the butcher's knife! If ye are men—follow me! Strike down yon guard, gain the mountain passes, and there do bloody work, as did your sires at old Thermopylae! Is Sparta dead? Is the old Grecian spirit frozen in your veins, that you do couch and cower like a belabored hound beneath his master's lash? O comrades! warriors! Thracians! —if we must fight, let us fight for ourselves! If we must slaughter, let us slaughter our oppressors! If we must die, let it be under the clear sky, by the bright waters, in noble, honorable battle!

I HAD BUT FIFTY CENTS

Anonymous

I took my girl to a fancy ball;
It was a social hop;
We waited till the folks got out,
And the music it did stop,
Then to a restaurant we went,
The best one on the street;
She said she wasn't hungry,

But this is what she eat:
A dozen raw, a plate of slaw,
A chicken and a roast,
Some applesass, and sparagrass,
And soft-shell crabs on toast,
A big box stew, and crackers too;
Her appetite was immense!
When she called for pie,
I thought I'd die,
For I had but fifty cents.

She said she wasn't hungry
And didn't care to eat,
But I've got money in my clothes
To bet she can't be beat;
She took it in so cozy,
She had an awful tank;
She said she wasn't thirsty,
But this is what she drank:
A whisky skin, a glass of gin,
Which made me shake with fear,
A ginger pop, with rum on top,
A schooner then of beer,
A glass of ale, a gin cocktail;
She should have had more sense;
When she called for more,
I fell on the floor,
For I had but fifty cents.

Of course I wasn't hungry,
And didn't care to eat,
Expecting every moment
To be kicked into the street;
She said she'd fetch her family round,
And some night we'd have fun;
When I gave the man the fifty cents,
This is what he done:
He tore my clothes,
He smashed my nose,
He hit me on the jaw,
He gave me a prize
Of a pair of black eyes
And with me swept the floor.

He took me where my pants hung loose,
And threw me over the fence;
Take my advice, don't try it twice
If you've got but fifty cents!

REMEMBER NOW THY CREATOR

Holy Bible, Ecclesiastes 12

1 Remember now thy Creator in the days of thy youth, while
the evil days come not, nor the years draw nigh, when thou shalt
say, I have no pleasure in them;

2 While the sun, or the light, or the moon, or the stars, be not
darkened, nor the clouds return after the rain:

3 In the day when the keepers of the house shall tremble, and
the strong men shall bow themselves, and the grinders cease because they are few, and those that look out of the windows be
darkened,

4 And the doors shall be shut in the streets, when the sound
of the grinding is low, and he shall rise up at the voice of the bird,
and all the daughters of musick shall be brought low;

5 Also when they shall be afraid of that which is high, and fears
shall be in the way, and the almond tree shall flourish, and the
grasshopper shall be a burden, and desire shall fail: because man
goeth to his long home, and the mourners go about the streets:

6 Or ever the silver cord be loosed, or the golden bowl be
broken, or the pitcher be broken at the fountain, or the wheel
broken at the cistern.

7 Then shall the dust return to the earth as it was: and the
spirit shall return unto God who gave it.

8 Vanity of vanities, saith the preacher; all is vanity.

9 And moreover, because the preacher was wise, he still taught
the people knowledge; yea, he gave good heed, and sought out,
and set in order many proverbs.

10 The preacher sought to find out acceptable words: and that
which was written was upright, even words of truth.

11 The words of the wise are as goads, and as nails fastened by
the masters of assemblies, which are given from one shepherd.

12 And further, by these, my son, be admonished: of making
many books there is no end; and much study is a weariness of the
flesh.

13 Let us hear the conclusion of the whole matter: Fear God, and keep his commandments: for this is the whole duty of man.

14 For God shall bring every work into judgment, with every secret thing, whether it be good, or whether it be evil.

"HOW DO I LOVE THEE?"

Elizabeth Barrett Browning

How do I love thee? Let me count the ways.
I love thee to the depth and breadth and height
My soul can reach, when feeling out of sight
For the ends of Being and ideal Grace.
I love thee to the level of every day's
Most quiet need, by sun and candle-light.
I love thee freely, as men strive for Right;
I love thee purely, as men turn from Praise.
I love thee with the passion put to use
In my old griefs, and with my childhood's faith.
I love thee with a love I seemed to lose
With my lost saints,—I love thee with the breath,
Smiles, tears, of all my life!—and, if God choose,
I shall but love thee better after death.
(From Sonnets from the Portuguese)

SONG OF MARION'S MEN

William Cullen Bryant

Our band is few, but true and tried,
　Our leader frank and bold;
The British soldier trembles
　When Marion's name is told.
Our fortress is the good greenwood,
　Our tent the cypress-tree;
We know the forest round us,
　As seamen know the sea;
We know its walls of thorny vines,
　Its glades of reedy grass,
Its safe and silent islands
　Within the dark morass.

Woe to the English soldiery
    That little dread us near!
On them shall light at midnight
    A strange and sudden fear;
When, waking to their tents on fire,
    They grasp their arms in vain,
And they who stand to face us
    Are beat to earth again;
And they who fly in terror deem
    A mighty host behind,
And hear the tramp of thousands
    Upon the hollow wind.

Then sweet the hour that brings release
    From danger and from toil;
We talk the battle over,
    And share the battle's spoil.
The woodland rings with laugh and shout,
    As if a hunt were up,
And woodland flowers are gathered
    To crown the soldier's cup.
With merry songs we mock the wind
    That in the pine-top grieves,
And slumber long and sweetly
    On beds of oaken leaves.

Well knows the fair and friendly moon
    The band that Marion leads,—
The glitter of their rifles,
    The scampering of their steeds.
'Tis life to guide the fiery barb
    Across the moonlight plain;
'Tis life to feel the night-wind
    That lifts his tossing mane.
A moment in the British camp—
    A moment—and away
Back to the pathless forest,
    Before the peep of day.

Grave men there are by broad Santee,
    Grave men with hoary hairs;
Their hearts are all with Marion,
    For Marion are their prayers.

And lovely ladies greet our band
  With kindliest welcoming,
With smiles like those of summer,
  And tears like those of spring.
For them we wear these trusty arms,
  And lay them down no more
Till we have driven the Briton
  Forever from our shore.

THE GLORIOUS WHITEWASHER

Mark Twain

Saturday morning was come, and all the summer world was
bright and fresh, and brimming with life. There was a song in
every heart; and if the heart was young the music issued at the
lips. There was cheer in every face and a spring in every step. The
locust trees were in bloom and the fragrance of the blossoms
filled the air. Cardiff Hill, beyond the village and above it, was
green with vegetation, and it lay just far enough away to seem
a Delectable Land, dreamy, reposeful, and inviting.

Tom appeared on the sidewalk with a bucket of whitewash
and a long-handled brush. He surveyed the fence, and all gladness left him and a deep melancholy settled down upon his
spirit. Thirty yards of board fence nine feet high. Life to him
seemed hollow, and existence but a burden. Sighing he dipped
his brush and passed it along the topmost plank; repeated the
operation; did it again; compared the insignificant whitewashed
streak with the far-reaching continent of unwhitewashed fence,
and sat down on a tree-box discouraged. Jim came skipping
out at the gate with a tin pail, and singing "Buffalo Gals." Bringing water from the town pump had always been hateful work in
Tom's eyes, before, but now it did not strike him so. He remembered that there was company at the pump. White, mulatto, and
Negro boys and girls were always there waiting their turns, resting, trading playthings, quarreling, fighting, skylarking. And he
remembered that although the pump was only a hundred and fifty
yards off, Jim never got back with a bucket of water under an
hour—and even then somebody generally had to go after him.
Tom said:

"Say, Jim, I'll fetch the water if you'll whitewash some."

Jim shook his head and said:

"Can't, Mars Tom. Ole missis, she tole me I got to go an' git dis water an' not stop foolin' roun' wid anybody. She says she spec' Mars Tom gwine to ax me to whitewash, an' so she tole me go 'long an' tend to my own business—she 'lowed *she'd* 'tend to de whitewashin'.''

"O, never you mind what she said, Jim. That's the way she always talks. Gimme the bucket—I won't be gone only a minute. *She* won't ever know."

"Oh, I dasn't, Mars Tom. Ole missis she'd take an' tar de head off'n me. Deed she would."

"*She!* She never licks anybody—whacks 'em over the head with her thimble—and who cares for that, I'd like to know. She talks awful, but talk don't hurt—anyways it don't if she don't cry. Jim, I'll give you a marvel. I'll give you a white alley!"

Jim began to waver.

"White alley, Jim! And it's a bully taw."

"My! Dat's a mighty gay marvel, I tell you! But Mars Tom I's powerful fraid ole missis—"

"And, besides, if you will I'll show you my sore toe."

Jim was only human—this attraction was too much for him. He put down the pail, took the white alley, and bent over the toe with absorbing interest while the bandage was being unwound. In another moment he was flying down the street with his pail and a tingling rear, Tom was whitewashing with vigor, and Aunt Polly was retiring from the field with a slipper in her hand and triumph in her eye.

But Tom's energy did not last. He began to think of the fun he had planned for this day, and his sorrows multiplied. Soon the free boys would come tripping along on all sorts of delicious expeditions, and they would make a world of fun of him for having to work—the very thought of it burnt him like fire. He got out his worldly wealth and examined it—bits of toys, marbles, and trash; enough to buy an exchange of *work*, maybe, but not half enough to buy so much as half an hour of pure freedom. So he returned his straitened means to his pocket, and gave up the idea of trying to buy the boys. At this dark and hopeless moment an inspiration burst upon him! Nothing less than a great, magnificent inspiration.

He took up his brush and went tranquilly to work. Ben Rogers hove in sight presently—the very boy, of all boys, whose ridicule he had been dreading. Ben's gait was the hop-skip-and-jump—proof enough that his heart was light and his anticipations high. He was eating an apple, and giving a long, melodious whoop, at intervals, followed by a deep-toned ding-dong-dong, for he was personating a steamboat. As he drew near, he slackened speed, took the middle of the street, leaned far over to starboard and rounded to ponderously and with laborious pomp and circumstance—for he was personating the *Big Missouri,* and considered himself to be drawing nine feet of water. He was boat and captain and engine-bells combined, so he had to imagine himself standing on his own hurricane-deck giving the orders and executing them:

"Stop her, sir! Ting-a-ling-ling!" The headway ran almost out and he drew up slowly toward the sidewalk.

"Ship up to back! Ting-a-ling-ling!" His arms straightened and stiffened down his sides.

"Set her back on the starboard! Ting-a-ling-ling! Chow! ch-chow-wow! Chow!" His right hand, meantime, describing stately circles—for it was representing a forty-foot wheel.

"Let her go back on the labboard! Ting-a-ling-ling! Chow-ch-chow-chow!" The left hand began to describe circles.

"Stop the stabboard! Ting-a-ling-ling! Stop the labboard! Come ahead on the stabboard! Stop her! Let your outside turn over slow! Ting-a-ling-ling! Chow-ow-ow! Get out that head-line! *Lively* now! Come—out with your spring-line—what're you about there! Take a turn round that stump with the bight of it! Stand by that stage, now—let her go! Done with the engines, sir! Ting-a-ling-ling! Sh't! Sh't!" (trying the gauge-cocks.)

Tom went on whitewashing—paid no attention to the steamboat. Ben stared a moment and then said:

"Hi-*yi! You're* up a stump, ain't you!"

No answer. Tom surveyed his last touch with the eye of an artist, then he gave his brush another gentle sweep and surveyed the result, as before. Ben ranged up alongside of him. Tom's mouth watered for the apple, but he stuck to his work. Ben said:

"Hello, old chap, you got to work, hey?"

Tom wheeled suddenly and said:

"Why, it's you, Ben! I warn't noticing."

"Say—I'm going in a-swimming, I am. Don't you wish you could? But of course you'd druther *work*—wouldn't you? Course you would!"

Tom contemplated the boy a bit, and said:

"What do you call work?"

"Why, ain't *that* work?"

Tom resumed his whitewashing and answered carelessly:

"Well, maybe it is, and maybe it ain't. All I know is, it suits Tom Sawyer."

"Oh come, now, you don't mean to let on that you *like* it?"

The brush continued to move.

"Like it? Well, I don't see why I oughtn't to like it. Does a boy get a chance to whitewash a fence every day?"

That put the thing in a new light. Ben stopped nibbling his apple. Tom swept his brush daintily back and forth—stepped back to note the effect—added a touch here and there—criticized the effect again—Ben watching every move and getting more and more interested, more and more absorbed. Presently he said:

"Say, Tom, let *me* whitewash a little."

Tom considered, was about to consent; but he altered his mind: "No—no—I reckon it wouldn't hardly do, Ben. You see, Aunt Polly's awful particular about this fence—right here on the street, you know—but if it was the back fence I wouldn't mind and *she* wouldn't. Yes, she's awful particular about this fence; it's got to be done very careful; I reckon there ain't one boy in a thousand, maybe two thousand, that can do it the way it's got to be done."

"No—is that so? Oh, come, now—lemme just try. Only just a little—I'd let *you*, if you was me, Tom."

"Ben, I'd like to, honest injun; but Aunt Polly—well, Jim wanted to do it, but she wouldn't let him; Sid wanted to do it, and she wouldn't let Sid. Now don't you see how I'm fixed? If you was to tackle this fence and anything was to happen to it—"

"Oh, shucks, I'll be just as careful. Now lemme try. Say—I'll give you the core of my apple."

"Well, here— No, Ben, now don't. I'm afeard—"

"I'll give you *all* of it!"

Tom gave up the brush with reluctance in his face, but alacrity in his heart. And while the late steamer *Big Missouri* worked and sweated in the sun, the retired artist sat on a barrel in the shade close by, dangled his legs, munched his apple, and planned the slaughter of more innocents. There was no lack of material; boys happened along every little while; they came to jeer, but remained to whitewash. By the time Ben was fagged out, Tom had traded the next chance to Billy Fisher for a kite, in good repair; and when *he* played out, Johnny Miller bought in for a dead rat and a string to swing it with—and so on, and so on, hour after hour. And when the middle of the afternoon came, from being a poor poverty-stricken boy in the morning, Tom was literally rolling in wealth. He had beside the things before mentioned, twelve marbles, part of a jew's-harp, a piece of blue bottle-glass to look through, a spool cannon, a key that wouldn't unlock anything, a fragment of chalk, a glass stopper of a decanter, a tin soldier, a couple of tadpoles, six firecrackers, a kitten with only one eye, a brass door-knob, a dog-collar—but no dog—the handle of a knife, four pieces of orange-peel, and a dilapidated old window-sash.

He had had a nice, good, idle time all the while—plenty of company—and the fence had three coats of whitewash on it! If he hadn't run out of whitewash, he would have bankrupted every boy in the village.

Tom said to himself that it was not such a hollow world, after all. He had discovered a great law of human action, without knowing it—namely, that in order to make a man or boy covet a thing, it is only necessary to make the thing difficult to attain. If he had been a great and wise philosopher, like the writer of this book, he would now have comprehended that Work consists of whatever a body is *obliged* to do, and that Play consists of whatever a body is not obliged to do. And this would help him to understand why constructing artificial flowers or performing on a treadmill is work, while rolling tenpins or climbing Mont Blanc is only amusement. There are wealthy gentlemen in England who drive four-horse passenger-coaches twenty or thirty miles on a daily line, in the summer, because the privilege costs them considerable money; but if they are offered wages for the service, that would turn it into work and then they would resign.

The boy mused awhile over the substantial change which had taken place in his worldly circumstances, and then wended toward headquarters to report.

(From The Adventures of Tom Sawyer)

GOOD-BYE

Ralph Waldo Emerson

Good-bye, proud world! I'm going home:
Thou art my friend, and I'm not thine.
Long through thy weary crowds I roam;
A river-ark on the ocean brine,
Long I've been tossed like the driven foam;
But now, proud world! I'm going home.

Good-bye to Flattery's fawning face;
To Grandeur with his wise grimace;
To upstart Wealth's averted eye;
To supple Office, low and high;

To crowded halls, to court and street;
To frozen hearts and hasting feet;
To those who go, and those who come;
Good-bye, proud world! I'm going home.

I am going to my own hearth-stone,
Bosomed to yon green hills alone,—
A secret nook in a pleasant land,
Whose groves the frolic fairies planned;
Where arches green, the livelong day,
Echo the blackbird's roundelay,
And vulgar feet have never trod
A spot that is sacred to thought and God.

O, when I am safe in my sylvan home,
I tread on the pride of Greece and Rome;
And when I am stretched beneath the pines,
Where the evening star so holy shines,
I laugh at the lore and the pride of man,
At the sophist schools and the learned clan;
For what are they all, in their high conceit,
When man in the bush with God may meet?

FOR, LO, THE WINTER IS PAST

Holy Bible, Song of Solomon 2:10–13

10 My beloved spake, and said unto me, Rise up, my love, my
fair one, and come away.

11 For, lo, the winter is past, the rain is over and gone;

12 The flowers appear on the earth; the time of the singing of
birds is come, and the voice of the turtle is heard in our land;

13 The fig tree putteth forth her green figs, and the vines with
the tender grape give a good smell. Arise, my love, my fair one,
and come away.

THE MOURNING BRIDE

William Congreve

Thus grief still treads upon the heels of pleasure,
Married in haste, we may repent at leisure.

133

THE ETERNAL GOODNESS

John Greenleaf Whittier

I know not what the future hath
  Of marvel or surprise;
Assured alone that life and death
  His mercy underlies.

And if my heart and flesh are weak
  To bear an untried pain,
The bruisèd reed He will not break,
  But strengthen and sustain.

No offerings of my own I have,
  No works my faith to prove;
I can but give the gifts He gave,
  And plead His love for love.

And so, beside the silent sea,
  I wait the muffled oar;
No harm from Him can come to me
  On ocean or on shore.

I know not where His islands lift
  Their fronded palms in air;
I only know I cannot drift
  Beyond His love and care.

PORTIA'S PLEA FOR MERCY

William Shakespeare

The quality of mercy is not strain'd,
It droppeth as the gentle rain from heaven
Upon the place beneath: it is twice blest;
It blesseth him that gives and him that takes:
'Tis mightiest in the mightiest: it becomes
The thronèd monarch better than his crown;
His sceptre shows the force of temporal power,
The attribute to awe and majesty,
Wherein doth sit the dread and fear of kings;

But mercy is above this sceptred sway;
It is enthroned in the hearts of kings,
It is an attribute to God himself;
And earthly power doth then show likest God's
When mercy seasons justice. Therefore, Jew,
Though justice be thy plea, consider this,
That, in the course of justice, none of us
Should see salvation: we do pray for mercy;
And that same prayer doth teach us all to render
The deeds of mercy. I have spoke thus much
To mitigate the justice of thy plea;
Which if thou follow, this strict court of Venice
Must needs give sentence 'gainst the merchant there.

(From The Merchant of Venice)

THE FLYING TRAPEZE

George Lebourne

O once I was happy but now I'm forlorn,
Like an old coat that is tatter'd and torn,
Left on this wide world to fret and to mourn,
Betray'd by a maid in her teens.
The girl that I lov'd she was handsome,
I tried all I knew, her to please.
But I could not please her one quarter so well,
Like that man upon the Trapeze.

Chorus:

He'd fly through the air with the greatest of ease,
A daring young man on the flying Trapeze,
His movements were graceful all girls he could please,
And my love he purloin'd away.

This young man by name was Signor Bona Slang.
Tall, big, and handsome, as well made as Chang,
Where'er he appeared, the Hall loudly rang
With ovation from all people there.
He'd smile from the bar on the people below
And one night he smil'd on my love
She wink'd back on him and shouted *Bravo!*
As he hung by his nose up above!

Her father and mother were both on my side,
And very hard tried to make her my own bride,
Her father he sigh'd, and her mother she cried,
To see her throw herself away.
'Twas all no avail, she went there ev'ry night,
And would throw him Bouquets on the stage.
Which caus'd him to meet her, how he ran me down,
To tell you would take a whole page.

One night I as usual went to her dear home,
Found there her father and mother alone,
I asked for my love, and soon they made known
To my horror, that she'd run away,
She'd pack'd up her box, and elop'd in the night
With him, with the greatest of ease,
From two stories high, he had lower'd her down
To the ground, on his flying Trapeze!

Some months after this I went to a Hall,
Was greatly surprised to see on the Wall
A bill in red letters, which did my heart gall,
That she was appearing with him.
He taught her gymnastics and dress'd her in tights
To help him to live at his ease,
And made her assume a masculine name,
And now she goes on the Trapeze.

Second Chorus:
> She floats through the air with the greatest of ease,
> You'd think her a man on the flying Trapeze,
> She does all the work, while he takes his ease,
> And that's what's become of my love.

WHEN LOVELY WOMAN STOOPS TO FOLLY

Oliver Goldsmith

When lovely woman stoops to folly
And finds too late that men betray,—
What charm can soothe her melancholy,
What art can wash her guilt away?

The only art her guilt to cover,
To hide her shame from every eye,
To give repentance to her lover
And wring his bosom, is—to die.

I CANNOT SING THE OLD SONGS

Anonymous

I cannot sing the old songs
I sang long years ago,
For heart and voice would fail me,
And foolish tears would flow;
Far by-gone hours come o'er my heart
With each familiar strain.
I cannot sing the old songs,
Or dream those dreams again.

I cannot sing the old songs,
Their charm is sad and deep;
Their melodies would waken
Old sorrows from their sleep.
And though all unforgotten still,
And sadly sweet they be,
I cannot sing the old songs,
They are too dear to me!

I cannot sing the old songs,
For visions come again
Of golden dreams departed
And years of weary pain;
Perhaps when earthly fetters shall
Have set my spirit free
My voice shall know the old songs
For all eternity.

* * *

You can fool some of the people all of the time and all of the
people some of the time: but you can't fool all of the people all
of the time.

—Attributed to Lincoln

THE STAR-SPANGLED BANNER

Francis Scott Key

O! say can you see by the dawn's early light,
What so proudly we hail'd at the twilight's last gleaming,
Whose broad stripes and bright stars, through the perilous fight,
O'er the ramparts we watched were so gallantly streaming?
And the rocket's red glare, the bombs bursting in air,
Gave proof through the night that our flag was still there;
O! say does that star-spangled banner yet wave,
O'er the land of the free, and the home of the brave?

On the shore dimly seen through the mists of the deep,
Where the foe's haughty host in dread silence reposes,
What is that which the breeze, o'er the towering steep,
As it fitfully blows, half conceals, half discloses?
Now it catches the gleam of the morning's first beam,
In full glory reflected now shines in the stream.
'Tis the star-spangled banner, O! long may it wave
O'er the land of the free, and the home of the brave.

And where is that band who so vauntingly swore
That the havoc of war and the battle's confusion,
A home and a country, shall leave us no more?
Their blood has wash'd out their foul footsteps pollution;
No refuge could save the hireling and slave,
From the terror of flight, or the gloom of the grave;
And the star-spangled banner in triumph doth wave,
O'er the land of the free, and the home of the brave.

O, thus be it ever when freemen shall stand,
Between their lov'd home and the war's desolation,
Blest with vict'ry and peace, may the heav'n-rescued land,
Praise the Power that hath made and preserved us a nation.
Then conquer we must, when our cause it is just,
And this be our motto,—"In God is our trust,"
And the star-spangled banner in triumph shall wave,
O'er the land of the free, and the home of the brave.

* * *

'Tis more brave to live than to die.
                                          —Meredith

SERMON TO THE BIRDS

St. Francis of Assisi

My little sisters, the birds, much bounden are ye unto God, your Creator, and always in every place ought ye to praise Him, for that He hath given you liberty to fly about everywhere, and hath also given you double and triple raiment; moreover, He preserved your seed in the ark of Noah, that your race might not perish out of the world; still more are ye beholden to Him for the element of the air which He hath appointed for you; beyond all this, ye sow not, neither do you reap; and God feedeth you, and giveth you the streams and fountains for your drink; the mountains and the valleys for your refuge and the high trees whereon to make your nests; and because ye know not how to spin or sew, God clotheth you, you and your children; wherefore your Creator loveth you much, seeing that He hath bestowed on you so many benefits; and therefore, my little sisters, beware of the sin of ingratitude, and study always to give praises unto God.

NEARER HOME

Phoebe Cary

One sweetly solemn thought
  Comes to me o'er and o'er;
I'm nearer my home today
  Than I ever have been before;

Nearer my Father's house,
  Where the many mansions be;
Nearer the great white throne,
  Nearer the crystal sea.

Nearer the bound of life,
  Where we lay our burdens down;
Nearer leaving the cross,
  Nearer gaining the crown!

But lying darkly between,
  Winding down thro' the night,
Is the silent, unknown stream,
  That leads at last to the night.

139

Oh, if my mortal feet
   Have almost gained the brink;
If it be I am nearer home
   Even today than I think,—

Father, perfect my trust!
   Let my spirit feel, in death,
That her feet are firmly set
   On the Rock of a living faith!

THE STAR

Jane Taylor

Twinkle, twinkle, little star,
How I wonder what you are!
Up above the world so high,
Like a diamond in the sky.

When the blazing sun is set,
When the grass with dew is wet,
Then you show your little light,
Twinkle, twinkle, all the night.

Then the traveler in the dark,
Thanks you for your tiny spark;
He could not see which way to go
If you did not twinkle so.

In the dark blue sky you keep,
And often through my curtains peep,
For you never shut your eye
Till the sun is in the sky.

As your bright and shiny spark,
Lights the traveler in the dark,
Though I know not what you are,
Twinkle, twinkle, little star.

* * *

The blood of the martyrs is the seed of the Church.
                    —Tertullian

"THROW HIM DOWN M'CLOSKEY"

John W. Kelly

'Twas down at Dan McDevitt's at the corner of this street,
There was to be a prize fight and both parties were to meet;
To make all the arrangements and see everything was right,
McCloskey and a nagur were to have a finish fight;
The rules were London Prize Ring and McCloskey said he'd try,
To bate the nagur wid one punch or in the ring he'd die;
The odds were on McCloskey though the betting it was small,
'Twas on McCloskey ten to one, on the nagur none at all.

Chorus:

    "Throw him down McCloskey," was to be the battle cry,
    "Throw him down McCloskey, you can lick him if you try,"
    And future generations, with wonder and delight,
    Will read on hist'ry's pages of the great McCloskey fight.

The fighters were to start in at a quarter after eight,
But the nagur did not show up and the hour was getting late;
He sent around a messenger who then went on to say,
That the Irish crowd would jump him and he couldn't get fair play;
Then up steps Pete McCracken, and said that he would fight,
Stand up or rough and tumble if McCloskey didn't bite?
McCloskey says I'll go you, then the seconds got in place,
And the fighters started in to decorate each others face. *(Chorus.)*

They fought like two hyenas 'till the forty-seventh round,
They scattered blood enough around by gosh, to paint the town,
McCloskey got a mouthful of poor McCracken's jowl.
McCracken hollered 'murthur' and his seconds hollered "foul!"
The friends of both the fighters that instant did begin,
To fight and ate each other the whole party started in.
You couldn't tell the difference in the fighters if you'd try,
McCracken lost his upper lip, McCloskey lost an eye. *(Chorus.)*

THE MOURNING BRIDE

William Congreve

Heaven hath no rage like love to hatred turned,
Nor hell a fury like a woman scorned.

ON THE PROSPECT OF PLANTING ARTS AND LEARNING IN AMERICA

George Berkeley

The Muse, disgusted at an age and clime
Barren of every glorious theme,
In distant lands now waits a better time,
Producing subjects worthy fame:

In happy climes, where from the genial sun
And virgin earth such scenes ensue,
The force of art by nature seems outdone,
And fancied beauties by the true:

In happy climes the seat of innocence,
Where nature guides and virtue rules,
Where men shall not impose for truth and sense
The pedantry of courts and schools:

There shall be sung another golden age,
The rise of empire and of arts,
The good and great inspiring epic rage,
The wisest heads and noblest hearts.

Not such as Europe breeds in her decay;
Such as she bred when fresh and young,
When heavenly flame did animate her clay,
By future poets shall be sung.

Westward the course of empire takes its way;
The first four Acts already past,
A fifth shall close the Drama with the day;
Time's noblest offspring is the last.

BELSHAZZAR'S FEAST

Holy Bible, Daniel 5

1 Belshazzar the king made a great feast to a thousand of his lords, and drank wine before the thousand.

2 Belshazzar, whiles he tasted the wine, commanded to bring the golden and silver vessels which his father Nebuchadnezzar

had taken out of the temple which was in Jerusalem; that the king, and his princes, his wives, and his concubines, might drink therein.

3 Then they brought the golden vessels that were taken out of the temple of the house of God which was at Jerusalem; and the king, and his princes, his wives, and his concubines, drank in them.

4 They drank wine, and praised the gods of gold, and of silver, of brass, of iron, of wood, and of stone.

5 In the same hour came forth fingers of a man's hand, and wrote over against the candlestick upon the plaister of the wall of the king's palace: and the king saw the part of the hand that wrote.

6 Then the king's countenance was changed, and his thoughts troubled him, so that the joints of his loins were loosed, and his knees smote one against another.

7 The king cried aloud to bring in the astrologers, the Chaldeans, and the soothsayers. And the king spake, and said to the wise men of Babylon, Whosoever shall read this writing, and shew me the interpretation thereof, shall be clothed with scarlet, and have a chain of gold about his neck, and shall be the third ruler in the kingdom.

8 Then came in all the king's wise men: but they could not read the writing, nor make known to the king the interpretation thereof.

9 Then was king Belshazzar greatly troubled, and his countenance was changed in him, and his lords were astonied.

10 Now the queen, by reason of the words of the king and his lords, came into the banquet house: and the queen spake and said, O king, live for ever: let not thy thoughts trouble thee, nor let thy countenance be changed:

11 There is a man in thy kingdom, in whom is the spirit of the holy gods; and in the days of thy father light and understanding and wisdom, like the wisdom of the gods, was found in him; whom the king Nebuchadnezzar thy father, the king, I say, thy father, made master of the magicians, astrologers, Chaldeans, and soothsayers;

12 Forasmuch as an excellent spirit, and knowledge, and understanding, interpreting of dreams, and shewing of hard sentences, and dissolving of doubts, were found in the same Daniel, whom the king named Belteshazzar: now let Daniel be called, and he will shew the interpretation.

13 Then was Daniel brought in before the king. And the king spake and said unto Daniel, Art thou that Daniel, which art of the children of the captivity of Judah, whom the king my father brought out of Jewry?

14 I have even heard of thee, that the spirit of the gods is in thee and that light and understanding and excellent wisdom is found in thee.

15 And now the wise men, the astrologers, have been brought in before me, that they should read this writing, and make known unto me the interpretation thereof: but they could not shew the interpretation of the thing:

16 And I have heard of thee, that thou canst make interpretations, and dissolve doubts: now if thou canst read the writing, and make known to me the interpretation thereof, thou shalt be clothed with scarlet, and have a chain of gold about thy neck, and shalt be the third ruler in the kingdom.

17 Then Daniel answered and said before the king, Let thy gifts be to thyself, and give thy rewards to another; yet I will read the writing unto the king, and make known to him the interpretation.

18 O thou king, the most high God gave Nebuchadnezzar thy father a kingdom, and majesty, and glory, and honour:

19 And for the majesty that he gave him, all people, nations, and languages, trembled and feared before him: whom he would he slew; and whom he would he kept alive; and whom he would he set up; and whom he would he put down.

20 But when his heart was lifted up, and his mind hardened in pride, he was deposed from his kingly throne, and they took his glory from him:

21 And he was driven from the sons of men; and his heart was made like the beasts, and his dwelling was with the wild asses: they fed him with grass like oxen, and his body was wet with the dew of heaven; till he knew that the most high God ruled in the kingdom of men, and that he appointeth over it whomsoever he will.

22 And thou his son, O Belshazzar, hast not humbled thine heart, though thou knewest all this;

23 But hast lifted up thyself against the Lord of heaven; and they have brought the vessels of his house before thee, and thou, and thy lords, thy wives, and thy concubines, have drunk wine in them; and thou hast praised the gods of silver, and gold, of brass, iron, wood, and stone, which see not, nor hear, nor know: and the God in whose hand thy breath is, and whose are all thy ways, hast thou not glorified:

24 Then was the part of the hand sent from him; and this writing was written.

25 And this is the writing that was written, MENE, MÉNE, TEKEL, UPHARSIN.

26 This is the interpretation of the thing: MENE; God hath numbered thy kingdom, and finished it.

27 TEKEL; Thou art weighed in the balances, and art found wanting.

28 PERES; Thy kingdom is divided, and given to the Medes and Persians.

29 Then commanded Belshazzar, and they clothed Daniel with scarlet, and put a chain of gold about his neck, and made a proclamation concerning him, that he should be the third ruler in the kingdom.

30 In that night was Belshazzar the king of the Chaldeans slain.

31 And Darius the Median took the kingdom, being about threescore and two years old.

A PSALM OF LIFE

Henry Wadsworth Longfellow

Tell me not, in mournful numbers,
Life is but an empty dream!—
For the soul is dead that slumbers,
And things are not what they seem.

Life is real! Life is earnest!
And the grave is not its goal;
Dust thou art, to dust returnest,
Was not spoken of the soul.

Not enjoyment, and not sorrow
Is our destined end or way;
But to act, that each tomorrow
Find us farther than today.

Art is long, and Time is fleeting,
And our hearts, though stout and brave,
Still, like muffled drums, are beating
Funeral marches to the grave.

In the world's broad field of battle,
In the bivouac of life,
Be not like dumb, driven cattle!
Be a hero in the strife!

Trust no Future, howe'er pleasant!
Let the dead Past bury its dead!
Act,—act in the living Present!
Heart within, and God o'erhead!

Lives of great men all remind us
We can make our lives sublime,
And, departing, leave behind us
Footprints on the sand of time—

Footprints, that perhaps another,
Sailing o'er life's solemn main,
A forlorn and shipwrecked brother,
Seeing, shall take heart again.

Let us, then, be up and doing,
With a heart for any fate;
Still achieving, still pursuing,
Learn to labor and to wait.

GEORGE WASHINGTON AND THE CHERRY-TREE

Mason Locke ("Parson") Weems

The following anecdote is a case in point. It is too valuable to be lost, and too true to be doubted; for it was communicated to me by the same excellent lady to whom I am indebted for the last.

"When George," said she, "was about six years old, he was made the wealthy master of a hatchet! of which, like most little boys, he was immoderately fond, and was constantly going about chopping every thing that came in his way. One day, in the garden, where he often amused himself hacking his mother's pea-sticks, he unluckily tried the edge of his hatchet on the body of a beautiful young cherry-tree, which he barked so terribly, that I don't believe the tree ever got the better of it. The next morning the old gentleman, finding out what had befallen his tree, which, by the by, was a great favourite, came into the house; and with much warmth asked for the mischievous author, declaring at the same time, that he would not have taken five guineas for his tree. Nobody could tell him anything about it. Presently George and his hatchet made their appearance. 'George,' said his father, 'do you know who killed that beautiful little cherry-tree yonder in the garden?' This was a tough question; and George staggered under it for a moment; but quickly recovered himself; and looking at his father, with the sweet face of youth brightened with the inexpressible charm of all-conquering truth, he bravely cried out, 'I can't tell a lie. I did cut it with my hatchet.'—'Run to my arms, you dearest boy,' cried his father in transports, 'run to my arms; glad am I, George, that you killed my tree; for you have paid me for it a thousand fold. Such an act of heroism in my son is more worth than a thousand trees, though blossomed with silver, and their fruits of purest gold.' "

(From The Life of George Washington)

THE LIGHT OF OTHER DAYS

Thomas Moore

Oft in the stilly night
  Ere slumber's chain has bound me,
Fond Memory brings the light
  Of other days around me:
    The smiles, the tears,
    Of boyhood's years,
  The words of love then spoken;
    The eyes that shone,
    Now dimmed and gone,
  The cheerful hearts now broken!
Thus in the stilly night
  Ere slumber's chain has bound me,
Sad Memory brings the light
  Of other days around me.

When I remember all
  The friends so linked together
I've seen around me fall
  Like leaves in wintry weather,
    I feel like one
    Who treads alone
  Some banquet-hall deserted,
    Whose lights are fled,
    Whose garlands dead,
  And all but he departed!
Thus in the stilly night
  Ere slumber's chain has bound me,
Sad Memory brings the light
  Of other days around me.

HERACLITUS

William (Johnson) Cory

They told me, Heraclitus, they told me you were dead,
They brought me bitter news to hear and bitter tears to shed
I wept as I remember'd how often you and I
Had tired the sun with talking and sent him down the sky.

And now that thou art lying, my dear old Carian guest,
A handful of gray ashes, long, long ago at rest,
Still are thy pleasant voices, thy nightingales, awake;
For Death, he taketh all away, but them he cannot take.

LONDON, 1802

William Wordsworth

Milton! thou should'st be living at this hour;
England hath need of thee: she is a fen
Of stagnant waters: altar, sword, and pen,
Fireside, the heroic wealth of hall and bower,
Have forfeited their ancient English dower
Of inward happiness. We are selfish men;
Oh! raise us up, return to us again;
And give us manners, virtue, freedom, power.
Thy soul was like a Star, and dwelt apart:
Thou hadst a voice whose sound was like the sea:
Pure as the naked heavens, majestic, free,
So didst thou travel on life's common way,
In cheerful godliness; and yet thy heart
The lowliest duties on herself did lay.

'OSTLER JOE

George R. Sims

I stood at eve, as the sun went down, by a grave where a woman
    lies,
Who lured men's souls to the shores of sin with the light of her
    wanton eyes;

Who sang the song that the Siren sang on the treacherous Lurley
  height,
Whose face was as fair as a summer day, and whose heart was as
  black as night.

Yet a blossom I fain would pluck today from the garden above her
  dust—
Not the languorous lily of soulless sin, nor the blood-red rose of
  lust,
But a pure white blossom of holy love that grew in the one green
  spot
In the arid desert of Phryne's life, where all was parched and hot.

In the summer, when the meadows were aglow with blue and red,
Joe, the hostler of the "Magpie," and fair Annie Smith were wed.
Plump was Annie, plump and pretty, with cheek as white as snow;
He was anything but handsome, was the "Magpie" hostler, Joe.

But he won the winsome lassie. They'd a cottage and a cow;
And her matronhood sat lightly on the village beauty's brow.
Sped the months and came a baby—such a blue-eyed baby boy;
Joe was working in the stables when they told him of his joy.

He was rubbing down the horses, and he gave them then and there
All a special feed of clover, just in honor of the heir.
It had been his great ambition, and he told the horses so,
That the Fates would send a baby who might bear the name of Joe.

Little Joe the child was christened, and, like babies, grew apace,
He'd his mother's eyes of azure and his father's honest face.
Swift the happy years went over, years of blue and cloudless sky;
Love was lord of that small cottage, and the tempest passed them
  by.

Passed them by for years, then swiftly burst in fury o'er their home.
Down the lane by Annie's cottage chanced a gentleman to roam;
Thrice he came and saw her sitting by the window with her child,
And he nodded to the baby, and the baby laughed and smiled.

So at last it grew to know him—little Joe was nearly four—
He would call the "pretty gemlum" as he passed the open door;
And one day he ran and caught him, and in child's play pulled
  him in,
And the baby Joe had prayed for brought about the mother's sin.

'Twas the same old wretched story that for ages bards had sung,
'Twas a woman weak and wanton, and a villain's tempting tongue;
'Twas a picture deftly painted for a silly creature's eyes
Of the Babylonian wonders, and the joy that in them lies.

Annie listened and was tempted—she was tempted and she fell,
As the angel fell from heaven to the blackest depths of hell;
She was promised wealth and splendour, and a life of guilty sloth,
Yellow gold for child and husband—and the woman left them both.

Home one eve came Joe the hostler, with a cheery cry of "Wife,"
Finding that which blurred forever all the story of his life.
She had left a silly letter,—through the cruel scrawl he spelt;
Then he sought his lonely bedroom, joined his horny hands, and
    knelt.

"Now, O Lord, O God, forgive her, for she ain't to blame," he
    cried;
"For I owt to seen her trouble, and 'a' gone away and died.
Why, a wench like her—God bless her! 'twasn't likely as her'd rest
With that bonnie head forever on a hostler's rugged breast.

"It was kind o' her to bear me all this long and happy time;
So, for my sake please to bless her, though you count her deed a
    crime;
If so be I don't pray proper, Lord, forgive me; for you see
I can talk all right to 'osses; but I'm nervous like with Thee."

Ne'er a line came to the cottage, from the woman who had flown;
Joe, the baby, died that winter, and the man was left alone.
Ne'er a bitter word he uttered, but in silence kissed the rod,
Saving what he told the horses—saving what he told his God

Far away, in mighty London, rose the woman into fame,
For her beauty won men's homage, and she prospered in her
    shame.
Quick from lord to lord she flitted, higher still each prize she won,
And her rivals paled beside her, as the stars beside the sun.

Next she trod the stage half naked, and she dragged a temple down
To the level of a market for the women of the town.
And the kisses she had given to poor hostler Joe for naught
With their gold and priceless jewels rich and titled roués bought.

Went the years with flying footsteps while her star was at its height,
Then the darkness came on swiftly, and the gloaming turned to
  night.
Shattered strength and faded beauty tore the laurels from her
  brow;
Of the thousands who had worshipped never one came near her
  now.

Broken down in health and fortune, men forgot her very name,
Till the news that she was dying woke the echoes of her fame;
And the papers, in their gossip, mentioned how an actress lay
Sick to death in humble lodgings, growing weaker every day.

One there was who read the story in a far-off country place,
And that night the dying woman woke and looked upon his face.
Once again the strong arms clasped her that had clasped her years
  ago,
And the weary head lay pillowed on the breast of hostler Joe.

All the past had he forgiven, all the sorrow and the shame;
He had found her sick and lonely, and his wife he now could
  claim,
Since the grand folks who had known her, one and all, had slunk
  away,
He could clasp his long-lost darling, and no man would say him
  nay.

In his arms death found her lying, in his arms her spirit fled;
And his tears came down in torrents as he knelt beside her dead.
Never once his love had faltered, through her base, unhallowed
  life,
And the stone above her ashes bears the honored name of wife.

That's the blossom I fain would pluck today, from the garden
  above her dust;
Not the languorous lily of soulless sin, nor the blood-red rose of
  lust;
But a sweet white blossom of holy love, that grew in the one green
  spot
In the arid desert of Phryne's life, where all was parched and hot.

* * *

Virtue, though in rags, will keep me warm.
                              —Dryden

AN ELEGY ON THE DEATH OF A MAD DOG

Oliver Goldsmith

Good people all, of every sort,
Give ear unto my song;
And if you find it wondrous short—
It cannot hold you long.

In Islington there was a man,
Of whom the world might say
That still a godly race he ran—
Whene'er he went to pray.

A kind and gentle heart he had,
To comfort friends and foes;
The naked every day he clad—
When he put on his clothes.

And in that town a dog was found,
As many dogs there be,
Both mongrels, puppy, whelp, and hound,
And curs of low degree.

This dog and man at first were friends;
But when a pique began,
The dog, to gain some private ends,
Went mad, and bit the man.

Around from all the neighboring streets,
The wondering neighbors ran,
And swore the dog had lost his wits
To bite so good a man!

The wound it seemed both sore and sad
To every Christian eye;
And while they swore the dog was mad,
They swore the man would die.

But soon a wonder came to light,
That showed the rogues they lied;
The man recovered of the bite,
The dog it was that died!

THE FOURTEEN POINTS

Woodrow Wilson

The program of the world's peace is our program, and that program, the only possible program, as we see it, is this:

I. Open covenants of peace must be arrived at, after which there will surely be no private international action or rulings of any kind, but diplomacy shall proceed always frankly and in the public view.

II. Absolute freedom of navigation upon the seas, outside territorial waters, alike in peace and in war, except as the seas may be closed in whole or in part by international action for the enforcement of international covenants.

III. The removal, so far as possible, of all economic barriers and the establishment of an equality of trade conditions among all the nations consenting to the peace and associating themselves for its maintenance.

IV. Adequate guaranties given and taken that national armaments will reduce to the lowest point consistent with domestic safety.

V. Free, open-minded, and absolutely impartial adjustment of all colonial claims, based upon a strict observance of the principle that in determining all such questions of sovereignty the interests of the population concerned must have equal weight with the equitable claims of the government whose title is to be determined.

VI. The evacuation of all Russian territory and such a settlement of all questions affecting Russia as will secure the best and freest coöperation of the other nations of the world in obtaining for her an unhampered and unembarrassed opportunity for the independent determination of her own political development and national policy, and assure her of a sincere welcome into the society of free nations under institutions of her own choosing; and, more than a welcome, assistance also of every kind that she may need and may herself desire. The treatment accorded Russia by her sister nations in the months to come will be the acid test of their good-will, of their comprehension of her needs as distinguished from their own interests, and of their intelligent and unselfish sympathy.

VII. Belgium, the whole world will agree, must be evacuated and restored, without any attempt to limit the sovereignty which she enjoys in common with all other free nations. No other single act will serve as this will serve to restore confidence among the nations in the laws which they have themselves set and determined for the government of their relations with one another. Without this healing act the whole structure and validity of international law is forever impaired.

VIII. All French territory should be freed and the invaded portions restored, and the wrong done to France by Prussia in 1871 in the matter of Alsace-Lorraine, which has unsettled the peace of the world for nearly fifty years, should be righted, in order that peace may once more be made secure in the interest of all.

IX. A readjustment of the frontiers of Italy should be effected along clearly recognizable lines of nationality.

X. The peoples of Austria-Hungary, whose place among the nations we wish to see safeguarded and assured, should be accorded the freest opportunity of autonomous development.

XI. Roumania, Serbia, and Montenegro should be evacuated; occupied territories restored; Serbia accorded free and secure access to the sea; and the relations of the several Balkan States to one another determined by friendly counsel along historically established lines of allegiance and nationality; and international guaranties of the political and economic independence and territorial integrity of the several Balkan States should be entered into.

XII. The Turkish portions of the present Ottoman Empire should be assured a secure sovereignty, but the other nationalities which are now under Turkish rule should be assured an undoubted security of life and an absolutely unmolested opportunity of autonomous development, and the Dardanelles should be permanently opened as a free passage to the ships and commerce of all nations under international guaranties.

XIII. An independent Polish state should be erected which should include the territories inhabited by indisputably Polish populations, which should be assured a free and secure access to the sea, and whose political and economic independence and territorial integrity should be guaranteed by international covenant.

XIV. A general association of nations must be formed under specific covenants for the purpose of affording mutual guaranties of political independence and territorial integrity to great and small states alike.

In regard to these essential rectifications of wrong and assertions of right, we feel ourselves to be intimate partners of all the Governments and peoples associated together against the imperialists.

We cannot be separated in interest or divided in purpose. We stand together until the end.

For such arrangements and covenants we are willing to fight and to continue to fight until they are achieved; but only because we wish the right to prevail and desire a just and stable peace, such as can be secured only by removing the chief provocations to war, which this program does remove. We have no jealousy of German greatness, and there is nothing in this program that impairs it. We grudge her no achievement or distinction of learning or of pacific enterprise such as have made her record very bright and very enviable. We do not wish to injure her or to block in any way her legitimate influence or power. We do not wish to fight her either with arms or with hostile arrangements of trade, if she is willing to associate herself with us and the other peace-loving nations of the world in covenants of justice and law and fair dealing. We wish her only to accept a place of equality among the peoples of the world—the new world in which we now live—instead of a place of mastery.

Neither do we presume to suggest to her any alteration or modification of her institutions. But it is necessary, we must frankly say, and necessary as a preliminary to any intelligent dealings with her on our part, that we should know whom her spokesmen speak for when they speak to us, whether for the Reichstag majority or for the military party and the men whose creed is imperial domination.

We have spoken now, surely, in terms too concrete to admit of any further doubt or question. An evident principle runs through the whole program I have outlined. It is the principle of justice to all peoples and nationalities, and their right to live on equal terms of liberty and safety with one another, whether they be strong or weak. Unless this principle be made its foundation, no part of the structure of international justice can stand. The people of the United States could act upon no other principle, and to the vindication of this principle they are ready to devote their lives, their honor, and everything that they possess. The moral climax of this, the culminating and final war for human liberty, has come, and they are ready to put their own strength, their own highest purpose, their own integrity and devotion to the test.

* * *

The Spartans do not enquire how many the enemy are, but where they are.

—Agis II, 427 B.C.

155

WHAT IS GOOD?

John Boyle O'Reilly

"What is the real good?"
I ask in musing mood.

"Order," said the law court;
"Knowledge," said the school;
"Truth," said the wise man;
"Pleasure," said the fool;
"Love," said the maiden;
"Beauty," said the page;
"Freedom," said the dreamer;
"Home," said the sage;
"Fame," said the soldier;
"Equity," said the seer.
Spake my heart fully sad:
"The answer is not here."

Then within my bosom
Softly this I heard:
"Each heart holds the secret:
'Kindness' is the word."

EVEN SUCH IS TIME

Sir Walter Raleigh

Even such is Time, that takes in trust our youth, our joys, our all
  we have,
And pays us but with earth and dust;
Who in the dark and silent grave,
When we have wandered all our ways,
Shuts up the story of our days;
But from this earth, this grave, this dust,
My God shall raise me up, I trust.

(From his History of the World)

* * *

The cynic is one who knows the price of everything and the
value of nothing.

—Oscar Wilde

PERICLES' FUNERAL ORATION

Most of those who have spoken here before me have commended the lawgiver who added this oration to our other funeral customs; it seemed to them a worthy thing that such an honor should be given at their burial to the dead who had fallen on the field of battle. But I should have preferred that, when men's deeds have been brave, they should be honored in deed only, and with such an honor as this public funeral, which you are now witnessing. Then the reputation of many would not have been imperilled on the eloquence or want of eloquence of one, and their virtues believed or not, as he spoke well or ill. For it is difficult to say neither too little or too much; and even moderation is apt not to give the impression of truthfulness. The friend of the dead who know the facts is likely to think that the words of the speaker fall short of his knowledge and of his wishes; another who is not so well informed, when he hears of anything which surpasses his own powers, will be envious and will suspect exaggeration. Mankind is tolerant of the praises of others so long as each hearer thinks that he can do as well or nearly as well himself; but, when the speaker rises above him, jealousy is aroused, and he begins to be incredulous. However, since our ancestors have set the seal of their approval upon the practice, I must obey, and to the utmost of my power shall endeavor to satisfy the wishes and beliefs of all who hear me. . . .

I have dwelt upon the greatness of Athens because I want to show you that we are contending for a higher prize than those who enjoy none of these privileges, and to establish by manifest proof the merit of these men whom I am now commemorating. Their loftiest praise has been already spoken. For in magnifying the city I have magnified them, and men like them whose virtues made her glorious. And of how few Hellenes can it be said, as of them, that their deeds when weighed in the balance have been found equal to their fame! Methinks that a death such as theirs has been gives the true measure of a man's worth; it may be the first revelation of his virtues, but is at any rate their final seal. For even those who come short in other ways may justly plead the valor with which they fought for their country; they have blotted out the evil with the good, and have benefited the State more by their public services than they have injured her by their private actions. None of these men were enervated by wealth or hesitated to resign the pleasures of life; none of them put off the evil day in the hope, natural to poverty, that a man, though poor, may one day become rich. But deeming that the punishment of their enemies was sweeter than any of these things, and that they could fall in no nobler cause, they determined at the hazard of their lives to be honorably avenged, and to leave the rest. They resigned to hope their unknown chance of happiness; but in the face of death they resolved to rely upon themselves alone. And when the moment came they were minded to resist and suffer, rather than to fly and save their lives; they ran away from the world of dishonor, but on the battle-field their feet stood fast, and in an instant, at the height of their fortune, they passed away from the scene, not of their fear, but of their glory.

Such was the end of these men; they were worthy of Athens, and the living need not desire to have a more heroic spirit, although they may pray for a less fatal issue. The value of such a spirit is not to be expressed in words. Anyone can discourse to you forever about the advantages of a brave defense which you know already. But instead of listening to him I would have you day by day fix your eyes upon the greatness of Athens, until you become filled with the love of her; and when you are impressed by the spectacle of her glory, reflect that this empire has been acquired by men who knew their duty and had the courage to do it, who in the hour of conflict had the fear of dishonor always present to them, and who, if they ever failed in an enterprise, would not allow their virtues to be lost to their country, but freely gave their lives to her as the fairest offering which they could present at her feast. The sacrifice which they collectively made was individually repaid to them; for they received again each one for himself a praise which grows not old, and the noblest of all sepulchres—I speak not of that in which their remains are laid, but of that in which their glory survives and is proclaimed always and on every fitting occasion both in word and deed. For the whole earth is the sepulchre of famous men; not only are they commemorated by famous columns and inscriptions in their own country, but in foreign lands there dwells also an unwritten memorial to them, graven, not on stone, but in the hearts of men. Make them your examples, and, esteeming courage to be freedom and freedom to be happiness, do not weigh too nicely the perils of war. The unfortunate who has no hope of a change for the better has less reason to throw away his life than the prosperous who, if he survives, is always liable to a change for the worse, and to whom any accidental fall makes the most serious difference. To a man of spirit, cowardice and disaster coming together are far more bitter than death striking him unperceived at a time when he is full of courage and animated by the general hope.

Wherefore I do not now commiserate the parents of the dead who stand here; I would rather comfort them. You know that your life has been passed amid manifold vicissitudes; and that they may be deemed fortunate who have gained most honor, whether an honorable death like theirs, or an honorable sorrow like yours, and whose days have been so ordered that the term of their happiness is likewise the term of their life. I know how hard it is to make you feel this, when the good fortunes of others will too often remind you of the gladness which once lightened your hearts. And sorrow is felt at the want of those blessings, not which a man never knew, but which were a part of his life before they were taken from him. Some [of you] are of an age at which they may hope to have other children, and they ought to bear their sorrow better; not only will the children who may hereafter be born make them forget their own lost ones, but the city will be doubly a gainer. She will not be left desolate, and she will be safer. For a man's counsel cannot have equal weight or worth, when he alone has no children to risk in the general danger. To those of you who have passed their prime, I say: Congratulate yourselves that you have been happy during the greater part of your days; remember that your life of sorrow will not last long, and be comforted by the glory of those who are gone. For the love of honor alone is ever young, and not riches, as some say, but honor is the delight of men when they are old and useless.

To you who are the sons and brothers of the departed, I see that the struggle to emulate them will be an arduous one. For all men praise the dead, and, however preeminent your virtues may be, hardly will you be thought, I do not say equal, but even to approach them. The living have their rivals and detractors, but when a man is out of the way, the honor and good-will which he receives is unalloyed. And, if I am to speak of womanly virtues to those of you who will henceforth be widows, let me sum them up in one short admonition: To a woman not to show more weakness than is natural to her sex is a great glory, and not to be talked about for good or for evil among men. I have paid the required tribute, in obedience to the law, making use of such fitting words as I had. The tribute in deeds has been paid in part; for the dead have been honorably interred, and it remains only that their children should be maintained at the public charge until they are grown up; this is the solid prize with which, as with a garland, Athens crowns her sons living and dead, after a struggle like theirs. For where the rewards of virtue are greatest, there the noblest citizens are enlisted in the service of the State. And now, when you have duly lamented, every one his own dead, you may depart.

THE FOOL'S PRAYER

Edward Rowland Sill

The royal feast was done; the King
Sought some new sport to banish care,
And to his jester cried: "Sir Fool,
Kneel now, and make for us a prayer!"

The jester doffed his cap and bells,
And stood the mocking court before;
They could not see the bitter smile
Behind the painted grin he wore.

He bowed his head, and bent his knee
Upon the monarch's silken stool;
His pleading voice arose: "O Lord,
Be merciful to me, a fool!

"No pity, Lord, could change the heart
From red with wrong to white as wool;
The rod must heal the sin; but, Lord,
Be merciful to me, a fool!

" 'Tis not by guilt, the onward sweep
Of truth and right, O Lord, we stay;
'Tis by our follies that so long
We hold the earth from heaven away.

"These clumsy feet, still in the mire,
Go crushing blossoms without end;
These hard, well-meaning hands we thrust
Among the heart-strings of a friend.

"The ill-timed truth we might have kept—
Who knows how sharp it pierced and stung!
The words we had not sense to say—
Who knows how grandly it had rung!

"Our faults no tenderness should ask,
The chastening strips must cleanse them all;
But for our blunders—oh, in shame
Before the eyes of heaven we fall.

"Earth bears no balsam for mistakes;
Men crown the knave, and scourge the tool
That did his will; but Thou, O Lord,
Be merciful to me, a fool!"

The room was hushed; in silence rose
The King, and sought his gardens cool,
And walked apart, and murmured low,
"Be merciful to me, a fool!"

FRANKIE AND JOHNNY

Anonymous

Frankie and Johnny were lovers,
Oh, Lordy, how they could love!
They swore to be true to each other,
Just as true as the stars above,
He was her man, but he done her wrong.

Frankie and Johnny went walking,
Johnny in his brand new suit.
"Oh, good Lord," says Frankie,
"Don't my Johnny look cute."
He was her man but he done her wrong.

Johnny said, "I've got to leave you,
But I won't be very long,
Don't you wait up for me honey,
Nor worry while I'm gone."
He was her man, but he done her wrong.

Frankie went down to the corner,
Stopped in to buy her some beer,
Says to the fat bar-tender,
"Has my Johnny man been here?"
He was her man, but he done her wrong.

"Well, I ain't going to tell you no story,
Ain't going to tell you no lie.
Johnny went by, 'bout an hour ago,
With a girl named Nellie Blye,
He was your man, but he's doin' you wrong."

Frankie went home in a hurry,
She didn't go there for fun.
She hurried home to get a-hold,
Of Johnny's shottin' gun.
He was her man, but he's doin' her wrong.

Frankie took a cab at the corner,
Says "Driver, step on this can."
She was just a desperate woman,
Gettin' two-timed by her man.
He was her man, but he's doin' her wrong.

Frankie got out at South Clark Street,
Looked in a window so high,
Saw her Johnny man a-lovin' up,
That high brown Nellie Blye.
He was her man, but he's doin' her wrong.

Johnny saw Frankie a-comin',
Out the back door he did scoot,
But Frankie took aim with her pistol;
And the gun went "Root atoot-toot!"
He was her man, but he done her wrong.

"Oh roll me over so easy,
Roll me over so slow,
Roll me over easy boys,
'Cause my wounds they hurt me so.
I was her man, but I done her wrong."

Bring out your long black coffin,
Bring out your funeral clo'es,
Johnny's gone and cashed his checks,
To the graveyard Johnny goes.
He was her man, but he done her wrong.

Drive out your rubber-tired carriage,
Drive out your rubber-tired hack;
There's twelve men going to the graveyard,
And eleven coming back,
He was her man, but he done her wrong.

The sheriff arrested poor Frankie,
Took her to jail that same day
He locked her up in a dungeon cell,
And threw the key away,
She shot her man, though he done her wrong.

Note: This is one of three hundred versions of the story of Frankie and Johnny

MARCO BOZZARIS

[Marco Bozzaris, the Epaminondas of modern Greece, fell
in a night attack upon the Turkish camp at Laspi, the site of
the ancient Platæa, August 20, 1823, and expired in the moment of victory. His last words were: "To die for liberty is a
pleasure, and not a pain."]

Fitz-Greene Halleck

At midnight, in his guarded tent,
    The Turk was dreaming of the hour
When Greece, her knee in suppliance bent,
    Should tremble at his power.
In dreams, through camp and court, he bore
The trophies of a conqueror;
    In dreams his song of triumph heard;
Then wore his monarch's signet-ring,
Then pressed that monarch's throne—a king;
As wild his thoughts, and gay of wing,
    As Eden's garden bird.

At midnight, in the forest shades,
    Bozzaris ranged his Suliote band,—
True as the steel of their tried blades,
    Heroes in heart and hand.
There had the Persian's thousands stood,
There had the glad earth drunk their blood,
    On old Platæa's day;

163

And now there breathed that haunted air
The sons of sires who conquered there,
With arms to strike, and soul to dare,
   As quick, as far, as they.

An hour passed on, the Turk awoke:
   That bright dream was his last;
He woke—to hear his sentries shriek,
   "To arms! they come! the Greek! the Greek!"
He woke—to die midst flame, and smoke,
And shout, and groan, and sabre-stroke,
   And death-shots falling thick and fast
As lightnings from the mountain-cloud;
And heard, with voice as trumpet loud,
   Bozzaris cheer his band:
"Strike—till the last armed foe expires;
   Strike—for your altars and your fires;
Strike—for the green graves of your sires,
   God, and your native land!"

They fought—like brave men, long and well;
   They piled that ground with Moslem slain:
They conquered—but Bozzaris fell,
   Bleeding at every vein.
His few surviving comrades saw
His smile when rang their proud hurrah,
   And the red field was won;
Then saw in death his eyelids close
Calmly, as to a night's repose.
   Like flowers at set of sun.

Come to the bridal chamber, death,
   Come to the mother's, when she feels,
For the first time, her first-born's breath;
   Come when the blessed seals
That close the pestilence are broke,
And crowded cities wail its stroke;
Come in consumption's ghastly form,
The earthquake shock, the ocean storm;
Come when the heart beats high and warm,
   With banquet song and dance and wine,—

And thou art terrible; the tear,
The groan, the knell, the pall, the bier,
And all we know, or dream, or fear
    Of agony, are thine.

But to the hero, when his sword
    Has won the battle for the free,
Thy voice sounds like a prophet's word,
And in its hollow tones are heard
    The thanks of millions yet to be.
Come when his task of fame is wrought;
Come with her laurel-leaf, blood-bought;
    Come in her crowning hour,—and then
Thy sunken eye's unearthly light
To him is welcome as the sight
    Of sky and stars to prisoned men;
Thy grasp is welcome as the hand
Of brother in a foreign land;
Thy summons welcome as the cry
That told the Indian isles were nigh
    To the world-seeking Genoese,
When the land-wind, from woods of palm,
And orange-groves, and fields of balm,
    Blew o'er the Haytian seas.

Bozzaris! with the storied brave
    Greece nurtured in her glory's time,
Rest thee; there is no prouder grave,
    Even in her own proud clime.
She wore no funeral weeds for thee,
    Nor bade the dark hearse wave its plume,
Like torn branch from death's leafless tree,
In sorrow's pomp and pageantry,
    The heartless luxury of the tomb.
But she remembers thee as one
Long loved, and for a season gone.
For thee her poet's lyre is wreathed,
Her marble wrought, her music breathed;
For thee she rings the birthday bells;
Of thee her babes' first lisping tells;
For thine her evening prayer is said
At palace couch and cottage bed.
Her soldier, closing with the foe,

Gives for thy sake a deadlier blow;
His plighted maiden, when she fears
For him, the joy of her young years,
Thinks of thy fate, and checks her tears.

And she, the mother of thy boys,
Though in her eye and faded cheek
Is read the grief she will not speak,
The memory of her buried joys,—
And even she who gave thee birth,—
Will, by her pilgrim-circled hearth,
Talk of thy doom without a sigh;
For thou art freedom's now, and fame's,—
One of the few, the immortal names
That were not born to die.

SEVEN AGES OF MAN

William Shakespeare

All the world's a stage,
And all the men and women merely players:
They have their exits and their entrances;
And one man in his time plays many parts,
His acts being seven ages. At first the infant,
Mewling and puking in the nurse's arms.
And then the whining school-boy, with his satchel
And shining morning face, creeping like snail
Unwillingly to school. And then the lover,
Sighing like furnace, with a woeful ballad
Made to his mistress' eyebrow. Then a soldier,
Full of strange oaths and bearded like the pard,
Jealous in honour, sudden and quick in quarrel,
Seeking the bubble reputation
Even in the cannon's mouth. And then the justice,
In fair round belly with good capon lined,
With eyes severe and beard of formal cut,
Full of wise saws and modern instances;
And so he plays his part. The sixth age shifts
Into the lean and slipper'd pantaloon,
With spectacles on nose and pouch on side,
His youthful hose, well saved, a world too wide
For his shrunk shank; and his big manly voice,

Turning again toward childish treble, pipes
And whistles in his sound. Last scene of all,
That ends this strange eventful history,
Is second childishness and mere oblivion,
Sans teeth, sans eyes, sans taste, sans every thing.

(From As You Like It)

WHAT ONE MAY AND MAY NOT CALL A WOMAN

Anonymous

You may call a woman a kitten, but you must not call her a cat.
You may call her a mouse, but you must not call her a rat.
You may call her a chicken, but you must not call her a hen.
You may call her a duck, but you must not call her a goose.
You may call her a vision, but you must not call her a sight.

I REMEMBER, I REMEMBER

Thomas Hood

I remember, I remember,
  The house where I was born,
The little window where the sun
  Came peeping in at morn:
He never came a wink too soon,
  Nor brought too long a day;
But now, I often wish the night
  Had borne my breath away.

I remember, I remember,
  The roses, red and white;
The violets, and the lily-cups,
  Those flowers made of light!
The lilacs where the robin built,
  And where my brother set
The laburnum on his birthday,—
  The tree is living yet!

I remember, I remember,
  Where I used to swing;
And thought the air must rush as fresh
  To swallows on the wing:

My spirit flew in feathers then,
        That is so heavy now,
And summer pools could hardly cool
        The fever on my brow!

I remember, I remember,
        The firtrees dark and high;
I used to think their slender tops
        Were close against the sky:
It was a childish ignorance,
        But now 'tis little joy
To know I'm farther off from heaven
        Than when I was a boy.

EMMY

Arthur Symons

Emmy's exquisite youth and her virginal air,
Eyes and teeth in the flash of a musical smile,
Come to me out of the past, and I see her there
As I saw her once for a while.

Emmy's laughter rings in my ears, as bright,
Fresh and sweet as the voice of a mountain brook,
And still I hear her telling us tales that night,
Out of Boccaccio's book.

There, in the midst of the villainous dancing-hall,
Leaning across the table, over the beer,
While the music madden'd the whirling skirts of the ball,
As the midnight hour drew near,

There with the women, haggard, painted and old,
One fresh bud in a garland wither'd and stale,
She, with the innocent voice and her clear eyes, told
Tale after shameless tale.

And ever the witching smile, to her face beguiled,
Paused and broaden'd, and broke in a ripple of fun,
And the soul of a child look'd out of the eyes of a child,
Or ever the tale was done.

O my child, who wrong'd you first, and began
First the dance of death that you dance so well?
Soul for soul: and I think the soul of a man
Shall answer for yours in hell.

RULE BRITANNIA!

James Thomson

When Britain first, at Heaven's command,
    Arose from out the azure main,
This was the charter of the land,
    And guardian angels sing the strain:
        Rule Britannia! Britannia rules the waves!
        Britons never will be slaves.

The nations not so blest as thee,
    Must, in their turn, to tyrants fall;
Whilst thou shalt flourish, great and free,
    The dread and envy of them all.
        Rule Britannia! etc.

Still more majestic shalt thou rise,
    More dreadful from each foreign stroke;
As the loud blasts that tear thy skies
    Serve but to root thy native oak.
        Rule Britannia! etc.

Thee haughty tyrants ne'er shall tame;
    All their attempts to hurl thee down
Will but arouse thy generous flame,
    And work their woe—but thy renown.
        Rule Britannia! etc.

To thee belongs the rural reign;
    Thy cities shall with commerce shine;
All thine shall be the subject main,
    And every shore encircle thine.
        Rule Britannia! etc.

The Muses, still with Freedom found,
    Shall to thy happy coast repair;
Blest Isle! with matchless beauty crowned,
    And manly hearts to guard the fair.
        Rule Britannia! etc.

AND THEY SHALL BEAT THEIR SWORDS INTO PLOWSHARES

Holy Bible, Micah 4:1–5

1 But in the last days it shall come to pass, that the mountain of the house of the Lord shall be established in the top of the mountains, and it shall be exalted above the hills; and people shall flow unto it.

2 And many nations shall come, and say, Come, and let us go up to the mountain of the Lord, and to the house of the God of Jacob; and he will teach us of his ways, and we will walk in his paths: for the law shall go forth of Zion, and the word of the Lord from Jerusalem.

3 And he shall judge among many people, and rebuke strong nations afar off; and they shall beat their swords into plowshares, and their spears into pruninghooks: nation shall not lift up a sword against nation, neither shall they learn war any more.

4 But they shall sit every man under his vine and under his fig tree; and none shall make them afraid: for the mouth of the Lord of hosts hath spoken it.

5 For all people will walk every one in the name of his god, and we will walk in the name of the Lord our God for ever and ever.

KATHLEEN MAVOURNEEN

Louisa Macartney Crawford

Kathleen Mavourneen! the grey dawn is breaking,
The horn of the hunter is heard on the hill;
The lark from her light wing, the bright dew is shaking,—
Kathleen Mavourneen! what, slumbering still?
Oh, hast thou forgotten how soon we must sever?
Oh, hast thou forgotten this day we must part?
It may be for years, and it may be for ever!
Oh, why art thou silent, thou voice of my heart?
Oh, why art thou silent, Kathleen Mavourneen?

Kathleen Mavourneen, awake from thy slumbers!
The blue mountains glow in the sun's golden light;
Ah, where is the spell that once hung on my numbers?
Arise in thy beauty, thou star of my night!

Mavourneen, Mavourneen, my sad tears are falling,
To think that from Erin and thee I must part!
It may be for years, and it may be for ever!
Then why art thou silent, thou voice of my heart?
Then why art thou silent, Kathleen Mavourneen?

LINCOLN'S SECOND INAUGURAL ADDRESS

FELLOW-COUNTRYMEN:

At this second appearing to take the oath of the presidential office, there is less occasion for an extended address than there was at first. Then a statement, somewhat in detail, of a course to be pursued seemed very fitting and proper. Now, at the expiration of four years, during which public declarations have been constantly called forth on every point and phase of the great contest which still absorbs the attention and engrosses the energies of the nation, little that is new could be presented.

The progress of our arms, upon which all else chiefly depends, is as well known to the public as to myself, and it is, I trust, reasonably satisfactory and encouraging to all. With high hope for the future, no prediction in regard to it is ventured.

On the occasion corresponding to this four years ago, all thoughts were anxiously directed to an impending civil war. All dreaded it, all sought to avoid it. While the inaugural address was being delivered from this place, devoted altogether to saving the Union without war, insurgent agents were in the city seeking to destroy it with war—seeking to dissolve the Union and divide the effects by negotiation. Both parties deprecated war, but one of them would make war rather than let the nation survive, and the other would accept war rather than let it perish, and the war came. One-eighth of the whole population were colored slaves, not distributed generally over the Union, but localized in the Southern part of it. These slaves constituted a peculiar and powerful interest. All knew that this interest was somehow the cause of the war. To strengthen, perpetuate, and extend this interest was the object for which the insurgents would rend the Union by war, while the government claimed no right to do more than to restrict the territorial enlargement of it.

Neither part expected for the war the magnitude or the duration which it has already attained. Neither anticipated that the cause of the conflict might cease when, or even before the conflict itself should cease. Each looked for an easier triumph, and a result less fundamental and astounding. Both read the same Bible and pray to the same God, and each invokes His aid against the other. It may seem strange that any men should dare to ask a just God's assistance in wringing their bread from the sweat of other men's faces, but let us judge not that we be not judged. The prayer of both could not be answered. That of neither has been answered fully. The Almighty has His own purposes. Woe unto the world because of offences, for it must needs be that offences come, but woe to that man by whom the offence cometh. If we shall suppose that American slavery is one of those offences which, in the providence of God, must needs come, but which having continued through His appointed time, He now wills to remove, and that He gives to both North and South this terrible war as the woe due to those by whom the offence came, shall we discern there any departure from those divine attributes which the believers in a living God always ascribe to Him? Fondly do we hope, fervently do we pray, that this mighty scourge of war may speedily pass away. Yet if God wills that it continue until all the wealth piled by the bondman's two hundred and fifty years of unrequited toil shall be sunk, and until every drop of blood drawn with the lash shall be paid by another drawn with the sword, as was said three thousand years ago, so still it must be said, that the judgments of the Lord are true and righteous altogether.

With malice toward none, with charity for all, with firmness in the right as God gives us to see the right, let us finish the work we are in, to bind up the nation's wounds, to care for him who shall have borne the battle, and for his widow and orphans, to do all which may achieve and cherish a just and lasting peace among ourselves and with all nations.

THE ARROW AND THE SONG

Henry Wadsworth Longfellow

I shot an arrow into the air,
It fell to earth, I knew not where;
For, so swiftly it flew, the sight
Could not follow it in its flight.

I breathed a song into the air,
It fell to earth, I knew not where;
For who has sight so keen and strong,
That it can follow the flight of song?

Long, long, afterward, in an oak
I found the arrow, still unbroke;
And the song, from beginning to end,
I found again in the heart of a friend.

NEWS ITEM

Dorothy Parker

Men seldom make passes
At girls who wear glasses.

THE MINSTREL BOY

Thomas Moore

The minstrel boy to the war is gone,
  In the ranks of death you'll find him,
His father's sword he has girded on,
  And his wild harp slung behind him.
"Land of song!" said the warrior bard,
  "Though all the world betrays thee,
One sword, at least, thy rights shall guard,
  One faithful harp shall praise thee!"

The minstrel fell!—but the foeman's chain
  Could not bring his proud soul under;
The harp he loved ne'er spoke again,
  For he tore its chords asunder,
And said, "No chains shall sully thee,
  Thou soul of love and bravery!
Thy songs were made for the pure and free,
  They shall never sound in slavery!"

MAN PROPOSES

Man proposes, but God disposes.
When he is out of sight, quickly also is he out of mind.
Of two evils, the less is always to be chosen.

(From Thomas à Kempis' *Imitation of Christ*)

OH! WHY SHOULD THE SPIRIT OF MORTAL BE PROUD?

William Knox

Oh! why should the spirit of mortal be proud?
Like a swift-fleeting meteor, a fast-flying cloud,
A flash of the lightning, a break of the wave,
Man passeth from life to his rest in the grave.

The leaves of the oak and the willow shall fade,
Be scattered around, and together be laid;
And the young and the old, and the low and the high
Shall moulder to dust and together shall die.

The infant a mother attended and loved;
The mother that infant's affection who proved;
The husband that mother and infant have blessed,—
Each, all, are away to their dwellings of rest.

The maid on whose cheek, on whose brow, in whose eye,
Shone beauty and pleasure—her triumphs are by;
And the memory of those who loved her and praised
Are alike from the minds of the living erased.

The hand of the king that the sceptre hath borne;
The brow of the priest that the mitre hath worn;
The eye of the sage, and the heart of the brave,
Are hidden and lost in the depth of the grave.

The peasant whose lot was to sow and to reap;
The herdsman who climbed with his goats up the steep;
The beggar who wandered in search of his bread,
Have faded away like the grass that we tread.

The saint who enjoyed the communion of heaven;
The sinner who dared to remain unforgiven;
The wise and the foolish, the guilty and just,
Have quietly mingled their bones in the dust.

So the multiude goes, like the flowers or the weed
That withers away to let others succeed;
So the multitude comes, even those we behold,
To repeat every tale that has often been told.

For we are the same our fathers have been;
We see the same sights our fathers have seen;
We drink the same stream, and view the same sun,
And run the same course our fathers have run.

The thoughts we are thinking our fathers would think;
From the death we are shrinking our fathers would shrink;
To the life we are clinging they also would cling;
But it speeds for us all, like a bird on the wing.

They loved, but the story we cannot unfold;
They scorned, but the heart of the haughty is cold;
They grieved, but no wail from their slumbers will come;
They joyed, but the tongue of their gladness is dumb.

They died, aye! they died: and we things that are now,
Who walk on the turf that lies over their brow,
Who make in their dwelling a transient abode,
Meet the things that they met on their pilgrimage road.

Yea! hope and despondency, pleasure and pain,
We mingle together in sunshine and rain;
And the smiles and the tears, the song and the dirge,
Still follow each other, like surge upon surge.

'Tis the wink of an eye, 'tis the draught of a breath,
From the blossom of health to the paleness of death,
From the gilded saloon to the bier and the shroud,
Oh! why should the spirit of mortal be proud?

THE AMERICAN STANDARD

Booker T. Washington

MR. PRESIDENT AND GENTLEMEN:
It would in some measure relieve my embarrassment if I could,
even in a slight degree, feel myself worthy of the great honor which
you do me to-day. Why you have called me from the Black Belt of
the South, from among my humble people, to share in the honors
of this occasion, is not for me to explain; and yet it may not be
inappropriate for me to suggest that it seems to me that one of the
most vital questions that touch our American life, is how to bring

the strong, wealthy, and learned into helpful touch with the poorest, most ignorant, and humble, and at the same time make the one appreciate the vitalizing, strengthening influence of the other. How shall we make the mansions on yon Beacon Street feel and see the need of the spirits in the lowliest cabin in Alabama cotton fields or Louisiana sugar bottoms? This problem Harvard University is solving, not by bringing itself down, but by bringing the masses up.

If through me, a humble representative, seven millions of my people in the South might be permitted to send a message to Harvard—Harvard that offered up on death's altar, young Shaw, and Russell, and Lowell and scores of others, that we might have a free and united country—that message would be, "Tell them that the sacrifice was not in vain. Tell them that by the way of the shop, the field, the skilled hand, habits of thrift and economy, by way of industrial school and college, we are coming. We are crawling up, working up, yea, bursting up. Often through oppression, unjust discrimination, and prejudice, but through them we are coming up, and with proper habits, intelligence, and property, there is no power on earth that can permanently stay our progress."

If my life in the past has meant anything in the lifting up of my people and the bringing about of better relations between your race and mine, I assure you from this day it will mean doubly more. In the economy of God, there is but one standard by which an individual can succeed—there is but one for a race. This country demands that every race measure itself by the American standard. By it a race must rise or fall, succeed or fail, and in the last analysis mere sentiment counts for little. During the next half century and more, my race must continue passing through the severe American crucible. We are to be tested in our patience, our forbearance, our perseverance, our power to endure wrong, to withstand temptations, to economize, to acquire and use skill; our ability to compete, to succeed in commerce, to disregard the superficial for the real, the appearance for the substance, to be great and yet small, learned and yet simple, high and yet the servant of all. This, this is the passport to all that is best in the life of our Republic, and the Negro must possess it, or be debarred.

While we are thus being tested, I beg of you to remember that wherever our life touches yours, we help or hinder. Wherever your life touches ours, you make us stronger or weaker. No member of your race in any part of our country can harm the meanest member of mine, without the proudest and bluest blood in Massachusetts being degraded. When Mississippi commits crime, New England commits crime, and in so much lowers the standard of your civilization. There is no escape—man drags man down, or man lifts man up.

In working out our destiny, while the main burden and center of activity must be with us, we shall need in a large measure in the years that are to come as we have in the past, the help, the encouragement, the guidance that the strong can give the weak. Thus helped, we of both races in the South soon shall throw off the shackles of racial and sectional prejudices and rise as Harvard University has risen and as we all should rise, above the clouds of ignorance, narrowness, and selfishness, into that atmosphere, that pure sunshine, where it will be our highest ambition to serve man, our brother, regardless of race or previous condition.

HOW THEY BROUGHT THE GOOD NEWS FROM GHENT TO AIX

Robert Browning

I sprang to the stirrup, and Joris and he;
I galloped, Dirck galloped, we galloped all three;
"Good speed!" cried the watch as the gate-bolts undrew,
"Speed!" echoed the wall to us galloping through.
Behind shut the postern, the lights sank to rest,
And into the midnight we galloped abreast.

Not a word to each other; we kept the great pace
Neck by neck, stride by stride, never changing our place;
I turned in my saddle and made its girths tight,
Then shortened each stirrup and set the pique right,
Rebuckled the cheek-strap, chained slacker the bit,
Nor galloped less steadily Roland a whit.

'Twas a moonset at starting; but while we drew near
Lokeren, the cocks crew and twilight dawned clear;
At Boom a great yellow star came out to see;
At Düffeld 'twas morning as plain as could be;
And from Mecheln church-steeple we heard the half-chime,—
So Joris broke silence with "Yet there is time!"

At Aerschot up leaped of a sudden the sun,
And against him the cattle stood black every one,
To stare through the mist at us galloping past;
And I saw my stout galloper Roland at last,
With resolute shoulders, each butting away
The haze, as some bluff river headland its spray;

And his low head and crest, just one sharp ear bent back
For my voice, and the other pricked out on his track;
And one eye's black intelligence,—ever that glance
O'er its white edge at me, his own master, askance;
And the thick heavy spume-flakes, which aye and anon
His fierce lips shook upward in galloping on.

By Hasselt Dirck groaned; and cried Joris, "Stay spur!
Your Roos galloped bravely, the fault's not in her;
We'll remember at Aix,"—for one heard the quick wheeze
Of her chest, saw the stretched neck, and staggering knees,
And sunk tail, and horrible heave of the flank,
As down on her haunches she shuddered and sank.

So we were left galloping, Joris and I,
Past Looz and past Tongres, no cloud in the sky;
The broad sun above laughed a pitiless laugh;
'Neath our feet broke the brittle, bright stubble like chaff;
Till over by Dalhem a dome-spire sprang white,
And "Gallop," gasped Joris, "for Aix is in sight!"

"How they'll greet us!"—and all in a moment his roan
Rolled neck and croup over, lay dead as a stone;
And there was my Roland to bear the whole weight
Of the news which alone could save Aix from her fate,
With his nostrils like pits full of blood to the brim,
And with circles of red for his eye-sockets' rim.

Then I cast loose my buff-coat, each holster let fall,
Shook off both my jack-boots, let go belt and all,
Stood up in the stirrup, leaned, patted his ear,
Called my Roland his pet name, my horse without peer,—
Clapped my hands, laughed and sung, any noise, bad or good,
Till at length into Aix Roland galloped and stood.

And all I remember is friends flocking round,
As I sat with his head 'twixt my knees on the ground;
And no voice but was praising this Roland of mine,
As I poured down his throat our last measure of wine,
Which (the burgesses voted by common consent)
Was no more than his due who brought good news from Ghent.

CHARTLESS

Emily Dickinson

I never saw a moor,
I never saw the sea;
Yet know I how the heather looks,
And what a wave must be.

I never spoke with God,
Nor visited in heaven;
Yet certain am I of the spot
As if the chart were given.

THE DAYS GONE BY

James Whitcomb Riley

Oh, the days gone by! Oh, the days gone by!
The apples in the orchard, and the pathway through the rye;
The chirrup of the robin, and the whistle of the quail
As he piped across the meadows sweet as any nightingale;
When the bloom was on the clover and the blue was in the sky,
And my happy heart brimmed over in the days gone by.

In the days gone by, when my naked feet were tripped
By the honeysuckle tangles where the water lilies dripped,
And the ripples of the river lipped the moss along the brink
Where the placid-eyed and lazy-footed cattle came to drink,
And the tilting snipe stood fearless of the truant's wayward cry
And the splashing of the swimmer, in the days gone by.

Oh, the days gone by! Oh, the days gone by!
The music of the laughing lip, the luster of the eye;

The childish faith in fairies, and Aladdin's magic ring—
The simple, soul-reposing glad belief in everything—
When life was like a story, holding neither sob nor sigh,
In the golden olden glory of the days gone by.

WORTH WHILE

Ella Wheeler Wilcox

It is easy enough to be pleasant,
When life flows by like a song,
But the man worth while is one who will smile,
When everything goes dead wrong.
For the test of the heart is trouble,
And it always comes with the years,
And the smile that is worth the praises of earth
Is the one that shines through tears.

It is easy enough to be prudent
When nothing tempts you to stray,
When without or within no voice of sin
Is luring your soul away;
But it's only a negative virtue
Until it is tried by fire,
And the life that is worth the honor of earth
Is the one that resists desire.

By the cynic, the sad, the fallen,
Who had no strength for the strife,
The world's highway is cumbered today;
They make up the sum of life.
But the virtue that conquers passion,
And the sorrow that hides in a smile,—
It is these that are worth the homage of earth,
For we find them but once in a while.

REASON

Anonymous

He that will not reason is a bigot,
He that cannot reason is a fool,
He that does not reason is a slave.

THE EVE OF ST. AGNES

John Keats

I

St. Agnes' Eve,—ah, bitter chill it was!
The owl, for all his feathers, was a-cold;
The hare limped trembling through the frozen grass,
And silent was the flock in woolly fold:
Numb were the beadsman's fingers while he told
His rosary, and while his frosted breath,
Like pious incense from a censer old,
Seemed taking flight for heaven without a death,
Past the sweet virgin's picture, while his prayer he saith.

II

His prayer he saith, this patient, holy man;
Then takes his lamp, and riseth from his knees,
And back returneth, meagre, barefoot, wan,
Along the chapel aisle by slow degrees;
The sculptured dead, on each side seem to freeze,
Emprisoned in black, purgatorial rails;
Knights, ladies, praying in dumb orat'ries,
He passed by; and his weak spirit fails
To think how they may ache in icy hoods and mails.

III

Northward he turneth through a little door,
And scarce three steps, ere music's golden tongue
Flattered to tears this aged man and poor;
But no,—already had his death-bell rung;
The joys of all his life were said and sung;
His was harsh penance on St. Agnes' Eve;
Another way he went, and soon among
Rough ashes sat he for his soul's reprieve,
And all night kept awake, for sinners' sake to grieve.

IV

That ancient beadsman heard the prelude soft:
And so it chanced, for many a door was wide,
From hurry to and fro. Soon, up aloft,
The silver, snarling trumpets 'gan to chide;
The level chambers, ready with their pride,

Were glowing to receive a thousand guests;
The carved angels, ever eager-eyed,
Stared, where upon their heads the cornice rests,
With hair blown back, and wings put crosswise on
    their breasts.

V

At length burst in the argent revelry,
With plume, tiara, and all rich array,
Numerous as shadows haunting fairily
The brain, new-stuffed, in youth, with triumphs gay
Of old romance. These let us wish away;
And turn, sole-thoughted, to one lady there,
Whose heart had brooded, all that wintry day,
On love, and winged St. Agnes' saintly care,
As she had heard old dames full many times declare.

VI

They told her how, upon St. Agnes' Eve,
Young virgins might have visions of delight,
And soft adorings from their loves receive
Upon the honeyed middle of the night,
If ceremonies due they did aright;
As, supperless to bed they must retire,
And couch supine their beauties, lily white;
Nor look behind, nor sideways, but require
Of heaven with upward eyes for all that they desire.

VII

Full of this whim was thoughtful Madeline;
The music, yearning like a god in pain,
She scarcely heard; her maiden eyes divine,
Fixed on the floor, saw many a sweeping train
Pass by,—she heeded not at all; in vain
Came many a tiptoe, amorous cavalier,
And back retired; not cooled by high disdain,
But she saw not; her heart was otherwhere;
She sighed for Agnes' dreams, the sweetest of the year.

VIII

She danced along with vague, regardless eyes,
Anxious her lips, her breathing quick and short;
The hallowed hour was near at hand; she sighs
Amid the timbrels, and the thronged resort

Of whispers in anger, or in sport;
'Mid looks of love, defiance, hate, and scorn,
Hoodwinked with faery fancy; all amort
Save to St. Agnes and her lambs unshorn,
And all the bliss to be before to-morrow morn.

IX

So, purposing each moment to retire,
She lingered still. Meantime, across the moors,
Had come young Porphyro, with heart on fire
For Madeline. Beside the portal doors,
Buttressed from moonlight, stands he, and implores
All saints to give him sight of Madeline;
But for one moment in the tedious hours,
That he might gaze and worship all unseen;
Perchance speak, kneel, touch, kiss,—in sooth such
    things have been.

X

He ventures in; let no buzzed whisper tell;
All eyes he muffled, or a hundred swords
Will storm his heart, love's feverous citadel;
For him, those chambers held barbarian hordes,
Hyena foemen, and hot-blooded lords,
Whose very dogs would execrations howl
Against his lineage; not one breast affords
Him any mercy, in that mansion foul,
Save one old beldame, weak in body and in soul.

XI

Ah, happy chance! the aged creature came,
Shuffling along with ivory-headed wand,
To where he stood, hid from the torch's flame,
Behind a broad hall-pillar, far beyond
The sound of merriment and chorus bland.
He startled her; but soon she knew his face,
And grasped his fingers in her palsied hand,
Saying, "Mercy, Porphyro! hie thee from this place;
They are all here to-night, the whole bloodthirsty race!

XII

"Get hence! get hence! there's dwarfish Hildebrand;
He had a fever late, and in the fit
He cursed thee and thine, both house and land;

Then there's that old Lord Maurice, not a whit
More tame for his gray hairs—Alas me! flit!
Flit like a ghost away!"—"Ah, gossip dear,
We're safe enough; here in this arm-chair sit,
And tell me how"—"Good saints, not here, not here;
Follow me, child, or else these stones will be thy bier."

XIII

He followed through a lowly arched way,
Brushing the cobwebs with his lofty plume;
And as she muttered "Well-a—well-a-day!"
He found him in a little moonlight room,
Pale, latticed, chill, and silent as a tomb.
"Now tell me where is Madeline," said he,
"O, tell me, Angela, by the holy loom
Which none but secret sisterhood may see,
When they St. Agnes' wool are weaving piously."

XIV

"St. Agnes! Ah! it is St. Agnes' Eve,—
Yet men will murder upon holy days;
Thou must hold water in a witch's sieve,
And be liege-lord of all the elves and fays,
To venture so. It fills me with amaze
To see thee, Porphyro!—St. Agnes' Eve!
God's help! my lady fair the conjurer plays
This very night; good angels her deceive!
But let me laugh awhile, I've mickle time to grieve."

XV

Feebly she laughed in the languid moon,
While Porphyro upon her face doth look,
Like puzzled urchin on an aged crone
Who keepeth closed a wondrous riddle-book,
As spectacled she sits in chimney nook.
But soon his eyes grew brilliant, when she told
His lady's purpose; and he scarce could brook
Tears, at the thought of those enchantments cold,
And Madeline asleep in lap of legends old.

XVI

Sudden a thought came like a full-blown rose,
Flushing his brow, and in his pained heart
Made purple riot; then doth he propose

184

A stratagem, that makes the beldame start:
"A cruel man and impious thou art!
Sweet lady, let her pray, and sleep and dream
Alone with her good angels, far apart
From wicked men like thee. Go, go! I deem
Thou canst not surely be the same that thou didst
    seem."

XVII

"I will not harm her, by all saints I swear!"
Quoth Porphyro; "O, may I ne'er find grace
When my weak voice shall whisper its last prayer,
If one of her soft ringlets I displace,
Or look with ruffian passion in her face;
Good Angela, believe me by these tears;
Or I will, even in a moment's space,
Awake, with horrid shout, my foemen's ears,
And beard them, though they be more fanged than
    wolves and bears."

XVIII

"Ah! why wilt thou affright a feeble soul?
A poor, weak, palsy-stricken, church-yard thing,
Whose passing-bell may ere the midnight toll;
Whose prayers for thee, each morn and evening,
Were never missed." Thus plaining, doth she bring
A gentler speech from burning Porphyro;
So woful, and of such deep sorrowing,
That Angela gives promise she will do
Whatever he shall wish, betide her weal or woe.

XIX

Which was, to lead him, in close secrecy,
Even to Madeline's chamber, and there hide
Him in a closet, of such privacy
That he might see her beauty unespied,
And win perhaps that night a peerless bride;
While legioned fairies paced the coverlet,
And pale enchantment held her sleepy-eyed.
Never on such a night have lovers met,
Since Merlin paid his demon all the monstrous debt.

185

XX

"It shall be as thou wishest," said the dame;
"All cates and dainties shall be stored there
Quickly on this feast-night; by the tambour frame
Her own lute thou wilt see; no time to spare,
For I am slow and feeble, and scarce dare
On such a catering trust my dizzy head.
Wait here, my child, with patience kneel in prayer
The while. Ah! thou must needs the lady wed,
Or may I never leave my grave among the dead."

XXI

So saying, she hobbled off with busy fear.
The lover's endless minutes slowly passed:
The dame returned, and whispered in his ear
To follow her; with aged eyes aghast
From fright of dim espial. Safe at last,
Through many a dusky gallery, they gain
The maiden's chamber, silken, hushed and chaste;
Where Porphyro took covert, pleased amain.
His poor guide hurried back with agues in her brain.

XXII

Her faltering hand upon the balustrade,
Old Angela was feeling for the stair,
When Madeline, St. Agnes' charmed maid,
Rose, like a missioned spirit, unaware;
With silver taper's light, and pious care,
She turned, and down the aged gossip led
To a safe level matting. Now prepare,
Young Porphyro, for gazing on that bed!
She comes, she comes again, like a ring-dove frayed and
    fled.

XXIII

Out went the taper as she hurried in;
Its little smoke, in pallid moonshine, died;
She closed the door, she panted, all akin
To spirits of the air, and visions wide;
No uttered syllable, or, woe betide!

But to her heart, her heart was voluble,
Paining with eloquence her balmy side;
As though a tongueless nightingale should swell
Her throat in vain, and die, heart-stifled in her dell.

XXIV

A casement high and triple-arched there was,
All garlanded with carven imageries
Of fruits, and flowers, and bunches of knot-grass,
And diamonded with panes of quaint device,
Innumerable of stains and splendid dyes,
As are the tiger-moth's deep-damasked wings;
And in the midst, 'mong thousand heraldries,
And twilight saints, and dim emblazonings,
A shielded scutcheon blushed with blood of queens
  and kings.

XXV

Full on this casement shone the wintry moon,
And threw warm gules on Madeline's fair breast,
As down she knelt for heaven's grace and boon;
Rose-bloom fell on her hands, together prest,
And on her silver cross soft amethyst,
And on her hair a glory, like a saint;
She seemed a splendid angel, newly drest,
Save wings, for heaven. Porphyro grew faint:
She knelt, so pure a thing, so free from mortal taint.

XXVI

Anon his heart revives; her vespers done,
Of all its wreathed pearls her hair she frees;
Unclasps her warmed jewels one by one;
Loosens her fragrant bodice; by degrees
Her rich attire creeps rustling to her knees;
Half hidden, like a mermaid in sea-weed,
Pensive awhile she dreams awake, and sees,
In fancy, fair St. Agnes in her bed,
But dares not look behind, or all the charm is fled.

XXVII

Soon, trembling in her soft and chilly nest,
In sort of wakeful swoon, perplexed she lay,
Until the poppied warmth of sleep oppressed

Her soothed limbs, and soul fatigued away;
Flown like a thought, until the morrow-day;
Blissfully havened both from joy and pain;
Clasped like a missal where swart Paynims pray;
Blinded alike from sunshine and from rain,
As though a rose should shut, and be a bud again.

XXVIII

Stolen to this paradise, and so entranced,
Prophyro gazed upon her empty dress,
And listened to her breathing, if it chanced
To wake into a slumberous tenderness;
Which when he heard, that minute did he bless,
And breathed himself; then from the closet crept,
Noiseless as fear in a wide wilderness,
And over the hushed carpet, silent, stept,
And 'tween the curtains peeped, where, lo!—how fast
   she slept.

XXIX

Then by the bedside, where the faded moon
Made a dim, silver twilight, soft he set
A table, and, half anguished, threw thereon
A cloth of woven crimson, gold, and jet:—
O for some drowsy Morphean amulet!
The boisterous, midnight, festive clarion,
The kettle-drum, and far-heard clarionet,
Affray his ears, though but in dying tone:—
The hall-door shuts again, and all the noise is gone.

XXX

And still she slept an azure-lidded sleep,
In blanched linen, smooth, and lavendered;
While he from forth the closet brought a heap
Of candied apple, quince, and plum, and gourd;
With jellies soother than the creamy curd,
And lucent syrops, tinct with cinnamon;
Manna and dates, in argosy transferred
From Fez; and spiced dainties, every one,
From silken Samarcand to cedared Lebanon.

XXXI

These delicates he heaped with glowing hand
On golden dishes and in baskets bright

Of wreathed silver. Sumptuous they stand
In the retired quiet of the night,
Filling the chilly room with perfume light.—
"And now, my love, my seraph fair awake!
Thou art in my heaven, and I thine eremite;
Open thine eyes, for meek St. Agnes' sake,
Or I shall drowse beside thee, so my soul doth ache."

XXXII

Thus whispering, his warm, unnervéd arm
Sank in her pillow. Shaded was her dream
By the dusk curtains;—'twas a midnight charm
Impossible to melt as iced stream:
The lustrous salvers in the moonlight gleam;
Broad golden fringe upon the carpet lies;
It seemed he never, never could redeem
From such a steadfast spell his lady's eyes;
So mused awhile, entoiled in woofed phantasies.

XXXIII

Awakening up, he took her hollow lute,—
Tumultuous,—and, in chords that tenderest be,
He played an ancient ditty, long since mute,
In Provence called "La belle dame sans mercy";
Close to her ear touching the melody;—
Wherewith disturbed, she uttered a soft moan:
He ceased—she panted quick—and suddenly
Her blue affrayed eyes wide open shone;
Upon his knees he sank, pale as smooth-sculptured
    stone.

XXXIV

Her eyes were open, but she still beheld,
Now wide awake, the vision of her sleep.
There was a painful change, that nigh expelled
The blisses of her dream so pure and deep;
At which fair Madeline began to weep,
And moan forth witless words with many a sigh;
While still her gaze on Porphyro would keep.
Who knelt, with joined hands and piteous eye,
Fearing to move or speak, she looked so dreamingly.

XXXV

"Ah, Porphyro!" said she, "but even now
Thy voice was at sweet tremble in mine ear,
Made tunable with every sweetest vow;
And those sad eyes were spiritual and clear;
How changed thou art! how pallid, chill, and drear!
Give me that voice again, my Porphyro,
Those looks immortal, those complainings dear!
O, leave me not in this eternal woe,
For if thou diest, my love, I know not where to go."

Beyond a mortal man impassioned far
At these voluptuous accents, he arose,
Ethereal, flushed, and like a throbbing star
Seen mid the sapphire heaven's deep repose;
Into her dream he melted, as the rose
Blendeth its odor with the violet,—
Solution sweet; meantime the frost-wind blows
Like love's alarum pattering the sharp sleet
Against the window-panes; St. Agnes' moon hath set.

XXXVII

'Tis dark; quick pattereth the flaw-blown sleet;
"This is no dream, my bride, my Madeline!"
'Tis dark; the iced gusts still rave and beat:
"No dream, alas! alas! and woe is mine!
Porphyro will leave me here to fade and pine.—
Cruel! what traitor could thee hither bring?
I curse not, for my heart is lost in thine,
Though thou forsakest a deceived thing;—
A dove forlorn and lost, with sick, unpruned wing."

"My Madeline! sweet dreamer! lovely bride!
Say, may I be for aye thy vassal blest?
Thy beauty's shield, heart-shaped and vermeil dyed?
Ah, silver shrine, here will I take my rest
After so many hours of toil and quest,
A famished pilgrim,—saved by miracle.
Though I have found, I will not rob thy nest,
Saving of thy sweet self; if thou think'st well
To trust, fair Madeline, to no rude infidel.

"Hark! 'tis an elfin-storm from faery land,
Of haggard seeming, but a boon indeed:
Arise—arise! the morning is at hand;—
The bloated wassaillers will never heed:—
Let us away, my love, with happy speed;
There are no ears to hear, or eyes to see,—
Drown'd all in Rhenish and the sleepy mead:
Awake! arise! my love, and fearless be,
For o'er the southern moors I have a home for thee."

XL

She hurried at his words, beset with fears,
For there were sleeping dragons all around,
At glaring watch, perhaps, with ready spears—
Down the wide stairs a darkling way they found.—
In all the house was heard no human sound.
A chain-droop'd lamp was flickering by each door;
The arras, rich with horseman, hawk, and hound,
Flutter'd in the besieging wind's uproar;
And the long carpets rose along the gusty floor.

XLI

They glide, like phantoms, into the wide hall!
Like phantoms to the iron porch they glide,
Where lay the porter, in uneasy sprawl,
With a huge empty flagon by his side;
The wakeful bloodhound rose, and shook his hide,
But his sagacious eye an inmate owns;
By one, and one, the bolts full easy slide;
The chains lie silent on the footworn stones;
The key turns, and the door upon its hinges groans.

XLII

And they are gone! ay, ages long ago
These lovers fled away into the storm.
That night the baron dreamt of many a woe,
And all his warrior-guests, with shade and form
Of witch, and demon, and large coffin-worm,
Were long be-nightmared. Angela the old
Died palsy-twitched, with meagre face deform;
The beadsman, after thousand aves told,
For aye unsought-for slept among his ashes cold.

THE OLD BROWN SCHOOLHOUSE

Anonymous

It stood on a bleak country corner,
  The houses were distant and few,
A meadow lay back in the distance,
  Beyond rose the hills to our view.
The roads crossing there at right angles,
  Untraversed by pomp and array,
Were cropped by the cows in the summer;
  I've watched them there many a day.

In memory's hall hangs the picture,
  And though years of sad care are between,
It hangs with a beautiful gilding,
  And well do I love it, I ween.
It stood on a bleak country corner,
  But boyhood's young heart made it warm.
It gloried in the sunshine of summer;
  'Twas cheerful in winter and storm.

The teacher, oh, well I remember;
  My heart has long kept him a place;
Perhaps by the world he's forgotten,
  His memory no time can efface.
He met us with smiles on the threshold,
  And in that rude temple of art,
He left with the skill of a workman
  His touch on the mind and the heart.

Oh, gay were the sports of the noontide,
  When winter winds frolicked with snow;
We laughed at the freaks of the storm king,
  And shouted him on, all aglow.
We dashed at his beautiful sculptures,
  Regardless of all its array,
We plunged in the feathery snowdrift
  And sported the winter away.

We sat on the old-fashioned benches,
  Beguiled with our pencils and slate;
We thought of the opening future,
  And dreamed of our manhood's estate.

O days of my boyhood! I bless you;
  While looking from life's busy prime,
The treasures are lingering with me
  I gathered in life's early time.

O still to that bleak country corner
  Turns my heart in its weariness yet,
Where leading my gentle young sisters
  With youthful companions I met.
I cast a fond glance o'er the meadow;
  The hills just behind it I see
Away in the charm of the distance,
  Old schoolhouse! a blessing on thee!

FATHER WILLIAM

(AFTER SOUTHEY)

Lewis Carroll

"You are old, Father William," the young man said,
  "And your hair has become very white;
And yet you incessantly stand on your head—
  Do you think, at your age, it is right?"

"In my youth," Father William replied to his son,
  "I feared it might injure the brain;
But, now that I'm perfectly sure I have none,
  Why, I do it again and again."

"You are old," said the youth, "as I mentioned before,
  And have grown most uncommonly fat;
Yet you turn a back-somersault in at the door—
  Pray, what is the reason of that?"

"In my youth," said the sage, as he shook his gray locks,
  "I kept all my limbs very supple
By the use of this ointment—one shilling the box—
  Allow me to sell you a couple?"

"You are old," said the youth, "and your jaws are too weak
  For anything tougher than suet;
Yet you finished the goose, with the bones and the beak—
  Pray, how did you manage to do it?"

193

"In my youth," said his father, "I took to the law,
    And argued each case with my wife;
And the muscular strength which it gave to my jaw
    Has lasted the rest of my life."

"You are old," said the youth, "one would hardly suppose
    That your eye was as steady as ever;
Yet you balanced an eel on the end of your nose—
    What made you so awfully clever?"

"I have answered three questions, and that is enough,"
    Said his father. "Don't give yourself airs!
Do you think I can listen all day to such stuff?
    Be off, or I'll kick you down-stairs!"

THE GIRL I LEFT BEHIND ME

Anonymous

The dames of France are fond and free,
And Flemish lips are willing,
And soft the maids of Italy,
And Spanish eyes are thrilling;
Still, though I bask beneath their smile,
Their charms fail to bind me.
And my heart falls back to Erin's Isle,
To the girl I left behind me.

For she's as fair as Shannon's side,
And purer than its water,
But she refused to be my bride
Though many years I sought her;
Yet since to France I sailed away,
Her letters oft remind me,
That I promised never to gainsay
The girl I left behind me.

She says, "My own dear love come home,
My friends are rich and many,
Or else, abroad with you I'll roam,
A soldier stout as any;

If you'll not come, nor let me go,
I'll think you have resigned me."
My heart nigh broke when I answered "No,"
To the girl I left behind me.

For never shall my true love brave
A life of war and toiling,
And never as a skulking slave
I'll tread my native soil on;
But were it free or to be freed,
The battle's close would find me
To Ireland bound, nor message need
From the girl I left behind me.

FROM THE RUBÁIYÁT OF OMAR KHAYYÁM

Edward Fitzgerald

VII

Come, fill the Cup, and in the fire of Spring
Your Winter-garment of Repentance fling:
    The Bird of Time has but a little way
To flutter—and the Bird is on the Wing.

VIII

Whether at Naishápúr or Babylon,
Whether the Cup with sweet or bitter run,
    The Wine of Life keeps oozing drop by drop,
The Leaves of Life keep falling one by one.

XII

A Book of Verses underneath the Bough,
A Jug of Wine, a Loaf of Bread—and Thou
    Beside me singing in the Wilderness—
Oh, Wilderness were Paradise enow!

XIII

Some for the Glories of this World; and some
Sigh for the Prophet's Paradise to come;
    Ah, take the Cash, and let the Credit go,
Nor heed the rumble of a distant Drum!

I sometimes think that never blows so red
The Rose as where some buried Caesar bled;
   That every Hyacinth the Garden wears
Dropt in her Lap from some once lovely Head.

XXI

Ah, my Beloved, fill the Cup that clears
To-day of past Regrets and future Fears:
   To-morrow!—Why, To-morrow I may be
Myself with Yesterday's Sev'n thousand Years.

XXII

For some we loved, the loveliest and the best
That from his Vintage rolling Time hath prest,
   Have drunk their Cup a Round or two before.
And one by one crept silently to rest.

XXIII

And we, that now make merry in the Room
They left, and Summer dresses in new bloom,
   Ourselves must we beneath the Couch of Earth
Descend—ourselves to make a couch—for whom?

XXIV

Ah, make the most of what we yet may spend,
Before we too into the Dust descend;
   Dust into Dust, and under Dust to lie,
Sans Wine, sans Song, sans Singer, and—sans End!

XXVI

Why, all the Saints and Sages who discuss'd
Of the Two Worlds so wisely—they are thrust
   Like foolish Prophets forth; their Words to Scorn
Are scatter'd, and their Mouths are stopt with Dust.

XXVIII

With them the seed of Wisdom did I sow,
And with mine own hand wrought to make it grow;
   And this was all the Harvest that I reap'd—
"I came like Water, and like Wind I go."

XXIX

Into this Universe, and *Why* not knowing
Nor *Whence,* like Water willy-nilly flowing;
   And out of it, as Wind along the Waste,
I know not *Whither,* willy-nilly blowing.

XXX

What, without asking, hither hurried *Whence?*
And, without asking, *whither* hurried hence?
   Oh, many a Cup of this forbidden Wine
Must drown the memory of that insolence!

LXVI

I sent my Soul through the Invisible,
Some letter of that After-life to spell:
   And by and by my Soul return'd to me,
And answered "I Myself and Heav'n and Hell:"

LXX

The Ball no question makes of Ayes and Noes,
But Here or There as strikes the Player goes;
   And He that toss'd you down into the Field,
He knows about it all—HE knows—HE knows!

LXXI

The Moving Finger writes; and, having writ,
Moves on: nor all your Piety nor Wit
   Shall lure it back to cancel half a Line,
Nor all your Tears wash out a Word of it.

LXXX

Oh Thou, who didst with pitfall and with gin
Beset the Road I was to wander in,
   Thou wilt not with Predestined Evil round
Enmesh, and then impute my Fall to Sin!

LXXXI

Oh Thou, who Man of baser Earth didst make,
And ev'n with Paradise devise the Snake:
   For all the Sin wherewith the Face of Man
Is blacken'd—Man's forgiveness give—and take!

Ah, with the Grape my fading Life provide,
And wash the Body whence the Life has died,
   And lay me, shrouded in the living Leaf,
By some not unfrequented Garden-side.

XCII

That ev'n my buried Ashes such as snare
Of Vintage shall fling up into the Air
   As not a True-believer passing by
But shall be overtaken unaware.

XCVI

Yet Ah, that Spring should vanish with the Rose!
That Youth's sweet-scented manuscript should close!
   The Nightingale that in the branches sang,
Ah whence, and whither flown again, who knows!

XCIX

Ah, Love! could you and I with Him conspire
To grasp this sorry Scheme of Things Entire,
   Would not we shatter it to bits—and then
Re-mould it nearer to the Heart's desire!

C

Yon rising Moon that looks for us again—
How oft hereafter will she wax and wane;
   How oft hereafter rising look for us
Through this same Garden—and for *one* in vain!

CI

And when like her, oh Sákí, you shall pass
Among the Guests Star-scatter'd on the Grass,
   And in your joyous errand reach the spot
Where I made One—turn down an empty Glass!

*   *   *

Variety's the very spice of life,
That gives it all its flavour.
—William Cowper

AGAINST CENSORSHIP

John Milton

I deny not, but that it is of greatest concernment in the church and commonwealth, to have a vigilant eye how books demean themselves, as well as men; and thereafter to confine, imprison, and do sharpest justice on them as malefactors; for books are not absolutely dead things, but do contain a potency of life in them to be as active as that soul was whose progeny they are; nay, they do preserve as in a vial the purest efficacy and extraction of that living intellect that bred them. I know they are as lively, and as vigorously productive, as those fabulous dragon's teeth: and being sown up and down, may chance to spring up armed men. And yet, on the other hand, unless wariness be used, as good almost kill a man as kill a good book: who kills a man kills a reasonable creature, God's image; but he who destroys a good book, kills reason itself, kills the image of God, as it were, in the eye. Many a man lives a burden to the earth; but a good book is the precious lifeblood of a master-spirit, embalmed and treasured up on purpose to a life beyond life. It is true, no age can restore a life, whereof, perhaps, there is no great loss; and revolutions of ages do not oft recover the loss of a rejected truth, for the want of which whole nations fare the worse. We should be wary, therefore, what persecution we raise against the living labours of public men, how we spill that seasoned life of man, preserved and stored up in books; since we see a kind of homicide may be thus committed, sometimes a martyrdom; and if it extend to the whole impression, a kind of massacre, whereof the execution ends not in the slaying of an elemental life, but strikes at the ethereal and fifth essence, the breath of reason itself; slays an immortality rather than a life.

(From Areopagitica)

PAUL REVERE'S RIDE

Henry Wadsworth Longfellow

Listen, my children, and you shall hear
Of the midnight ride of Paul Revere,
On the eighteenth of April, in Seventy-five;
Hardly a man is now alive
Who remembers that famous day and year.

He said to his friend, "If the British march
By land or sea from the town tonight,
Hang a lantern aloft in the belfry arch
Of the North Church tower as a signal light,—
One, if by land, and two, if by sea;
And I on the opposite shore will be,
Ready to ride and spread the alarm
Through every Middlesex village and farm,
For the country folk to be up and to arm."

Then he said, "Good night!" and with muffled oar
Silently rowed to the Charlestown shore,
Just as the moon rose over the bay,
Where swinging wide at her moorings lay
The *Somerset*, British man-of-war;
A phantom ship, with each mast and spar
Across the moon like a prison bar,
And a huge black hulk, that was magnified
By its own reflection in the tide.

Meanwhile, his friend through alley and street
Wanders and watches, with eager ears,
Till in the silence around him he hears
The muster of men at the barrack door,
The sound of arms, and the tramp of feet,
And the measured tread of the grenadiers,
Marching down to their boats on the shore.

Then he climbed the tower of the Old North Church,
By the wooden stairs, with stealthy tread,
To the belfry-chamber overhead,
And startled the pigeons from their perch
On the sombre rafters, that round him made
Masses and moving shapes of shade,—
By the trembling ladder, steep and tall,
To the highest window in the wall,
Where he paused to listen and look down
A moment on the roofs of the town
And the moonlight flowing over all.

Beneath in the churchyard, lay the dead,
In their night-encampment on the hill,
Wrapped in silence so deep and still
That he could hear, like a sentinel's tread,

The watchful night-wind, as it went
Creeping along from tent to tent,
And seeming to whisper, "All is well!"
A moment only he feels the spell
Of the place and the hour, and the secret dread
Of the lonely belfry and the dead;
For suddenly all his thoughts are bent
On a shadowy something far away,
Where the river widens to meet the bay,—
A line of black that bends and floats
On the rising tide, like a bridge of boats.

Meanwhile, impatient to mount and ride,
Booted and spurred, with a heavy stride
On the opposite shore walked Paul Revere.
Now he patted his horse's side,
Now gazed at the landscape far and near,
Then, impetuous, stamped the earth,
And turned and tightened his saddle girth;
But mostly he watched with eager search
The belfrey's tower of the Old North Church,
As it rose above the graves on the hill,
Lonely and spectral and sombre and still.
And lo! as he looks, on the belfry height
A glimmer, and then a gleam of light!
He springs to the saddle, the bridle he turns,
But lingers and gazes, till full on his sight
A second lamp in the belfry burns!

A hurry of hoofs in a village street,
A shape in the moonlight, a bulk in the dark,
And beneath, from the pebbles, in passing, a spark
Struck out by a steed flying fearless and fleet;
That was all! And yet, through the gloom and the light,
The fate of a nation was riding that night;
And the spark struck out by that steed, in his flight,
Kindled the land into flame with its heat.
He has left the village and mounted the steep,
And beneath him, tranquil and broad and deep,
Is the Mystic, meeting the ocean tides;
And under the alders that skirt its edge,
Now soft on the sand, now loud on the ledge,
Is heard the tramp of his steed as he rides.

It was twelve by the village clock,
When he crossed the bridge into Medford town.
He heard the crowing of the cock,
And the barking of the farmer's dog,
And he felt the damp of the river fog,
That rises after the sun goes down.

It was one by the village clock,
When he galloped into Lexington.
He saw the gilded weathercock
Swim in the moonlight as he passed,
And the meeting-house windows, blank and bare,
Gaze at him with a spectral glare,
As if they already stood aghast
At the bloody work they would look upon.

It was two by the village clock,
When he came to the bridge in Concord town.
He heard the bleating of the flock,
And the twitter of birds among the trees,
And felt the breath of the morning breeze
Blowing over the meadows brown.
And one was safe and asleep in his bed
Who at the bridge would be first to fall,
Who that day would be lying dead,
Pierced by a British musket-ball.

You know the rest. In books you have read,
How the British Regulars fired and fled,—
How the farmers gave them ball for ball,
From behind each fence and farmyard wall,
Chasing the redcoats down the lane,
Then crossing the fields to emerge again
Under the trees at the turn of the road,
And only pausing to fire and load.

So through the night rode Paul Revere;
And so through the night went his cry of alarm
To every Middlesex village and farm,—
A cry of defiance, and not of fear,
A voice in the darkness, a knock at the door,
And a word that shall echo for evermore!
For, borne on the night-wind of the Past,

Through all our history, to the last,
In the hour of darkness and peril and need,
The people will waken and listen to hear
The hurrying hoof-beats of that steed,
And the midnight message of Paul Revere.

THE SUICIDE'S GRAVE

Sir W. S. Gilbert

On a tree, by a river, a little tom-tit
Sang "Willow, titwillow, titwillow!"
And I said to him, "Dicky-bird, why do you sit
Singing 'Willow, titwillow, titwillow?' "
"Is it weakness of intellect, birdie?" I cried,
"Or a rather tough worm in your little inside?"
With a shake of his poor little head, he replied,
"Oh, willow, titwillow, titwillow!"

He slapped at his chest as he sat on that bough,
Singing "Willow, titwillow, titwillow!"
And a cold perspiration bespangled his brow,
Oh, willow, titwillow, titwillow!
He sobbed and he sighed, and a gurgle he gave,
Then he threw himself into the billowy wave,
And an echo arose from the suicide's grave—
"Oh, willow, titwillow, titwillow!"

Now I feel just as sure as I'm sure that my name
Isn't Willow, titwillow, titwillow,
That 'twas blighted affection that made him exclaim,
"Oh, willow, titwillow, titwillow!"
And if you remain callous and obdurate, I
Shall perish as he did, and you will know why,
Though I probably shall not exclaim as I die,
"Oh, willow, titwillow, titwillow!"

* * *

They never taste who always drink;
They never talk who always think.
—Matthew Prior

OPPORTUNITY

John James Ingalls

Master of human destinies am I!
Fame, love, and fortune on my footsteps wait.
Cities and fields I walk; I penetrate
Deserts and seas remote, and passing by
Hovel and mart, and palace—soon or late
I knock unbidden once at every gate!

If sleeping, wake—if feasting, rise before
I turn away. It is the hour of fate,
And they who follow me reach every state
Mortals desire, and conquer every foe
Save death; but those who doubt or hesitate,
Condemned to failure, penury and woe,
Seek me in vain and uselessly implore.
I answer not, and I return no more.

"BELIEVE ME, IF ALL THOSE ENDEARING YOUNG CHARMS"

Thomas Moore

Believe me, if all those endearing young charms,
Which I gaze on so fondly to-day,
Were to change by to-morrow, and fleet in my arms,
Like fairy-gifts fading away,
Thou wouldst still be adored, as this moment thou art,
Let thy loveliness fade as it will,
And around the dear ruin each wish of my heart
Would entwine itself verdantly still.

It is not while beauty and youth are thine own,
And thy cheeks unprofaned by a tear,
That the fervor and faith of a soul may be known,
To which time will but make thee more dear!
No, the heart that has truly loved never forgets,
But as truly loves on to the close,
As the sunflower turns on her god when he sets
The same look which she turned when he rose!

5

1 And seeing the multitudes, he went up into a mountain: and when he was set, his disciples came unto him:

2 And he opened his mouth, and taught them, saying,

3 Blessed are the poor in spirit: for theirs is the kingdom of heaven.

4 Blessed are they that mourn: for they shall be comforted.

5 Blessed are the meek: for they shall inherit the earth.

6 Blessed are they which do hunger and thirst after righteousness: for they shall be filled.

7 Blessed are the merciful: for they shall obtain mercy.

8 Blessed are the pure in heart: for they shall see God.

9 Blessed are the peacemakers: for they shall be called the children of God.

10 Blessed are they which are persecuted for righteousness' sake: for theirs is the kingdom of heaven.

11 Blessed are ye, when men shall revile you, and persecute you, and shall say all manner of evil against you falsely, for my sake.

12 Rejoice, and be exceeding glad: for great is your reward in heaven: for so persecuted they the prophets which were before you.

13 Ye are the salt of the earth: but if the salt have lost his savour, wherewith shall it be salted? it is thenceforth good for nothing, but to be cast out, and to be trodden under foot of men.

14 Ye are the light of the world. A city that is set on an hill cannot be hid.

15 Neither do men light a candle, and put it under a bushel, but on a candlestick; and it giveth light unto all that are in the house.

16 Let your light so shine before men, that they may see your good works, and glorify your Father which is in heaven.

17 Think not that I am come to destroy the law, or the prophets: I am not come to destroy, but to fulfil.

18 For verily I say unto you, Till heaven and earth pass, one jot or one tittle shall in no wise pass from the law, till all be fulfilled.

19 Whosoever therefore shall break one of these least command-

ments, and shall teach men so, he shall be called the least in the kingdom of heaven: but whosoever shall do and teach them, the same shall be called great in the kingdom of heaven.

20 For I say unto you, That except your righteousness shall exceed the righteousness of the scribes and Pharisees, ye shall in no case enter into the kingdom of heaven.

21 Ye have heard that it was said by them of old time, Thou shall not kill; and whosoever shall kill shall be in danger of the judgment:

22 But I say unto you, That whosoever is angry with his brother without a cause shall be in danger of the judgment: and whosoever shall say to his brother, Raca, shall be in danger of the council: but whosoever shall say, Thou fool, shall be in danger of hell fire.

23 Therefore if thou bring thy gift to the altar, and there rememberest that thy brother hath ought against thee;

24 Leave there thy gift before the altar, and go thy way; first be reconciled to thy brother, and then come and offer thy gift.

25 Agree with thine adversary quickly, whiles thou art in the way with him; lest at any time the adversary deliver thee to the judge, and the judge deliver thee to the officer, and thou be cast into prison.

26 Verily I say unto thee, Thou shalt by no means come out thence, till thou hast paid the uttermost farthing.

27 Ye have heard that it was said by them of old time, Thou shalt not commit adultery:

28 But I say unto you, That whosoever looketh on a woman to lust after her hath committed adultery with her already in his heart.

29 And if thy right eye offend thee, pluck it out, and cast it from thee: for it is profitable for thee that one of thy members should perish, and not that thy whole body should be cast into hell.

30 And if thy right hand offend thee, cut it off, and cast it from thee: for it is profitable for thee that one of thy members should perish, and not that thy whole body should be cast into hell.

31 It hath been said, Whosoever shall put away his wife, let him give her a writing of divorcement:

32 But I say unto you, That whosoever shall put away his wife, saving for the cause of fornication, causeth her to commit adultery: and whosoever shall marry her that is divorced committeth adultery.

33 Again, ye have heard that it hath been said by them of old time, Thou shall not forswear thyself, but shalt perform unto the Lord thine oaths:

34 But I say unto you, Swear not at all; neither by heaven; for it is God's throne:

35 Nor by the earth; for it is his footstool: neither by Jerusalem; for it is the city of the great King.

36 Neither shalt thou swear by thy head, because thou canst not make one hair white or black.

37 But let your communication be, Yea, yea; Nay, nay: for whatsoever is more than these cometh of evil.

38 Ye have heard that it hath been said, An eye for an eye, and a tooth for a tooth:

39 But I say unto you, That ye resist not evil: but whosoever shall smite thee on thy right cheek, turn to him the other also.

40 And if any man will sue thee at the law, and take away thy coat, let him have thy cloke also.

41 And whosoever shall compel thee to go a mile, go with him twain.

42 Give to him that asketh thee, and from him that would borrow of thee turn not thou away.

43 Ye have heard that it hath been said, Thou shalt love thy neighbour, and hate thine enemy.

44 But I say unto you, Love your enemies, bless them that curse you, do good to them that hate you, and pray for them which despitefully use you, and persecute you;

45 That ye may be the children of your Father which is in heaven: for he maketh his sun to rise on the evil and on the good, and sendeth rain on the just and on the unjust.

46 For if ye love them which love you, what reward have ye? do not even the publicans the same?

47 And if ye salute your brethren only, what do ye more than others? do not even the publicans so?

48 Be ye therefore perfect, even as your Father which is in heaven is perfect.

6

1 Take heed that ye do not your alms before men, to be seen of them: otherwise ye have no reward of your Father which is in heaven.

2 Therefore when thou doest thine alms, do not sound a trumpet before thee, as the hypocrites do in the synagogues and

in the streets, that they may have glory of men. Verily I say unto you, They have their reward.

3 But when thou doest alms, let not thy left hand know what thy right hand doeth:

4 That thine alms may be in secret: and thy Father which seeth in secret himself shall reward thee openly.

5 And when thou prayest, thou shalt not be as the hypocrites are: for they love to pray standing in the synagogues and in the corners of the streets, that they may be seen of men. Verily I say unto you, They have their reward.

6 But thou, when thou prayest, enter into thy closet, and when thou hast shut thy door, pray to thy Father which is in secret; and thy Father which seeth in secret shall reward thee openly.

7 But when ye pray, use not vain repetitions, as the heathen do: for they think that they shall be heard for their much speaking.

8 Be not ye therefore like unto them: for your Father knoweth what things ye have need of, before ye ask him.

9 After this manner therefore pray ye: Our Father which art in heaven, Hallowed be thy name.

10 Thy kingdom come. Thy will be done in earth, as it is in heaven.

11 Give us this day our daily bread.

12 And forgive us our debts, as we forgive our debtors.

13 And lead us not into temptation, but deliver us from evil: For thine is the kingdom, and the power, and the glory, for ever. Amen.

14 For if ye forgive men their trespasses, your heavenly Father will also forgive you:

15 But if ye forgive not men their trespasses, neither will your Father forgive your trespasses.

16 Moreover when ye fast, be not, as the hypocrites, of a sad countenance: for they disfigure their faces, that they may appear unto men to fast. Verily I say unto you, They have their reward.

17 But thou, when thou fastest, anoint thine head, and wash thy face;

18 That thou appear not unto men to fast, but unto thy Father which is in secret: and thy Father, which seeth in secret, shall reward thee openly.

19 Lay not up for yourselves treasures upon earth, where moth and rust doth corrupt, and where thieves break through and steal:

20 But lay up for yourselves treasures in heaven, where neither moth nor rust doth corrupt, and where thieves do not break through nor steal:

21 For where your treasure is, there will your heart be also.

22 The light of the body is the eye: if therefore thine eye be single, thy whole body shall be full of light.

23 But if thine eye be evil, thy whole body shall be full of darkness. If therefore the light that is in thee be darkness, how great is that darkness!

24 No man can serve two masters: for either he will hate the one, and love the other; or else he will hold to the one, and despise the other. Ye cannot serve God and mammon.

25 Therefore I say unto you, Take no thought for your life, what ye shall eat, or what ye shall drink; nor yet for your body, what ye shall put on. Is not the life more than meat, and the body than raiment?

26 Behold the fowls of the air: for they sow not, neither do they reap, nor gather into barns; yet your heavenly Father feedeth them. Are ye not much better than they?

27 Which of you by taking thought can add one cubit unto his stature?

28 And why take ye thought for raiment? Consider the lilies of the field, how they grow, they toil not, neither do they spin:

29 And yet I say unto you, That even Solomon in all his glory was not arrayed like one of these.

30 Wherefore, if God so clothe the grass of the field, which to day is, and to morrow is cast into the oven, shall he not much more clothe you, O ye of little faith?

31 Therefore take no thought, saying, What shall we eat? or, What shall we drink? or, Wherewithal shall we be clothed?

32 (For after all these things do the Gentiles seek:) for your heavenly Father knoweth that ye have need of all these things.

33 But seek ye first the kingdom of God, and his righteousness; and all these things shall be added unto you.

34 Take therefore no thought for the morrow: for the morrow shall take thought for the things of itself. Sufficient unto the day is the evil thereof.

7

1 Judge not, that ye be not judged.

2 For with what judgment ye judge, ye shall be judged: and with what measure ye mete, it shall be measured to you again.

3 And why beholdest thou the mote that is in thy brother's eye, but considerest not the beam that is in thine own eye?

4 Or how wilt thou say to thy brother, Let me pull out the mote out of thine eye; and, behold, a beam is in thine own eye?

5 Thou hypocrite, first cast out the beam out of thine own eye; and then shalt thou see clearly to cast out the mote out of thy brother's eye.

6 Give not that which is holy unto the dogs, neither cast ye your pearls before swine, lest they trample them under their feet and turn again and rend you.

7 Ask, and it shall be given you; seek, and ye shall find; knock and it shall be opened unto you:

8 For every one that asketh receiveth; and he that seeketh findeth; and to him that knocketh it shall be opened.

9 Or what man is there of you, whom if his son ask bread, will he give him a stone?

10 Or if he ask a fish, will he give him a serpent?

11 If ye then, being evil, know how to give good gifts unto your children, how much more shall your Father which is in heaven give good things to them that ask him?

12 Therefore all things whatsoever ye would that men should do to you, do ye even so to them: for this is the law and the prophets.

13 Enter ye in at the strait gate: for wide is the gate, and broad is the way, that leadeth to destruction, and many there be which go in thereat:

14 Because strait is the gate, and narrow is the way, which leadeth unto life, and few there be that find it.

15 Beware of false prophets, which come to you in sheep's clothing, but inwardly they are ravening wolves.

16 Ye shall know them by their fruits. Do men gather grapes of thorns, or figs of thistles?

17 Even so every good tree bringeth forth good fruit; but a corrupt tree bringeth forth evil fruit.

18 A good tree cannot bring forth evil fruit, neither can a corrupt tree bring forth good fruit.

19 Every tree that bringeth not forth good fruit is hewn down and cast into the fire.

20 Wherefore by their fruits ye shall know them.

21 Not every one that saith unto me, Lord, Lord, shall enter into the kingdom of heaven; but he that doeth the will of my Father which is in heaven.

22 Many will say to me in that day, Lord, Lord, have we not prophesied in thy name? and in thy name have cast out devils? and in thy name done many wonderful works?

23 And then will I profess unto them, I never knew you: depart from me, ye that work iniquity.

24 Therefore whosoever heareth these sayings of mine, and doeth them, I will liken him unto a wise man, which built his house upon a rock:

25 And the rain descended, and the floods came, and the winds blew, and beat upon that house; and it fell not: for it was founded upon a rock.

26 And every one that heareth these sayings of mine, and doeth them not, shall be likened unto a foolish man, which built his house upon the sand:

27 And the rain descended, and the floods came, and the winds blew, and beat upon that house; and it fell: and great was the fall of it.

28 And it came to pass, when Jesus had ended these sayings, the people were astonished at his doctrine:

29 For he taught them as one having authority, and not as the scribes.

WARREN'S ADDRESS AT BUNKER HILL

John Pierpont

Stand! the ground's your own, my braves!
Will ye give it up to slaves?
Will ye look for greener graves?
    Hope ye mercy still?
What's the mercy despots feel?
Hear it in that battle-peal!
Read it on yon bristling steel!
    Ask it,—ye who will.

Fear ye foes who kill for hire?
Will ye to your *homes* retire?
Look behind you!—they're afire!
    And, before you, see
Who have done it! From the vale
On they come!—and will ye quail?
Leaden rain and iron hail
    Let their welcome be!

In the God of battles trust!
Die we may,—and die we must:
But, O, where can dust to dust
    Be consigned so well,

As where heaven its dews shall shed
On the martyred patriot's bed,
And the rocks shall raise their head,
    Of his deeds to tell?

TO ALTHEA, FROM PRISON

Richard Lovelace

When Love with unconfinèd wings
    Hovers within my gates,
And my divine Althea brings
    To whisper at the grates;
When I lie tangled in her hair
    And fettered to her eye,
The birds that wanton in the air
    Know no such liberty.

When flowing cups run swiftly round
    With no allaying Thames,
Our careless heads with roses bound,
    Our hearts with loyal flames;
When thirsty grief in wine we steep,
    When healths and draughts go free,
Fishes that tipple in the deep
    Know no such liberty.

When, like committed linnets, I
    With shriller throat will sing
The sweetness, mercy, majesty,
    And glories of my king;
When I shall voice aloud how good
    He is, how great should be,
Enlargèd winds, that curl the flood,
    Know no such liberty.

Stone walls do not a prison make,
    Nor iron bars a cage;
Minds innocent and quiet take
    That for an hermitage;
If I have freedom in my love
    And in my soul am free,
Angels alone, that soar above,
    Enjoy such liberty.

IF I WERE A VOICE

Charles Mackay

If I were a Voice—a persuasive Voice—
　That could travel the wide world through,
I would fly on the beams of the morning light
And speak to men with a gentle might.
　And tell them to be true.
I'd fly, I'd fly o'er land and sea,
Wherever a human heart might be,
　Telling a tale, or singing a song,
　In praise of the Right—in blame of the Wrong.

If I were a Voice—a consoling Voice—
　I'd fly on the wings of the air;
The home of Sorrow and Guilt I'd seek,
And calm and truthful words I'd speak,
　To save them from Despair.
I'd fly, I'd fly o'er the crowded town,
And drop, like the happy sunlight, down
　Into the hearts of suffering men,
　And teach them to rejoice again.

If I were a Voice—a controlling Voice—
　I'd travel with the wind;
And, whenever I saw the nations torn
By warfare, jealousy or scorn,
　Or hatred of their kind,
I'd fly, I'd fly on the thunder crash,
And into their blinded bosoms flash;
　And, all their evil thoughts subdued,
　I'd teach them a Christian Brotherhood.

If I were a Voice—an immortal Voice—
　I'd speak in the people's ear;
And whenever they shouted "Liberty"
Without deserving to be free,
　I'd make their error clear.
I'd fly, I'd fly on the wings of day,
Rebuking wrong on my world-wide way,
　And making all the Earth rejoice—
　If I were a Voice—an immortal Voice.

If I were a Voice—a pervading Voice—
  I'd seek the kings of Earth;
I'd find them alone on their beds at night,
And whisper words that should guide them right,
  Lessons of priceless worth.
I'd fly more swift than the swiftest bird,
And tell them things they never heard—
  Truths which the ages for aye repeat,
  Unknown to the statesmen at their feet.

HOME, SWEET HOME

John Howard Payne

Mid pleasures and palaces though we may roam,
Be it ever so humble, there's no place like home;
A charm from the sky seems to hallow us there,
Which, seek through the world, is ne'er met with elsewhere
Home, home, sweet, sweet home!
There's no place like home, oh, there's no place like home!

An exile from home, splendor dazzles in vain;
Oh, give me my lowly thatched cottage again!
The birds singing gayly, that came at my call—
Give me them—and the peace of mind, dearer than all!
Home, home, sweet, sweet home!
There's no place like home, oh, there's no place like home!

I gaze on the moon as I tread the drear wild,
And feel that my mother now thinks of her child,
As she looks on that moon from our own cottage door
Thro' the woodbine, whose fragrance shall cheer me no more
Home, home, sweet, sweet home!
There's no place like home, oh, there's no place like home!

How sweet 'tis to sit 'neath a fond father's smile,
And the caress of a mother to soothe and beguile!
Let others delight mid new pleasures to roam,
But give me, oh, give me, the pleasures of home,
Home, home, sweet, sweet home!
There's no place like home, oh, there's no place like home!

To thee I'll return, overburdened with care;
The heart's dearest solace will smile on there;
No more from that cottage again will I roam;
Be it ever so humble, there's no place like home.
Home, home, sweet, sweet home!
There's no place like home, oh, there's no place like home!

PROSPERO ENDS THE REVELS

William Shakespeare

Our revels now are ended. These our actors,
As I foretold you, were all spirits and
Are melted into air, into thin air:
And, like the baseless fabric of this vision,
The cloud-capp'd towers, the gorgeous palaces,
The solemn temples, the great globe itself,
Yea, all which it inherit, shall dissolve
And, like this insubstantial pageant faded,
Leave not a rack behind. We are such stuff
As dreams are made on, and our little life
Is rounded with a sleep.

(From The Tempest)

THE VILLAGE BLACKSMITH

Henry Wadsworth Longfellow

Under a spreading chestnut-tree
The village smithy stands;
The smith, a mighty man is he,
With large and sinewy hands;
And the muscles of his brawny arms
Are strong as iron bands.

His hair is crisp, and black, and long,
His face is like the tan;
His brow is wet with honest sweat,
He earns what'er he can,
And looks the whole world in the face,
For he owes not any man.

Week in, week out, from morn till night,
You can hear his bellows blow;
You can hear him swing his heavy sledge,
With measured beat and slow,
Like a sexton ringing the village bell,
When the evening sun is low.

And children coming home from school
Look in at the open door;
They love to see the flaming forge,
And hear the bellows roar,
And catch the burning sparks that fly
Like chaff from a threshing-floor.

He goes on Sunday to the church,
And sits among his boys;
He hears the parson pray and preach,
He hears his daughter's voice
Singing in the village choir,
And it makes his heart rejoice.

It sounds to him like her mother's voice,
Singing in Paradise!
He needs must think of her once more,
How in the grave she lies;
And with his hard, rough hand he wipes
A tear out of his eyes.

Toiling—rejoicing—sorrowing,
Onward through life he goes;
Each morning sees some task begin,
Each evening sees it close;
Something attempted, something done,
Has earned a night's repose.

Thanks, thanks to thee, my worthy friend,
For the lesson thou hast taught!
Thus at the flaming forge of life
Our fortunes must be wrought;
Thus on its sounding anvil shaped
Each burning deed and thought!

THE BRIDGE OF SIGHS

Thomas Hood

One more Unfortunate,
Weary of breath,
Rashly importunate,
Gone to her death!

Take her up tenderly,
Lift her with care;
Fashion'd so slenderly,
Young, and so fair.

Look at her garments
Clinging like cerements;
Whilst the wave constantly
Drips from her clothing;
Take her up instantly,
Loving, not loathing.

Touch her not scornfully;
Think of her mournfully,
Gently and humanly;
Not of the stains of her,
All that remains of her
Now is pure womanly.

Make no deep scrutiny
Into her mutiny
Rash and undutiful:
Past all dishonour,
Death has left on her
Only the beautiful.

Still, for all slips of hers,
One of Eve's family—
Wipe those poor lips of hers
Oozing so clammily.

Loop up her tresses
Escaped from the comb,
Her fair auburn tresses;
Whilst wonderment guesses
Where was her home?

Who was her father?
Who was her mother?
Had she a sister?
Had she a brother?
Or was there a dearer one
Still, and a nearer one
Yet, than all others?

Alas! for the rarity
Of Christian charity
Under the sun!
O, it was pitiful!
Near a whole city full,
Home she had none!

Sisterly, brotherly,
Fatherly, motherly
Feelings had changed:
Love, by harsh evidence,
Thrown from its eminence;
Even God's providence
Seeming estranged.

Where the lamps quiver
So far in the river,
With many a light
From window and casement,
From garret to basement,
She stood, with amazement,
Houseless by night.

The bleak wind of March
Made her tremble and shiver;
But not the dark arch,
Or the black flowing river:
Mad from life's history,
Glad to death's mystery,
Swift to be hurl'd—
Anywhere, anywhere
Out of the world!

In she plunged boldly—
No matter how coldly
The rough river ran—
Over the brink of it,
Picture it—think of it,
Dissolute Man!
Lave in it, drink of it,
Then, if you can!

Take her up tenderly,
Lift her with care;
Fashion'd so slenderly,
Young, and so fair!

Ere her limbs frigidly
Stiffen too rigidly,
Decently, kindly,
Smooth and compose them;
And her eyes, close them,
Staring so blindly!

Dreadfully staring
Thro' muddy impurity,
As when with the daring
Last look of despairing
Fix'd on futurity.

Perishing gloomily,
Spurr'd by contumely,
Cold inhumanity,
Burning insanity,
Into her rest.—
Cross her hands humbly
As if praying dumbly,
Over her breast!

Owning her weakness,
Her evil behavior,
And leaving, with meekness,
Her sins to her Savior!

THE RICH MAN AND THE KINGDOM OF HEAVEN
Holy Bible, Matthew 19:13–30

13 Then were there brought unto him little children, that he should put his hands on them, and pray: and the disciples rebuked them.

14 But Jesus said, Suffer little children, and forbid them not, to come unto me: for of such is the kingdom of heaven.

15 And he laid his hands on them, and departed thence.

16 And, behold, one came and said unto him, Good Master, what good thing shall I do, that I may have eternal life?

17 And he said unto him, Why callest thou me good? there is none good but one, that is, God: but if thou wilt enter into life, keep the commandments.

18 He saith unto him, Which? Jesus said, Thou shalt do no murder, Thou shalt not commit adultery, Thou shalt not steal, Thou shalt not bear false witness,

19 Honour thy father and thy mother: and, Thou shalt love thy neighbour as thyself.

20 The young man saith unto him, All these things have I kept from my youth up: what lack I yet?

21 Jesus said unto him, If thou wilt be perfect, go and sell that thou hast, and give to the poor, and thou shalt have treasure in heaven: and come and follow me.

22 But when the young man heard that saying, he went away sorrowful: for he had great possessions.

23 Then said Jesus unto his disciples, Verily I say unto you, That a rich man shall hardly enter into the kingdom of heaven.

24 And again I say unto you, It is easier for a camel to go through the eye of a needle, than for a rich man to enter into the kingdom of God.

25 When his disciples heard it, they were exceedingly amazed, saying, Who then can be saved?

26 But Jesus beheld them, and said unto them, With men this is impossible; but with God all things are possible.

27 Then answered Peter and said unto him, Behold, we have forsaken all, and followed thee; what shall we have therefore?

28 And Jesus said unto them, Verily I say unto you, That ye which have followed me, in the regeneration when the Son of man shall sit in the throne of his glory, ye also shall sit upon twelve thrones, judging the twelve tribes of Israel.

29 And every one that hath forsaken houses, or brethren, or sisters, or father, or mother, or wife, or children, or lands, for my name's sake, shall receive an hundredfold, and shall inherit everlasting life.

30 But many that are first shall be last; and the last shall be first.

WOODMAN, SPARE THAT TREE

George P. Morris

Woodman, spare that tree!
Touch not a single bough!
In youth it sheltered me,
And I'll protect it now.
'Twas my forefather's hand
That placed it near his cot;
There, woodman, let it stand
Thy ax shall harm it not!

That old familiar tree,
Whose glory and renown
Are spread o'er land and sea,
And wouldst thou hew it down?

Woodman, forbear thy stroke!
Cut not its earth-bound ties!
Oh! spare that aged oak,
Now towering to the skies.

When but an idle boy
I sought its grateful shade;
In all their gushing joy
Here too my sisters played.
My mother kissed me here;
My father pressed my hand—
Forgive this foolish tear,
But let that old oak stand!

My heart-strings round thee cling,
Close as thy bark, old friend!
Here shall the wild-bird sing,
And still thy branches bend.
Old tree, the storm still brave!
And, woodman, leave the spot!
While I've a hand to save,
Thy ax shall harm it not.

THE THIRTEEN SISTERS

Stephen Vincent Benét

Thirteen sisters beside the sea,
(Have a care, my son.)
Builded a house called Liberty
And locked the doors with a stately key.
None should enter it but the free.
(Have a care, my son.)

The walls are solid as Plymouth Rock.
(Rock can crumble, my son.)
The door of seasoned New England stock.
Before it a Yankee fighting-cock
Pecks redcoat kings away from the lock.
(Fighters can die, my son.)

The hearth is a corner where sages sit.
(Sages pass, my son.)
Washington's heart lies under it.
And the long roof-beams are chiseled and split
From hickory tough as Jackson's wit.
(Bones in the dust, my son.)

The trees in the garden are fair and fine.
(Trees blow down, my son.)
Connecticut elm and Georgia pine.
The warehouse groans with cotton and swine.
The cellar is full of scuppernong-wine.
(Wine turns sour, my son.)

Surely a house so strong and bold,
(The wind is rising, my son,)
Will last till Time is a pinch of mould!
There is a ghost, when the night is old.
There is a ghost, who walks in the cold.
(The trees are shaking, my son.)

The sisters sleep on Liberty's breast,
(The thunder thunders, my son,)
Like thirteen swans in a single nest.
But the ghost is naked and will not rest
Until the sun rise out of the West.
(The lightning lightens, my son.)

All night long like a moving stain,
(The trees are breaking, my son,)
The black ghost wanders his house of pain.
There is blood where his hand has lain.
It is wrong he should wear a chain.
(The sky is falling, my son.)

(From John Brown's Body)

STILL THE WONDER GREW

Oliver Goldsmith

While words of learned strength and thundering sound
Amazed the gazing rustics gathered round,
And still they gazed, and still the wonder grew
That one small head could carry all he knew.

HOW SLEEP THE BRAVE

William Collins

How sleep the brave, who sink to rest
By all their country's wishes blest!
When Spring, with dewy fingers cold,
Returns to deck their hallowed mould,
She there shall dress a sweeter sod
Than Fancy's feet have ever trod.

By fairy hands their knell is rung;
By forms unseen their dirge is sung;
There Honour comes, a pilgrim grey,
To bless the turf that wraps their clay;
And Freedom shall awhile repair
To dwell, a weeping hermit, there!

FROM DON JUAN

Lord Byron

Man's love is of man's life a thing apart,
'Tis woman's whole existence; man may range
The court, camp, church, the vessel, and the mart,
Sword, gown, gain, glory, offer in exchange
Pride, fame, ambition, to fill up his heart,
And few there are whom these can not estrange:
Men have all these resources, we but one,
To love again, and be again undone.

RICHARD CORY

Edward Arlington Robinson

Whenever Richard Cory went down town,
  We people on the pavement looked at him:
He was a gentleman from sole to crown,
  Clean favored, and imperially slim.

And he was always quietly arrayed,
  And he was always human when he talked;
But still he fluttered pulses when he said,
  "Good-morning," and he glittered when he walked.

And he was rich—yes, richer than a king—
  And admirably schooled in every grace:
In fine, we thought that he was everything
  To make us wish that we were in his place.

So on we worked, and waited for the light,
  And went without the meat, and cursed the bread;
And Richard Cory, one calm summer night,
  Went home and put a bullet through his head.

MASSA'S IN DE COLD, COLD GROUND

Stephen Foster

Round de meadows am a-ringing
  De darkies' mournful song,
While de mocking-bird am singing,
  Happy as de day am long.
Where de ivy am a-creeping,
  O'er de grassy mound,
Dere old massa am a-sleeping,
  Sleeping in de cold, cold ground.

      Down in de corn-field
        Hear dat mournful sound:
      All de darkies am a-weeping,—
        Massa's in de cold, cold ground.

When de autumn leaves were falling,
  When de days were cold,
'Twas hard to hear old massa calling,
  Cayse he was so weak and old.
Now de orange tree am blooming
  On de sandy shore,
Now de summer days am coming,—
  Massa nebber calls no more.

Massa make de darkies love him,
  Cayse he was so kind;
Now dey sadly weep above him,
  Mourning cayse he leave dem behind.

I cannot work before tomorrow,
  Cayse de tear-drop flow;
I try to drive away my sorrow,
  Pickin' on de old banjo.

SHERIDAN'S RIDE

Thomas Buchanan Read

Up from the South at break of day,
Bringing to Winchester fresh dismay,
The affrighted air with a shudder bore,
Like a herald in haste, to the chieftain's door,
The terrible grumble, and rumble, and roar,
Telling the battle was on once more,
And Sheridan twenty miles away.

And wider still those billows of war
Thundered along the horizon's bar;
And louder yet into Winchester rolled
The roar of that red sea uncontrolled,
Making the blood of the listener cold,
As he thought of the stake in that fiery fray,
With Sheridan twenty miles away.

But there is a road from Winchester town,
A good, broad highway leading down;
And there, through the flush of the morning light,
A steed as black as the steeds of night
Was seen to pass, as with eagle flight;
As if he knew the terrible need,
He stretched away with the utmost speed;
Hills rose and fell; but his heart was gay,
With Sheridan fifteen miles away.

Still sprung from those swift hoofs, thundering South,
The dust, like smoke from the cannon's mouth;
Or the trail of a comet, sweeping faster and faster,
Foreboding to traitors the doom of disaster,
The heart of the steed and the heart of the master
Were beating like prisoners assaulting their walls,
Impatient to be where the battlefield calls;
Every nerve of the charger was strained to full play,
With Sheridan only ten miles away.

Under his spurning feet the road
Like an arrowy Alpine river flowed,
And the landscape sped away behind
Like an ocean flying before the wind,
And the steed, like a barque fed with furnace ire,
Swept on, with his wild eye full of fire.
But lo! he is nearing his heart's desire;
He is snuffing the smoke of the roaring fray,
With Sheridan only five miles away.

The first that the general saw were the groups
Of stragglers, and then the retreating troops;
What was done? What to do? A glance told him both,
Then striking his spurs, with a terrible oath,
He dashed down the line 'mid a storm of huzzas,
And the wave of retreat checked its course there, because
The sight of the master compelled it to pause.
With foam and with dust the black charger was gray;
By the flash of his eye and the red nostril's play,
He seemed to the whole great army to say,
"I have brought you Sheridan all the way
From Winchester down to save the day!"

Hurrah! Hurrah for Sheridan!
Hurrah! Hurrah for horse and man!
And when their statues are placed on high,
Under the dome of the Union sky,
The American soldier's Temple of Fame;
There with the glorious general's name,
Be it said, in letters both bold and bright,
"Here is the steed that saved the day,
By carrying Sheridan into the fight,
From Winchester, twenty miles away!"

THE HEIGHTS

The heights by great men reached and kept
Were not attained by sudden flight,
But they, while their companions slept
Were toiling upward in the night.

(From Longfellow's
The Ladder of St. Augustine)

THE WONDERFUL TAR-BABY STORY

Joel Chandler Harris

"Didn't the fox *never* catch the rabbit, Uncle Remus?" asked the little boy next evening.

"He come mighty nigh it, honey, sho's you born—Brer Fox did. One day atter Brer Rabbit fool 'im wid dat calamus root, Brer Fox went ter wuk en got 'im some tar, en mix it wid some turkentime, en fix up a contrapshun w'at he call a Tar-Baby, en he tuck dish yer Tar-Baby en he sot 'er in de big road, en den he lay off in de bushes fer to see w'at de news wuz gwineter be. En he didn't hatter wait long, nudder, kaze bimeby here come Brer Rabbit pacin' down de road—lippity-clippity, clippity-lippity—des ez sassy ez a jay-bird. Brer Fox, he lay low. Brer Rabbit come prancin' 'long twel he spy de Tar-Baby, en den he fotch up on his behime legs like he wuz 'stonished. De Tar-Baby, she sot dar, she did, en Brer Fox, he lay low.

"'Mawnin'!' sez Brer Rabbit, sezee—'nice wedder dis mawnin',' sezee.

"Tar-Baby ain't sayin' nothin', en Brer Fox, he lay low.

"'How duz yo' sym'tums seem ter segashuate?' sez Brer Rabbit, sezee.

"Brer Fox, he wink his eye slow, en lay low, en de Tar-Baby, she ain't sayin' nothin'.

"'How you come on, den? Is you deaf?' sez Brer Rabbit, sezee. 'Kaze if you is, I kin holler loder,' sezee.

"Tar-Baby stay still, en Brer Fox, he lay low.

"'You'er stuck up, dat's w'at you is,' says Brer Rabbit, sezee, 'en I'm gwineter kyore you, dat's w'at I'm gwineter do,' sezee.

"Brer Fox, he sorter chuckle in his stummuck, he did, but Tar-Baby ain't sayin' nothin'.

"'I'm gwineter larn you how ter talk ter 'specttubble fokes ef hit's de las' ack,' sez Brer Rabbit, sezee. 'Ef you don't take off dat hat en tell me howdy, I'm gwineter bu' you wide open,' sezee.

"Tar-Baby stay still, en Brer Fox, he lay low.

"Brer Rabbit keep on axin' 'im, en de Tar-Baby, she keep on sayin' nothin', 'twel present'y Brer Rabbit draw back wid his fis', he did, en blip he tuck 'er side 'er de head. His fis' stuck, en he can't pull loose. De tar hilt 'im. But Tar-Baby, she stay still, en Brer Fox, he lay low.

" 'Ef you don't lemme loose, I'll knock you agin,' sez Brer Rabbit, sezee, en wid dat he fotch 'er a wipe wid de udder han', en dat stuck. Tar-Baby, she ain't sayin' nothin', en Brer Fox, he lay low.

" 'Tu'n me loose, fo' I kick de natal stuffin' outen you,' sez Brer Rabbit, sezee, but de Tar-Baby, she ain't sayin' nothin'. She des hilt on, en den Brer Rabbit lose de use er his feet in de same way. Brer Fox, he lay low. Den Brer Rabbit squall out dat ef de Tar-Baby don't tu'n 'im loose he butt'er cranksided. En den he butted, en his head got stuck. Den Brer Fox, he sa'ntered fort', lookin' des ez innercent ez one er yo' mammy's mockin'-birds.

" 'Howdy, Brer Rabbit,' sez Brer Fox, sezee. 'You look sorter stuck up dis mawnin',' sezee, en den he rolled on de groun' en laughed en laughed twel he couldn't laugh no mo'. 'I speck you'll take dinner wid me dis time, Brer Rabbit. I done laid in some calamus root, en ain't gwineter take no skuse,' sez Brer Fox, sezee."

Here Uncle Remus paused, and drew a two-pound yam out of the ashes.

"Did the fox eat the rabbit?" asked the little boy to whom the story had been told.

"Dat's all de fur de tale goes," replied the old man. "He mout, en den agin he moutent. Some say Jedge B'ar come 'long en loosed 'im—some say he didn't. I hear Miss Sally callin'. You better run 'long."

HOW MR. RABBIT WAS TOO SHARP FOR MR. FOX

"Uncle Remus," said the little boy one evening, when he found the old man with little or nothing to do, "did the fox kill and eat the rabbit when he caught him with the Tar-Baby?"

"Law, honey, ain't I tell you 'bout dat?" replied the old darkey, chuckling slyly. "I 'clar ter grashus I ought er tole you dat, but old man Nod wuz ridin' on my eyeleds 'twel a leetle mo'n I'd a dis'member'd my own name, en den on to dat her come yo' mammy hollerin' atter you.

"W'at I tell you w'en I fus' begin? I tole you Brer Rabbit wuz a monstus soon creetur; leas' ways dat's w'at I laid out fer ter tell you. Well den, honey, don't you go en make no udder calkalashuns, kaze in dem days Brer Rabbit en his family wuz at de head er de gang w'en enny racket wuz on han', en dar dey stayed. Fo' you begins ter wipe yo' eyes 'bout Brer Rabbit, you wait and see whar'bouts Brer Rabbit gwineter fetch up at. But dat needer yer ner dar.

"W'en Brer Fox fine Brer Rabbit mixt up wid de Tar-Baby, he feel mighty good, en he roll on de groun' en laff. Mimeby he up'n say, sezee:

" 'Well, I speck I got you distime, Brer Rabbit,' sezee; 'maybe I ain't, but I speck I is. You been runnin' roun' her sassin' atter me a mightly long time, but I speck you done come ter de een' er de row. You bin cuttin' up yo' capers en bouncin' 'roun' in dis neighberhood ontwel you come ter b'leeve yo'self de boss er de whole gang. En den youer allers some'ers whar you got no bizness,' sez Brer Rabbit, sezee. 'Who ax you fer ter come en strike up a 'quaintance wid dish yer Tar-Baby? En who stuck you up dar what you iz? Nobody in de roun' worril. You des tuck en jam yo'-self on dat Tar-Baby widout waitin' fer enny invite,' sez Brer Fox, sezee, 'en dar you is, en dar you'll stay twel I fixes up a bresh-pile and fires her up, kaze I'm gwineter bobbycue you dis day, sho,' sez Brer Fox, sezee.

"Den Brer Rabbit talk mighty 'umble.

" 'I don't keer w'at you do wid me, Brer Fox,' sezee, 'so you don't fling me in dat brier-patch. Roas'me, Brer Fox,' sezee, 'but don't fling me in dat brier-patch,' sezee.

" 'Het's so much trouble fer ter kindle a fier,' sez Brer Fox, sezee, 'dat I speck I'll hatter hang you,' sezee.

" 'Hang me des ez high as you please, Brer Fox,' sez Brer Rabbit, sezee, 'but do fer de Lord's sake don't fling me in dat brier-patch,' sezee.

" 'I ain't got no string,' sez Brer Fox, sezee, 'en now I speck I'll hatter drown you,' sezee.

" 'Drown me des ez deep ez you please, Brer Fox,' sez Brer Rabbit, sezee, 'but do don't fling me in dat brier-patch,' sezee.

" 'Dey ain't no water nigh,' sez Brer Fox, sezee, 'en now I speck I'll hatter skin you,' sezee.

" 'Skin me, Brer Fox,' sez Brer Rabbit, sezee, 'snatch out my eyeballs, t'ar out my years by de roots, en cut off my legs,' sezee, 'but do please, Brer Fox, don't fling me in dat brier-patch,' sezee.

"Co'se Brer Fox wanter hurt Brer Rabbit bad ez he kin, so he cotch 'im by de behime legs en slung 'im right in de middle er de brier-patch. Dar wuz a considerbul flutter whar Brer Rabbit struck de bushes, en Brer Fox sorter hang roun' fer ter see w'at wuz gwineter happen. Bimeby he hear somebody call 'im, en way up de hill he see Brer Rabbit settin' cross-legged on a chinkapin log koamin' de pitch outen his har wid a chip. Den Brer Fox know dat he bin swop off mighty bad. Brer Rabbit wuz bleedzed fer ter fling back some er his sass, en he holler out:

" 'Bred en bawn in a brier-patch, Brer Fox—bred en bawn in a brier-patch!' en wid dat he skip out des ez a cricket in de embers."

(From Uncle Remus: His Songs and His Sayings)

HOW DOTH THE LITTLE BUSY BEE

Isaac Watts

How doth the little busy bee
Improve each shining hour,
And gather honey all the day
From every opening flower!

How skilfully she builds her cell!
How neat she spreads the wax!
And labors hard to store it well
With the sweet food she makes.

In works of labor or of skill
I would be busy too;
For Satan finds some mischief still
For idle hands to do.

In books, or work, or healthful play,
Let my first years be passed,
That I may give for every day
Some good account at last.

WHEN OTHER LIPS AND OTHER HEARTS

Alfred Bunn

When other lips and other hearts
Their tales of love shall tell,
In language whose excess imparts
The power they feel so well,
There may perhaps in such a scene
A recollection be,
Of days that have as happy been,
And you'll remember me.

229

When coldness and deceit shall slight
　The beauty they now prize,
And deem it but a hollow light
　That beams within your eyes,
When hollow hearts shall wear a mask,
　'Twill break your own to see,
In such a moment I but ask
　That you'll remember me.
　　　　　(From The Bohemian Girl)

THE PICTURE THAT IS TURNED TOWARD
THE WALL

Charles Graham

Far away beyond the glamor of the city and its strife,
There's a quiet little homestead by the sea,
Where a tender loving lassie used to live a happy life
Contented in her home as she could be;
Not a shadow ever seemed to cloud the sunshine of her youth,
And they thought no sorrow could her life befall.
But she left them all one evening and their sad hearts knew the
　truth,
When her father turned her picture to the wall.

Chorus:
　　There's a name that's never spoken and a mother's heart half
　　　broken,
　　There is just another missing from the old home, that is all;
　　There is still a memory living, there's a father unforgiving,
　　And a picture that is turned toward the wall.

They have laid away each token of the one who ne'er returns,
Every trinket, every ribbon that she wore,
Though it seems so long ago now, yet the lamp of hope still burns,
And her mother prays to see her child once more,
Though no tidings ever reach them what her life or lot may be,
Though they sometimes think she's gone beyond recall,
There's a tender recollection of a face they never see,
In the picture that is turned toward the wall. (*Chorus.*)

BURIAL OF SIR JOHN MOORE

Charles Wolfe

Not a drum was heard, not a funeral note,
  As his corse to the rampart we hurried;
Not a soldier discharged his farewell shot
  O'er the grave where our hero we buried.

We buried him darkly, at dead of night,
  The sods with our bayonets turning;
By the struggling moonbeams' misty light,
  And the lantern dimly burning.

No useless coffin inclosed his breast,
  Not in sheet nor in shroud we wound him;
But he lay, like a warrior taking his rest,
  With his martial cloak around him.

Few and short were the prayers we said,
  And we spoke not a word of sorrow;
But we steadfastly gazed on the face that was dead,
  And we bitterly thought of the morrow.

We thought, as we hollowed his narrow bed,
  And smoothed down his lonely pillow,
That the foe and the stranger would tread o'er his head,
  And we far away on the billow!

Lightly they'll talk of the spirit that's gone,
  And o'er his cold ashes upbraid him;
But little he'll reck, if they let him sleep on,
  In the grave where a Briton has laid him!

But half of our heavy task was done,
  When the clock struck the hour for retiring
And we heard the distant and random gun
  That the foe was sullenly firing.

Slowly and sadly we laid him down,
  From the field of his fame fresh and gory!
We carved not a line, we raised not a stone,
  But we left him alone with his glory.

THE THINGS THAT ARE CAESAR'S

Holy Bible, Matthew 22:15–22

15 Then went the Pharisees, and took counsel how they might entangle him in his talk.

16 And they sent out unto him their disciples with the Herodians, saying, Master, we know that thou art true, and teachest the way of God in truth, neither carest thou for any man: for thou regardest not the person of men.

17 Tell us therefore, What thinkest thou? Is it lawful to give tribute unto Caesar, or not?

18 But Jesus perceived their wickedness, and said, Why tempt ye me, ye hypocrites?

19 Shew me the tribute money. And they brought unto him a penny.

20 And he saith unto them, Whose is this image and superscription?

21 They say unto him, Caesar's. Then saith he unto them, Render therefore unto Caesar the things which are Caesar's; and unto God the things that are God's.

22 When they had heard these words, they marvelled, and left him, and went their way.

MAUD MULLER

John Greenleaf Whittier

Maud Muller on a summer's day
Raked the meadows sweet with hay.

Beneath her torn hat glowed the wealth
Of simple beauty and rustic health.

Singing, she wrought, and her merry glee
The mock-bird echoed from his tree.

But when she glanced to the far-off town,
White from its hill-slope looking down,

The sweet song died, and a vague unrest
And a nameless longing filled her breast,—

A wish that she hardly dared to own,
For something better than she had known.

The Judge rode slowly down the lane,
Smoothing his horse's chestnut mane.

He drew his bridle in the shade
Of the apple-trees, to greet the maid,

And ask a draught from the spring that flowed
Through the meadow across the road.

She stooped where the cool spring bubbled up,
And filled for him her small tin cup,

And blushed as she gave it, looking down
On her feet so bare, and her tattered gown.

"Thanks!" said the Judge, "a sweeter draught
From a fairer hand was never quaffed."

He spoke of the grass and flowers and trees,
Of the singing birds and humming bees;

Then talked of the haying, and wondered whether
The cloud in the west would bring foul weather.

And Maud forgot her brier-torn gown,
And her graceful ankles bare and brown;

And listened, while a pleased surprise
Looked from her long-lashed hazel eyes.

At last, like one who for delay
Seeks a vain excuse, he rode away.

Maud Muller looked and sighed: "Ah me!
That I the Judge's bride might be!

"He would dress me up in silks so fine,
And praise and toast me at his wine.

"My father should wear a broadcloth coat,
My brother should sail a painted boat.

"I'd dress my mother so grand and gay,
And the baby should have a new toy each day.

"And I'd feed the hungry and clothe the poor,
And all should bless me who left our door."

The Judge looked back as he climbed the hill,
And saw Maud Muller standing still.

"A form more fair, a face more sweet,
Ne'er hath it been my lot to meet.

"And her modest answer and graceful air
Show her wise and good as she is fair.

"Would she were mine, and I to-day,
Like her, a harvester of hay:

"No doubtful balance of rights and wrongs,
Nor weary lawyers with endless tongues,

"But low of cattle and song of birds,
And health and quiet and loving words."

But he thought of his sister, proud and cold,
And his mother, vain of her rank and gold.

So, closing his heart, the Judge rode on,
And Maud was left in the field alone.

But the lawyers smiled that afternoon,
When he hummed in court an old love tune;

And the young girl mused beside the well,
Till the rain on the unraked clover fell.

He wedded a wife of richest dower,
Who lived for fashion, as he for power.

Yet oft, in his marble hearth's bright glow,
He watched a picture come and go;

And sweet Maud Muller's hazel eyes
Looked out in their innocent surprise.

Oft, when the wine in his glass was red,
He longed for the wayside well instead;

And closed his eyes on his garnished rooms,
To dream of meadows and clover-blooms.

And the proud man sighed, with a secret pain,
"Ah, that I were free again!

"Free as when I rode that day
Where the barefoot maiden raked her hay."

She wedded a man unlearned and poor,
And many children played round her door.

But care and sorrow, and child-birth pain,
Left their traces on heart and brain.

And oft, when the summer sun shone hot
On the new-mown hay in the meadow lot,

And she heard the little spring brook fall
Over the roadside, through the wall,

In the shade of the apple-tree again
She saw a rider draw his rein;

And, gazing down with a timid grace,
She felt his pleased eyes read her face.

Sometimes her narrow kitchen walls
Stretched away into stately halls;

The weary wheel to a spinnet turned,
The tallow candle an astral burned,

And for him who sat by the chimney lug,
Dozing and grumbling o'er pipe and mug,

A manly form at her side she saw,
And joy was duty and love was law.

Then she took up her burden of life again,
Saying only, "It might have been."

Alas for maiden, alas for judge,
For rich repiner and household drudge!

God pity them both! and pity us all,
Who vainly the dreams of youth recall.

For of all sad words of tongue or pen,
The saddest are these: "It might have been!"

Ah, well! for us all some sweet hope lies
Deeply buried from human eyes;

And, in the hereafter, angels may
Roll the stone from its grave away!

THE COLUMBIAN ORATION

Chauncey Mitchell Depew

This day belongs not to America, but to the world. The results of the event it commemorates are the heritage of the peoples of every race and clime. We celebrate the emancipation of man. The preparation was the work of almost countless centuries; the realization was the revelation of one. The Cross on Calvary was hope; the cross raised on San Salvador was opportunity. But for the first, Columbus would never have sailed; but for the second, there would have been no place for the planting, the nurture, and the expansion of civil and religious liberty.

The spirit of Columbus hovers over us to-day. Only by celestial intelligence can it grasp the full significance of this spectacle and ceremonial.

From the first century to the fifteenth counts for little in the history of progress, but in the period between the fifteenth and twentieth is crowded the romance and reality of human development. Life has been prolonged, and its enjoyment intensified. The powers of the air and the water, the resistless forces of the elements, which in the time of the discoverer were the visible terrors of the wrath of God, have been subdued to the service of man. Arts and luxuries which could be possessed and enjoyed only by the rich and noble, the works of genius which were read and understood only by the learned few, domestic comforts and surroundings beyond the reach of lord or bishop, now adorn and illumine the homes of our citizens. Serfs are sovereigns and the people are kings. The trophies and splendors of their reign are commonwealths, rich in every attribute of great states, and united in a Republic whose power and prosperity and liberty and enlightment are the wonder and admiration of the world.

All hail, Columbus, discoverer, dreamer, hero, and apostle! We, here, of every race and country, recognize the horizon which bounded his vision and the infinite scope of his genius. The voice of gratitude and praise for all the blessings which have been showered upon mankind by his adventure is limited to no language, but is uttered in every tongue. Neither marble nor brass can fitly form his statue. Continents are his monument, and unnumbered millions present and to come, who enjoy in their liberties and their happiness the fruits of his faith, will reverently guard and preserve, from century to century, his name and fame.

HIAWATHA'S CHILDHOOD

Henry Wadsworth Longfellow

By the shores of Gitchee Gumee,
By the shining Big-Sea-Water,
Stood the wigwam of Nokomis,
Daughter of the Moon, Nokomis.
Dark behind it rose the forest,
Rose the black and gloomy pine-trees,
Rose the firs with cones upon them;
Bright before it beat the water,
Beat the clear and sunny water,
Beat the shining Big-Sea-Water.
    There the wrinkled old Nokomis
Nursed the little Hiawatha,
Rocked him in his linden cradle,
Bedded soft in moss and rushes,
Safely bound with reindeer sinews;
Stilled his fretful wail by saying,
"Hush! the Naked Bear will hear thee!"
Lulled him into slumber, singing,
"Ewa-yea! my little owlet!
Who is this, that lights the wigwam?
With his great eyes lights the wigwam?
Ewa-yea! my little owlet!"

Many things Nokomis taught him
Of the stars that shine in heaven;
Showed him Ishkoodah, the comet,
Ishkoodah, with fiery tresses;
Showed the Death-Dance of the spirits,
Warriors with their plumes and war-clubs,
Flaring far away to northward
In the frosty nights of Winter;
Showed the broad white road in heaven,
Pathway of the ghosts, the shadows,
Running straight across the heavens,
Crowded with the ghosts, the shadows.

At the door on summer evenings
Sat the little Hiawatha;
Heard the whispering of the pine-trees,
Heard the lapping of the waters,
Sounds of music, words of wonder;
"Minne-wawa!" said the pine-trees,
"Mudway-aushka!" said the water.

Saw the fire-fly, Wah-wah-taysee,
Flitting through the dusk of evening,
With the twinkle of its candle
Lighting up the brakes and bushes,
And he sang the song of children,
Sang the song Nokomis taught him:
"Wah-wah-taysee, little fire-fly,
Little, flitting, white-fire insect,
Little, dancing, white-fire creature,
Light me with your little candle,
Ere upon my bed I lay me,
Ere in sleep I close my eye-lids!"

Saw the moon rise from the water,
Rippling, rounding from the water,
Saw the flecks and shadows on it,
Whispered, "What is that, Nokomis?"
And the good Nokomis answered:
"Once a warrior, very angry,
Seized his grandmother, and threw her
Up into the sky at midnight;
Right against the moon he threw her;
'Tis her body that you see there." . . .

Then the little Hiawatha
Learned of every bird its language,

Learned their names and all their secrets,
How they built their nests in Summer,
Where they hid themselves in Winter,
Talked with them whene'er he met them,
Called them "Hiawatha's Chickens."
Of all beasts he learned the language,
Learned their names and all their secrets,
How the beavers built their lodges,
Where the squirrels hid their acorns,
How the reindeer ran so swiftly,
Why the rabbit was so timid,
Talked with them whene'er he met them,
Called them "Hiawatha's Brothers." . . .

(From The Song of Hiawatha)

HOPE

Alexander Pope

Hope springs eternal in the human breast:
Man never is, but always to be blest.
The soul, uneasy, and confined from home,
Rests and expatiates in a life to come.

(From Essay on Man)

THE SHEPHERD'S BOY

A certain Shepherd's Boy kept his sheep upon a common, and in sport and wantonness would often cry out, The wolf! the wolf! By this means he several times drew the husbandmen in an adjoining field from their work; who, finding themselves deluded, resolved for the future to take no notice of his alarm. Soon after the wolf came indeed. The Boy cried out in earnest; but no heed being given to his cries, the sheep are devoured by the wolf.

(From Aesop's Fables)

LOST

Lost, yesterday, somewhere between sunrise and sunset, two golden hours, each set with sixty diamond minutes. No reward is offered for they are gone forever.

(Anonymous)

THE SPELL OF THE YUKON

Robert W. Service

I wanted the gold, and I sought it;
  I scrabbled and mucked like a slave.
Was it famine or scurvy—I fought it;
  I hurled my youth into a grave.
I wanted the gold, and I got it—
  Came out with a fortune last fall—
Yet somehow life's not what I thought it,
  And somehow the gold isn't all.

No! There's the land. (Have you seen it?)
  It's the cussedest land that I know,
From the big, dizzy mountains that screen it
  To the deep, deathlike valleys below.
Some say God was tired when He made it;
  Some say it's a fine land to shun;
Maybe; but there's some as would trade it
  For no land on earth—and I'm one.

You come to get rich (damned good reason);
  You feel like an exile at first;
You hate it like hell for a season,
  And then you are worse than the worst.
It grips you like some kinds of sinning;
  It twists you from foe to a friend;
It seems it's been since the beginning;
  It seems it will be to the end.

I've stood in some mighty-mouthed hollow
  That's plumb-full of hush to the brim;
I've watched the big, husky sun wallow
  In crimson and gold, and grow dim,
Till the moon set the pearly peaks gleaming,
  And the stars tumbled out, neck and crop;
And I've thought that I surely was dreaming,
  With the peace o' the world piled on top.

The summer—no sweeter was ever;
  The sunshiny woods all athrill;
The grayling aleap in the river,
  The bighorn asleep on the hill.

The strong life that never knows harness;
    The wilds where the caribou call;
The freshness, the freedom, the farness—
    O God! how I'm stuck on it all.

The winter! the brightness that blinds you,
    The white land locked tight as a drum,
The cold fear that follows and finds you,
    The silence that bludgeons you dumb.
The snows that are older than history,
    The woods where the weird shadows slant;
The stillness, the moonlight, the mystery,
    I've bade 'em good-bye—but I can't.

There's a land where the mountains are nameless,
    And the rivers all run God knows where;
There are lives that are erring and aimless,
    And deaths that just hang by a hair;
There are hardships that nobody reckons;
    There are valleys unpeopled and still;
There's a land—oh, it beckons and beckons,
    And I want to go back—and I will.

They're making my money diminish;
    I'm sick of the taste of champagne.
Thank God! when I'm skinned to a finish
    I'll pike to the Yukon again.
I'll fight—and you bet it's no sham-fight;
    It's hell!—but I've been there before;
And it's better than this by a damsite—
    So me for the Yukon once more.

There's gold, and it's haunting and haunting;
    It's luring me on as of old;
Yet it isn't the gold that I'm wanting
    So much as just finding the gold.
It's the great, big, broad land 'way up yonder,
    It's the forests where silence has lease;
It's the beauty that thrills me with wonder,
    It's the stillness that fills me with peace.

* * *

Fear not that thy life shall come to an end, but rather fear that
it shall never have a beginning.
                                    —Cardinal Newman

THE ONE-HOSS SHAY

(THE DEACON'S MASTERPIECE)

Oliver Wendell Holmes

Have you heard of the wonderful one-hoss shay,
That was built in such a logical way
It ran a hundred years to a day,
And then, of a sudden, it—ah, but stay,
I'll tell you what happened without delay,
Scaring the parson into fits,
Frightening people out of their wits,—
'Iave you ever heard of that, I say?

Seventeen hundred and fifty-five.
Georgius Secundus was then alive,—
Snuffy old drone from the German hive.
That was the year when Lisbon-town
Saw the earth open and gulp her down,
And Braddock's army was done so brown,
Left without a scalp to its crown.
It was on the terrible Earthquake-day
That the Deacon finished the one-hoss shay.

Now in building of chaises, I tell you what,
There is always *somewhere* a weaker spot,—
In hub, tire, felloe, in spring or thill,
In panel, or crossbar, or floor, or sill,
In screw, bolt, thoroughbrace,—lurking still,
Find it somewhere you must and will,—
Above or below, or within or without,—
And that's the reason, beyond a doubt,
A chaise *breaks down*, but doesn't *wear out*.

But the Deacon swore (as Deacons do),
With an "I dew vum," or an "I tell yeou,"
He would build one shay to beat the taown
'N' the keounty 'n' all the kentry raoun';
It should be so built that it *couldn'* break daown:
—"Fur," said the Deacon, " 't's mighty plain
Thut the weakes' place mus' stan' the strain;
'N' the way t' fix it, uz I maintain,
                              Is only jest
T' make that place uz strong uz the rest."

242

So the Deacon inquired of the village folk
Where he could find the strongest oak,
That couldn't be split nor bent nor broke,—
That was for spokes and floor and sills;
He sent for lancewood to make the thills;
The crossbars were ash, from the straightest trees,
The panels of white-wood, that cuts like cheese,
But lasts like iron for things like these;
The hubs of logs from the "Settler's ellum,"—
Last of its timber,—they couldn't sell 'em,
Never an axe had seen their chips,
And the wedges flew from between their lips,
Their blunt ends frizzled like celery tips;
Step and prop-iron, bolt and screw,
Spring, tire, axle, and linchpin too,
Steel of the finest, bright and blue;
Thoroughbrace bison-skin, thick and wide;
Boot, top, dasher, from tough old hide
Found in the pit when the tanner died.
That was the way he "put her through."—
"There!" said the Deacon, "naow she'll dew!"

Do! I tell you, I rather guess
She was a wonder, and nothing less!
Colts grew horses, beards turned gray,
Deacon and Deaconess dropped away,
Children and grandchildren—where were they?
But there stood the stout old one-hoss shay
As fresh as on Lisbon-earthquake-day!

EIGHTEEN HUNDRED;—it came and found
The Deacon's masterpiece strong and sound.
Eighteen hundred increased by ten;—
"Hahnsum kerridge" they called it then.
Eighteen hundred and twenty came;—
Running as usual; much the same.
Thirty and forty at last arrive,
And then come fifty, and FIFTY-FIVE.

Little of all we value here
Wakes on the morn of its hundredth year
Without both feeling and looking queer.
In fact, there's nothing that keeps its youth,
So far as I know, but a tree and truth.

243

(This is a moral that runs at large;
Take it.—You're welcome.—No extra charge.)
FIRST OF NOVEMBER—the-Earthquake-day,—
There are traces of age in the one-hoss-shay,
A general flavor of mild decay,
But nothing local, as one may say.
There couldn't be,—for the Deacon's art
Had made it so like in every part
That there wasn't a chance for one to start.
For the wheels were just as strong as the thills,
And the floor was just as strong as the sills,
And the panels just as strong as the floor,
And the whipple-tree neither less nor more,
And the back-cross bar as strong as the fore,
And spring and axle and hub *encore*.
And yet, as *a whole,* it is past a doubt
In another hour it will be *worn out!*

First of November, 'Fifty-five!
This morning the parson takes a drive.
Now, small boys, get out of the way!
Here comes the wonderful one-hoss shay,
Drawn by a rat-tailed, ewe-necked bay.
"Huddup!" said the parson. Off went they.
The parson was working his Sunday text,—
Had got to *fifthly,* and stopped perplexed
At what the—Moses—was coming next.
All at once the horse stood still,
Close by the meet'n'-house on the hill.
—First a shiver, and then a thrill,
Then something decidedly like a spill,—
And the parson was sitting up on a rock,
At half-past nine by the meet'n'-house clock,—
Just the hour of the Earthquake shock!
—What do you think the parson found,
When he got up and stared around?
The poor old chaise in a heap or mound,
As if it had been to the mill and ground!
You see, of course, if you're not a dunce,
How it went to pieces all at once,—
All at once, and nothing first,—
Just as bubbles do when they burst.

End of the wonderful one-hoss shay,
Logic is logic. That's all I say.

KISSIN'

Some say kissin's ae sin,
  But I say, not at a';
For it's been in the warld
  Ever sin' there were twa.
If it werena lawfu',
  Lawyers wadna' 'low it;
If it werena haly,
  Meenisters wadna' dae it;
If it werena modest,
  Maidens wadna' taste it;
If it werena plenty,
  Puir folk couldna' hae it.
      (A Scottish saying)

THE DECLARATION OF INDEPENDENCE

When in the Course of human Events, it becomes necessary for one People to dissolve the Political Bands which have connected them with another, and to assume among the Powers of the Earth, the separate and equal Station to which the Laws of Nature and of Nature's God entitle them, a decent Respect to the Opinions of Mankind requires that they should declare the causes which impel them to the Separation.

WE hold these Truths to be self-evident, that all Men are created equal, that they are endowed by their Creator with certain unalienable Rights, that among these are Life, Liberty, and the Pursuit of Happiness—That to secure these Rights, Governments are instituted among Men, deriving their just Powers from the Consent of the Governed, that whenever any Form of Government becomes destructive of these Ends, it is the Right of the People to alter or to abolish it, and to institute new Government, laying its Foundation on such Principles, and organizing its Powers in such Form, as to them shall seem most likely to effect their Safety and Happiness. Prudence, indeed, will dictate that Governments long established should not be changed for light and transient Causes; and accordingly all Experience hath shewn, that Mankind are more disposed to suffer, while Evils are sufferable, than to right themselves by abolishing the Forms to which they are accustomed. But when a long Train of Abuses and Usurpations, pursuing invariably the same Object, evinces a Design to reduce them under absolute Despotism, it is their Right, it is their Duty, to throw off such Government, and to provide new Guards for their future Security. Such has been the patient Sufferance of these Colonies; and such is now the Necessity which constrains them to alter their former Systems of Government. The History of the present King of Great-Britain is a History of repeated Injuries and Usurpations, all having in direct Object the Establishment of an absolute Tyranny over these States. To prove this, let Facts be submitted to a candid World.

HE has refused his Assent to Laws, the most wholesome and necessary for the public Good.

HE has forbidden his Governors to pass Laws of immediate and pressing Importance, unless suspended in their Operation till his Assent should be obtained; and when so suspended, he has utterly neglected to attend to them.

HE has refused to pass other Laws for the Accommodation of large Districts of People, unless those People would relinquish the Right of Representation in the Legislature, a Right inestimable to them, and formidable to Tyrants only.

HE has called together Legislative Bodies at Places unusual, uncomfortable, and distant from the Depository of their public Records, for the sole Purpose of fatiguing them into Compliance with his Measures.

HE has dissolved Representative Houses repeatedly, for opposing with manly Firmness his Invasions on the Rights of the People.

HE has refused for a long Time, after such Dissolutions, to cause others to be elected; whereby the Legislative Powers, incapable of Annihilation, have returned to the People at large for their exercise; the State remaining in the mean time exposed to all the Dangers of Invasion from without, and Convulsions within.

HE has endeavoured to prevent the Population of these States; for that Purpose obstructing the Laws for Naturalization of Foreigners; refusing to pass others to encourage their Migrations hither, and raising the Conditions of new Appropriations of Lands.

HE has obstructed the Administration of Justice, by refusing his Assent to Laws for establishing Judiciary Powers.

HE has made Judges dependent on his Will alone, for the Tenure of their Offices, and the Amount and Payment of their Salaries.

HE has erected a Multitude of new Offices, and sent hither Swarms of Officers to harass our People, and eat out their Substance.

HE has kept among us, in Times of Peace, Standing Armies, without the consent of our Legislatures.

246

HE has affected to render the Military independent of and superior to the Civil Power.

HE has combined with others to subject us to a Jurisdiction foreign to our Constitution, and unacknowledged by our Laws; giving his Assent to their Acts of pretended Legislation:

FOR quartering large Bodies of Armed Troops among us:

FOR protecting them, by a mock Trial, from Punishment for any Murders which they should commit on the Inhabitants of these States:

FOR cutting off our Trade with all Parts of the World:

FOR imposing Taxes on us without our Consent:

FOR depriving us, in many Cases, of the Benefits of Trial by Jury:

FOR transporting us beyond Seas to be tried for pretended Offences:

FOR abolishing the free System of English Laws in a neighbouring Province, establishing therein an arbitrary Government, and enlarging its Boundaries, so as to render it at once an Example and fit Instrument for introducing the same absolute Rule into these Colonies:

FOR taking away our Charters, abolishing our most valuable Laws, and altering fundamentally the Forms of our Governments:

FOR suspending our own Legislatures, and declaring themselves invested with Power to legislate for us in all Cases whatsoever.

HE has abdicated Government here, by declaring us out of his Protection and waging War against us.

HE has plundered our Seas, ravaged our Coasts, burnt our Towns, and destroyed the Lives of our People.

HE is, at this Time, transporting large Armies of foreign Mercenaries to compleat the Works of Death, Desolation, and Tyranny, already begun with circumstances of Cruelty and Perfidy, scarcely paralleled in the most barbarous Ages, and totally unworthy the Head of a civilized Nation.

HE has constrained our fellow Citizens taken Captive on the high Seas to bear Arms against their Country, to become the Executioners of their Friends and Brethren, or to fall themselves by their Hands.

HE has excited domestic Insurrections amongst us, and has endeavoured to bring on the Inhabitants of our Frontiers, the merciless Indian Savages, whose known Rule of Warfare, is an undistinguished Destruction, of all Ages, Sexes and Conditions.

IN every stage of these Oppressions we have Petitioned for Redress in the most humble Terms: Our repeated Petitions have been answered only by repeated Injury. A Prince, whose Character is thus marked by every act which may define a Tyrant, is unfit to be the Ruler of a free People.

Nor have we been wanting in Attentions to our British Brethren. We have warned them from Time to Time of Attempts by their Legislature to extend an unwarrantable Jurisdiction over us. We have reminded them of the Circumstances of our Emigration and Settlement here. We have appealed to their native Justice and Magnanimity, and we have conjured them by the Ties of our common Kindred to disavow these Usurpations, which, would inevitably interrupt our Connections and Correspondence. They too have been deaf to the Voice of Justice and of Consanguinity. We must, therefore, acquiesce in the Necessity, which denounces our Separation, and hold them, as we hold the rest of Mankind, Enemies in War, in Peace, Friends.

We, therefore, the Representatives of the UNITED STATES OF AMERICA, in General Congress, Assembled, appealing to the Supreme Judge of the World for the Rectitude of our Intentions, do, in the Name, and by Authority of the good People of these Colonies, solemnly Publish and Declare, That these United Colonies are, and of Right ought to be, Free and Independent States; that they are absolved from all Allegiance to the British Crown, and that all political Connection between them and the State of Great-Britain, is and ought to be totally dissolved; and that as Free and Independent States, they have full Power to levy War, conclude Peace, contract Alliances, establish Commerce, and to do all other Acts and Things which Independent States may of right do. And for the support of this Declaration, with a firm Reliance on the Protection of divine Providence, we mutually pledge to each other our Lives, our Fortunes, and our sacred Honor.

Signed by Order *and in* Behalf *of the* Congress,
JOHN HANCOCK, President.

Attest.
Charles Thomson, Secretary.

SIGNERS OF THE DECLARATION OF INDEPENDENCE

ACCORDING TO THE AUTHENTICATED LIST PRINTED BY
ORDER OF CONGRESS OF JANUARY 18, 1777 *

John Hancock.

NEW-HAMPSHIRE.	Josiah Bartlett, Wm. Whipple, Matthew Thornton.†	**DELAWARE**	Cæsar Rodney, Geo. Read, (Tho M:Kean.)‡
MASSACHUSETTS-BAY.	Saml. Adams, John Adams, Robt. Treat Paine, Elbridge Gerry.	**MARYLAND.**	Samuel Chase, Wm. Paca, Thos. Stone, Charles Carroll, of Carrollton.
RHODE-ISLAND AND PROVIDENCE, &c.	Step. Hopkins, William Ellery.		
CONNECTICUT.	Roger Sherman, Saml. Huntington, Wm. Williams, Oliver Wolcott.	**VIRGINIA.**	George Wythe, Richard Henry Lee, Ths. Jefferson, Benja. Harrison, Thos. Nelson, jr. Francis Lightfoot Lee, Carter Braxton.
NEW-YORK	Wm. Floyd, Phil. Livingston, Frans. Lewis, Lewis Morris.	**NORTH-CAROLINA.**	Wm. Hooper, Joseph Hewes, John Penn.
NEW-JERSEY.	Richd. Stockton, Jno. Witherspoon, Fras. Hopkinson, John Hart, Abra. Clark.	**SOUTH-CAROLINA.**	Edward Rutledge, Thos. Heyward, junr. Thomas Lynch, junr. Arthur Middleton.
PENNSYLVANIA.	Robt. Morris, Benjamin Rush, Benja. Franklin, John Morton, Geo. Clymer, Jas. Smith, Geo. Taylor, James Wilson, Geo. Ross.	**GEORGIA.**	Button Gwinnett, Lyman Hall, Geo. Walton.

* Braces, spelling, and abbreviation of names conform to original printed list.

† Matthew Thornton's name was signed on the engrossed copy following the Connecticut Members, but was transferred in the printed copy to its proper place with the other New Hampshire Members.

‡ Thomas McKean's name was not included in the list of signers printed by order of Congress on January 18, 1777, as he did not sign the engrossed copy until some time thereafter, probably in 1781.

RIME OF THE ANCIENT MARINER

IN SEVEN PARTS

Samuel Taylor Coleridge

PART I

An ancient mariner
meeteth three gal-
lants bidden to a
wedding feast, and
detaineth one.

It is an ancient mariner,
And he stoppeth one of three.
"By thy long gray beard and glittering eye,
Now wherefore stopp'st thou me?

The bridegroom's doors are opened wide,
And I am next of kin;
The guests are met, the feast is set,—
May'st hear the merry din."

He holds him with his skinny hand:
"There was a ship," quoth he.
"Hold off! unhand me, graybeard loon!"—
Eftsoons his hand dropt he.

The wedding-guest
is spellbound by the
eye of the old sea-
faring man, and con-
strained to hear
his tale.

He holds him with his glittering eye,—
The wedding-guest stood still;
He listens like a three years' child;
The mariner hath his will.

The wedding-guest sat on a stone,—
He cannot choose but hear;
And thus spake on that ancient man,
The bright-eyed mariner:

"The ship was cheered, the harbor cleared;
Merrily did we drop
Below the kirk, below the hill,
Below the lighthouse top.

The mariner tells
how the ship sailed
southward, with a
good wind and fair
weather, till it
reached the line.

The sun came up upon the left,
Out of the sea came he;
And he shone bright, and on the right
Went down into the sea.

Higher and higher every day,
Till over the mast at noon—"
The wedding-guest here beat his breast,
For he heard the loud bassoon.

The bride hath paced into the hall,—
Red as a rose is she;
Nodding their heads before her goes
The merry minstrelsy.

The wedding-guest heareth the bridal music; but the mariner continueth his tale.

The wedding-guest he beat his breast,
Yet he cannot choose but hear;
And thus spake on that ancient man,
The bright-eyed mariner:

"And now the storm-blast came, and he
Was tyrannous and strong;
He struck with his o'ertaking wings,
And chased us south along.

The ship drawn by a storm toward the south pole.

With sloping masts and dipping prow,—
As who pursued with yell and blow
Still treads the shadow of his foe,
And forward bends his head,—
The ship drove fast; loud roared the blast,
And southward aye we fled.

And now there came both mist and snow,
And it grew wondrous cold;
And ice, mast-high, came floating by,
As green as emerald.

And through the drifts the snowy clifts
Did send a dismal sheen;
Nor shapes of men nor beasts we ken,—
The ice was all between.

The land of ice and of fearful sounds, where no living thing was to be seen.

The ice was here, the ice was there,
The ice was all around;
It cracked and growled, and roared and howled,
Like noises in a swound!

Till a great sea-bird, called the albatross, came through the snow-fog, and was received with great joy and hospitality.
At length did cross an albatross,—
Thorough the fog it came;
As if it had been a Christian soul,
We hailed it in God's name.

It ate the food it ne'er had eat,
And round and round it flew.
The ice did split with a thunder-fit;
The helmsman steered us through!

And lo! the albatross proveth a bird of good omen, and followeth the ship as it returned northward through fog and floating ice.
And a good south wind sprung up behind;
The albatross did follow,
And every day, for food or play,
Came to the mariners' hollo!

In mist or cloud, on mast or shroud,
It perched for vespers nine;
Whiles all the night, through fog-smoke white,
Glimmered the white moonshine."

The ancient mariner inhospitably killed the pious bird of good omen.
"God save thee, ancient mariner!
From the fiends that plague thee thus!—
Why look'st thou so?"—"With my cross-bow
I shot the albatross."

PART II

"The sun now rose upon the right,—
Out of the sea came he,
Still hid in mist, and on the left
Went down into the sea.

And the good south wind still blew behind;
But no sweet bird did follow.
Nor any day for food or play
Came to the mariners' hollo.

His shipmates cry out against the ancient mariner, for killing the bird of good luck.
And I had done a hellish thing,
And it would work 'em woe;
For all averred I had killed the bird
That made the breeze to blow:
Ah, wretch! said they, the bird to slay,
That made the breeze to blow!

252

Nor dim nor red, like God's own head
The glorious sun uprist;
Then all averred I had killed the bird
That brought the fog and mist:
'Twas right, said they, such birds to slay,
That bring the fog and mist.

But when the fog cleared off, they justify the same, and thus make themselves accomplices in the crime.

The fair breeze blew, the white foam flew,
The furrow followed free;
We were the first that ever burst
Into that silent sea.

The fair breeze continues; the ship enters the Pacific Ocean, and sails northward, even till it reaches the line.

Down dropt the breeze, the sails dropt down,—
'Twas sad as sad could be;
And we did speak only to break
The silence of the sea.

The ship hath been suddenly becalmed.

All in a hot and copper sky
The bloody sun, at noon,
Right up above the mast did stand,
No bigger than the moon.

Day after day, day after day,
We stuck,—nor breath nor motion;
As idle as a painted ship
Upon a painted ocean.

Water, water everywhere,
And all the boards did shrink;
Water, water everywhere,
Nor any drop to drink.

And the albatross begins to be avenged.

The very deep did rot: O Christ!
That ever this should be!
Yea, slimy things did crawl with legs
Upon the slimy sea!

About, about, in reel and rout,
The death-fires danced at night;
The water, like a witch's oils,
Burnt green, and blue, and white.

A spirit had followed them,—one of the invisible inhabitants of this planet, neither departed souls nor angels; concerning whom the learned Jew, Josephus, and the Platonic Constantinopolitan, Michael Psellus, may be consulted. They are very numerous, and there is no climate or element without one or more.

And some in dreams assured were
Of the spirit that plagued us so;
Nine fathom deep he had followed us
From the land of mist and snow.

And every tongue, through utter drought,
Was withered at the root;
We could not speak, no more than if
We had been choked with soot.

The shipmates, in their sore distress, would fain throw the whole guilt on the ancient mariner: in sign whereof they hang the dead seabird round his neck.

Ah! well-a-day! what evil looks
Had I from old and young!
Instead of the cross, the albatross
About my neck was hung.

PART III

There passed a weary time. Each throat
Was parched, and glazed each eye,—
A weary time! a weary time!
How glazed each weary eye!—
The ancient mariner beholdeth a sign in the element afar off.
When, looking westward, I beheld
A something in the sky.

At first it seemed a little speck,
And then it seemed a mist;
It moved and moved, and took at last
A certain shape, I wist,—

A speck, a mist, a shape, I wist!
And still it neared and neared;
As if it dodged a water-sprite,
It plunged, and tacked, and veered.

At its nearer approach it seemeth him to be a ship; and at a dear ransom he freeth his speech from the bonds of thirst.

With throats unslaked, with black lips baked,
We could not laugh nor wail;
Through utter drought all dumb we stood;
I bit my arm, I sucked the blood,
And cried, A sail! a sail!

With throats unslaked, with black lips baked,
Agape they heard me call;

254

Gramercy! they for joy did grin,
And all at once their breath drew in,
As they were drinking all.

A flash of joy.

See! see! I cried, she tacks no more!
Hither, to work us weal,—
Without a breeze, without a tide,
She steadies with upright keel!

And horror follows;
for can it be a ship
that comes onward
without wind or
tide?

The western wave was all aflame;
The day was well-nigh done;
Almost upon the western wave
Rested the broad bright sun,—
When that strange shape drove suddenly
Betwixt us and the sun.

And straight the sun was flecked with bars,
(Heaven's mother send us grace!)
As if through a dungeon grate he peered
With broad and burning face.

It seemeth him but
the skeleton of a
ship.

Alas! thought I—and my heart beat loud—
How fast she nears and nears!
Are those her sails that glance in the sun
Like restless gossameres?

Are those her ribs through which the sun
Did peer, as through a grate?
And is that woman all her crew?
Is that a Death? and are there two?
Is Death that woman's mate?

And its ribs are seen
as bars on the face
of the setting sun.
The spectre-woman
and her death-mate,
and no other, on
board the skeleton
ship.

Her lips were red, her looks were free,
Her locks were yellow as gold;
Her skin was as white as leprosy:
The nightmare Life-in-death was she,
Who thicks man's blood with cold.

Like vessel, like
crew!

The naked hulk alongside came,
And the twain were casting dice:
'The game is done! I've won! I've won!'
Quoth she, and whistles thrice.

Death and Life-in-
Death have diced for
the ship's crew, and
she (the latter)
winneth the ancient
mariner.

The sun's rim dips, the stars rush out,
At one stride comes the dark;
With far-heard whisper, o'er the sea
Off shot the spectre bark.

At the rising of the
moon,

We listened, and looked sideways up;
Fear at my heart, as at a cup,
My life-blood seemed to sip;
The stars were dim, and thick the night,—
The steersman's face by his lamp gleamed white;
From the sails the dew did drip,—
Till clomb above the eastern bar
The hornéd moon, with one bright star
Within the nether tip.

One after another

One after one, by the star-dogged moon,
Too quick for groan or sigh,
Each turneth his face, with a ghastly pang,
And cursed me with his eye.

His shipmates drop
down dead;

Four times fifty living men,
(And I heard nor sigh nor groan!)
With heavy thump, a lifeless lump,
They dropped down one by one.

But Life-in-Death
begins her work on
the ancient mariner.

The souls did from their bodies fly,—
They fled to bliss or woe!
And every soul it passed me by,
Like the whiz of my cross-bow!"

PART IV

The wedding-guest
feareth that a spirit
is talking to him;

"I fear thee, ancient mariner!
I fear thy skinny hand!
And thou art long, and lank, and brown,
As is the ribbed sea-sand.

I fear thee and thy glittering eye,
And thy skinny hand so brown."

But the ancient
mariner assureth
him of his bodily
life, and proceedeth
to relate his horrible
penance.

"Fear not, fear not, thou wedding-guest!
This body dropt not down.

256

Alone, alone, all, all alone,
Alone on a wide, wide sea!
And never a saint took pity on
My soul in agony.

The many men, so beautiful!
And they all dead did lie;
And a thousand thousand slimy things
Lived on,—and so did I.

He despiseth the
creatures of the
calm;

I looked upon the rotting sea,
And drew my eyes away;
I looked upon the rotting deck,
And there the dead men lay.

And envieth that
they should live, and
so many lie dead.

I looked to heaven and tried to pray;
But or ever a prayer had gusht
A wicked whisper came, and made
My heart as dry as dust.

I closed my lids, and kept them close,
And the balls like pulses beat;
For the sky and the sea, and the sea and the sky
Lay like a load on my weary eye,
And the dead were at my feet.

The cold sweat melted from their limbs,—
Nor rot nor reek did they;
The look with which they looked on me
Had never passed away.

But the curse liveth
for him in the eye of
the dead men.

An orphan's curse would drag to hell
A spirit from on high;
But O, more horrible than that
Is the curse in a dead man's eye!
Seven days, seven nights, I saw that curse,—
And yet I could not die.

The moving moon went up the sky,
And nowhere did abide;
Softly she was going up,
And a star or two beside.

In his loneliness
and fixedness he
yearneth towards the
journeying moon,
and the stars that
still sojurn, yet still
move onward; and
everywhere the blue
sky belongs to them,
and is their ap-

257

Her beams bemocked the sultry main,
Like April hoar-frost spread;
But where the ship's huge shadow lay
The charmèd water burnt alway
A still and awful red.

pointed rest, and
their native country,
and their own natu-
ral homes, which
they enter unan-
nounced, as lords
that are certainly
expected; and yet
there is a silent joy
at their arrival.

By the light of the
moon he beholdeth
God's creatures of
the great calm.

Beyond the shadow of the ship
I watched the water-snakes;
They moved in tracks of shining white;
And when they reared, the elfish light
Fell off in hoary flakes.

Within the shadow of the ship
I watched their rich attire,—
Blue, glossy green, and velvet black,
They coiled and swam; and every track
Was a flash of golden fire.

Their beauty and
their happiness.

O happy living things! no tongue
Their beauty might declare;
A spring of love gushed from my heart,

He blesseth them in
his heart.

And I blessed them unaware,—
Sure my kind saint took pity on me,
And I blessed them unaware.

The spell begins to
break.

The selfsame moment I could pray;
And from my neck so free
The albatross fell off, and sank
Like lead into the sea.

PART V

O sleep! it is a gentle thing,
Beloved from pole to pole!
To Mary Queen the praise be given!
She sent the gentle sleep from heaven
That slid into my soul.

By grace of the Holy
Mother, the ancient
mariner is refreshed
with rain.

The silly buckets on the deck,
That had so long remained,
I dreamt that they were filled with dew;
And when I woke, it rained.

258

My lips were wet, my throat was cold,
My garments all were dank;
Sure I had drunken in my dreams,
And still my body drank.

I moved, and could not feel my limbs;
I was so light—almost
I thought that I had died in sleep,
And was a blesséd ghost.

And soon I heard a roaring wind,—
It did not come anear;
But with its sound it shook the sails,
That were so thin and sere.

He heareth sounds
and seeth strange
sights and com-
motions in the sky
and the element.

The upper air burst into life;
And a hundred fire-flags sheen,
To and fro they were hurried about;
And to and fro, and in and out,
The wan stars danced between.

And the coming wind did roar more loud,
And the sails did sigh like sedge;
And the rain poured down from one black cloud,—
The moon was at its edge.

The thick black cloud was cleft, and still
The moon was at its side;
Like waters shot from some high crag,
The lightning fell with never a jag,
A river steep and wide.

The loud wind never reached the ship,
Yet now the ship moved on!
Beneath the lightning and the moon
The dead men gave a groan.

The bodies of the
ship's crew are in-
spired, and the ship
moves on.

They groaned, they stirred, they all uprose,
Nor spake, nor moved their eyes;
It had been strange, even in a dream,
To have seen those dead men rise.

The helmsman steered, the ship moved on;
Yet never a breeze upblew;
The mariners all 'gan work the ropes,
Where they were wont to do;
They raised their limbs like lifeless tools,—
We were a ghastly crew.

The body of my brother's son
Stood by me, knee to knee;
The body and I pulled at one rope,
But he said naught to me."

But not by the souls
of the men, nor by
demons of earth or
middle air, but by a
blessed troop of an-
gelic spirits sent
down by the invoca-
tion of the guardian
saint.

"I fear thee, ancient mariner!"
"Be calm, thou wedding-guest!
'Twas not those souls that fled in pain,
Which to their corses came again,
But a troop of spirits blest.

For when it dawned they dropped their arms,
And clustered round the mast;
Sweet sounds rose slowly through their mouths,
And from their bodies passed.

Around, around flew each sweet sound,
Then darted to the sun;
Slowly the sounds came back again,
Now mixed, now one by one.

Sometimes, a-dropping from the sky,
I heard the skylark sing;
Sometimes all little birds that are,—
How they seemed to fill the sea and air
With their sweet jargoning!

And now 'twas like all instruments,
Now like a lonely flute;
And now it is an angel's song,
That makes the heavens be mute.

It ceased; yet still the sails made on
A pleasant noise till noon,—

A noise like of a hidden brook
In the leafy month of June,
That to the sleeping woods all night
Singeth a quiet tune.

Till noon we quietly sailed on,
Yet never a breeze did breathe;
Slowly and smoothly went the ship,
Moved onward from beneath.

Under the keel nine fathom deep,
From the land of mist and snow,
The spirit slid; and it was he
That made the ship to go.
The sails at noon left off their tune,
And the ship stood still also.

The lonesome spirit from the south pole carries on the ship as far as the line in obedience to the angelic troop; but still requireth vengeance.

The sun, right up above the mast,
Had fixed her to the ocean;
But in a minute she 'gan to stir,
With a short uneasy motion,—
Backwards and forwards half her length,
With a short uneasy motion.

Then like a pawing horse let go,
She made a sudden bound,—
It flung the blood into my head,
And I fell down in a swound.

How long in that same fit I lay
I have not to declare;
But ere my living life returned
I heard, and in my soul discerned,
Two voices in the air;

The polar spirit's fellow-demons, the invisible inhabitants of the element, take part in his wrong; and two of them relate, one to the other, that penance, long and heavy for the ancient mariner, hath been accorded to the polar spirit, who returneth southward.

'Is it he?' quoth one, 'Is this the man?
By him who died on cross,
With his cruel bow he laid full low
The harmless albatross!

The spirit who bideth by himself
In the land of mist and snow,

261

He loved the bird that loved the man
Who shot him with his bow.'

The other was a softer voice,
As soft as honey-dew:
Quoth he, 'The man hath penance done,
And penance more will do.'

PART VI

FIRST VOICE

'But tell me, tell me! speak again,
Thy soft response renewing,—
What makes that ship drive on so fast?
What is the ocean doing?'

SECOND VOICE

'Still as a slave before his lord,
The ocean hath no blast;
His great bright eye most silently
Up to the moon is cast,—

If he may know which way to go;
For she guides him smooth or grim.
See, brother, see! how graciously
She looketh down on him.'

The mariner hath been cast into a trance; for the angelic power causeth the vessel to drive northward faster than human life could endure.

FIRST VOICE

'But why drives on that ship so fast,
Without or wave or wind?'

SECOND VOICE

'The air is cut away before,
And closes from behind.

Fly, brother, fly! more high, more high!
Or we shall be belated;
For slow and slow that ship will go,
When the mariner's trance is abated.'

The supernatural motion is retarded; the mariner awakes, and his penance begins anew.

I woke, and we were sailing on
As in a gentle weather;
'Twas night, calm night,—the moon was high;
The dead men stood together.

262

All stood together on the deck,
For a charnel-dungeon fitter;
All fixed on me their stony eyes,
That in the moon did glitter.

The pang, the curse, with which they died,
Had never passed away;
I could not draw my eyes from theirs,
Nor turn them up to pray.

And now this spell was snapt; once more
I viewed the ocean green,
And looked far forth, yet little saw
Of what had else been seen,—

The curse is finely expiated.

Like one that on a lonesome road
Doth walk in fear and dread,
And, having once turned round, walks on,
And turns no more his head;
Because he knows a frightful fiend
Doth close behind him tread.

But soon there breathed a wind on me,
Nor sound nor motion made;
Its path was not upon the sea,
In ripple or in shade.

It raised my hair, it fanned my cheek,
Like a meadow-gale of spring,—
It mingled strangely with my fears,
Yet it felt like a welcoming.

Swiftly, swiftly flew the ship,
Yet she sailed softly too;
Sweetly, sweetly blew the breeze,—
On me alone it blew.

O dream of joy! is this indeed
The lighthouse top I see?
Is this the hill? is this the kirk?
Is this mine own countree?

And the ancient mariner beholdeth his native country.

We drifted o'er the harbor-bar,
And I with sobs did pray,—
O, let me be awake, my God!
Or let me sleep alway.

The harbor-bay was clear as glass,
So smoothly it was strewn!
And on the bay the moonlight lay,
And the shadow of the moon.

The rock shone bright, the kirk no less,
That stands above the rock;
The moonlight steeped in silentness
The steady weathercock.

The angelic spirits leave the dead bodies,

And the bay was white with silent light,
Till, rising from the same,
Full many shapes, that shadows were,
In crimson colors came.

And appear in their own forms of light.

A little distance from the prow
Those crimson shadows were;
I turned my eyes upon the deck,—
O Christ! what saw I there!

Each corse lay flat, lifeless and flat;
And, by the holy rood!
A man all light, a seraph man,
On every corse there stood.

This seraph band, each waved his hand,—
It was a heavenly sight!
They stood as signals to the land,
Each one a lovely light;

This seraph band each waved his hand;
No voice did they impart,—
No voice; but O, the silence sank
Like music on my heart!

But soon I heard the dash of oars,
I heard the pilot's cheer;

My head was turned perforce away,
And I saw a boat appear.

The pilot and the pilot's boy,
I heard them coming fast;
Dear Lord in heaven! it was a joy
The dead men could not blast.

I saw a third,—I heard his voice;
It is the hermit good!
He singeth loud his godly hymns
That he makes in the wood;
He'll shrieve my soul,—he'll wash away
The albatross's blood.

PART VII

This hermit good lives in that wood
Which slopes down to the sea.
How loudly his sweet voice he rears!
He loves to talk with marineres
That come from a far countree.

The hermit of the wood

He kneels at morn and noon and eve,—
He hath a cushion plump;
It is the moss that wholly hides
The rotted old oak-stump.

The skiff-boat neared,—I heard them talk:
'Why, this is strange, I trow!
Where are those lights, so many and fair,
That signal made but now?'

'Strange, by my faith!' the hermit said,—
'And they answered not our cheer!
The planks looked warped! and see those sails,
How thin they are and sere!
I never saw aught like to them,
Unless perchance it were

Approacheth the ship with wonder.

Brown skeletons of leaves that lag
My forest-brook along,

When the ivy-tod is heavy with snow,
And the owlet whoops to the wolf below,
That eats the she-wolf's young.'

'Dear Lord! it hath a fiendish look,'
The pilot made reply,—
'I am a-feared.'—'Push on, push on!'
Said the hermit cheerily.

The boat came closer to the ship,
But I nor spake nor stirred;
The boat came close beneath the ship,
And straight a sound was heard:

The ship suddenly sinketh. Under the water it rumbled on,
Still louder and more dread;
It reached the ship, it split the bay;
The ship went down like lead.

The ancient mariner is saved in the pilot's boat. Stunned by that loud and dreadful sound,
Which sky and ocean smote,
Like one that hath been seven days drowned,
My body lay afloat;
But, swift as dreams, myself I found
Within the pilot's boat.

Upon the whirl where sank the ship
The boat spun round and round;
And all was still, save that the hill
Was telling of the sound.

I moved my lips,—the pilot shrieked,
And fell down in a fit;
The holy hermit raised his eyes,
And prayed where he did sit.

I took the oars; the pilot's boy,
Who now doth crazy go,
Laughed loud and long; and all the while
His eyes went to and fro:
'Ha! ha!' quoth he, 'full plain I see,
The Devil knows how to row.'

And now, all in my own countree,
I stood on the firm land!
The hermit stepped forth from the boat,
And scarcely he could stand.

'O, shrieve me, shrieve me, holy man!'—
The hermit crossed his brow:
'Say quick,' quoth he, 'I bid thee say,—
What manner of man art thou?'

The ancient mariner earnestly entreateth the hermit to shrieve him; and the penance of life falls on him.

Forthwith this frame of mine was wrenched
With a woful agony,
Which forced me to begin my tale,—
And then it left me free.

Since then, at an uncertain hour,
That agony returns;
And till my ghastly tale is told,
This heart within me burns.

And ever and anon, throughout his future life, an agony constraineth him to travel from land to land.

I pass, like night, from land to land;
I have strange power of speech;
That moment that his face I see
I know the man that must hear me,—
To him my tale I teach.

What loud uproar bursts from that door!
The wedding-guests are there;
But in the garden bower the bride
And bridemaids singing are;
And hark the little vesper bell,
Which biddeth me to prayer!

O wedding-guest! this soul hath been
Alone on a wide, wide sea,—
So lonely 'twas, that God himself
Scarce seemèd there to be.

O, sweeter than the marriage-feast,
'Tis sweeter far to me
To walk together to the kirk
With a goodly company!—

To walk together to the kirk,
And all together pray,
While each to his great Father bends,—
Old men, and babes, and loving friends,
And youths and maidens gay!

Farewell! farewell! but this I tell
To thee, thou wedding-guest!
He prayeth well who loveth well
Both man and bird and beast.

He prayeth best who loveth best
All things both great and small;
For the dear God who loveth us,
He made and loveth all."

The mariner, whose eye is bright,
Whose beard with age is hoar,
Is gone. And now the wedding-guest
Turned from the bridegroom's door.

He went like one that hath been stunned,
And is of sense forlorn;
A sadder and a wiser man
He rose the morrow morn.

A FAREWELL

Charles Kingsley

My fairest child, I have no song to give you;
   No lark could pipe to skies so dull and gray;
Yet, ere we part, one lesson I can leave you
    For every day.

Be good, sweet maid, and let who will be clever;
   Do noble things, not dream them, all day long:
And so make life, death, and that vast forever
    One grand, sweet song.

*   *   *

A conservative government is an organized hypocrisy.
            —Benjamin Disraeli

DOUGLAS, DOUGLAS, TENDER AND TRUE

Dinah Maria Mulock Craik

Could ye come back to me, Douglas, Douglas,
  In the old likeness that I knew,
I would be so faithful, so loving, Douglas,
  Douglas, Douglas, tender and true.

Never a scornful word should grieve ye,
  I'd smile on ye sweet as the angels do;—
Sweet as your smile on me shone ever,
  Douglas, Douglas, tender and true.

O, to call back the days that are not!
  My eyes were blinded, your words were few;
Do you know the truth now up in heaven
  Douglas, Douglas, tender and true?

I never was worthy of you, Douglas;
  Not half worthy the like of you:
Now all men beside seem to me like shadows—
  I love *you*, Douglas, tender and true.

Stretch out your hand to me, Douglas, Douglas,
  Drop forgiveness from heaven like dew;
As I lay my heart on your dead heart, Douglas,
  Douglas, Douglas, tender and true.

ODE

Arthur O'Shaughnessy

We are the music-makers,
  And we are the dreamers of dreams,
Wandering by lone sea-breakers,
  And sitting by desolate streams;
World-losers and world-forsakers,
  On whom the pale moon gleams:
Yet we are the movers and shakers
  Of the world for ever, it seems.

With wonderful deathless ditties
  We build up the world's great cities,
And out of a fabulous story
  We fashion an empire's glory:
One man with a dream, at pleasure,
  Shall go forth and conquer a crown;
And three with a new song's measure
  Can trample an empire down.

We, in the ages lying,
  In the buried past of the earth,
Built Nineveh with our sighing,
  And Babel itself with our mirth;
And o'erthrew them with prophesying
  To the old of the new world's worth;
For each age is a dream that is dying,
  Or one that is coming to birth.

INDEPENDENCE FOREVER

Daniel Webster

The oration wherein Webster imagines some states
have objected to the Declaration of Independence, and
gives his version of the answer John Adams would have
made.

SINK OR SWIM, live or die, survive or perish, I give my hand and
my heart to this vote. It is true, indeed, that in the beginning, we
aimed not at independence. But there is a divinity which shapes
our ends. The injustice of England has driven us to arms; and
blinded to her own interests, she has obstinately persisted, till
independence is now within our grasp. We have but to reach
forth to it, and it is ours. Why, then, should we defer the Declaration? Is any man so weak as now to hope for a reconciliation with
England, which shall leave either safety to the country and its
liberties, or security to his own life and his own honour? Are not
you, sir, who sit in that chair,—is not he, our venerable colleague,
near you—are you not both already proscribed and predestined
objects of punishment and of vengeance? Cut off from all hope of
royal clemency, what are you, what can you be, while the power
of England remains, but outlaws? If we postpone independence,

do we mean to carry on or to give up the war? Do we mean to submit to the measures of Parliament, Boston Port Bill and all? Do we mean to submit, and consent that we ourselves shall be ground to powder, and our country and its rights trodden down in the dust? I know we do not mean to submit. Do we intend to violate that most solemn obligation ever entered into by men,— that plighting, before God, of our sacred honour to Washington, when, putting him forth to incur the dangers of war, as well as the political hazards of the times, we promise to adhere to him, in every extremity, with our fortunes and our lives? I know there is not a man here who would not rather see a general conflagration sweep over the land, or an earthquake sink it, than one jot or tittle of that plighted faith fall to the ground. For myself, having twelve months ago, in this place, moved you, that George Washington be appointed commander of the forces raised, or to be raised, for defence of American liberty, may my right hand forget her cunning, and my tongue cleave to the roof of my mouth, if I hesitate or waver in the support I give him. The war, then, must go on. We must fight it through. And if the war must go on, why put off longer the Declaration of Independence? That measure will strengthen us. It will give us character abroad. The nations then will treat with us, which they can never do while we acknowledge ourselves subjects in arms against our sovereign. Nay, I maintain that England herself will sooner treat for peace with us on the footing of independence, than consent, by repealing her acts, to acknowledge that her whole conduct towards us has been a course of injustice and oppression. Her pride will be less wounded by submitting to that course of things which now predestinates our independence, than by yielding the points in controversy to her rebellious subjects. The former she would feel as her own deep disgrace. Why, then, do we not, as soon as possible, change this from a civil to a national war? And since we must fight it through, why not put ourselves in a state to enjoy all the benefits of victory, if we gain the victory? If we fail, it can be no worse for us. But we shall not fail. The cause will raise up armies; the cause will create navies. The people, the people, if we are true to them, will carry us, and will carry themselves, gloriously through this struggle. I care not how fickle other people have been found. I know the people of these colonies; and I know that resistance to British aggression is deep and settled in their hearts, and cannot be eradicated.

The Declaration of Independence will inspire the people with increased courage. Instead of a long and bloody war for the restoration of privileges, for redress of grievances, for chartered immunities, held under a British king, set before them the glorious object of entire independence, and it will breathe into them anew the spirit of life. Read this declaration at the head of the army; every sword will be drawn from its scabbard, and the solemn vow uttered to maintain it, or perish on the field of honour. Publish it from the pulpit; religion will approve it, and the love of religious liberty will cling around it, resolved to stand with it, or fall with it. Send it to the public halls; proclaim it there; let them hear it who heard the first roar of the enemy's cannon—let them see it, who saw their brothers and their sons fall on the field of Bunker Hill, and in the streets of Lexington and Concord,—and the very walls will cry out in its support.

Sir, I know the uncertainty of human affairs, but I see, I see clearly, through this day's business. You and I, indeed, may rue it. We may not live to see the time when this Declaration shall be made good. We may die; die colonists; die slaves; die, it may be ignominiously and on the scaffold. Be it so. If it be the pleasure of Heaven that my country shall require the poor offering of my life, the victim shall be ready at the appointed hour of sacrifice, come when that hour may. But while I do live, let me have a country, or at least the hope of a country, and that a free country.

But whatever may be our fate, be assured, be assured that this Declaration will stand. It may cost treasure, and it may cost blood; but it will stand, and it will richly compensate for both. Through the thick gloom of the present, I see the brightness of the future, as the sun in heaven. We shall make this a glorious, an immortal day. When we are in our graves, our children will honour it. They will celebrate it with thanksgiving, with festivity, with bonfires and illuminations. On its annual return, they will shed tears, copious, gushing tears; not of subjection and slavery, not of agony and distress, but of exultation, of gratitude, and of joy.

Sir, before God, I believe the hour is come. My judgment approves this measure, and my whole heart is in it. All that I have, and all that I am, and all that I hope in this life, I am now ready here to stake upon it; and I leave off as I began, that, live or die, survive or perish, I am for the Declaration. It is my living sentiment, and by the blessing of God, it shall be my dying sentiment—Independence *now*, and INDEPENDENCE FOREVER.

THE DOG AND THE SHADOW

A Dog, crossing a little rivulet with a piece of flesh in his mouth, saw his own shadow represented in the clear mirror of the limpid stream; and, believing it to be another dog, who was carrying another piece of flesh, he could not forbear catching at it; but was so far from getting anything by his greedy design, that he dropped the piece he had in his mouth, which immediately sunk to the bottom, and was irrecoverably lost.

(From Aesop's Fables)

THE LADY OF SHALOTT

Alfred, Lord Tennyson

PART I

On either side the river lie
Long fields of barley and of rye,
That clothe the wold and meet the sky;
And thro' the field the road runs by
      To many-tower'd Camelot;
And up and down the people go,
Gazing where the lilies blow
Round an island there below,
      The island of Shalott.

Willows whiten, aspens quiver,
Little breezes dusk and shiver
Thro' the wave that runs for ever
By the island in the river
      Flowing down to Camelot.
Four gray walls, and four gray towers,
Overlook a space of flowers,
And the silent isle imbowers
      The Lady of Shalott.

By the margin, willow-veil'd,
Slide the heavy barges trail'd
By slow horses; and unhail'd
The shallop flitteth silken-sail'd
      Skimming down to Camelot:

But who hath seen her wave her hand?
Or at the casement seen her stand?
Or is she known in all the land,
        The Lady of Shalott?

Only reapers, reaping early
In among the bearded barley,
Hear a song that echoes cheerly
From the river winding clearly,
        Down to tower'd Camelot;
And by the moon the reaper weary,
Piling sheaves in uplands airy,
Listening, whispers " 'Tis the fairy
        Lady of Shalott."

PART II

There she weaves by night and day
A magic web with colors gay.
She has heard a whisper say,
A curse is on her if she stay
        To look down to Camelot.
She knows not what the curse may be,
And so she weaveth steadily,
And little other care hath she,
        The Lady of Shalott.

And moving thro' a mirror clear
That hangs before her all the year,
Shadows of the world appear.
There she sees the highway near
        Winding down to Camelot;
There the river eddy whirls,
And there the surly village-churls,
And the red cloaks of market girls,
        Pass onward from Shalott.

Sometimes a troop of damsels glad,
An abbot or an ambling pad,
Sometimes a curly shepherd-lad,
Or long-hair'd page in crimson clad,
        Goes by to tower'd Camelot;

And sometimes thro' the mirror blue
The knights come riding two and two:
She hath no loyal knight and true,
   The Lady of Shalott.

But in her web she still delights
To weave the mirror's magic sights,
For often thro' the silent nights
A funeral, with plumes and lights
   And music, went to Camelot;
Or when the moon was overhead,
Came two young lovers lately wed:
"I am half sick of shadows," said
   The Lady of Shalott.

PART III

A bow-shot from her bower-eaves,
He rode between the barley-sheaves,
The sun came dazzling thro' the leaves,
And flamed upon the brazen greaves
   Of bold Sir Lancelot.
A red-cross knight for ever kneel'd
To a lady in his shield,
That sparkled on the yellow field,
   Beside remote Shalott.

The gemmy bridle glitter'd free,
Like to some branch of stars we see
Hung in the Golden Galaxy.
The bridle bells rang merrily
   As he rode down to Camelot;
And from his blazon'd baldric slung
A mighty silver bugle hung,
And as he rode his armor rung,
   Beside remote Shalott.

All in the blue unclouded weather
Thick-jewell'd shone the saddle-leather,
The helmet and the helmet-feather
Burn'd like one burning flame together,
   As he rode down to Camelot;

As often thro' the purple night,
Below the starry clusters bright,
Some bearded meteor, trailing light,
      Moves over still Shalott.

His broad clear brow in sunlight glow'd;
On burnish'd hooves his war-horse trode;
From underneath his helmet flow'd
His coal-black curls as on he rode,
      As he rode down to Camelot.
From the bank and from the river
He flash'd into the crystal mirror,
"Tirra lirra", by the river
      Sang Sir Lancelot.

She left the web, she left the loom,
She made three paces thro' the room,
She saw the water-lily bloom,
She saw the helmet and the plume,
      She look'd down to Camelot.
Out flew the web and floated wide;
The mirror crack'd from side to side:
"The curse is come upon me," cried
      The Lady of Shalott.

PART IV

In the stormy east-wind straining,
The pale yellow woods were waning,
The broad stream in his banks complaining,
Heavily the low sky raining
      Over tower'd Camelot;
Down she came and found a boat
Beneath a willow left afloat,
And round about the prow she wrote
      The Lady of Shalott.

And down the river's dim expanse
Like some bold seër in a trance,
Seeing all his own mischance—
With a glassy countenance
      Did she look to Camelot.

And at the closing of the day
She loosed the chain, and down she lay,
The broad stream bore her far away,
      The Lady of Shalott.

Lying, robed in snowy white
That loosely flew to left and right—
The leaves upon her falling light—
Thro' the noises of the night
      She floated down to Camelot;
And as the boat-head wound along
The willowing hills and fields among,
They heard her singing her last song,
      The Lady of Shalott.

Heard a carol, mournful, holy,
Chanted loudly, chanted lowly,
Till her blood was frozen slowly,
And her eyes were darken'd wholly,
      Turn'd to tower'd Camelot.
For ere she reach'd upon the tide
The first house by the water-side,
Singing in her song she died,
      The Lady of Shalott.

Under tower and balcony,
By garden-wall and gallery,
A gleaming shape she floated by,
Dead-pale between the houses high,
      Silent into Camelot.
Out upon the wharfs they came,
Knight and burgher, lord and dame,
And round the prow they read her name,
      The Lady of Shalott.

Who is this? and what is here?
And in the lighted palace near
Died the sound of royal cheer;
And they cross'd themselves for fear,
      All the knights at Camelot:
But Lancelot mused a little space;
He said, "She has a lovely face;
God in his mercy lend her grace,
      The Lady of Shalott."

CASEY AT THE BAT

Ernest Lawrence Thayer

It looked extremely rocky for the Mudville nine that day;
The score stood two to four, with but one inning left to play.
So, when Cooney died at second, and Burrows did the same,
A pallor wreathed the features of the patrons of the game.

A straggling few got up to go, leaving there the rest,
With that hope which springs eternal within the human breast.
For they thought: "If only Casey could get a whack at that,"
They'd put even money now, with Casey at the bat.

But Flynn preceded Casey, and likewise so did Blake,
And the former was a pudd'n, and the latter was a fake.
So on that stricken multitude a deathlike silence sat;
For there seemed but little chance of Casey's getting to the bat.

But Flynn let drive a "single," to the wonderment of all.
And the much-despisèd Blakey "tore the cover off the ball."
And when the dust had lifted, and they saw what had occurred,
There was Blakey safe at second, and Flynn a-huggin' third.

Then from the gladdened multitude went up a joyous yell—
It rumbled in the mountaintops, it rattled in the dell;
It struck upon the hillside and rebounded on the flat;
For Casey, mighty Casey, was advancing to the bat.

There was ease in Casey's manner as he stepped into his place,
There was pride in Casey's bearing and a smile on Casey's face;
And when responding to the cheers he lightly doffed his hat,
No stranger in the crowd could doubt 'twas Casey at the bat.

Ten thousand eyes were on him as he rubbed his hands with dirt,
Five thousand tongues applauded when he wiped them on his
    shirt;
Then when the writhing pitcher ground the ball into his hip,
Defiance glanced in Casey's eye, a sneer curled Casey's lip.

And now the leather-covered sphere came hurtling through the air,
And Casey stood a-watching it in haughty grandeur there.
Close by the sturdy batsman the ball unheeded sped;
"That ain't my style," said Casey. "Strike one," the umpire said.

From the benches, black with people, there went up a muffled roar,
Like the beating of the storm waves on the stern and distant shore.
"Kill him! kill the umpire!" shouted someone on the stand;
And it's likely they'd have killed him had not Casey raised his hand.

With a smile of Christian charity great Casey's visage shone;
He stilled the rising tumult, he made the game go on;
He signaled to the pitcher, and once more the spheroid flew;
But Casey still ignored it, and the umpire said, "Strike two."

"Fraud!" cried the maddened thousands, and the echo answered
   "Fraud!"
But one scornful look from Casey and the audience was awed;
They saw his face grow stern and cold, they saw his muscles strain,
And they knew that Casey wouldn't let the ball go by again.

The sneer is gone from Casey's lips, his teeth are clenched in hate,
He pounds with cruel vengeance his bat upon the plate;
And now the pitcher holds the ball, and now he lets it go,
And now the air is shattered by the force of Casey's blow.

Oh, somewhere in this favored land the sun is shining bright,
The band is playing somewhere, and somewhere hearts are light;
And somewhere men are laughing, and somewhere children shout,
But there is no joy in Mudville—Mighty Casey has struck out.

VITAÏ LAMPADA

Sir Henry Newbolt

There's a breathless hush in the Close tonight—
   Ten to make and the match to win—
A bumping pitch and a blinding light,
   An hour to play and the last man in.
And it's not for the sake of a ribboned coat,
   Or the selfish hope of a season's fame,
But his Captain's hand on his shoulder smote
   "Play up! play up! and play the game!"

The sand of the desert is sodden red,—
   Red with the wreck of a square that broke;—
The Gatling's jammed and the colonel dead,
   And the regiment blind with dust and smoke.

The river of death has brimmed his banks,
    And England's far, and Honor a name,
But the voice of a schoolboy rallies the ranks,
    "Play up! play up! and play the game!"

This is the word that year by year
    While in her place the School is set
Every one of her sons must hear,
    And none that hears it dare forget.
This they all with a joyful mind
    Bear through life like a torch in a flame,
And falling fling to the host behind—
    "Play up! play up! and play the game!"

THE LAST LEAF

Oliver Wendell Holmes

I saw him once before,
As he passed by the door,
        And again
The pavement stones resound
As he totters o'er the ground
        With his cane.

They say that in his prime,
Ere the pruning-knife of Time
        Cut him down,
Not a better man was found
By the crier on his round
        Through the town.

But now he walks the streets,
And he looks at all he meets
        Sad and wan,
And he shakes his feeble head,
That it seems as if he said,
        "They are gone."

The mossy marbles rest
On the lips that he has pressed
        In their bloom,

And the names he loved to hear
Have been carved for many a year
    On the tomb.

My grandmamma has said—
Poor old lady, she is dead
    Long ago—
That he had a Roman nose,
And his cheek was like a rose
    In the snow.

But now his nose is thin,
And it rests upon his chin
    Like a staff,
And a crook is in his back,
And a melancholy crack
    In his laugh.

I know it is a sin
For me to sit and grin
    At him here;
But the old three-cornered hat,
And the breeches, and all that,
    Are so queer!

And if I should live to be
The last leaf upon the tree
    In the spring,
Let them smile, as I do now,
At the old forsaken bough
    Where I cling.

NON SUM QUALIS ERAM BONAE SUB REGNO CYNARAE

Ernest Dowson

Last night, ah, yesternight, betwixt her lips and mine
There fell thy shadow, Cynara! thy breath was shed
Upon my soul between the kisses and the wine;
And I was desolate and sick of an old passion,
    Yea, I was desolate and bowed my head:
I have been faithful to thee, Cynara! in my fashion.

All night upon mine heart I felt her warm heart beat,
Night-long within mine arms in love and sleep she lay;
Surely the kisses of her bought red mouth were sweet;
But I was desolate and sick of an old passion,
    When I awoke and found the dawn was grey:
I have been faithful to thee, Cynara! in my fashion.

I have forgot much, Cynara! gone with the wind,
Flung roses, roses riotously with the throng,
Dancing, to put thy pale, lost lilies out of mind;
But I was desolate and sick of an old passion,
    Yea, all the time, because the dance was long:
I have been faithful to thee, Cynara! in my fashion.

I cried for madder music and for stronger wine,
But when the feast is finished and the lamps expire,
Then falls thy shadow, Cynara! the night is thine;
And I am desolate and sick of an old passion,
    Yea, hungry for the lips of my desire:
I have been faithful to thee, Cynara! in my fashion.

"OVER THE HILLS AND FAR AWAY"

W. E. Henley

Where forlorn sunsets flare and fade
    On desolate sea and lonely sand,
Out of the silence and the shade
    What is the voice of strange command
Calling you still, as friend calls friend
    With love that cannot brook delay,
To rise and follow the ways that wend
    Over the hills and far away?

Hark in the city, street on street
    A roaring reach of death and life,
Of vortices that clash and fleet
    And ruin in appointed strife,
Hark to it calling, calling clear,
    Calling until you cannot stay
From dearer things than your own most dear
    Over the hills and far away.

Out of the sound of the ebb-and-flow,
  Out of the sight of lamp and star,
It calls you where the good winds blow,
  And the unchanging meadows are:
From faded hopes and hopes agleam,
  It calls you, calls you night and day
Beyond the dark into the dream
  Over the hills and far away.

THE TIME I'VE LOST IN WOOING

Thomas Moore

The time I've lost in wooing,
In watching and pursuing
    The light that lies
    In woman's eyes,
Has been my heart's undoing.
Tho' Wisdom oft has sought me,
I scorn'd the lore she brought me,
    My only books
    Were women's looks,
And folly's all they taught me.

Her smile when Beauty granted,
I hung with gaze enchanted,
    Like him the Sprite
    Whom maids by night
Oft meet in glen that's haunted.
Like him, too, Beauty won me;
But when the spell was on me,
    If once their ray
    Was turn'd away,
O! winds could not outrun me.

And are those follies going?
And is my proud heart growing
    Too cold or wise
    For brilliant eyes
Again to set it glowing?

No—vain, alas! th' endeavour
From bonds so sweet to sever;—
Poor Wisdom's chance
Against a glance
Is now as weak as ever.

DOWN WENT McGINTY

Joseph Flynn

Sunday morning just at nine,
Dan McGinty dressed so fine,
Stood looking up at every high stone wall;
When his friend young Pat McCann,
Says "I'll bet five dollars, Dan,
I could carry you to the top without a fall";
So on his shoulders he took Dan;
To climb the ladder he began,
And he soon commenced to reach up near the top;
When McGinty, cute old rogue,
To win the five he did let go,
Never thinking just how far he'd have to drop.

Chorus:
    Down went McGinty to the bottom of the wall,
    And though he won the five, he was more dead than alive,
    Sure his ribs, and nose and back were broke from getting such
       a fall,
    Dress'd in his best suit of clothes.

From the hospital Mac went home,
When they fix'd his broken bone,
To find he was the father of a child;
So to celebrate it right,
His friend he went to invite,
And he soon was drinking whiskey fast and wild;
Then he waddled down the street
In his Sunday suit so neat
Holding up his head as proud as John the Great;
But in the sidewalk was a hole,
To receive a ton of coal,
That McGinty never saw till just too late.

Chorus:

> Down went McGinty to the bottom of the hole,
> Then the driver of the cart give the load of coal a start,
> And it took us half an hour to dig McGinty from the coal,
> Dress'd in his best suit of clothes.

Now McGinty raved and swore,
About his clothes he felt so sore,
And an oath he took he'd kill the man or die;
So he tightly grabbed his stick
And hit the driver a lick,
Then he raised a little shanty on his eye;
But two policemen saw the muss
And they soon join'd in the fuss,
Then they ran McGinty in for being drunk;
And the Judge says with a smile.
We will keep you for a while
In a cell to sleep upon a prison bunk.

Chorus:

> Down went McGinty to the bottom of the jail,
> Where his board would cost him nix, and he stay'd exactly six,
> They were big long months he stopped, for no one went his bail,
> Dress'd in his best suit of clothes.

Now the Ginty thin and pale,
One fine day got out of jail,
And with joy to see his boy was nearly wild;
To his home he quickly ran
To meet his wife Bedaley Ann,
But she'd skipped away and took along the child;
Then he gave up in despair,
And he madly pull'd his hair,
As he stood one day upon the river shore,
Knowing well he couldn't swim,
He did foolishly jump in,
Although water he had never took before.

Chorus:

> Down went McGinty to the bottom of the say,
> And he must be very wet for they haven't found him yet,
> But they say his ghost comes round the docks before the break of day,
> Dress'd in his best suit of clothes.

THE LADY, OR THE TIGER

Frank R. Stockton

In the very olden time, there lived a semi-barbaric king, whose ideas, though somewhat polished and sharpened by the progressiveness of distant Latin neighbors, were still large, florid, and untrammeled, as became the half of him which was barbaric. He was a man of exuberant fancy, and, withal, of an authority so irresistible that, at his will, he turned his fancies into facts. He was greatly given to self-communing; and, when he and himself agreed upon anything, the thing was done. When every member of his domestic and political systems moved smoothly in its appointed course, his nature was bland and genial; but whenever there was a little hitch, and some of his orbs got out of their orbits, he was blander and more genial still, for nothing pleased him so much as to make the crooked straight, and crush down uneven places.

Among the borrowed notions by which his barbarism had become semified was that of the public arena, in which, by exhibitions of manly and beastly valor, the minds of his subjects were refined and cultured.

But even here the exuberant and barbaric fancy asserted itself. The arena of the king was built, not to give the people an opportunity of hearing the rhapsodies of dying gladiators, nor to enable them to view the inevitable conclusion of a conflict between religious opinions and hungry jaws, but for purposes far better adapted to widen and develop the mental energies of the people. This vast amphitheater, with its encircling galleries, its mysterious vaults, and its unseen passages, was an agent of poetic justice, in which crime was punished, or virtue rewarded, by the decrees of an impartial and incorruptible chance.

When a subject was accused of a crime of sufficient importance to interest the king, public notice was given that on an appointed day the fate of the accused person would be decided in the king's arena—a structure which well deserved its name; for, although its form and plan were borrowed from afar, its purpose emanated solely from the brain of this man, who, every barleycorn a king, knew no tradition to which he owed more allegiance than pleased his fancy, and who ingrafted on every adopted form of human thought and action the rich growth of his barbaric idealism.

When all the people had assembled in the galleries, and the king, surrounded by his court, sat high up on his throne of royal state on one side of the arena, he gave a signal, a door beneath him opened, and the accused subject stepped out into the amphitheater. Directly opposite him, on the other side of the enclosed space, were two doors, exactly alike and side by side. It was the duty and the privilege of the person on trial, to walk directly to these doors and open one of them. He could open either door he pleased; he was subject to no guidance or influence but that of the aforementioned impartial and incorruptible chance. If he opened the one, there came out of it a hungry tiger, the fiercest and most cruel that could be found, which immediately sprang upon him and tore him to pieces, as a punishment for his guilt. The moment that the case of the criminal was thus decided, doleful iron bells were clanged, great wails went up from the hired mourners posted on the outer rim of the arena, and the vast audience, with bowed heads and downcast hearts, wended slowly their homeward way, mourning greatly that one so young and fair, or so old and respected, should have merited so dire a fate.

But, if the accused person opened the other door, there came forth from it a lady, the most suitable to his years and station that His Majesty could select among his fair subjects; and to this lady he was immediately married, as a reward of his innocence. It mattered not that he might already possess a wife and family, or that his affections might be engaged upon an object of his own selection; the king allowed no such subordinate arrangements to interfere with his great scheme of retribution and reward. The exercise, as in the other instance, took place immediately and in the arena. Another door opened beneath the king, and a priest, followed by a band of choristers, and dancing maidens blowing joyous airs on golden horns and treading an epithalamic measure, advanced to where the pair stood, side by side; and the wedding was promptly and cheerily solemnized. Then the gay brass bells rang forth their merry peals, the people shouted glad hurrahs, and the innocent man, preceded by children strewing flowers on his path, led his bride to his home.

This was the king's semi-barbaric method of administering justice. Its perfect fairness is obvious. The criminal could not know out of which door would come the lady; he opened either he pleased, without having the slightest idea whether, in the next instant, he was to be devoured or married. On some occasions the tiger came out one door, and on some out of the other. The decisions of this tribunal were not only fair, they were positively determinate; the accused person was instantly punished if he found himself guilty; and, if innocent, he was rewarded on the spot, whether he liked it or not. There was no escape from the judgments of the king's arena.

The institution was a very popular one. When the people gathered together on one of the great trial days, they never knew whether they were to witness a bloody slaughter or a hilarious wedding. This element of uncertainty lent an interest to the occasion which it could not otherwise have attained. Thus, the masses were entertained and pleased, and the thinking part of the community could bring no charge of unfairness against this plan; for did not the accused person have the whole matter in his own hands?

This semi-barbaric king had a daughter as blooming as his most florid fancies, and with a soul as fervent and impervious as his own. As is usual in such cases, she was the apple of his eye, and was loved by him above all humanity. Among his courtiers was a young man of that firmness of blood and lowness of station common to the conventional heroes of romance who love royal maidens. This royal maiden was well satisfied with her lover, for he was handsome and brave to a degree unsurpassed in all this kingdom; and she loved him with an ardor that had enough of barbarism in it to make it exceedingly warm and strong. This love affair moved on happily for many months, until one day the king happened to discover its existence. He did not hesitate nor waver in regard to his duty in the premises. The youth was immediately cast into prison, and a day was appointed for his trial in the king's arena. This, of course, was an especially important occasion; and His Majesty, as well as all the people, was greatly interested in the workings and development of this trial. Never before had such a case occurred; never before had a subject dared to love the daughter of a king. In after-years such things became common-place enough; but then they were, in no slight degree, novel and startling.

The tiger-cages of the kingdom were searched for the most savage and relentless beasts, from which the fiercest monster might be selected for the arena; and the ranks of maiden youth and beauty throughout the land were carefully surveyed by competent judges in order that the young man might have a fitting bride in case fate did not determine for him a different destiny. Of course, everybody knew that the deed with which the accused was charged had been done. He had loved the princess, and neither he, she, nor anyone else though of denying the fact; but the king would not think of allowing any fact of this kind to interfere with the working of the tribunal, in which he took such great delight and satisfaction. No matter how the affair turned out, the youth would be disposed of; and the king would take an aesthetic pleasure in watching the course of events, which would determine whether or not the young man had done wrong in allowing himself to love the princess.

The appointed day arrived. From far and near the people gathered, and thronged the great galleries of the arena; and crowds, unable to gain admittance, massed themselves against its outside walls. The king and his court were in their places, opposite the twin doors—those fateful portals, so terrible in their similarity.

All was ready. The signal was given. A door beneath the royal party opened, and the lover of the princess walked into the arena. Tall, beautiful, fair, his appearance was greeted with a low hum of admiration and anxiety. Half the audience had not known so grand a youth had lived among them. No wonder the princess loved him! What a terrible thing for him to be there!

As the youth advanced into the arena, he turned, as the custom was, to bow to the king; but he did not think at all of that royal personage; his eyes were fixed upon the princess who sat to the right of her father. Had it not been for the moiety of barbarism in her nature, it is probable that lady would not have been there; but her intense and fervid soul would not allow her to be absent on an occasion in which she was so terribly interested. From the moment that the decree had gone forth, that her lover should decide his fate in the king's arena, she had thought of nothing, night or day, but this great event and the various subjects connected with it. Possessed of more power, influence, and force of character than anyone who had ever before been interested in such a case, she had done what no other person had done—she had possessed herself of the secret of the doors. She knew in which of the two rooms that lay behind those doors stood the cage of the tiger, with its open front, and in which waited the lady. Through these thick doors, heavily curtained with skins on the inside, it was impossible that any noise or suggestion should come from within to the person who should approach to raise the latch of one of them; but gold, and the power of a woman's will, had brought the secret to the princess.

And not only did she know in which room stood the lady ready to emerge, all blushing and radiant, should her door he opened, but she knew who the lady was. It was one of the fairest and loveliest of the damsels of the court who had been selected as the reward of the accused youth, should he be proved innocent of the crime of aspiring to one so far above him, and the princess hated her.

Often had she seen, or imagined that she had seen, this fair creature throwing glances of admiration upon the person of her lover, and sometimes she thought these glances were perceived and even returned. Now and then she had seen them talking together; it was but for a moment or two, but much can be said in a brief space; it may have been on most unimportant topics, but how could she know that? The girl was lovely, but she had dared to raise her eyes to the loved one of the princess; and, with all the intensity of the savage blood transmitted to her through long lines of wholly barbaric ancestors, she hated the woman who blushed and trembled behind the silent door.

When her lover turned and looked at her, and his eyes met hers as she sat there paler and whiter than anyone in the vast ocean of anxious faces about her, he saw, by that power of quick perception which is given to those whose souls are one, that she knew behind which door crouched the tiger, and behind which stood the lady. He had expected her to know it. He understood her nature, and his soul was assured that she would never rest until she had made plain to herself this thing, hidden to all other lookers-on, even to the king. The only hope for the youth in which there was any element of certainty was based upon the success of the princess in discovering this mystery; and the moment he looked upon her, he saw she had succeeded, as in his soul he knew she would succeed.

Then it was his quick and anxious glance asked the question: "Which?" It was as plain to her as if he shouted it from where he stood. There was not an instant to be lost. The question was asked in a flash; it must be answered in another.

Her right arm lay on the cushioned parapet before her. She raised her hand, and made a slight, quick movement toward the right. No one but her lover saw her. Every eye but his was fixed on the man in the arena.

He turned, and with a firm and rapid step he walked across the empty space. Every heart stopped beating, every breath was held, every eye was fixed immovable upon that man. Without the slightest hesitation, he went to the door on the right, and opened it.

Now, the point of the story is this: Did the tiger come out of that door, or did the lady?

The more we reflect upon this question the harder it is to answer. It involves a study of the human heart which leads us through devious mazes of passion, out of which it is difficult to find our way. Think of it, fair reader, not as if the decision of the question depended upon yourself, but upon that hot-blooded, semi-barbaric princess, her soul at a white heat beneath the combined fires of despair and jealousy. She had lost him, but who should have him?

How often, in her waking hours and in her dreams, had she started in wild horror, and covered her face with her hands as she thought of her lover opening the door on the other side of which waited the cruel fangs of the tiger!

But how much oftener had she seen him at the other door! How in her grievous reveries had she gnashed her teeth, and torn her hair, when she saw his start of rapturous delight as he opened the door of the lady! How her soul had burned in agony when she had seen him rush to meet that woman, with her flushing cheek and sparkling eye of triumph; when she had seen him lead her forth, his whole frame kindled with the joy of recovered life; when she had heard the loud shouts from the multitude and the wild ringing of the happy bells; when she had seen the priest with his joyous followers advance to the couple, and make them man and wife before her very eyes; and when she had seen them walk away together upon their path of flowers, followed by the tremendous shouts of the hilarious multitude, in which her one despairing shriek was lost and drowned!

Would it not be better for him to die at once and go to wait for her in the blessed regions of semi-barbaric futurity?

And yet, that awful tiger, those shrieks, that blood!

Her decision had been indicated in an instant, but it had been made after days and nights of anguished deliberation. She had known she would be asked, she had decided what she would answer, and without the slightest hesitation, she had moved her hand to the right.

The question of her decision is not one to be lightly considered, and it is not for me to presume to set myself up as the one person able to answer it. And so I leave it all with you: Which came out of the opened door—the lady, or the tiger?

CARGOES

John Masefield

Quinquireme of Nineveh from distant Ophir,
Rowing home to haven in sunny Palestine,
With a cargo of ivory,
And apes and peacocks,
Sandalwood, cedarwood, and sweet white wine.

Stately Spanish galleon coming from the Isthmus,
Dipping through the Tropics by the palm-green shores,
With a cargo of diamonds,
Emeralds, amethysts,
Topazes, and cinnamon, and gold moidores.

Dirty British coaster with a salt-caked smoke stack,
Butting through the Channel in the mad March days,
With a cargo of Tyne coal,
Road-rails, pig-lead,
Firewood, iron-ware, and cheap tin trays.

THE DYING CHRISTIAN TO HIS SOUL

Alexander Pope

Vital spark of heavenly flame!
Quit, O quit this mortal frame!
Trembling, hoping, lingering, flying,
O! the pain, the bliss of dying!
Cease, fond nature, cease thy strife,
And let me languish into life!

Hark! they whisper: angels say,
Sister spirit, come away!
What is this absorbs me quite?
Steals my senses, shuts my sight,
Drowns my spirit, draws my breath?
Tell me, my soul, can this be death?

The world recedes; it disappears!
Heaven opens on my eyes! my ears
With sounds seraphic ring!
Lend, lend your wings! I mount! I fly!
O Grave! where is thy victory?
O Death! where is thy sting?

* * *

Lord, reform thy world, beginning with me.
> (Prayer of a Chinese Christian, quoted
> by President Roosevelt in press confer-
> ence, Dec. 17, 1941)

THE WISE AND FOOLISH VIRGINS

Holy Bible, Matthew 25:1–13

1 Then shall the kingdom of heaven be likened unto ten virgins, which took their lamps, and went forth to meet the bridegroom.

2 And five of them were wise, and five were foolish.

3 They that were foolish took their lamps, and took no oil with them:

4 But the wise took oil in their vessels with their lamps.

5 While the bridegroom tarried, they all slumbered and slept.

6 And at midnight there was a cry made, Behold, the bridegroom cometh; go ye out to meet him.

7 Then all those virgins arose, and trimmed their lamps.

8 And the foolish said unto the wise, Give us of your oil; for our lamps are gone out.

9 But the wise answered, saying, Not so; lest there be not enough for us and you: but go ye rather to them that sell, and buy for yourselves.

10 And while they went to buy, the bridegroom came; and they that were ready went in with him to the marriage: and the door was shut.

11 Afterward came also the other virgins, saying, Lord, Lord, open to us.

12 But he answered and said, Verily I say unto you, I know you not.

13 Watch therefore, for ye know neither the day nor the hour wherein the Son of man cometh.

LANDING OF THE PILGRIM FATHERS

Felicia Dorothea Hemans

The breaking waves dashed high
On a stern and rock-bound coast;
And the woods against a stormy sky,
Their giant branches tossed;
And the heavy night hung dark
The hills and waters o'er—
When a band of exiles moored their bark
On a wild New England shore.

Not as the conqueror comes,
They, the true-hearted, came;—
Not with the roll of stirring drums,
And the trumpets that sing of fame;—
Not as the flying come,
In silence and in fear;
They shook the depths of the desert's gloom
With their hymns of lofty cheer.

Amidst the storm they sang,
And the stars heard, and the sea!
And the sounding aisles of the dim woods rang
To the anthem of the free;
The ocean eagle soared
From his nest by the white wave's foam,
And the rocking pines of the forest roared:—
This was their welcome home!

There were men with hoary hair
Amidst that pilgrim band;
Why had they come to wither there,
Away from their childhood's land?
There was woman's fearless eye,
Lit by her deep love's truth;
There was manhood's brow serenely high,
And the fiery heart of youth.

What sought they thus afar?
Bright jewels of the mine?
The wealth of seas? the spoils of war?
They sought a faith's pure shrine!
Ay, call it holy ground,
The soil where first they trod!
They left unstained what there they found
Freedom to worship God!

THE VOICE OF GOD

Louis I. Newman

I sought to hear the voice of God,
And climbed the topmost steeple.
But God declared: "Go down again,
I dwell among the people."

OZYMANDIAS OF EGYPT

Percy Bysshe Shelley

I met a traveller from an antique land
Who said: Two vast and trunkless legs of stone
Stand in the desert . . . Near them, on the sand,
Half sunk, a shattered visage lies, whose frown,
And wrinkled lip, and sneer of cold command,
Tell that its sculptor well those passions read
Which yet survive, stamped on these lifeless things,
The hand that mocked them and the heart that fed:
And on the pedestal these words appear:
"My name is Ozymandias, king of kings:
Look on my works, ye Mighty, and despair!"
Nothing beside remains. Round the decay
Of that colossal wreck, boundless and bare,
The lone and level sands stretch far away.

MACBETH LEARNS OF HIS WIFE'S DEATH

William Shakespeare

Tomorrow, and tomorrow, and tomorrow,
Creeps in this petty pace from day to day
To the last syllable of recorded time,
And all our yesterdays have lighted fools
The way to dusty death. Out, out, brief candle!
Life's but a walking shadow, a poor player
That struts and frets his hour upon the stage
And then is heard no more; it is a tale
Told by an idiot, full of sound and fury,
Signifying nothing.

THE OLD OAKEN BUCKET

Samuel Woodworth

How dear to my heart are the scenes of my childhood,
  When fond recollection presents them to view!
The orchard, the meadow, the deep-tangled wildwood,
  And every loved spot which my infancy knew,

The wide-spreading pond and the mill which stood by it,
 The bridge and the rock where the cataract fell;
The cot of my father, the dairy house nigh it,
 And e'en the rude bucket which hung in the well.
The old oaken bucket, the iron-bound bucket,
The moss-covered bucket which hung in the well.

That moss-covered vessel I hail as a treasure;
 For often at noon, when returned from the field,
I found it the source of an exquisite pleasure,
 The purest and sweetest that nature can yield.
How ardent I seized it with hands that were glowing!
 And quick to the white-pebbled bottom it fell;
Then soon, with the emblem of truth overflowing,
 And dripping with coolness it rose from the well;
The old oaken bucket, the iron-bound bucket,
The moss-covered bucket, arose from the well.

How sweet from the green mossy brim to receive it,
 As poised on the curb, it inclined to my lips!
Not a full blushing goblet could tempt me to leave it,
 Though filled with the nectar that Jupiter sips.
And now, far removed from the loved situation,
 The tear of regret will intrusively swell,
As fancy reverts to my father's plantation,
 And sighs for the bucket which hangs in the well;
The old oaken bucket, the iron-bound bucket,
The moss-covered bucket which hangs in the well.

WAITING

John Burroughs

Serene, I fold my hands and wait,
Nor care for wind, or tide, or sea;
I rave no more 'gainst Time or Fate,
For, lo! my own shall come to me.

I stay my haste, I make delays,
For what avails this eager pace?
I stand amid the eternal ways,
And what is mine shall know my face.

Asleep, awake, by night or day,
The friends I seek are seeking me;
No wind can drive my bark astray,
Nor change the tide of destiny.

What matter if I stand alone?
I wait with joy the coming years;
My heart shall reap where it has sown,
And garner up its fruits of tears.

The waters know their own and draw
The brook that springs in yonder height;
So flows the good with equal law
Unto the soul of pure delights.

The stars come nightly to the sky;
The tidal wave unto the sea;
Nor time, nor space, nor deep, nor high,
Can keep my own away from me.

WHAT WE MAY LIVE WITHOUT

Owen Meredith *

We may live without poetry, music and art;
We may live without conscience and live without heart;
We may live without friends; we may live without books;
But civilized man cannot live without cooks.

He may live without books,—what is knowledge but grieving?
He may live without hope,—what is hope but deceiving?
He may live without love,—what is passion but pining?
But where is the man that can live without dining?

(From Lucile, Pt. I, Canto II)

THE WOMAN I LOVE

At long last I am able to say a few words of my own. I have
never wanted to withhold anything, but until now it has not been
constitutionally possible for me to speak.

* Edward Lytton.

A few hours ago I discharged my last duty as King and Emperor, and now that I have been succeeded by my brother, the Duke of York, my first words must be to declare my allegiance to him. This I do with all my heart.

You all know the reasons which have impelled me to renounce the throne. But I want you to understand that in making up my mind I did not forget the country or the empire, which, as Prince of Wales and lately as King, I have for twenty-five years tried to serve.

But you must believe me when I tell you that I have found it impossible to carry the heavy burden of responsibility and to discharge my duties as King as I would wish to do without the help and support of the woman I love.

And I want you to know that the decision I have made has been mine and mine alone. This was a thing I had to judge entirely for myself. The other person most nearly concerned has tried up to the last to persuade me to take a different course.

I have made this, the most serious decision of my life, only upon the single thought of what would, in the end, be best for all.

This decision has been made less difficult to me by the sure knowledge that my brother, with his long training in the public affairs of this country and with his fine qualities, will be able to take my place forthwith without interruption or injury to the life and progress of the empire. And he has one matchless blessing, enjoyed by so many of you, and not bestowed on me—a happy home with his wife and children.

During these hard days I have been comforted by her majesty my mother and by my family. The ministers of the crown, and in particular, Mr. Baldwin, the Prime Minister, have always treated me with full consideration. There has never been any constitutional difference between me and them, and between me and Parliament. Bred in the constitutional tradition by my father, I should never have allowed any such issue to arise.

Ever since I was Prince of Wales, and later on when I occupied the throne, I have been treated with the greatest kindness by all classes of the people wherever I have lived or journeyed throughout the empire. For that I am very grateful.

I now quit altogether public affairs and I lay down my burden. It may be some time before I return to my native land, but I shall always follow the fortunes of the British race and empire with profound interest, and if at any time in the future I can be found of service to his majesty in a private station, I shall not fail.

And now, we all have a new King. I wish him and you, his people, happiness and prosperity with all my heart. God bless you all! God save the King!

December 11, 1936.   EDWARD VIII

SILVER

Walter de la Mare

Slowly, silently, now the moon
Walks the night in her silver shoon;
This way, and that, she peers, and sees
Silver fruit upon silver trees;
One by one the casements catch
Her beams beneath the silvery thatch;
Couched in his kennel, like a log,
With paws of silver sleeps the dog;
From their shadowy cote the white breasts peep
Of doves in a silver-feathered sleep;
A harvest mouse goes scampering by,
With silver claws and a silver eye;
And moveless fish in the water gleam,
By silver reeds in a silver stream.

CASABIANCA

Felicia Dorothea Hemans

In the battle of the Nile, thirteen-year-old Casabianca, son of the Admiral of the Orient, remained at his post after the ship had taken fire and all the guns had been abandoned. He perished when the vessel exploded.

The boy stood on the burning deck,
Whence all but he had fled;
The flame that lit the battle's wreck,
Shone round him o'er the dead.

Yet beautiful and bright he stood,
As born to rule the storm;
A creature of heroic blood,
A proud though childlike form.

The flames rolled on; he would not go
Without his father's word;
That father, faint in death below,
His voice no longer heard.

He called aloud, "Say, Father, say,
If yet my task is done!"
He knew not that the chieftain lay
Unconscious of his son.

"Speak, Father!" once again he cried,
"If I may yet be gone!"
—And but the booming shots replied,
And fast the flames rolled on.

Upon his brow he felt their breath,
And in his waving hair;
And looked from that lone post of death
In still yet brave despair;

And shouted but once more aloud,
"My Father! must I stay?"
While o'er him fast, through sail and shroud,
The wreathing fires made way.

They wrapt the ship in splendor wild,
They caught the flag on high,
And streamed above the gallant child,
Like banners in the sky.

There came a burst of thunder sound;
The boy—Oh! where was *he?*
—Ask of the winds, that far around
With fragments strewed the sea;—

With shroud, and mast, and pennon fair,
That well had borne their part,—
But the noblest thing that perished there
Was that young, faithful heart.

* * *

Speech is the index of the mind.
                                        —Seneca

FROM EVANGELINE

Henry Wadsworth Longfellow

PRELUDE

This is the forest primeval. The murmuring pines and the hem-
  locks,
Bearded with moss, and in garments green, indistinct in the twi
  light,
Stand like Druids of eld, with voices sad and prophetic,
Stand like harpers hoar, with beards that rest on their bosoms.
Loud from its rocky caverns, the deep-voiced neighboring ocean
Speaks, and in accents disconsolate answers the wail of the forest.

This is the forest primeval; but where are the hearts that be-
  neath it
Leaped like the roe, when he hears in the woodland the voice of
  the huntsman?
Where is the thatched-roofed village, the home of Acadian farm-
  ers,—
Men whose lives glided on like rivers that water the woodlands,
Darkened by shadows of earth, but reflecting an image of heaven?
Waste are those pleasant farms, and the farmers forever departed!
Scattered like dust and leaves, when the mighty blasts of October
Seize them, and whirl them aloft, and sprinkle them far o'er the
  ocean.
Naught but tradition remains of the beautiful village of Grand-
  Pré.

Ye who believe in affection that hopes, and endures, and is patient,
Ye who believe in the beauty and strength of woman's devotion,
List to the mournful tradition still sung by the pines of the forest;
List to a Tale of Love in Acadie, home of the happy.

* * *

THE CHURCH SCENE

So passed the morning away. And lo! with a summons sonorous
Sounded the bell from its tower, and over the meadows a drum
  beat.
Thronged erelong was the church with men. Without, in the
  churchyard,

Waited the women. They stood by the graves, and hung on the headstones
Garlands of autumn-leaves and evergreens fresh from the forest.
Then came the guard from the ships and marching proudly among them
Entered the sacred portal. With loud and dissonant clangor
Echoed the sound of their brazen drums from ceiling and casement—
Echoed a moment only, and slowly the ponderous portal
Closed, and in silence the crowd awaited the will of the soldiers.
Then uprose their commander, and spake from the steps of the altar,
Holding aloft in his hands, with its seals, the royal commission.
"You are convened this day," he said, "by his Majesty's orders,
Clement and kind has he been; but how you have answered his kindness,
Let your own hearts reply! To my natural make and my temper
Painful the task is I do, which to you I know must be grievous.
Yet must I bow and obey, and deliver the will of our monarch:
Namely, that all your lands, and dwellings, and cattle of all kinds
Forfeited be to the crown; and that you yourselves from this province
Be transported to other lands. God grant you may dwell there
Ever as faithful subjects, a happy and peaceable people!
Prisoners now I declare you, for such is his Majesty's pleasure!"

As, when the air is serene in sultry solstice of summer,
Suddenly gathers a storm, and the deadly sling of the hailstones
Beats down the farmer's corn in the field, and shatters his windows,
Hiding the sun, and strewing the ground with thatch from the house-roofs,
Bellowing fly the herds, and seek to break their enclosures;
So on the hearts of the people descended the words of the speaker.
Silent a moment they stood in speechless wonder, and then rose
Louder and ever louder a wail of sorrow and anger,
And, by one impulse moved, they madly rushed to the doorway.
Vain was the hope of escape; and cries and fierce imprecations
Rang through the house of prayer; and high o'er the heads of the others
Rose, with his arms uplifted, the figure of Basil the blacksmith,
As, on a stormy sea, a spar is tossed by the billows.
Flushed was his face and distorted with passion; and wildly he shouted—

"Down with the tyrants of England! we never have sworn them
   allegiance!
Death to these foreign soldiers, who seize on our homes and our
   harvests!"
More he fain would have said, but the merciless hand of a soldier
Smote him upon the mouth, and dragged him down to the pavement.

In the midst of the strife and tumult of angry contention,
Lo! the door of the chancel opened, and Father Felician
Entered, with serious mien, and ascended the steps of the altar.
Raising his reverend hand, with a gesture he awed into silence
All that clamorous throng; and thus he spake to his people;
Deep were his tones and solemn; in accents measured and mourn-
   ful
Spake he, as, after the tocsin's alarum, distinctly the clock strikes.
"What is that ye do, my children? what madness has seized you?
Forty years of my life have I labored among you, and taught you,
Not in word alone, but in deed, to love one another!
Is this the fruit of my toils, of my vigils and prayers and priva-
   tions?
Have you so soon forgotten all lessons of love and forgiveness?
This is the house of the Prince of Peace, and would you profane it
Thus with violent deeds and hearts overflowing with hatred?
Lo! where the crucified Christ from His cross is gazing upon you!
See! in those sorrowful eyes what meekness and holy compassion!
Hark! how those lips still repeat the prayer, 'O Father, forgive
   them!'
Let us repeat that prayer in the hour when the wicked assail us,
Let us repeat it now, and say, 'O Father, forgive them!'"
Few were his words of rebuke, but deep in the hearts of his people
Sank they, and sobs of contrition succeeded the passionate out-
   break,
While they repeated his prayer, and said, "O Father, forgive
   them!"

* * *

He that fights and runs away
May turn and fight another day;
But he that is in battle slain
Will never rise to fight again.
                              —Anonymous

WHEN THE SON OF MAN SHALL COME
IN HIS GLORY

Holy Bible, Matthew 25:31–46

31 When the Son of man shall come in his glory, and all the holy angels with him, then shall he sit upon the throne of his glory:

32 And before him shall be gathered all nations: and he shall separate them one from another, as a shepherd divideth his sheep from the goats:

33 And he shall set the sheep on his right hand, but the goats on the left.

34 Then shall the King say unto them on his right hand, Come, ye blessed of my Father, inherit the kingdom prepared for you from the foundation of the world:

35 For I was an hungred, and ye gave me meat: I was thirsty, and ye gave me drink: I was a stranger, and ye took me in:

36 Naked, and ye clothed me: I was sick, and ye visited me: I was in prison, and ye came unto me.

37 Then shall the righteous answer him, saying, Lord, when saw we thee an hungred, and fed thee? or thirsty, and gave thee drink?

38 When saw we thee a stranger, and took thee in? or naked, and clothed thee?

39 Or when saw we thee sick, or in prison, and came unto thee?

40 And the King shall answer and say unto them, Verily I say unto you, Inasmuch as ye have done it unto one of the least of these my brethren, ye have done it unto me.

41 Then shall he say also unto them on the left hand, Depart from me, ye cursed, into everlasting fire, prepared for the devil and his angels:

42 For I was an hungred, and ye gave me no meat: I was thirsty, and ye gave me no drink:

43 I was a stranger and ye took me not in: naked, and ye clothed me not: sick and in prison, and ye visited me not.

44 Then shall they also answer him, saying, Lord, when saw we thee an hungred, or athirst, or a stranger, or naked, or sick, or in prison, and did not minister unto thee?

45 Then shall he answer them, saying, Verily I say unto you, Inasmuch as ye did it not to one of the least of these, ye did it not to me.

46 And these shall go away into everlasting punishment: but the righteous into life eternal.

IN TIME OF "THE BREAKING OF NATIONS"

Thomas Hardy

Only a man harrowing clods
    In a slow silent walk,
With an old horse that stumbles and nods
    Half asleep as they stalk.

Only thin smoke without flame
    From the heaps of couch grass:
Yet this will go onward the same
    Though Dynasties pass.

Yonder a maid and her wight
    Come whispering by;
War's annals will fade into night
    Ere their story die.

A LETTER TO CONGRESS FROM VALLEY FORGE

23 December 1777.

The Continental Congress,
Philadelphia, Pa.

SIR:

Full as I was in my representation of the matters in the commissary's department yesterday, fresh and more powerful reasons oblige me to add, that I am now convinced beyond a doubt, that unless some great and capital change suddenly takes place in that line, this army must inevitably be reduced to one or other of these three things: starve, dissolve, or disperse in order to obtain subsistence in the best manner they can. Rest assured, Sir, this is not an exaggerated picture, and that I have abundant reason to suppose what I say.

Yesterday afternoon, receiving information that the enemy in force had left the city, and were advancing towards Derby with the apparent design to forage, and draw subsistence from that part of the country, I ordered the troops to be in readiness, that I might give every opposition in my power; when behold, to my great mortification, I was not only informed, but convinced, that the men were unable to stir on account of provision, and that a dangerous mutiny, begun the night before, and which with difficulty was suppressed by the spirited exertions of some officers, was still much to be apprehended for want of this article. This brought forth the only commissary in the purchasing line in this camp; and, with him, this melancholy and alarming truth, that he had not a single hoof of any kind to slaughter, and not more than twenty-five barrels of flour! From hence form an opinion of our situation when I add that he could not tell when to expect any.

All I could do, under these circumstances, was to send out a few light parties to watch and harass the enemy, whilst other parties were instantly detached different ways to collect, if possible, as much provision as would satisfy the present pressing wants of the soldiery. But will this answer? No, Sir; three or four days of bad weather would prove our destruction. What then is to become of the army this winter? And if we are so often without provisions now, what is to become of us in the spring, when our force will be collected, with the aid perhaps of militia, to take advantage of an early campaign, before the enemy can be reinforced? These are considerations of great magnitude, meriting the closest attention; and they will, when my own reputation is so intimately connected with the event and to be effected by it, justify my saying that the present commissaries are by no means equal to the execution of the office, or that the disaffection of the people is past all belief. The misfortune, however, does in my opinion proceed from both causes; and, though I have been tender heretofore of giving any opinion, or lodging complaints, as the change in that department took place contrary to my judgment, and the consequences thereof were predicted, yet, finding that the inactivity of the army, whether for want of provisions, clothes, or other essentials, is charged to my account, not only by the common vulgar but by those in power, it is time to speak plain in exculpation of myself. With truth, then, I can declare, that no man, in my opinion, ever had his measures more impeded than I have, by every department of the army.

Since the month of July we have had no assistance from the quartermaster-general, and to want of assistance from this department the commissary general charges great part of his deficiency. To this I am to add, that, notwithstanding it is a standing order, and often repeated, that the troops shall always have two days' provisions by them, that they might be ready at any sudden call; yet an opportunity has scarcely ever offered, of taking an advantage of the enemy, that has not been either totally obstructed, or greatly impeded, on this account. And this, the great and crying evil, is not all. The soap, vinegar, and other articles allowed by Congress, we see none of, nor have we seen them, I believe, since the battle of Brandywine. The first, indeed, we have now little occasion for; few men having more than one shirt, many only the moiety of one, and some none at all. In addition to which, as a proof of the little benefit received from a clothier-general, and as a further proof of the inability of an army, under the circumstances of this, to perform the common duties of soldiers, (besides a number of men confined to hospitals for want of shoes, and others in farmers' houses on the same account,) we have, by a field-return this day made, no less than two thousand eight hundred and ninety-eight men in camp unfit for duty, because they are barefoot and otherwise naked. By the same return it appears that our whole strength in Continental troops, including the eastern brigades, which have joined us since the surrender of General Burgoyne, exclusive of the Maryland troops sent to Wilmington, amounts to no more than eight thousand two hundred in camp fit for duty. Notwithstanding which, and that since the 4th instant, our numbers fit for duty, from the harships and exposures they have undergone, particularly on account of blankets (numbers having been obliged, and still are, to sit up all night by fires, instead of taking comfortable rest in a natural and common way), have decreased near two thousand men.

We find, gentlemen, without knowing whether the army was really going into winter-quarters or not (for I am sure no resolution of mine would warrant the remonstrance), reprobating the measure as much as if they thought the soldiers were made of stocks or stones, and equally insensible of frost and snow; and moreover, as if they conceived it easily practicable for an inferior army, under the disadvantages I have described ours to be, which are by no means exaggerated, to confine a superior one, in all respects well-appointed for a winter's campaign, within the city of Philadelphia, and to cover from depredation and waste the States of Pennsylvania and Jersey. But what makes this matter still more extraordinary in my eye is that these very gentlemen—who were well apprized of the nakedness of the troops from ocular demonstration, who thought their own soldiers worse clad than others, and who advised me near a month ago to postpone the execution of a plan I was about to adopt, in consequence of a resolve of Congress for seizing clothes, under strong assurances that an ample supply would be collected in ten days agreeably to a decree of the State (not one article of which, by the by, is yet come to hand)—should think a winter's campaign, and the covering of these States from the invasion of an enemy, so easy and practicable a business I can assure those gentlemen it is a much easier and less distressing thing to draw remonstrances in a comfortable room by a good fireside, than to occupy a cold bleak hill, and sleep under frost and snow, without clothes or blankets. However, although they seem to have little feeling for the naked and distressed soldiers, I feel superabundantly for them, and from my soul, I pity those miseries, which it is neither in my power to relieve or prevent.

It is for these reasons, therefore, that I have dwelt upon the subject; and it adds not a little to my other difficulties and distress to find that much more is expected of me than is possible to be performed, and that upon the ground of safety and policy I am obliged to conceal the true state of the army from public view, and thereby expose myself to detraction and calumny. The honorable committee of Congress went from camp fully possessed of my sentiments respecting the establishment of this army, the necessity of auditors of accounts, the appointment of officers, and new arrangements. I have no need, therefore, to be prolix upon these subjects, but I refer to the committee. I shall add a word or two to show, first, the necessity of some better provision for binding the officers by the tie of interest to the service, as no day or scarce an hour passes without the offer of a resigned commission.

GEORGE WASHINGTON

MAN

William Shakespeare

What a piece of work is a man! how noble in reason! how infinite in faculty! in form and moving how express and admirable! in action how like an angel! in apprehension how like a god! the beauty of the world! the paragon of animals!

(From Hamlet)

IF I SHOULD DIE TONIGHT

Arabella Eugenia Smith

If I should die tonight,
My friends would look upon my quiet face
Before they laid it in its resting place,
And deem that death had left it almost fair;

And laying snow-white flowers against my hair,
Would smooth it down with tearful tenderness,
And fold my hands with lingering caress;
Poor hands, so empty and so cold tonight!

If I should die tonight,
My friends would call to mind with loving thought,
Some kindly deed the icy hand had wrought,
Some gentle word the frozen lips had said;
Errands on which the willing feet had sped.
The memory of my selfishness and pride,
My hasty words, would all be put aside,
And so I should be loved and mourned tonight.

If I should die tonight,
Even hearts estranged would turn once more to me,
Recalling other days remorsefully.
The eyes that chill me with averted glance
Would look upon me as of yore, perchance,
Would soften in the old, familiar way;
For who could war with dumb, unconscious clay?
So I might rest, forgiven of all, tonight.

O friends, I pray tonight,
Keep not your kisses for my dead, cold brow.
The way is lonely; let me feel them now.
Think gently of me; I am travel-worn;
My faltering feet are pierced with many a thorn.
Forgive, O hearts estranged, forgive, I plead!
When dreamless rest is mine I shall not need
The tenderness for which I long tonight.

LORD RANDAL

Anonymous

"O where ha'e ye been, Lord Randal, my son?
O where ha'e ye been, my handsome young man?"
"I ha'e been to the wild wood; mother make my bed soon;
For I'm weary wi' hunting, and fain wald lie down."

"Where gat ye your dinner, Lord Randal, my son?
Where gat ye your dinner, my handsome young man?"
"I dined wi' my true-love; mother make my bed soon;
For I'm weary wi' hunting, and fain wald lie down."

"What gat ye your dinner, Lord Randal, my son?
What gat ye your dinner, my handsome young man?"
"I gat eels boild in broo'; mother, make my bed soon;
For I'm weary wi' hunting, and fain wald lie down."

"What became of your bloodhounds, Lord Randal, my son?
What became of your bloodhounds, my handsome young man?"
"O they swelled and they died; mother, make my bed soon;
For I'm weary wi' hunting, and fain wald lie down."

"O I fear ye are poisoned, Lord Randal, my son!
I fear ye are poisoned, my handsome young man!"
"Oh yes! I am poisoned; mother, make my bed soon;
For I'm sick at the heart, and I fain wald lie down."

THE RAVEN

Edgar Allan Poe

Once upon a midnight dreary, while I pondered, weak and weary
Over many a quaint and curious volume of forgotten lore—
While I nodded, nearly napping, suddenly there came a tapping
As of some one gently rapping, rapping at my chamber door.
" 'Tis some visitor," I muttered, "tapping at my chamber door:
    Only this, and nothing more."

Ah, distinctly I remember, it was in the bleak December,
And each separate dying ember wrought its ghost upon the floor
Eagerly I wished the morrow; vainly I had sought to borrow
From my books surcease of sorrow—sorrow for the lost Lenore—
For the rare and radiant maiden whom the angels name Lenore—
    Nameless here for evermore.

And the silken, sad, uncertain rustling of each purple curtain,
Thrilled me—filled me with fantastic terrors never felt before;
So that now, to still the beating of my heart, I stood repeating,
" 'Tis some visitor entreating entrance at my chamber door—
Some late visitor entreating entrance at my chamber door:
    This it is, and nothing more."

Presently my soul grew stronger: hesitating then no longer,
"Sir," said I, "or Madam, truly your forgiveness I implore;
But the fact is, I was napping, and so gently you came rapping,
And so faintly you came tapping, tapping at my chamber door,
That I scarce was sure I heard you"—here I opened wide the
    door;—
        Darkness there, and nothing more!

Deep into that darkness peering, long I stood there, wondering,
    fearing,
Doubting, dreaming dreams no mortal ever dared to dream before;
But the silence was unbroken, and the darkness gave no token,
And the only word there spoken was the whispered word, "Le-
    nore!"
This I whispered, and an echo murmured back the word "Le-
    nore!"
        Merely this, and nothing more.

Back into the chamber turning, all my soul within me burning,
Soon again I heard a tapping, somewhat louder than before.
"Surely," said I, "surely that is something at my window-lattice;
Let me see then what thereat is, and this mystery explore—
Let my heart be still a moment, and this mystery explore;—
        'Tis the wind, and nothing more!"

Open here I flung the shutter, when, with many a flirt and flutter,
In there stepped a stately Raven of the saintly days of yore.
Not the least obeisance made he; not an instant stopped or stayed
    he;
But, with mien of lord or lady, perched above my chamber door—
Perched upon a bust of Pallas, just above my chamber door—
        Perched, and sat, and nothing more.

Then this ebony bird beguiling my sad fancy into smiling,
By the grave and stern decorum of the countenance it wore,
"Though thy crest be shorn and shaven, thou," I said, "art sure no
    craven,
Ghastly, grim, and ancient Raven, wandering from the nightly
    shore!
Tell me what thy lordly name is on the night's Plutonian shore!"
        Quoth the Raven, "Nevermore!"

Much I marveled this ungainly fowl to hear discourse so plainly,
Though its answer little meaning—little relevancy bore:

For we cannot help agreeing that no living human being
Ever yet was blessed with seeing bird above his chamber door—
Bird or beast upon the sculptured bust above his chamber door,
　　　　With such name as "Nevermore!"

But the Raven, sitting lonely on the placid bust, spoke only
That one word, as if his soul in that one word he did outpour.
Nothing further then he uttered—not a feather then he fluttered—
Till I scarcely more than muttered, "Other friends have flown be-
　　　fore—
On the morrow *he* will leave me, as my hopes have flown before."
　　　　Then the bird said, "Nevermore!"

Startled at the stillness broken by reply so aptly spoken,
"Doubtless," said I, "what it utters is its only stock and store,
Caught from some unhappy master, whom unmerciful Disaster
Followed fast and followed faster, till his songs one burden bore—
Till the dirges of his Hope one melancholy burden bore
　　　　Of 'Never—nevermore.'"

But the Raven still beguiling all my sad soul into smiling,
Straight I wheeled a cushioned seat in front of bird, and bust, and
　　　door;
Then, upon the velvet sinking, I betook myself to linking
Fancy unto fancy, thinking what this ominous bird of yore—
What this grim, ungainly, ghastly, gaunt, and ominous bird of
　　　yore—
　　　　Meant in croaking "Nevermore!"

This I sat engaged in guessing, but no syllable expressing
To the fowl whose fiery eyes now burned into my bosom's core
This and more I sat divining, with my head at ease reclining
On the cushion's velvet lining that the lamplight gloated o'er,
But whose velvet violet lining, with the lamplight gloating o'er,
　　　　She shall press, ah! nevermore!

Then methought the air grew denser, perfumed from an unseen
　　　censer,
Swung by seraphim, whose footfalls tinkled on the tufted floor.
"Wretch," I cried, "thy God hath lent thee—by these angels he
　　　hath sent thee
Respite—respite and nepenthe from the memories of Lenore!
Quaff, Oh, quaff this kind nepenthe, and forget this lost Lenore!"
　　　　Quoth the raven, "Nevermore!"

"Prophet!" said I, "thing of evil!—prophet still, if bird or devil!
Whether tempter sent, or whether tempest tossed thee here ashore,
Desolate yet all undaunted, on this desert land enchanted—
On this home by horrors haunted—tell me truly, I implore—
Is there—*is* there balm in Gilead?—tell me—tell me, I implore!"
      Quoth the raven, "Nevermore!"

"Prophet!" said I, "thing of evil!—prophet still, if bird or devil!
By that heaven that bends above us—by that God we both adore,
Tell this soul with sorrow laden if, within the distant Aidenn,
It shall clasp a sainted maiden, whom the angels name Lenore—
Clasp a fair and radiant maiden, whom the angels name Lenore!"
      Quoth the raven, "Nevermore!"

"Be that word our sign of parting, bird or fiend!" I shrieked, up-
   starting—
"Get thee back into the tempest and the night's Plutonian shore!
Leave no black plume as a token of that lie thy soul hath spoken!
Leave my loneliness unbroken!—quit the bust above my door!
Take thy beak from out my heart, and take thy form from off my
   door!"
      Quoth the raven, "Nevermore!"

And the raven, never flitting, still is sitting, still is sitting
On the pallid bust of Pallas, just above my chamber door;
And his eyes have all the seeming of a demon that is dreaming,
And the lamplight o'er him streaming throws his shadow on the
   floor;
And my soul from out that shadow that lies floating on the floor
      Shall be lifted—*nevermore!*

THE MARINES' HYMN

Anonymous

From the Halls of Montezuma
To the shores of Tripoli
We fight our country's battles
On the land as on the sea.
First to fight for right and freedom
And to keep our honor clean;
We are proud to claim the title
Of United States Marine.

Our flag's unfurled to every breeze
From dawn to setting sun;
We have fought in every clime and place
Where we could take a gun;
In the snow of far-off Northern lands
And in sunny tropic scenes;
You will find us always on the job
The United States Marines.

Here's health to you and to our Corps
Which we are proud to serve;
In many a strife we've fought for life
And never lost our nerve;
If the Army and the Navy
Ever look on Heaven's scenes,
They will find the streets are guarded
By United States Marines.

PIPPA'S SONG

Robert Browning

The year's at the spring
The day's at the morn;
Morning's at seven;
The hillside's dew pearled;
The lark's on the wing;
The snail's on the thorn;
God's in his heaven—
All's right with the world!
(From Pippa Passes)

WHEN YOU AND I WERE YOUNG, MAGGIE

George W. Johnson

I wander'd today to the hill, Maggie,
To watch the scene below,
The creek and the creaking old mill, Maggie,
As we used to, long ago.
The green grove is gone from the hill, Maggie,
Where first the daisies sprung,

The creaking old mill is still, Maggie,
Since you and I were young,
And now we are aged and gray, Maggie,
And the trials of life nearly done;
Let us sing of the days that are gone, Maggie,
When you and I were young.

THE SIEGE OF BELGRADE

Alaric Alexander Watts

An Austrian army, awfully arrayed,
Boldly by battery besieged Belgrade.
Cossack commanders cannonading come,
Dealing destruction's devastating doom.
Every endeavor engineers essay,
For fame, for fortune fighting—furious fray!
Generals 'gainst general grapple—gracious God!
How honors Heaven heroic hardihood!
Infuriate, indiscriminate in ill,
Kindred kill kinsmen, kinsmen kindred kill.
Labor low levels longest, loftiest lines;
Men march 'mid mounds, 'mid moles, 'mid murderous mines;
Now noxious, noisy numbers nothing, naught
Of outward obstacles, opposing ought;
Poor patriots, partly purchased, partly pressed,
Quite quaking, quickly "Quarter! Quarter!" quest.
Reason returns, religious right redounds,
Suwarrow stops such sanguinary sounds.
Truce to thee, Turkey! Triumph to thy train,
Unwise, unjust, unmerciful Ukraine!
Vanish, vain victory! vanish, victory vain!
Why wish we warfare? Wherefore welcome were
Xerxes, Ximenes, Xanthus, Xavier?
Yield, yield, ye youths! ye yeomen, yield your yell!
Zeus', Zarpater's, Zoroaster's zeal,
Attracting all, arms against acts appeal!

* * *

When Greeks joined Greeks, then was the tug of war.
(From Nathaniel Lee's Alexander the Great)

TO AN ATHLETE DYING YOUNG

A. E. Housman

The time you won your town the race
We chaired you through the market-place;
Man and boy stood cheering by,
And home we brought you shoulder-high.

To-day, the road all runners come,
Shoulder-high we bring you home,
And set you at your threshold down,
Townsman of a stiller town.

Smart lad, to slip betimes away
From fields where glory does not stay
And early though the laurel grows,
It withers quicker than the rose.

Eyes the shady night has shut
Cannot see the record cut,
And silence sounds no worse than cheers
After earth has stopped the ears:

Now you will not swell the rout
Of lads that wore their honours out,
Runners whom renown outran
And the name died before the man.

So set, before its echoes fade,
The fleet foot on the sill of shade,
And hold to the low lintel up
The still-defended challenge-cup.

And round that early-laurelled head
Will flock to gaze the strengthless dead,
And find unwithered on its curls
The garland briefer than a girl's.

* * *

You can always get the truth from an American statesman after
he has turned seventy, or given up all hope for the Presidency.
—Wendell Phillips

EASTER MORNING

Holy Bible, Matthew 28:1–10

1 In the end of the sabbath, as it began to dawn toward the first day of the week, came Mary Magdalene and the other Mary to see the sepulchre.

2 And, behold, there was a great earthquake: for the angel of the Lord descended from heaven, and came and rolled back the stone from the door, and sat upon it.

3 His countenance was like lightning, and his raiment white as snow:

4 And for fear of him the keepers did shake, and became as dead men.

5 And the angel answered and said unto the women, Fear not ye: for I know that ye seek Jesus, which was crucified.

6 He is not here: for he is risen, as he said. Come, see the place where the Lord lay.

7 And go quickly, and tell his disciples that he is risen from the dead; and, behold, he goeth before you into Galilee; there shall ye see him: lo, I have told you.

8 And they departed quickly from the sepulchre with fear and great joy; and did run to bring his disciples word.

9 And as they went to tell his disciples, behold, Jesus met them, saying, All hail. And they came and held him by the feet, and worshipped him.

10 Then said Jesus unto them, Be not afraid: go tell my brethren that they go into Galilee, and there shall they see me.

THE MAN HE KILLED

Thomas Hardy

"Had he and I but met
By some old ancient inn,
We should have sat us down to wet
Right many a nipperkin!

"But ranged as infantry,
And staring face to face,
I shot at him as he at me,
And killed him in his place.

"I shot him dead because—
Because he was my foe,
Just so: my foe of course he was;
That's clear enough; although

"He thought he'd 'list, perhaps,
Off-hand-like—just as I—
Was out of work—had sold his traps—
No other reason why.

"Yes; quaint and curious war is!
You shoot a fellow down
You'd treat, if met where any bar is,
Or help to half-a-crown."

BREATHES THERE THE MAN WITH SOUL SO DEAD

Sir Walter Scott

Breathes there the man with soul so dead
Who never to himself hath said,
This is my own, my native land!
Whose heart hath ne'er within him burned,
As home his footsteps he hath turned
From wandering on a foreign strand?
If such there breathe, go, mark him well;
For him no minstrel raptures swell;
High though his titles, proud his name,
Boundless his wealth as wish can claim,
Despite those titles, power, and pelf,
The wretch, concentred all in self,
Living, shall forfeit fair renown,
And, doubly dying, shall go down
To the vile dust from whence he sprung,
Unwept, unhonored, and unsung.
(From The Lay of the Last Minstrel)

* * *

Now that is the wisdom of a man, in every instance of his labour
to hitch his wagon to a star, and see his chore done by the gods
themselves.

—R. W. Emerson

THE WEARIN' O' THE GREEN

Anonymous

Oh, Paddy dear! and did ye hear the news that's goin' round?
The shamrock is forbid by law to grow on Irish ground!
No more St. Patrick's day we'll keep; his color can't be seen,
For there's a cruel law ag'n the Wearin' o' the Green!

I met with Napper Tandy, and he took me by the hand,
And he said, "How's poor ould Ireland, and how does she stand?"
"She's the most distressful country that ever yet was seen,
For they're hanging men and women there for the Wearin' o' the
  Green."

An' if the color we must wear is England's cruel red,
Let it remind us of the blood that Ireland has shed;
Then pull the shamrock from your hat, and throw it on the sod,
An' never fear, 'twill take root there, though under foot 'tis trod.

When law can stop the blades of grass from growin' as they grow,
An' when the leaves in summer time their color dare not show,
Then I will change the color, too, I wear in my caubeen;
But till that day, plaise God, I'll stick to the Wearin' o' the Green.

REQUIESCAT

Oscar Wilde

> Tread lightly, she is near
>   Under the snow,
> Speak gently, she can hear
>   The daisies grow.
>
> All her bright golden hair
>   Tarnished with rust,
> She that was young and fair
>   Fallen to dust.
>
> Lily-like, white as snow,
>   She hardly knew
> She was a woman, so
>   Sweetly she grew.

Coffin-board, heavy stone,
  Lie on her breast,
I vex my heart alone,
  She is at rest.

Peace, Peace, she cannot hear
  Lyre or sonnet,
All my life's buried here,
  Heap earth upon it.

A DISSERTATION UPON ROAST PIG

Charles Lamb

MANKIND, says a Chinese manuscript, which my friend M——
was obliging enough to read and explain to me, for the first
seventy thousand ages ate their meat raw, clawing or biting it
from the living animal, just as they do in Abyssinia to this day.
This period is not obscurely hinted at by their great Confucius in
the second chapter of his Mundane Mutations, where he desig-
nates a kind of golden age by the term Cho-fang, literally the
Cooks' Holiday. The manuscript goes on to say, that the art of
roasting, or rather broiling (which I take to be the elder brother)
was accidentally discovered in the manner following. The swine-
herd Ho-ti, having gone out into the woods one morning, as his
manner was, to collect mast for his hogs, left his cottage in the care
of his eldest son, Bo-bo, a great lubberly boy, who being fond of
playing with fire, as younkers of his age commonly are, let some
sparks escape into a bundle of straw, which kindling quickly,
spread the conflagration over every part of their poor mansion,
till it was reduced to ashes. Together with the cottage, (a sorry
antediluvian make-shift of a building, you may think it,) what was
of much more importance, a fine litter of new-farrowed pigs, no
less than nine in number, perished. China pigs have been esteemed
a luxury all over the East, from the remotest period that we read
of. Bo-bo was in the utmost consternation, as you may think, not
so much for the sake of the tenement, which his father and he
could easily build up again with a few dry branches, and the
labour of an hour or two at any time, as for the loss of the pigs.
While he was thinking what he should say to his father, and wringing his hands over the smoking remnants of one of those untimely

sufferers, an odour assailed his nostrils, unlike any scent which he had before experienced. What could it proceed from? Not from the burnt cottage: he had smelt that smell before; indeed this was by no means the first accident of the kind which had occurred through the negligence of this unlucky young fire-brand. Much less did it resemble that of any known herb, weed, or flower. A premonitory moistening at the same time overflowed his nether lip. He knew not what to think. He next stooped down to feel the pig, if there were any signs of life in it. He burnt his fingers, and to cool them he applied them in his booby fashion to his mouth. Some of the crumbs of the scorched skin had come away with his fingers, and for the first time in his life, (in the world's life indeed, for before him no man had known it,) he tasted *crackling!* Again he felt and fumbled at the pig. It did not burn him so much now, still he licked his fingers from a sort of habit. The truth at length broke into his slow understanding, that it was the pig that smelt so, and the pig that tasted so delicious; and surrendering himself up to the new-born pleasure, he fell to tearing up whole handfuls of the scorched skin with the flesh next it, and was cramming it down his throat in his beastly fashion, when his sire entered amid the smoking rafters, armed with retributory cudgel, and finding how affairs stood, began to rain blows upon the young rogue's shoulders as thick as hail-stones, which Bo-bo heeded not any more than if they had been flies. The tickling pleasure which he experienced in his lower regions had rendered him quite callous to any inconveniences he might feel in those remote quarters. His father might lay on, but he could not beat him from his pig, till he had fairly made an end of it, when, becoming a little more sensible of his situation, something like the following dialogue ensued:—

"You graceless whelp, what have you got there devouring? Is it not enough that you have burnt me down three houses with your dog's tricks, and be hanged to you! but you must be eating fire, and I know not what. What have you got there, I say?"

"O father, the pig, the pig! do come and taste how nice the burnt pig eats."

The ears of Ho-ti tingled with horror. He cursed his son, and he cursed himself that ever he should beget a son that should eat burnt pig.

Bo-bo, whose scent was wonderfully sharpened since morning, soon raked out another pig, and fairly rending it asunder, thrust the lesser half by main force into the fists of Ho-ti, still shouting out, "Eat, eat, eat the burnt pig, father, only taste—O Lord!"—

with such-like barbarous ejaculations, cramming all the while as if he would choke.

Ho-ti trembled every joint while he grasped the abominable thing, wavering whether he should not put his son to death for an unnatural young monster, when the crackling scorching his fingers, as it had done his son's, and applying the same remedy to them, he in his turn tasted some of its flavour, which, make what sour mouths he would for a pretence, proved not altogether displeasing to him. In conclusion, (for the manuscript here is a little tedious,) both father and son fairly sat down to the mess, and never left off till they had despatched all that remained of the litter.

Bo-bo was strictly enjoined not to let the secret escape, for the neighbours would certainly have stoned them for a couple of abominable wretches, who could think of improving upon the good meat which God had sent them. Nevertheless, strange stories got about. It was observed that Ho-ti's cottage was burnt down now more frequently than ever. Nothing but fires from this time forward. Some would break out in broad day, others in the night time. As often as the sow farrowed, so sure was the house of Ho-ti to be in a blaze; and Ho-ti himself, which was the more remarkable, instead of chastising his son, seemed to grow more indulgent to him than ever. At length they were watched, the terrible mystery discovered, and father and son summoned to take their trial at Pekin, then an inconsiderable assize town. Evidence was given, the obnoxious food itself produced in court, and verdict about to be pronounced, when the foreman of the jury begged that some of the burnt pig, of which the culprits stood accused, might be handed into the box. He handled it, and they all handled it; and burning their fingers, as Bo-bo and his father had done before them, and nature prompting to each of them the same remedy, against the face of all the facts, and the clearest charge which judge had ever given,—to the surprise of the whole court, townsfolk, strangers, reporters, and all present—without leaving the box, or any manner of consultation whatever, they brought in a simultaneous verdict of Not Guilty.

The judge, who was a shrewd fellow, winked at the manifest iniquity of the decision: and when the court was dismissed, went privily and bought up all the pigs that could be had for love or money. In a few days his lordship's town-house was observed to be on fire. The thing took wing, and now there was nothing to be seen but fire in every direction. Fuel and pigs grew enormously dear all over the district. The insurance-offices, one and all, shut up shop. People built slighter and slighter every day, until it was feared that the very science of architecture would in no long time be lost to the world. Thus this custom of firing houses continued, till in process of time, says my manuscript, a sage arose, like our Locke, who made a discovery that the flesh of swine, or indeed of any other animal, might be cooked (*burnt*, as they called it,) without the necessity of consuming a whole house to dress it. Then first began the rude form of a gridiron. Roasting by the string or spit came in a century or two later, I forget in whose dynasty. By such slow degrees, concludes the manuscript, do the most useful and seemingly the most obvious, arts make their way among mankind.

Without placing too implicit faith in the account above given, it must be agreed that if a worthy pretext for so dangerous an experiment as setting houses on fire (especially in these days) could be assigned in favour of any culinary object, that pretext and excuse might be found in ROAST PIG.

Of all the delicacies in the whole *mundus edibilis,* I will maintain it to be the most delicate—*princeps obsoniorum.*

I speak not of your grown porkers—things between pig and pork, those hobbydehoys—but a young and tender suckling, under a moon old, guiltless as yet of the sty, with no original speck of the *amor immunditiae,* the herditary failing of the first parent, yet manifest—his voice as yet not broken, but something between a childish treble and a grumble—the mild fore-runner or *praeludium* of a grunt.

He must be roasted. I am not ignorant that our ancestors ate them seethed, or boiled; but what a sacrifice of the exterior tegument!

There is no flavour comparable, I will contend, to that of the crisp, tawny, well-watched, not over-roasted, *crackling,* as it is well called. The very teeth are invited to their share of the pleasure at this banquet in overcoming the coy, brittle resistance—with the adhesive oleaginous—O call it not fat! but an indefinable sweetness growing up to it—the tender blossoming of fat—fat cropped in the bud—taken in the shoot—in the first innocence—the cream and quintessence of the child-pig's yet pure food—the lean, no lean, but a kind of animal manna—or, rather, fat and lean (if it must be so) so blended and running into each other, that both together make but one embrosian result, or common substance.

Behold him, while he is "doing"—it seemeth rather a refreshing warmth than a scorching heat that he is so passive to. How equably he twirleth round the string!—Now he is just done. To see the extreme sensibility of that tender age! he hath wept out his pretty eyes—radiant jellies—shooting stars.—

See him in the dish, his second cradle, how meek he lieth!—Wouldst thou have had this innocent grow up to the grossness and indocility which too often accompany maturer swine-hood? Ten to one he would have proved a glutton, a sloven, an obstinate, disagreeable animal, wallowing in all manner of filthy conversation. From these sins he is happily snatched away.

> Ere sin could blight or sorrow fade,
> Death came with timely care.

His memory is odouriferous. No clown curseth, while his stomach half rejecteth, the rank bacon; no coal-heaver bolteth him in reeking sausages; he hath a fair sepulchre in the grateful stomach of the judicious epicure, and for such a tomb might be content to die. He is the best of sapors. Pine-apple is great. She is indeed almost too transcendent,—a delight, if not sinful, yet so like to sinning that really a tender-conscienced person would do well to pause,—too ravishing for mortal taste, she woundeth and excoriateth the lips that approach her. Like lovers' kisses, she biteth: she is a pleasure bordering on pain from the fierceness and insanity of her relish; but she stoppeth at the palate; she meddleth not with the appetite; and the coarsest hunger might barter her consistently for a mutton-chop.

Pig (let me speak his praise) is no less provocative of the appetite than he is satisfactory to the criticalness of the censorious palate. The strong man may batten on him, and the weakling refuseth not his mild juices.

Unlike to mankind's mixed characters, a bundle of virtues and vices, inexplicably inter-twisted, and not to be unravelled without hazard, he is good throughout. No part of him is better or worse than another. He helpeth, as far as his little means extend, all around. He is the least envious of banquets. He is all neighbours' fare.

I am one of those who freely and ungrudgingly impart a share of the good things of this life which fall to their lot (few as mine are in this kind) to a friend, I protest I take as great an interest in my friend's pleasures, his relishes, and proper satisfactions, as in mine own. "Presents," I often say, "endear Absents." Hares, pheasants, partridges, snipes, barn-door chickens, (those "tame villatic fowl,") capons, plovers, brawn, barrels of oysters, I dispense as freely as I receive them. I love to taste them, as it were, upon the tongue of my friend. But a stop must be put somewhere. One would not, like Lear, "give everything." I make my stand upon pig. Methinks it is an ingratitude to the giver of all good flavours to extra-domiciliate, or send out of the house slightingly (under pretext of friendship, or I know not what,) a blessing so particularly adapted, predestined, I may say, to my individual palate.—It argues an insensibility.

I remember a touch of conscience in this kind at school. My good old aunt, who never parted from me at the end of a holiday without stuffing a sweetmeat, or some nice thing into my pocket, had dismissed me one evening with a smoking plum-cake, fresh from the oven. In my way to school (it was over London Bridge) a grey-headed old beggar saluted me. (I have no doubt, at this time of day, that he was a counterfeit.) I had no pence to console him with, and in the vanity of self-denial, and the very coxcombry of charity, schoolboy-like, I made him a present of the whole cake. I walked on a little, buoyed up, as one is on such occasions, with a sweet soothing of self-satisfaction; but before I had got to the end of the bridge my better feelings returned, and I burst into tears, thinking how ungrateful I had been to my good aunt, to go and give her good gift away to a stranger that I had never seen before, and who might be a bad man for aught I knew; and then I thought of the pleasure my aunt would be taking in thinking that I (I myself, and not another) would eat her nice cake. And what should I say to her the next time I saw her?—how naughty I was to part with her pretty present!—and the odour of that spicy cake came back upon my recollection, and the pleasure and the curiosity I had taken in seeing her make it, and her joy when she sent it to the oven, and how disappointed she would feel that I had never had a bit of it in my mouth at last. And I blamed my impertinent spirit of alms-giving, and out-of-place hypocrisy of goodness; and above all, I wished never to see the face again of that insidious, good-for-nothing, old grey impostor.

Our ancestors were nice in their method of sacrificing these tender victims. We read of pigs whipt to death with something of a shock, as we hear of any other obsolete custom. The age of discipline is gone by, or it would be curious to inquire (in a philosophical light merely) what effect this process might have towards intenerating and dulcifying a substance naturally so mild and dulcet as the flesh of young pigs. It looks like refining a violet. Yet we should be cautious, while we condemn the inhumanity how we censure the wisdom of the practice. It might impart a gusto.

I remember an hypothesis, argued upon by the young students when I was at St. Omer's, and maintained with much learning and pleasantry on both sides, "Whether, supposing that the flavour of a pig who obtained his death by whipping (*per flagellationem extremam*) superadded a pleasure upon the palate of a man more intense than any possible suffering we can conceive in the animal, is man justified in using that method of putting the animal to death?" I forget the decision.

His sauce should be considered: decidedly, a few bread crumbs, done up with his liver and brains, and a dash of mild sage. But banish, dear Mrs. Cook, I beseech you, the whole onion tribe. Barbecue your whole hogs to your palate, steep them in shalots, stuff them out with plantations of the rank and guilty garlic; you cannot poison them, or make them stronger than they are; but consider, he is a weakling—a flower.

THE HAND THAT ROCKS THE CRADLE IS THE HAND THAT RULES THE WORLD

William Ross Wallace

Blessings on the hand of women!
Angels guard its strength and grace,
In the palace, cottage, hovel,
Oh, no matter where the place;
Would that never storms assailed it,
Rainbows ever gently curled;
For the hand that rocks the cradle
Is the hand that rules the world.

Infancy's the tender fountain,
Power may with beauty flow,
Mother's first to guide the streamlets,
From them souls unresting grow—
Grow on for the good or evil,
Sunshine streamed or evil hurled;
For the hand that rocks the cradle
Is the hand that rules the world.

Woman, how divine your mission
Here upon our natal sod!
Keep, oh, keep the young heart open
Always to the breath of God!

All true trophies of the ages
Are from mother-love impearled;
For the hand that rocks the cradle
Is the hand that rules the world.

Blessings on the hand of women!
Fathers, sons, and daughters cry,
And the sacred song is mingled
With the worship in the sky—
Mingles where no tempest darkens,
Rainbows evermore are hurled;
For the hand that rocks the cradle
Is the hand that rules the world.

FROM IN MEMORIAM

Alfred, Lord Tennyson

Strong Son of God, immortal Love,
    Whom we, that have not seen thy face,
    By faith, and faith alone, embrace,
Believing where we cannot prove;

Thine are these orbs of light and shade;
    Thou madest Life in man and brute;
    Thou madest Death; and lo, thy foot
Is on the skull which thou hast made.

Thou wilt not leave us in the dust;
    Thou madest man, he knows not why,
    He thinks he was not made to die;
And thou hast made him: thou art just.

Thou seemest human and divine,
    The highest, holiest manhood, thou.
    Our wills are ours, we know not how;
Our wills are ours, to make them thine.

Our little systems have their day;
    They have their day and cease to be;
    They are but broken lights of thee,
And thou, O Lord, art more than they.

We have but faith: we cannot know,
    For knowledge is of things we see;
    And yet we trust it comes from thee,
A beam in darkness: let it grow.

Let knowledge grow from more to more,
    But more of reverence in us dwell;
    That mind and soul, according well,
May make one music as before,

But vaster. We are fools and slight;
    We mock thee when we do not fear:
    But help thy foolish ones to bear;
Help thy vain worlds to bear thy light.

Forgive what seem'd my sin in me,
    What seem'd my worth since I began;
    For merit lives from man to man,
And not from man, O Lord, to thee.

Forgive my grief for one removed,
    Thy creature, whom I found so fair.
    I trust he lives in thee, and there
I find him worthier to be loved.

Forgive these wild and wandering cries,
    Confusions of a wasted youth;
    Forgive them where they fail in truth,
And in thy wisdom make me wise.

HAMLET CONTEMPLATES SUICIDE

William Shakespeare

To be, or not to be; that is the question;
Whether 'tis nobler in the mind to suffer
The slings and arrows of outrageous fortune,
Or to take arms against a sea of troubles,
And by opposing end them. To die: to sleep;
No more; and by a sleep to say we end
The heart-ache and the thousand natural shocks
That flesh is heir to; 'tis a consummation

Devoutly to be wished. To die; to sleep;
To sleep: perchance to dream; aye, there's the rub;
For in that sleep of death what dreams may come
When we have shuffled off this mortal coil,
Must give us pause: there's the respect
That makes calamity of so long life;
For who would bear the whips and scorns of time,
The oppressor's wrong, the proud man's contumely,
The pangs of despised love, the law's delay,
The insolence of office, and the spurns
That patient merit of the unworthy takes,
When he himself might his quietus make
With a bare bodkin? Who would fardels bear,
To grunt and sweat under a weary life,
But that the dread of something after death—
The undiscover'd country from whose bourn
No traveler returns—puzzles the will
And makes us rather bear those ills we have
Than fly to others that we know not of?
Thus conscience does make cowards of us all,
And thus the native hue of resolution
Is sicklied o'er with the pale cast of thought,
And enterprises of great pith and moment
With this regard their currents turn awry,
And lose the name of action.

(From Hamlet)

SONG

William Watson

April, April,
Laugh thy girlish laughter;
Then, the moment after,
Weep thy girlish tears,
April, that mine ears
Like a lover greetest,
If I tell thee, sweetest,
All my hopes and fears.
April, April,
Laugh thy golden laughter,
But, the moment after,
Weep thy golden tears!

329

EULOGY AT HIS BROTHER'S FUNERAL

Robert G. Ingersoll

DEAR FRIENDS: I am going to do that which the dead oft promised he would do for me.

The loved and loving brother, husband, father, friend, died where manhood's morning almost touches noon, and while the shadows still were falling toward the west.

He had not passed on life's highway the stone that marks the highest point; but being weary for a moment, he lay down by the wayside, and using his burden for a pillow, fell into that dreamless sleep that kisses down his eyelids still. While yet in love with life and raptured with the world, he passed to silence and pathetic dust.

Yet, after all, it may be best, just in the happiest, sunniest hour of all the voyage, while eager winds are kissing every sail, to dash against the unseen rock, and in an instant hear the billows roar above a sunken ship. For whether in mid-sea or 'mong the breakers of the farther shore, a wreck at last must mark the end of each and all. And every life, no matter if its every hour is rich with love and every moment jeweled with a joy, will, at its close, become a tragedy as sad and deep and dark as can be woven of the warp and woof of mystery and death.

This brave and tender man in every storm of life was oak and rock; but in the sunshine he was vine and flower. He was the friend of all heroic souls. He climbed the heights, and left all superstitions far below, while on his forehead fell the golden dawning of the grander day.

He loved the beautiful, and was with color, form and music touched to tears. He sided with the weak, the poor, the wronged, and lovingly gave alms. With loyal heart and with the purest hands he faithfully discharged all public trusts.

He was a worshiper of liberty, a friend of the oppressed. A thousand times I have heard him quote these words: *"For Justice all places a temple, and all seasons, summer."* He believed that happiness was the only good, reason the only torch, justice the only worship, humanity the only religion, and love the only priest. He added to the sum of human joy; and were every one to whom he did some loving service to bring a blossom to his grave, he would sleep tonight beneath a wilderness of flowers.

Life is a narrow vale between the cold and barren **peaks of two** eternities. We strive in vain to look beyond the heights. We cry aloud, and the only answer is the echo of our wailing cry. From the voiceless lips of the unreplying dead there comes no word; but in the night of death hope sees a star and listening love can hear the rustle of a wing.

He who sleeps here, when dying, mistaking the approach of death for the return of health, whispered with his latest breath, "I am better now." Let us believe, in spite of doubts and dogmas, of fears and tears, that these dear words are true of all the countless dead.

The record of a generous life runs like a vine around the memory of our dead, and every sweet, unselfish act is now a perfumed flower.

And now, to you, who have been chosen, from among the many men he loved, to do the last sad office for the dead, we give his sacred dust.

Speech cannot contain our love. There was, there is, no gentler, stronger, manlier man.

THE LEAK IN THE DIKE

Phoebe Cary

The good dame looked from her cottage
    At the close of the pleasant day,
And cheerily called to her little son
    Outside the door at play:
"Come, Peter! come! I want you to go,
    While there is light to see,
To the hut of the blind old man who lives
    Across the dike, for me;
And take these cakes I made for him—
    They are hot and smoking yet;
You have time enough to go and come
    Before the sun is set."

Then the good wife turned to her labor,
    Humming a simple song,
And thought of her husband working hard
    At the sluices all day long;
And set the turf a-blazing,
    And brought the coarse black bread:
That he might find a fire at night,
    And find the table spread.

331

And Peter left the brother,
   With whom all day he had played,
And the sister who had watched their sports
   In the willow's tender shade;
And told them they'd see him back before
   They saw a star in sight,
Though he wouldn't be afraid to go
   In the very darkest night!
For he was a brave, bright fellow,
   With eye and conscience clear;
He could do whatever a boy might do,
   And he had not learned to fear.
Why, he wouldn't have robbed a bird's nest,
   Nor brought a stork to harm,
Though never a law in Holland
   Had stood to stay his arm!

And now with his face all glowing,
   And eyes as bright as the day
With the thoughts of his pleasant errand,
   He trudged along the way;
And soon his joyous prattle
   Made glad a lonesome place—
Alas! if only the blind old man
   Could have seen that happy face!
Yet he somehow caught the brightness
   Which his voice and presence lent
And he felt the sunshine come and go
   As Peter came and went.

And now, as the day was sinking,
   And the winds began to rise,
The mother looked from her door again,
   Shading her anxious eyes,
And saw the shadows deepen
   And birds to their homes come back,
But never a sign of Peter
   Along the level track.
But she said: "He will come at morning,
   So I need not fret or grieve—
Though it isn't like my boy at all
   To stay without my leave."

But where was the child delaying?
 On the homeward way was he,
And across the dike while the sun was up
 An hour above the sea.
He was stopping now to gather flowers,
 Now listening to the sound,
As the angry waters dashed themselves
 Against their narrow bound.
"Ah! well for us," said Peter,
 "That the gates are good and strong,
And my father tends them carefully,
 Or they would not hold you long!
You're a wicked sea," said Peter;
 "I know why you fret and chafe;
You would like to spoil our lands and homes;
 But our sluices keep you safe."

But hark! through the noise of waters
 Comes a low, clear, trickling sound;
And the child's face pales with terror,
 And his blossoms drop to the ground.
He is up the bank in a moment,
 And, stealing through the sand,
He sees a stream not yet so large
 As his slender, childish hand.

'Tis a leak in the dike!—He is but a boy,
 Unused to fearful scenes;
But, young as he is, he has learned to know
 The dreadful thing that means.
A leak in the dike! The stoutest heart
 Grows faint that cry to hear,
And the bravest man in all the land
 Turns white with mortal fear.
For he knows the smallest leak may grow
 To a flood in a single night;
And he knows the strength of the cruel sea
 When loosed in its angry might.

And the Boy! he has seen the danger
 And, shouting a wild alarm,
He forces back the weight of the sea
 With the strength of his single arm!

He listens for the joyful sound
    Of a footstep passing nigh;
And lays his ear to the ground, to catch
    The answer to his cry.
And he hears the rough winds blowing,
    And the waters rise and fall,
But never an answer comes to him
    Save the echo of his call.
He sees no hope, no succor,
    His feeble voice is lost;
Yet what shall he do but watch and wait
    Though he perish at his post!

So, faintly calling and crying
    Till the sun is under the sea;
Crying and moaning till the stars
    Come out for company;
He thinks of his brother and sister,
    Asleep in their safe warm bed;
He thinks of his father and mother,
    Of himself as dying—and dead;
And of how, when the night is over,
    They must come and find him at last;
But he never thinks he can leave the place
    Where duty holds him fast.

The good dame in the cottage
    Is up and astir with the light,
For the thought of her little Peter
    Has been with her all night.
And now she watches the pathway,
    As yester-eve she had done;
But what does she see so strange and black
    Against the rising sun?
Her neighbors are bearing between them
    Something straight to her door;
Her child is coming home, but not
    As he ever came before!

"He is dead!" she cries, "my darling!"
    And the startled father hears,
And comes and looks the way she looks,
    And fears the thing she fears;

Till a glad shout from the bearers
   Thrills the stricken man and wife—
"Give thanks, for your son has saved our land,
   And God has saved his life!"
So, there in the morning sunshine
   They knelt about the boy;
And every head was bared and bent
   In tearful, reverent joy.

'Tis many a year since then; but still,
   When the sea roars like a flood,
The boys are taught what a boy can do
   Who is brave and true and good;
For every man in that country
   Takes his son by the hand
And tells him of little Peter,
   Whose courage saved the land.

They have many a valiant hero,
   Remembered through the years;
But never one whose name so oft
   Is named with loving tears.
And his deed shall be sung by the cradle,
   And told to the child on the knee,
So long as the dikes of Holland
   Divide the land from the sea!

THAT NANTUCKET LIMERICK, AND WHAT FOLLOWED

There once was a man from Nantucket
Who kept all his cash in a bucket;
   But his daughter, named Nan,
   Ran away with a man,
And as for the bucket, Nantucket.

(Princeton Tiger)

But he followed the pair to Pawtucket—
The man and the girl with the bucket;
   And he said to the man
   He was welcome to Nan,
But as for the bucket, Pawtucket.

(Chicago Tribune)

Then the pair followed Pa to Manhasset,
Where he still held the cash as an asset;
But Nan and the man
Stole the money and ran,
And as for the bucket, Manhasset.

(New York Press)

HOHENLINDEN

Thomas Campbell

On Linden, when the sun was low,
All bloodless lay the untrodden snow;
And dark as winter was the flow
Of Iser, rolling rapidly.

But Linden saw another sight,
When the drum beat at dead of night,
Commanding fires of death to light
The darkness of her scenery.

By torch and trumpet fast arrayed,
Each horseman drew his battle-blade,
And furious every charger neighed
To join the dreadful revelry.

Then shook the hills with thunder riven,
Then rushed the steed to battle driven,
And louder than the bolts of heaven
Far flashed the red artillery.

But redder yet that light shall glow
On Linden's hills of stainèd snow,
And bloodier yet the torrent flow
Of Iser, rolling rapidly.

'Tis morn; but scarce yon level sun
Can pierce the war-clouds, rolling dun
Where furious Frank and fiery Hun
Shout in their sulphurous canopy.

The combat deepens. On, ye brave,
Who rush to glory, or the grave!
Wave, Munich! all thy banners wave,
And charge with all thy chivalry!

Few, few shall part where many meet!
The snow shall be their winding-sheet,
And every turf beneath their feet
Shall be a soldier's sepulchre.

ECHOES

To W. A.

William Ernest Henley

Or ever the knightly years were gone
    With the old world to the grave,
I was a King in Babylon
    And you were a Christian Slave.

I saw, I took, I cast you by,
    I bent and broke your pride.
You loved me well, or I heard them lie,
    But your longing was denied.
Surely I knew that by and by
    You cursed your gods and died.

And a myriad suns have set and shone
    Since then upon the grave
Decreed by the King in Babylon
    To her that had been his Slave.

The pride I trampled is now my scathe,
    For it tramples me again.
The old resentment lasts like death,
    For you love, yet you refrain.
I break my heart on your hard unfaith,
    And I break my heart in vain.

Yet not for an hour do I wish undone
    The deed beyond the grave,
When I was a King in Babylon
    And you were a Virgin Slave.

337

WORDS FOR ARMY BUGLE CALLS

REVEILLE

I can't get 'em up, I can't get 'em up,
I can't get 'em up in the morning.
I can't get 'em up, I can't get 'em up,
I can't get 'em up at all.
The corp'ral's worse than privates;
The sergeant's worse than corp'rals;
Lieutenant's worse than sergeants;
An' the captain's worst of all!

SICK CALL

Come and get your quinine, and come and get your pills;
Oh! Come and get your quinine,
And cure, and cure, all your ills, and cure your ills.

MESS CALL

Soupy, soupy, soupy, without a single bean;
Porky, porky, porky, without a streak of lean;
Coffee, coffee, coffee, without any cream.

STABLE CALL

Come off to the stable, all you who are able,
And give your horses some oats and some corn;
For if you don't do it, your colonel will know it,
And then you will rue it, as sure as you're born.

FATIGUE CALL

With a pick and with a shovel, and with a hoe;
With a sentry at your back you won't say no;
With a pick and with a shovel, and with a hoe,
Down in the ditch you go!

TAPS

Fading light
Dims the sight,
And a star gems the sky,
Gleaming bright,
From a-far,
Drawing nigh,
Falls the night.

Dear one, rest!
In the west
Sable night
Lulls the day on her breast.
Sweet, good night!
Now away
To thy rest.

Love, sweet dreams!
Lo, the beams
Of the light
Fairy moon kiss the streams.
Love, good night!
Ah, so soon!
Peaceful dreams!

SHE IS MORE TO BE PITIED THAN CENSURED

William B. Gray

At the old concert hall on the Bowery
Round the table were seated one night
A crowd of young fellows carousing;
With them life seemed cheerful and bright.
At the very next table was seated
A girl who had fallen to shame.
All the young fellows jeered at her weakness
Till they heard an old woman exclaim:

Chorus:
　　She is more to be pitied than censured,
　　She is more to be helped than despised,
　　She is only a lassie who ventured
　　On life's stormy path ill-advised.
　　Do not scorn her with words fierce and bitter,
　　Do not laugh at her shame and downfall;
　　For a moment just stop and consider
　　That a man was the cause of it all.

There's an old-fashioned church round the corner,
Where the neighbors all gathered one day
While the parson was preaching a sermon
O'er a soul that had just passed away.

'Twas the same wayward girl from the Bow'ry,
Who a life of adventure had led—
Did the clergyman jeer at her downfall?
No—he asked for God's mercy and said: (*Chorus.*)

WHICH SHALL IT BE?

Ethel L. Beers

Which shall it be? Which shall it be?
I look'd at John—John look'd at me
(Dear, patient John, who loves me yet
As well as though my locks were jet);
And when I found that I must speak,
My voice seem'd strangely low and weak:
"Tell me again what Robert said?"
And then I, listening, bent my head.
"This is his letter:

     " 'I will give
A house and land while you shall live,
If, in return, from out your seven,
One child to me for aye is given.' "
I look'd at John's old garments worn,
I thought of all that John had borne
Of poverty, and work, and care,
Which I, though willing, could not share;
I thought of seven mouths to feed,
Of seven little children's need,
And then of this.

     "Come, John," said I,
"We'll choose among them as they lie
Asleep"; so, walking hand in hand,
Dear John and I survey'd our band.
First to the cradle lightly stepp'd,
Where Lilian the baby slept,
A glory 'gainst the pillow white.
Softly the father stooped to lay
His rough hand down in loving way,
When dream or whisper made her stir,
And huskily he said: "Not her!"

We stooped beside the trundle-bed,
And one long ray of lamp-light shed
Athwart the boyish faces there,
In sleep so pitiful and fair;
I saw on Jamie's rough, red cheek,
A tear undried. Ere John could speak,
"He's but a baby, too," said I,
And kissed him as we hurried by.

Pale, patient Robbie's angel face
Still in his sleep bore suffering's trace;
"No, for a thousand crowns, not him,"
He whispered, while our eyes were dim.

Poor Dick! bad Dick! our wayward son,
Turbulent, reckless, idle one—
Could he be spared? "Nay, He who gave,
Bade us befriend him to the grave;
Only a mother's heart can be
Patient enough for such as he;
And so," said John, "I would not dare
To send him from her bedside prayer."

Then stole we softly up above
And knelt by Mary, child of love.
"Perhaps for her 'twould better be,"
I said to John. Quite silently
He lifted up a curl that lay
Across her cheek in willful way,
And shook his head. "Nay, love, not thee,"
The while my heart beat audibly.

Only one more, our eldest lad,
Trusty and truthful, good and glad—
So like his father. "No, John, no—
I can not, will not let him go."

And so we wrote in courteous way.
We could not drive one child away.
And afterward, toil lighter seemed,
Thinking of that of which we dreamed;

Happy, in truth, that not one face
We missed from its accustomed place;
Thankful to work for all the seven,
Trusting the rest to One in heaven!

IF I WERE KING

Justin Huntly McCarthy

If I were king—ah, love, if I were king—
    What tributary nations would I bring
To stoop before your sceptre and to swear
Allegiance to your lips and eyes and hair;
Beneath your feet what treasures I would fling:—
The stars should be your pearls upon a string,
The world a ruby for your finger ring,
And you should have the sun and moon to wear,
            If I were king.
Let these wild dreams and wilder words take wing,
Deep in the woods I hear a shepherd sing
A simple ballad, to a sylvan air,
Of love that ever finds your face more fair;
I could not give you any goodlier thing
            If I were king.

THE HARE AND THE TORTOISE

A Hare insulted a Tortoise upon account of his slowness, and
vainly boasted of her own great speed in running. "Let us make a
match," replied the Tortoise; "I will run with you five miles for
five pounds, and the fox yonder shall be the umpire of the race."
The Hare agreed; and away they both started together. But the
Hare, by reason of her exceeding swiftness, outran the Tortoise to
such a degree, that she made a jest of the matter; and, finding herself a little tired, squatted in a tuft of fern that grew by the way,
and took a nap; thinking that, if the Tortoise went by, she could
at any time fetch him up with all the ease imaginable. In the
meantime while the Tortoise came jogging on with slow but continued motion and the Hare, out of a too great security and confidence of victory, oversleeping herself, the Tortoise arrived at the
end of the race first.

(From Aesop's Fables)

THE CLOUD

Percy Bysshe Shelley

I bring fresh showers for the thirsting flowers,
    From the seas and the streams;
I bear light shade for the leaves when laid
    In their noonday dreams.
From my wings are shaken the dews that waken
    The sweet buds every one,
When rocked to rest on their mother's breast,
    As she dances about the sun.
I wield the flail of the lashing hail,
    And whiten the green plains under,
And then again I dissolve it in rain,
    And laugh as I pass in thunder.

I sift the snow on the mountains below,
    And their great pines groan aghast,
And all the nights 'tis my pillow white,
    While I sleep in the arms of the blast.
Sublime on the towers of my skiey bowers,
    Lightning, my pilot, sits,
In a cavern under is fettered the thunder,
    It struggles and howls at fits;
Over earth and ocean, with gentle motion,
    This pilot is guiding me,
Lured by the love of the genii that move
    In the depths of the purple sea;
Over the rills, and the crags, and the hills,
    Over the lakes and the plains,
Wherever he dream, under mountain or stream,
    The Spirit he loves remains;
And I all the while bask in heaven's blue smile,
    Whilst he is dissolving in rains.

The sanguine sunrise, with his meteor eyes,
    And his burning plumes outspread,
Leaps on the back of my sailing rack,
    When the morning star shines dead,
As on the jag of a mountain crag,
    Which an earthquake rocks and swings,

An eagle alit one moment may sit
   In the light of its golden wings.
And when sunset may breathe, from the lit sea beneath,
   Its ardours of rest and of love,
And the crimson pall of eve may fall
   From the depth of heaven above,
With wings folded I rest, on mine airy nest,
   As still as a brooding dove.

That orbèd maiden with white fire laden,
   Whom mortals call the moon,
Glides glimmering o'er my fleece-like floor,
   By the midnight breezes strewn:
And wherever the beat of her unseen feet,
   Which only the angels hear,
May have broken the woof of my tent's thin roof,
   The stars peep behind her and peer;
And I laugh to see them whirl and flee,
   Like a swarm of golden bees,
When I widen the rent in my wind-built tent,
   Till the calm rivers, lakes, and seas,
Like strips of the sky fallen through me on high,
   Are each paved with the moon and these.

I bind the sun's throne with a burning zone,
   And the moon's with a girdle of pearl;
The volcanoes are dim, and the stars reel and swim,
   When the whirlwinds my banner unfurl.
From cape to cape, with a bridge-like shape,
   Over a torrent sea,
Sunbeam-proof, I hang like a roof,
   The mountains its columns be.
The triumphal arch through which I march
   With hurricane, fire, and snow,
When the powers of the air are chained to my chair,
   Is the million-coloured bow;
The sphere-fire above its soft colours wove,
   While the moist earth was laughing below.

I am the daughter of earth and water,
   And the nursling of the sky;
I pass through the pores of the ocean and shores;
   I change, but I cannot die.

For after the rain, when with never a stain
   The pavilion of heaven is bare,
And the winds and sunbeams, with their convex gleams,
   Build up the blue dome of air,
I silently laugh at my own cenotaph,
   And out of the caverns of rain,
Like a child from the womb, like a ghost from the tomb,
   I arise and unbuild it again.

THE GOOD SAMARITAN

Holy Bible, Luke 10:25–37

25 And, behold, a certain lawyer stood up, and tempted him, saying, Master, what shall I do to inherit eternal life?

26 He said unto him, What is written in the law? how readest thou?

27 And he answering said, Thou shalt love the Lord thy God with all thy heart, and with all thy soul, and with all thy strength, and with all thy mind; and thy neighbour as thyself.

28 And he said unto him, Thou hast answered right: this do, and thou shalt live.

29 But he, willing to justify himself, said unto Jesus, And who is my neighbour?

30 And Jesus answering said, A certain man went down from Jerusalem to Jericho, and fell among thieves, which stripped him of his raiment, and wounded him, and departed, leaving him half dead.

31 And by chance there came down a certain priest that way: and when he saw him, he passed by on the other side.

32 And likewise a Levite, when he was at the place, came and looked on him, and passed by on the other side.

33 But a certain Samaritan, as he journeyed, came where he was: and when he saw him, he had compassion on him,

34 And went to him, and bound up his wounds, pouring in oil and wine, and set him on his own beast, and brought him to an inn, and took care of him.

35 And on the morrow when he departed, he took out two pence, and gave them to the host, and said unto him, Take care of him; and whatsoever thou spendest more, when I come again, I will repay thee.

36 Which now of these three, thinkest thou, was neighbour
unto him that fell among the thieves?

37 And he said, He that shewed mercy on him. Then said Jesu
unto him, Go, and do thou likewise.

TO AN INSECT

Oliver Wendell Holmes

I love to hear thine earnest voice,
  Wherever thou art hid,
Thou testy like dogmatist,
  Thou pretty Katydid!
Thou mindest me of gentlefolks,—
  Old gentlefolks are they,—
Thou say'st an undisputed thing
  In such a solemn way.

Thou art a female, Katydid!
  I know it by the trill
That quivers through thy piercing notes,
  So petulant and shrill;
I think there is a knot of you
  Beneath the hollow tree,—
A knot of spinster Katydids,—
  Do Katydids drink tea?

O, tell me where did Katy live,
  And what did Katy do?
And was she very fair and young,
  And yet so wicked too?
Did Katy love a naughty man,
  Or kiss more cheeks than one?
I warrant Katy did no more
  Than many a Kate has done.

* *

Wherever God erects a house of prayer,
The Devil always builds a chapel there;
And 'twill be found upon examination,
The latter has the largest congregation.
                              —Daniel Defoe

FAREWELL TO NANCY

Robert Burns

Ae fond kiss, and then we sever!
Ae fareweel, alas, for ever!
Deep in heart-wrung tears I'll pledge thee,
Warring sighs and groans I'll wage thee.
Who shall say that fortune grieves him
While the star of hope she leaves him?
Me, nae cheerfu' twinkle lights me,
Dark despair around benights me.

I'll ne'er blame my partial fancy,
Naething could resist my Nancy;
But to see her, was to love her;
Love but her, and love for ever.
Had we never lov'd sae kindly,
Had we never lov'd sae blindly,
Never met—or never parted,
We had ne'er been broken hearted.

Fare thee weel, thou first and fairest!
Fare thee weel, thou best and dearest!
Thine be ilka joy and treasure,
Peace, enjoyment, love, and pleasure.
Ae fond kiss, and then we sever;
Ae fareweel, alas, for ever!
Deep in heart-wrung tears I pledge thee,
Warring sighs and groans I'll wage thee.

ODE ON INTIMATIONS OF IMMORTALITY FROM RECOLLECTIONS OF EARLY CHILDHOOD

William Wordsworth

There was a time when meadow, grove, and stream,
The earth, and every common sight,
To me did seem
Apparelled in celestial light,

The glory and the freshness of a dream.
It is not now as it hath been of yore;—
      Turn whereso'er I may,
        By night or day,
The things which I have seen I now can see no more.
      The Rainbow comes and goes,
      And lovely is the Rose,
      The Moon doth with delight
Look round her when the heavens are bare;
      Waters on a starry night
      Are beautiful and fair;
    The sunshine is a glorious birth;
    But yet I know, where'er I go,
That there hath past away a glory from the earth.

               *   *   *

Our birth is but a sleep and a forgetting:
The Soul that rises with us, our life's Star,
      Hath had elsewhere its setting,
        And cometh from afar:
    Not in entire forgetfulness,
    And not in utter nakedness,
But trailing clouds of glory do we come
      From God, who is our home:
Heaven lies about us in our infancy!
Shades of the prison-house begin to close
      Upon the growing Boy,
But he beholds the light, and whence it flows,
      He sees it in his joy;
The Youth, who daily farther from the east
      Must travel, still is Nature's Priest,
      And by the vision splendid
      Is on his way attended;
At length the Man perceives it die away,
And fade into the light of common day.

               *   *   *

    O joy! that in our embers
    Is something that doth live,
    That nature yet remembers
    What was so fugitive!
The thought of our past years in me doth breed
Perpetual benediction: not indeed

For that which is most worthy to be blest—
Delight and liberty, the simple creed
Of Childhood, whether busy or at rest,
With new-fledged hope still fluttering in his breast: ·
    Not for these I raise
    The song of thanks and praise;
  But for those obstinate questionings
  Of sense and outward things,
  Fallings from us, vanishings;
  Blank misgivings of a Creature
Moving about in worlds not realized,
High instincts before which our mortal Nature
Did tremble like a guilty Thing surprised:
    But for those first affections,
      Those shadowy recollections,
  Which, be they what they may,
Are yet the fountain light of all our day,
Are yet a master light of all our seeing;
  Uphold us, cherish, and have power to make
Our noisy years seem moments in the being
Of the eternal Silence: truths that wake,
    To perish never;
Which neither listlessness, nor mad endeavour,
    Nor Man nor Boy,
Nor all that is at enmity with joy,
Can utterly abolish or destroy!
    Hence in a season of calm weather
    Though inland far we be,
Our Souls have sight of that immortal sea
    Which brought us hither,
    Can in a moment travel thither,
And see the Children sport upon the shore,
And hear the mighty waters rolling evermore.

Then sing, ye Birds, sing, sing a joyous song!
    And let the young Lambs bound
    As to the tabor's sound!
We in thought will join your throng,
    Ye that pipe and ye that play,
    Ye that through your hearts to-day
    Feel the gladness of the May!
What though the radiance which was once so bright

Be now forever taken from my sight,
   Though nothing can bring back the hour
Of splendour in the grass, of glory in the flower;
   We will grieve not, rather find
   Strength in what remains behind;
   In the primal sympathy
   Which having been must ever be;
   In the soothing thoughts that spring
   Out of human suffering;
   In the faith that looks through death,
In years that bring the philosophic mind.

And O ye Fountains, Meadows, Hills, and Groves,
Forebode not any severing of our loves!
Yet in my heart of hearts I feel your might;
I only have relinquished one delight
To live beneath your more habitual sway.
I love the Brooks which down their channels fret,
Even more than when I tripped lightly as they;
The innocent brightness of a new-born Day
      Is lovely yet;
The Clouds that gather round the setting sun
Do take a sober colouring from an eye
That hath kept watch o'er man's mortality;
Another race hath been, and other palms are won.
Thanks to the human heart by which we live,
Thanks to its tenderness, its joys, and fears,
To me the meanest flower that blows can give
Thoughts that do often lie too deep for tears.

WORDS OF A GREAT ADMIRAL

Lord Nelson

When I don't know whether to fight or not, I always fight.

I owe all my success in life to having been always a quarter of
an hour beforehand.

England expects every man to do his duty. (Signal to the English fleet before Trafalgar, 1805.)

Before this time tomorrow I shall have gained a peerage or
Westminster Abbey. (Rising from table before the Battle of the
Baltic, March, 1801.)

MY GARDEN

Thomas Edward Brown

A Garden is a lovesome thing, God wot!
Rose plot,
Fringed pool,
Fern'd grot—
The veriest school
Of peace; and yet the fool
Contends that God is not—
Not God! in gardens! when the eve is cool?
Nay, but I have a sign;
'Tis very sure God walks in mine.

CONTENTMENT

"Man wants but little here below"

Oliver Wendell Holmes

Little I ask; my wants are few;
    I only wish a hut of stone
(A *very plain* brownstone will do),
    That I may call my own:—
And close at hand is such a one,
In yonder street that fronts the sun.

Plain food is quite enough for me;
    Three courses are as good as ten;—
If Nature can subsist on three,
    Thank Heaven for three. Amen!
I always thought cold victual nice;—
My *choice* would be vanilla-ice.

I care not much for gold or land;—
    Give me a mortgage here and there,—
Some good bank-stock, some note of hand,
    Or trifling railroad share,—
I only ask that Fortune send
A *little* more than I shall spend.

Honors are silly toys, I know,
    And titles are but empty names;
I would, *perhaps,* be Plenipo,—
    But only near St. James;
I'm very sure I should not care
To fill our Gubernator's chair.

Jewels are bawbles; 'tis a sin
    To care for such unfruitful things;—
One good-sized diamond in a pin,—
    Some, *not so large,* in rings,
A ruby, and a pearl, or so,
Will do for me;—I laugh at show.

My dame should dress in cheap attire;
    (Good, heavy silks are never dear;)
I own perhaps I *might* desire
    Some shawls of true Cashmere,—
Some marrowy crapes of China silk,
Like wrinkled skins on scalded milk.

I would not have the horse I drive
    So fast that folks must stop and stare;
And easy gait—two, forty-five—
    Suits me; I do not care;—
Perhaps, for just a *single spurt,*
Some seconds less would do no hurt.

Of pictures, I should like to own
    Titians and Raphaels three or four,—
I love so much their style and tone,—
    One Turner, and no more,
(A landscape,—foreground golden dirt,—
The sunshine painted with a squirt.)

Of books but few,—some fifty score
    For daily use, and bound for wear;
The rest upon an upper floor;—
    Some *little* luxury *there*
Of red morocco's gilded gleam,
And vellum rich as country cream.

Busts, cameos, gems,—such things as these
    Which others often show for pride,

I value for their power to please,
    And selfish churls deride;—
One Stradivarius, I confess,
Two meerschaums, I would fain possess.

Wealth's wasteful tricks I will not learn
    Nor ape the glittering upstart fool;—
Shall not carved tables serve my turn,
    But all must be of buhl?
Give grasping pomp its double share,—
I ask but one recumbent chair.

Thus humble let me live and die,
    Nor long for Midas's golden touch;
If Heaven more generous gifts deny,
    I shall not miss them *much,*—
Too grateful for the blessing lent
Of simple tastes and mind content!

SOMEBODY'S DARLING

Marie Ravenal De Lacoste

Into a ward of the whitewashed halls,
Where the dead and dying lay,
Wounded by bayonets, shells, and balls,
Somebody's darling was borne one day;

Somebody's darling, so young and brave,
Wearing yet on his pale, sweet face,
Soon to be hid by the dust of the grave,
The lingering light of his boyhood's grace.

Matted and damp are the curls of gold,
Kissing the snow of that fair young brow;
Pale are the lips of delicate mold—
Somebody's darling is dying now.

Back from his beautiful blue-veined brow,
Brush all the wandering waves of gold;
Cross his hands on his bosom now;
Somebody's darling is still and cold.

Kiss him once for somebody's sake,
Murmur a prayer soft and low;
One bright curl from its fair mates take;
They were somebody's pride, you know;

Somebody's hand has rested there;
Was it a mother's, soft and white?
And have the lips of a sister fair
Been baptized in the waves of light?

God knows best! he was somebody's love:
Somebody's heart enshrined him there;
Somebody wafted his name above,
Night and morn, on the wings of prayer.

Somebody wept when he marched away,
Looking so handsome, brave, and grand;
Somebody's kiss on his forehead lay;
Somebody clung to his parting hand.

Somebody's watching and waiting for him,
Yearning to hold him again to her heart;
And there he lies, with his blue eyes dim,
And the smiling, child-like lips apart.

Tenderly bury the fair young dead,
Pausing to drop on his grave a tear;
Carve on the wooden slab at his head,
"Somebody's darling slumbers here."

OF LOVE OF SILENCE AND OF SOLITUDE

Thomas À Kempis

Seek a convenient time to take heed to thyself and think oft-times of the benefits of God.

Leave curious things and read such matters that rather give compunction than occupation.

If thou withdraw thyself from void speakings and idle circuits and from vanities and hearing of tidings thou shalt find time sufficient and convenient to have sweet meditations.

The great holy men where they might, fled men's fellowship and chose to live to God in secret places.

354

One said 'as ofttimes as I was among men I came back a less man' that is to say less holy: this we find by experience when we talk any while.

It is easier for a man always to be still than not to exceed in words. It is easier for a man to abide privily at home than well to keep himself being away from home.

Wherefore whoever purposeth to come to inward and to spiritual things it behoveth him to decline from the company of people —with Jesu.

No man appeareth safely away from home but he that loveth gladly to abide at home.

No man speaketh safely but he that is glad to hold his peace.

No man is safe above but he that will gladly be beneath.

No man commandeth safely but he that hath learned to obey.

No man rejoiceth safely but he that hath the witness of a good conscience.

Nevertheless the safety of holy men was never without dread of God; nor were they the less busy and meek in themselves though they had great virtues and grace.

The safety of shrews (wicked men) groweth from pride and presumption and in the end it turneth into deceit.

Promise thyself safety in this world never, though thou seem a good religious man or a devout hermit: Ofttimes they that are best in man's estimation fall most perilously for their trust in themselves.

Wherefore it is not profitable that they lack temptations utterly but they should ofttimes be attacked lest they be too secure and lest they be left up by pride and lightly decline to outer consolations.

O he that never sought transitory gladness, he that never occupied him in the world, how good a conscience would he keep.

O he that would cut away all manner of vain business and would think all only on ghostly and godly things and set all his hope in God how great peace and quiet should he have.

There is no man worthy heavenly comfort unless he diligently exercise himself in holy compunction. If thou heartily be sorry enter into thy closet, exclude all worldly noise as it is written 'Be ye sorry in your chambers'; thou shalt find there what outside thou shalt ofttimes lose.

The cell well continued waxeth sweet and the cell evil kept engendreth weariness. If in the beginning of thy conversion thou keep thy cell and dwell well therein it shall be to thee afterwards as a dear and well beloved friend and most pleasant solace.

In silence and quiet the devout soul profiteth and learneth the secrets of the scriptures: there he findeth the floods of tears wherewith every night he may wash and cleanse himself that he may be the more familiar to his creator the more he withdraweth him far from secular noise.

He that withdraweth himself from friends and known men, God shall come nigh unto him with his holy angels.

Better it is for a man to be hid and take care of himself than, taking no heed of himself, to work wonders.

It is commendable for a man of religion seldom to go out, to fly from being seen and not wish to see men; why wilt thou see what is not lawful for thee to have?

The world passeth and his concupiscence.

The desires of sensuality draw men to walk about; but when the hour is past what cometh thereof but grudging (murmuring) of conscience and dispersion of heart?

A glad going out ofttimes bringeth forth a sorrowful coming home and a glad watching over evening bringeth forth a sorry morning; so every fleshly joy entereth in pleasantly but in the end he biteth and slayeth.

What canst thou see elsewhere that thou canst not see here? Lo here heaven earth and all elements and of these all things are made.

What canst thou see elsewhere that may long abide under the sun? peradventure thou waitest to be filled; but thou shalt never come thereto.

If thou sawest all things that are present what were that but a vain sight? Lift up thine eyes to God on high and pray God for thy sins and negligence; leave vain things to the vain and take thou heed to the things that God commandeth thee.

Shut thy door upon thee and call to thee Jesu thy love: dwell with him in thy cell for thou shalt not find elsewhere so great peace.

If thou hadst not gone out nor heard no tidings thou wouldst the better have abided in peace; and since it delighteth thee sometimes to hear new tidings it behoveth, following this, that thou suffer turbation of heart.

(From Imitation of Christ)

* * *

Young men think old men fools, and old men know young men to be so.

—Anonymous

THE CAISSON SONG *

Major Edmund L. Gruber

Over hill, over dale, we have hit the dusty trail,
And those caissons go rolling along.
In and out, hear them shout, "Counter march and right about!"
And those caissons go rolling along.

Chorus:
>   Then it's hi! hi! hi! hee! in the field artillery,
>   Sound off your numbers loud and strong
>   Where e'er you go you will always know
>   That those caissons are rolling along.
>   Keep them rolling! And those caissons go rolling along
>   Then it's Battery Halt!

Through the storm, through the night, up to where the dough-
>   boys fight,
All our caissons go rolling along.
At zero we'll be there, answering every call and flare,
While our caissons go rolling along.

Cavalry, boot to boot, we will join in the pursuit,
While the caissons go rolling along.
Action front, at a trot; volley fire with shell and shot,
While those caissons go rolling along.

But if fate me should call, and in action I should fall,
And those caissons go rolling along.
Fire at will, lay 'em low, never stop for any foe,
While those caissons go rolling along.

But if fate me should call, and in action I should fall,
Keep those caissons a-rolling along.
Then in peace I'll abide when I take my final ride
On a caisson that's rolling along.

* * *

When a man assumes a public trust, he should consider himself
as public property.

—Thomas Jefferson

OVER THE HILL TO THE POOR-HOUSE

Will M. Carleton

Over the hill to the poor-house I'm trudgin' my weary way,—
I, a woman of seventy, and only a trifle gray,—
I, who am smart and chipper, for all the years I've told,
As many another woman that's only half as old.

Over the hill to the poor-house,—I can't quite make it clear!
Over the hill to the poor-house,—it seems so horrid queer!
Many a step I've taken a toilin' to and fro,
But this is a sort of journey I never thought to go.

What is the use of heapin' on me a pauper's shame?
Am I lazy or crazy? am I blind or lame?
True, I am not so supple, nor yet so awful stout;
But charity ain't no favor, if one can live without.

I am willin' and anxious an' ready any day
To work for a decent livin', and pay my honest way;
For I can earn my victuals, an' more too, I'll be bound,
If anybody only is willin' to have me round.

Once I was young and handsome,—I was, upon my soul,—
Once my cheeks were roses, my eyes as black as coal;
And I can't remember, in them days, of hearin' people say,
For any kind of a reason, that I was in their way.

'Taint no use of boastin', or talkin' over free,
But many a house an' home was open then to me;
Many a han'some offer I had from likely men,
And nobody ever hinted that I was a burden then.

And when to John I was married, sure he was good and smart,
But he and all the neighbors would own I done my part;
For life was all before me, an' I was young an' strong,
And I worked the best that I could in tryin' to get along.

And so we worked together; and life was hard, but gay,
With now and then a baby for to cheer us on our way;
Till we had half a dozen, an' all growed clean an' neat,
All went to school like others, an' had enough to eat.

So we worked for the childr'n, and raised 'em every one;
Worked for 'em summer and winter, just as we ought to've **done**;
Only perhaps we humored 'em, which some goods folks condemn,
But every couple's childr'n's a heap the best to them.

Strange how much we think of our blessed little ones!—
I'd have died for my daughters, I'd have died for my sons;
And God He made that rule of love; but when we're old and gray,
I've noticed it sometimes somehow fails to work the other way.

Strange, another thing; when our boys and girls was grown,
And when, exceptin' Charley, they'd left us there alone;
When John he nearer an' nearer come, and dearer seemed to be,
The Lord of Hosts He come one day an' took him away from me.

Still I was bound to struggle, an' never to cringe or fall,—
Still I worked for Charley, for Charley was now my all;
And Charley was pretty good to me, with scarce a word or frown,
Till at last he went a courtin', and brought a wife from town.

She was somewhat dressy, an' hadn't a pleasant smile,—
She was quite conceity, and carried a heap o' style;
But if ever I tried to be friends, I did with her, I know;
But she was hard and proud, an' I couldn't make it go.

She had an edication, an' that was good for her;
But when she twitted me on mine, 'twas carryin' things too fur;
An' I told her once, 'fore company (an' it almost made her sick),
That I never swallowed a grammar, or 'et a 'rithmetic.

So 'twas only a few days before the thing was done,—
They was a family of themselves, and I another one;
And a very little cottage one family will do,
But I never have seen a house that was big enough for two.

An' I never could speak to suit her, never could please her eye,
An' it made me independent, an' then I didn't try;
But I was terribly staggered, an' felt it like a blow,
When Charley turned ag'in me, an' told me I could go.

I went to live with Susan, but Susan's house was small,
And she was always a hintin' how snug it was for us all;
And what with her husband's sisters, and what with childr'n three,
'Twas easy to discover that there wasn't room for me.

An' then I went to Thomas, the oldest son I've got,
For Thomas's buildings'd cover the half of an acre lot;
But all the childr'n was on me—I couldn't stand their sauce—
And Thomas said I needn't think I was comin' there to boss.

An' then I wrote to Rebecca, my girl who lives out West,
And to Isaac, not far from her—some twenty miles at best;
And one of 'em said 'twas too warm there for any one so old,
And t'other had an opinion the climate was too cold.

So they have shirked and slighted me, an' shifted me about—
So they have well-nigh soured me, an' wore my old heart out;
But still I've born up pretty well, an' wasn't much put down,
Till Charley went to the poor-master, an' put me on the town.

Over the hill to the poor-house—my childr'n dear, goodbye!
Many a night I've watched you when only God was nigh;
And God'll judge between us; but I will al'ays pray
That you shall never suffer the half I do to-day.

LABOR

Abraham Lincoln

Inasmuch as most good things are produced by labor, it follows that all such things ought to belong to those whose labor has produced them. But it has happened in all ages of the world that some have labored, and others, without labor, have enjoyed a larger proportion of the fruits. This is wrong, and should not continue. To secure to each laborer the whole product of his labor as nearly as possible is a worthy object of any good government.

(From First Annual Message to Congress, Dec. 3, 1861)

THE LOST SHEEP

Holy Bible, St. Luke 15:4-7

4 What man of you, having an hundred sheep, if he lose one of them, doth not leave the ninety and nine in the wilderness, and go after that which is lost, until he find it?

5 And when he hath found it, he layeth it on his shoulders, rejoicing.

6 And when he cometh home, he calleth together his friends and neighbours, saying unto them, Rejoice with me; for I have found my sheep which was lost.

7 I say unto you, that likewise joy shall be in heaven over one sinner that repenteth, more than over ninety and nine just persons which need no repentance.

PRAYER

Alfred, Lord Tennyson

More things are wrought by prayer
Than this world dreams of. Wherefore, let thy voice
Rise like a fountain for me night and day.
For what are men better than sheep or goats
That nourish a blind life within the brain,
If, knowing God, they lift not hands of prayer
Both for themselves and those who call them friend?
For so the whole round earth is every way
Bound by gold chains about the feet of God.

(From Idylls of the King)

WHY I WENT TO THE WOODS

Henry David Thoreau

When first I took up my abode in the woods, that is, began to spend my nights as well as days there, which, by accident, was on Independence Day, on the 4th of July, 1845, my house was not finished for winter, but was merely a defence against the rain, without plastering or chimney, the walls being of rough weather-stained boards, with wide chinks, which made it cool at night. The upright white hewn studs and freshly planed door and window-casings gave it a clean and airy look, especially in the morning, when its timbers were saturated with dew, so that I fancied that by noon some sweet gum would exude from them. To my imagination it retained throughout the day more or less of this auroral character, reminding me of a certain house on a mountain which I had visited the year before. This was an airy, an unplastered cabin, fit to entertain a travelling god, and where a goddess might trail her garments. The winds which passed over my dwelling were such as sweep over the ridges of mountains, bearing the broken strains, or celestial parts only, of terrestrial music. The morning wind forever blows, the poem of creation is uninterrupted; but few are the ears that hear it. Olympus is but the outside of the earth everywhere.

The only house I had been the owner of before, if I except a boat, was a tent, which I used occasionally when making excursions in the summer, and this is still rolled up in my garret; but the boat, after passing from hand to hand, has gone down the stream of time. With this more substantial shelter about me, I had made some progress toward settling in the world. This frame, so slightly clad, was a sort of crystallisation around me, and reacted on the builder. It was suggestive somewhat as a picture in outlines. I did not need to go out doors to take the air, for the atmosphere within had lost none of its freshness. It was not so much within doors as behind a door where I sat, even in the rainiest weather. The Harivansa says: 'An abode without birds is like a meat without seasoning.' Such was not my abode, for I found myself suddenly neighbour to the birds; not by having imprisoned one, but having caged myself near them. I was not only nearer to some of those which commonly frequent the garden and the orchard, but to those wilder and more trilling songsters of the forest which never, or rarely, serenade a villager—the woodthrush, the veery, the scarlet tanager, the field-sparrow, the whip-poor-will, and many others.

I was seated by the shore of a small pond, about a mile and a half south of the village of Concord and somewhat higher than it, in the midst of an extensive wood between that town and Lincoln, and about two miles south of that our only field known to fame, Concord battle ground; but I was so low in the woods that opposite shore, half a mile off, like the rest, covered with wood, was my most distant horizon. For the first week, whenever I looked out on the pond, it impressed me like a tarn high up on the one side of a mountain, its bottom far above the surface of other lakes, and as the sun arose, I saw it throwing off its nightly clothing of mist, and here and there, by degrees, its soft ripples or its smooth reflecting surface was revealed, while the mists, like ghosts, were stealthily withdrawing in every direction into the woods, as at the breaking up of some nocturnal conventicle. The very dew seemed to hang upon the trees later into the day than usual, as on the sides of mountains.

This small lake was of most value as a neighbour in the intervals of a gentle rain-storm in August, when, both air and water being perfectly still, but the sky overcast, mid-afternoon had all the serenity of evening, and the woodthrush sang around, and was heard from shore to shore. A lake like this is never smoother than at such a time; and the clear portion of the air above it being shallow and darkened by clouds, the water, full of light and re-flections, becomes a lower heaven itself so much the more impor-tant. From a hill-top near by, where the wood had been recently cut off, there was a pleasing vista southward across the pond, through a wide indentation in the hills which form the shore there, where their opposite sides sloping toward each other sug-gested a stream flowing out in that direction through a wooded valley, but stream there was none. That way I looked between and over the near green hills to some distant and higher ones in the horizon, tinged with blue. Indeed, by standing on tiptoe I could catch a glimpse of some of the peaks of the still bluer and more distant mountain ranges in the northwest, those true-blue coins from heaven's own mint, and also of some portion of the village. But in other directions, even from this point, I could not see over or beyond the woods which surrounded me. It is well to have some water in your neighbourhood, to give buoyancy to and float the earth. One value even of the smallest well is, that when you look into it you see that earth is not continent but insular. This is as important as that it keeps butter cool. When I looked across the pond from this peak toward the Sudbury meadows, which in time of flood I distinguished elevated perhaps by a mirage in their seething valley, like a coin in a basin, all the earth beyond the pond appeared like a thin crust insulated and floated even by this small sheet of intervening water, and I was reminded that this on which I dwelt was but dry land.

Though the view from my door was still more contracted, I did not feel crowded or confined in the least. There was pasture enough for my imagination. The low shrub-oak plateau to which the opposite shore arose, stretched away toward the prairies of the West and the steppes of Tartary, affording ample room for all the roving families of men. 'There are none happy in the world but beings who enjoy freely a vast horizon,' said Damodara, when his herds required new and larger pastures.

I went to the woods because I wish to live deliberately, to front only the essential facts of life, and see if I could not learn what it had to teach, and not, when I came to die, discover that I had not lived. I did not wish to live what was not life, living is so dear; nor did I wish to practise resignation, unless it was quite neces-sary. I wanted to live deep and suck out all the marrow of life, to live so sturdily and Spartan-like as to put to rout all that was not life, to cut a broad swath and shave close, to drive life into a corner, and reduce it to its lowest terms, and, if it proved to be mean, why then to get the whole and genuine meanness of it, and publish its meanness to the world; or if it were sublime, to know it by experience, and be able to give a true account of it in my next excursion. For most men, it appears to me, are in a strange uncertainty about it, whether it is of the devil or of God, and have somewhat hastily concluded that it is the chief end of man here to 'glorify God and enjoy Him forever.'

Still we live meanly, like ants; though the fable tells us that we were long ago changed into men; like pygmies we fight with cranes; it is error upon error, and clout upon clout, and our best virtue has for its occasion a superfluous and evitable wretchedness. Our life is frittered away by detail. An honest man has hardly need to count more than his ten fingers, or in extreme cases he may add his ten toes, and lump the rest. Simplicity, simplicity, simplicity! I say, let your affairs be as two or three, and not a hundred or a thousand; instead of a million count half-a-dozen, and keep your accounts on your thumb-nail. In the midst of this chopping sea of civilised life, such are the clouds and storms and quicksands and thousand-and-one items to be allowed for, that a man has to live, if he would not founder and go to the bottom and not make his port at all, by dead reckoning, and he must be a great calculator indeed who succeeds. Simplify, simplify. Instead of three meals a-day, if it be necessary eat but one; instead of a hundred dishes, five; and reduce other things in proportion. Our life is like a German Confederacy, made up of petty states, with its boundary forever fluctuating, so that even a German cannot tell you how it is bounded at any moment. The nation itself, with all its so-called internal improvements, which, by the way, are all external and superficial, is just such an unwieldy and overgrown establishment, cluttered with furniture and tripped up by its own traps, ruined by luxury and heedless expense, by want of calculation and a worthy aim, as the million households in the land; and the only cure for it as for them is in a rigid economy, a stern and more than Spartan simplicity of life and elevation of purpose. It lives too fast. Men think that it is essential that the Nation have commerce, and export ice, and talk through a telegraph, and ride thirty miles an hour, without a doubt, whether they do or not; but whether we should live like baboons or like men, is a little uncertain. If we do not get out sleepers and forge rails, and devote days and nights to the work, but go to tinkering upon our lives to improve them, who will build railroads? And if railroads are not built, how shall we get to heaven in season? But if we stay at home and mind our business, who will want railroads? We do not ride on the railroad; it rides upon us. Did you ever think what those sleepers are that underlie the railroad? Each one is a man, an Irishman or a Yankee man. The rails are laid on them and they are covered with sand, and the cars run smoothly over them. They are sound sleepers, I assure you. And every few years a new lot is laid down and run over; so that, if some have the pleasure of riding on a rail, others have the misfortune to be ridden upon. And when they run over a man that is walking in his sleep, a supernumerary sleeper in the wrong position, and wake him up, they suddenly stop the cars, and make a hue and cry about it, as if this were an exception. I am glad to know that it takes a gang of men for every five miles to keep the sleepers down and level in their beds as it is, for this is a sign that they may sometime get up again.

Why should we live with such hurry and waste of life? We are determined to be starved before we are hungry. Men say that a stitch in time saves nine, and so they take a thousand stitches to-day to save nine to-morrow. As for work, we haven't any of any consequence. We have the Saint Vitus' dance, and cannot possibly keep our heads still. If I should only give a few pulls at the parish bell-rope, as for a fire, that is, without setting the bell, there is hardly a man on his farm in the outskirts of Concord, not with-standing that press of engagements which was his excuse so many times this morning, nor a boy, nor a woman, I might almost say, but would forsake all and follow that sound, not mainly to save property from the flames, but, if we will confess the truth, much more to see it burn, since burn it must, and we, be it known, did not set it on fire—or to see it put out, and have a hand in it, if that is done as handsomely; yes, even if it were the parish church itself. Hardly a man takes a half-hour's nap after dinner, but when he wakes he holds up his head and ask 'What's the news?' as if the rest of mankind had stood his sentinels. Some give directions to be waked every half-hour, doubtless for no other purpose; and then to pay for it, they tell what they have dreamed. After a night's sleep the news is as indispensable as the breakfast. 'Pray, tell me anything new that has happened to a man anywhere on this globe'—and he reads it over his coffee and rolls, that a man has had his eyes gouged out this morning on the Wachito River;

never dreaming the while that he lives in the dark unfathomed mammoth cave of this world, and has but the rudiment of an eye himself.

For my part, I could easily do without the post office. I think that there are very few important communications made through it. To speak critically, I never received more than one or two letters in my life—I wrote this some years ago—that were worth the postage. The penny-post is commonly an institution through which you seriously offer a man that penny for his thoughts which is so often safely offered in jest. And I am sure that I never read any memorable news in a newspaper. If we read of one man robbed, or murdered, or killed by accident, or one house burned, or one vessel wrecked, or one steam-boat blown-up or one cow run over on the Western Railroad, or one mad dog killed, or one lot of grass-hoppers in the winter—we never need read of another. One is enough. If you are acquainted with the principle, what do you care for a myriad instances and applications? To a philosopher all news, as it is called, is gossip, and they who edit and read it are old women over their tea. Yet not a few are greedy after this gossip. There was such a rush, as I hear, the other day at one of the offices to learn the foreign news by the last arrival, that several large squares of plate glass belonging to the establishment were broken by the pressure—news which I seriously think a ready wit might write a twelvemonth or twelve years beforehand with sufficient accuracy. As for Spain, for instance, if you know how to throw in Don Carlos and the Infanta, and Don Pedro and Seville and Granada, from time to time in the right proportions—they may have changed the names a little since I saw the papers—and serve up a bull-fight when other entertainments fail, it will be true to the letter, and give us as good an idea of the exact state or ruin of things in Spain as the most succinct and lucid reports under this head in the newspapers; and as for England, almost the last significant scrap of news from that quarter was the Revolution of 1649; and if you have learned the history of her crops for an average year, you never need attend to that thing again, unless your speculations are of a merely pecuniary character. If one may judge who rarely looks into the newspapers, nothing new does ever happen in foreign parts, a French Revolution not excepted.

Let us spend one day as deliberately as Nature, and not be thrown off the track by every nutshell and mosquito's wing that falls on the rails. Let us rise early and fast, or break fast, gently and without perturbation; let company come and let company go, let the bells ring and the children cry—determined to make a day of it. Why should we knock under and go with the stream? Let us not be upset and overwhelmed in that terrible rapid and whirlpool called a dinner, situated in the meridian shallows. Weather this danger and you are safe, for the rest of the way is down hill. With unrelaxed nerves, with morning vigour, sail by it, looking another way, tied to the mast like Ulysses. If the engine whistles, let it whistle till it is hoarse for its pains. If the bell rings, why should we run? We will consider what kind of music they are like. Let us settle ourselves, and work and wedge our feet downward through the mud and slush of opinion, and prejudice, and tradition, and delusion, and appearance, that alluvion which covers the globe, through Paris and London, through New York and Boston and Concord, through church and state, through poetry and philosophy and religion, till we come to a hard bottom and rocks in place, which we call reality, and say, This is, and no mistake; and then begin, having a point d'appui, below freshet and frost and fire, a place where you might found a wall or a state, or set a lamp-post safely, or perhaps a gauge, not a Nilometer, but a Realometer, that future ages might know how deep a freshet of shams and appearances had gathered from time to time. If you stand right fronting and face to face to a fact, you will see the sun glimmer on both its surfaces, as if it were a cimeter, and feel its sweet edge dividing you through the heart and marrow, and so you will happily conclude your mortal career. Be it life or death, we crave only reality. If we are really dying, let us hear the rattle in our throats and feel cold in the extremities; if we are alive, let us go about our business.

Time is but the stream I go a-fishing in. I drink at it; but while I drink I see the sandy bottom and detect how shallow it is. Its thin current slides away, but eternity remains. I would drink deeper; fish in the sky, whose bottom is pebbly with stars. I cannot count one. I know not the first letter of the alphabet. I have always been regretting that I was not as wise as the day I was born. The intellect is a cleaver; it discerns and rifts its way into the secret of things. I do not wish to be any more busy with my hands than is necessary. My head is hands and feet. I feel all my best faculties concentrated in it. My instinct tells me that my head is an organ for burrowing, as some creatures use their snout and forepaws, and with it I would mine and burrow my way through these hills. I think that the richest vein is somewhere hereabouts; so by the divining rod and thin rising vapours I judge; and here I will begin to mine.

(From Walden)

CASEY JONES

Anonymous

Come all you rounders for I want you to hear
The story told of a brave engineer;
Casey Jones was the rounder's name
On a heavy six-wheeler he rode to fame.

Caller called Jones about half past four,
Jones kissed his wife at the station door,
Climbed into the cab with the orders in his hand,
Says, "This is my trip to the promised land."

Through South Memphis yards on the fly,
He heard the fireman say, "You've got a white eye."
All the switchmen knew by the engine's moans,
That the hogger at the throttle was Casey Jones.

Fireman says, "Casey, you're runnin' too fast,
You run the block signal the last station you passed."
Jones says, "Yes, I think we can make it, though,
For she steams much better than ever I know."

Jones says, "Fireman, don't you fret,
Keep knockin' at the firedoor, don't give up yet;
I'm goin' to run her till she leaves the rail
Or make it on time with the southbound mail."

Around the curve and a-down the dump,
Two locomotives were a-bound to bump,
Fireman hollered, "Jones, it's just ahead,
We might jump and make it but we'll all be dead."

'Twas around this curve he saw the passenger train,
Something happened in Casey's brain;
Fireman jumped off, but Jones stayed on,
He's a good engineer but he's dead and gone.

Poor Casey Jones was always all right,
He stuck to his post both day and night;
They loved to hear the whistle of old Number Three
As he came into Memphis on the old K.C.

Headaches and Heartaches and all kinds of pain
Are not apart from a railroad train;
Tales that are earnest, noble and gran'
Belong to the life of a railroad man.

FROM THE VISION OF SIR LAUNFAL

James Russell Lowell

Earth gets its price for what Earth gives us;
   The beggar is taxed for a corner to die in,
The priest hath his fee who comes and shrives us,
   We bargain for the graves we lie in;
At the Devil's booth are all things sold,
Each ounce of dross costs its ounce of gold;
   For a cap and bells our lives we pay,
Bubbles we buy with a whole soul's tasking:
   'Tis heaven alone that is given away,
'Tis only God may be had for the asking;
There is no price set on the lavish summer;
And June may be had by the poorest comer.

And what is so rare as a day in June?
   Then, if ever, come perfect days;
Then Heaven tries earth if it be in tune,
   And over it softly her warm ear lays;
Whether we look, or whether we listen,
We hear life murmur, or see it glisten;
   Every clod feels a stir of might,
   An instinct within it that reaches and towers,
And, groping blindly above it for light,
   Climbs to a soul in grass and flowers;
The flush of life may well be seen
   Thrilling back over hills and valleys;

The cowslip startles in meadows green,
   The buttercup catches the sun in its chalice,
And there's never a leaf nor a blade too mean
   To be some happy creature's palace;
The little bird sits at his door in the sun,
   Atilt like a blossom among the leaves,

And lets his illumined being o'errun
    With the deluge of summer it receives;
His mate feels the eggs beneath her wings,
And the heart in her dumb breast flutters and sings;
He sings to the wide world, and she to her nest,—
In the nice ear of Nature which song is the best?

* * *

PRELUDE TO PART SECOND

Down swept the chill wind from the mountain peak,
    From the snow five thousand summers old;
On open wold and hill-top bleak
    It had gathered all the cold,
And whirled it like sleet on the wanderer's cheek;
It carried a shiver everywhere
From the unleafed boughs and pastures bare;
The little brook heard it and built a roof
'Neath which he could house him, winter-proof;
All night by the white stars' frosty gleams
He groined his arches and matched his beams;
Slender and clear were his crystal spars
As the lashes of light that trim the stars:
He sculptured every summer delight
In his halls and chambers out of sight;
Sometimes his tinkling waters slipt
Down through a frost-leaved forest-crypt,
Long, sparkling aisles of steel-stemmed trees
Bending to counterfeit a breeze;
Sometimes the roof no fretwork knew
But silvery mosses that downward grew;
Sometimes it was carved in sharp relief
With quaint arabesques of ice-fern leaf;
Sometimes it was simply smooth and clear
For the gladness of heaven to shine through, and here
He had caught the nodding bulrush-tops
And hung them thickly with diamond drops,
That crystalled the beams of moon and sun,
And made a star of every one:
No mortal builder's most rare device
Could match this winter-palace of ice;
'Twas as if every image that mirrored lay
In his depths serene through the summer day,

370

Each fleeting shadow of earth and sky,
  Lest the happy model should be lost,
Had been mimicked in fairy masonry
  By the elfin builders of the frost.

* * *

"Lo, it is I, be not afraid!
In many climes, without avail,
Thou hast spent thy life for the Holy Grail;
Behold, it is here,—this cup which thou
Didst fill at the streamlet for me but now;
This crust is my body broken for thee,
This water His blood that died on the tree;
The Holy Supper is kept, indeed,
In whatso we share with another's need;
Not what we give, but what we share,—
For the gift without the giver is bare;
Who gives himself with his alms feeds three,
Himself, his hungering neighbor, and me."

CURFEW MUST NOT RING TONIGHT

Rosa Hartwick Thorpe

England's sun was slowly setting
O'er the hills so far away,
Filling all the land with beauty
At the close of one sad day;
And the last rays kissed the forehead
Of a man and maiden fair—
He with a step so slow and weakened,
She with sunny, floating hair;
He with sad bowed head, and thoughtful,
She with lips so cold and white,
Struggling to keep back the murmur,
"Curfew must not ring tonight."

"Sexton," Bessie's white lips faltered,
Pointing to the prison old,
With its walls so dark and gloomy—
Walls so dark, and damp, and cold—

"I've a lover in that prison,
Doomed this very night to die,
At the ringing of the curfew,
And no earthly help is nigh.
Cromwell will not come till sunset";
And her face grew strangely white,
As she spoke in husky whispers,
"Curfew must not ring tonight."

"Bessie," calmly spoke the sexton—
Every word pierced her young heart
Like a thousand gleaming arrows,
Like a deadly poisoned dart—
"Long, long years I've rung the curfew
From that gloomy shadowed tow'r;
Every evening, just at sunset,
It has told the twilight hour.
I have done my duty ever.
Tried to do it just and right;
Now I'm old, I will not miss it;
Girl, the curfew rings tonight!"

Wild her eyes and pale her features,
Stern and white her thoughtful brow,
And within her heart's deep center,
Bessie made a solemn vow.
She had listened while the judges
Read, without a tear or sigh,
"At the ringing of the curfew
Basil Underwood must die."
And her breath came fast and faster,
And her eyes grew large and bright;
One low murmur, scarcely spoken—
"Curfew must not ring tonight."

She with light step bounded forward,
Sprang within the old church door,
Left the old man coming slowly,
Paths he'd often trod before;
Not one moment paused the maiden,
But with cheek and brow aglow,
Staggered up the gloomy tower,
Where the bell swung to and fro;

Then she climbed the slimy ladder,
Dark, without one ray of light,
Upward still, her pale lips saying,
"Curfew shall not ring tonight."

She has reached the topmost ladder,
O'er her hangs the great dark bell,
And the awful gloom beneath her,
Like the pathway down to Hell.
See, the ponderous tongue is swinging,
'Tis the hour of curfew now;
And the sight has chilled her bosom,
Stopped her breath, and paled her brow.
Shall she let it ring? No, never!
Her eyes flash with sudden light,
As she springs and grasps it firmly—
"Curfew shall not ring tonight."

Out she swung, far out, the city
Seemed a tiny speck below;
There twixt heaven and earth suspended,
As the bell swung to and fro;
And the half-deaf sexton ringing
(Years he had not heard the bell)
And he thought the twilight curfew
Rang young Basil's funeral knell;
Still the maiden clinging firmly,
Cheek and brow so pale and white,
Stilled her frightened heart's wild beating—
"Curfew shall not ring tonight."

It was o'er—the bell ceased swaying,
And the maiden stepped once more
Firmly on the damp old ladder,
Where for hundred years before
Human foot had not been planted;
And what she this night had done
Should be told in long years after:
As the rays of setting sun
Light the sky with mellow beauty,
Aged sires with heads of white,
Tell the children why the curfew
Did not ring that one sad night.

O'er the distant hills came Cromwell;
Bessie saw him, and her brow,
Lately white with sickening terror,
Glows with sudden beauty now.
At his feet she told her story,
Showed her hands all bruised and torn;
And her sweet young face so haggard,
With a look so sad and worn,
Touched his heart with sudden pity,
Lit his eyes with misty light;
"Go, your lover lives!" cried Cromwell;
"Curfew shall not ring tonight."

JEANIE WITH THE LIGHT BROWN HAIR

Stephen Foster

I dream of Jeanie with the light brown hair,
Borne, like a vapor, on the summer air;
I see her tripping where the bright streams play,
Happy as the daisies that dance on her way.
Many were the wild notes her merry voice would pour,
Many were the blithe birds that warbled them o'er:
Oh! I dream of Jeanie with the light brown hair,
Floating, like a vapor, on the summer air.

I long for Jeanie with the day-dawn smile,
Radiant in gladness, warm with winning guile;
I hear her melodies, like joys gone by,
Sighing round my heart o'er the fond hopes that die:—

Sighing like the wind and sobbing like the rain,—
Wailing for the lost one that comes not again:
Oh! I long for Jeanie, and my heart bows low,
Never more to find her where the bright waters flow.

* * *

This house, where once a lawyer dwelt,
Is now a smith's, Alas!
How rapidly the iron age
Succeeds the age of brass!
—William Erskine

374

LOVE ME LITTLE, LOVE ME LONG

Anonymous

Love me little, love me long,
Is the burden of my song:
Love that is too hot and strong
   Burneth soon to waste.
I am with little well content,
And a little from thee sent
Is enough, with true intent,
   To be steadfast friend.
Love me little, love me long,
Is the burden of my song.

Say thou lov'st me while thou live,
I to thee my love will give,
Never dreaming to deceive
   While that life endures:
Nay, and after death in sooth,
I to thee will keep my truth,
As now when in my May of youth,
   This my love assures.
Love me little, love me long,
Is the burden of my song.

Constant love is moderate ever,
And it will through life persever,
Give to me that with true endeavor
   I will it restore:
A suit of durance let it be,
For all weathers, that for me,
For the land or for the sea,
   Lasting evermore.
Love me little, love me long,
Is the burden of my song.

ON A BAD SINGER

Samuel Taylor Coleridge

Swans sing before they die: 'twere no bad thing,
Should certain persons die before they sing.

SIR PATRICK SPENS

Anonymous

The King sits in Dunfermline town,
    Drinking the blude-red wine:
"O whaur will I get a skeely skipper
    To sail this new ship o' mine?"

O up and spake an eldern knight,
    Sat at the King's right knee:
"Sir Patrick Spens is the best sailor
    That ever sailed the sea."

Our King has written a braid letter
    And sealed it wi' his hand,
And sent it to Sir Patrick Spens,
    Was walking on the strand.

"To Noroway, to Noroway,
    To Noroway o'er the faem;
The King's daughter to Noroway,
    'Tis thou maun bring her hame."

The first word that Sir Patrick read,
    Sae loud, loud lauchèd he;
The neist word that Sir Patrick read,
    The tear blinded his ee.

"O wha is this has done this deed,
    And tauld the King of me,
To send us out at this time o' year
    To sail upon the sea?

Be it wind, be it weet, be it hail, be it sleet,
    Our ship must sail the faem;
The King's daughter to Noroway,
    'Tis we must bring her hame."

They hoysed their sails on Monday morn
    Wi' a' the speed they may;
They hae landed in Noroway
    Upon a Wodensday.

They hadna been a week, a week,
   In Noroway but twae,
When that the lords of Noroway
   Began aloud to say:

"Ye Scottishmen spend a' our King's goud
   And a' our Queenis fee."
"Ye lie, ye lie, ye liars loud,
   Fu' loud I hear ye lie!

For I brought as mickle white monie
   As gane my men and me,
And I brought a half-fou o' gude red goud
   Out-o'er the sea wi' me.

Mak' ready, mak' ready, my merry men a'!
   Our gude ship sails the morn."
"Now, ever alake, my master dear,
   I fear a deadly storm.

I saw the new moon late yestreen
   Wi' the auld moon in her arm;
And, if we gang to sea, master,
   I fear we'll come to harm."

They hadna sailed a league, a league,
   A league but barely three,
When the lift grew dark, and the wind blew loud,
   And gurly grew the sea

"O where will I get a gude sailor
   To tak' my helm in hand,
Till I gae up to the tall topmast
   To see if I can spy land?"

"O here am I, a sailor gude,
   To tak' the helm in hand,
Till you gae up to the tall topmast;
   But I fear you'll ne'er spy land."

He nadna gone a step, a step,
   A step but barely ane,
When a bolt flew out o' our goodly ship,
   And the salt sea it came in.

"Gae fetch a web o' the silken claith,
    Anither o' the twine,
And wap them into our ship's side,
    And letna the sea come in."

They fetched a web o' the silken claith,
    Anither o' the twine,
And they wapped them round that gude ship's side,
    But still the sea cam' in.

O laith, laith were our gude Scots lords
    To weet their milk-white hands;
But lang ere a' the play was ower
    They wat their gowden bands.

O laith, laith were our gude Scots lords
    To weet their cork-heeled shoon;
But lang ere a' the play was played
    They wat their hats aboon.

O lang, lang may the ladies sit
    Wi' their fans intill their hand,
Before they see Sir Patrick Spens
    Come sailing to the strand!

And lang, lang may the maidens sit
    Wi' their goud kaims in their hair,
A' waiting for their ain dear loves!
    For them they'll see nae mair.

Half ower, half ower to Aberdour,
    It's fifty fathoms deep,
And there lies gude Sir Patrick Spens
    Wi' the Scots lords at his feet.

THE FIRST SNOW-FALL

James Russell Lowell

The snow had begun in the gloaming,
    And busily all the night
Had been heaping field and highway
    With a silence deep and white.

Every pine and fir and hemlock
   Wore ermine too dear for an earl,
And the poorest twig on the elm-tree
   Was ridged inch deep with pearl.

From sheds new-roofed with Carrara
   Came Chanticleer's muffled crow,
The stiff rails were softened to swan's-down,
   And still fluttered down the snow.

I stood and watched by the window
   The noiseless work of the sky,
And the sudden flurries of snow-birds,
   Like brown leaves whirling by.

I thought of a mound in sweet Auburn
   Where a little headstone stood;
How the flakes were folding it gently,
   As did robins the babes in the wood.

Up spoke our own little Mabel,
   Saying, "Father, who makes it snow?"
And I told of the good All-father
   Who cares for us here below.

Again I looked at the snow-fall,
   And thought of the leaden sky
That arched o'er our first great sorrow,
   When that mound was heaped so high.

I remembered the gradual patience
   That fell from that cloud like snow,
Flake by flake, healing and hiding
   The scar that renewed our woe.

And again to the child I whispered,
   "The snow that husheth all,
Darling, the merciful Father
   Alone can make it fall!"

Then, with eyes that saw not, I kissed her;
   And she, kissing back, could not know
That *my* kiss was given to her sister,
   Folded close under deepening snow.

Holy Bible, St. Luke 15:11–32

11 And he said, A certain man had two sons:

12 And the younger of them said to his father, Father, give me the portion of goods that falleth to me. And he divided unto them his living.

13 And not many days after the younger son gathered all together, and took his journey into a far country, and there wasted his substance with riotous living.

14 And when he had spent all, there arose a mighty famine in that land; and he began to be in want.

15 And he went and joined himself to a citizen of that country; and he sent him into his fields to feed swine.

16 And he would fain have filled his belly with the husks that the swine did eat: and no man gave unto him.

17 And when he came to himself, he said, How many hired servants of my father's have bread enough and to spare, and I perish with hunger!

18 I will arise and go to my father, and will say unto him, Father, I have sinned against heaven, and before thee,

19 And am no more worthy to be called thy son: make me as one of thy hired servants.

20 And he arose, and came to his father. But when he was yet a great way off, his father saw him, and had compassion, and ran, and fell on his neck, and kissed him.

21 And the son said unto him, Father, I have sinned against heaven, and in thy sight, and am no more worthy to be called thy son.

22 But the father said to his servants, Bring forth the best robe, and put it on him; and put a ring on his hand, and shoes on his feet:

23 And bring hither the fatted calf, and kill it; and let us eat, and be merry:

24 For this my son was dead, and is alive again; he was lost, and is found. And they began to be merry.

25 Now his elder son was in the field: and as he came and drew nigh to the house, he heard musick and dancing.

26 And he called one of the servants, and asked what these things meant.

27 And he said unto him, Thy brother is come; and thy father

hath killed the fatted calf, because he hath received him safe and sound.

28 And he was angry, and would not go in: therefore came his father out, and intreated him.

29 And he answering said to his father, Lo, these many years do I serve thee, neither transgressed I at any time thy commandment: and yet thou never gavest me a kid, that I might make merry with my friends:

30 But as soon as this thy son was come, which hath devoured thy living with harlots, thou hast killed for him the fatted calf.

31 And he said unto him, Son, thou art ever with me, and all that I have is thine.

32 It was meet that we should make merry, and be glad: for this thy brother was dead, and is alive again; and was lost, and is found.

POLONIUS' ADVICE TO HIS SON

William Shakespeare

These few precepts in thy memory
See thou character. Give thy thoughts no tongue,
Nor any unproportion'd thought his act.
Be thou familiar, but by no means vulgar:
The friends thou hast, and their adoption tried,
Grapple them to thy soul with hoops of steel;
But do not dull thy palm with entertainment
Of each new-hatch'd, unfledg'd comrade. Beware
Of entrance to a quarrel: but being in,
Bear't that th' opposed may beware of thee.
Give every man thine ear, but few thy voice:
Take each man's censure, but reserve thy judgment.
Costly thy habit as thy purse can buy,
But not express'd in fancy: rich, not gaudy;
For the apparel oft proclaims the man.
Neither a borrower nor a lender be;
For loan oft loses both itself and friend,
And borrowing dulls the edge of husbandry.
This above all: to thine own self be true;
And it must follow, as the night the day,
Thou canst not then be false to any man.

(From Hamlet)

ABDUL A-BUL-BUL A-MIR

Anonymous

The sons of the prophet are brave men and bold,
And quite unaccustomed to fear,—
But the bravest by far in the ranks of the Shah
Was Abdul A-bul-bul A-mir.

If you wanted a man to encourage the van
Or harass the foe from the rear,
Storm fort or redoubt, you had only to shout
For Abdul A-bul-bul A-mir.

Now the heroes were plenty and well known to fame
In the troops that were led by the Czar,
And the bravest of these was a man by the name
Of Ivan Skavinsky Skavar.

He could imitate Irving, play poker and pool,
And strum on the Spanish guitar,
In fact quite the cream of the Muscovite team
Was Ivan Skavinsky Skavar.

One day this bold Russian had shouldered his gun,
And donned his most truculent sneer,
Downtown he did go, where he trod on the toe
Of Abdul A-bul-bul A-mir.

"Young man," quoth Abdul, "has life grown so dull
That you wish to end your career?
Vile infidel, know, you have trod on the toe
Of Abdul A-bul-bul A-mir."

Said Ivan, "My friend, your remarks in the end
Will avail you but little, I fear,
For you ne'er will survive to repeat them alive,
Mr. Abdul A-bul-bul A-mir.

"So take your last look at sunshine and brook,
And send your regrets to the Czar—
For by this I imply, you are going to die,
Count Ivan Skavinsky Skavar!"

Then this bold Mameluke drew his trusty skibouk,
With a cry of "Allah Akbar,"
And with murderous intent he ferociously went
For Ivan Skavinsky Skavar.

They parried and thrust, they sidestepped and cussed,
Of blood they spilled a great part;
The philologist blokes, who seldom crack jokes,
Say that hash was first made on that spot.

They fought all that night, 'neath the pale yellow moon,
The din, it was heard from afar,
And huge multitudes came, so great was the fame,
Of Abdul and Ivan Skavar.

As Abdul's long knife was extracting the life,
In fact he was shouting "Huzzah,"
He felt himself struck by that wily Calmuck,
Count Ivan Skavinsky Skavar.

The Sultan drove by in his red-breasted fly,
Expecting the victor to cheer,
But he only drew nigh to hear the last sigh
Of Abdul A-bul-bul A-mir.

Czar Petrovitch too, in his spectacles blue,
Rode up in his new-crested car.
He arrived just in time to exchange a last line,
With Ivan Skavinsky Skavar.

There's a tomb rises up where the Blue Danube rolls,
And 'graved there in characters clear,
Are, "Stranger, when passing, oh pray for the soul
Of Abdul A-bul-bul A-mir."

A splash in the Black Sea one dark moonless night,
Caused ripples to spread wide and far,
It was made by a sack fitting close to the back
Of Ivan Skavinsky Skavar.

A Muscovite maiden her love vigil keeps,
'Neath the light of the pale polar star,
And the name that she murmurs so oft as she weeps
Is Ivan Skavinsky Skavar.

GRANDFATHER'S CLOCK

Henry Clay Work

My grandfather's clock was too large for the shelf,
  So it stood ninety years on the floor;
It was taller by half than the old man himself,
  Though it weighed not a pennyweight more.
It was bought on the morn of the day that he was born
  And was always his treasure and pride.
But it stopped short—never to go again—
  When the old man died.

        Ninety years without slumbering
          Tick, tick, tick, tick.
        His life-seconds numbering
          Tick, tick, tick, tick.
        It stopped short—never to go again—
          When the old man died.

In watching its pendulum swing to and fro
  Many hours had he spent while a boy;
And in childhood and manhood the clock seemed to know
  And to share both his grief and his joy,
For it struck twenty-four when he entered the door
  With a blooming and beautiful bride,
But it stopped short—never to go again—
  When the old man died.

My grandfather said of those he could hire,
  Not a servant so faithful he found,
For it wasted no time and had but one desire—
  At the close of each week to be wound.
And it kept in its place—not a frown upon its face,
  And its hands never hung by its side;
But it stopped short—never to go again—
  When the old man died.

It rang an alarm in the dead of night—
  An alarm that for years had been dumb.
And we knew that his spirit was pluming for flight
  That his hour for departure had come.

384

Still the clock kept the time with a soft and muffled chime
    As we silently stood by his side;
But it stopped short—never to go again—
    When the old man died.

WHEN JOHNNY COMES MARCHING HOME

Patrick S. Gilmore

When Johnny comes marching home again,
Hurrah! Hurrah!
We'll give him a hearty welcome then,
Hurrah! Hurrah!
The men will cheer, the boys will shout,
The ladies they will all turn out,
And we'll all feel gay
When Johnny comes marching home.

The old church bell will peal with joy,
Hurrah! Hurrah!
To welcome home our darling boy,
Hurrah! Hurrah!
The village lads and lassies say
With roses they will strew the way,
And we'll all feel gay
When Johnny comes marching home.

Get ready for the Jubilee,
Hurrah! Hurrah!
We'll give the hero three times three,
Hurrah! Hurrah!
The laurel wreath is ready now
To place upon his loyal brow
And we'll all feel gay
When Johnny comes marching home.

In eighteen hundred and sixty-one,
Hurrah! Hurrah!
That was when the war begun,
Hurrah! Hurrah!

In eighteen hundred and sixty-two,
Both sides were falling to
And we'll all drink stone wine,
When Johnny comes marching home.

In eighteen hundred and sixty-four,
Hurrah! Hurrah!
Abe called for five hundred thousand more,
Hurrah! Hurrah!
In eighteen hundred and sixty-five,
They talked rebellion—strife;
And we'll all drink some wine
When Johnny comes marching home.

CHRISTMAS DAY IN THE WORKHOUSE

George R. Sims

It is Christmas Day in the workhouse, and the cold, bare walls are
    bright
With garlands of green and holly, and the place is a pleasant sight;
For with clean-washed hands and faces in a long and hungry line
The paupers sit at the table, for this is the hour they dine.

And the guardians and their ladies, although the wind is east,
Have come in their furs and wrappers to watch their charges feast;
To smile and be condescending, putting on pauper plates.
To be hosts at the workhouse banquet they've paid for—with the
    rates.

O, the paupers are meek and lowly with their "Thank'ee kindly,
    mums!"
So long as they fill their stomachs what matter it whence it comes?
But one of the old men mutters and pushes his plate aside,
"Great God!" he cries, "but it chokes me; for this is the day she
    died!"

The guardians gazed in horror, the master's face went white;
"Did a pauper refuse their pudding? Could that their ears believe
    aright?"
Then the ladies clutched their husbands, thinking the man would
    die,
Struck by a bolt, or something, by the outraged One on high.

But the pauper sat for a moment, then rose 'mid silence grim,
For the others had ceased to chatter and trembled in every limb:
He looked at the guardians' ladies, then, eyeing their lords, he
   said;
"I eat not the food of villains whose hands are foul and red;

"Whose victims cry for vengeance from their dark, unhallowed
   graves."
"He's drunk," said the workhouse master, "or else he's mad and
   raves."
"Not drunk or mad," cried the pauper, "but only a haunted beast,
Who, torn by the hounds and mangled, declines the vulture's feast.

"I care not a curse for the guardians, and I won't be dragged away;
Just let me have the fit out, it's only on Christmas Day
That the black past comes to goad me and prey on my burning
   brain;
I'll tell you the rest in a whisper—I swear I won't shout again.

"Keep your hands off me, curse you! Hear me right out to the end.
You come here to see how paupers the season of Christmas spend;
You come here to watch us feeding, as they watched the captured
   beast;
Here's why a penniless pauper spits on your paltry feast.

"Do you think I will take your bounty and let you smile and think
You're doing a noble action with the parish's meat and drink?
Where is my wife, you traitors—the poor old wife you slew?
Yes, by the God above me, my Nance was killed by you.

"Last Winter my wife lay dying, starved in a filthy den.
I had never been to the parish—I came to the parish then;
I swallowed my pride in coming! for ere the ruin came
I held up my head as a trader, and I bore a spotless name.

"I came to the parish, craving bread for a starving wife—
Bread for the woman who'd loved me thro' fifty years of life;
And what do you think they told me, mocking my awful grief,
That the house was open to us, but they wouldn't give out relief.

"I slunk to the filthy alley—'twas a cold, raw Christmas Eve—
And the bakers' shops were open, tempting a man to thieve;
But I clenched my fists together, holding my head awry,
So I came to her empty-handed and mournfully told her why.

"Then I told her the house was open; she had heard of the ways
  of that,
For her bloodless cheeks went crimson, and up in her rags she sat,
Crying, 'Bide the Christmas here, John, we've never had one apart;
I think I can bear the hunger—the other would break my heart.'

"All through that eve I watched her, holding her hand in mine,
Praying the Lord and weeping till my lips were salt as brine;
I asked her once if she hungered, and she answered 'No.'
The moon shone in at the window, set in a wreath of snow.

"Then the room was bathed in glory, and I saw in my darling's
  eyes
The faraway look of wonder that comes when the spirit flies;
And her lips were parched and parted, and her reason came and
  went.
For she rav'd of our home in Devon, where our happiest years
  were spent.

"And the accents, long forgotten, came back to the tongue once
  more.
For she talked like the country lassie I woo'd by the Devon shore;
Then she rose to her feet and trembled, and fell on the rags and
  moaned,
And, 'Give me a crust—I'm famished—for the love of God,' she
  groaned.

"I rushed from the room like a madman and flew to the workhouse gate,
Crying, 'Food for a dying woman!' and the answer came, 'Too
  late;'
They drove me away with curses; then I fought with a dog in the
  street
And tore from the mongrel's clutches a crust he was trying to eat.

"Back through the filthy byways! Back through the trampled
  slush!
Up to the crazy garret, wrapped in an awful hush;
My heart sank down at the threshold, and I paused with a sudden
  thrill,
For there, in the silv'ry moonlight, my Nance lay cold and still.

"Up to the blackened ceiling the sunken eyes were cast—
I knew on those lips, all bloodless, my name had been the last;
She called for her absent husband—O God! Had I known—
Had called in vain, and, in anguish, had died in that den alone.

"Yes, there in a land of plenty, lay a loving woman dead.
Cruelly starved and murdered for a loaf of the parish bread;
At yonder gate, last Christmas, I craved for a human life,
You, who would feed us paupers, what of my murdered wife?

"There, get ye gone to your dinners, don't mind me in the least;
Think of the happy paupers eating your Christmas feast;
And when you recount their blessings in your parochial way,
Say what you did for me, too, only last Christmas Day."

EXCELSIOR

Henry Wadsworth Longfellow

The shades of night were falling fast,
As through an Alpine village passed
A youth, who bore, 'mid snow and ice,
A banner with the strange device—
　　Excelsior!

His brow was sad; his eye beneath
Flashed like a falchion from its sheath;
And like a silver clarion rung
The accents of that unknown tongue—
　　Excelsior!

In happy homes he saw the light
Of household fires gleam warm and bright,
Above, the spectral glaciers shone,
And from his lips escaped a groan—
　　Excelsior!

"Try not the pass," the old man said:
"Dark lowers the tempest overhead;
The roaring torrent is deep and wide."
And loud that clarion voice replied,
　　Excelsior!

"Oh, stay," the maiden said, "and rest
Thy weary head upon this breast!"
A tear stood in his bright blue eye,
But still he answered with a sigh,
       Excelsior!

"Beware the pine-tree's withered branch!
Beware the awful avalanche!"
This was the peasant's last Good-night:
A voice replied, far up the height:
       Excelsior!

At break of day, as heavenward
The pious monks of Saint Bernard
Uttered the oft-repeated prayer,
A voice cried through the startled air,
       Excelsior!

A traveller, by the faithful hound,
Half-buried in the snow was found,
Still grasping in his hand of ice
That banner with the strange device,
       Excelsior!

There in the twilight cold and gray,
Lifeless, but beautiful, he lay,
And from the sky, serene and far,
A voice fell, like a falling star—
       Excelsior!

THE BATTLE OF WATERLOO

Lord Byron

There was a sound of revelry by night,
And Belgium's capital had gathered then
Her beauty and her chivalry, and bright
The lamps shone o'er fair women and brave men;
A thousand hearts beat happily; and when
Music arose with its voluptuous swell,
Soft eyes looked love to eyes which spake again,
And all went merry as a marriage-bell;
But hush! hark! a deep sound strikes like a rising knell!

Did ye not hear it?—No; 'twas but the wind,
Or the car rattling o'er the stony street;
On with the dance! let joy be unconfined;
No sleep till morn, when Youth and Pleasure meet
To chase the glowing Hours with flying feet.
But hark! that heavy sound breaks in once more,
As if the clouds its echo would repeat;
And nearer, clearer, deadlier than before!
Arm! arm! it is—it is—the cannon's opening roar!

Within a windowed niche of that high hall
Sate Brunswick's fated chieftain; he did hear
That sound, the first amidst the festival,
And caught its tone with Death's prophetic ear;
And when they smiled because he deemed it near,
His heart more truly knew that peal too well
Which stretched his father on a bloody bier,
And roused the vengeance blood alone could quell:
He rushed into the field, and, foremost fighting, fell.

Ah! then and there was hurrying to and fro,
And gathering tears, and tremblings of distress,
And cheeks all pale, which but an hour ago
Blushed at the praise of their own loveliness;
And there were sudden partings, such as press
The life from out young hearts, and choking sighs
Which ne'er might be repeated: who would guess
If evermore should meet those mutual eyes,
Since upon night so sweet such awful morn could rise!

And there was mounting in hot haste: the steed,
The mustering squadron, and the clattering car,
Went pouring forward with impetuous speed,
And swiftly forming in the ranks of war;
And the deep thunder peal on peal afar;
And near, the beat of the alarming drum
Roused up the soldier ere the morning star;
While thronged the citizens with terror dumb,
Or whispering with white lips,—"The foe! they come!
they come!"

And wild and high the "Cameron's gathering" rose,
The war-note of Lochiel, which Albyn's hills

Have heard,—and heard, too, have her Saxon foes;
How in the noon of night that pibroch thrills
Savage and shrill! But with the breath which fills
Their mountain pipe, so fill the mountaineers
With the fierce native daring which instils
The stirring memory of a thousand years,
And Evan's, Donald's fame rings in each clansman's ears!

And Ardennes waves above them her green leaves,
Dewy with nature's tear-drops, as they pass,
Grieving, if aught inanimate e'er grieves,
Over the unreturning brave,—alas!
Ere evening to be trodden like the grass
Which now beneath them, but above shall grow
In its next verdure, when this fiery mass
Of living valor, rolling on the foe,
And burning with high hope, shall moulder cold and
    low.

Last noon beheld them full of lusty life,
Last eve in Beauty's circle proudly gay,
The midnight brought the signal-sound of strife,
The morn the marshalling in arms—the day
Battle's magnificently stern array!
The thunder-clouds close o'er it, which when rent
The earth is covered thick with other clay,
Which her own clay shall cover, heaped and pent,
Rider and horse,—friend, foe,—in one red burial blent!

Their praise is hymned by loftier harps than mine;
Yet one I would select from that proud throng,
Partly because they blend me with his line,
And partly that I did his sire some wrong,
And partly that bright names will hallow song!
And his was of the bravest, and when showered
The death-bolts deadliest the thinned files along,
Even where the thickest of war's tempest lowered,
They reached no nobler breast than thine, young, gal-
    lant Howard!

There have been tears and breaking hearts for thee,
And mine were nothing, had I such to give;

But when I stood beneath the fresh green tree,
Which living waves where thou didst cease to live,
And saw around me the wide field revive
With fruits and fertile promise, and the Spring
Come forth her work of gladness to contrive,
With all her reckless birds upon the wing,
I turned from all she brought to those she could not
    bring.

I turned to thee, to thousands, of whom each
And one as all a ghastly gap did make
In his own kind and kindred, whom to teach
Forgetfulness were mercy for their sake;
The Archangel's trump, not glory's, must awake
Those whom they thirst for; though the sound of Fame
May for a moment soothe, it cannot slake
The fever of vain longing, and the name
So honored, but assumes a stronger, bitterer claim.

They mourn, but smile at length; and, smiling, mourn;
The tree will wither long before it fall;
The hull drives on, though mast and sail be torn;
The roof-tree sinks, but moulders on the hall
In massy hoariness; the ruined wall
Stands when its wind-worn battlements are gone;
The bars survive the captive they inthrall;
The day drags through though storms keep out the
    sun;
And thus the heart will break, yet brokenly live on:

Even as a broken mirror, which the glass
In every fragment multiplies; and makes
A thousand images of one that was,
The same, and still the more, the more it breaks;
And thus the heart will do which not forsakes,
Living in shattered guise, and still, and cold,
And bloodless, with its sleepless sorrow aches,
Yet withers on till all without is old,
Showing no visible sign, for such things are untold.

                    (From Childe Harold)

THE LISTENERS

Walter de la Mare

"Is there anybody there?" said the Traveller,
  Knocking on the moonlit door;
And his horse in the silence champed the grasses
  Of the forest's ferny floor:
And a bird flew up out of the turret,
  Above the Traveller's head:
And he smote upon the door again a second time;
  "Is there anybody there?" he said.
But no one descended to the Traveller;
  No head from the leaf-fringed sill
Leaned over and looked into his grey eyes,
  Where he stood perplexed and still.
But only a host of phantom listeners
  That dwelt in the lone house then
Stood listening in the quiet of the moonlight
  To that voice from the world of men:
Stood thronging the faint moon beams on the dark stair,
  That goes down to the empty hall,
Hearkening in an air stirred and shaken
  By the lonely Traveller's call.
And he felt in his heart their strangeness,
  Their stillness answering his cry,
While his horse moved, cropping the dark turf,
  'Neath the starred and leafy sky;
For he suddenly smote on the door, even
  Louder, and lifted his head:—
"Tell them I came, and no one answered,
  That I kept my word," he said.
Never the least stir made the listeners,
  Though every word he spake
Fell echoing through the shadowiness of the still house
  From the one man left awake:
Ay, they heard his foot upon the stirrup,
  And the sound of iron on stone
And how the silence surged softly backward
  When the plunging hoofs were gone.

* * *

There is always room at the top—after the investigation.
                                        —Oliver Herford

THE DEATH OF JESUS

Holy Bible, Luke 23:1–46

1 And the whole multitude of them arose, and led him unto Pilate.

2 And they began to accuse him, saying, We found this fellow perverting the nation, and forbidding to give tribute to Caesar, saying that he himself is Christ a king.

3 And Pilate asked him, saying, Art thou the King of the Jews? And he answered him, and said, Thou sayest it.

4 Then said Pilate to the chief priests and to the people, I find no fault in this man.

5 And they were the more fierce, saying, He stirreth up the people, teaching, throughout all Jewry, beginning from Galilee to this place.

6 When Pilate heard of Galilee, he asked whether the man were a Galilean.

7 And as soon as he knew that he belonged unto Herod's jurisdiction, he sent him to Herod, who himself also was at Jerusalem at that time.

8 And when Herod saw Jesus, he was exceeding glad: for he was desirous to see him of a long season, because he had heard many things of him; and he hoped to have seen some miracles done by him.

9 Then he questioned with him in many words; but he answered him nothing.

10 And the chief priests and scribes stood and vehemently accused him.

11 And Herod with his men of war set him at nought, and mocked him, and arrayed him in a gorgeous robe, and sent him again to Pilate.

12 And the same day Pilate and Herod were made friends together: for before they were at enmity between themselves.

13 And Pilate, when he had called together the chief priests and the rulers and the people.

14 Said unto them, Ye have brought this man unto me, as one that perverteth the people; and, behold, I having examined him before you, have found no fault in this man, touching those things whereof ye accuse him:

15 No, nor yet Herod: for I sent you to him; and lo, nothing worthy of death is done unto him.

16 I will therefore chastise him, and release him.

17 (For of necessity he must release one unto them at the feast.)

18 And they cried out all at once, saying, Away with this man, and release unto us Barabbas:

19 (Who for a certain sedition made in the city, and for murder, was cast into prison.)

20 Pilate, therefore, willing to release Jesus, spake again to them.

21 But they cried, saying, Crucify him, crucify him.

22 And he said unto them the third time, Why, what evil hath he done? I have found no cause of death in him: I will therefore chastise him, and let him go.

23 And they were instant with loud voices, requiring that he might be crucified. And the voices of them and of the chief priests prevailed.

24 And Pilate gave sentence that it should be as they required.

25 And he released unto them him that for sedition and murder was cast into prison, whom they had desired; but he delivered Jesus to their will.

26 And as they led him away, they laid hold upon one Simon, a Cyrenian, coming out of the country, and on him they laid the cross, that he might bear it after Jesus.

27 And there followed him a great company of people, and of women, which also bewailed and lamented him.

28 But Jesus turning unto them, said, Daughters of Jerusalem, weep not for me, but weep for yourselves, and for your children.

29 For, behold, the days are coming, in the which they shall say, Blessed are the barren, and the wombs that never bare, and the paps which never gave suck.

30 Then shall they begin to say to the mountains, Fall on us; and to the hills, cover us.

31 For if they do these things in a green tree, what shall be done in the dry?

32 And there were also two other, malefactors, led with him to be put to death.

33 And when they were come to the place, which is called Calvary, there they crucified him, and the malefactors, one on the right hand, and the other on the left.

34 Then said Jesus, Father, forgive them; for they know not what they do. And they parted his raiment, and cast lots.

35 And the people stood beholding. And the rulers also with them derided him, saying He saved others; let him save himself, if he be Christ, the chosen of God.

36 And the soldiers also mocked him, coming to him, and offering him vinegar,

37 And saying, If thou be the king of the Jews, save thyself.

38 And a superscription also was written over him, in letters of Greek, and Latin, and Hebrew, THIS IS THE KING OF THE JEWS.

39 And one of the malefactors which were hanged railed on him, saying, If thou be Christ, save thyself and us.

40 But the other answering, rebuked him, saying, Dost not thou fear God, seeing thou art in the same condemnation?

41 And we indeed justly; for we receive the due reward of our deeds: but this man hath done nothing amiss.

42 And he said unto Jesus, Lord, remember me when thou comest into thy kingdom.

43 And Jesus said unto him, Verily I say unto thee, Today shalt thou be with me in paradise.

44 And it was about the sixth hour, and there was a darkness over all the earth until the ninth hour.

45 And the sun was darkened, and the veil of the temple was rent in the midst.

46 And when Jesus had cried with a loud voice, he said, Father, into thy hands I commend my spirit: and having said thus, he gave up the ghost.

ROCK OF AGES

August M. Toplady

Rock of Ages, cleft for me,
Let me hide myself in Thee!
Let the water and the blood
From Thy riven side which flowed,
Be of sin the double cure,
Save from guilt and make me pure.

Could my tears forever flow;
Could my zeal no languor know;
These for sin could not atone,
Thou must save, and Thou alone.
Rock of Ages, cleft for me,
Let me hide myself in Thee.

Not the labors of my hands
Can fulfill Thy law's demands;
Could my zeal no respite know,
Could my tears forever flow,
All for sin could not atone;
Thou must save and Thou alone.

Nothing in my hand I bring;
Simply to Thy cross I cling.
Naked, come to Thee for dress,
Helpless, look to Thee for grace.
Foul, I to the Fountain fly,
Wash me, Saviour, or I die.

While I draw this fleeting breath,
When mine eyes shall close in death,
When I rise to worlds unknown,
See Thee on Thy judgment throne—
Rock of Ages, cleft for me,
Let me hide myself in Thee.

ROCK ME TO SLEEP

Elizabeth Akers Allen

Backward, turn backward, O Time, in your flight,
Make me a child again just for tonight!
Mother, come back from the echoless shore,
Take me again to your heart as of yore;
Kiss from my forehead the furrows of care,
Smooth the few silver threads out of my hair;
Over my slumbers your loving watch keep;—
Rock me to sleep, mother,—rock me to sleep!

Backward, flow backward, O tide of the years!
I am so weary of toil and of tears—
Toil without recompense, tears all in vain—
Take them, and give me my childhood again!
I have grown weary of dust and decay—
Weary of flinging my soul-wealth away;
Weary of sowing for others to reap;—
Rock me to sleep, mother,—rock me to sleep!

Tired of the hollow, the base, the untrue,
Mother, O mother, my heart calls to you!
Many a summer the grass has grown green,
Blossomed and faded, our faces between;
Yet with strong yearning and passionate pain,
Long I to-night for your presence again.
Come from the silence so long and so deep;—
Rock me to sleep, mother,—rock me to sleep!

Over my heart, in the days that are flown,
No love like mother-love ever has shone;
No other worship abides and endures—
Faithful, unselfish, and patient like yours:
None like a mother can charm away pain
From the sick soul and the world-weary brain.
Slumber's soft calms o'er my heavy lips creep;—
Rock me to sleep, mother,—rock me to sleep!

Come, let your brown hair, just lighted with gold,
Fall on your shoulders again as of old;
Let it drop over my forehead to-night,
Shading my faint eyes away from the light;
For with its sunny-edged shadows once more
Haply will throng the sweet visions of yore;
Lovingly, softly, its bright billows sweep:—
Rock me to sleep, mother,—rock me to sleep!

Mother, dear mother, the years have been long
Since I last listened your lullaby songs:
Sing, then, and unto my soul it shall seem
Womanhood's years have been only a dream.
Clasped to your heart in a loving embrace,
With your light lashes just sweeping my face,
Never hereafter to wake or to weep;—
Rock me to sleep, mother,—rock me to sleep!

YE MARINERS OF ENGLAND

Thomas Campbell

Ye mariners of England
That guard our native seas;
Whose flag has braved, a thousand years,
The battle and the breeze!

Your glorious standard launch again
To match another foe,
And sweep through the deep,
While the stormy winds do blow;
While the battle rages loud and long,
And the stormy winds do blow.

The spirits of your fathers
Shall start from every wave,
For the deck it was their field of fame,
And ocean was their grave:
Where Blake and mighty Nelson fell,
Your manly hearts shall glow,
As ye sweep through the deep,
While the stormy winds do blow;
While the battle rages loud and long,
And the stormy winds do blow.

Britannia needs no bulwarks,
No towers along the steep;
Her march is o'er the mountain-waves,
Her home is on the deep.
With thunders from her native oak,
She quells the floods below,—
As they roar on the shore,
When the stormy winds do blow;
When the battle rages loud and long
And the stormy winds do blow.

The meteor flag of England
Shall yet terrific burn;
Till danger's troubled night depart,
And the star of peace return.
Then, then, ye ocean warriors,
Our song and feast shall flow
To the fame of your name,
When the storm has ceased to blow;
When the fiery fight is heard no more,
And the storm has ceased to blow.

*   *   *

There is nothing more frightful than a bustling ignorance.
—Goethe

EVOLUTION

Langdon Smith

When you were a tadpole and I was a fish
   In the Paleozoic time,
And side by side on the ebbing tide
   We sprawled through the ooze and slime,
Or skittered with many a caudal flip
   Through the depths of the Carbrian fen,
My heart was rife with the joy of life,
   For I loved you even then.

Mindless we lived and mindless we loved
   And mindless at last we died;
And deep in the rift of the Caradoc drift
   We slumbered side by side.
The world turned on in the lathe of time,
   The hot lands heaved amain,
Till we caught our breath from the womb of death
   And crept into light again.

We were amphibians, scaled and tailed,
   And drab as a dead man's hand;
We coiled at ease 'neath the dripping trees
   Or trailed through the mud and sand.
Croaking and blind, with our three-clawed feet
   Writing a language dumb,
With never a spark in the empty dark
   To hint at a life to come.

Yet happy we lived and happy we loved,
   And happy we died once more;
Our forms were rolled in the clinging mold
   Of a Neocomian shore.
The eons came and the eons fled
   And the sleep that wrapped us fast
Was riven away in a newer day
   And the night of death was past.

Then light and swift through the jungle trees
   We swung in our airy flights,
Or breathed in the balms of the fronded palms
   In the hush of the moonless nights;

And, oh! what beautiful years were there
   When our hearts clung each to each;
When life was filled and our senses thrilled
   In the first faint dawn of speech.

Thus life by life and love by love
   We passed through the cycles strange,
And breath by breath and death by death
   We followed the chain of change.
Till there came a time in the law of life
   When over the nursing side
The shadows broke and the soul awoke
   In a strange, dim dream of God.

I was thewed like an Auroch bull
   And tusked like the great cave bear;
And you, my sweet, from head to feet
   Were gowned in your glorious hair.
Deep in the gloom of a fireless cave,
   When the night fell o'er the plain
And the moon hung red o'er the river bed
   We mumbled the bones of the slain.

I flaked a flint to a cutting edge
   And shaped it with brutish craft;
I broke a shank from the woodland lank
   And fitted it, head and haft;
Then I hid me close to the reedy tarn,
   Where the mammoth came to drink;
Through the brawn and bone I drove the stone
   And slew him upon the brink.

Loud I howled through the moonlit wastes,
   Loud answered our kith and kin;
From west and east to the crimson feast
   The clan came tramping in.
O'er joint and gristle and padded hoof
   We fought and clawed and tore,
And cheek by jowl with many a growl
   We talked the marvel o'er.

I carved that fight on a reindeer bone
   With rude and hairy hand;

I pictured his fall on the cavern wall
    That men might understand.
For we lived by blood and the right of might
    Ere human laws were drawn,
And the age of sin did not begin
    Till our brutal tush were gone.

And that was a million years ago
    In a time that no man knows;
Yet here tonight in the mellow light
    We sit at Delmonico's.
Your eyes are deep as the Devon springs,
    Your hair is dark as jet,
Your years are few, your life is new,
    Your soul untried, and yet—

Our trail is on the Kimmeridge clay
    And the scarp of the Purbeck flags;
We have left our bones in the Bagshot stones
    And deep in the Coralline crags;
Our love is old, our lives are old,
    And death shall come amain;
Should it come today, what man may say
    We shall not live again?

God wrought our souls from the Tremadoc beds
    And furnished them wings to fly;
He sowed our spawn in the world's dim dawn,
    And I know that it shall not die,
Though cities have sprung above the graves
    Where the crook-bone men make war
And the oxwain creaks o'er the buried caves
    Where the mummied mammoths are.

Then as we linger at luncheon here
    O'er many a dainty dish,
Let us drink anew to the time when you
    Were a tadpole and I was a fish.

* * *

The Right Honorable Gentleman is indebted to his memory
for his jests and to his imagination for his facts.
                    (R. B. Sheridan's reply to Mr. Dundas)

TO A WATERFOWL

William Cullen Bryant

Whither, midst falling dew,
While glow the heavens with the last steps of day,
Far through their rosy depths dost thou pursue
    Thy solitary way?

Vainly the fowler's eye
Might mark thy distant flight, to do thee wrong,
As, darkly painted on the crimson sky,
    Thy figure floats along.

Seek'st thou the plashy brink
Of weedy lake, or marge of river wide,
Or where the rocking billows rise and sink
    On the chafed ocean-side?

There is a Power whose care
Teaches thy way along that pathless coast—
The desert and illimitable air—
    Lone wandering, but not lost.

All day thy wings have fanned,
At that far height, the cold, thin atmosphere;
Yet stoop not, weary, to the welcome land,
    Though the dark night is near.

And soon that toil shall end;
Soon shalt thou find a summer home, and rest,
And scream among thy fellows; reeds shall bend
    Soon o'er thy sheltered nest.

Thou'rt gone; the abyss of Heaven
Hath swallowed up thy form; yet on my heart
Deeply hath sunk the lesson thou hast given,
    And shall not soon depart.

He, who from zone to zone
Guides through the boundless sky thy certain flight,
In the long way that I must tread alone,
    Will lead my steps aright.

FROM THOMAS JEFFERSON'S INAUGURAL
ADDRESS

FRIENDS AND FELLOW CITIZENS:

Called upon to undertake the duties of the first executive office of the country, I will avail myself of that portion of my fellow citizens which is here assembled to express my grateful thanks for the favor with which they have been pleased to look toward me, to declare a sincere consciousness that the task is above my talents, and that I approach it with those anxious and awful presentiments which the greatness of the charge and the weakness of my powers so justly inspire. A rising nation, spread over a wide and fruitful land, traversing all the seas with the rich productions of their industry, engaged in commerce with nations who feel power and forget right, advancing rapidly to destinies beyond the reach of mortal eye—when I contemplate these transcendent objects, and see the honor, the happiness, and the hopes of this beloved country committed to the issue and the auspices of this day, I shrink from the contemplation, and humble myself before the magnitude of the undertaking . . .

During the contest of opinion through which we have passed the animation of discussions and of exertions has sometimes worn an aspect which might impose on strangers unused to think freely and to speak and to write what they think; but this being now decided by the voice of the nation, announced according to the rules of the Constitution, all will, of course, arrange themselves under the will of the law, and unite in common efforts for the common good. All, too, will bear in mind the sacred principle, that though the will of the majority is in all cases to prevail, that will to be rightful must be reasonable; that the minority possesses their equal rights, which equal law must protect, and to violate would be oppression. Let us, then, fellow citizens, unite with one heart and one mind. Let us restore to social intercourse that harmony and affection without which liberty and even life itself are but dreary things. And let us reflect that, having banished from our land that religious intolerance under which mankind so long bled and suffered, we have yet gained little if we countenance a political intolerance as despotic, as wicked, and capable of as bitter and bloody persecutions. During the throes and convulsions of the ancient world, during the agonized spasms of infuriated man, seeking through blood and slaughter his long-lost liberty, it was not wonderful that the agitation of the billows should reach even this distant and peaceful shore; that this should be more felt and feared by some and less by others, and should divide opinions as to measures of safety. But every difference of opinion is not a difference of principle. We have called by different names brethren of the same principle. We are all Republicans, we are all Federalists. If there be any among us who would wish to dissolve this Union or to change its republican form, let them stand undisturbed as monuments of the safety with which error of opinion may be tol· erated where reason is left free to combat it. I know, indeed, that some honest men fear that a republican government cannot be strong, that this government is not strong enough; but would the honest patriot, in the full tide of successful experiment, abandon a government which has so far kept us free and firm on the theoretic and visionary fear that this government, the world's best hope, may by possibility want energy to preserve itself? I trust not. I believe this, on the contrary, the strongest government on earth. I believe it is the only one where every man, at the call of the law, would fly to the standard of the law, and would meet invasions of the public order as his own personal concern. Sometimes it is said that man cannot be trusted with the government of himself. Can he, then, be trusted with the government of others? Or have we found angels in the form of kings to govern him? Let history answer this question.

Let us, then, with courage and confidence pursue our own Federal and Republican principles, our attachment to union and representative government. Kindly separated by nature and a wide ocean from the exterminating havoc of one quarter of the globe; too high-minded to endure the degradations of the others; possessing a chosen country, with room enough for our descendants to the thousandth and thousandth generation; entertaining a due sense of our equal right to the use of our faculties, to the acquisitions of our own industry, to honor and confidence from our fellow citizens, resulting not from birth, but from our actions and their sense of them; enlightened by a benign religion, professed, indeed, and practiced in various forms, yet all of them inculcating honesty, truth, temperance, gratitude, and the love of man; acknowledging and adoring an over-ruling Providence, which by all its dispensations proves that it delights in the happiness of man here and his greater happiness hereafter—with all these blessings, what more is necessary to make us a happy and a prosperous people? Still one thing more, fellow citizens—a wise and frugal government, which shall restrain men from injuring one another, shall leave them otherwise free to regulate their own pursuits of industry and improvement, and shall not take from the mouth of labor the bread it has earned. This is the sum of good government, and this is necessary to close the circle of our felicities. . . .

BARBARA FRIETCHIE

John Greenleaf Whittier

Up from the meadows rich with corn,
Clear in the cool September morn,

The clustered spires of Frederick stand
Green-walled by the hills of Maryland.

Round about them orchards sweep,
Apple and peach-tree fruited deep,

Fair as a garden of the Lord
To the eyes of the famished rebel horde,

On that pleasant morn of the early fall
When Lee marched over the mountain wall;

Over the mountains winding down,
Horse and foot, into Frederick town.

Forty flags with their silver stars,
Forty flags with their crimson bars,

Flapped in the morning wind: the sun
Of noon looked down, and saw not one.

Up rose old Barbara Frietchie then,
Bowed with her fourscore years and ten;

Bravest of all in Frederick town,
She took up the flag the men hauled down;

In her attic window the staff she set,
To show that one heart was loyal yet.

Up the street came the rebel tread,
Stonewall Jackson riding ahead.

Under his slouched hat left and right
He glanced; the old flag met his sight.

"Halt!"—the dust-brown ranks stood fast.
"Fire!"—out blazed the rifle blast.

It shivered the window, pane and sash;
It rent the banner with seam and gash.

Quick, as it fell, from the broken staff
Dame Barbara snatched the silken scarf.

She leaned far out on the window-sill,
And shook it forth with a royal will.

"Shoot, if you must, this old grey head,
But spare your country's flag," she said.

A shade of sadness, a blush of shame,
Over the face of the leader came;

The nobler nature within him stirred
To life at that woman's deed and word;

"Who touches a hair of yon grey head
Dies like a dog! March on!" he said.

All day long through Frederick street
Sounded the tread of marching feet:

All day long that free flag tost
Over the heads of the rebel host.

Ever its torn folds rose and fell
On the loyal winds that loved it well;

And through the hill-gaps sunset light
Shone over it with a warm good-night.

Barbara Frietchie's work is o'er,
And the rebel rides on his raids no more.

Honor to her! and let a tear
Fall, for her sake, on Stonewall's bier.

Over Barbara Frietchie's grave,
Flag of freedom and union, wave!

Peace, and order, and beauty draw
Round thy symbol of light and law;

And ever the stars above look down
On thy stars below in Frederick town!

THE GREATEST BATTLE THAT EVER WAS FOUGHT

Joaquin Miller

The greatest battle that ever was fought—
  Shall I tell you where and when?
On the maps of the world you will find it not:
  It was fought by the Mothers of Men.

Not with cannon or battle shot,
  With sword or nobler pen;
Not with eloquent word or thought
  From the wonderful minds of men;

But deep in a walled up woman's heart;
  A woman that would not yield;
But bravely and patiently bore her part;
  Lo! there is that battlefield.

No marshalling troops, no bivouac song,
  No banner to gleam and wave;
But Oh these battles they last so long—
  From babyhood to the grave!

But faithful still as a bridge of stars
  She fights in her walled up town;
Fights on, and on, in the endless wars;
  Then silent, unseen goes down!

Ho! ye with banners and battle shot,
  With soldiers to shout and praise,
I tell you the kingliest victories fought
  Are fought in these silent ways.

THE DEATH OF THE FLOWERS

William Cullen Bryant

The melancholy days are come, the saddest of the year,
Of wailing winds, and naked woods, and meadows brown and sere.
Heaped in the hollows of the grove, the autumn leaves lie dead;
They rustle to the eddying gust, and to the rabbit's tread;
The robin and the wren are flown, and from the shrubs the jay,
And from the wood-top calls the crow through all the gloomy day.

Where are the flowers, the fair young flowers, that lately sprang
   and stood
In brighter light and softer airs, a beauteous sisterhood?
Alas! they all are in their graves, the gentle race of flowers
Are lying in their lowly beds, with the fair and good of ours.
The rain is falling where they lie but the cold November rain
Calls not from out the gloomy earth the lovely ones again.

The wind-flower and the violet, they perished long ago,
And the brier-rose and the orchis died amid the summer glow;
But on the hill the golden-rod, and the aster in the wood,
And the yellow sun-flower by the brook in autumn beauty stood,
Till fell the frost from the clear cold heaven, as falls the plague
   on men,
And the brightness of their smile was gone, from upland, glade,
   and glen.

And now, when comes the calm mild day, as still such days will
   come,
To call the squirrel and the bee from out their winter home;
When the sound of dropping nuts is heard, though all the trees
   are still,
And twinkle in the smoky light the waters of the rill,
The south-wind searches for the flowers whose fragrance late he
   bore,
And sighs to find them in the wood and by the stream no more.

And then I think of one who in her youthful beauty died,
The fair meek blossom that grew up and faded by my side.
In the cold moist earth we laid her, when the forests cast the leaf
And we wept that one so lovely should have a life so brief:
Yet not unmeet it was that one, like that young friend of ours,
So gentle and so beautiful, should perish with the flowers.

A LOST CHORD

Adelaide Anne Procter

Seated one day at the Organ,
I was weary and ill at ease,
And my fingers wandered idly
Over the noisy keys.

I do not know what I was playing,
Or what I was dreaming then;
But I struck one chord of music,
Like the sound of a great Amen.

It flooded the crimson twilight
Like the close of an angel's Psalm,
And it lay on my fevered spirit
With a touch of infinite calm.

It quieted pain and sorrow,
Like love overcoming strife;
It seemed the harmonious echo
From our discordant life.

It linked all perplexèd meanings
Into one perfect peace,
And trembled away into silence,
As if it were loath to cease.

I have sought, but I seek it vainly,
That one lost chord divine,
That came from the soul of the Organ
And entered into mine.

It may be that Death's bright angel
Will speak in that chord again,—
It may be that only in Heaven
I shall hear that grand Amen.

*   *   *

"The spear that knows no brother," said Theodore Roosevelt in
referring to the attitude of his Administration toward what he
termed "the malefactors of great wealth."

WHEN A MAN BUILDS BETTER MOUSETRAPS

Ralph Waldo Emerson

If a man can write a better book, preach a better sermon, or make a better mousetrap, than his neighbors, though he builds his house in the woods, the world will make a beaten path to his door.

STRICTLY GERM-PROOF

Arthur Guiterman

The Antiseptic Baby and the Prophylactic Pup
Were playing in the garden when the Bunny gamboled up;
They looked upon the Creature with a loathing undisguised;—
It wasn't Disinfected and it wasn't Sterilized.

They said it was a Microbe and a Hotbed of Disease;
They steamed it in a vapor of a thousand-odd degrees;
They froze it in a freezer that was cold as Banished Hope
And washed it in permanganate with carbolated soap.

In sulphureted hydrogen they steeped its wiggly ears;
They trimmed its frisky whiskers with a pair of hard-boiled shears;
They donned their rubber mittens and they took it by the hand
And 'lected it a member of the Fumigated Band.

There's not a Micrococcus in the garden where they play;
They bathe in pure iodoform a dozen times a day;
And each imbibes his rations from a Hygienic Cup—
The Bunny and the Baby and the Prophylactic Pup.

THE SOLITARY REAPER

William Wordsworth

Behold her, single in the field,
Yon solitary Highland Lass!
Reaping and singing by herself;
Stop here, or gently pass!

Alone she cuts and binds the grain,
And sings a melancholy strain;
O listen! for the Vale profound
Is overflowing with the sound.

No Nightingale did ever chant
More welcome notes to weary bands
Of travellers in some shady haunt,
Among Arabian sands:
A voice so thrilling ne'er was heard
In spring-time from the Cuckoo-bird,
Breaking the silence of the seas
Among the farthest Hebrides.

Will no one tell me what she sings?—
Perhaps the plaintive numbers flow
For old, unhappy, far-off things,
And battles long ago:
Or is it some more humble lay,
Familiar matter of to-day?
Some natural sorrow, loss, or pain,
That has been, and may be again?

Whate'er the theme, the maiden sang
As if her song could have no ending;
I saw her singing at her work,
And o'er the sickle bending;—
I listened, motionless and still;
And, as I mounted up the hill,
The music in my ear I bore
Long after it was heard no more.

WHEN FATHER CARVES THE DUCK

E. V. Wright

We all look on with anxious eyes
  When father carves the duck,
And mother almost always sighs
  When father carves the duck;

Then all of us prepare to rise,
And hold our bibs before our eyes,
And be prepared for some surprise,
    When father carves the duck.

He braces up and grabs a fork
    Whene'er he carves a duck,
And won't allow a soul to talk
    Until he's carved the duck.
The fork is jabbed into the sides,
Across the breast the knife he slides,
While every careful person hides
    From flying chips of duck.

The platter's always sure to slip
    When father carves a duck,
And how it makes the dishes skip!
    Potatoes fly amuck!
The squash and cabbage leap in space,
We get some gravy in our face,
And father mutters Hindoo grace
    Whene'er he carves a duck.

We then have learned to walk around
    The dining-room and pluck
From off the window-sills and walls
    Our share of father's duck.
While father growls and blows and jaws
And swears the knife was full of flaws,
And mother laughs at him because
    He couldn't carve a duck.

BEAUTIFUL HANDS

Ellen M. H. Gates

Such beautiful, beautiful hands,
    They're neither white nor small;
And you, I know, would scarcely think
    That they were fair at all.

I've looked on hands whose form and hue
   A sculptor's dream might be,
Yet are these aged wrinkled hands
   Most beautiful to me.

Such beautiful, beautiful hands!
   Though heart were weary and sad
These patient hands kept toiling on
   That the children might be glad.
I almost weep when looking back
   To childhood's distant day!
I think how these hands rested not
   When mine were at their play.

Such beautiful, beautiful hands!
   They're growing feeble now,
And time and pain have left their mark
   On hand, and heart and brow.
Alas! alas! the nearing time—
   And the sad, sad day to me,
When 'neath the daisies, out of sight,
   These hands must folded be.

But, oh! beyond the shadowy lands,
   Where all is bright and fair,
I know full well these dear old hands
   Will palms of victory bear;
When crystal streams, through endless years,
   Flow over golden sands,
And where the old are young again,
   I'll clasp my mother's hands.

THERE IS A TAVERN IN THE TOWN

Anonymous

There is a tavern in the town,
And there my dear love sits him down, sits him down,
And drinks his wine mid laughter free,
And never, never thinks of me.

   Fare thee well for I must leave thee,
   Do not let this parting grieve thee,
   And remember that the best of friends must part, must part.

Adieu, adieu, kind friends, adieu,
I can no longer stay with you, stay with you,
I'll hang my harp on the weeping willow tree
And may the world go well with thee.

He left me for a damsel dark, damsel dark,
Each Friday night they used to spark, used to spark,
And now my love once true to me
Takes that dark damsel on his knee.

O dig my grave both wide and deep, wide and deep,
Put tombstones at my head and feet, head and feet,
And on my breast carve a turtle dove
To signify I died of love.

THE CHAMBERED NAUTILUS

Oliver Wendell Holmes

This is the ship of pearl, which, poets feign,
    Sails the unshadowed main,—
    The venturous bark that flings
On the sweet summer wind its purpled wings
In gulfs enchanted, where the Siren sings,
    And coral reefs lie bare,
Where the cold sea-maids rise to sun their streaming hair.

Its webs of living gauze no more unfurl;
    Wrecked is the ship of pearl!
    And every chambered cell,
Where its dim dreaming life was wont to dwell,
As the frail tenant shaped his growing shell,
    Before thee lies revealed,—
Its irised ceiling rent, its sunless crypt unsealed!

Year after year beheld the silent toil
    That spread his lustrous coil;
    Still, as the spiral grew,
He left the past year's dwelling for the new,
Stole with soft step its shining archway through,
    Built up its idle door,
Stretched in his last-found home, and knew the old no more.

Thanks for the heavenly message brought by thee,
    Child of the wandering sea,
    Cast from her lap, forlorn!
From thy dead lips a clearer note is born
Than ever Triton blew from wreathèd horn!
    While on mine ear it rings,
Through the deep caves of thought I hear a voice that sings—

Build thee more stately mansions, O my soul,
    As the swift seasons roll!
    Leave thy low-vaulted past!
Let each new temple, nobler than the last,
Shut thee from heaven with a dome more vast,
    Till thou at length art free,
Leaving thine outgrown shell by life's unresting sea!

THE FACE ON THE FLOOR

Hugh D'Arcy

'Twas a balmy summer evening, and a goodly crowd was there,
Which well-nigh filled Joe's bar-room, on the corner of the square;
And as songs and witty stories came through the open door,
A vagabond crept slowly in and posed upon the floor.

"Where did it come from?" someone said. "The wind has blown
    it in."
"What does it want?" another cried. "Some whiskey, rum or gin?"
"Here, Toby, seek 'em, if your stomach's equal to the work—
I wouldn't touch him with a fork, he's filthy as a Turk."

This badinage the poor wretch took with stoical good grace;
In fact, he smiled as tho' he thought he'd struck the proper place.
"Come, boys, I know there's kindly hearts among so good a crowd—
To be in such good company would make a deacon proud."

"Give me a drink—that's what I want—I'm out of funds, you know,
When I had the cash to treat the gang this hand was never slow.
What? You laugh as if you thought this pocket never held a sou;
I once was fixed as well, my boys, as any one of you."

"There, thanks, that's braced me nicely; God bless you one and all;
Next time I pass this good saloon I'll make another call.
Give you a song? No, I can't do that; my singing days are past;
My voice is cracked, my throat's worn out, and my lungs are going
    fast.

"Say! Give me another whiskey, and I'll tell you what I'll do—
I'll tell you a funny story, and a fact, I promise, too,
That ever I was a decent man not one of you would think;
But I was, some four or five years back. Say, give me another
    drink.

"Fill her up, Joe, I want to put some life into my frame—
Such little drinks to a bum like me are miserably tame;
Five fingers—there, that's the scheme—and corking whiskey, too.
Well, here's luck, boys, and landlord, my best regards to you.

"You've treated me pretty kindly and I'd like to tell you how
I came to be the dirty sot you see before you now.
As I told you, once I was a man, with muscle, frame and health,
And, but for a blunder ought to have made considerable wealth.

"I was a painter—not one that daubed on bricks and wood,
But an artist, and for my age, was rated pretty good.
I worked hard at my canvas, and was bidding fair to rise,
For gradually I saw the star of fame before my eyes.

"I made a picture perhaps you've seen, 'tis called the 'Chase of
    Fame'.
It brought me fifteen hundred pounds and added to my name.
And then I met a woman—now comes the funny part—
With eyes that petrified my brain, and sunk into my heart.

"Why don't you laugh? 'Tis funny that the vagabond you see
Could ever love a woman, and expect her love for me;
But 'twas so, and for a month or two, her smiles were freely given,
And when her loving lips touched mine, it carried me to heaven.

"Boys, did you ever see a girl for whom your soul you'd give,
With a form like the Milo Venus, too beautiful to live;
With eyes that would beat the Koh-i-noor, and a wealth of chest-
    nut hair?
If so, 'twas she, for there never was another half so fair.

418

"I was working on a portrait, one afternoon in May,
Of a fair-haired boy, a friend of mine, who lived across the way;
And Madeline admired it, and, much to my surprise,
She said she'd like to know the man that had such dreamy eyes.

"It didn't take long to know him, and before the month had flown
My friend had stole my darling, and I was left alone;
And ere a year of misery had passed above my head,
The jewel I had treasured so had tarnished and was dead.

"That's why I took to drink, boys. Why, I never saw you smile,
I thought you'd be amused, and laughing all the while.
Why, what's the matter, friend? There's a tear-drop in your eye,
Come, laugh like me; 'tis only babes and women that should cry.

"Say, boys, if you give me just another whiskey I'll be glad,
And I'll draw right here a picture of the face that drove me mad.
Give me that piece of chalk with which you mark the baseball
    score—
You shall see the lovely Madeline upon the bar-room floor."

Another drink, and with chalk in hand, the vagabond began
To sketch a face that might well buy the soul of any man.
Then, as he placed another lock upon the shapely head,
With a fearful shriek, he leaped and fell across the picture—dead.

APPOINTMENT IN SAMARRA

Somerset Maugham

DEATH SPEAKS:

There was a merchant in Bagdad who sent his servant to market
to buy provisions and in a little while the servant came back,
white and trembling, and said, "Master, just now when I was in
the market place I was jostled by a woman in the crowd and when
I turned I saw it was Death that jostled me. She looked at me and
made a threatening gesture; now, lend me your horse and I will
ride away from this city and avoid my fate. I will go to Samarra
and there Death will not find me." The merchant lent him his
horse, and he dug his spurs in its flanks and as fast as the horse
could gallop he went. Then the merchant went down to the market place and he saw me standing in the crowd and he came to me
and said, "Why did you make a threatening gesture to my servant

when you saw him this morning?" "That was not a threatening gesture," I said, "it was only a start of surprise. I was astonished to see him in Bagdad, for I had an appointment with him tonight in Samarra."

(From Sheppy)

UPON WESTMINSTER BRIDGE

William Wordsworth

Earth has not anything to show more fair:
Dull would he be of soul who could pass by
A sight so touching in its majesty:
This City now doth, like a garment, wear
The beauty of the morning; silent, bare,
Ships, towers, domes, theatres and temples lie
Open unto the fields, and to the sky;
All bright and glittering in the smokeless air.
Never did sun more beautifully steep
In his first splendour, valley, rock, or hill;
Ne'er saw I, never felt, a calm so deep!
The river glideth at his own sweet will:
Dear God! the very houses seem asleep;
And all that mighty heart is lying still!

ROCKED IN THE CRADLE OF THE DEEP

Emma Willard

Rocked in the cradle of the deep,
I lay me down in peace to sleep;
Secure I rest upon the wave,
For Thou, O Lord, hast power to save.

I know Thou wilt not slight my call,
For Thou dost mark the sparrow's fall;
And calm and peaceful is my sleep,
Rocked in the cradle of the deep.

And such the trust that still were mine,
Though stormy winds swept o'er the brine,
Or though the tempest's fiery breath
Roused me from sleep to wreck and death.

In ocean's caves still safe with Thee,
The germ of immortality;
And calm and peaceful in my sleep,
Rocked in the cradle of the deep.

SPEECH AT HARPERS FERRY

John Brown

I have, may it please the Court, a few words to say.

In the first place, I deny everything but what I have all along admitted—the design on my part to free the slaves. I intended certainly to have made a clean thing of that matter, as I did last winter (1858), when I went into Missouri and there took slaves without the snapping of a gun on either side, moved them through the country, and finally left them in Canada. I designed to have done the same thing again, on a larger scale. That was all I intended. I never did intend murder, or treason, or the destruction of property, or to excite or incite slaves to rebellion, or to make insurrection.

I have another objection; and that is, it is unjust that I should suffer such a penalty. Had I interfered in the manner which I admit, and which I admit has been fairly proved . . . had I so interfered in behalf of the rich, the powerful, the intelligent, the so-called great, or in behalf of any of their friends—either father, mother, brother, sister, wife, or children, or any of that class—and suffered and sacrificed what I have in this interference, it would have been all right; and every man in this court would have deemed it an act worthy of reward rather than punishment.

This court acknowledges, as I suppose, the validity of the law of God. I see a book kissed here which I suppose to be the Bible, or at least the New Testament. That teaches me that all things whatsoever I would that men should do to me, I should do even to to them. It teaches me, further, to "remember them that are in bonds, as bound with them." I endeavored to act up to that instruction. I say, I am yet too young to understand that God is any respecter of persons. I believe that to have interfered as I have done—as I have always freely admitted I have done—in behalf of His despised poor, was not wrong but right. Now if it is deemed necessary that I should forfeit my life for the furtherance of the ends of justice and mingle my blood further with the blood of my children and with the blood of millions in this slave country whose rights are disregarded by wicked, cruel, and unjust enactments—I submit; so let it be done!

Let me say one word further.

I feel entirely satisfied with the treatment I have received on my trial. Considering all the circumstances, it has been more generous than I expected. But I feel no consciousness of guilt. I have stated from the first what was my intention and what was not. I never had any design against the life of any person, nor any disposition to commit treason, or incite slaves to rebel, or make any general insurrection. I never encouraged any man to do so, but always discouraged any idea of that kind.

Let me also say a word in regard to the statements made by some of those connected with me. I hear it has been stated by some of them that I have induced them to join me. But the contrary is true. I do not say this to injure them, but as regretting their weakness. There is not one of them but joined me of his own accord, and the greater part of them at their own expense. A number of them I never saw and never had a word of conversation with till the day they came to me, and that was for the purpose I have stated. Now I have done.

OLD IRONSIDES

Oliver Wendell Holmes

Ay, tear her tattered ensign down!
Long has it waved on high,
And many an eye has danced to see
That banner in the sky;
Beneath it rung the battle shout,
And burst the cannon's roar;—
The meteor of the ocean air
Shall sweep the clouds no more!

Her deck, once red with heroes' blood,
Where knelt the vanquished foe,
When winds were hurrying o'er the flood,
And waves were white below,
No more shall feel the victor's tread,
Or know the conquered knee;—
The harpies of the shore shall pluck
The eagle of the sea!

O, better that her shattered hulk
  Should sink beneath the wave;
Her thunders shook the mighty deep,
  And there should be her grave;
Nail to the mast her holy flag,
  Set every threadbare sail,
And give her to the god of storms,
  The lightning and the gale!

ENGLAND, MY ENGLAND

William Ernest Henley

What have I done for you,
  England, my England?
What is there I would not do,
  England, my own?
With your glorious eyes austere,
As the Lord were walking near,
Whispering terrible things and dear
    As the Song on your bugles blown,
      England——
    Round the world on your bugles blown!

Where shall the watchful sun,
  England, my England,
Match the master-work you've done,
  England, my own?
When shall he rejoice again
Such a breed of mighty men
As come forward, one to ten,
    To the Song on your bugles blown,
      England——
    Down the years on your bugles blown?

Ever the faith endures,
  England, my England:
"Take and break us: we are yours,
  England, my own!
Life is good, and joy runs high
Between English earth and sky:

Death is death; but we shall die
  To the Song on your bugles blown,
    England——
  To the stars on your bugle blown!"

They call you proud and hard,
  England, my England:
You with worlds to watch and ward,
  England, my own!
You whose mail'd hand keeps the keys
Of such teeming destinies,
You could know nor dread nor ease
  Were the Song on your bugles blown,
    England——
  Round the Pit on your bugles blown!

Mother of Ships whose might,
  England, my England,
Is the fierce old Sea's delight,
  England, my own,
Chosen daughter of the Lord,
Spouse-in-chief of the ancient Sword,
There's the menace of the Word
  In the Song on your bugles blown,
    England——
  Out of heaven on your bugles blown!

THIS WAS THEIR FINEST HOUR

Winston Churchill

What General Weygand called the Battle of France is over.
The Battle of Britain is about to begin. On this battle depends
the survival of Christian civilization.

Upon it depends our own British life and the long continuity
of our institutions and our empire. The whole fury and might of
the enemy must very soon be turned upon us. Hitler knows he
will have to break us in this island or lose the war.

If we stand up to him all Europe may be freed and the life of
the world may move forward into broad sunlit uplands; but if
we fail, the whole world, including the United States and all that
we have known and cared for, will sink into the abyss of a new

dark age made more sinister and perhaps more prolonged by the lights of a perverted science.

Let us therefore brace ourselves to our duty and so bear ourselves that if the British Commonwealth and Empire last for a thousand years, men will still say, "This was their finest hour."
(From the Speech of June 18, 1940)

ANNIE LAURIE

William Douglas

Maxwelton's braes are bonnie
Where early fa's the dew,
And it's there that Annie Laurie
Gie'd me her promise true;
Gie'd me her promise true,
Which ne'er forgot will be;
And for bonnie Annie Laurie
I'd lay me doun and dee.

Her brow is like the snaw drift;
Her throat is like the swan;
Her face it is the fairest
That e'er the sun shone on—
That e'er the sun shone on—
And dark blue is her ee;
And for bonnie Annie Laurie
I'd lay me doun and dee.

Like dew on the gowan lying
Is the fa' o' her fairy feet;
And like the winds in summer sighing,
Her voice is low and sweet—
Her voice is low and sweet—
And she's a' the world to me;
And for bonnie Annie Laurie
I'd lay me doun and dee.

* * *

Public office is a public trust.
(Grover Cleveland, in accepting the mayoralty nomination of Buffalo, N. Y.)

DAISY BELL

Harry Dacre

There is a flower within my heart,
Daisy, Daisy!
Planted one day by a glancing dart,
Planted by Daisy Bell!
Whether she loves me or loves me not
Sometimes it's hard to tell;
Yet I am longing to share the lot
Of beautiful Daisy Bell!

Chorus:
>   Daisy, Daisy, Give me your answer, do!
>   I'm half crazy, All for the love of you!
>   It won't be a stylish marriage,
>   I can't afford a carriage,
>   But you'll look sweet on the seat
>   Of a bicycle built for two!

We will go "tandem" as man and wife,
Daisy, Daisy!
"Ped'ling" away down the road of life,
I and my Daisy Bell!
When the road's dark we can both despise
P'licemen and "lamps" as well;
There are "bright lights" in the dazzling eyes
Of beautiful Daisy Bell!   (*Chorus.*)

I will stand by you in "wheel" or woe,
Daisy, Daisy!
You'll be the bell(e) which I'll ring, you know!
Sweet little Daisy Bell!
You'll take the "lead" in each "trip" we take,
Then, if I don't do well
I will permit you to use the brake,
My beautiful Daisy Bell!   (*Chorus.*)

*   *   *

The highest and most lofty trees have the most reason to dread the thunder.

—Charles Rollin

ON FIRST LOOKING INTO CHAPMAN'S HOMER

John Keats

Much have I travell'd in the realms of gold,
  And many goodly states and kingdoms seen;
  Round many western islands have I been
Which bards in fealty to Apollo hold.
Oft of one wide expanse had I been told
  That deep-brow'd Homer ruled as his demesne:
  Yet did I never breathe its pure serene
Till I heard Chapman speak out loud and bold:
Then felt I like some watcher of the skies
  When a new planet swims into his ken;
Or like stout Cortez when with eagle eyes
  He star'd at the Pacific—and all his men
Look'd at each other with a wild surmise—
  Silent, upon a peak in Darien.

MY LAST WALK WITH THE SCHOOLMISTRESS

Oliver Wendell Holmes

I can't say how many walks she and I had taken together before
this one. I found the effect of going out every morning was decidedly favorable on her health. Two pleasing dimples, the places
or which were just marked when she came, played, shadowy, in
her freshening cheeks when she smiled and nodded good-morning
o me from the school-house steps.

I am afraid I did the greater part of the talking. At any rate, if
should try to report all that I said during the first half-dozen
walks we took together, I fear that I might receive a gentle hint
rom my friends the publishers, that a separate volume, at my own
isk and expense, would be the proper method of bringing them
before the public.

I would have a woman as true as Death. At the first real lie
which works from the heart outward, she should be tenderly
chloroformed into a better world, where she can have an angel
for a governess, and feed on strange fruits which will make her
all over again, even to her bones and marrow.—Whether gifted with
he accident of beauty or not, she should have been moulded in
he rose-red clay of Love, before the breath of life made a moving

mortal of her. Love-capacity is a congenital endowment; and I think, after a while, one gets to know the warm-hued natures it belongs to from the pretty pipe-clay counterfeits of them.—Proud she may be, in the sense of respecting herself; but pride, in the sense of contemning others less gifted than herself, deserves the two lowest circles of a vulgar woman's Inferno, where the punishments are Smallpox and Bankruptcy.—She who nips off the end of a brittle courtesy, as one breaks the tips of an icicle, to bestow upon those whom she ought cordially and kindly to recognize, proclaims the fact that she comes not merely of low blood, but of bad blood. Consciousness of unquestioned position makes people gracious in proper measure to all; but if a woman put on airs with her real equals, she has something about herself, or her family she is ashamed of, or ought to be. Middle, and more than middle-aged people, who know family histories, generally see through it. An official of standing was rude to me once. Oh, that is the maternal grandfather,—said a wise old friend to me,—he was a boor. Better too few words from the woman we love, than too many; while she is silent, Nature is working for her; while she talks, she is working for herself.—Love is sparingly soluble in the words of men; therefore they speak much of it; but one syllable of woman's speech can dissolve more of it than a man's heart can hold.

Whether I said any or all of these things to the schoolmistress or not,—whether I stole them out of Lord Bacon,—whether I cribbed them from Balzac,—whether I dipped them from the ocean of Tupperian wisdom,—or whether I have just found them in my head, laid there by that solemn fowl, Experience (who, according to my observation, cackles oftener than she drops real live eggs), I cannot say. Wise men have said more foolish things,—and foolish men, I don't doubt, have said as wise things. Anyhow, the schoolmistress and I had pleasant walks and long talks, all of which I do not feel bound to report. . . .

Books we talked about, and education. It was her duty to know something of these, and of course she did. Perhaps I was somewhat more learned than she, but I found that the difference between her reading and mine was like that of a man's and a woman's dusting a library. The man flaps about with a bunch of feathers; the woman goes to work softly with a cloth. She does not raise half the dust, nor fill her own eyes and mouth with it,—but she goes into all the corners and attends to the leaves as much as to the covers.—Books are the *negative* pictures of thought, and the more sensitive the mind that receives their images, the more nicely the finest lines are reproduced. A woman (of the right kind), reading after a man, follows him as Ruth followed the reapers of Boaz, and her gleanings are often the finest of the wheat.

But it was in talking of Life that we came most nearly together. I thought I knew something about that,—that I could speak or write about it somewhat to the purpose.

To take up this fluid earthly being of ours as a sponge sucks up water,—to be steeped and soaked in its realities as a hide fills its pore lying seven years in a tan-pit,—to have winnowed every wave of it as a mill-wheel works up the stream that runs through the flume upon its float-boards,—to have curled up in the keenest spasms and flattened out in the laxest languors of this breathing-sickness, which keeps certain parcels of matter uneasy for three or four score years,—to have fought all the devils and clasped all the angels of its delirium,—and then, just at the point when the white-hot passions have cooled down to a cherry-red, plunge our experi-ence into the ice-cold stream of some human language or other, one might think would end in a rhapsody with something of spring and temper in it. All this I thought my power and province.

The schoolmistress had tried life, too. Once in a while one meets with a single soul greater than all the living pageant which passes before it. As the pale astronomer sits in his study with sunken eyes and thin fingers, and weighs Uranus or Neptune as in a bal-ance, so there are meek, slight women who have weighed all which this planetary life can offer, and hold it like a bauble in the palm of their slender hands. This was one of them. Fortune had left her, sorrow had baptized her; the routine of labor and the loneli-ness of almost friendless city-life were before her. Yet, as I looked upon her tranquil face, gradually regaining a cheerfulness which was often sprightly, as she became interested in the various mat-ters we talked about and places we visited, I saw that eye and lip and every shifting lineament were made for love,—unconscious of their sweet office as yet, and meeting the cold aspect of Duty with the natural graces which were meant for the reward of nothing less than the Great Passion.

I never addressed one word of love to the schoolmistress in the course of these pleasant walks. It seemed to me we talked of every-thing but love on that particular morning. There was, perhaps, a little more timidity and hesitancy on my part than I have com-monly shown among our people at the boarding-house. In fact, I considered myself the master at the breakfast-table; but, somehow,

I could not command myself just then so well as usual. The truth is, I had secured a passage to Liverpool in the steamer which was to leave at noon,—with the condition, however, of being released in case circumstances occurred to detain me. The schoolmistress knew nothing of all this, of course, as yet.

It was on the Common that we were walking. The *mall*, or boulevard of our Common, you know, has various branches leading from it in different directions. One of these runs down from opposite Joy Street southward across the whole length of the Common to Boylston Street. We called it the long path, and were fond of it.

I felt very weak indeed (though of a tolerably robust habit) as we came opposite the head of this path on that morning. I think I tried to speak twice without making myself distinctly audible. At last I got out the question,—Will you take the long path with me? —Certainly,—said the schoolmistress,—with much pleasure.—Think, —I said—before you answer; if you take the long path with me now, I shall interpret it that we are to part no more!—The schoolmistress stepped back with a sudden movement, as if an arrow had struck her.

One of the long granite blocks used as seats was hard by,—the one you may still see close by the Gingko-tree.—Pray, sit down,— I said.—No, no, she answered, softly,—I will walk the *long path* with you!

The old gentleman who sits opposite met us walking, arm in arm, about the middle of the long path, and said, very charmingly,—"Good morning, my dears!"

(From the Autocrat of the Breakfast Table)

HORATIUS AT THE BRIDGE

Thomas Babington Macaulay

Lars Porsena of Clusium,
  By the Nine Gods he swore
That the great house of Tarquin
  Should suffer wrong no more.
By the Nine Gods he swore it,
  And named a trysting-day,
And bade his messengers ride forth,
East and west and south and north,
  To summon his array.

East and west and south and north
    The messengers ride fast,
And tower and town and cottage
    Have heard the trumpet's blast.
Shame on the false Etruscan
    Who lingers in his home,
When Porsena of Clusium
    Is on the march for Rome!

The horsemen and the footmen
    Are pouring in amain
From many a stately market-place,
    From many a fruitful plain,
From many a lonely hamlet,
    Which, hid by beech and pine,
Like an eagle's nest hangs on the crest
    Of purple Apennine:

From lordly Volaterræ,
    Where scowls the far-famed hold
Piled by the hands of giants
    For godlike kings of old;
From sea-girt Populonia,
    Whose sentinels descry
Sardinia's snowy mountain-tops
    Fringing the southern sky;

From the proud mart of Pisæ,
    Queen of the western waves,
Where ride Massilia's triremes,
    Heavy with fair-haired slaves;
From where sweet Clanis wanders
    Through corn and vines and flowers,
From where Cortona lifts to heaven
    Her diadem of towers.

Tall are the oaks whose acorns
    Drop in dark Auser's rill;
Fat are the stags that champ the boughs
    Of the Ciminian hill;
Beyond all streams, Clitumnus
    Is to the herdsman dear;
Best of all pools the fowler loves
    The great Volsinian mere.

But now no stroke of woodman
  Is heard by Auser's rill;
No hunter tracks the stag's green path
  Up to Ciminian hill;
Unwatched along Clitumnus
  Grazes the milk-white steer;
Unharmed the water-fowl may dip
  In the Volsinian mere.

The harvests of Arretium,
  This year, old men shall reap;
This year, young boys in Umbro
  Shall plunge the struggling sheep;
And in the vats of Luna,
  This year, the must shall foam
Round the white feet of laughing girls
  Whose sires have marched to Rome.

There be thirty chosen prophets,
  The wisest of the land,
Who always by Lars Porsena
  Both morn and evening stand.
Evening and morn the Thirty
  Have turned the verses o'er,
Traced from the right on linen white
  By mighty seers of yore;

And with one voice the Thirty
  Have their glad answer given:
"Go forth, go forth, Lars Porsena,—
  Go forth, beloved of Heaven!
Go, and return in glory
  To Clusium's royal dome,
And hang round Nurscia's altars
  The golden shields of Rome!"

And now hath every city
  Sent up her tale of men;
The foot are fourscore thousand,
  The horse are thousands ten.
Before the gates of Sutrium
  Is met the great array;
A proud man was Lars Porsena
  Upon the trysting-day.

For all the Etruscan armies
    Were ranged beneath his eye,
And many a banished Roman,
    And many a stout ally;
And with a mighty following,
    To join the muster, came
The Tusculan Mamilius,
    Prince of the Latian name.

But by the yellow Tiber
    Was tumult and affright;
From all the spacious champaign
    To Rome men took their flight.
A mile around the city
    The throng stopped up the ways;
A fearful sight it was to see
    Through two long nights and days.

For aged folk on crutches,
    And women great with child,
And mothers, sobbing over babes
    That clung to them and smiled,
And sick men borne in litters
    High on the necks of slaves,
And troops of sunburned husbandmen
    With reaping-hooks and staves,

And droves of mules and asses
    Laden with skins of wine,
And endless flocks of goats and sheep,
    And endless herds of kine,
And endless trains of wagons,
    That creaked beneath the weight
Of corn-sacks and of household goods,
    Choked every roaring gate.

Now, from the rock Tarpeian,
    Could the wan burghers spy
The line of blazing villages
    Red in the midnight sky.
The Fathers of the City,
    They sat all night and day,
For every hour some horseman came
    With tidings of dismay.

To eastward and to westward
  Have spread the Tuscan bands,
Nor house, nor fence, nor dovecote
  In Crustumerium stands.
Verbenna down to Ostia
  Hath wasted all the plain;
Astur hath stormed Janiculum,
  And the stout guards are slain.

I wis, in all the Senate
  There was no heart so bold
But sore it ached, and fast it beat,
  When that ill news was told.
Forthwith up rose the Consul,
  Up rose the Fathers all;
In haste they girded up their gowns,
  And hied them to the wall.

They held a council, standing
  Before the River-gate;
Short time was there, ye well may guess,
  For musing or debate.
Out spake the Consul roundly:
  "The bridge must straight go down;
For, since Janiculum is lost,
  Naught else can save the town."

Just then a scout came flying,
  All wild with haste and fear:
"To arms! to arms! Sir Consul,—
  Lars Porsena is here."
On the low hills to westward
  The Consul fixed his eye,
And saw the swarthy storm of dust
  Rise fast along the sky.

And nearer fast and nearer
  Doth the red whirlwind come;
And louder still, and still more loud,
From underneath that rolling cloud,
Is heard the trumpets' war-note proud,
  The trampling and the hum.
And plainly and more plainly
  Now through the gloom appears,

Far to left and far to right,
In broken gleams of dark-blue light,
The long array of helmets bright,
    The long array of spears.

And plainly and more plainly,
    Above that glimmering line,
Now might ye see the banners
    Of twelve fair cities shine;
But the banner of proud Clusium
    Was highest of them all,—
The terror of the Umbrian,
    The terror of the Gaul.

And plainly and more plainly
    Now might the burghers know,
By port and vest, by horse and crest,
    Each warlike Lucumo:
There Cilnius of Arretium
    On his fleet roan was seen;
And Astur of the fourfold shield,
Girt with the brand none else may wield;
Tolumnius with the belt of gold,
And dark Verbenna from the hold
    By reedy Thrasymene.

Fast by the royal standard,
    O'erlooking all the war,
Lars Porsena of Clusium
    Sat in his ivory car.
By the right wheel rode Mamilius,
    Prince of the Latian name;
And by the left false Sextus,
    That wrought the deed of shame.

But when the face of Sextus
    Was seen among the foes,
A yell that rent the firmament
    From all the town arose.
On the house-tops was no woman
    But spat towards him and hissed,
No child but screamed out curses,
    And shook its little fist.

But the Consul's brow was sad,
    And the Consul's speech was low,
And darkly looked he at the wall,
    And darkly at the foe:
"Their van will be upon us
    Before the bridge goes down;
And if they once may win the bridge,
    What hope to save the town?"

Then out spake brave Horatius,
    The Captain of the gate:
"To every man upon this earth
    Death cometh soon or late.
And how can man die better
    Than facing fearful odds
For the ashes of his fathers
    And the temples of his gods,

"And for the tender mother
    Who dandled him to rest,
And for the wife who nurses
    His baby at her breast,
And for the holy maidens
    Who feed the eternal flame,—
To save them from false Sextus
    That wrought the deed of shame?

"Hew down the bridge, Sir Consul,
    With all the speed ye may;
I, with two more to help me,
    Will hold the foe in play.
In yon strait path a thousand
    May well be stopped by three:
Now who will stand on either hand,
    And keep the bridge with me?"

Then out spake Spurius Lartius,—
    A Ramnian proud was he:
"Lo, I will stand at thy right hand,
    And keep the bridge with thee."
And out spake strong Herminius,—
    Of Titian blood was he:
"I will abide on thy left side,
    And keep the bridge with thee."

"Horatius," quoth the Consul,
  "As thou sayest so let it be."
And straight against that great array
  Went forth the dauntless three.
For Romans in Rome's quarrel
  Spared neither land nor gold,
Nor son nor wife, nor limb nor life,
  In the brave days of old.

Then none was for a party—
  Then all were for the state;
Then the great man helped the poor,
  And the poor man loved the great;
Then lands were fairly portioned!
  Then spoils were fairly sold:
The Romans were like brothers
  In the brave days of old.

Now Roman is to Roman
  More hateful than a foe,
And the tribunes beard the high,
  And the fathers grind the low.
As we wax hot in faction,
  In battle we wax cold;
Wherefore men fight not as they fought
  In the brave days of old.

Now while the three were tightening
  Their harness on their backs,
The Consul was the foremost man
  To take in hand an axe;
And fathers, mixed with commons,
  Seized hatchet, bar, and crow,
And smote upon the planks above,
  And loosed the props below.

Meanwhile the Tuscan army,
  Right glorious to behold,
Came flashing back the noonday light,
Rank behind rank, like surges bright
  Of a broad sea of gold.
Four hundred trumpets sounded
  A peal of warlike glee,

As that great host with measured tread,
And spears advanced, and ensigns spread
Rolled slowly towards the bridge's head,
    Where stood the dauntless three.

The three stood calm and silent,
    And looked upon the foes,
And a great shout of laughter
    From all the vanguard rose;
And forth three chiefs came spurring
    Before that deep array;
To earth they sprang, their swords they drew,
And lifted high their shields, and flew
    To win the narrow way.

Aunus, from green Tifernum,
    Lord of the Hill of Vines;
And Seius, whose eight hundred slaves
    Sicken in Ilva's mines;
And Picus, long to Clusium
    Vassal in peace and war,
Who led to fight his Umbrian powers
From that gray crag where, girt with towers,
The fortress of Nequinum lowers
    O'er the pale waves of Nar.

Stout Lartius hurled down Aunus
    Into the stream beneath;
Herminius struck at Seius,
    And clove him to the teeth;
At Picus brave Horatius
    Darted one fiery thrust,
And the proud Umbrian's gilded arms
    Clashed in the bloody dust.

Then Ocnus of Falerii
    Rushed on the Roman three;
And Lausulus of Urgo,
    The rover of the sea;
And Aruns of Volsinium,
    Who slew the great wild boar,—

The great wild boar that had his den
Amidst the reeds of Cosa's fen,
And wasted fields, and slaughtered men,
  Along Albinia's shore.

Herminius smote down Aruns;
  Lartius laid Ocnus low;
Right to the heart of Lausulus
  Horatius sent a blow:
"Lie there," he cried, "fell pirate!
  No more, aghast and pale,
From Ostia's walls the crowd shall mark
The track of thy destroying bark;
No more Campania's hinds shall fly
To woods and caverns, when they spy
  Thy thrice-accursèd sail!"

But now no sound of laughter
  Was heard among the foes;
A wild and wrathful clamor
  From all the vanguard rose.
Six spears' length from the entrance,
  Halted that deep array,
And for a space no man came forth
  To win the narrow way.

But, hark! the cry is Astur:
  And lo! the ranks divide;
And the great lord of Luna
  Comes with his stately stride.
Upon his ample shoulders
  Clangs loud the fourfold shield,
And in his hand he shakes the brand
  Which none but he can wield.

He smiled on those bold Romans,
  A smile serene and high;
He eyed the flinching Tuscans,
  And scorn was in his eye.
Quoth he, "The she-wolf's litter
  Stand savagely at bay;
But will ye dare to follow,
  If Astur clears the way?"

Then, whirling up his broadsword
    With both hands to the height,
He rushed against Horatius,
    And smote with all his might.
With shield and blade Horatius
    Right deftly turned the blow.
The blow, though turned, came yet too nigh;
It missed his helm, but gashed his thigh.
The Tuscans raised a joyful cry
    To see the red blood flow.

He reeled, and on Herminius
    He leaned one breathing-space,
Then, like a wild-cat mad with wounds,
    Sprang right at Astur's face.
Through teeth and skull and helmet
    So fierce a thrust he sped,
The good sword stood a handbreadth out
    Behind the Tuscan's head.

And the great lord of Luna
    Fell at that deadly stroke,
As falls on Mount Avernus
    A thunder-smitten oak.
Far o'er the crashing forest
    The giant arms lie spread;
And the pale augurs, muttering low
    Gaze on the blasted head.

On Astur's throat Horatius
    Right firmly pressed his heel,
And thrice and four times tugged amain,
    Ere he wrenched out the steel.
And "See," he cried, "the welcome,
    Fair guests, that waits you here!
What noble Lucumo comes next
    To taste our Roman cheer?"

But at his haughty challenge
    A sullen murmur ran,
Mingled with wrath and shame and dread,
    Along that glittering van.

There lacked not men of prowess,
    Nor men of lordly race,
For all Etruria's noblest
    Were round the fatal place.

But all Etruria's noblest
    Felt their hearts sink to see
On the earth the bloody corpses,
    In the path of the dauntless three;
And from the ghastly entrance,
    Where those bold Romans stood,
All shrank,—like boys who, unaware,
Ranging the woods to start a hare,
Come to the mouth of the dark lair
Where, growling low, a fierce old bear
    Lies amidst bones and blood.

Was none who would be foremost
    To lead such dire attack;
But those behind cried "Forward!"
    And those before cried "Back!"
And backward now and forward
    Wavers the deep array;
And on the tossing sea of steel
To and fro the standards reel,
And the victorious trumpet-peal
    Dies fitfully away.

Yet one man for one moment
    Strode out before the crowd;
Well known was he to all the three,
    And they gave him greeting loud:
"Now welcome, welcome, Sextus!
    Now welcome to thy home!
Why dost thou stay, and turn away?
    Here lies the road to Rome."

Thrice looked he at the city;
    Thrice looked he at the dead;
And thrice came on in fury,
    And thrice turned back in dread;

And, white with fear and hatred,
   Scowled at the narrow way
Where, wallowing in a pool of blood,
   The bravest Tuscans lay.

But meanwhile axe and lever
   Have manfully been plied;
And now the bridge hangs tottering
   Above the boiling tide.
"Come back, come back, Horatius!"
   Loud cried the Fathers all,—
"Back, Lartius! back, Herminius!
   Back, ere the ruin fall!"

Back darted Spurius Lartius,—
   Herminius darted back;
And, as they passed, beneath their feet
   They felt the timbers crack.
But when they turned their faces,
   And on the farther shore
Saw brave Horatius stand alone,
   They would have crossed once more;

But with a crash like thunder
   Fell every loosened beam,
And, like a dam, the mighty wreck
   Lay right athwart the stream;
And a long shout of triumph
   Rose from the walls of Rome,
As to the highest turret-tops
   Was splashed the yellow foam.

And like a horse unbroken,
   When first he feels the rein,
The furious river struggled hard,
   And tossed his tawny mane,
And burst the curb, and bounded,
   Rejoicing to be free;
And whirling down, in fierce career,
Battlement and plank and pier,
   Rushed headlong to the sea.

Alone stood brave Horatius,
  But constant still in mind,—
Thrice thirty thousand foes before.
  And the broad flood behind.
"Down with him!" cried false Sextus,
  With a smile on his pale face;
"Now yield thee," cried Lars Porsena,
  "Now yield thee to our grace!"

Round turned he, as not deigning
  Those craven ranks to see;
Naught spake he to Lars Porsena,
  To Sextus naught spake he;
But he saw on Palatinus
  The white porch of his home;
And he spake to the noble river
  That rolls by the towers of Rome:

"O Tiber! Father Tiber!
  To whom the Romans pray,
A Roman's life, a Roman's arms,
  Take thou in charge this day!"
So he spake, and, speaking, sheathed
  The good sword by his side,
And, with his harness on his back,
  Plunged headlong in the tide.

No sound of joy or sorrow
  Was heard from either bank,
But friends and foes in dumb surprise,
With parted lips and straining eyes,
  Stood gazing where he sank;
And when above the surges
  They saw his crest appear,
All Rome sent forth a rapturous cry,
And even the ranks of Tuscany
  Could scarce forbear to cheer.

But fiercely ran the current,
  Swollen high by months of rain;
And fast his blood was flowing,
  And he was sore in pain,

And heavy with his armor,
    And spent with changing blows;
And oft they thought him sinking,
    But still again he rose.

Never, I ween, did swimmer,
    In such an evil case,
Struggle through such a raging flood
    Safe to the landing-place;
But his limbs were borne up bravely
    By the brave heart within,
And our good Father Tiber
    Bare bravely up his chin.

"Curse on him!" quoth false Sextus,—
    "Will not the villain drown?
But for this stay, ere close of day
    We should have sacked the town!"
"Heaven help him!" quoth Lars Porsena,
    "And bring him safe to shore;
For such a gallant feat of arms
    Was never seen before."

And now he feels the bottom;
    Now on dry earth he stands;
Now round him throng the Fathers
    To press his gory hands;
And now, with shouts and clapping,
    And noise of weeping loud,
He enters through the River-gate,
    Borne by the joyous crowd.

They gave him of the corn-land,
    That was of public right,
As much as two strong oxen
    Could plough from morn till night;
And they made a molten image,
    And set it up on high,—
And there it stands unto this day
    To witness if I lie.

It stands in the Comitium,
    Plain for all folk to see,—

Horatius in his harness,
    Halting upon one knee;
And underneath is written,
    In letters all of gold,
How valiantly he kept the bridge
    In the brave days of old.

And still his name sounds stirring
    Unto the men of Rome,
As the trumpet-blast that cries to them
    To charge the Volscian home;
And wives still pray to Juno
    For boys with hearts as bold
As his who kept the bridge so well
    In the brave days of old.

And in the nights of winter,
    When the cold north-winds blow,
And the long howling of the wolves
    Is heard amidst the snow;
When round the lonely cottage
    Roars loud the tempest's din,
And the good logs of Algidus
    Roar louder yet within;

When the oldest cask is opened,
    And the largest lamp is lit;
When the chestnuts glow in the embers,
    And the kid turns on the spit;
When young and old in circle
    Around the firebrands close;
When the girls are weaving baskets,
    And the lads are shaping bows;

When the goodman mends his armor,
    And trims his helmet's plume;
When the goodwife's shuttle merrily
    Goes flashing through the loom;
With weeping and with laughter
    Still is the story told,
How well Horatius kept the bridge
    In the brave days of old.

CAPTAIN JINKS

Anonymous

I'm Captain Jinks of the Horse Marines,
I feed my horse on corn and beans,
And sport young ladies in their teens,
   Though a captain in the army.
I teach young ladies how to dance,
How to dance, how to dance,
I teach young ladies how to dance,
   For I'm the pet of the army.

Chorus:
   Captain Jinks of the Horse Marines,
   I feed my horse on corn and beans,
   And often live beyond my means,
      Though a captain in the army.

I joined my corps when twenty-one,
Of course I thought it capital fun;
When the enemy came, of course I ran,
   For I'm not cut out for the army.
When I left home, mama she cried,
Mama she cried, mama she cried,
When I left home, mama she cried:
   "He's not cut out for the army."

The first time I went out to drill,
The bugle sounding made me ill;
Of the battle field I'd had my fill,
   For I'm not cut out for the army.
The officers they all did shout,
They all did shout, they all did shout,
The officers they all did shout:
   "Why, kick him out of the army."

* * *

If all our misfortunes were laid in one common heap, whence every one must take an equal portion, most people would be contented to take their own and depart.

                                               —Solon

ON HIS BLINDNESS

John Milton

When I consider how my light is spent
Ere half my days in this dark world and wide,
And that one talent which is death to hide
Lodged with me useless, though my soul more bent

To serve therewith my Maker, and present
My true account, lest he returning chide,
'Doth God exact day-labor, light denied?'
I fondly ask. But Patience, to prevent

That murmur, soon replies, 'God doth not need
Either man's work or his own gifts. Who best
Bear his mild yoke, they serve him best. His state
Is kingly: thousands at his bidding speed,
And post o'er land and ocean without rest;
They also serve who only stand and wait.'

BIRCHES

Robert Frost

When I see birches bend to left and right
Across the lines of straighter darker trees,
I like to think some boy's been swinging them.
But swinging doesn't bend them down to stay.
Ice-storms do that. Often you must have seen them
Loaded with ice a sunny winter morning
After a rain. They click upon themselves
As the breeze rises, and turn many-colored
As the stir cracks and crazes their enamel.
Soon the sun's warmth makes them shed crystal shells
Shattering and avalanching on the snow-crust—
Such heaps of broken glass to sweep away
You'd think the inner dome of heaven had fallen.
They are dragged to the withered bracken by the load,
And they seem not to break; though once they are bowed
So low for long, they never right themselves:
You may see their trunks arching in the woods

447

Years afterwards, trailing their leaves on the ground
Like girls on hands and knees that throw their hair
Before them over their heads to dry in the sun.
But I was going to say when Truth broke in
With all her matter-of-fact about the ice-storm
(Now am I free to be poetical?)
I should prefer to have some boy bend them
As he went out and in to fetch the cows—
Some boy too far from town to learn baseball,
Whose only play was what he found himself,
Summer or winter, and could play alone.
One by one he subdued his father's trees
By riding them down over and over again
Until he took the stiffness out of them,
And not one but hung limp, not one was left
For him to conquer. He learned all there was
To learn about not launching out too soon
And so not carrying the tree away
Clear to the ground. He always kept his poise
To the top branches, climbing carefully
With the same pains you use to fill a cup
Up to the brim, and even above the brim.
Then he flung outward, feet first, with a swish,
Kicking his way down through the air to the ground.
So was I once myself a swinger of birches.
And so I dream of going back to be.
It's when I'm weary of considerations,
And life is too much like a pathless wood
Where your face burns and tickles with the cobwebs
Broken across it, and one eye is weeping
From a twig's having lashed across it open.
I'd like to get away from earth awhile
And then come back to it and begin over.
May no fate wilfully misunderstand me
And half grant what I wish and snatch me away
Not to return. Earth's the right place for love:
I don't know where it's likely to go better.
I'd like to go by climbing a birch tree,
And climb black branches up a snow-white trunk
Toward heaven, till the tree could bear no more,
But dipped its top and set me down again.
That would be good both going and coming back.
One could do worse than be a swinger of birches.

HOW TO TELL BAD NEWS

Anonymous

MR. H. Ha! Steward, how are you, my old boy? How do things go on at home?

STEWARD. Bad enough, your honor; the magpie's dead.

H. Poor Mag! So he's gone. How came he to die?

S. Overeat himself, sir.

H. Did he? A greedy dog; why, what did he get he liked so well?

S. Horseflesh, sir; he died of eating horseflesh.

H. How came he to get so much horseflesh?

S. All your father's horses, sir.

H. What! are they dead, too?

S. Ay, sir; they died of overwork.

H. And why were they overworked, pray?

S. To carry water, sir.

H. To carry water! and what were they carrying water for?

S. Sure, sir, to put out the fire.

H. Fire! what fire?

S. O, sir, your father's house is burned to the ground.

H. My father's house burned down! and how came it to set on fire?

S. I think, sir, it must have been the torches.

H. Torches! what torches?

S. At your mother's funeral.

H. My mother dead!

S. Ah, poor lady! she never looked up, after it.

H. After what?

S. The loss of your father.

H. My father gone, too?

S. Yes, poor gentleman! he took to his bed as soon as he heard of it.

H. Heard of what?

S. The bad news, sir, and please your honor.

H. What! more miseries! more bad news!

S. Yes, sir; your bank has failed, and your credit is lost, and you are not worth a shilling in the world. I make bold, sir, to wait on you about it, for I thought you would like to hear the news.

* * *

Socrates died like a philosopher, but Jesus Christ like a God—
(From McGuffey's Reader)

COMIN' THRO' THE RYE

Robert Burns

Gin a body meet a body
Comin' thro' the rye,
Gin a body kiss a body,
Need a body cry?
Every lassie has her laddie—
Ne'er a ane hae I;
Yet a' the lads they smile at me
When comin' thro' the rye.
Amang the train there is a swain
I dearly lo'e mysel';
But whaur his hame, or what his name,
I dinna care to tell.

Gin a body meet a body
Comin' frae the town,
Gin a body greet a body,
Need a body frown?
Every lassie has her laddie—
Ne'er a ane hae I;
Yet a' the lads they smile at me
When comin' thro' the rye.
Amang the train there is a swain
I dearly lo'e mysel';
But whaur his hame, or what his name,
I dinna care to tell.

EPITAPH PLACED ON HIS DAUGHTER'S TOMB

Warm summer sun,
Shine kindly here.
Warm southern wind,
Blow softly here.

Green sod above,
Lie light, lie light.
Good night, dear heart,
Good night, good night.
(Mark Twain, adapted from
Robert Richardson)

TEARS, IDLE TEARS

Alfred, Lord Tennyson

Tears, idle tears, I know not what they mean,
Tears from the depth of some divine despair
Rise in the heart, and gather to the eyes,
In looking on the happy autumn-fields,
And thinking of the days that are no more.

Fresh as the first beam glittering on a sail,
That brings our friends up from the underworld,
Sad as the last which reddens over one
That sinks with all we love below the verge;
So sad, so fresh, the days that are no more.

Ah, sad and strange as in dark summer dawns
The earliest pipe of half-awaken'd birds
To dying ears, when unto dying eyes
The casement slowly grows a glimmering square;
So sad, so strange, the days that are no more.

Dear as remember'd kisses after death,
And sweet as those by hopeless fancy feign'd
On lips that are for others; deep as love,
Deep as first love, and wild with all regret;
O Death in Life, the days that are no more!

(From The Princess)

SALUTE TO OUR FLAG

I pledge allegiance to the flag of the United States and to the Republic for which it stands; one nation, indivisible, with liberty and justice for all.

ON CONCILIATION WITH AMERICA

Edmund Burke

America, gentlemen say, is a noble object. It is an object well worth fighting for. Certainly it is, if fighting a people be the best way of gaining them. Gentlemen in this respect will be led to their choice of means by their complexions and their habits. Those who understand the military art will, of course, have some predilection for it. Those who wield the thunder of the State may have more confidence in the efficacy of arms. But I confess, possibly for want of this knowledge, my opinion is much more in favor of prudent management than of force, considering force not as an odious, but a feeble, instrument for preserving a people so numerous, so active, so growing, so spirited as this, in a profitable and subordinate connection with us.

First, sir, permit me to observe, the use of force alone is but temporary. It may subdue for a moment, but it does not remove the necessity of subduing again; and a nation is not governed which is perpetually to be conquered.

My next objection is its uncertainty. Terror is not always the effect of force; and an armament is not a victory. If you do not succeed you are without resource, for conciliation failing, force remains, but force failing, no further hope of reconciliation is left. Power and authority are sometimes bought by kindness, but they can never be begged as alms by an impoverished and defeated violence.

A further objection to force is, that you impair the object by your very endeavors to preserve it. The thing you fought for is not the thing which you recover; but depreciated, sunk, wasted, and consumed in the contest. Nothing less will content me than whole America. I do not choose to consume its strength along with our own, because it is in all parts the British strength that I consume. I do not choose to be caught by a foreign enemy at the end of this exhausting conflict, and still less in the midst of it. I may escape; but I can make no insurance against such an event. Let me add, that I do not choose wholly to break the American spirit, because it is the spirit that has made the country.

Lastly, we have no sort of experience in favor of force as an instrument in the rule of our colonies. Their growth and their utility has been owing to methods altogether different. Our ancient indulgence has been said to be pursued to a fault. It may be so; but we know, if feeling is evidence, that our fault was more tolerable than our attempt to mend it, and our sin far more salutary than our penitence.

These, sir, are my reasons for not entertaining that high opinion of untried force, by which many gentlemen, for whose sentiments in other particulars I have great respect, seem to be so greatly captivated.

But there is still behind a third consideration concerning this object, which serves to determine my opinion on the sort of policy which ought to be pursued in the management of America, even more than its population and its commerce,—I mean its temper and character. In this character of the Americans a love of freedom is the predominating feature, which marks and distinguishes the whole; and, as an ardent is always a jealous affection, your colonies become suspicious, restive, and untractable, whenever they see the least attempt to wrest from them by force, or shuffle from them by chicane, what they think the only advantage worth living for. This fierce spirit of liberty is stronger in the English colonies, probably, than in any other people of the earth, and this from a variety of powerful causes, which, to understand the true temper of their minds, and the direction which this spirit takes, it will not be amiss to lay open somewhat more largely. . . .

The Americans will have no interest contrary to the grandeur and glory of England, when they are not oppressed by the weight of it; and they will rather be inclined to respect the acts of a superintending legislature, when they see them the acts of that power which is itself the security, not the rival, of their secondary importance. In this assurance my mind most perfectly acquiesces, and I confess I feel not the least alarm from the discontents which are to arise from putting people at their ease; nor do I apprehend the destruction of this empire from giving, by an act of free grace and indulgence, to two million of my fellow-citizens, some share of the rights upon which I have always been taught to value myself. . . .

My hold of the colonies is in the close affection which grows from common names, from kindred blood, from similar privileges, and equal protection. These are the ties which, though light as air, are as strong as links of iron. Let the colonies always keep the idea of their civil rights associated with your government; they will cling and grapple to you, and no force under heaven will be of power to tear them from their allegiance. But let it once be understood that your government may be one thing and their privileges another; that these two things may exist without any mutual relation; the cement is gone; the cohesion is loosened; and everything hastens to decay and dissolution. As long as you have the wisdom to keep the sovereign authority of this country as the sanctuary of liberty, the sacred temple, consecrated to our common faith, wherever the chosen race and sons of England worship freedom, they will turn their faces toward you. The more they multiply, the more friends you will have. The more ardently they love freedom, the more perfect will be their obedience. Slavery they can have anywhere. It is a weed that grows in every soil. They may have it in Spain; they may have it from Prussia; but, until you become lost to all feeling of your true interest and your natural dignity, freedom they can have from none but you. This is the commodity price of which you have the monopoly. This is the true Act of Navigation, which binds to you the commerce of the colonies, and through them secures to you the wealth of the world. Deny them this participation of freedom, and you break the sole bond which originally made, and must still preserve, the unity of the empire. . . .

All this, I know well enough, will sound wild and chimerical to the profane herd of those vulgar and mechanical politicians, who have no place among us; a sort of people who think that nothing exists but what is gross and material, and who, therefore, far from being qualified to be directors of the great movement of the empire are not fit to turn a wheel in the machine. But to men truly initiated and rightly taught, these ruling master principles, which in the opinion of such men as I have mentioned have no substantial existence, are, in truth, everything and all in all. Magnanimity in politics is not seldom the truest wisdom; and a great empire and little minds go ill together. If we are conscious of our situation, and glow with zeal to fill our place as becomes our station and ourselves, we ought to auspicate all our public proceedings in America with the warning of the church, *sursum corda*. We ought to elevate our minds to the greatness of that trust to which the order of providence has called us. By adverting to the dignity of this high calling, our ancestors have turned a savage wilderness into a glorious temple, and have made the most extensive and only honorable conquests not by destroying but by promoting the wealth, the number, the happiness of the human race. Let us get an American revenue as we have got an American empire. English privileges have made it all that it is; English privileges will make it all that it can be.

(From the Speech to the House of Commons, Mar. 22, 1775)

THE PURE HEART

My good blade carves the casques of men,
My tough lance thrusteth sure,
My strength is as the strength of ten,
Because my heart is pure.
                    (From Tennyson's Sir Galahad)

THANATOPSIS

William Cullen Bryant

To him who, in the love of Nature, holds
Communion with her visible forms, she speaks
A various language: for his gayer hours
She has a voice of gladness, and a smile
And eloquence of beauty; and she glides
Into his darker musings with a mild
And gentle sympathy, that steals away
Their sharpness, ere he is aware. When thoughts
Of the last bitter hour come like a blight
Over thy spirit, and sad images
Of the stern agony, and shroud, and pall,
And breathless darkness, and the narrow house,
Make thee to shudder, and grow sick at heart,
Go forth under the open sky, and list
To Nature's teachings, while from all around—
Earth and her waters, and the depths of air—
Comes a still voice,—Yet a few days, and thee
The all-beholding sun shall see no more
In all his course; nor yet in the cold ground,
Where thy pale form was laid, with many tears,
Nor in the embrace of ocean, shall exist
Thy image. Earth, that nourished thee, shall claim
Thy growth, to be resolved to earth again;
And, lost each human trace, surrendering up
Thine individual being, shalt thou go
To mix forever with the elements;
To be a brother to the insensible rock,
And to the sluggish clod, which the rude swain
Turns with his share, and treads upon. The oak
Shall send his roots abroad, and pierce thy mould.

Yet not to thine eternal resting-place
Shalt thou retire alone,—nor couldst thou wish
Couch more magnificent. Thou shalt lie down
With patriarchs of the infant world,—with kings,
The powerful of the earth,—the wise, the good,
Fair forms, and hoary seers of ages past,
All in one mighty sepulchre. The hills,
Rock-ribbed, and ancient as the sun; the vales
Stretching in pensive quietness between;

The venerable woods; rivers that move
In majesty, and the complaining brooks,
That make the meadows green; and, poured round all,
Old ocean's gray and melancholy waste,—
Are but the solemn decorations all
Of the great tomb of man! The golden sun,
The planets, all the infinite host of heaven,
Are shining on the sad abodes of death,
Through the still lapse of ages. All that tread
The globe are but a handful to the tribes
That slumber in its bosom. Take the wings
Of morning, traverse Barca's desert sands,
Or lose thyself in the continuous woods
Where rolls the Oregon, and hears no sound
Save his own dashings,—yet the dead are there!
And millions in those solitudes, since first
The flight of years began, have laid them down
In their last sleep,—the dead reign there alone!
So shalt thou rest; and what if thou withdraw
In silence from the living; and no friend
Take note of thy departure? All that breathe
Will share thy destiny. The gay will laugh
When thou art gone, the solemn brood of care
Plod on, and each one, as before, will chase
His favorite phantom; yet all these shall leave
Their mirth and their employments, and shall come
And make their bed with thee. As the long train
Of ages glide away, the sons of men—
The youth in life's green spring, and he who goes
In the full strength of years, matron and maid,
The speechless babe, and the gray-headed man—
Shall, one by one, be gathered to thy side
By those who in their turn shall follow them.

So live, that when thy summons comes to join
The innumerable caravan that moves
To the pale realms of shade, where each shall take
His chamber in the silent halls of death,
Thou go not, like the quarry-slave at night,
Scourged to his dungeon, but, sustained and soothed
By an unfaltering trust, approach thy grave
Like one who wraps the drapery of his couch
About him, and lies down to pleasant dreams.

GIFTS

James Thompson

Give a man a horse he can ride,
Give a man a boat he can sail;
And his rank and wealth, his strength and health,
On sea nor shore shall fail.

Give a man a pipe he can smoke,
Give a man a book he can read:
And his home is bright with a calm delight,
Though the room be poor indeed.

Give a man a girl he can love,
As I, O my love, love thee;
And his heart is great with the pulse of Fate,
At home, on land, on sea.

LOVE'S NOT TIME'S FOOL

William Shakespeare

Let me not to the marriage of true minds
Admit impediments. Love is not love
Which alters when it alteration finds,
Or bends with the remover to remove:
O, no! it is an ever-fixed mark
That looks on tempests and is never shaken;
It is the star to every wandering bark,
Whose worth's unknown, although his height be taken.
Love's not Time's fool, though rosy lips and cheeks
Within his bending sickle's compass come;
Love alters not with his brief hours and weeks,
But bears it out even to the edge of doom.
  If this be error and upon me proved,
  I never writ, nor no man ever loved.

(From the Sonnets)

* * *

Not to go back is somewhat to advance,
And men must walk, at least, before they dance,
—Alexander Pope

JUST FOR TODAY

Samuel Wilberforce

Lord, for tomorrow and its needs
   I do not pray:
Keep me, my God, from stain of sin
   Just for today.

Let me both diligently work
   And duly pray,
Let me be kind in word and deed
   Just for today.

Let me be slow to do my will,
   Prompt to obey,
Help me to mortify my flesh
   Just for today.

Let me no wrong or idle word
   Unthinking say:
Set Thou a seal upon my lips
   Just for today.

Let me in season, Lord, be grave,
   In season gay,
Let me be faithful to Thy grace,
   Just for today.

And if today my tide of life
   Should ebb away,
Give me Thy sacraments divine,
   Sweet Lord, today.

So for tomorrow and its needs
   I do not pray:
But keep me, guide me, love me, Lord,
   Just for today.

*   *   *

Put your trust in God, my boys, and keep your powder dry.
                         (Attributed to Oliver Cromwell)

IN THE BEGINNING WAS THE WORD

Holy Bible, John 1:1-17

1 In the beginning was the Word, and the Word was with God, and the Word was God.

2 The same was in the beginning with God.

3 All things were made by him; and without him was not any thing made that was made.

4 In him was life; and the life was the light of men.

5 And the light shineth in darkness; and the darkness comprehended it not.

6 There was a man sent from God, whose name was John.

7 The same came for a witness, to bear witness of the Light, that all men through him might believe.

8 He was not that Light, but was sent to bear witness of that Light.

9 That was the true Light, which lighteth every man that cometh into the world.

10 He was in the world, and the world was made by him, and the world knew him not.

11 He came unto his own, and his own received him not.

12 But as many as received him, to them gave he power to become the sons of God, even to them that believe on his name:

13 Which were born, not of blood, nor of the will of the flesh, nor of the will of man, but of God.

14 And the Word was made flesh, and dwelt among us, (and we beheld his glory, the glory as of the only begotten of the Father,) full of grace and truth.

15 John bare witness of him, and cried, saying, This was he of whom I spake, He that cometh after me is preferred before me: for he was before me.

16 And of his fulness have all we received, and grace for grace.

17 For the law was given by Moses, but grace and truth came by Jesus Christ.

EPIGRAM

Samuel Taylor Coleridge

Sir, I admit your general rule,
That every poet is a fool,
But you yourself may serve to show it,
That every fool is not a poet.

THE WORLD IS TOO MUCH WITH US

William Wordsworth

The world is too much with us; late and soon,
Getting and spending, we lay waste our powers:
Little we see in Nature that is ours;
We have given our hearts away, a sordid boon!
The Sea that bares her bosom to the moon;
The winds that will be howling at all hours,
And are up-gathered now like sleeping flowers;
For this, for everything, we are out of tune;
It moves us not.—Great God! I'd rather be
A Pagan, suckled in a creed outworn,
So might I, standing on this pleasant lea,
Have glimpses that would make me less forlorn;
Have sight of Proteus rising from the sea;
Or hear old Triton blow his wreathèd horn.

OLD SUPERSTITIONS

Anonymous

See a pin and pick it up,
All the day you'll have good luck.
See a pin and let it lay,
Bad luck you will have all day.

The maid who, on the first of May,
Goes to the fields at break of day,
And washes in dew from the hawthorn tree,
Will ever after handsome be.

Friday night's dream on a Saturday told,
Is sure to come true, be it never so old.

Monday's child is fair of face,
Tuesday's child is full of grace,
Wednesday's child is full of woe,
Thursday's child has far to go,
Friday's child is loving and giving,
Saturday's child works hard for its living,
And a child that is born on the Sabbath day
Is fair and wise and good and gay.

Marry Monday, marry for wealth;
Marry Tuesday, marry for health;
Marry Wednesday, the best day of all;
Marry Thursday, marry for crosses;
Marry Friday, marry for losses;
Marry Saturday, no luck at all.

They that wash on Monday
Have all the week to dry;
They that wash on Tuesday
Are not so much awry;
They that wash on Wednesday
Are not so much to blame;
They that wash on Thursday
Wash for shame;
They that wash on Friday
Wash for need;
And they that wash on Saturday
Oh, slovens are indeed!

Sneeze on a Monday, you sneeze for danger;
Sneeze on a Tuesday, you'll kiss a stranger;
Sneeze on a Wednesday, you sneeze for a letter;
Sneeze on a Thursday, for something better;
Sneeze on a Friday, you sneeze for sorrow;
Sneeze on a Saturday, your sweetheart tomorrow;
Sneeze on a Sunday, your safety seek,
For you will have trouble the whole of the week.

THE MOTH AND THE FLAME

George Taggert

At a gay reception given in a mansion grand and old,
A young man met the girl he used to know;
And once again the story of his honest love he told,
The love he'd cherished long years ago.
But she sighed and sadly murmured that her childhood love was
    past,
That soon another man she was to wed.
The lover knew the other man already had a wife.
He bade farewell, but as he went, he said:

        "The Moth and the Flame play'd a game, one day,
        The game of a woman's heart;
        And the Moth that play'd was a maid, they say,
        The Flame was a bad man's art.
        The Moth never knew, as she flew so near,
        That Flame was the light of shame:
        But she flutter'd away just in time, so they say,
        That's the tale of the Moth and the Flame!"

The maiden did not understand the fable that he told,
A church was soon arranged in holy state,
A couple at the altar stood before the crowd of guests.
When a woman screamed, "Stop! ere it is too late."
The villain turned and saw his wife and rudely struck her down,
Denouncing her as an impostor bold;
But the girl threw off the bridal wreath; "You coward," then she
    cried,
"My true love warned me when this tale he told:" (*Chorus.*)

THE BAREFOOT BOY

John Greenleaf Whittier

        Blessings on thee, little man,
        Barefoot boy, with cheek of tan!
        With thy turned-up pantaloons,
        And thy merry whistled tunes;
        With thy red lip, redder still
        Kissed by strawberries on the hill;
        With the sunshine on thy face,
        Through thy torn brim's jaunty grace;
        From my heart I give thee joy,—
        I was once a barefoot boy!

        Prince thou art,—the grown-up man
        Only is republican.
        Let the million-dollared ride!
        Barefoot, trudging at his side,
        Thou hast more than he can buy
        In the reach of ear and eye,—
        Outward sunshine, inward joy:
        Blessings on thee, barefoot boy!

Oh for boyhood's painless play,
Sleep that wakes in laughing day,
Health that mocks the doctor's ruies,
Knowledge never learned of schools,
Of the wild bee's morning chase,
Of the wild-flower's time and place,
Flight of fowl and habitude
Of the tenants of the wood;
How the tortoise bears his shell,
How the woodchuck digs his cell,
And the ground-mole sinks his well;
How the robin feeds her young,
How the oriole's nest is hung;
Where the whitest lilies blow,
Where the freshest berries grow,
Where the ground-nut trails its vine,
Where the wood-grape's clusters shine;
Of the black wasp's cunning way,
Mason of his walls of clay,
And the architectural plans
Of gray hornet artisans!
For, eschewing books and tasks,
Nature answers all he asks;
Hand in hand with her he walks,
Face to face with her he talks,
Part and parcel of her joy,—
Blessings on the barefoot boy!

Oh for boyhood's time of June,
Crowding years in one brief moon,
When all things I heard or saw,
Me, their master, waited for.
I was rich in flowers and trees,
Humming-birds and honey-bees;
For my sport the squirrel played,
Plied the snouted mole his spade;
For my taste the blackberry cone
Purpled over hedge and stone;
Laughed the brook for my delight
Through the day and through the night,
Whispering at the garden wall,·
Talked with me from fall to fall;
Mine the sand-rimmed pickerel pond,

Mine the walnut slopes beyond,
Mine, on bending orchard trees,
Apples of Hesperides!
Still as my horizon grew,
Larger grew my riches too;
All the world I saw or knew
Seemed a complex Chinese toy,
Fashioned for a barefoot boy!

Oh for festal dainties spread,
Like my bowl of milk and bread;
Pewter spoon and bowl of wood,
On the door-stone, gray and rude!
O'er me, like a regal tent,
Cloudy-ribbed, the sunset bent,
Purple-curtained, fringed with gold,
Looped in many a wind swung fold;
While for music came the play
Of the pied frogs' orchestra;
And, to light the noisy choir,
Lit the fly his lamp of fire.
I was monarch: pomp and joy
Waited on the barefoot boy!

Cheerily, then, my little man,
Live and laugh, as boyhood can!
Though the flinty slopes be hard,
Stubble-speared the new-mown sward,
Every morn shall lead thee through
Fresh baptisms of the dew;
Every evening from thy feet
Shall the cool wind kiss the heat:
All too soon these feet must hide
In the prison cells of pride,
Lose the freedom of the sod,
Like a colt's for work be shod,
Made to tread the mills of toil,
Up and down in ceaseless moil:
Happy if their track be found
Never on forbidden ground;
Happy if they sink not in
Quick and treacherous sands of sin.
Ah! that thou couldst know thy joy,
Ere it passes, barefoot boy!

WHERE IS MY WANDERING BOY TONIGHT?

Anonymous

Where is my wandering boy tonight? the boy of my tend'rest care:
The boy that was once my joy and light, the child of my love and
  prayer.

Chorus:
    Oh, where is my boy tonight? where is my boy tonight?
    My heart o'erflows, for I love him, he knows,
    Oh, where is my boy tonight?

Once he was pure as the morning dew, as he knelt at his mother's
  knee;
No face was so bright, no heart more true, and none was as sweet
  as he. (*Chorus.*)

Oh, could I see him now, my boy, as fair as in olden time,
When prattle and smile made home a joy, and life was a merry
  chime. (*Chorus.*)

Go, for my wandering boy tonight, go search for him where you
  will:
But bring him to me with all his blight, and tell him I love him
  still. (*Chorus.*)

THE MERMAID

Anonymous

'Twas a Friday morn when we set sail, and we were not far from
  the land,
When the captain spied a lovely mermaid with a comb and a glass
  in her hand.

Chorus:
    Oh the ocean waves may roll, may roll, and the stormy winds
      may blow,
    While we poor sailors go skipping through the tops, and the
      landlubbers lie down below, below.
    And the landlubbers lie down below.

Then up spoke the captain of our gallant ship, and a well-spoken
man was he.
"I have married a wife in Salem town; and tonight she a widow
will be." (*Chorus.*)

Then up spoke the boy of our gallant ship, and a well-spoken lad
was he,
"I've a father and mother in Boston City, and tonight they child-
less will be." (*Chorus.*)

"Oh, the moon shines bright, and the stars give light; oh, my
mother'll be looking for me;
She may look, she may weep, she may look to the deep, she may
look to the bottom of the sea." (*Chorus.*)

Then up spoke the cook of our gallant ship, and a red-hot cook
was he,
"I care more for my kettles and pots than I care for the bottom
of the sea." (*Chorus.*)

Then three times round went our gallant ship, and three times
round went she;
Then three times round went our gallant ship, and she went to
the bottom of the sea. (*Chorus.*)

THE WIFE OF USHER'S WELL

Anonymous

There lived a wife at Usher's Well,
  And a wealthy wife was she;
She had three stout and stalwart sons,
  And sent them o'er the sea.

They hadna been a week from her,
  A week but barely ane,
Whan word came to the carline wife,
  That her three sons were gane.

They hadna been a week from her,
  A week but barely three,
Whan word came to the carline wife,
  That her sons she'd never see.

"I wish the wind may never cease,
  Nor fishes in the flood,
Till my three sons come hame to me,
  In earthly flesh and blood!"

It fell about the Martinmas,
  When nights are lang and mirk,
The carline wife's three sons came hame,
  And their hats were o' the birk.

It neither grew in syke nor ditch,
  Nor yet in ony sheugh;
But at the gates o' Paradise,
  That birk grew fair eneugh.

"Blow up the fire, my maidens!
  Bring water from the well!
For a' my house shall feast this night,
  Since my three sons are well."

And she has made to them a bed,
  She's made it large and wide;
And she's ta'en her mantle her about,
  Sat down at the bed-side.

Up then crew the red, red cock,
  And up and crew the grey;
The eldest to the youngest said,
  " 'Tis time we were awa'."

The cock he hadna crawed but once,
  And clapped his wings at a'
Whan the youngest to the eldest said,
  "Brother, we must awa'.

"The cock doth craw, the day doth daw',
  The channerin' worm doth chide;
Gin we be missed out o' our place,
  A sair pain we maun bide."

"Lie still, lie still, a little wee while,
  Lie still but if we may;
Gin my mother should miss us when she wakes,
  She'll go mad ere it be day."

O they've ta'en up their mother's mantle
   And they've hinged it on the pin:
"O lang may ye hing, my mother's mantle,
   Ere ye hap us again!

"Fare-ye-weel, my mother dear!
   Fareweel to barn and byre!
And fare-ye-weel, the bonny lass
   That kindles my mother's fire."

I SHALL NOT PASS AGAIN THIS WAY

Anonymous

The bread that bringeth strength I want to give,
The water pure that bids the thirsty live:
I want to help the fainting day by day;
I'm sure I shall not pass again this way.

I want to give the oil of joy for tears,
The faith to conquer crowding doubts and fears.
Beauty for ashes may I give alway:
I'm sure I shall not pass again this way.

I want to give some measure running o'er,
And into angry hearts I want to pour
The answer soft that turneth wrath away;
I'm sure I shall not pass again this way.

I want to give to others hope and faith,
I want to do all that the Master saith;
I want to live aright from day to day;
I'm sure I shall not pass again this way.

THE CROW AND THE PITCHER

A Crow, ready to die with thirst, flew with joy to a Pitcher, which he beheld at some distance. When he came, he found water in it indeed, but so near the bottom, that, with all his stooping and straining, he was not able to reach it. Then he endeavored to over-turn the Pitcher, that so at least he might be able to get a little of it. But his strength was not sufficient for this. At last, seeing some pebbles lie near the place, he cast them one by one into the Pitcher; and thus, by degrees, raised the water up to the very brim, and satisfied his thirst.

(From Aesop's Fables)

ULYSSES

Alfred, Lord Tennyson

It little profits that an idle king,
By this still hearth, among these barren crags,
Match'd with an agèd wife, I mete and dole
Unequal laws unto a savage race,
That hoard, and sleep, and feed, and know not me.
I cannot rest from travel: I will drink
Life to the lees: all times I have enjoy'd
Greatly, have suffer'd greatly, both with those
That loved me, and alone; on shore, and when
Thro' scudding drifts the rainy Hyades
Vext the dim sea; I am become a name;
For always roaming with a hungry heart
Much have I seen and known; cities of men,
And manners, climates, councils, governments,
Myself not least, but honour'd of them all;
And drunk delight of battle with my peers,
Far on the ringing plains of windy Troy.
I am a part of all that I have met.
Yet all experience is an arch where-thro'
Gleams that untravell'd world, whose margin fades
Forever and forever when I move.
How dull it is to pause, to make an end,
To rust unburnish'd, not to shine in use!
As tho' to breathe were life. Life piled on life
Were all too little, and of one to me
Little remains: but every hour is saved
From that eternal silence, something more,
A bringer of new things; and vile it were
For some three suns to store and hoard myself,
And this grey spirit yearning in desire
To follow knowledge like a sinking star,
Beyond the utmost bound of human thought.

This is my son, mine own Telemachus,
To whom I leave the sceptre and the isle—
Well-loved of me, discerning to fulfil
This labour, by slow prudence to make mild
A rugged people, and thro' soft degrees
Subdue them to the useful and the good.
Most blameless is he, centred in the sphere
Of common duties, decent not to fail
In offices of tenderness, and pay
Meet adoration to my household gods,
When I am gone. He works his work, I mine.
   There lies the port; the vessel puffs her sail:
There gloom the dark broad seas. My mariners,
Souls that have toil'd, and wrought, and thought with me—
That ever with a frolic welcome took
The thunder and the sunshine, and opposed
Free hearts, free foreheads—you and I are old;
Old age hath yet his honour and his toil;
Death closes all: but something ere the end,
Some work of noble note, may yet be done,
Not unbecoming men that strove with Gods.
The lights begin to twinkle from the rocks:
The long day wanes: the slow moon climbs: the deep
Moans round with many voices. Come, my friends
'Tis not too late to seek a newer world.
Push off, and sitting well in order smite
The sounding furrows; for my purpose holds
To sail beyond the sunset, and the baths
Of all the western stars, until I die.
It may be that the gulfs will wash us down:
It may be we shall touch the Happy Isles,
And see the great Achilles, whom we knew.
Tho' much is taken, much abides; and tho'
We are not now that strength which in old days
Moved earth and heaven; that which we are, we are;
One equal temper of heroic hearts,
Made weak by time and fate, but strong in will
To strive, to seek, to find, and not to yield.

*   *   *

Let us all be happy and live within our means, even if we have
to borrow money to do it with.

—Artemus Ward

BREDON HILL

A. E. Housman

In summertime on Bredon
  The bells they sound so clear;
Round both the shires they ring them
  In steeples far and near,
  A happy noise to hear.

Here of a Sunday morning
  My love and I would lie,
And see the coloured counties,
  And hear the larks so high
  About us in the sky.

The bells would ring to call her
  In valleys miles away:
"Come all to church, good people;
  Good people, come and pray."
  But here my love would stay.

And I would turn and answer
  Among the springtime thyme,
"Oh, peal upon our wedding,
  And we will hear the chime,
  And come to church in time."

But when the snows at Christmas
  On Bredon top were strown,
My love rose up so early
  And stole out unbeknown
  And went to church alone.

They tolled the one bell only,
  Groom there was none to see,
The mourners followed after,
  And to church went she,
  And would not wait for me.

The bells they sound on Bredon,
  And still the steeples hum.
"Come all to church, good people,"—
  Oh, noisy bells, be dumb;
  I hear you, I will come.

THE D.L. AND W.'S PHOEBE SNOW

Says Phoebe Snow
About to go,
Upon a trip
To Buffalo,
"My gown stays white
From morn till night
Upon the Road of Anthracite."

With dimpling face
All full of grace
Fair Phoebe pictures
In a daze
That journey bright
When clad in white
She used the Road of Anthracite.

Says Phoebe—"You
Have travelled too,
On many roads—
And find it true
That all that's bright
And best, unite
Upon the Road of Anthracite."

Yes, Phoebe, I
Can now see why
The praises of
This road you cry.
My gloves are white
As when last night
We took the Road of Anthracite.

When "Made" they say
"In U.S.A."
They mean the Maid
Who's made away
With travel's blight
Both day and night
In Using Simply Anthracite.

Miss Snow draws near
The cab to cheer
The level-headed
Engineer,
Whose wonderful sight
Makes safe her flight
Upon the Road of Anthracite.

A birch canoe
And Phoebe too,
Already there
To welcome you.
The season's right
The distance slight
Upon the Road of Anthracite.

INSCRIPTION ON GENERAL POST OFFICE, NEW YORK, N. Y.

Neither Snow, Nor Rain, Nor Heat, Nor Gloom
of Night Stops These Couriers From the
Swift Completion of Their Appointed Rounds.
(From Herodotus)

BEN BOLT

Thomas Dunn English

Don't you remember sweet Alice, Ben Bolt,—
Sweet Alice whose hair was so brown,
Who wept with delight when you gave her a smile,
And trembled with fear at your frown?
In the old church-yard in the valley, Ben Bolt,
In a corner obscure and alone,
They have fitted a slab of the granite so gray,
And Alice lies under the stone.

Under the hickory tree, Ben Bolt,
Which stood at the foot of the hill,
Together we've lain in the noonday shade,
And listened to Appleton's mill.

The mill-wheel has fallen to pieces, Ben Bolt,
The rafters have tumbled in,
And a quiet which crawls round the walls as you gaze
Has followed the olden din.

Do you mind of the cabin of logs, Ben Bolt,
At the edge of the pathless wood,
And the button-ball tree with its motley limbs,
Which nigh by the doorstep stood?
The cabin to ruin has gone, Ben Bolt,
The tree you would seek for in vain;
And where once the lords of the forest waved
Are grass and golden grain.

And don't you remember the school, Ben Bolt,
With the master so cruel and grim,
And the shaded nook in the running brook
Where the children went to swim?
Grass grows on the master's grave, Ben Bolt,
The spring of the brook is dry,
And of all the boys who were schoolmates then
There are only you and I.

There is a change in the things I loved, Ben Bolt,
They have changed from the old to the new;
But I feel in the deeps of my spirit the truth,
There never was change in you.
Twelve months twenty have past, Ben Bolt,
Since first we were friends—yet I hail
Your presence a blessing, your friendship a truth,
Ben Bolt of the salt-sea gale.

"WHEN, IN DISGRACE——"

William Shakespeare

When, in disgrace with fortune and men's eyes,
I all alone beweep my outcast state
And trouble deaf heaven with my bootless cries
And look upon myself and curse my fate,
Wishing me like to one more rich in hope,
Featured like him, like him with friends possess'd,

474

Desiring this man's art and that man's scope,
With what I most enjoy contented least;
Yet in these thoughts myself almost despising,
Haply I think on thee, and then my state,
Like to the lark at break of day arising
From sullen earth, sings hymns at heaven's gate;
 For thy sweet love remember'd such wealth brings
 That then I scorn to change my state with kings.

(From his Sonnets)

THE CHARGE OF THE LIGHT BRIGADE *

Alfred, Lord Tennyson

Half a league, half a league,
Half a league onward,
All in the valley of Death
 Rode the six hundred.
 "Forward, the Light Brigade!
Charge for the guns!" he said.
Into the valley of Death
 Rode the six hundred.

"Forward, the Light Brigade!"
Was there a man dismayed?
Not though the soldier knew
 Some one had blundered.
Theirs not to make reply,
Theirs not to reason why,
Theirs but to do and die.
Into the valley of Death
 Rode the six hundred.

Cannon to right of them,
Cannon to left of them,
Cannon in front of them
 Volleyed and thundered;
Stormed at with shot and shell,
Boldly they rode and well,
Into the jaws of Death,
Into the mouth of Hell
 Rode the six hundred.

* To commemorate the cavalry charge at Balaclava in the Crimean War.

Flashed all their sabres bare,
Flashed as they turned in air
Sabring the gunners there,
Charging an army, while
   All the world wondered:
Plunged in the battery-smoke
Right through the line they broke;
Cossack and Russian
Reeled from the sabre-stroke
   Shattered and sundered.
Then they rode back, but not,
   Not the six hundred.

Cannon to right of them,
Cannon to left of them,
Cannon behind them
   Volleyed and thundered;
Stormed at with shot and shell,
While horse and hero fell,
They that had fought so well
Came through the jaws of Death,
Back from the mouth of Hell,
All that was left of them,
   Left of six hundred.

When can their glory fade?
O the wild charge they made!
   All the world wondered.
Honor the charge they made!
Honor the Light Brigade,
   Noble six hundred!

SOURCE OF NEWS

Anonymous

Absolute knowledge I have none,
But my niece's washerwoman's son
Heard a policeman on his beat
Say to a laborer in the street
That he had a letter last week
Written in the finest Greek,

From a Chinese coolie in Timbuctoo,
Who said that the niggers in Cuba knew
Of a colored man in a Texas town,
Who got it straight from a circus clown,
That a man in the Klondike heard the news
From a gang of South American Jews,
Who heard of a society female rake,
Whose mother-in-law will undertake
To prove that her husband's sister knows,
As stated in a printed piece,
That she has a son, who has a friend
Who knows when the war is going to end!

THE SKELETON IN ARMOR

Henry Wadsworth Longfellow

"Speak! speak! thou fearful guest!
    Who, with thy hollow breast
Still in rude armor drest,
    Comest to daunt me!
Wrapt not in Eastern balms,
But with thy fleshless palms
Stretched, as if asking alms,
    Why dost thou haunt me?"

Then, from those cavernous eyes
Pale flashes seemed to rise,
As when the Northern skies
    Gleam in December;
And, like the water's flow
Under December's snow,
Came a dull voice of woe
    From the heart's chamber.

"I was a Viking old!
My deeds, though manifold,
No Skald in song has told,
    No Saga taught thee!
Take heed, that in thy verse
Thou dost the tale rehearse,
Else dread a dead man's curse;
    For this I sought thee.

"Far in the Northern Land,
By the wild Baltic's strand,
I, with my childish hand,
    Tamed the gerfalcon;
And, with my skates fast-bound,
Skimmed the half-frozen Sound,
That the poor whimpering hound
    Trembled to walk on.

"Oft to his frozen lair
Tracked I the grisly bear,
While from my path the hare
    Fled like a shadow;
Oft through the forest dark
Followed the were-wolf's bark,
Until the soaring lark
    Sang from the meadow.

"But when I older grew,
Joining a corsair's crew,
O'er the dark sea I flew
    With the marauders.
Wild was the life we led;
Many the souls that sped,
Many the hearts that bled,
    By our stern orders.

"Many a wassail-bout
Wore the long Winter out;
Often our midnight shout
    Set the cocks crowing,
As we the Berserk's tale
Measured in cups of ale,
Draining the oaken pail,
    Filled to o'erflowing.

"Once as I told in glee
Tales of the stormy sea,
Soft eyes did gaze on me,
    Burning yet tender;
And as the white stars shine
On the dark Norway pine,
On that dark heart of mine
    Fell their soft splendor.

478

"I wooed the blue-eyed maid,
Yielding, yet half afraid,
And in the forest's shade
  Our vows were plighted.
Under its loosened vest
Fluttered her little breast,
Like birds within their nest
  By the hawk frighted.

"Bright in her father's hall
Shields gleamed upon the wall,
Loud sang the minstrels all,
  Chanting his glory;
When of old Hildebrand
I asked his daughter's hand,
Mute did the minstrels stand
  To hear my story.

"While the brown ale he quaffed,
Loud then the champion laughed,
And as the wind-gusts waft
  The sea-foam brightly,
So the loud laugh of scorn,
Out of those lips unshorn,
From the deep drinking-horn
  Blew the foam lightly.

"She was a Prince's child,
I but a Viking wild,
And though she blushed and smiled,
  I was discarded!
Should not the dove so white
Follow the sea-mew's flight,
Why did they leave that night
  Her nest unguarded?

"Scarce had I put to sea,
Bearing the maid with me,
Fairest of all was she
  Among the Norsemen!
When on the white sea-strand,
Waving his armèd hand,
Saw we old Hildebrand,
  With twenty horsemen.

"Then launched they to the blast,
Bent like a reed each mast,
Yet we were gaining fast,
   When the wind failed us;
And with a sudden flaw
Came round the gusty Skaw,
So that our foe we saw
   Laugh as he hailed us.

"And as to catch the gale
Round veered the flapping sail,
" 'Death!' was the helmsman's hail,
   " 'Death without quarter!'
Mid-ships with iron keel
Struck we her ribs of steel;
Down her black hulk did reel
   Through the black water!

"As with his wings aslant,
Sails the fierce cormorant,
Seeking some rocky haunt,
   With his prey laden,—
So toward the open main,
Beating to sea again,
Through the wild hurricane,
   Bore I the maiden.

"Three weeks we westward bore,
And when the storm was o'er,
Cloud-like we saw the shore
   Stretching to leeward;
There for my lady's bower
Built I the lofty tower,
Which, to this very hour,
 ⸱ Stands looking seaward.

"There lived we many years;
Time dried the maiden's tears;
She had forgot her fears,
   She was a mother;
Death closed her mild blue eyes,
Under that tower she lies;
Ne'er shall the sun arise
   On such another!

"Still grew my bosom then,
Still as a stagnant fen!
Hateful to me were men,
  The sunlight hateful!
In the vast forest here,
Clad in my warlike gear,
Fell I upon my spear,
  Oh, death was grateful!

"Thus, seamed with many scars,
Bursting these prison bars,
Up to its native stars
  My soul ascended!
There from the flowing bowl
Deep drinks the warrior's soul,
Skoal! to the Northland! *Skoal!*"
  Thus the tale ended.

WE ARE SEVEN

William Wordsworth

          A simple child,
That lightly draws its breath,
And feels its life in every limb,
    What should it know of death?

I met a little cottage girl:
    She was eight years old, she said;
Her hair was thick with many a curl
    That clustered round her head.

She had a rustic, woodland air,
    And she was wildly clad;
Her eyes were fair, and very fair;—
    Her beauty made me glad.

"Sisters and brothers, little maid,
    How many may you be?"
"How many? Seven in all," she said,
    And wondering looked at me.

481

"And where are they? I pray you tell."
  She answered, "Seven are we;
And two of us at Conway dwell,
  And two are gone to sea;

"Two of us in the churchyard lie,
  My sister and my brother;
And, in the churchyard cottage, I
  Dwell near them with my mother."

"You say that two at Conway dwell,
  And two are gone to sea,
Yet ye are seven! I pray you tell,
  Sweet maid, how this may be."

Then did the little maid reply,
  "Seven boys and girls are we;
Two of us in the churchyard lie
  Beneath the churchyard tree."

"You run about, my little maid;
  Your limbs they are alive;
If two are in the churchyard laid,
  Then ye are only five."

"Their graves are green, they may be seen,"
  The little maid replied:
"Twelve steps or more from my mother's door,
  And they are side by side.

"My stockings there I often knit;
  My kerchief there I hem;
And there upon the ground I sit,
  And sing a song to them.

"And often after sunset, sir,
  When it is light and fair,
I take my little porringer,
  And eat my supper there.

"The first that died was Sister Jane;
  In bed she moaning lay,
Till God released her of her pain;
  And then she went away.

"So in the churchyard she was laid;
  And, when the grass was dry,
Together round her grave we played,
  My brother John and I.

"And when the ground was white with snow,
  And I could run and slide,
My brother John was forced to go,
  And he lies by her side."

"How many are you, then," said I,
  "If they two are in heaven?"
Quick was the little maid's reply:
  "O Master! we are seven."

"But they are dead; those two are dead!
  Their spirits are in heaven!"—
'Twas throwing words away; for still
The little maid would have her will,
  And said, "Nay, we are seven!"

THE AMERICAN FLAG

Joseph Rodman Drake

When Freedom, from her mountain height,
  Unfurled her standard to the air,
She tore the azure robe of night,
  And set the stars of glory there!
She mingled with its gorgeous dyes
The milky baldric of the skies,
And striped its pure, celestial white
With streakings of the morning light;
Then, from his mansion in the sun,
She called her eagle-bearer down,
And gave into his mighty hand
  The symbol of her chosen land!

Majestic monarch of the cloud!
  Who rear'st aloft thy regal form,
To hear the tempest trumping loud,
And see the lightning lances driven,
  When strive the warriors of the storm,
And rolls the thunder-drum of heaven,—

Child of the Sun! to thee 't is given
   To guard the banner of the free,
To hover in the sulphur smoke,
To ward away the battle-stroke,
And bid its blendings shine afar,
Like rainbows on the cloud of war,
   The harbingers of victory!

Flag of the brave! thy folds shall fly,
The sign of hope and triumph high!
When speaks the signal-trumpet tone,
And the long line comes gleaming on,
Ere yet the life-blood, warm and wet,
Has dimmed the glistening bayonet,
Each soldier's eye shall brightly turn
To where thy sky-born glories burn,
And, as his springing steps advance,
   Catch war and vengeance from the glance.

And when the cannon-mouthings loud
Heave in wild wreaths the battle shroud,
And gory sabres rise and fall
Like shoots of flame on midnight's pall,
Then shall thy meteor glances glow,
   And cowering foes shall shrink beneath
Each gallant arm that strikes below
   That lovely messenger of death.

Flag of the seas! on ocean wave
Thy stars shall glitter o'er the brave;
When death, careering on the gale,
Sweeps darkly round the bellied sail,
And frighted waves rush wildly back
Before the broadside's reeling rack,
Each dying wanderer of the sea
Shall look at once to heaven and thee,
And smile to see thy splendors fly
   In triumph o'er his closing eye.

Flag of the free heart's hope and home,
   By angel hands to valor given!
Thy stars have lit the welkin dome,
   And all thy hues were born in heaven.

Forever float that standard sheet!
    Where breathes the foe but falls before us,
With Freedom's soil beneath our feet,
    And Freedom's banner streaming o'er us!

I'VE BEEN WORKIN' ON THE RAILROAD

Anonymous

I've been workin' on the railroad
All the livelong day.
I've been workin' on the railroad
Just to pass the time away.
Don't you hear the whistle blowing?
Rise up so early in the morn.
Don't you hear the Captain shouting:
"Dinah, blow your horn."

LASCA

Frank Desprez

I want free life and I want fresh air;
And I sigh for the canter after the cattle,
The crack of the whips like shots in a battle,
The medley of horns and hoofs and heads
That wars and wrangles and scatters and spreads;
The green beneath and the blue above,
And dash and danger, and life and love.

And Lasca!

      Lasca used to ride
On a mouse-gray mustang close to my side,
With blue serape and bright-belled spur;
I laughed with joy as I looked at her!
Little knew she of books or of creeds;
An Ave Maria sufficed her needs;
Little she cared, save to be by my side,
To ride with me, and ever to ride,
From San Saba's shore to Lavaca's tide.

She was as bold as the billows that beat,
She was as wild as the breezes that blow;
From her little head to her little feet
She was swayed in her suppleness to and fro
By each gust of passion; a sapling pine,
That grows on the edge of a Kansas bluff,
And wars with the wind when the weather is rough,
Is like this Lasca, this love of mine.
She would hunger that I might eat,
Would take the bitter and leave me the sweet;
But once, when I made her jealous for fun,
At something I'd whispered, or looked, or done,
One Sunday, in San Antonio,
To a glorious girl on the Alamo,
She drew from her garter a dear little dagger,
And—sting of a wasp!—it made me stagger!
An inch to the left, or an inch to the right,
And I shouldn't be maundering here tonight;
But she sobbed, and, sobbing, so swiftly bound
Her torn reboso about the wound,
That I quite forgave her. Scratches don't count
            In Texas, down by the Rio Grande.

Her eye was brown—a deep, deep brown;
Her hair was darker than her eye;
And something in her smile and frown,
Curled crimson lip and instep high,
Showed that there ran in each blue vein,
Mixed with the milder Aztec strain,
The vigorous vintage of Old Spain.
She was alive in every limb
With feeling, to the finger tips;
And when the sun is like a fire,
And sky one shining, soft sapphire,
One does not drink in little sips.

The air was heavy, the night was hot,
I sat by her side, and forgot—forgot;
Forgot the herd that were taking their rest,
Forgot that the air was close opprest,
That the Texas norther comes sudden and soon,
In the dead of night or the blaze of noon;

That once let the herd at its breath take fright,
Nothing on earth can stop the flight;
And woe to the rider, and woe to the steed,
Who falls in front of their mad stampede!

Was that thunder? I grasped the cord
Of my swift mustang without a word.
I sprang to the saddle, and she clung behind.
Away! on a hot chase down the wind!
But never was fox hunt half so hard,
And never was steed so little spared.
For we rode for our lives. You shall hear how we fared
       In Texas, down by the Rio Grande.

The mustang flew, and we urged him on;
There was one chance left, and you have but one;
Halt, jump to ground, and shoot your horse;
Crouch under his carcass, and take your chance;
And, if the steers in their frantic course
Don't batter you both to pieces at once,
You may thank your star; if not, good-by
To the quickening kiss and the long-drawn sigh,
And the open air and the open sky,
       In Texas, down by the Rio Grande!

The cattle gained on us, and, just as I felt
For my old six-shooter behind in my belt,
Down came the mustang, and down came we,
Clinging together, and—what was the rest—
A body that spread itself on my breast.
Two arms that shielded my dizzy head,
Two lips that hard on my lips were prest;
Then came thunder in my ears,
As over us surged the sea of steers,
Blows that beat blood into my eyes,
And when I could rise—
Lasca was dead!

I gouged out a grave a few feet deep,
And there in Earth's arms I laid her to sleep;
And there she is lying, and no one knows,
And the summer shines and the winter snows;
For many a day the flowers have spread

A pall of petals over her head;
And the little gray hawk hangs aloft in the air,
And the sly coyote trots here and there,
And the black snake glides and glitters and slides
Into a rift in a cottonwood tree;
And the buzzard sails on,
And comes and is gone,
Stately and still like a ship at sea;
And I wonder why I do not care
For the things that are like the things that were.
Does half my heart lie buried there
        In Texas, down by the Rio Grande.

SILVER THREADS AMONG THE GOLD

Eben E. Rexford

Darling, I am growing old,
Silver threads among the gold,
Shine upon my brow today,
Life is fading fast away;
But, my darling, you will be
Always young and fair to me.
Yes! my darling, you will be
Always young and fair to me.

Chorus:

    Darling, I am growing old,
    Silver threads among the gold,
    Shine upon my brow today;
    Life is fading fast away.

When your hair is silver white,
And your cheeks no longer bright,
With the roses of the May,
I will kiss your lips and say;
Oh! my darling mine alone,
You have never older grown. (*Chorus.*)

Love can never more grow old,
Locks may lose their brown and gold,

Cheeks may fade and hollow grow,
But the hearts that love will know;
Never, never, winter's frost and chill,
Summer warmth is in them still. (*Chorus.*)

Love is always young and fair,
What to us is silver hair,
Faded cheeks or steps grown slow,
To the heart that beats below?
Since I kissed you mine alone,
You have never older grown. (*Chorus.*)

LOCHINVAR

Sir Walter Scott

Oh, young Lochinvar is come out of the west:
Through all the wide border his steed was the best;
And save his good broadsword he weapons had none;
He rode all unarmed and he rode all alone.
So faithful in love, and so dauntless in war,
There never was knight like the young Lochinvar!

He stayed not for brake, and he stopped not for stone;
He swam the Esk River where ford there was none:
But ere he alighted at Netherby gate,
The bride had consented, the gallant came late;
For a laggard in love, and a dastard in war,
Was to wed the fair Ellen of brave Lochinvar.

So boldly he entered the Netherby Hall,
Among bridesmen, and kinsmen, and brothers, and all:
Then spoke the bride's father, his hand on his sword
(For the poor craven bridegroom said never a word),
"O come ye in peace here, or come ye in war,
Or to dance at our bridal, young Lord Lochinvar?"—

"I long wooed your daughter, my suit you denied;—
Love swells like the Solway, but ebbs like its tide!
And now am I come, with this lost love of mine,
To lead but one measure, drink one cup of wine:
There are maidens in Scotland more lovely by far,
That would gladly be bride to the young Lochinvar."

The bride kissed the goblet: the knight took it up,
He quaffed off the wine, and he threw down the cup.
She looked down to blush, and she looked up to sigh,
With a smile on her lips, and a tear in her eye.
He took her soft hand, ere her mother could bar,—
"Now tread we a measure!" said young Lochinvar.

So stately his form, and so lovely her face,
That never a hall such a galliard did grace:
While her mother did fret, and her father did fume,
And the bridegroom stood dangling his bonnet and plume;
And the bride-maidens whispered, " 'Twere better far
To have matched our fair cousin with young Lochinvar."

One touch to her hand, and one word in her ear,
When they reached the hall door, and the charger stood near;
So light to the croupe the fair lady he swung,
So light to the saddle before her he sprung!
"She is won! we are gone, over bank, bush, and scaur:
They'll have fleet steeds that follow," quoth young Lochinvar.

There was mounting 'mong Graemes of the Netherby clan:
Forsters, Fenwicks, and Musgraves, they rode and they ran;
There was racing and chasing on Canobie Lee,
But the lost bride of Netherby ne'er did they see.
So daring in love, and so dauntless in war,
Have ye e'er heard of gallant like young Lochinvar?

(From Marmion)

HENRY V AT HARFLEUR

William Shakespeare

Once more unto the breach, dear friends, once more;
Or close the wall up with our English dead.
In peace there's nothing so becomes a man
As modest stillness and humility:
But when the blast of war blows in our ears,
Then imitate the action of the tiger;
Stiffen the sinews, summon up the blood,
Disguise fair nature with hard-favour'd rage;
Then lend the eye a terrible aspect;

490

Let it pry through the portage of the head
Like the brass cannon; let the brow o'erwhelm it
As fearfully as doth a galled rock
O'erhang and jutty his confounded base,
Swill'd with the wild and wasteful ocean.
Now set the teeth and stretch the nostril wide,
Hold hard the breath and bend up every spirit
To his full height. On, on, you noblest English,
Whose blood is fet from fathers of war-proof!
Fathers that, like so many Alexanders,
Have in these parts from morn till even fought
And sheathed their swords for lack of argument:
Dishonour not your mothers; now attest
That those whom you call'd fathers did beget you.
Be copy now to men of grosser blood,
And teach them how to war. And you, good yeomen,
Whose limbs were made in England, show us here
The mettle of your pasture; let us swear
That you are worth your breeding; which I doubt not;
For there is none of you so mean and base,
That hath not noble lustre in your eyes.
I see you stand like greyhounds in the slips,
Straining upon the start. The game's afoot:
Follow your spirit, and upon this charge
Cry "God for Harry, England, and Saint George!"

(From King Henry V)

LINCOLN'S GETTYSBURG ADDRESS

November 19, 1863

Fourscore and seven years ago our fathers brought forth upon this continent a new nation, conceived in liberty, and dedicated to the proposition that all men are created equal. Now we are engaged in a great civil war, testing whether that nation, or any nation so conceived and so dedicated, can long endure. We are met on a great battlefield of that war. We have come to dedicate a portion of that field as a final resting-place for those who here gave their lives that that nation might live. It is altogether fitting and proper that we should do this. But in a larger sense we cannot dedicate, we cannot consecrate, we cannot hallow this ground.

The brave men, living and dead, who struggled here, have conse-crated it far above our poor power to add or detract. The world will little note, nor long remember, what we say here; but it can never forget what they did here. It is for us, the living, rather to be dedicated here to the unfinished work which they who fought here have thus far so nobly advanced. It is rather for us to be here dedicated to the great task remaining before us, that from these honored dead we take increased devotion to that cause for which they gave the last full measure of devotion; that we here highly resolve that these dead shall not have died in vain; that this nation, under God, shall have a new birth of freedom, and that government of the people, by the people, and for the people, shall not perish from the earth.

AMERICA

Samuel Francis Smith

My country, 'tis of thee,
Sweet land of liberty,
  Of thee I sing;
Land where my fathers died,
Land of the pilgrims' pride.
From every mountain-side
  Let Freedom ring.

My native country, thee,
Land of the noble free,—
  Thy name I love;
I love thy rocks and rills,
Thy woods and templed hills:
My heart with rapture thrills
  Like that above.

Let music swell the breeze,
And ring from all the trees,
  Sweet Freedom's song;
Let mortal tongues awake,
Let all that breathe partake,
Let rocks their silence break,—
  The sound prolong.

Our fathers' God, to Thee,
Author of liberty,
   To thee we sing;
Long may our land be bright
With Freedom's holy light;
Protect us by Thy might,
   Great God, our King.

IN SCHOOL-DAYS

John Greenleaf Whittier

Still sits the school-house by the road,
   A ragged beggar sunning;
Around it still the sumachs grow,
   And blackberry-vines are running.

Within, the master's desk is seen,
   Deep scarred by raps official;
The warping floor, the battered seats,
   The jack-knife's carved initial;

The charcoal frescoes on its wall;
   Its door's worn sill, betraying
The feet that, creeping slow to school,
   Went storming out to playing!

Long years ago a winter sun
   Shone over it at setting;
Lit up its western window-panes,
   And low eaves' icy fretting.

It touched the tangled golden curls,
   And brown eyes full of grieving,
Of one who still her steps delay
   When all the school were leaving.

For near her stood the little boy
   Her childish favor singled;
His cap pulled low upon a face
   Where pride and shame were mingled.

Pushing with restless feet the snow
  To right and left, he lingered;—
As restlessly her tiny hands
  The blue-checked apron fingered.

He saw her lift her eyes; he felt
  The soft hand's light caressing,
And heard the tremble of her voice,
  As if a fault confessing.

"I'm sorry that I spelt the word:
  I hate to go above you,
Because,"—the brown eyes lower fell,—
  "Because, you see, I love you!"

Still memory to a gray-haired man
  That sweet child-face is showing.
Dear girl! the grasses on her grave
  Have forty years been growing!

He lives to learn, in life's hard school,
  How few who pass above him
Lament their triumph and his loss,
  Like her,—because they love him.

SEEIN' THINGS

Eugene Field

I ain't afeard uv snakes, or toads, or bugs, or worms, or mice,
An' things 'at girls are skeered uv I think are awful nice!
I'm pretty brave, I guess; an' yet I hate to go to bed,
For, when I'm tucked up warm an' snug an' when my prayers are
    said,
Mother tells me, "Happy Dreams!" an' takes away the light,
An' leaves me lyin' all alone an' seein' things at night!

Sometimes they're in the corner, sometimes they're by the door,
Sometimes they're all a-standin' in the middle uv the floor;
Sometimes they are a-sittin' down, sometimes they're walkin'
    round

So softly and creepy like they never make a sound!
Sometimes they are as black as ink, an' other times they're white—
But the color ain't no difference when you see things at night!

Once when I licked a feller 'at had just moved on our street,
An' father sent me up to bed without a bite to eat,
I woke up in the dark an' saw things standin' in a row,
A-lookin' at me cross-eyed an' p'intin' at me—so!
Oh, my! I wuz so skeered that time I never slep' a mite—
It's almost alluz when I'm bad I see things at night!

Lucky thing I ain't a girl, or I'd be skeered to death!
Bein' I'm a boy, I duck my head an' hold my breath;
An' I am, oh, *so* sorry I'm a naughty boy, an' then
I promise to be better an' I say my prayers again!
Gran'ma tells me that's the only way to make it right
When a feller has been wicked an' sees things at night!

An' so when other naughty boys would coax me into sin,
I try to skwush the Tempter's voice 'at urges me within;
An' when they's pie for supper, or cakes 'at's big an' nice,
I want to—but I do not pass my plate f'r them things twice!
No, ruther let Starvation wipe me slowly out of sight
Than I should keep-a-livin' on an' seein' things at night!

DRAKE'S DRUM

Sir Henry Newbolt

Drake he's in his hammock an' a thousand miles away,
  (Capten, art tha sleepin' there below?)
Slung atween the round shot in Nombre Dios Bay,
  An' dreamin' arl the time o' Plymouth Hoe.
Yarnder lumes the Island, yarnder lie the ships,
  Wi' sailor lads a-dancin' heel-an'-toe,
An' the shore-lights flashin', an' the night-tide dashin',
  He see et arl so plainly as he saw et long ago.

Drake he was a Devon man, an' ruled the Devon seas,
  (Capten, art tha sleepin' there below?)
Rovin' tho' his death fell, he went wi' heart at ease,
  An' dreamin' arl the time o' Plymouth Hoe.

"Take my drum to England, hang et by the shore,
    Strike et when your powder's runnin' low;
If the Dons sight Devon, I'll quit the port o' Heaven,
    An' drum them up the Channel as we drumm'd them long ago."

Drake he's in his hammock till the great Armadas come,
    (Capten, art tha sleepin' there below?)
Slung atween the round shot, listenin' for the drum,
    An' dreamin' arl the time o' Plymouth Hoe.
Call him on the deep sea, call him up the Sound,
    Call him when ye sail to meet the foe;
Where the old trade's plyin' an' the old flag flyin'
    They shall find him ware an wakin', as they found him long ago!

THE GREAT LOVER

Rupert Brooke

I have been so great a lover: filled my days
So proudly with the splendor of Love's praise,
The pain, the calm, and the astonishment,
Desire illimitable, and still content,
And all dear names men use, to cheat despair,
For the perplexed and viewless streams that bear
Our hearts at random down the dark of life.
Now, ere the unthinking silence on that strife
Steals down, I would cheat drowsy Death so far,
My night shall be remembered for a star
That outshone all the suns of all men's days.
Shall I not crown them with immortal praise
Whom I have loved, who have given me, dared with me
High secrets, and in darkness knelt to see
The inenarrable godhead of delight?
Love is a flame:—we have beaconed the world's night.
A city:—and we have built it, these and I.
An emperor:—we have taught the world to die.
So, for their sakes I loved, ere I go hence,
And the high cause of Love's magnificence,
And to keep loyalties young, I'll write those names
Golden for ever, eagles, crying flames,
And set them as a banner, that men may know,
To dare the generations, burn, and blow

Out on the wind of Time, shining and streaming. . . .
These I have loved:
                    White plates and cups, clean-gleaming,
Ringed with blue lines; and feathery, faëry dust;
Wet roofs, beneath the lamp-light; the strong crust
Of friendly bread; and many-tasting food;
Rainbows; and the blue bitter smoke of wood;
And radiant raindrops couching in cool flowers;
And flowers themselves, that sway through sunny hours,
Dreaming of moths that drink them under the moon;
Then, the cool kindliness of sheets, that soon
Smooth away trouble; and the rough male kiss
Of blankets; grainy wood; live hair that is
Shining and free; blue-massing clouds; the keen
Unpassioned beauty of a great machine;
The benison of hot water; furs to touch;
The good smell of old clothes; and other such—
The comfortable smell of friendly fingers,
Hair's fragrance, and the musty reek that lingers
About dead leaves and last year's ferns. . . .
                                    Dear names,
And thousand others throng to me! Royal flames;
Sweet water's dimpling laugh from tap or spring;
Holes in the ground; and voices that do sing:
Voices in laughter, too; and body's pain;
Soon turned to peace; and the deep-panting train;
Firm sands; the little dulling edge of foam
That browns and dwindles as the waves go home;
And washen stones, gay for an hour; the cold
Graveness of iron; moist black earthen mold;
Sleep; and high places; footprints in the dew;
And oaks; and brown horse-chestnuts, glossy-new;
And new-peeled sticks; and shining pools on grass;—
All these have been my loves. And these shall pass,
Whatever passes not, in the great hour,
Nor all my passion, all my prayers, have power
To hold them with me through the gate of Death.
They'll play deserter, turn with the traitor breath,
Break the high bond we made, and sell Love's trust
And sacramental covenant to the dust.
—Oh, never a doubt but, somewhere, I shall wake,
And give what's left of love again, and make
New friends, now strangers. . . .

But the best I've known
Stays here, and changes, breaks, grows old, is blown
About the winds of the world, and fades from brains
Of living men, and dies.
                    Nothing remains.
O dear my loves, O faithless, once again
This one last gift I give: that after men
Shall know, and later lovers, far-removed
Praise you, "All these were lovely"; say, "He loved."

BEFORE SLEEPING

Anonymous

Matthew, Mark, Luke and John
Bless the bed that I lie on!
Four corners to my bed,
Four angels round my head,
One at head and one at feet,
And two to guard my soul asleep.

THE OLD FAMILIAR FACES

Charles Lamb

I have had playmates, I have had companions,
In my days of childhood, in my joyful school-days;
All, all are gone, the old familiar faces.

I have been laughing, I have been carousing,
Drinking late, sitting late, with my bosom cronies;
All, all are gone, the old familiar faces.

I loved a Love once, fairest among women:
Closed are her doors on me, I must not see her—
All, all are gone, the old familiar faces.

I have a friend, a kinder friend has no man:
Like an ingrate, I left my friend abruptly;
Left him, to muse on the old familiar faces.

498

Ghost-like I paced round the haunts of my childhood,
Earth seem'd a desert I was bound to traverse,
Seeking to find the old familiar faces.

Friend of my bosom, thou more than a brother,
Why wert not thou born in my father's dwelling?
So might we talk of the old familiar faces.

How some they have died, and some they have left me,
And some are taken from me; all are departed;
All, all are gone, the old familiar faces.

THE BATTLE OF BLENHEIM

Robert Southey

I.

It was a summer evening,—
   Old Kaspar's work was done,
And he before his cottage door
   Was sitting in the sun;
And by him sported on the green
His little grandchild Wilhelmine.

II.

She saw her brother Peterkin
   Roll something large and round,
Which he beside the rivulet,
   In playing there, had found;
He came to ask what he had found
That was so large and smooth and round.

III.

Old Kaspar took it from the boy,
   Who stood expectant by;
And then the old man shook his head,
   And, with a natural sigh,—
" 'Tis some poor fellow's skull," said he,
"Who fell in the great victory.

IV.

"I find them in the garden,
   For there's many hereabout;

And often, when I go to plough,
    The ploughshare turns them out;
For many thousand men," said he,
"Were slain in the great victory."

v.

"Now tell us what 'twas all about,"
    Young Peterkin he cries;
And little Wilhelmine looks up
    With wonder-waiting eyes,—
"Now tell us all about the war,
And what they fought each other for."

VI.

"It was the English," Kaspar cried,
    "Who put the French to rout;
But what they fought each other for
    I could not well make out;
But everybody said," quoth he,
"That 'twas a famous victory.

VII.

"My father lived at Blenheim then,
    Yon little stream hard by;
They burnt his dwelling to the ground,
    And he was forced to fly;
So with his wife and child he fled,
Nor had he where to rest his head.

VIII.

"With fire and sword the country round
    Was wasted far and wide;
And many a childing mother there,
    And new-born baby died;
But things like that, you know, must be
At every famous victory.

IX.

"They say it was a shocking sight
    After the field was won,—
For many thousand bodies here
    Lay rotting in the sun;
But things like that, you know, must be
After a famous victory.

"Great praise the Duke of Marlborough won,
 And our good Prince Eugene."
"Why, 'twas a very wicked thing!"
 Said little Wilhelmine.
"Nay, nay, my little girl!" quoth he,
"It was a famous victory."

"And everybody praised the Duke
 Who this great fight did win."
"But what good came of it at last?"
 Quoth little Peterkin.
"Why, that I cannot tell," said he;
"But 'twas a famous victory."

THE SHOOTING OF DAN McGREW

Robert W. Service

A bunch of the boys were whooping it up in the
 Malamute saloon;
The kid that handles the music-box was hitting
 a jag-time tune;
Back of the bar, in a solo game, sat Dangerous
 Dan McGrew;
And watching his luck was his light-o'-love, the
 lady that's known as Lou.

When out of the night, which was fifty below,
 and into the din and the glare,
There stumbled a miner fresh from the creeks,
 dog-dirty, and loaded for bear.
He looked like a man with a foot in the grave
 and scarcely the strength of a louse,
Yet he tilted a poke of dust on the bar, and he
 called for drinks for the house.
There was none could place the stranger's face,
 though we searched ourselves for a clue;
But we drank his health, and the last to drink
 was Dangerous Dan McGrew.

There's men that somehow just grip your eyes,
    and hold them hard like a spell;
And such was he, and he looked to me like a
    man who had lived in hell;
With a face most hair, and the dreary stare of
    a dog whose day is done,
As he watered the green stuff in his glass, and
    the drops fell one by one.
Then I got to figgering who he was, and won-
    dering what he'd do,
And I turned my head—and there watching
    him was the lady that's known as Lou.

His eyes went rubbering round the room, and
    he seemed in a kind of daze,
Till at last that old piano fell in the way of his
    wandering gaze.
The rag-time kid was having a drink: there
    was no one else on the stool,
So the stranger stumbles across the room, and
    flops down there like a fool.
In a buckskin shirt that was glazed with dirt
    he sat, and I saw him sway;
Then he clutched the keys with his talon hands
    —my God! but that man could play.

Were you ever out in the Great Alone, when the
    moon was awful clear,
And the icy mountains hemmed you in with a
    silence you most could *hear;*
With only the howl of a timber wolf, and you
    camped there in the cold,
A half-dead thing in a stark, dead world, clean
    mad for the muck called gold;
While high overhead, green, yellow and red,
    the North Lights swept in bars?—
Then you've a hunch what the music meant
    . . . hunger and night and the stars.

And hunger not of the belly kind, that's ban-
    ished with bacon and beans,
But the gnawing hunger of lonely men for a
    home and all that it means:

For a fireside far from the cares that are, four
    walls and a roof above;
But oh! so cramful of cosy joy, and crowned
    with a woman's love—
A woman dearer than all the world, and true
    as Heaven is true—
(God! how ghastly she looks through her
    rouge,—the lady that's known as Lou.)

Then on a sudden the music changed, so soft
    that you scarce could hear;
But you felt that your life had been looted clean
    of all that it once held dear;
That someone had stolen the woman you loved;
    that her love was a devil's lie;
That your guts were gone, and the best for you
    was to crawl away and die.
'Twas the crowning cry of a heart's despair,
    and it thrilled you through and through—
"I guess I'll make it a spread misere," said
    Dangerous Dan McGrew.

The music almost died away . . . then it burst
    like a pent-up flood;
And it seemed to say, "Repay, repay," and my
    eyes were blind with blood.
The thought came back of an ancient wrong,
    and it stung like a frozen lash,
And the lust awoke to kill, to kill . . . then
    the music stopped with a crash,
And the stranger turned, and his eyes they
    burned in a most peculiar way;
In a buckskin shirt that was glazed with dirt
    he sat, and I saw him sway;
Then his lips went in a kind of grin, and he
    spoke, and his voice was calm,
And "Boys," says he, "you don't know me,
    and none of you care a damn;
But I want to state, and my words are straight,
    and I'll bet my poke they're true,
That one of you is a hound of hell . . . and
    that one is Dan McGrew."

Then I ducked my head, and the lights went
    out, and two guns blazed in the dark,
And a woman screamed, and the lights went up,
    and two men lay stiff and stark.
Pitched on his head, and pumped full of lead,
    was Dangerous Dan McGrew,
While the man from the creeks lay clutched to
    the breast of the lady that's known as Lou.
These are the simple facts of the case, and I
    guess you ought to know.
They say that the stranger was crazed with
    "hooch", and I'm not denying it's so.
I'm not so wise as the lawyer guys, but strictly
    between us two—
The woman that kissed him and—pinched his
    poke—was the lady that's known as Lou.

PROPHECY

Alfred, Lord Tennyson

For I dipt into the future, far as human eye could see,
Saw the Vision of the world, and all the wonder that would be;

Saw the heavens fill with commerce, argosies of magic sails,
Pilots of the purple twilight, dropping down with costly bales;

Heard the heavens fill with shouting, and there rain'd a ghastly
    dew
From the nations' airy navies grappling in the central blue;

Far along the world-wide whisper of the south-wind rushing warm,
With the standards of the peoples plunging thro' the thunder-
    storm;

Till the war-drum throbb'd no longer, and the battle-flags were
    furl'd
In the Parliament of man, the Federation of the world.

There the common sense of most shall hold a fretful realm in awe,
And the kindly earth shall slumber, lapt in universal law.

                        (From Locksley Hall)

"WHERE IGNORANCE IS BLISS——"

Thomas Gray

To each his suffering; all are men,
Condemn'd alike to groan,
The tender for another's pain,
The unfeeling for his own.
Yet, ah! why should they know their fate,
Since sorrow never comes too late,
And happiness too swiftly flies?
Thought would destroy their paradise.
No more;—where ignorance is bliss,
'Tis folly to be wise.

> (From On A Distant Prospect
> of Eton College)

THE CARES OF MAJESTY

William Shakespeare

How many thousand of my poorest subjects
Are at this hour asleep! O sleep, O gentle sleep,
Nature's soft nurse, how have I frighted thee,
That thou no more wilt weigh my eyelids down
And steep my senses in forgetfulness?
Why rather, sleep, liest thou in smoky cribs,
Upon uneasy pallets stretching thee
And hush'd with buzzing night-flies to thy slumber,
Than in the perfumed chambers of the great,
Under the canopies of costly state,
And lull'd with sound of sweetest melody?
O thou dull god, why liest thou with the vile
In loathsome beds, and leavest the kingly couch
A watch-case or a common 'larum-bell?
Wilt thou upon the high and giddy mast
Seal up the ship-boy's eyes, and rock his brains
In cradle of the rude imperious surge
And in the visitation of the winds,
Who take the ruffian billows by the top,
Curling their monstrous heads and hanging them
With deafening clamour in the slippery clouds,

That, with the hurly, death itself awakes?
Canst thou, O partial sleep, give thy repose
To the wet sea-boy in an hour so rude,
And in the calmest and most stillest night,
With all appliances and means to boot,
Deny it to a king? Then happy low, lie down!
Uneasy lies the head that wears a crown.

(From King Henry IV, Pt. II)

THE LAND OF COUNTERPANE

Robert Louis Stevenson

When I was sick and lay a-bed,
I had two pillows at my head,
And all my toys beside me lay
To keep me happy all the day.

And sometimes for an hour or so
I watched my leaden soldiers go,
With different uniforms and drills,
Among the bed-clothes, through the hills.

And sometimes sent my ships in fleets
All up and down among the sheets;
Or brought my trees and houses out,
And planted cities all about.

I was the giant great and still
That sits upon the pillow-hill,
And sees before him, dale and plain
The pleasant Land of Counterpane.

MY MOTHER

Jane Taylor

Who fed me from her gentle breast
And hushed me in her arms to rest,
And on my cheek sweet kisses prest?
My mother.

When sleep forsook my open eye,
Who was it sung sweet lullaby
And rocked me that I should not cry?
    My mother.

Who sat and watched my infant head
When sleeping in my cradle bed,
And tears of sweet affection shed?
    My mother.

When pain and sickness made me cry,
Who gazed upon my heavy eye
And wept, for fear that I should die?
    My mother.

Who ran to help me when I fell
And would some pretty story tell,
Or kiss the part to make it well?
    My mother.

Who taught my infant lips to pray,
To love God's holy word and day,
And walk in wisdom's pleasant way?
    My mother.

And can I ever cease to be
Affectionate and kind to thee
Who wast so very kind to me,—
    My mother.

Oh no, the thought I cannot bear;
And if God please my life to spare
I hope I shall reward thy care,
    My mother.

When thou art feeble, old and gray,
My healthy arm shall be thy stay,
And I will soothe thy pains away,
    My mother.

And when I see thee hang thy head,
'Twill be my turn to watch thy bed,
And tears of sweet affection shed,—
    My mother.

ABIDE WITH ME

Henry F. Lyte

Abide with me: fast falls the eventide;
The darkness deepens; Lord, with me abide:
When other helpers fail, and comforts flee,
Help of the helpless, oh, abide with me!

Swift to its close ebbs our life's little day;
Earth's joys grow dim, its glories pass away;
Change and decay in all around I see:
O Thou Who changeth not, abide with me!

Not a brief glance, I beg, a passing word,
But, as Thou dwell'st with Thy disciples, Lord,
Familiar, condescending, patient, free,—
Come, not to sojourn, but abide with me!

Come not in terrors, as the King of kings;
But kind and good, with healing in Thy wings:
Tears for all woes, a heart for every plea;
Come, Friend of sinners, and abide with me!

Thou on my head in early youth didst smile,
And, though rebellious and perverse meanwhile,
Thou hast not left me, oft as I left Thee;
On to the close, O Lord, abide with me!

I need Thy presence every passing hour:
What but Thy grace can foil the tempter's power?
Who like Thyself my guide and stay can be?
Through cloud and sunshine, oh, abide with me!

I fear no foe with Thee at hand to bless;
Ills have no weights, and tears no bitterness;
Where is death's sting? where, grave thy victory?
I triumph still, if Thou abide with me.

Hold then Thy cross before my closing eyes;
Shine through the gloom, and point me to the skies:
Heaven's morning breaks, and earth's vain shadows flee—
In life and death, O Lord, abide with me!

INSCRIPTION ON THE TOMB OF THE UNKNOWN SOLDIER

Here Rests in
Honored Glory
An American
Soldier
Known But to God

DIXIE *

Daniel Decatur Emmett

I wish I was in de land ob cotton,
Old time dar am not forgotten;
   Look away, look away, look away, Dixie land!
In Dixie whar I was born in,
Early on one frosty mornin',
   Look away, look away, look away, Dixie land!

Chorus:
     Den I wish I was in Dixie! Hooray! Hooray!
     In Dixie land we'll take our stand, to lib an'
       die in Dixie,
     Away, away, away down south in Dixie!
     Away, away, away down south in Dixie!

Old missus marry Will de weaber,
William was a gay deceaber,
When he put his arm around 'er,
He looked as fierce as a forty-pounder. (*Chorus.*)

His face was sharp as a butcher cleaber,
But dat did not seem to greab 'er;
Will run away, missus took a decline, O,
Her face was the color of bacon rhine, O. (*Chorus.*)

While missus libbed, she libbed in clover,
When she died, she died all over;
How could she act de foolish part,
An' marry a man to break her heart? (*Chorus.*)

* The original version.

Buck wheat cakes an' stony batter
Makes you fat or a little fatter;
Here's a health to de next old missus,
An' all de gals dat want to kiss us. (*Chorus.*)

Now if you want to drive 'way sorrow,
Come an' hear dis song to-morrow;
Den hoe it down an' scratch your grabble,
To Dixie's land I'm bound to trabble. (*Chorus.*)

TAKE BACK YOUR GOLD

Louis W. Paitzakow

I saw a youth and maiden on a lonely city street,
And thought them lovers at their meeting place;
Until, as I drew near, I heard the girl's sad voice entreat
The one who heeded not her tear-stained face.
"I only ask you, Jack, to do your duty, that is all,
You know you promised that we should be wed."
And when he said, "You shall not want, whatever may befall,"
She spurned the gold he offered her and said—

Chorus:
    "Take back your gold, for gold can never buy me;
    Take back your bribe and promise you'll be true;
    Give me the love, the love that you'd deny me;
    Make me your wife, that's all I ask of you."

He drew her close unto him and to soothe her then he tried,
But she in pride and sorrow turned away,
And as he sought to comfort her, she wept and softly sighed,
"You'll rue your cruel actions, Jack, some day."
"Now, little one, don't cry," he said, "for though tonight we part,
And though another soon will be my bride,
This gold will help you to forget"; but with a breaking heart,
She scorned his gift and bitterly replied: (*Chorus.*)

* * *

Die when I may, I want it said by those who knew me best, that
I always plucked a thistle and planted a flower where I thought a
flower would grow.
           —Abraham Lincoln

BINGEN ON THE RHINE

Caroline E. Norton

A soldier of the Legion lay dying in Algiers,
There was lack of woman's nursing, there was dearth of woman's
    tears;
But a comrade stood beside him, while his life-blood ebbed away,
And bent, with pitying glances, to hear what he might say.
The dying soldier faltered, and he took that comrade's hand,
And he said, "I nevermore shall see my own, my native land;
Take a message, and a token, to some distant friends of mine,
For I was born at Bingen,—at Bingen on the Rhine.

"Tell my brothers and companions, when they meet and crowd
    around,
To hear my mournful story, in the pleasant vineyard ground,
That we fought the battle bravely, and when the day was done,
Full many a corse lay ghastly pale beneath the setting sun;
And, mid the dead and dying, were some grown old in wars,—
The death-wound on their gallant breasts, the last of many scars;
And some were young, and suddenly beheld life's morn decline,—
And one had come from Bingen,—fair Bingen on the Rhine.

"Tell my mother that her other son shall comfort her old age;
For I was still a truant bird, that thought his home a cage.
For my father was a soldier, and even as a child
My heart leaped forth to hear him tell of struggles fierce and wild;
And when he died, and left us to divide his scanty hoard,
I let them take whate'er they would,—but kept my father's sword;
And with boyish love I hung it where the bright light used to
    shine,
On the cottage wall at Bingen,—calm Bingen on the Rhine.

"Tell my sister not to weep for me, and sob with drooping head,
When the troops come marching home again with glad and gal-
    lant tread,
But to look upon them proudly, with a calm and steadfast eye,
For her brother was a soldier too, and not afraid to die;
And if a comrade seek her love, I ask her in my name
To listen to him kindly, without regret or shame,
And to hang the old sword in its place (my father's sword and
    mine)
For the honor of old Bingen,—dear Bingen on the Rhine.

"There's another,—not a sister; in the happy days gone by
You'd have known her by the merriment that sparkled in her eye
Too innocent for coquetry,—too fond for idle scorning,—
O friend! I fear the lightest heart makes sometimes heaviest
  mourning!
Tell her the last night of my life (for, ere the moon be risen,
My body will be out of pain, my soul be out of prison),—
I dreamed I stood with *her*, and saw the yellow sunlight shine
On the vine-clad hills of Bingen,—fair Bingen on the Rhine.

"I saw the blue Rhine sweep along,—I heard, or seemed to hear
The German songs we used to sing, in chorus sweet and clear;
And down the pleasant river, and up the slanting hill,
The echoing chorus sounded, through the evening calm and still
And her glad blue eyes were on me, as we passed, with friendly
  talk,
Down many a path beloved of yore, and well-remembered walk
And her little hand lay lightly, confidingly in mine,—
But we'll meet no more at Bingen,—loved Bingen on the Rhine."

His trembling voice grew faint and hoarse,—his grasp was child
  ish weak,—
His eyes put on a dying look,—he sighed and ceased to speak;
His comrade bent to lift him, but the spark of life had fled,—
The soldier of the Legion in a foreign land is dead!
And the soft moon rose up slowly, and calmly she looked down
On the red sand of the battle-field, with bloody corses strewn;
Yes, calmly on that dreadful scene her pale light seemed to shine
As it shone on distant Bingen,—fair Bingen on the Rhine.

THE PASSIONATE SHEPHERD TO HIS LOVE

Christopher Marlowe

Come live with me and be my Love,
And we will all the pleasures prove
That valleys, groves, hills and fields,
Woods or steepy mountain yields.

And we will sit upon the rocks
Seeing the shepherds feed their flocks.
By shallow rivers, to whose falls
Melodious birds sing madrigals.

And I will make thee beds of roses
And a thousand fragrant posies,
A cap of flowers, and a kirtle
Embroidered all with leaves of myrtle.

A gown made of the finest wool,
Which from our pretty lambs we pull,
Fair linèd slippers for the cold,
With buckles of the purest gold.

A belt of straw and ivy buds,
With coral clasps and amber studs:
And if these pleasures may thee move,
Come live with me and be my Love.

The shepherd swains shall dance and sing
For thy delight each May-morning:
If these delights thy mind may move,
Then live with me and be my Love.

SEVEN TIMES ONE

Jean Ingelow

There's no dew left on the daisies and clover,
    There's no rain left in heaven.
I've said my "seven times" over and over,—
    Seven times one are seven.

I am old,—so old I can write a letter;
    My birthday lessons are done.
The lambs play always,—they know no better;
    They are only one times one.

O Moon! in the night I have seen you sailing
    And shining so round and low.
You were bright—ah, bright—but your light is failing;
    You are nothing now but a bow.

You Moon! have you done something wrong in heaven,
    That God has hidden your face?
I hope, if you have, you will soon be forgiven,
    And shine again in your place.

O velvet Bee! you're a dusty fellow,—
    You've powdered your legs with gold.
O brave marsh Mary-buds, rich and yellow,
    Give me your money to hold!

O Columbine! open your folded wrapper,
    Where two twin turtle-doves dwell!
O Cuckoo-pint! toll me the purple clapper
    That hangs in your clear green bell!

And show me your nest, with the young ones in it,—
    I will not steal them away:
I am old! you may trust me, linnet, linnet!
    I am seven times one to-day.

ONWARD, CHRISTIAN SOLDIERS

Sabine Baring-Gould

Onward, Christian soldiers,
Marching as to war,
With the cross of Jesus
Going on before!
Christ, the royal Master,
Leads against the foe;
Forward into battle,
See his banners go.
Onward, Christian soldiers,
Marching as to war,
With the cross of Jesus
Going on before!

At the sign of triumph
Satan's host doth flee;
On, then, Christian soldiers,
On to victory!
Hell's foundations quiver
At the shout of praise;
Brothers, lift your voices,
Loud your anthems raise!

Like a mighty army
Moves the Church of God;
Brother, we are treading
Where the saints have trod;
We are not divided,
All one Body we,
One in hope and doctrine,
One in charity.

Crowns and thorns may perish,
Kingdoms rise and wane,
But the Church of Jesus
Constant will remain;
Gates of hell can never
'Gainst that Church prevail;
We have Christ's own promise,
And that cannot fail.

Onward, then, ye people!
Join our happy throng!
Blend with ours your voices
In the triumph song!
Glory, laud, and honor,
Unto Christ the King;
This through countless ages
Men and angels sing.
Onward, Christian soldiers,
Marching as to war,
With the cross of Jesus
Going on before!

SHE WALKS IN BEAUTY

Lord Byron

She walks in beauty, like the night
Of cloudless climes and starry skies,
And all that's best of dark and bright
Meet in her aspect and her eyes;
Thus mellow'd to that tender light
Which heaven to gaudy day denies.

One shade the more, one ray the less,
Had half impair'd the nameless grace
Which waves in every raven tress
Or softly lightens o'er her face,
Where thoughts serenely sweet express
How pure, how dear their dwelling-place.

And on that cheek and o'er that brow
So soft, so calm, yet eloquent,
The smiles that win, the tints that glow
But tell of days in goodness spent,
A mind at peace with all below,
A heart whose love is innocent.

YANKEE DOODLE

Anonymous

Father and I went down to camp,
Along with Cap'n Goodwin,
And there we saw the men and boys,
As thick as hasty puddin'!

Chorus:

    Yankee Doodle, keep it up,
    Yankee Doodle dandy,
    Mind the music and the step,
    And with the girls be handy!

And there we see a thousand men,
As rich as Squire David;
And what they wasted ev'ry day,
I wish it could be saved.

The 'lasses they eat ev'ry day,
Would keep a house a winter;
They have so much that, I'll be bound,
They eat it when they've mind ter.

And there I see a swamping gun,
Large as a log of maple,
Upon a deuced little cart,
A load for father's cattle.

And every time they shoot it off,
It takes a horn of powder,
And makes a noise like father's gun,
Only a nation louder.

I went as nigh to one myself
As 'Siah's underpinning;
And father went as nigh agin,
I thought the deuce was in him.

Cousin grew so bold,
I thought he would have cocked it,
It scared me so I shrinked it off
And hung by father's pocket.

And Cap'n Davis had a gun,
He kind of clapt his hand on't,
And stuck a crooked stabbing iron
Upon the little end of it.

And there I see a pumpkin shell
As big as mother's basin;
And every time they touched it off
They scampered like the nation.

And there they'd fife away like fun,
And play on corn-stalk fiddles,
And some had ribbons red as blood,
All bound around their middles.

The troopers, too, would gallop up,
And fire right in our faces,
It scared me almost half to death
To see them run such races.

Uncle Sam came there to change
Some pancakes and some onions,
For 'lasses cakes to carry home
To give his wife and young ones.

I see a little barrel too,
The heads were made of leather;
They knocked upon't with little clubs
And called the folks together.

And there was Cap'n Washington,
And gentle folks about him;
They say he's grown so 'tarnal proud,
He will not ride without 'em.

He got him on his meeting clothes
Upon a slapping stallion,
He sees the world along in rows,
In hundreds and in millions.

The flaming ribbons in his hat,
They looked so taring fine, ah,
I wanted dreadfully to get
To give to my Jemima.

I see another snarl of men
A-digging graves, they told me,
So 'tarnal long, so 'tarnal deep
They 'tended they should hold me.

It scared me so I hooked it off,
Nor stopped, as I remember,
Nor turned about till I got home,
Locked up in mother's chamber.

MAID OF ATHENS, ERE WE PART

Ζώη μοῦ, σάς ἀγαπῶ

Lord Byron

Maid of Athens, ere we part,
Give, oh give me back my heart!
Or, since that has left my breast,
Keep it now, and take the rest!
Hear my vow before I go,
Ζώη μοῦ, σάς ἀγαπῶ.

By those tresses unconfined,
Woo'd by each Ægean wind;
By those lids whose jetty fringe
Kiss thy soft cheeks' blooming tinge;
By those wild eyes like the roe,
Ζώη μοῦ, σάς ἀγαπῶ.

By that lip I long to taste;
By that zone-encircled waist;
By all the token-flowers that tell
What words can never speak so well;
By love's alternate joy and woe,
Ζώη μοῦ, σάς ἀγαπῶ.

Maid of Athens! I am gone;
Think of me, sweet! when alone.
Though I fly to Istambol,
Athens holds my heart and soul:
Can I cease to love thee? No!
Ζώη μοῦ, σάς ἀγαπῶ.

POLLY WOLLY DOODLE

Anonymous

Oh, I went down South for to see my Sal,
Sing Polly-wolly-doodle all the day;
My Sally am a spunky girl,
Sing Polly-wolly-doodle all the day.
Fare thee well, fare thee well,
Fare thee well, my fairy fay,
For I'm going to Louisiana
For to see my Susyanna
Sing Polly-wolly-doodle all the day.

Oh, I came to a river, and I couldn't get across,
Sing Polly-wolly-doodle all the day;
So I jumped on a nigga' an' I thought he was a hoss.
Sing Polly-wolly-doodle all the day.

A grasshopper sitting on a railroad track,
Sing Polly-wolly-doodle all the day;
And picking his teeth with a carpet tack,
Sing Polly-wolly-doodle all the day.

Behind the barn down on my knees,
Sing Polly-wolly-doodle all the day,
I think I heard a chicken sneeze,
Sing Polly-wolly-doodle all the day.

He sneezed so hard with the whooping cough,
Sing Polly-wolly-doodle all the day,
He sneezed his head and his tail right off,
Sing Polly-wolly-doodle all the day.

LONG, LONG AGO

Thomas H. Bayly

Tell me the tales that to me were so dear,
Long, long ago, Long, long ago.
Sing me the songs I delighted to hear,
Long, long ago, long ago.
Now you are come, all my grief is removed,
Let me forget that so long you have roved,
Let me believe that you love as you loved,
Long, long ago, long ago.

Do you remember the path where we met,
Long, long ago, Long, long ago?
Ah, yes, you told me you ne'er would forget,
Long, long ago, long ago.
Then, to all others, my smile you preferred,
Love, when you spoke, gave a charm to each word,
Still my heart treasures the praises I heard,
Long, long ago, long ago.

Tho' by your kindness my fond hopes were raised,
Long, long ago, Long, long ago.
You by more eloquent lips have been praised,
Long, long ago, long ago.
But by long absence your truth has been tried,
Still to your accents I listen with pride,
Blest as I was when I sat by your side,
Long, long ago, long ago.

INSCRIPTION TO SPARTANS DEAD AT THERMOPYLAE

Go, tell the Spartans, thou that passeth by,
That here obedient to their laws we lie.

IN THE GOOD OLD SUMMER TIME

Ren Shields

There's a time each year that we always hold dear,
Good old summer time;
With the birds and the trees and the sweet scented breezes,
Good old summer time,
When your day's work is over then you are in clover,
And life is one beautiful rhyme.
No trouble annoying each one is enjoying,
The good old summer time.

Chorus:

In the good old summer time,
In the good old summer time,
Strolling through the shady lanes,
With your baby mine;
You hold her hand, she holds yours.
And that's a very good sign
That she's your tootsey wootsey
In the good old summer time.

To swim in the pool, you'd play "hookey" from school,
Good old summer time;
You'd play "ring-a-rosie" with Jim, Kate and Josie,
Good old summer time,
Those days full of pleasure we now fondly treasure,
When we never thought it a crime,
To go stealing cherries, with faces brown as berries,
Good old summer time. (*Chorus.*)

THE FACE

Anthony Euwer

As a beauty I'm not a great star,
There are others more handsome by far,
But my face I don't mind it,
Because I'm behind it—
'Tis the folks in the front that I jar.

(Woodrow Wilson's favorite limerick)

CROSSING THE BAR

Alfred, Lord Tennyson

Sunset and evening star,
And one clear call for me!
And may there be no moaning of the bar,
When I put out to sea,

But such a tide as moving seems asleep,
Too full for sound and foam,
When that which drew from out the boundless deep
Turns again home.

Twilight and evening bell,
And after that the dark!
And may there be no sadness of farewell,
When I embark;

For tho' from out our bourne of Time and Place
The flood may bear me far,
I hope to see my Pilot face to face
When I have crossed the bar.

TALL OAKS FROM LITTLE ACORNS GROW

David Everett

You'd scarce expect one of my age
To speak in public on the stage,
And if I chance to fall below
Demosthenes or Cicero,
Don't view me with a critic's eye,
But pass my imperfections by.
Large streams from little fountains flow,
Tall oaks from little acorns grow;
And though now I am small and young,
Of judgment weak and feeble tongue,
Yet all great, learned men, like me
Once learned to read their ABC.
But why may not Columbia's soil
Rear men as great as Britain's Isle,
Exceed what Greece and Rome have done

Or any land beneath the sun?
Mayn't Massachusetts boast as great
As any other sister state?
Or where's the town, go far or near,
That does not find a rival here?
Or where's the boy but three feet high
Who's made improvement more than I?
These thoughts inspire my youthful mind
To be the greatest of mankind:
Great, not like Caesar, stained with blood,
But only great as I am good.

EVIL DESIGNS

William Shakespeare

Now is the winter of our discontent
Made glorious summer by this sun of York;
And all the clouds that lour'd upon our house
In the deep bosom of the ocean buried.
Now are our brows bound with victorious wreaths;
Our bruised arms hung up for monuments;
Our stern alarums changed to merry meetings,
Our dreadful marches to delightful measures.
Grim-visaged war hath smooth'd his wrinkled front;
And now, instead of mounting barbed steeds
To fright the souls of fearful adversaries,
He capers nimbly in a lady's chamber
To the lascivious pleasing of a lute,
But I, that am not shaped for sportive tricks,
Nor made to court an amorous looking-glass;
I, that am rudely stamp'd, and want love's majesty
To strut before a wanton ambling nymph;
I, that am curtail'd of this fair proportion,
Cheated of feature by dissembling nature,
Deform'd, unfinish'd, sent before my time
Into this breathing world, scarce half made up,
And that so lamely and unfashionable
That dogs bark at me as I halt by them;
Why, I, in this weak piping time of peace,
Have no delight to pass away the time,
Unless to spy my shadow in the sun

And descant on mine own deformity:
And therefore, since I cannot prove a lover,
To entertain these fair well-spoken days,
I am determined to prove a villain
And hate the idle pleasures of these days.
Plots have I laid, inductions dangerous,
By drunken prophecies, libels and dreams,
To set my brother Clarence and the king
In deadly hate the one against the other:
And if King Edward be as true and just
As I am subtle, false and treacherous,
This day should Clarence closely be mew'd
About a prophecy, which says that G
Of Edward's heirs the murderer shall be.
Dive, thoughts, down to my soul: here Clarence comes.

(From King Richard III)

THE LION AND THE MOUSE

A Lion, faint with heat, and weary with hunting, was laid down to take his repose under the spreading boughs of a thick shady oak. It happened that, while he slept, a company of scrambling mice ran over his back, and waked him; upon which, starting up, he clapped his paw upon one of them, and was just going to put it to death, when the little supplicant implored his mercy in a very moving manner, begging him not to stain his noble character with the blood of so despicable and small a beast. The Lion, considering the matter, thought proper to do as he was desired, and immediately released his little trembling prisoner. Not long after, traversing the forest in pursuit of his prey, he chanced to run into the toils of the hunters; from whence, not able to disengage himself, he set up a most hideous and loud roar. The Mouse, hearing the voice, and knowing it to be the Lion's, immediately repaired to the place, and bid him fear nothing, for that he was his friend. Then straight he fell to work, and, with his little sharp teeth, gnawing asunder the knots and fastenings of the toils, set the royal brute at liberty.

(From Aesop's Fables)

* * *

No one is a hero to his valet.
—Madame de Sévigné

CHICAGO

Carl Sandburg

Hog Butcher for the World,
Tool Maker, Stacker of Wheat,
Player with Railroads and the Nation's Freight Handler;
Stormy, husky, brawling,
City of the Big Shoulders:
They tell me you are wicked, and I believe them; for I have seen
   your painted women under the gas lamps luring the farm boys.
And they tell me you are crooked, and I answer: Yes, it is true
   I have seen the gunman kill and go free to kill again.
And they tell me you are brutal, and my reply is: On the faces
   of women and children I have seen the marks of wanton
   hunger.
And having answered so I turn once more to those who sneer
   at this my city, and I give them back the sneer and say to them:
Come and show me another city with lifted head singing so
   proud to be alive and coarse and strong and cunning.
Flinging magnetic curses amid the toil of piling job on job, here
   is a tall bold slugger set vivid against the little soft cities;
Fierce as a dog with tongue lapping for action, cunning as a savage pitted against the wilderness,
      Bareheaded,
      Shoveling,
      Wrecking,
      Planning,
      Building, breaking, rebuilding,
Under the smoke, dust all over his mouth, laughing with white
   teeth,
Under the terrible burden of destiny laughing as a young man
   laughs,
Laughing even as an ignorant fighter laughs who has never lost
   a battle,
Bragging and laughing that under his wrist is the pulse, and
   under his ribs the heart of the people,
                      Laughing!
Laughing the stormy, husky, brawling laughter of youth; half-
   naked, sweating, proud to be Hog-butcher, Tool-maker, Stacker
   of Wheat, Player with Railroads, and Freight Handler to the
   Nation.

THE BLUE AND THE GRAY

Francis Miles Finch

By the flow of the inland river,
Whence the fleets of iron have fled,
Where the blades of the grave-grass quiver,
Asleep are the ranks of the dead:—
Under the sod and the dew
Waiting the Judgment Day:—
Under the one, the Blue;
Under the other, the Gray.

These in the robings of glory,
Those in the gloom of defeat,
All 'vith the battle-blood gory,
In the dusk of eternity meet;—
Under the sod and the dew
Waiting the Judgment Day:—
Under the laurel, the Blue;
Under the willow, the Gray.

From the silence of sorrowful hours
The desolate mourners go,
Lovingly laden with flowers,
Alike for the friend and the foe:—
Under the sod and dew
Waiting the Judgment Day:—
Under the roses, the Blue;
Under the lilies, the Gray.

So with an equal splendor
The morning sun-rays fall,
With a touch impartially tender,
On the blossoms blooming for all;—
Under the sod and the dew
Waiting the Judgment Day:—
'Broidered with gold, the Blue;
Mellowed with gold, the Gray.

So when the summer calleth,
On forest and field of grain,
With an equal murmur falleth
The cooling drip of the rain;—

Under the sod and the dew
Waiting the Judgment Day:—
Wet with the rain, the Blue;
Wet with the rain, the Gray.

Sadly, but not with upbraiding
The generous deed was done.
In the storms of the years that are fading
No braver battle was won:—
Under the sod and the dew
Waiting the Judgment Day:—
Under the blossoms, the Blue;
Under the garlands, the Gray.

No more shall the war-cry sever,
Or the winding river be red;
They banish our anger forever
When they laurel the graves of our dead!
Under the sod and the dew
Waiting the Judgment Day:—
Love and tears for the Blue;
Tears and love for the Gray.

RING OUT, WILD BELLS

Alfred, Lord Tennyson

Ring out, wild bells, to the wild sky,
The flying cloud, the frosty light:
The year is dying in the night;
Ring out, wild bells, and let him die.

Ring out the old, ring in the new,
Ring, happy bells, across the snow:
The year is going, let him go;
Ring out the false, ring in the true.

Ring out the grief that saps the mind,
For those that here we see no more;
Ring out the feud of rich and poor,
Ring in redress to all mankind.

Ring out a slowly dying cause,
　　And ancient forms of party strife;
　　Ring in the nobler modes of life,
With sweeter manners, purer laws.

Ring out the want, the care, the sin,
　　The faithless coldness of the times;
　　Ring out, ring out my mournful rhymes,
But ring the fuller minstrel in.

Ring out false pride in place and blood,
　　The civic slander and the spite;
　　Ring in the love of truth and right,
Ring in the common love of good.

Ring out old shapes of foul disease;
　　Ring out the narrowing lust of gold;
　　Ring out the thousand wars of old,
Ring in the thousand years of peace.

Ring in the valiant man and free,
　　The larger heart, the kindlier hand;
　　Ring out the darkness of the land,
Ring in the Christ that is to be.

　　　　　　　　　(From In Memoriam)

PAUL ON THE ROAD TO DAMASCUS

Holy Bible, Acts 9:3–6

3 And as he journeyed, he came near Damascus: and suddenly there shined round about him a light from heaven:

4 And he fell to the earth, and heard a voice saying unto him, Saul, Saul, why persecutest thou me?

5 And he said, Who art thou, Lord? And the Lord said, I am Jesus whom thou persecutest: it is hard for thee to kick against the pricks.

6 And he trembling and astonished said, Lord, what wilt thou have me to do? And the Lord said unto him, Arise, and go into the city, and it shall be told thee what thou must do.

MINIVER CHEEVY

Edward Arlington Robinson

Miniver Cheevy, child of scorn,
  Grew lean while he assailed the seasons;
He wept that he was ever born,
  And he had reasons.

Miniver loved the days of old
  When swords were bright and steeds were prancing;
The vision of a warrior bold
  Would set him dancing.

Miniver sighed for what was not,
  And dreamed, and rested from his labors;
He dreamed of Thebes and Camelot,
  And Priam's neighbors.

Miniver mourned the ripe renown
  That made so many a name so fragrant;
He mourned Romance, now on the town,
  And Art, a vagrant.

Miniver loved the Medici,
  Albeit he had never seen one;
He would have sinned incessantly
  Could he have been one.

Miniver cursed the commonplace
  And eyed a khaki suit with loathing;
He missed the mediaeval grace
  Of iron clothing.

Miniver scorned the gold he sought,
  But sore annoyed was he without it;
Miniver thought, and thought, and thought,
  And thought about it.

Miniver Cheevy, born too late,
  Scratched his head and kept on thinking;
Miniver coughed, and called it fate,
  And kept on drinking.

DOWN IN LEHIGH VALLEY

Anonymous

Let me sit down a minute, stranger,
I ain't done a thing to you.
You needn't start your swearin',
A stone got in my shoe.

Yes, I'm a tramp, what of it?
Some folks think we're no good;
But a tramp has to live, I reckon,
Though they say we never should.

Once I was young and handsome,
Had plenty of cash and clothes,
But that was before I tripped,
And booze colored up my nose.

It was down in Lehigh Valley
Me and my people grew;
I was the village blacksmith,
Yes, and a good one, too.

Me and my daughter Nellie;
Nellie was just sixteen:
And she was the prettiest creature
The valley had ever seen.

Beaus, she had a dozen,
They came from near and far;
But most of them were farmers,
And none of them suited her.

Along came a stranger,
Young, handsome, straight and tall,
Damn him, I wish I had him,
Strangled against that wall.

He was the man for Nellie,
Nellie knew no ill,
Her mother tried to tell her,
But you know how young girls will.

Well, it's the same old story,
Common enough you'll say,
He was a smooth-tongued devil,
And he got her to run away.

It was less than a month later,
That we heard from the poor young thing;
He had gone away and left her,
Without a wedding ring.

Back to our home we brought her,
Back to her mother's side,
Filled with a raging fever,
She fell at our feet and died.

Frantic with grief and trouble,
Her mother began to sink,
Dead in less than a fortnight,
That's why I took to drink.

Give me a drink, bartender,
And I'll be on my way,
And I'll hunt the runt that stole my girl,
If it takes 'til judgment day.

THE BOY SCOUT OATH

On my honor I will do my best—
    To do my duty to God and my country, and to obey
      the scout law;
    To help other people at all times;
    To keep myself physically strong, mentally awake,
      and morally straight.

ON HIS SEVENTY-FIFTH BIRTHDAY

Walter Savage Landor

I strove with none, for none was worth my strife,
Nature I loved, and next to nature, art;
I warmed both hands before the fire of life,
It sinks, and I am ready to depart.

A FAMOUS TOAST

Richard Brinsley Sheridan

Here's to the maiden of bashful fifteen;
Here's to the widow of fifty;
Here's to the flaunting, extravagant queen,
And here's to the housewife that's thrifty.
      Let the toast pass;
      Drink to the lass;
I'll warrant she'll prove an excuse for the glass.
      (From School for Scandal)

ANTONY AND CLEOPATRA

William Haines Lytle

I am dying, Egypt, dying,
  Ebbs the crimson life-tide fast,
And the dark Plutonian shadows
  Gather on the evening blast;
Let thine arms, O Queen, enfold me,
  Hush thy sobs and bow thine ear;
Listen to the great heart-secrets,
  Thou, and thou alone, must hear.

Though my scarr'd and veteran legions
  Bear their eagles high no more,
And my wreck'd and scatter'd galleys
  Strew dark Actium's fatal shore,
Though no glittering guards surround me,
  Prompt to do their master's will,
I must perish like a Roman,
  Die the great Triumvir still.

Let not Cæsar's servile minions
  Mock the lion thus laid low;
'Twas no foeman's arm that fell'd him,
  'Twas his own that struck the blow;
His who, pillow'd on thy bosom,
  Turn'd aside from glory's ray,
His who, drunk with thy caresses,
  Madly threw a world away.

Should the base plebeian rabble
  Dare assail my name at Rome,
Where my noble spouse, Octavia,
  Weeps within her widow'd home,
Seek her; say the gods bear witness—
  Altars, augurs, circling wings—
That her blood, with mine commingled,
  Yet shall mount the throne of kings.

As for thee, star-eyed Egyptian,
  Glorious sorceress of the Nile,
Light the path to Stygian horrors
  With the splendors of thy smile.
Give the Cæsar crowns and arches,
  Let his brow the laurel twine;
I can scorn the Senate's triumphs,
  Triumphing in love like thine.

I am dying, Egypt, dying;
  Hark! the insulting foeman's cry.
They are coming! quick, my falchion,
  Let me front them ere I die.
Ah! no more amid the battle
  Shall my heart exulting swell;
Isis and Osiris guard thee!
  Cleopatra, Rome, farewell!

EPITAPH

Anonymous

Here lies a poor woman who always was tired,
She lived in a house where help wasn't hired.
The last words she said were: "Dear friends, I am going
Where washing ain't wanted, nor sweeping nor sewing;
And everything there is exact to my wishes,
For where folks don't eat there's no washing of dishes,
In heaven loud anthems forever are ringing,
But having no voice I'll keep clear of the singing.
Don't mourn for me now, don't mourn for me never;
I'm going to do nothing for ever and ever."

WHEN I WAS ONE-AND-TWENTY

A. E. Housman

When I was one-and-twenty
  I heard a wise man say,
"Give crowns and pounds and guineas
  But not your heart away;
Give pearls away and rubies
  But keep your fancy free."
But I was one-and-twenty,
  No use to talk to me.

When I was one-and-twenty
  I heard him say again,
"The heart out of the bosom
  Was never given in vain;
'Tis paid with sighs a-plenty
  And sold for endless rue."
And I am two-and-twenty,
  And oh, 'tis true, 'tis true.

MR. VALIANT-FOR-TRUTH CROSSES THE RIVER

John Bunyan

After this, it was noised abroad that Mr. *Valiant-for-truth* was taken with a Summons, by the same *Post* as the other, and had this for a Token that the Summons was true, *That his Pitcher was broken at the fountain*. When he understood it, he called for his Friends, and told them of it. Then said he, I am going to my Fathers, and though with great difficulty I am got hither, yet now I do not repent me of all the Trouble I have been to arrive where I am. *My Sword*, I give to him that shall succeed me in my Pilgrimage, and my *Courage* and *Skill*, to him that can get it. My *Marks* and *Scars* I carry with me, to be a Witness for me, that I have fought his Battles who now will be my Rewarder. When the Day that he must go hence, was come, many accompanied him to the River side, into which, as he went, he said, *Death, where is thy Sting?* And as he went down deeper, he said, *Grave, where is thy Victory?* So he passed over, and the Trumpets sounded for him on the other side.

(From Pilgrim's Progress)

BUGLE SONG

Alfred, Lord Tennyson

The splendor falls on castle walls
  And snowy summits old in story;
The long light shakes across the lakes,
  And the wild cataract leaps in glory.
Blow, bugle, blow, set the wild echoes flying,
Blow, bugle; answer, echoes, dying, dying, dying.

O, hark, O, hear! how thin and clear,
  And thinner, clearer, farther going!
O, sweet and far from cliff and scar
  The horns of Elfland faintly blowing!
Blow, let us hear the purple glens replying;
Blow, bugle; answer, echoes, dying, dying, dying.

O love, they die in yon rich sky,
  They faint on hill or field or river;
Our echoes roll from soul to soul,
  And grow for ever and for ever.
Blow, bugle, blow, set the wild echoes flying,
And answer, echoes, answer, dying, dying, dying.

OLD FOLKS AT HOME

Stephen Foster

'Way down upon de Swanee ribber,
Far, far away,
Dere's wha' my heart is turning ebber,
Dere's wha' de old folks stay.
All up and down de whole creation,
Sadly I roam,
Still longing for de old plantation,
And for de old folks at home.

All round de little farm I wander'd
When I was young,
Den many happy days I squander'd,
Many de songs I sung.

When I was playing wid my brudder,
Happy was I.
Oh! take me to my kind old mudder,
Dere let me live and die.

One little hut among de bushes,
One dat I love,
Still sadly to my mem'ry rushes,
No matter where I rove.
When will I see the bees a-humming,
All round de comb?
When will I hear de banjo tumming,
Down in my good old home?

Chorus:

All de world am sad and dreary,
Ebrywhere I roam,
Oh! darkies how my heart grows weary,
Far from de old folks at home.

TO HELEN

Edgar Allan Poe

Helen, thy beauty is to me
Like those Nicèan barks of yore
That gently, o'er a perfumed sea,
The weary way-worn wanderer bore
To his own native shore.

On desperate seas long wont to roam,
Thy hyacinth hair, thy classic face,
Thy Naiad airs have brought me home
To the glory that was Greece,
And the grandeur that was Rome.

Lo, in yon brilliant window-niche
How statue-like I see thee stand,
The agate lamp within thy hand,
Ah! Psyche, from the regions which
Are holy land!

A MESSAGE TO GARCIA

Elbert Hubbard

In all this Cuban business there is one man who stands out on the horizon of my memory like Mars at perihelion.

When war broke out between Spain and the United States, it was very necessary to communicate quickly with the leader of the insurgents. Garcia was somewhere in the mountain fastnesses of Cuba—no one knew where. No mail or telegraph message could reach him. The President must secure his co-operation, and quickly.

What to do!

Someone said to the President, "There is a fellow by the name of Rowan will find Garcia for you, if anybody can."

Rowan was sent for and given a letter to be delivered to Garcia. How "the fellow by the name of Rowan" took the letter, sealed it up in an oilskin pouch, strapped it over his heart, in four days landed by night off the coast of Cuba from an open boat, disappeared in the jungle, and in three weeks came out on the other side of the island, having traversed a hostile country on foot and delivered his letter to Garcia—are things I have no special desire now to tell in detail.

The point that I wish to make is this: McKinley gave Rowan a letter to be delivered to Garcia; Rowan took the letter and did not ask, "Where is he at?"

By the Eternal! there is a man whose form should be cast in deathless bronze and the statue placed in every college of the land. It is not book-learning young men need, nor instruction about this and that, but a stiffening of the vertebrae which will cause them to be loyal to a trust, to act promptly, concentrate their energies: do the thing—"Carry a message to Garcia."

General Garcia is dead now, but there are other Garcias. No man who has endeavored to carry out an enterprise where many hands were needed but has been well-nigh appalled at times by the imbecility of the average man—the inability or unwillingness to concentrate on a thing and do it. Slipshod assistance, foolish inattention, dowdy indifference, and half-hearted work seem the rule; and no man succeeds unless, by hook or crook, or threat, he forces or bribes other men to assist him; or mayhap, God in his goodness performs a miracle and sends him an Angel of Light for an assistant.

You, reader, put this matter to a test. You are sitting now in your office; six clerks are within call. Summon anyone and make this request: "Please look in the encyclopedia and make a brief memorandum for me concerning the life of Correggio."

Will the clerk quietly say, "Yes, sir," and go do the task?

On your life, he will not. He will look at you out of a fishy eye and ask one or more of the following questions:

Who was he?

Which encyclopedia?

Where is the encyclopedia?

Was I hired for that?

Don't you mean Bismarck?

What's the matter with Charlie doing it?

Is he dead?

Is there any hurry?

Shan't I bring you the book and let you look it up yourself?

What do you want to know for?

And I will lay you ten to one that after you have answered the questions, and explained how to find the information, and why you want it, the clerk will go off and get one of the other clerks to help him try to find Garcia—and then come back and tell you there is no such man. Of course I may lose my bet, but according to the law of averages, I will not.

Now if you are wise, you will not bother to explain to your "assistant" that Correggio is indexed under the C's, not in the K's, but you will smile sweetly and say, "Never mind," and go look it up yourself.

And this incapacity for independent action, this moral stupidity, this infirmity of the will, this unwillingness cheerfully to catch hold and lift—these are the things that put pure socialism so far into the future. If men will not act for themselves, what will they do when the benefit of their efforts is for all?

A first mate with a knotted club seems necessary; and the dread of getting "the bounce" Saturday night holds many a worker to his place.

Advertise for a stenographer, and nine out of ten who apply can neither spell nor punctuate—and do not think it necessary to. Can such a one write a letter to Garcia?

"You see the bookkeeper," said the foreman to me in a large factory.

"Yes, what about him?"

"Well, he's a fine accountant, but if I'd send him uptown on an errand, he might accomplish the errand all right and, on the

538

other hand, might stop at four saloons on the way, and when he got to Main street, would forget what he had been sent for."

Can such a man be entrusted to carry a message to Garcia?

We have recently been hearing much maudlin sympathy expressed for the "downtrodden denizens of the sweatshop" and the "homeless wanderer searching for honest employment" and with it all often go many hard words for men in power.

Nothing is said about the employer who grows old before his time in a vain attempt to get frowzy ne'er-do-wells to do intelligent work; and his long, patient striving with "help" that does nothing but loaf when his back is turned. In every store and factory there is a constant weeding-out process going on. The employer is constantly sending away "help" that have shown their incapacity to further the interests of the business, and others are being taken on. No matter how good times are, this sorting continues; only, if times are hard and work is scarce, the sorting is done finer—but out and forever out, the incompetent and unworthy go. It is the survival of the fittest. Self-interest prompts every employer to keep the best—those who can carry a message to Garcia.

I know one man of really brilliant parts who has not the ability to manage a business of his own, and yet who is absolute worthless to anyone else, because he carries with him constantly the insane suspicion that his employer is oppressing or intending to oppress him. He cannot give orders, and he will not receive them. Should a message be given him to take to Garcia, his answer would probably be, "Take it yourself."

Tonight this man walks the streets looking for work, the wind whistling through his threadbare coat. No one who knows him dares employ him, for he is a regular firebrand of discontent. He is impervious to reason, and the only thing that can impress him is the toe of a thick-soled number nine boot.

Of course I know that one so morally deformed is no less to be pitied than a physical cripple; but in our pitying, let us drop a tear too for the men who are striving to carry on a great enterprise, and whose working hours are not limited by the whistle; and whose hair is fast turning white through the struggle to hold in line dowdy indifference, slipshod imbecility, and the heartless ingratitude which, but for their enterprise, would be both hungry and homeless.

Have I put the matter too strongly? Possibly I have; but when all the world has gone a-slumming, I wish to speak a word of sympathy for the man who succeeds—the man who, against great odds, has directed the efforts of others and, having succeeded, finds there's nothing in it—nothing but bare board and clothes.

I have carried a dinner-pail and worked for day's wages, and I have also been an employer of labor, and I know there is something to be said on both sides. There is no excellence per se, in poverty; rags are no recommendation; and all employers are not rapacious and high-handed, any more than all men are virtuous.

My heart goes out to the man who does his work when the "boss" is away as well as when he is at home. And the man who, when given a letter to Garcia, quietly takes the missive, without asking any idiotic questions, and with no lurking intention of chucking it into the nearest sewer, or of doing aught else but deliver it, never gets "laid off" nor has to go on strike for higher wages. Civilization is one long, anxious search for just such individuals. Anything such a man asks shall be granted; his kind is so rare that no employer can afford to let him go. He is wanted in every city, town, and village—in every office, shop, store, and factory. The world cries out for such; he is needed and needed badly—the man who can "Carry a message to Garcia."

NOW I LAY ME DOWN TO TAKE MY SLEEP

> Now I lay me down to take my sleep,
> I pray The Lord my soul to keep;
> If I should die before I wake
> I pray The Lord my soul to take.
> (From the New England Primer 1777 ed.) *

MARK TWAIN DISCUSSES SATAN

Of course, Satan has some kind of a case, it goes without saying. It may be a poor one, but that is nothing; that can be said about any one of us.—We may not pay him reverence for that would be indiscreet; but we can at least respect his talents. A person who has for untold centuries maintained the imposing position of spiritual head of four fifths of the human race, and political head of the whole of it, must be granted the possession of executive abilities of the loftiest order.—I would like to see him. I would rather see him and shake him by the tail than any other member of the European Concert.

* The first record of this prayer is said to be found in the *Enchiridion Leonis*, A.D. 1160.

ODE TO A NIGHTINGALE

John Keats

My heart aches, and a drowsy numbness pains
  My sense, as though of hemlock I had drunk,
Or emptied some dull opiate to the drains
  One minute past, and Lethe-wards had sunk:
'Tis not through envy of thy happy lot,
  But being too happy in thine happiness.—
    That thou, light-wingèd Dryad of the trees,
      In some melodious plot
  Of beechen green, and shadows numberless,
    Singest of summer in full-throated ease.

O, for a draught of vintage! that hath been
  Cool'd a long age in the deep-delvèd earth,
Tasting of Flora and the country green,
  Dance, and Provençal song, and sunburnt mirth!
O for a beaker full of the warm South,
  Full of the true, the blushful Hippocrene,
    With beaded bubbles winking at the brim,
      And purple-stainèd mouth;
  That I might drink, and leave the world unseen,
    And with thee fade away into the forest dim:

Fade far away, dissolve, and quite forget
  What thou amongst the leaves hast never known,
The weariness, the fever, and the fret
  Here, where men sit and hear each other groan;
Where palsy shakes a few, sad, last gray hairs,
  Where youth grows pale, and spectre-thin, and dies;
    Where but to think is to be full of sorrow
      And leaden-eyed despairs,
  Where Beauty cannot keep her lustrous eyes,
    Or new Love pine at them beyond to-morrow.

Away! away! for I will fly to thee,
  Not charioted by Bacchus and his pards,
But on the viewless wings of Poesy,
  Though the dull brain perplexes and retards:

Already with thee! tender is the night,
  And haply the Queen-Moon is on her throne,
    Cluster'd around by all her starry Fays;
      But here there is no light,
  Save what from heaven is with the breezes blown
    Through verdurous glooms and winding mossy ways.

I cannot see what flowers are at my feet,
  Nor what soft incense hangs upon the boughs,
But, in embalmèd darkness, guess each sweet
  Wherewith the seasonable month endows
The grass, the thicket, and the fruit-tree wild;
  White hawthorn, and the pastoral eglantine;
    Fast fading violets cover'd up in leaves;
      And mid-May's eldest child,
  The coming musk-rose, full of dewy wine,
    The murmurous haunt of flies on summer eves.

Darkling I listen; and, for many a time
  I have been half in love with easeful Death,
Call'd him soft names in many a musèd rhyme,
  To take into the air my quiet breath;
Now more than ever seems it rich to die,
  To cease upon the midnight with no pain,
    While thou art pouring forth thy soul abroad
      In such an ecstasy!
  Still wouldst thou sing, and I have ears in vain—
    To thy high requiem become a sod.

Thou wast not born for death, immortal Bird!
  No hungry generations tread thee down;
The voice I hear this passing night was heard
  In ancient days by emperor and clown:
Perhaps the self-same song that found a path
  Through the sad heart of Ruth, when, sick for home,
    She stood in tears amid the alien corn;
      The same that oft-times hath
  Charm'd magic casements, opening on the foam
    Of perilous seas, in faery lands forlorn.

Forlorn! the very word is like a bell
  To toll me back from thee to my sole self!
Adieu! the fancy cannot cheat so well
  As she is fam'd to do, deceiving elf.

Adieu! adieu! thy plaintive anthem fades
  Past the near meadows, over the still stream,
    Up the hill-side; and now 'tis buried deep
      In the next valley-glades:
  Was it a vision, or a waking dream?
    Fled is that music:—Do I wake or sleep?

MY OLD KENTUCKY HOME

Stephen Foster

The sun shines bright in our old Kentucky home;
  'Tis summer, the darkeys are gay;
The corn top's ripe and the meadow's in the bloom,
  While the birds make music all the day;
The young folks roll on the little cabin floor,
  All merry, all happy, all bright;
By'm by hard times comes a knockin' at the door,—
  Then, my old Kentucky home, good night!

Chorus:

   Weep no more, my lady; O, weep no more today!
   We'll sing one song for my old Kentucky home,
   For our old Kentucky home far away.

They hunt no more for the possum and the coon,
  On the meadow, the hill, and the shore;
They sing no more by the glimmer of the moon,
  On the bench by the old cabin door;
The day goes by, like a shadow o'er the heart,
  With sorrow where all was delight;
The time has come, when the darkeys have to part,
  Then, my old Kentucky home, good night!
     Weep no more, my lady, &c.

The head must bow, and the back will have to bend,
  Wherever the darkey may go;
A few more days, and the troubles all will end,
  In the field where the sugar-cane grow;
A few more days to tote the weary load,
  No matter it will never be light;
A few more days till we totter on the road,
  Then, my old Kentucky home, good night!
     Weep no more, my lady, &c.

JABBERWOCKY

Lewis Carroll

'Twas brillig, and the slithy toves
   Did gyre and gimble in the wabe;
All mimsy were the borogoves,
   And the mome raths outgrabe.

"Beware the Jabberwock, my son!
   The jaws that bite, the claws that catch!
Beware the Jubjub bird, and shun
   The frumious Bandersnatch!"

He took his vorpal sword in hand:
   Long time the manxome foe he sought,—
So rested he by the Tumtum tree,
   And stood awhile in thought.

And as in uffish thought he stood,
   The Jabberwock, with eyes of flame,
Came whiffling through the tulgey wood,
   And burbled as it came!

One, two! One, two! And through and through
   The vorpal blade went snicker-snack!
He left it dead, and with his head
   He went galumphing back.

"And hast thou slain the Jabberwock?
   Come to my arms, my beamish boy!
O frabjous day! Callooh! Callay!"
   He chortled in his joy.

'Twas brillig, and the slithy toves
   Did gyre and gimble in the wabe;
All mimsy were the borogoves,
   And the mome raths outgrabe.

*   *   *

Life is a tragedy wherein we sit as spectators awhile, and then act our own part in it.

       —Jonathan Swift

MY MOTHER WAS A LADY, OR IF JACK WERE ONLY HERE

Edward B. Marks

Two drummers sat at dinner, in a grand hotel one day,
While dining they were chatting in a jolly sort of way,
And when a pretty waitress brought them a tray of food,
They spoke to her familiarly in a manner rather rude;
At first she did not notice them or make the least reply,
But one remark was passed that brought the tear drops to her eye,
And facing her tormentor, with cheeks now burning red,
She looked a perfect picture as appealingly she said:

Chorus:
"My mother was a lady—like yours you will allow,
And you may have a sister, who needs protection now,
I've come to this great city to find a brother dear,
And you wouldn't dare insult me, Sir, if Jack were only here."

It's true one touch of nature, it makes the whole world kin,
And ev'ry word she uttered seemed to touch their hearts within,
They sat there stunned and silent, until one cried in shame,
"Forgive me, Miss! I meant no harm, pray tell me what's your name?"
She told him and he cried again, "I know your brother, too,
Why we've been friends for many years and he often speaks of you,
He'll be glad to see you, and if you'll only wed,
I'll take you to him as my wife, for I love you since you said:
(*Chorus.*)

THE HARP THAT ONCE THROUGH TARA'S HALLS

Thomas Moore

The harp that once through Tara's halls
    The soul of music shed,
Now hangs as mute on Tara's walls
    As if that soul were fled.
So sleeps the pride of former days,
    So glory's thrill is o'er,
And hearts that once beat high for praise
    Now feel that pulse no more!

545

No more to chiefs and ladies bright
   The harp of Tara swells;
The chord alone that breaks at night
   Its tale of ruin tells.
Thus Freedom now so seldom wakes,
   The only throb she gives
Is when some heart indignant breaks,
   To show that still she lives.

GO DOWN, MOSES

Anonymous

Go down, Moses,
'Way down in Egypt's land;
Tell ole Pharaoh—
Let my people go.
When Israel was in Egypt's land,
Let my people go;
Oppressed so hard they could not stand,
Let my people go.

Thus saith the Lord, bold Moses said;
Let my people go;
If not I'll smite your first born dead,
Let my people go.
Chorus: Go down, Moses, etc.

No more shall they in bondage toil,
Let my people go;
Let them come out with Egypt's spoil,
Let my people go.
Chorus: Go down, Moses, etc.

The Lord told Moses what to do,
Let my people go;
To lead the people of Israel thro',
Let my people go.
Chorus: Go down, Moses, etc.

When they had reached the other shore,
Let my people go;
They sang a song of triumph o'er
Let my people go.
Chorus: Go down, Moses, etc.

THE LAMB

William Blake

Little lamb, who made thee?
Dost thou know who made thee,
Gave thee life and bade thee feed
By the stream and o'er the mead;
Gave thee clothing of delight,
Softest clothing, woolly, bright;
Gave thee such a tender voice,
Making all the vales rejoice?
    Little lamb, who made thee?
    Dost thou know who made thee?

Little lamb, I'll tell thee;
Little lamb, I'll tell thee.
He is callèd by thy name,
For He calls himself a Lamb;
He is meek and He is mild,
He became a little child.
I a child and thou a lamb,
We are callèd by His name.
    Little lamb, God bless thee!
    Little lamb, God bless thee!

BABY

George Macdonald

Where did you came from, Baby dear?
Out of the everywhere into here.

Where did you get your eyes so blue?
Out of the sky as I came through.

What makes the light in them sparkle and spin?
Some of the starry spikes left in.

Where did you get that little tear?
I found it waiting when I got here.

What makes your forehead so smooth and high?
A soft hand stroked it as I went by.

What makes your cheek like a warm white rose?
I saw something better than anyone knows.

Whence that three-cornered smile of bliss?
Three angels gave me at once a kiss.

Where did you get this pearly ear?
God spoke, and it came out to hear.

Where did you get those arms and hands?
Love made itself into hooks and bands.

Feet, whence did you come, you darling things?
From the same box as the cherubs' wings.

How did they all come to be you?
God thought about me, and so I grew.

But how did you come to us, you dear?
God thought about you, and so I am here.

THE MAN WHO BROKE THE BANK AT MONTE CARLO

Fred Gilbert

I've just got here, through Paris, from the sunny southern shore,
I to Monte Carlo went, just to raise my winter's rent;
Dame Fortune smiled upon me as she'd never done before,
And I've now such lots of money, I'm a gent;
Yes, I've now such lots of money I'm a gent.

Chorus:
    As I walk along the Bois-Boo-long
    With an independent air
    You can hear the girls declare
    "He must be a Millionaire."
    You can hear them sigh,
    And wish to die,
    You can see them wink the other eye
    At the man that broke the bank at Monte Carlo.

stay indoors till after lunch, and then my daily walk
o the great Triumphal Arch is one grand triumphal march.
bserv'd by each observer with the keenness of a hawk,
m a mass of money, linen, silk and starch,
m a mass of money, linen, silk and starch. (*Chorus.*)

patronized the tables at the Monte Carlo hell,
ill they hadn't got a sou for a Christian or a Jew;
I quickly went to Paris, for the charms of mademoiselle,
'ho's the lodestone of my heart what can I do,
'hen with twenty tongues she swears that she'll be true. (*Chorus.*)

SAY NOT THE STRUGGLE NOUGHT AVAILETH

Arthur Hugh Clough

Say not the struggle nought availeth,
  The labour and the wounds are vain,
The enemy faints not, nor faileth,
  And as things have been they remain.

If hopes were dupes, fears may be liars;
  It may be, in yon smoke concealed,
Your comrades chase e'en now the fliers,
  And, but for you, possess the field.

For while the tired waves, vainly breaking,
  Seem here no painful inch to gain,
Far back, through creeks and inlets making,
  Comes silent, flooding in, the main.

And not by eastern windows only,
  When daylight comes, comes in the light;
In front, the sun climbs slow, how slowly,
  But westward, look, the land is bright.

GENERAL JOFFRE TO HIS SOLDIERS

Soldiers, we are attacking. Advance as long as you can. When
u can no longer advance, hold your position. When you can no
nger hold it, die!

(First Battle of the Marne)

PRESIDENT ROOSEVELT ASKS CONGRESS TO DECLARE WAR ON JAPAN

MR. VICE PRESIDENT, MR. SPEAKER, MEMBERS OF THE SENATE AN THE HOUSE OF REPRESENTATIVES:

Yesterday, December 7, 1941—a date which will live in infam —the United States of America was suddenly and deliberatel attacked by naval and air forces of the empire of Japan.

The United States was at peace with that nation, and, at th solicitation of Japan, was still in conversation with its goverr ment and its Emperor looking toward the maintenance of peac in the Pacific.

Indeed, one hour after Japanese air squadrons had commence bombing in the Amercian island of Oahu the Japanese Amba sador to the United States and his colleague delivered to ou Secretary of State a formal reply to a recent American messag And, while this reply stated that it seemed useless to continu the existing diplomatic negotiations, it contained no threat c hint of war or of armed attack.

It will be recorded that the distance of Hawaii from Japa makes it obvious that the attack was deliberately planned man days or even weeks ago. During the intervening time the Japane: Government has deliberately sought to deceive the United State by false statements and expressions of hope for continued peac

The attack yesterday on the Hawaiian Islands has caused sever damage to American naval and military forces. I regret to tell yo that very many American lives have been lost. In addition, Ame ican ships have been reported torpedoed on the high seas betwee San Francisco and Honolulu.

Yesterday the Japanese Government also launched an attac against Malaya.

Last night Japanese forces attacked Hong Kong.

Last night Japanese forces attacked Guam.

Last night Japanese forces attacked the Philippine Islands.

Last night the Japanese attacked Wake Island.

And this morning the Japanese attacked Midway Island.

Japan has therefore undertaken a surprise offensive extendir throughout the Pacific area. The facts of yesterday and tod: speak for themselves. The people of the United States have a ready formed their opinions and well understand the implicatio: to the very life and safety of our nation.

As Commander in Chief of the Army and Navy I have directe

hat all measures be taken for our defense, that always will our
whole nation remember the character of the onslaught against us.

No matter how long it may take us to overcome this premedi-
ated invasion, the American people, in their righteous might,
will win through to absolute victory.

I believe that I interpret the will of the Congress and of the
people when I assert that we will not only defend ourselves to
the uttermost but will make it very certain that this form of
treachery shall never again endanger us.

Hostilities exist. There is no blinking at the fact that our people, our territory and our interests are in grave danger.

With confidence in our armed forces, with the unbounding
determination of our people, we will gain the inevitable triumph.
So help us God.

I ask that the Congress declare that since the unprovoked and
dastardly attack by Japan on Sunday, December 7, 1941, a state
of war has existed between the United States and the Japanese
Empire.

December 8, 1941

COLUMBUS

Joaquin Miller

Behind him lay the gray Azores,
Behind the Gates of Hercules;
Before him not the ghost of shores,
Before him only shoreless seas.
The good mate said: "Now must we pray,
For lo! the very stars are gone.
Brave Admiral, speak, what shall I say?"
"Why, say, 'Sail on! sail on! and on!'"

"My men grow mutinous day by day;
My men grow ghastly wan and weak."
The stout mate thought of home; a spray
Of salt wave washed his swarthy cheek.
"What shall I say, brave Admiral, say,
If we sigh but naught but seas at dawn?"
"Why, you shall say at break of day,
'Sail on! sail on! and on!'"

They sailed and sailed, as winds might blow,
Until at last the blanched mate said:
"Why, now not even God would know
Should I and all my men fall dead.
These very winds forget their way,
For God from these dread seas is gone.
Now speak, brave Admiral, speak and say"—
He said, "Sail on! sail on! and on!"

They sailed. They sailed. Then spake the mate:
"This mad sea shows his teeth tonight.
He curls his lip, he lies in wait,
With lifted teeth, as if to bite!
Brave Admiral, say but one good word:
What shall we do when hope is gone?"
The words leapt like a leaping sword:
"Sail on! sail on! sail on! and on!"

Then pale and worn, he kept his deck,
And peered through darkness. Ah, that night
Of all dark nights! And then a speck—
A light! a light! at last a light!
It grew, a starlit flag unfurled!
It grew to be Time's burst of dawn.
He gained a world; he gave that world
Its grandest lesson: "On! sail on!"

BREAK, BREAK, BREAK

Alfred, Lord Tennyson

Break, break, break,
On thy cold gray stones, O Sea!
And I would that my tongue could utter
The thoughts that arise in me.

O, well for the fisherman's boy,
That he shouts with his sister at play!
O, well for the sailor lad,
That he sings in his boat on the bay!

And the stately ships go on
To the haven under the hill;
But O, for the touch of a vanish'd hand,
And the sound of a voice that is still!

Break, break, break,
At the foot of thy crags, O Sea!
But the tender grace of a day that is dead
Will never come back to me.

THROW OUT THE LIFELINE

Edward Smith Ufford

Throw out the Life-Line across the dark wave,
There is a brother whom someone should save;
Somebody's brother! Oh, who then, will dare
To throw out the Life-Line, his peril to save?

Throw out the Life-Line! Someone is drifting away;
Throw out the Life-Line! Throw out the Life-Line!
Someone is sinking today.

UNFORTUNATE COINCIDENCE

Dorothy Parker

By the time you swear you're his,
Shivering and sighing,
And he vows his passion is
Infinite, undying—
Lady, make a note of this:
One of you is lying.

LITTLE THINGS

Julia Carney

Little drops of water,
Little grains of sand,
Make the mighty ocean
And the pleasant land.

Little deeds of kindness,
Little words of love,
Make our world an Eden
Like the Heaven above.

MANDALAY

Rudyard Kipling

By the old Moulmein Pagoda, lookin' eastward to the sea,
There's a Burma girl a-settin', an' I know she thinks o' me;
For the wind is in the palm-trees, an' the temple-bells they say
"Come you back, you British soldier; come you back to Mandalay!
    Come you back to Mandalay,
    Where the old Flotilla lay:
    Can't you 'ear their paddles chunkin' from Rangoon to
       Mandalay?
    On the road to Mandalay,
    Where the flyin'-fishes play,
    An' the dawn comes up like thunder outer China 'crost
       the Bay!

'Er petticoat was yaller an' 'er little cap was green,
An' 'er name was Supi-yaw-let—jes' the same as Theebaw's Queen,
An' I seed her fust a-smokin' of a whackin' white cheroot,
An' a-wastin' Christian kisses on an 'eathen idol's foot:
    Bloomin' idol made o' mud—
    What they called the Great Gawd Budd—
    Plucky lot she cared for idols when I kissed 'er where she
       stud!
    On the road to Mandalay—

When the mist was on the rice-fields an' the sun was droppin' slow,
She'd git 'er little banjo an' she'd sing *"Kulla-lo-lo!"*
With 'er arm upon my shoulder an' her cheek agin my cheek
We useter watch the steamers an' the *hathis* pilin' teak.
    Elephints a-pilin' teak
    In the sludgy, squdgy creek,
    Where the silence 'ung that 'eavy you was 'arf afraid to
       speak!
    On the road to Mandalay—

ut that's all shove be'ind me—long ago an' fur away,
n' there ain't no 'busses runnin' from the Bank to Mandalay;
n' I'm learnin' 'ere in London what the ten-year soldier tells:
f you've 'eard the East a-callin', why, you won't 'eed naught
   else."
         No! you won't 'eed nothin' else
         But them spicy garlic smells
         An' the sunshine an' the palm-trees an' the tinkly temple
            bells;
         On the road to Mandalay—

am sick o' wastin' leather on these gritty pavin'-stones,
n' the blasted Henglish drizzle wakes the fever in my bones;
ho' I walks with fifty 'ousemaids outer Chelsea to the Strand,
n' they talks a lot o' lovin', but wot do they understand?
         Beefy face an' grubby 'and—
         Law! wot *do* they understand?
         I've a neater, sweeter maiden in a cleaner, greener land!
         On the road to Mandalay—

ip me somewheres east of Suez where the best is like the worst,
here there aren't no Ten Commandments, an' a man can raise
   a thirst;
or the temple-bells are callin', an' it's there that I would be—
y the old Moulmein Pagoda, lookin' lazy at the sea—
         On the road to Mandalay,
         Where the old Flotilla lay,
         With our sick beneath the awnings when we went to
            Mandalay!
         Oh, the road to Mandalay,
         Where the flyin'-fishes play,
         An' the dawn comes up like thunder outer China 'crost
            the Bay!

                    KASHMIRI SONG

                    Laurence Hope

         Pale hands I love beside the Shalimar,
            Where are you now? Who lies beneath your spell?
         Whom do you lead on Rapture's Roadway, far,
            Before you agonize them in farewell?

Or, pale dispensers of my Joys and Pains,
  Holding the doors of Heaven and of Hell,
How the hot blood rushed wildly through the veins
  Beneath your touch, until you waved farewell.

Pale hands, pink-tipped, like Lotus buds that float
  On those cool waters where we used to dwell,
I would have rather felt you round my throat
  Crushing out life than waving me farewell!

REVEILLE

A. E. Housman

Wake: the silver dusk returning
Up the beach of darkness brims,
And the ship of sunrise burning
Strands upon the eastern rims.

Wake: the vaulted shadow shatters,
Trampled to the floor it spanned,
And the tent of night in tatters
Strews the sky-pavilioned land.

Up, lad, up, 'tis late for lying:
Hear the drums of morning play;
Hark, the empty highways crying
"Who'll beyond the hills away?"

Towns and countries woo together,
Forelands beacon, belfries call;
Never lad that trod on leather
Lived to feast his heart with all.

Up, lad: thews that lie and cumber
Sunlit pallets never thrive;
Morns abed and daylight slumber
Were not meant for man alive.

Clay lies still, but blood's a rover;
Breath's a ware that will not keep.
Up, lad: when the journey's over
There'll be time enough to sleep.

SEA FEVER

John Masefield

I must go down to the seas again, to the lonely sea and the sky,
And all I ask is a tall ship and a star to steer her by,
And the wheel's kick and the wind's song and the white sail's
    shaking,
And a gray mist on the sea's face, and a gray dawn breaking.

I must go down to the seas again, for the call of the running tide
Is a wild call and a clear call that may not be denied;
And all I ask is a windy day with the white clouds flying,
And the flung spray and the blown spume, and the sea-gulls crying.

I must go down to the seas again, to the vagrant gypsy life,
To the gull's way and the whale's way, where the wind's like a
    whetted knife;
And all I ask is a merry yarn from a laughing fellow-rover,
And quiet sleep and a sweet dream when the long trick's over.

HEAVEN WILL PROTECT THE WORKING GIRL

Edgar Smith

A village maid was leaving home, with tears her eyes were wet,
Her mother dear was standing near the spot;
She says to her: "Neuralgia dear, I hope you won't forget
That I'm the only mother you have got.
The city is a wicked place as anyone can see,
And cruel dangers 'round your path may hurl;
So ev'ry week you'd better send your wages back to me
For Heaven will protect a working girl.

Chorus:

    "You are going far away, but remember what I say,
    When you are in the city's giddy whirl,
    From temptations, crimes and follies, villains, taxicabs and
       trolleys,
    Oh! Heaven will protect the working girl."

Her dear old mother's words proved true, for soon the poor girl
  met
A man who on her ruin was intent;
He treated her respectful as those villains always do,
And she supposed he was a perfect gent.
But she found different when one night she went with him to dine
Into a table d'hôte so blithe and gay.
And he says to her: "After this we'll have a demitasse!"
Then to him these brave words the girl did say:

Chorus:
> "Stand back, villain, go your way! here I will no longer stay,
> Although you were a marquis or an earl;
> You may tempt the upper classes with your villainous demi-
>   tasses,
> But Heaven will protect the working girl."

THE CONGO

A STUDY OF THE NEGRO RACE

Vachel Lindsay

I. THEIR BASIC SAVAGERY

Fat black bucks in a wine-barrel room,
Barrel-house kings, with feet unstable,

A deep rolling bass. Sagged and reeled and pounded on the table,
Pounded on the table,
Beat an empty barrel with the handle of a broom,
Hard as they were able,
Boom, boom, BOOM.
With a silk umbrella and the handle of a broom,
Boomlay, boomlay, boomlay, BOOM.
THEN I had religion, THEN I had a vision.
I could not turn from their revel in derision.

More deliberate.
Solemnly chanted. THEN I SAW THE CONGO, CREEPING THROUGH THE
  BLACK,
CUTTING THROUGH THE FOREST WITH A GOLDEN
  TRACK.
Then along that riverbank
A thousand miles
Tattooed cannibals danced in files;

Then I heard the boom of the blood-lust song
And a thigh-bone beating on a tin-pan gong. *A rapidly piling climax of speed and racket.*
And "BLOOD" screamed the whistles and the fifes of
    the warriors,
"BLOOD" screamed the skull-faced, lean witch-
    doctors,
"Whirl ye the deadly voo-doo rattie,
Harry the uplands,
Steal all the cattle,
Rattle-rattle, rattle-rattle,
Bing.
Boomlay, boomlay, boomlay, BOOM,"
A roaring, epic, rag-time tune *With a philosophic pause.*
From the mouth of the Congo
To the Mountains of the Moon.
Death is an Elephant, *Shrilly and with a heavily accented metre.*
Torch-eyed and horrible,
Foam-flanked and terrible.
BOOM, steal the pygmies,
BOOM, kill the Arabs,
BOOM, kill the white men,
Hoo, Hoo, Hoo.
Listen to the yell of Leopold's ghost *Like the wind in the chimney.*
Burning in Hell for his hand-maimed host.
Hear how the demons chuckle and yell
Cutting his hands off, down in Hell.
Listen to the creepy proclamation,
Blown through the lairs of the forest-nation,
Blown past the white-ants' hill of clay,
Blown past the marsh where the butterflies play: *All the "o" sounds very golden. Heavy accents very heavy. Light accents very light. Last line whispered.*
"Be careful what you do,
Or Mumbo-Jumbo, God of the Congo,
And all of the other
Gods of the Congo,
Mumbo-Jumbo will hoo-doo you,
Mumbo-Jumbo will hoo-doo you,
Mumbo-Jumbo will hoo-doo you."

. . . .

III. THE HOPE OF THEIR RELIGION

A good old negro in the slums of the town *Heavy bass. With a literal imitation of camp-meeting racket, and trance.*
Preached at a sister for her velvet gown.

Howled at a brother for his low-down ways,
His prowling, guzzling, sneak-thief days.
Beat on the Bible till he wore it out
Starting the jubilee revival shout.
And some had visions, as they stood on chairs,
And sang of Jacob, and the golden stairs,
And they all repented, a thousand strong,
From their stupor and savagery and sin and wrong,
And slammed with their hymn books till they
    shook the room
With "Glory, glory, glory,"
And "Boom, boom, BOOM."

Exactly as in the first section. Begin with terror and power, and with joy.

THEN I SAW THE CONGO, CREEPING THROUGH THE
    BLACK,
CUTTING THROUGH THE JUNGLE WITH A GOLDEN
    TRACK.
And the gray sky opened like a new-rent veil
And showed the Apostles with their coats of mail.
In bright white steel they were seated round
And their fire-eyes watched where the Congo
    wound.
And the twelve Apostles, from their thrones on
    high,

Sung to the tune of "Hark, ten thousand harps and voices."

Thrilled all the forest with their heavenly cry:—
"Mumbo-Jumbo will die in the jungle;
Never again will he hoo-doo you,
Never again will he hoo-doo you."
Then along that river, a thousand miles,

With growing deliberation and joy.

The vine-snarled trees fell down in files.
Pioneer angels cleared the way
For a Congo paradise, for babes at play,
For sacred capitals, for temples clean.
Gone were the skull-faced witch-men lean.

In a rather high key —as delicately as possible.

There, where the wild-ghost-gods had wailed
A million boats of the angels sailed
With oars of silver, and prows of blue
And silken pennants that the sun shone through.
'Twas a land transfigured, 'twas a new creation.
Oh, a singing wind swept the negro nation
And on through the backwoods clearing flew:—

To the tune of "Hark, ten thousand harps and voices."

"Mumbo-Jumbo is dead in the jungle.
Never again will he hoo-doo you.
Never again will he hoo-doo you."

Redeemed were the forests, the beasts and the men,
And only the vulture dared again
By the far, lone mountains of the moon
To cry, in the silence, the Congo tune:—
Mumbo-Jumbo will hoo-doo you,
"Mumbo-Jumbo will hoo-doo you.
Mumbo . . . Jumbo . . . will . . . hoo-doo . . . you."

Dying down into a penetrating, terrified whisper.

FROM THE HOUND OF HEAVEN

Francis Thompson

I fled Him, down the nights and down the days;
　　I fled Him, down the arches of the years;
I fled Him, down the labyrinthine ways
　　Of my own mind; and in the mist of tears
I hid from Him, and under running laughter.
　　　　Up vistaed hopes I sped;
　　　　And shot, precipitated
Adown Titanic glooms of chasmed fears,
　　From those strong Feet that followed, followed after.
　　　　But with unhurrying chase,
　　　　And unperturbèd pace,
　　Deliberate speed, majestic instancy,
　　　　They beat—and a Voice beat
　　　　More instant than the Feet—
"All things betray thee, who betrayest Me."

HOME

Edgar A. Guest

It takes a heap o' livin' in a house t' make it home,
A heap o' sun an' shadder, an' ye sometimes have t' roam
Afore ye really 'preciate the things ye lef' behind,
An' hunger fer 'em somehow, with 'em allus on yer mind.
It don't make any differunce how rich ye get t' be,
How much yer chairs an' tables cost, how great yer luxury;
It ain't home t' ye, though it be the palace of a king,
Until somehow yer soul is sort o' wrapped round everything.

Home ain't a place that gold can buy or get up in a minute;
Afore it's home there's got t' be a heap o' livin' in it;
Within the walls there's got t' be some babies born, and then
Right there ye've got t' bring 'em up t' women good, an' men;
And gradjerly, as time goes on, ye find ye wouldn't part
With anything they ever used—they've grown into yer heart:
The old high chairs, the playthings, too, the little shoes they wore
Ye hoard; an' if ye could ye'd keep the thumb-marks on the door.

Ye've got t' weep t' make it home, ye've got t' sit an' sigh
An' watch beside a loved one's bed, an' know that Death is nigh;
An' in the stillness o' the night t' see Death's angel come,
An' close the eyes o' her that smiled, an' leave her sweet voice
    dumb.
For these are scenes that grip the heart, an' when yer tears are
    dried,
Ye find the home is dearer than it was, an' sanctified;
An' tuggin' at ye always are the pleasant memories
O' her that was an' is no more—ye can't escape from these.

Ye've got to sing an' dance fer years, ye've got t' romp an' play,
An' learn t' love the things ye have by usin' 'em each day;
Even the roses round the porch must blossom year by year
Afore they 'come a part o' ye, suggestin' someone dear
Who used t' love 'em long ago, and trained 'em just t' run
The way they do, so's they would get the early mornin' sun;
Ye've got to love each brick an' stone from cellar up t' dome:
It takes a heap o' livin' in a house t' make it home.

BLOOD, SWEAT AND TEARS

Winston Churchill

On Friday evening last I received from His Majesty the mission
to form a new administration.

It was the evident will of Parliament and the nation that this
should be conceived on the broadest possible basis and that it
should include all parties.

I have already completed the most important part of this task.
A war cabinet has been formed of five members, representing,
with the Labor, Opposition and Liberals, the unity of the nation.

It was necessary that this should be done in one single day on account of the extreme urgency and rigor of events. Other key positions were filled yesterday, I am submitting a further list to the king tonight. I hope to complete the appointment of principal Ministers during tomorrow.

The appointment of other Ministers usually takes a little longer. I trust when Parliament meets again this part of my task will be completed and that the administration will be complete in all respects.

I considered it in the public interest to suggest to the Speaker that the House should be summoned today. At the end of today's proceedings, the adjournment of the House will be proposed until May 21 with provision for earlier meeting if need be. Business for that will be notified to M. P.'s at the earliest opportunity.

I now invite the House by a resolution to record its approval of the steps taken and declare its confidence in the new government. The resolution:

"That this House welcomes the formation of a government representing the united and inflexible resolve of the nation to prosecute the war with Germany to a victorious conclusion."

To form an administration of this scale and complexity is a serious undertaking in itself. But we are in action at many other points—in Norway and in Holland—and we have to be prepared in the Mediterranean. The air battle is continuing, and many preparations have to be made here at home.

In this crisis I think I may be pardoned if I do not address the House at any length today, and I hope that any of my friends and colleagues or former colleagues who are affected by the political reconstruction will make all allowances for any lack of ceremony with which it has been necessary to act.

I say to the House as I said to Ministers who have joined this government, I have nothing to offer but blood, toil, tears and sweat. We have before us an ordeal of the most grievous kind. We have before us many, many months of struggle and suffering.

You ask, what is our policy? I say it is to wage war by land, sea and air. War with all our might and with all the strength God has given us, and to wage war against a monstrous tyranny never surpassed in the dark and lamentable catalogue of human crime. That is our policy.

You ask, what is our aim? I can answer in one word. It is victory. Victory at all costs—victory in spite of all terrors—victory, however long and hard the road may be, for without victory there is no survival.

Let that be realized. No survival for the British Empire, no survival for all that the British Empire has stood for, no survival for the urge, the impulse of the ages, that mankind shall move forward toward his goal.

I take up my task in buoyancy and hope. I feel sure that our cause will not be suffered to fail among men.

I feel entitled at this juncture, at this time, to claim the aid of all and to say, "Come then, let us go forward together with our united strength."

OUT WHERE THE WEST BEGINS

Arthur Chapman

Out where the handclasp's a little stronger,
Out where the smile dwells a little longer,
That's where the West begins;
Out where the sun is a little brighter,
Where the snows that fall are a trifle whiter,
Where the bonds of home are a wee bit tighter,—
That's where the West begins.

Out where the skies are a trifle bluer,
Out where friendship's a little truer,
That's where the West begins;
Out where a fresher breeze is blowing,
Where there's laughter in every streamlet flowing,
Where there's more of reaping and less of sowing,—
That's where the West begins.

Out where the world is in the making,
Where fewer hearts in despair are aching,
That's where the West begins;
Where there's more of singing and less of sighing,
Where there's more of giving and less of buying,
And a man makes friends without half trying—
That's where the West begins.

* * *

Here lies my wife; here let her lie!
Now she's at rest, and so am I.
—John Dryden

THE MAN WITH THE HOE

Edwin Markham

Written after seeing Millet's world-famous painting of
a brutalized toiler.
*God made man in his own image, in the image of God
made he him.*—Genesis.

Bowed by the weight of centuries he leans
Upon his hoe and gazes on the ground,
The emptiness of ages in his face,
And on his back the burden of the world.
Who made him dead to rapture and despair,
A thing that grieves not and that never hopes,
Stolid and stunned, a brother to the ox?
Who loosened and let down this brutal jaw?
Whose was the hand that slanted back this brow?
Whose breath blew out the light within this brain?

Is this the Thing the Lord God made and gave
To have dominion over sea and land;
To trace the stars and search the heavens for power;
To feel the passion of Eternity?
Is this the dream He dreamed who shaped the suns
And marked their ways upon the ancient deep?
Down all the caverns of Hell to their last gulf
There is no shape more terrible than this—
More tongued with censure of the world's blind greed—
More filled with signs and portents for the soul—
More packt with danger to the universe.

What gulfs between him and the seraphim!
Slave of the wheel of labor, what to him
Are Plato and the swing of Pleiades?
What the long reaches of the peaks of song,
The rift of dawn, the reddening of the rose?
Thru this dread shape the suffering ages look;
Time's tragedy is in that aching stoop;
Thru this dread shape humanity betrayed,
Plundered, profaned and disinherited,
Cries protest to the Judges of the world,
A protest that is also prophecy.

O masters, lords and rulers in all lands,
Is this the handiwork you give to God,
This monstrous thing distorted and soul-quenched?
How will you ever straighten up this shape;
Touch it again with immortality;
Give back the upward looking and the light;
Rebuild in it the music and the dream;
Make right the immemorial infamies,
Perfidious wrongs, immedicable woes?

O masters, lords and rulers in all lands,
How will the Future reckon with this Man?
How answer his brute question in that hour
When whirlwinds of rebellion shake all shores?
How will it be with kingdoms and with kings—
With those who shaped him to the thing he is—
When this dumb Terror shall rise to judge the world,
After the silence of the centuries?

THE ARKANSAS TRAVELER

This piece is intended to represent an Eastern man's experiences among the inhabitants of Arkansas, showing their hospitality and the mode of obtaining it. This was in the days when railroads and stage lines were limited.

One evening, at dusk, the Easterner, traveling afoot, comes to small log house, fifteen or twenty yards back from the road. In th doorway is a man playing a violin—the tune "The Arkansas Trav eler"—the most popular in that region.

The man in the cabin doorway keeps repeating the first part o the tune over and over again, as he could not play the second par All the while it is raining and the Easterner is anxious to obtai shelter. The house is covered with clapboards, and the rain is leak ing into every part of it. The old man's daughter, Sarah, appear to be getting supper while a small boy sets the table, and the ol lady sits in the doorway admiring the music.

The stranger stops in the road before the cabin and says, "Ho do you do?" The old man merely glances at him, and, continuin to play, replies, "I do as I please."

STRANGER—How long have you been living here?

OLD MAN—D'y' see that mountain thar? Well, that was thar when I come here.

STRANGER—Can I stay here tonight?

OLD MAN—No! ye can't stay here.

STRANGER—How long will it take me to get to the next tavern?

OLD MAN—Well, you'll not get thar at all, if you stand thar foolin' with me all night. (Continues playing.)

STRANGER—Well, how far do you call it to the next tavern?

OLD MAN—I reckon it's upwards of some distance.

STRANGER—I am very dry—do you keep any spirits in your house?

OLD MAN—Do you think my house is haunted? They say, thar's plenty down in the graveyard.

STRANGER—How do they cross the river ahead?

OLD MAN—The ducks all swim across. (Plays on as before.)

STRANGER—How far is it to the fork of the road?

OLD MAN—I've been livin' here nigh on twenty years, and no road ain't forked yet.

STRANGER—Give me some satisfaction, if you please, sir? Where does the road go?

OLD MAN—Well, it hain't moved a step since I've moved here.

STRANGER—Why don't you cover your house?

OLD MAN—'Cause it's rainin'.

STRANGER—Then why don't you cover it when it's not raining?

OLD MAN—'Cause it don't leak.

STRANGER—Why don't you play the second part of that tune?

OLD MAN—If you're a better player than I am, you can play it yourself. I'll bring the fiddle out to you— I don't want you in here. (Stranger plays the second part of the tune.)

OLD MAN—Git over the fence, and come in and sit down— I didn't know you could play. You can board here if you want to. Kick that dog off that stool, and set down and play it over— I want to hear it again. (Stranger plays second part of tune again.)

OLD MAN—Our supper is ready now; won't you have some with us?

STRANGER—If you please.

OLD MAN—What will you take, tea or coffee?

STRANGER—A cup of tea, if you please.

OLD MAN—Sall, git the grubbin'-hoe, and go dig some sassafras, quick! (Old Man plays the first part of the tune.)

STRANGER (to the little boy)—Bub, give me a knife and fork, if you please.

Boy—We hain't got no knives and forks, sir.
Stranger—Then give me a spoon.
Boy—We hain't got no spoons neither.
Stranger—Well, then how do you do?
Boy—Tolerable, thank you; how do you do, sir? (Old Man plays
the first part of the tune again.)

The stranger, finding such poor accommodations, departs for
the next tavern.

SALLY IN OUR ALLEY

Henry Carey

Of all the girls that are so smart
  There's none like pretty Sally;
She is the darling of my heart,
  And she lives in our alley.
There is no lady in the land
  Is half so sweet as Sally;
She is the darling of my heart,
  And she lives in our alley.

Her father he makes cabbage-nets,
  And through the streets does cry 'em;
Her mother she sells laces long
  To such as please to buy 'em:
But sure such folks could ne'er beget
  So sweet a girl as Sally!
She is the darling of my heart,
  And she lives in our alley.

When she is by, I leave my work,
  I love her so sincerely;
My master comes like any Turk,
  And bangs me most severely:
But let him bang his bellyful,
  I'll bear it all for Sally;
She is the darling of my heart,
  And she lives in our alley.

Of all the days that's in the week
　I dearly love but one day—
And that's the day that comes **betwixt**
　A Saturday and Monday;
For then I'm drest all in my best
　To walk abroad with Sally;
She is the darling of my heart,
　And she lives in our alley.

My master carries me to church,
　And often am I blamèd
Because I leave him in the lurch
　As soon as text is namèd;
I leave the church in sermon-time
　And slink away to Sally;
She is the darling of my heart,
　And she lives in our alley.

When Christmas comes about again,
　O, then I shall have money;
I'll hoard it up, and box it all,
　I'll give it to my honey:
I would it were ten thousand pound,
　I'd give it all to Sally;
She is the darling of my heart,
　And she lives in our alley.

My master and the neighbours all
　Make game of me and Sally,
And, but for her, I'd better be
　A slave and row a galley;
But when my seven long years are out,
　O, then I'll marry Sally;
O, then we'll wed, and then we'll bed—
　But not in our alley!

THE DESTRUCTION OF SENNACHERIB

Lord Byron

The Assyrian came down like the wolf on the fold,
And his cohorts were gleaming in purple and gold;
And the sheen of their spears was like stars on the sea,
When the blue wave rolls nightly on deep Galilee.

Like the leaves of the forest when summer is green,
That host with their banners at sunset were seen;
Like the leaves of the forest when Autumn hath blown,
That host on the morrow lay withered and strown.

For the Angel of Death spread his wings on the blast,
And breathed in the face of the foe as he passed;
And the eyes of the sleepers waxed deadly and chill,
And their hearts but once heaved, and forever grew still!

And there lay the steed with his nostril all wide,
But through it there rolled not the breath of his pride:
And the foam of his gasping lay white on the turf,
And cold as the spray of the rock-beating surf.

And there lay the rider distorted and pale,
With the dew on his brow and the rust on his mail;
And the tents were all silent, the banners alone,
The lances unlifted, the trumpet unblown.

And the widows of Ashur are loud in their wail,
And the idols are broke in the temple of Baal;
And the might of the Gentile, unsmote by the sword,
Hath melted like snow in the glance of the Lord!

THE WOLF IN SHEEP'S CLOTHING

A Wolf, clothing himself in the skin of a Sheep, and getting in among the flock, by this means took the opportunity to devour many of them. At last the shepherd discovered him, and cunningly fastened a rope about his neck, tied him up to a tree which stood hard by. Some other shepherds happening to pass that way, and observing what he was about, drew near, and expressed their admiration at it. "What," says one of them, "brother, do you make hanging of Sheep?" "No," replies the other, "but I make hanging of a Wolf whenever I catch him, though in the habit and garb of a Sheep." Then he showed them their mistake, and they applauded the justice of the execution.

(From Aesop's Fables)

* * *

All history is but the lengthened shadow of great men.
—R. W. Emerson

BURY ME NOT ON THE LONE PRAIRIE

Anonymous

"O bury me not on the lone prairie!"
These words came low and mournfully
From the pallid lips of a youth who lay
On his dying bed at the close of day.

"O bury me not on the lone prairie,
Where the wild coyotes will howl o'er me,
Where the buzzards beat and the wind goes free;
O bury me not on the lone prairie!

"O bury me not on the lone prairie,
In a narrow grave six foot by three,
Where the buffalo paws o'er a prairie sea;
O bury me not on the lone prairie!

"O bury me not on the lone prairie,
Where the wild coyotes will howl o'er me,
Where the rattlesnakes hiss and the crow flies free;
O bury me not on the lone prairie!

"O bury me not," and his voice faltered there,
But we took no heed of his dying prayer;
In a narrow grave just six by three
We buried him there on the lone prairie.

LOVE'S NOBILITY

Ralph Waldo Emerson

Not to scatter bread and gold,
Goods and raiment bought and sold;
But to hold fast his simple sense
And speak the speech of innocence;
And with hand and body and blood,
To make his bosom counsel good.
He that feeds men serveth few;
He serves all who dares be true.

THE NINETY AND NINE

I. D. Sankey

There were ninety and nine that safely lay
In the shelter of the fold,
But one was out on the hills away,
Far off from the gates of gold—
Away on the mountains wild and bare,
Away from the tender Shepherd's care.

"Lord, thou hast here thy ninety and nine;
Are they not enough for thee?"
But the Shepherd made answer:
"This of mine has wandered away from me
And although the road be rough and steep
I go to the desert to find my sheep."

But none of the ransomed ever knew
How deep were the waters crossed;
Nor how dark was the night that the Lord passed thro'
Ere he found his sheep that was lost.
Out in the desert he heard its cry—
Sick and helpless, and ready to die.

But all through the mountains, thunder-riven,
And up from the rocky steep,
There arose a cry to the gate of heaven,
"Rejoice! I have found my sheep!"
And the angels echoed around the throne,
"Rejoice, for the Lord brings back his own!"

— FOR WHOM THE BELL TOLLS —

No man is an Iland, intire of it selfe; every man is a peece of
the Continent, a part of the maine; if a Clod bee washed away by
the Sea, Europe is the lesse, as well as if a Promontorie were, as
well as if a Mannor of thy friends or of thine owne were; any
mans death diminishes me, because I am involved in Mankinde;
and therefore never send to know for whom the bell tolls; It tolls
for thee.

(From John Donne's The Tolling Bell—A Devotion)

DUTY

Ralph Waldo Emerson

So nigh is grandeur to our dust,
So near is God to man,
When Duty whispers low, "Thou must,"
The youth replies, "I can."

ANNABEL LEE

Edgar Allan Poe

It was many and many a year ago,
   In a kingdom by the sea,
That a maiden there lived, whom you may know
   By the name of Annabel Lee;
And this maiden she lived with no other thought
   Than to love, and be loved by me.

I was a child and she was a child,
   In this kingdom by the sea;
But we loved with a love that was more than love,
   I and my Annabel Lee,—
With a love that the wingèd seraphs of heaven
   Coveted her and me.

And this was the reason that long ago,
   In this kingdom by the sea,
A wind blew out of a cloud, chilling
   My beautiful Annabel Lee;
So that her high-born kinsmen came,
   And bore her away from me,
To shut her up in a sepulchre,
   In this kingdom by the sea.

The angels, not so happy in heaven,
   Went envying her and me.
Yes! that was the reason (as all men know)
   In this kingdom by the sea,
That the wind came out of the cloud by night,
   Chilling and killing my Annabel Lee.

But our love it was stronger by far than the love
  Of those who were older than we,
  Of many far wiser than we;
And neither the angels in heaven above,
  Nor the demons down under the sea,
Can ever dissever my soul from the soul
  Of the beautiful Annabel Lee.

For the moon never beams without bringing me dreams
  Of the beautiful Annabel Lee,
And the stars never rise but I feel the bright eyes
  Of the beautiful Annabel Lee.
And so, all the night-tide I lie down by the side
Of my darling, my darling, my life, and my bride,
  In her sepulchre there by the sea,
  In her tomb by the sounding sea.

THE HISTORY OF THE U.S.

Winifred Sackville Stoner

In fourteen hundred ninety-two, Columbus sailed the ocean blu
And found this land, land of the Free, beloved by you, belove
  by me.

And in the year sixteen and seven, good Captain Smith thoug
  he'd reach Heav'n,
And then he founded Jamestown City, alas, 'tis gone, oh, what
  pity.

'Twas in September sixteen nine, with ship, Half Moon, a re
  Dutch sign,
That Henry Hudson found the stream, the Hudson River of o
  dream.

In sixteen twenty pilgrims saw our land that had no unjust la
Their children here in this day, proud citizens of U.S.A.

In sixteen hundred eighty-three, good William Penn stood 'nea
  a tree
And swore that unto his life's end he would be the Indian's frien

In seventeen hundred seventy-five good Paul Revere was then
   alive;
He rode like wild throughout the night, and called the Minute
   Men to fight.

Year seventeen hundred seventy-six, July the fourth, this date
   please fix
Within your minds, my children dear, for that was Independence
   Year.

In that same year, on a bitter night at Trenton was an awful fight,
But by our brave George Washington the battle was at last well
   won.

Two other dates in your mind fix—Franklin born in seventeen six,
And Washington first said "Boo-Hoo" in seventeen hundred
   thirty-two.

In seventeen hundred seventy-nine, Paul Jones, who was a captain
   fine,
Gained our first naval victory fighting on the big, wide sea.

And in the year eighteen and four, Lewis and Clark both went
   before,
And blazed for us the Oregon trail where men go now in ease by
   rail.

In eighteen hundred and thirteen on great Lake Erie could be
   seen
Our Perry fight the Union Jack and drive it from our shores far
   back.

In eighteen hundred and sixty-one an awful war was then begun
Between the brothers of our land, who now together firmly stand.

In eighteen hundred sixty-three each slave was told that he was
   free
By Lincoln with whom few compare in being kind and just and
   fair.

In eighteen hundred eighty-one at Panama there was begun
By good De Lesseps, wise and great, the big canal, now our ships'
   gate.

At San Juan, eighteen ninety-eight, our brave Rough Riders lay
in wait,
And on the land brought victory, while Dewey won it on the sea.

In nineteen hundred and fifteen was shown a panoramic screen
At San Francisco's wondrous fair; all people were invited there.

But cruel war in that same year kept strangers from our land o'
cheer,
And nineteen seventeen brought here the war that filled our
hearts with fear.

Thank God in nineteen eighteen Peace on the earth again was
seen,
And we are praying that she'll stay forever in our U.S.A.

EULOGY OF THE DOG

George G. Vest

Gentlemen of the jury, the best friend a man has in this world
may turn against him and become his enemy. His son or daughter
whom he has reared with loving care may prove ungrateful. Those
who are nearest and dearest to us—those whom we trust with our
happiness and our good name—may become traitors to their faith.
The money that a man has he may lose. It flies away from him,
perhaps when he needs it most. A man's reputation may be sacrificed in a moment of ill-considered action. The people who are
prone to fall on their knees to do us honor when success is with us
may be the first to throw the stone of malice when failure settles
its clouds upon our heads. The one absolutely unselfish friend that
man can have in this selfish world—the one that never deserts him,
the one that never proves ungrateful or treacherous—is his dog.

Gentlemen of the jury, a man's dog stands by him in prosperity
and in poverty, in health and in sickness. He will sleep on the cold
ground, where the wintry winds blow and the snow drives fiercely,
if only he can be near his master's side. He will kiss the hand that
has no food to offer, he will lick the wounds and sores that come
in encounter with the roughness of the world. He guards the sleep
of his pauper master as if he were a prince. When all other friends
desert, he remains. When riches take wings and reputation falls to
pieces he is as constant in his love as the sun in its journey through

the heavens. If fortune drives the master forth an outcast in the world, friendless and homeless, the faithful dog asks no higher privilege than that of accompanying him to guard against danger, to fight against his enemies. And when the last scene of all comes, and death takes the master in its embrace, and his body is laid away in the cold ground, no matter if all other friends pursue their way, there by his graveside will the noble dog be found, his head between his paws, his eyes sad but open in alert watchfulness, faithful and true even to death.

THE CREMATION OF SAM McGEE

Robert W. Service

There are strange things done in the midnight sun
By the men who moil for gold;
The Arctic trails have their secret tales
That would make your blood run cold;
The Northern Lights have seen queer sights,
But the queerest they ever did see
Was that night on the marge of Lake Lebarge
I cremated Sam McGee.

Now Sam McGee was from Tennessee, where the cotton blooms and blows.
Why he left his home in the South to roam 'round the Pole, God only knows.
He was always cold, but the land of gold seemed to hold him like a spell;
Though he'd often say in his homely way that "he'd sooner live in hell."

On a Christmas day we were mushing our way over the Dawson trail.
Talk of your cold! through the parka's fold it stabbed like a driven nail.
If our eyes we'd close, then the lashes froze till sometimes we couldn't see;
It wasn't much fun, but the only one to whimper was Sam McGee.

And that very night, as we lay packed tight in our robes beneath the snow,

And the dogs were fed, and the stars o'erhead were dancing heel and toe,

He turned to me, and "Cap," says he, "I'll cash in this trip, I guess;

And if I do, I'm asking that you won't refuse my last request."

Well, he seemed so low that I couldn't say no; then he says with a sort of moan:

"It's the cursed cold, and it's got right hold till I'm chilled clean through to the bone.

Yet 'tain't being dead—it's my awful dread of the icy grave that pains;

So I want you to swear that, foul or fair, you'll cremate my last remains."

A pal's last need is a thing to heed, so I swore I would not fail;

And we started on at the streak of dawn; but God! he looked ghastly pale.

He crouched on the sleigh, and he raved all day of his home in Tennessee;

And before nightfall a corpse was all that was left of Sam McGee.

There wasn't a breath in that land of death, and I hurried, horror-driven,

With a corpse half-hid that I couldn't get rid, because of a promise given;

It was lashed to the sleigh, and it seemed to say: "You may tax your brawn and brains,

But you promised true, and it's up to you to cremate these last remains."

Now a promise made is a debt unpaid, and the trail has its own stern code.

In the days to come, though my lips were dumb, in my heart how I cursed that load.

In the long, long night, by the lone firelight, while the huskies, round in a ring,

Howled out their woes to the homeless snows—O God! how I loathed the thing.

And every day that quiet clay seemed to heavy and heavier grow;

And on I went, though the dogs were spent and the grub was getting low;

he trail was bad, and I felt half mad, but I swore I would not
  give in;
nd I'd often sing to the hateful thing, and it harkened with a
  grin.

ill I came to the marge of Lake Lebarge, and a derelict there lay;
  was jammed in the ice, but I saw in a trice it was called the
  "Alice May."
nd I looked at it, and I thought a bit, and I looked at my frozen
  chum;
hen "Here," said I, with a sudden cry, "is my cre-ma-to-re-um."

)me planks I tore from the cabin floor, and I lit the boiler fire;
)me coal I found that was lying around, and I heaped the fuel
  higher;
he flames just soared, and the furnace roared—such a blaze you
  seldom see;
nd I burrowed a hole in the glowing coal, and I stuffed in Sam
  McGee.

hen I made a hike, for I didn't like to hear him sizzle so;
nd the heavens scowled, and the huskies howled, and the wind
  began to blow.
  was icy cold, but the hot sweat rolled down my cheeks, and I
  don't know why;
nd the greasy smoke in an inky cloak went streaking down the
  sky.

do not know how long in the snow I wrestled with grisly fear;
ut the stars came out and they danced about ere again I ventured
  near;
  was sick with dread, but I bravely said: "I'll just take a peep
  inside.
guess he's cooked, and it's time I looked"; . . . then the door I
  opened wide.

nd there sat Sam, looking cool and calm, in the heart of the
  furnace roar;
nd he wore a smile you could see a mile, and he said: "Please
  close that door.
's fine in here, but I greatly fear you'll let in the cold and storm—
ince I left Plumtree down in Tennessee, it's the first time I've
  been warm."

There are strange things done in the midnight sun
By the men who moil for gold;
The Arctic trails have their secret tales
That would make your blood run cold;
The Northern Lights have seen queer sights,
But the queerest they ever did see
Was that night on the marge of Lake Lebarge
I cremated Sam McGee.

Ode TO A LOUSE

ON SEEING ONE ON A LADY'S BONNET AT CHURCH

Robert Burns

Ha! Whare ye gaun, ye crawlin' ferlie?
Your impudence protects you sairly:
I canna say but ye strunt rarely
   Owre gauze an' lace;
Though, faith! I fear ye dine but sparely
   On sic a place.

Ye ugly, creepin', blastit wonner,
Detested, shunned by saunt an' sinner,
How dare you set your fit upon her,
   Sae fine a lady?
Gae somewhere else, and seek your dinner
   On some poor body.

Swith, in some beggar's haffet squattle;
There ye may creep and sprawl and sprattle
Wi' ither kindred, jumping cattle,
   In shoals and nations:
Whare horn nor bane ne'er daur unsettle
   Your thick plantations.

Now haud you there, ye're out o' sight,
Below the fatt'rels, snug an' tight;
Na, faith ye yet! ye'll no be right
   Till ye've got on it,
The very tapmost tow'ring height
   O' Miss's bonnet.

My sooth; right bauld ye set your nose out,
As plump and gray as ony grozet;
O for some rank, mercurial rozet,
    Or fell, red smeddum!
I'd gie you sic a hearty dose o't,
    Wad dress your droddum!

I wad na been surprised to spy
You on an auld wife's flannen toy;
Or aiblins some bit duddie boy,
    On's wyliecoat;
But Miss's fine Lunardi, fie!
    How daur ye do't?

O Jenny, dinna toss your head,
An' set your beauties a' abread!
Ye little ken what cursed speed
    The blastie's makin'!
Thae winks and finger-ends, I dread,
    Are notice takin'!

O wad some power the giftie gie us
To see oursel's as ithers see us!
It wad frae monie a blunder free us,
    And foolish notion:
What airs in dress an' gait wad lea'e us,
    And ev'n devotion!

FINNIGIN TO FLANNIGAN

Strickland Gillilan

Superintindint wuz Flannigan;
Boss av the siction wuz Finnigin;
Whiniver the kyars got offen th' thrack
An' muddled up things t' th' divil an' back
Finnigin writ it to Flannigan,
Afther the wrick wuz all on agin:
That is, this Finnigin
Repoorted to Flannigan.

Whin Finnigin furst writ to Flannigan,
He writ tin pages—did Finnigin.
An' he tould jist how the smash occurred;
Full minny a tajus, blunderin' wurrd
Did Finnigin write to Flannigan
Afther the cars had gone on agin.
That's th' way Finnigin
Repoorted to Flannigan.

Now Flannigan knowed more than Finnigin—
He'd more idjucation—had Flannigan;
An' it wore 'm clane an' complately out
To tell what Finnigin writ about
In his writin' to Muster Flannigan.
So he writed this here: Masther Finnigin:
Don't do sich a sin agin;
Make 'em brief, Finnigin!"

Whin Finnigin got this from Flannigan,
He blushed rosy rid—did Finnigin;
An' he said: "I'll gamble a whole month's pa-ay
That it'll be minny an' minny a da-ay
Befoore Sup'rintindint—that's Flannigan—
Gits a whack at that very same sin agin.
From Finnigin to Flannigan
Repoorts won't be so long agin."

Wan da-ay on the siction av Finnigin,
On the road sup'rintinded be Flannigan,
A rail give way on a bit av a curve
An' some kyars went off as they made th' shwerrve.
"There's nobody hurted," sez Finnigin,
"But repoorts must be made to Flannigan,"
An' he winked at Mike Corrigan,
As married a Finnigin.

He wuz shantyin' thin, wuz Finnigin,
As minny a railroader's been agin,
An' his shmoky ol' lamp wuz burnin' bright
In Finnigin's shanty all that night—
Bilin' down his repoort was Finnigin
An' he writed this here: "Muster Flannigan:
Off agin, on agin,
Gone agin.—Finnigin."

TREES

Joyce Kilmer

I think that I shall never see
A poem lovely as a tree.

A tree whose hungry mouth is prest
Against the earth's sweet flowing breast;

A tree that looks at God all day
And lifts her leafy arms to pray;

A tree that may in summer wear
A nest of robins in her hair;

Upon whose bosom snow has lain;
Who intimately lives with rain.

Poems are made by fools like me,
But only God can make a tree.

THE DUTIES OF MAN

Holy Bible, Romans 12:3–21

3 For I say, through the grace given unto me, to every man that is among you, not to think of himself more highly than he ought to think; but to think soberly, according as God hath dealt to every man the measure of faith.

4 For as we have many members in one body, and all members have not the same office:

5 So we, being many, are one body in Christ, and every one members one of another.

6 Having then gifts differing according to the grace that is given to us, whether prophecy, let us prophesy according to the proportion of faith;

7 Or ministry, let us wait on our ministering: or he that teacheth, on teaching;

8 Or he that exhorteth, on exhortation: he that giveth, let him do it with simplicity; he that ruleth, with diligence; he that sheweth mercy, with cheerfulness.

9 Let love be without dissimulation. Abhor that which is evil; cleave to that which is good.

10 Be kindly affectioned one to another with brotherly love; in honour preferring one another;

11 Not slothful in business; fervent in spirit; serving the Lord;

12 Rejoicing in hope; patient in tribulation; continuing instant in prayer;

13 Distributing to the necessity of saints; given to hospitality.

14 Bless them which persecute you: bless, and curse not.

15 Rejoice with them that do rejoice, and weep with them that weep.

16 Be of the same mind one toward another. Mind not high things, but condescend to men of low estate. Be not wise in your own conceits.

17 Recompense to no man evil for evil. Provide things honest in the sight of all men.

18 If it be possible, as much as lieth in you, live peaceably with all men.

19 Dearly beloved, avenge not yourselves, but rather give place unto wrath: for it is written, Vengeance is mine; I will repay, saith the Lord.

20 Therefore if thine enemy hunger, feed him; if he thirst, give him drink: for in so doing thou shalt heap coals of fire on his head.

21 Be not overcome of evil, but overcome evil with good.

THE LAKE ISLE OF INNISFREE

William Butler Yeats

I will arise and go now, and go to Innisfree,
And a small cabin build there, of clay and wattles made:
Nine bean rows will I have there, a hive for the honey bee,
And live alone in the bee-loud glade.

And I shall have some peace there, for peace comes dropping slow,
Dropping from the veils of the morning to where the cricket sings;
There midnight's all a glimmer, and noon a purple glow,
And evening full of the linnet's wings.

I will arise and go now, for always night and day
I hear lake water lapping with low sounds by the shore;
While I stand on the roadway, or on the pavements gray,
I hear it in the deep heart's core.

THE DEAD

Rupert Brooke

Blow out, you bugles, over the rich Dead!
    There's none of these so lonely and poor of old,
    But, dying, has made us rarer gifts than gold.
These laid the world away; poured out the red
Sweet wine of youth; gave up the years to be
    Of work and joy, and that unhoped serene
    That men call age; and those who would have been,
Their sons, they gave, their immortality.
Blow, bugles, blow! They brought us, for our dearth,
    Holiness, lacked so long, and Love and Pain.
Honor has come back, as a king, to earth,
    And paid his subjects with a royal wage;
And Nobleness walks in our ways again;
    And we have come into our heritage.

JINGLE BELLS

J. Pierpont

Dashing thro' the snow in a one-horse open sleigh,
O'er the fields we go, laughing all the way;
Bells on bob-tail ring, making spirits bright;
What fun it is to ride and sing a sleighing song tonight!

Chorus:
    Jingle bells! Jingle bells! Jingle all the way!
    Oh! what fun it is to ride in a one-horse open sleigh!

A day or two ago I thought I'd take a ride,
And soon Miss Fanny Bright was seated by my side;
The horse was lean and lank, misfortunes seemed his lot,
He got into a drifted bank, and we, we got upsot. (*Chorus.*)

Now the ground is white, go it while you're young,
Take the girls tonight, and sing this sleighing song;
Just get a bob-tailed nag, two-forty for his speed,
Then hitch him to an open sleigh, and crack! you'll take the lead.
                                                    (*Chorus.*)

THE BAND PLAYED ON

John F. Palmer

Matt Casey formed a social club that beat the town for style,
And hired for a meeting place a hall;
When pay day came around each week they greased the floor with
  wax,
And danced with noise and vigor at the ball.
Each Saturday you'd see them dressed up in Sunday clothes,
Each lad would have his sweetheart by his side.
When Casey led the first grand march they all would fall in line,
Behind the man who was their joy and pride.
  For—

Chorus:

  Casey would waltz with a strawberry blonde,
  And the band played on,
  He'd glide 'cross the floor with the girl he ador'd.
  And the band played on,
  But his brain was so loaded it nearly exploded,
  The poor girl would shake with alarm.
  He'd never leave the girl with the strawberry curl,
  And the band played on.

Such kissing in the corner and such whispering in the hall,
And telling tales of love behind the stairs—
As Casey was the favorite and he that ran the ball,
Of kissing and love-making did his share.
At twelve o'clock exactly they all would fall in line,
Then march down to the dining hall and eat.
But Casey would not join them although everything was fine,
But he stayed upstairs and exercised his feet.
  For—(*Chorus.*)

Now when the dance was over and the band played "Home Sweet
  Home",
They played a tune at Casey's own request.
He thanked them very kindly for the favors they had shown,
Then he'd waltz once with the girl he loved best.
Most all the friends are married that Casey used to know,
And Casey too has taken him a wife.
The blonde he used to waltz and glide with on the ball-room floor,
Is happy Missis Casey now for life.
  For—(*Chorus.*)

COME INTO THE GARDEN, MAUD

Alfred, Lord Tennyson

Come into the garden, Maud,
  For the black bat, night, has flown,
Come into the garden, Maud,
  I am here at the gate alone;
And the woodbine spices are wafted abroad,
  And the musk of the roses blown.

For a breeze of morning moves,
  And the planet of Love is on high,
Beginning to faint in the light that she loves
  On a bed of daffodil sky,
To faint in the light of the sun she loves,
  To faint in its light, and to die.

All night have the roses heard
  The flute, violin, bassoon;
All night has the casement jessamine stirr'd
  To the dancers dancing in tune;
Till a silence fell with the waking bird,
  And a hush with the setting moon.

I said to the lily, "There is but one
  With whom she has heart to be gay.
When will the dancers leave her alone?
  She is weary of dance and play."
Now half to the setting moon are gone,
  And half to the rising day;
Low on the sand and loud on the stone
  The last wheel echoes away.

I said to the rose, "The brief night goes
  In babble and revel and wine.
O young lord-lover, what sighs are those,
  For one that will never be thine?
But mine, but mine," so I sware to the rose,
  "For ever and ever mine."

And the soul of the rose went into my blood,
  As the music clash'd in the hall;
And long by the garden lake I stood,
  For I heard your rivulet fall

From the lake to the meadow and on to the wood,
  Our wood, that is dearer than all;

From the meadow your walks have left so sweet
  That whenever a March-wind sighs,
He sets the jewel-print of your feet
  In violets blue as your eyes,
To the woody hollows in which we meet
  And the valleys of Paradise.

The slender acacia would not shake
  One long milk-bloom on the tree;
The white lake-blossom fell into the lake
  As the pimpernel dozed on the lea;
But the rose was awake all night for your sake,
  Knowing your promise to me;
The lilies and roses were all awake,
  They sigh'd for the dawn and thee.

Queen rose of the rosebud garden of girls,
  Come hither, the dances are done,
In gloss of satin and glimmer of pearls,
  Queen lily and rose in one;
Shine out, little head, sunning over with curls,
  To the flowers, and be their sun.

There has fallen a splendid tear
  From the passion-flower at the gate.
She is coming, my dove, my dear;
  She is coming, my life, my fate.
The red rose cries, "She is near, she is near;"
  And the white rose weeps, "She is late;"
The larkspur listens, "I hear, I hear;"
  And the lily whispers, "I wait."

She is coming, my own, my sweet;
  Were it ever so airy a tread,
My heart would hear her and beat,
  Were it earth in an earthy bed;
My dust would hear her and beat,
  Had I lain for a century dead,
Would start and tremble under her feet,
  And blossom in purple and red.

O CAPTAIN! MY CAPTAIN!

Walt Whitman

1

O Captain! my Captain! our fearful trip is done;
The ship has weather'd every rack, the prize we sought is won;
The port is near, the bells I hear, the people all exulting,
While follow eyes the steady keel, the vessel grim and daring:
But O heart! heart! heart!
O the bleeding drops of red,
Where on the deck my Captain lies,
Fallen cold and dead.

2

O Captain! my Captain! rise up and hear the bells;
Rise up—for you the flag is flung—for you the bugle trills;
For you bouquets and ribbon'd wreaths—for you the shores a-crowd-
ing;
For you they call, the swaying mass, their eager faces turning:
Here Captain! dear father!
The arm beneath your head!
It is some dream that on the deck,
You've fallen cold and dead.

3

My Captain does not answer, his lips are pale and still;
My father does not feel my arm, he has no pulse nor will;
The ship is anchor'd safe and sound, its voyage closed and done;
From fearful trip, the victor ship comes in with object won:
Exult, O shores, and ring, O bells!
But I, with mournful tread,
Walk the deck my Captain lies,
Fallen cold and dead.

* * *

When I was a boy of fourteen, my father was so ignorant I could
hardly stand to have the old man around. But when I got to be
twenty-one I was astonished at how much the old man had learned
in seven years.

—Mark Twain

JEST 'FORE CHRISTMAS

Eugene Field

Father calls me William, sister calls me Will,
Mother calls me Willie, but the fellers call me Bill!
Mighty glad I ain't a girl—ruther be a boy,
Without them sashes, curls, an' things that's worn by Fauntleroy!
Love to chawnk green apples an' go swimmin' in the lake—
Hate to take the castor-ile they give for belly-ache!
'Most all the time, the whole year round, there ain't no flies on me,
But jest 'fore Christmas I'm as good as I kin be!

Got a yeller dog named Sport, sick him on the cat;
First thing she knows she doesn't know where she is at!
Got a clipper sled, an' when us kids goes out to slide,
'Long comes the grocery cart, an' we all hook a ride!
But sometimes when the grocery man is worrited an' cross,
He reaches at us with his whip, an' larrups up his hoss,
An' then I laff and holler, "Oh, ye never teched *me!*"
But jest 'fore Christmas I'm as good as I kin be!

Gran'ma says she hopes that when I git to be a man,
I'll be a missionarer like her oldest brother, Dan,
As was et up by the cannibuls that lives in Ceylon's Isle,
Where every prospeck pleases, an' only man is vile!
But gran'ma she has never been to see a Wild West show,
Nor read the Life of Daniel Boone, or else I guess she'd know
That Buff'lo Bill an' cowboys is good enough for me!
Excep' jest 'fore Christmas when I'm as good as I kin be!

And then old Sport he hangs around, so solemn-like an' still
His eyes they keep a-sayin': "What's the matter, little Bill?"
The old cat sneaks down off her perch an' wonders what's become
Of them two enemies of hern that used to make things hum!
But I am so perlite an' tend so earnestly to biz,
That mother says to father: "How improved our Willie is!"
But father, havin' been a boy hisself, suspicions me
When, jest 'fore Christmas I'm as good as I kin be!

For Christmas, with its lots an' lots of candies, cakes, an' toys,
Was made, they say, for proper kids an' not for naughty boys;
So wash yer face an' bresh yer hair, an' mind yer p's an' q's,
An' don't bust out yer pantaloons, an' don't wear out yer shoes;

Say "Yessum" to the ladies, and "Yessur" to the men,
An' when they's company, don't pass yer plate for pie again;
But, thinkin' of the things yer'd like to see upon that tree,
Jest 'fore Christmas be as good as yer kin be!

NEARER, MY GOD, TO THEE

Sarah Flower Adams

Nearer, my God, to Thee,
Nearer to Thee!
E'en though it be a cross
That raiseth me;
Still all my song shall be,
Nearer, my God, to Thee,
Nearer to Thee!

Though like the wanderer,
The sun gone down,
Darkness be over me,
My rest a stone;
Yet in my dreams I'd be
Nearer, my God, to Thee,
Nearer to Thee!

There let the way appear
Steps unto Heaven,
All that Thou send'st me
In mercy given;
Angels to beckon me
Nearer, my God, to Thee,
Nearer to Thee!

Then, with my waking thoughts
Bright with Thy praise,
Out of my stony griefs,
Bethel I'll raise;
So by my woes to be
Nearer, my God, to Thee,
Nearer to Thee!

Or if, on joyful wing,
Cleaving the sky,
Sun, moon and stars forgot,
Upward I fly,
Still all my song shall be,
Nearer, my God, to Thee,
Nearer to Thee!

ROBERT E. LEE'S FAREWELL TO HIS ARMY

Headquarters Army of Northern Virginia
April 10, 1865

After four years of arduous service marked by unsurpassed courage and fortitude, the Army of Northern Virginia has been compelled to yield to overwhelming numbers and resources.

I need not tell the survivors of so many hard-fought battles who have remained steadfast to the last that I have consented to this result from no distrust of them; but feeling that valor and devotion could accomplish nothing that would compensate for the loss that must have attended the continuance of the contest, I determined to avoid the useless sacrifice of those whose past services have endeared them to their countrymen. By the terms of the agreement, officers and men can return to their homes and remain until exchanged.

You may take with you the satisfaction that proceeds from the consciousness of duty faithfully performed, and I earnestly pray that a merciful God will extend to you His blessing and protection.

With an unceasing admiration of your constancy and devotion to your country, and a grateful remembrance of your kind and generous consideration of myself, I bid you all an affectionate farewell.

R. E. LEE, *General*

T.R. ON WAR VETERANS

A man who is good enough to shed his blood for his country is good enough to be given a square deal afterward. More than that no man is entitled to, and less than that no man shall have.

—Theodore Roosevelt, Springfield, Ill., 1903

THERE IS PLEASURE IN THE PATHLESS WOODS

Lord Byron

There is a pleasure in the pathless woods,
There is a rapture on the lonely shore,
There is society where none intrudes,
By the deep Sea, and music in its roar:
I love not man the less, but Nature more,
From these our interviews, in which I steal
From all I may be, or have been before,
To mingle with the Universe, and feel
What I can ne'er express, yet cannot all conceal.

(From Childe Harold)

THE BOWERY

Charles H. Hoyt

Oh! the night that I struck New York,
I went out for a quiet walk;
Folks who are "on to" the city say,
Better by far that I took Broadway;
But I wasn't out to enjoy the sights,
There was the Bowery ablaze with lights;
I had one of the devil's own nights!
I'll never go there anymore!

Chorus:

The Bowery, the Bowery! They say such things, and they do
strange things on
The Bowery! The Bowery! I'll never go there anymore!

I had walked but a block or two,
When up came a fellow and me he knew;
Then a policeman came walking by,
Chased him away, and I asked him why?
"Wasn't he pulling your leg," said he;
Said I, "He never laid hands on me!"
"Get off the Bowery, you Yap!" said he,
I'll never go there anymore! (*Chorus.*)

I went into an auction store,
I never saw any thieves before;
First he sold me a pair of socks,
Then said he how much for the box?
Someone said "Two dollars!" I said "Three!"
He emptied the box and gave it to me,
"I sold you the box, not the socks," said he,
I'll never go there anymore! (*Chorus.*)

I went into a concert hall,
I didn't have a good time at all;
Just the minute that I sat down,
Girls began singing, "New Coon in town."
I got up mad and spoke out free,
"Somebody put that man out," said she;
A man called a bouncer attended to me,
I'll never go there anymore! (*Chorus.*)

I struck a place that they called a "dive",
I was in luck to get out alive;
When the policeman heard my woes,
Saw my black eyes and my battered nose;
"You've been held up!" said the "copper" fly!
"No, sir! but I've been knocked down!" said I,
Then he laughed, though I couldn't see why!
I'll never go there anymore! (*Chorus.*)

RECESSIONAL

Rudyard Kipling

God of our fathers, known of old—
Lord of our far-flung battle line—
Beneath Whose awful hand we hold
Dominion over palm and pine—
Lord God of Hosts, be with us yet,
Lest we forget—lest we forget!

The tumult and shouting dies;
The captains and the kings depart:
Still stands Thine ancient Sacrifice,
An humble and a contrite heart.

594

Lord God of Hosts, be with us yet,
Lest we forget—lest we forget!

Far-called, our navies melt away;
On dune and headland sinks the fire:
Lo, all our pomp of yesterday
Is one with Nineveh and Tyre!
Judge of the Nations, spare us yet,
Lest we forget—lest we forget!

If, drunk with sight of power, we loose
Wild tongues that have not Thee in awe—
Such boasting as the Gentiles use
Or lesser breeds without the Law—
Lord God of Hosts, be with us yet,
Lest we forget—lest we forget!

For heathen heart that puts her trust
In reeking tube and iron shard—
All valiant dust that builds on dust,
And guarding, calls not on Thee to guard—
For frantic boast and foolish word,
Thy mercy on Thy people, Lord!
Amen.

WHEN LILACS LAST IN THE DOORYARD BLOOM'D

Walt Whitman

When lilacs last in the dooryard bloom'd,
And the great star early droop'd in the western sky in the night,
I mourn'd, and yet shall mourn with ever-returning spring.
Ever-returning spring, trinity sure to me you bring,
Lilac blooming perennial and drooping star in the west,
And thought of him I love.

O powerful western fallen star!
O shades of night—O moody, tearful night!
O great star disappear'd—O the black murk that hides the star!
O cruel hands that hold me powerless—O helpless soul of me!
O harsh surrounding cloud that will not free my soul.

In the dooryard fronting an old farm-house near the whitewash'd
    palings,
Stands the lilac-bush tall-growing with heart-shaped leaves of rich
    green,
With many a pointed blossom rising delicate, with the perfume
    strong I love,
With every leaf a miracle—and from this bush in the dooryard,
With delicate-color'd blossoms and heart-shaped leaves of rich
    green,
A sprig with its flower I break.

In the swamp in secluded recesses,
A shy and hidden bird is warbling a song.
Solitary the thrush,
The hermit withdrawn to himself, avoiding the settlements,
Sings by himself a song.
Song of the bleeding throat,
Death's outlet song of life, (for well dear brother I know,
If thou wast not granted to sing thou would'st surely die.)

Over the breast of the spring, the land, amid cities,
Amid lanes and through old woods, where lately the violets peep'd
    from the ground, spotting the gray debris,
Amid the grass in the fields each side of the lanes, passing the end-
    less grass,
Passing the yellow-spear'd wheat, every grain from its shroud in the
    dark-brown fields uprisen,
Passing the apple-tree blows of white and pink in the orchards,
Carrying a corpse to where it shall rest in the grave,
Night and day journeys a coffin.

Coffin that passes through lanes and streets,
Through day and night with the great cloud darkening the land,
With the pomp of the inloop'd flags with the cities draped in black,
With the show of the States themselves as of crape-veil'd women
    standing,
With processions long and winding and the flambeaus of the night,
With the countless torches lit, with the silent sea of faces and the
    unbared heads,
With the waiting depot, the arriving coffin, and the sombre faces,
With dirges through the night, with the thousand voices rising
    strong and solemn,

With all the mournful voices of the dirges pour'd around the
    coffin,
The dim-lit churches and the shuddering organs—where amid
    these you journey,
With the tolling tolling bells' perpetual clang,
Here, coffin that slowly passes,
    give you my sprig of lilac.

Nor for you, for one alone,
Blossoms and branches green to coffins all I bring,
For fresh as the morning, thus would I chant a song for you O
    sane and sacred death.
All over bouquets of roses,
O death, I cover you over with roses and early lilies,
But mostly and now the lilac that blooms the first,
Copious I break, I break the sprigs from the bushes,
With loaded arms I come, pouring for you,
For you and the coffins all of you O death.)

O western orb sailing the heaven,
Now I know what you must have meant as a month since I walk'd,
As I walk'd in silence the transparent shadowy night,
As I saw you had something to tell as you bent to me night after
    night,
As you droop'd from the sky low down as if to my side, (while the
    other stars all look'd on,)
As we wander'd together the solemn night, (for something I know
    not what kept me from sleep,)
As the night advanced, and I saw on the rim of the west how full
    you were of woe,
As I stood on the rising ground in the breeze in the cool trans-
    parent night,
As I watch'd where you pass'd and was lost in the netherward black
    of the night,
As my soul in its trouble dissatisfied sank, as where yon sad orb,
Concluded, dropt in the night, and was gone.

Sing on there in the swamp,
O singer bashful and tender, I hear your notes, I hear your call,
I hear, I come presently, I understand you,
But a moment I linger, for the lustrous star has detain'd me,
The star my departing comrade holds and detains me.

O how shall I warble myself for the dead one there I loved?
And how shall I deck my song for the large sweet soul that ha
    gone?
And what shall my perfume be for the grave of him I love?
Sea-winds blown from east and west,
Blown from the Eastern sea and blown from the Western sea, til
    there on the prairies meeting,
These and with these and the breath of my chant,
I'll perfume the grave of him I love.

O what shall I hang on the chamber walls?
And what shall the pictures be that I hang on the walls,
To adorn the burial-house of him I love?
Pictures of growing spring and farms and homes,
With the Fourth-month eve at sundown, and the gray smoke luci‹
    and bright,
With floods of the yellow gold of the gorgeous, indolent, sinkin
    sun, burning, expanding the air,
With the fresh sweet herbage under foot, and the pale green leave
    of the trees prolific,
In the distance the flowing glaze, the breast of the river, with
    wind-dapple here and there,
With ranging hills on the banks, with many a line against the sky
    and shadows,
And the city at hand with dwellings so dense, and stacks of chim
    neys,
And all the scenes of life and the workshops, and the workmei
    homeward returning.

Lo, body and soul—this land,
My own Manhattan with spires, and the sparkling and hurryin
    tides, and the ships,
The varied and ample land, the South and the North in the light
    Ohio's shores and flashing Missouri,
And ever the far-spreading prairies cover'd with grass and corn
Lo, the most excellent sun so calm and haughty,
The violet and purple morn with just-felt breezes,
The gentle soft-born measureless light,
The miracle, spreading, bathing all, the fulfill'd noon,
The coming eve delicious, the welcome night and the stars,
Over my cities shining all, enveloping man and land.
Sing on, sing on you gray-brown bird,

Sing from the swamps, the recesses, pour your chant from the
  bushes,
Limitless out of the dusk, out of the cedars and pines.
Sing on dearest brother, warble your reedy song,
Loud human song, with voice of uttermost woe.
O liquid and free and tender!
O wild and loose to my soul—O wondrous singer!
You only I hear—yet the star holds me, (but will soon depart,)
Yet the lilac with mastering odor holds me.

Now while I sat in the day and look'd forth,
In the close of the day with its light and the fields of spring, and
  the farmers preparing their crops,
In the large unconscious scenery of my land with its lakes and
  forests,
In the heavenly aerial beauty, (after the perturb'd winds and the
  storms,)
Under the arching heavens of the afternoon swift passing, and the
  voices of children and women,
The many-moving sea-tides, and I saw the ships how they sail'd,
And the summer approaching with richness, and the fields all busy
  with labor,
And the infinite separate houses, how they all went on, each with
  its meals and minutia of daily usages,
And the streets how their throbbings throbb'd, and the cities pent
  —lo, then and there,
Falling upon them all and among them all, enveloping me with
  the rest,
Appear'd the cloud, appear'd the long black trail,
And I knew death, its thought, and the sacred knowledge of death.

Then with the knowledge of death as walking one side of me,
And the thought of death close-walking the other side of me,
And I in the middle as with companions, and as holding the hands
  of companions,
I fled forth to the hiding receiving night that talks not,
Down to the shores of the water, the path by the swamp in the
  dimness,
To the solemn shadowy cedars and ghostly pines so still.

And the singer so shy to the rest receiv'd me,
The gray-brown bird I know receiv'd us comrades three,
And he sang the carol of death, and a verse for him I love.

From deep secluded recesses,
From the fragrant cedars and the ghostly pines so still,
Came the carol of the bird.
And the charm of the carol rapt me,
As I held as if by their hands my comrades in the night,
And the voice of my spirit tallied the song of the bird.

Come lovely and soothing death,
Undulate round the world, serenely arriving, arriving,
In the day, in the night, to all, to each,
Sooner or later delicate death.

Prais'd be the fathomless universe,
For life and joy, and for objects and knowledge curious,
And for love, sweet love—but praise! praise! praise!
For the sure-enwinding arms of cool-enfolding death.

Dark mother always gliding near with soft feet,
Have none chanted for thee a chant of fullest welcome?
Then I chant it for thee, I glorify thee above all,
I bring thee a song that when thou must indeed come, come un-
   falteringly.

Approach strong deliveress,
When it is so, when thou hast taken them I joyously sing the dead,
Lost in the loving floating ocean of thee,
Laved in the flood of thy bliss O death.

From me to thee glad serenades,
Dances for thee I propose saluting thee, adornments and feastings
   for thee,
And the sights of the open landscape and the high-spread sky are
   fitting,
And life and the fields, and the huge and thoughtful night.

The night in silence under many a star,
The ocean shore and the husky whispering wave whose voice I
   know,
And the soul turning to thee O vast and well-veil'd death,
And the body gratefully nestling close to thee.
Over the tree-tops I float thee a song,
Over the rising and sinking waves, over the myriad fields and the
   prairies wide,

Over the dense-pack'd cities all and the teeming wharves and ways,
I float this carol with joy, with joy to thee O death.

To the tally of my soul,
Loud and strong kept up the gray-brown bird,
With pure deliberate notes spreading filling the night.
Loud in the pines and cedars dim,
Clear in the freshness moist and the swamp-perfume,
And I with my comrades there in the night.
While my sight that was bound in my eyes unclosed,
As to long panoramas of visions.

And I saw askant the armies,
I saw as in noiseless dreams hundreds of battle-flags,
Borne through the smoke of the battles and pierc'd with missiles
     I saw them,
And carried hither and yon through the smoke, and torn and
     bloody,
And at last but a few shreds left on the staffs, (and all in silence,)
And the staffs all splinter'd and broken.
I saw battle-corpses, myriads of them,
And the white skeletons of young men, I saw them,
I saw the debris and debris of all the slain soldiers of the war,
But I saw they were not as was thought,
They themselves were fully at rest, they suffer'd not,
The living remain'd and suffer'd, the mother suffer'd,
And the wife and the child and the musing comrade suffer'd,
And the armies that remain'd suffer'd.

Passing the visions, passing the night,
Passing, unloosing the hold of my comrades' hands,
Passing the song of the hermit bird and the tallying song of my
     soul,
Victorious song, death's outlet song, yet varying ever-altering song,
As low and wailing, yet clear the notes, rising and falling, flooding
     the night,
Sadly sinking and fainting, as warning and warning, and yet again
     bursting with joy,
Covering the earth and filling the spread of the heaven,
As that powerful psalm in the night I heard from recesses,
Passing, I leave thee lilac with heart-shaped leaves,
I leave thee there in the dooryard, blooming, returning with
     spring.

I cease from my song for thee,
From my gaze on thee in the west, fronting the west, communing
    with thee,
O comrade lustrous with silver face in the night.
Yet each to keep and all, retrievements out of the night,
The song, the wondrous chant of the gray-brown bird,
And the tallying chant, the echo arous'd in my soul,
With the lustrous and drooping star with the countenance full of
    woe,
With the holders holding my hand hearing the call of the bird,
Comrades mine and I in the midst, and their memory ever to
    keep, for the dead I loved so well,
For the sweetest, wisest soul of all my days and lands—and this for
    his dear sake,
Lilac and star and bird twined with the chant of my soul,
There in the fragrant pines and the cedars dusk and dim.

THE ROSARY

Robert Cameron Rogers

The hours I spent with thee, dear heart,
Are as a string of pearls to me;
I count them over, every one apart,
    My rosary.

Each hour a pearl, each pearl a prayer;
To still a heart in absence wrung;
I tell each bead unto the end and there
    A cross is hung.

Oh, memories that bless—and burn!
O barren gain—and bitter loss!
I kiss each bead, and strive at last to learn,
    To kiss the cross,
      Sweetheart,
      To kiss the cross.

* * *

Every step of progress the world has made has been from scaffold
to scaffold, and from stake to stake.

—Wendell Phillips

LITTLE BOY BLUE

Eugene Field

The little toy dog is covered with dust,
    But sturdy and stanch he stands;
And the little toy soldier is red with rust,
    And his musket molds in his hands.
Time was when the little toy dog was new
    And the soldier was passing fair,
And that was the time when our Little Boy Blue
    Kissed them and put them there.

"Now, don't you go till I come," he said,
    "And don't you make any noise!"
So toddling off to his trundle-bed
    He dreamed of the pretty toys.
And as he was dreaming, an angel song
    Awakened our Little Boy Blue—
Oh, the years are many, the years are long,
    But the little toy friends are true.

Aye, faithful to Little Boy Blue they stand,
    Each in the same old place,
Awaiting the touch of a little hand,
    And the smile of a little face.
And they wonder, as waiting these long years through,
    In the dust of that little chair,
What has become of our Little Boy Blue
    Since he kissed them and put them there.

BIGOTRY EXPLAINED

Daniel O'Connell

Bigotry has no head and cannot think, no heart and cannot feel. When she moves it is in wrath; when she pauses it is amid ruin. Her prayers are curses, her god is a demon, her communion is death, her vengeance is eternity, her decalogue is written in the blood of her victims, and if she stops for a moment in her infernal flight it is upon a kindred rock to whet her vulture fang for more sanguinary desolation.

IN FLANDERS FIELDS

Captain John D. McCrae

In Flanders fields the poppies blow
Between the crosses, row on row,
That mark our place; and in the sky
The larks, still bravely singing, fly
Scarce heard amid the guns below.

We are the Dead. Short days ago
We lived, felt dawn, saw sunset glow,
Loved and were loved, and now we lie
    In Flanders fields.

Take up our quarrel with the foe!
To you from failing hands, we throw
The torch— Be yours to hold it high!
If ye break faith with us who die
We shall not sleep, though poppies grow
    In Flanders fields.

THE WEST WIND

John Masefield

It's a warm wind, the west wind, full of birds' cries;
I never hear the west wind, but tears are in my eyes.
For it comes from the west lands, the old brown hills,
And April's in the west wind, and daffodils.

It's a fine land, the west land, for hearts as tired as mine;
Apple orchards blossom there, and the air's like wine.
There is cool green grass there, where men may lie at rest;
And the thrushes are in song there, fluting from the nest.

"Will you not come home, brother? You have been long away.
It's April, and blossom time, and white is the spray:
And bright is the sun, brother, and warm is the rain;
Will you not come home, brother, home to us again?

"The young corn is green, brother, where the rabbits run;
It's blue sky, and white clouds, and warm rain and sun.
It's song to a man's soul, brother, fire to a man's brain,
To hear the wild bees and see the merry spring again.

"Larks are singing in the west, brother, above the green wheat,
So will you not come home, brother, and rest your tired feet?
I've a balm for bruised hearts, brother, sleep for aching eyes,"
Says the warm wind, the west wind, full of birds' cries.

It's the white road westwards is the road I must tread
To the green grass, the cool grass, and rest for heart and head,
To the violets and the brown brooks and the thrushes' song
In the fine land, the west land, the land where I belong.

O LITTLE TOWN OF BETHLEHEM

Phillips Brooks

O little town of Bethlehem,
How still we see thee lie!
Above thy deep and dreamless sleep
The silent stars go by:
Yet in thy dark streets shineth
The everlasting Light;
The hopes and fears of all the years
Are met in thee tonight.

For Christ is born of Mary;
And gathered all above,
While mortals sleep, the angels keep
Their watch of wondering love.
O morning stars together
Proclaim thy holy birth;
And praises sing to God the King,
And peace to men on earth.

How silently, how silently,
The wondrous Gift is given!
So God imparts to human hearts
The blessings of His heaven.
No ear may hear His coming,
But in this world of sin,
Where meek souls will receive Him still,
The dear Christ enters in.

O holy Child of Bethlehem,
Descend to us, we pray;
Cast out our sins, and enter in,
Be born in us today.
We hear the Christmas angels
The great glad tidings tell;
O come to us, abide with us,
Our Lord Emmanuel.

THERE IS NO DEATH

John Luckey McCreary

There is no death! The stars go down
To rise upon some fairer shore;
And bright, in heaven's jeweled crown,
They shine for evermore.

There is no death! The dust we tread
Shall change beneath the summer showers
To golden grain or mellow fruit,
Of rainbow-tinted flowers.

The granite rocks disorganize,
And feed the hungry moss they bear;
The forest-leaves drink daily life
From out the viewless air.

There is no death! The leaves may fall,
And flowers may fade and pass away;
They only wait through wintry hours
The coming of May-day.

There is no death! An angel-form
Walks o'er the earth with silent tread;
And bears our best-beloved things away,
And then we call them "dead."

He leaves our hearts all desolate,
He plucks our fairest, sweetest flowers;
Transplanted into bliss, they now
Adorn immortal bowers.

The bird-like voice, whose joyous tones
Made glad the scenes of sin and strife,
Sings now an everlasting song
Around the tree of life.

Where'er he sees a smile too bright,
Or heart too pure for taint and vice,
He bears it to that world of light,
To dwell in Paradise.

Born unto that undying life,
They leave us but to come again;
With joy we welcome them the same,
Except their sin and pain.

And ever near us, though unseen,
The dear immortal spirits tread;
For all the boundless universe
Is life—there is no dead!

CLEOPATRA AND HER BARGE

William Shakespeare

The barge she sat in, like a burnish'd throne,
Burn'd on the water: the poop was beaten gold;
Purple the sails, and so perfumed that
The winds were love-sick with them; the oars were silver,
Which to the tune of flutes kept stroke, and made
The water which they beat to follow faster,
As amorous of their strokes. For her own person,
It beggar'd all description: she did lie
In her pavilion—cloth-of-gold of tissue—
O'er-picturing that Venus where we see
The fancy outwork nature: on each side her
Stood pretty dimpled boys, like smiling Cupids,
With divers-colour'd fans, whose wind did seem
To glow the delicate cheeks which they did cool,
And what they undid did.

Age cannot wither her, nor custom stale
Her infinite variety: other women cloy

The appetites they feed; but she makes hungry
Where most she satisfies: for vilest things
Become themselves in her; that the holy priests
Bless her when she is riggish.

(From Antony and Cleopatra)

WEATHER WISDOM

Anonymous

A sunshiny shower
Won't last half an hour.

Rain before seven,
Fair by eleven.

The South wind brings wet weather,
The North wind wet and cold together;
The West wind always brings us rain,
The East wind blows it back again.

March winds and April showers
Bring forth May flowers.

Evening red and morning gray
Set the traveler on his way;
But evening gray and morning red
Bring the rain upon his head.

Rainbow at night is the sailor's delight;
Rainbow at morning, sailors, take warning.

If bees stay at home,
Rain will soon come;
If they fly away,
Fine will be the day.

When clouds appear like rocks and towers,
The earth's refreshed by frequent showers.

* * *

Defend me from my friends; I can defend myself from my enemies.

—Villars

WHOOPEE TI YI YO, GIT ALONG, LITTLE DOGIES

From the Collection by John A. Lomax and Alan Lomax

As I was a-walking one morning for pleasure,
I spied a cow-puncher a-riding along;
His hat was throwed back and his spurs were a-jinglin',
As he approached me a-singin' this song:

    Whoopee ti yi yo, git along, little dogie,
    It's your misfortune and none of my own;
    Whoopee ti yi yo, git along, little dogies,
    For you know Wyoming will be your new home.

Early in the springtime we'll round up the dogies,
Slap on their brands, and bob off their tails;
Round up our horses, load up the chuck wagon,
Then throw those dogies upon the trail.

It's whooping and yelling and driving the dogies,
Oh, how I wish you would go on;
It's whooping and punching and go on, little dogies,
For you know Wyoming will be your new home.

Some of the boys goes up the trail for pleasure,
But that's where they git it most awfully wrong;
For you haven't any idea the trouble they give us
When we go driving them dogies along.

When the night comes on and we hold them on the bed-ground,
These little dogies that roll on so slow;
Roll up the herd and cut out the strays,
And roll the little dogies that never rolled before.

Your mother she was raised way down in Texas,
Where the jimson weed and sand-burrs grow;
Now we'll fill you up on prickly pear and cholla
Till you are ready for the trail to Idaho.

Oh, you'll be soup for Uncle Sam's Injuns;
"It's beef, heap beef," I hear them cry.
Git along, git along, git along, little dogies,
You're going to be beef steers by and by.

WHAT FOLKS ARE MADE OF

Anonymous

What are little boys made of, made of?
What are little boys made of?
Piggins and pails and little puppy tails,
That's what little boys are made of.

What are little girls made of? etc.
Sugar and spice and all things nice
And that's what little girls are made of.

What's young men made of? etc.
Thorns and briars, they're all bad liars,
And that's what young men are made of.

What's young women made of? etc.
Rings and jings and all fine things
And that's what young women are made of.

What's old men made of? etc.
Whiskey and brandy and sugar and candy,
And that's what old men are made of.

THE DUEL

Eugene Field

The gingham dog and the calico cat
Side by side on the table sat;
'Twas half past twelve, and (what do you think!)
Nor one nor t'other had slept a wink!
   The old Dutch clock and the Chinese plate
   Appeared to know as sure as fate
There was going to be a terrible spat.
     (I wasn't there; I simply state
     What was told to me by the Chinese plate!)

The gingham dog went "Bow-wow-wow!"
And the calico cat replied "Mee-ow!"
The air was littered, an hour or so,
With bits of gingham and calico,

While the old Dutch clock in the chimney place
Up with its hands before its face,
For it always dreaded a family row!
        (*Now mind: I'm only telling you*
        What the old Dutch clock declares is true!)

The Chinese plate looked very blue,
And wailed, "Oh, dear! what shall we do!"
But the gingham dog and the calico cat
Wallowed this way and tumbled that,
        Employing every tooth and claw
        In the awfullest way you ever saw—
And, oh! how the gingham and calico flew!
        (*Don't fancy I exaggerate—*
        I got my news from the Chinese plate!)

Next morning where the two had sat
They found no trace of dog or cat:
And some folks think unto this day
That burglars stole that pair away!
        But the truth about the cat and pup
        Is this: they ate each other up!
Now what do you really think of that!
        (*The old Dutch clock it told me so,*
        And that is how I came to know.)

OUR LIPS AND EARS

Anonymous

If you your lips would keep from slips,
Five things observe with care:
Of whom you speak, to whom you speak,
And how and when and where.

If you your ears would save from jeers,
These things keep mildly hid:
Myself and I, and mine and my,
And how I do and did.

        *   *   *

It is not possible to found a lasting power upon injustice.
                                        —Demosthenes

THE BELLS

Edgar Allan Poe

I

Hear the sledges with the bells—
    Silver bells!
What a world of merriment their melody foretells!
    How they tinkle, tinkle, tinkle,
      In the icy air of night!
    While the stars that oversprinkle
    All the heavens, seem to twinkle
      With a crystalline delight;
    Keeping time, time, time,
    In a sort of Runic rhyme,
To the tintinnabulation that so musically wells
    From the bells, bells, bells, bells,
      Bells, bells, bells—
From the jingling and the tinkling of the bells.

II

    Hear the mellow wedding bells—
      Golden bells!
What a world of happiness their harmony foretells!
    Through the balmy air of night
    How they ring out their delight!—
    From the molten-golden notes,
      And all in tune,
    What a liquid ditty floats
To the turtle-dove that listens, while she gloats
      On the moon!
    Oh, from out the sounding cells,
What a gush of euphony voluminously wells!
      How it swells!
      How it dwells
    On the Future!—how it tells
    Of the rapture that impels
    To the swinging and the ringing
      Of the bells, bells, bells—
    Of the bells, bells, bells, bells,
      Bells, bells, bells—
To the rhyming and the chiming of the bells!

Hear the loud alarum bells—
 Brazen bells!
What a tale of terror, now their turbulency tells!
 In the startled ear of night
 How they scream out their affright!
  Too much horrified to speak,
  They can only shriek, shriek,
   Out of tune,
In a clamorous appealing to the mercy of the fire,
In a mad expostulation with the deaf and frantic fire,
  Leaping higher, higher, higher,
  With a desperate desire,
  And a resolute endeavor
  Now—now to sit, or never,
 By the side of the pale-faced moon.
  Oh, the bells, bells, bells!
  What a tale their terror tells
   Of Despair!
 How they clang, and clash, and roar!
 What a horror they outpour
 On the bosom of the palpitating air!
  Yet the ear, it fully knows,
   By the twanging,
   And the clanging,
  How the danger ebbs and flows;
  Yet the ear distinctly tells,
   In the jangling,
   And the wrangling,
  How the danger sinks and swells,
By the sinking or the swelling in the anger of the bells—
   Of the bells—
  Of the bells, bells, bells, bells,
   Bells, bells, bells—
 In the clamor and the clanging of the bells!

IV

 Hear the tolling of the bells—
  Iron bells!
What a world of solemn thought their monody compels!
  In the silence of the night,
  How we shiver with affright
 At the melancholy menace of their tone!

For every sound that floats
From the rust within their throats
  Is a groan.
And the people—ah, the people—
They that dwell up in the steeple,
  All alone,
And who, tolling, tolling, tolling,
In that muffled monotone,
Feel a glory in so rolling
On the human heart a stone—
They are neither man nor woman—
They are neither brute nor human—
  They are Ghouls:—
And their king it is who tolls:—
And he rolls, rolls, rolls,
  Rolls
A pæan from the bells!
And his merry bosom swells
With the pæan of the bells!
And he dances, and he yells;
Keeping time, time, time,
In a sort of Runic rhyme,
To the pæan of the bells:—
  Of the bells:
Keeping time, time, time,
In a sort of Runic rhyme,
To the throbbing of the bells:—
Of the bells, bells, bells—
To the sobbing of the bells:—
Keeping time, time, time,
As he knells, knells, knells,
In a happy Runic rhyme,
To the rolling of the bells—
Of the bells, bells, bells:—
To the tolling of the bells—
Of the bells, bells, bells, bells,
  Bells, bells, bells—
To the moaning and the groaning of the bells.

* * *

I never knew any man in my life who could not bear another's
misfortune perfectly like a Christian.
                                        —Alexander Pope

INDIAN SERENADE

Percy Bysshe Shelley

I arise from dreams of thee
  In the first sweet sleep of night,
When the winds are breathing low,
  And the stars are shining bright.
I arise from dreams of thee,
  And a spirit in my feet
Hath led me—who knows how?—
  To thy chamber-window, Sweet!

The wandering airs they faint
  On the dark, the silent stream,—
The Champak odors fail
  Like sweet thoughts in a dream;
The nightingale's complaint,
  It dies upon her heart;—
As I must die on thine,
  Oh, beloved as thou art!

Oh, lift me from the grass!
  I die! I faint! I fail!
Let thy love in kisses rain
  On my lips and eyelids pale.
My cheek is cold and white, alas!
  My heart beats loud and fast;—
Oh! press it to thine own again,
  Where it will break at last!

THE BRIDGE

Henry Wadsworth Longfellow

I stood on the bridge at midnight,
As the clocks were striking the hour,
And the moon rose o'er the city,
Behind the dark church-tower.

I saw her bright reflection
In the waters under me,
Like a golden goblet falling
And sinking into the sea.

And far in the hazy distance
Of that lovely night in June,
The blaze of the flaming furnace
Gleamed redder than the moon.

Among the long, black rafters
The wavering shadows lay,
And the current that came from the ocean
Seemed to lift and bear them away;

As sweeping and eddying through them,
Rose the belated tide,
And, streaming into the moonlight,
The seaweed floated wide.

And like those waters rushing
Among the wooden piers,
A flood of thoughts came o'er me,
That filled my eyes with tears.

How often, oh, how often,
In the days that had gone by,
I had stood on the bridge at midnight
And gazed on that wave and sky!

How often, oh, how often,
I had wished that the ebbing tide
Would bear me away on its bosom
O'er the ocean wild and wide!

For my heart was hot and restless,
And my life was full of care,
And the burden laid upon me
Seemed greater than I could bear.

But now it has fallen from me,
It is buried in the sea;
And only the sorrow of others
Throws its shadow over me.

Yet whenever I cross the river
On its bridge with wooden piers,
Like the odor of brine from the ocean
Come the thought of other years.

And I think how many thousands
Of care-encumbered men,
Each bearing his burden of sorrow,
Have crossed the bridge since then.

I see the long procession
Still passing to and fro,
The young heart hot and restless,
And the old subdued and slow!

And forever and forever,
As long as the river flows,
As long as the heart has passions,
As long as life has woes.

The moon and its broken reflection
And its shadows shall appear,
As the symbol of love in heaven,
And its wavering image here.

OH, MY DARLING CLEMENTINE

Anonymous

In a cavern, in a canyon,
Excavating for a mine,
Dwelt a miner, 'Forty-Niner,
And his daughter Clementine.

Chorus:
> Oh, my darling, Oh, my darling,
> Oh, my darling Clementine,
> You are lost and gone forever,
> Dreadful sorry, Clementine.

Light she was and like a fairy,
And her shoes were number nine;
Herring boxes, without topses
Sandals were for Clementine. (*Chorus.*)

Drove she ducklings to the water,
Every morning just at nine;
Hit her foot against a splinter,
Fell into the foaming brine. (*Chorus.*)

Ruby lips above the water,
Blowing bubbles soft and fine;
Alas for me! I was no swimmer,
So I lost my Clementine. (*Chorus.*)

In a churchyard, near the canyon,
Where the myrtle doth entwine,
There grow roses and other posies,
Fertilized by Clementine. (*Chorus.*)

Then the miner, 'Forty-Niner,
Soon began to peak and pine,
Thought he oughter jine his daughter,
Now he's with his Clementine. (*Chorus.*)

In my dreams she still doth haunt me,
Robed in garments soaked in brine,
Though in life I used to hug her,
Now she's dead, I'll draw the line. (*Chorus.*)

LINCOLN'S LETTER TO MRS. BIXBY

November 21, 1864

DEAR MADAM:

I have been shown in the files of the War Department a statement of the Adjutant General of Massachusetts that you are the mother of five sons who have died gloriously on the field of battle. I feel how weak and fruitless must be any words of mine which should attempt to beguile you from the grief of a loss so overwhelming, but I cannot refrain from tendering to you the consolation that may be found in the thanks of the Republic that they died to save. I pray that the Heavenly Father may assuage the anguish of your bereavement, and leave you only the cherished memory of the loved and lost, and the solemn pride that must be yours to have laid so costly a sacrifice upon the altar of freedom.

Yours very sincerely and respectfully,

Abraham Lincoln

* * *

A man is rich in proportion to the number of things which he can afford to let alone.

—Henry David Thoreau

EVOLUTION

John Bannister Tabb

Out of the dusk a shadow,
Then a spark;
Out of the cloud a silence,
Then a lark;

Out of the heart a rapture,
Then a pain;
Out of the dead, cold ashes,
Life again.

MY SHADOW

Robert Louis Stevenson

I have a little shadow that goes in and out with me,
And what can be the use of him is more than I can see.
He is very, very like me, from the heels up to the head;
And I see him jump before me, when I jump into bed.

The funniest thing about him is the way he likes to grow—
Not at all like proper children, which is always very slow;
For he sometimes shoots up taller, like an india-rubber ball,
And he sometimes gets so little that there's none of him at all.

He hasn't got a notion of how children ought to play,
And can only make a fool of me in every sort of way.
He stays so close beside me, he's a coward you can see;
I'd think shame to stick to nursie as that shadow sticks to me!

One morning, very early, before the sun was up,
I 'rose and found the shining dew on every buttercup;
But my lazy little shadow, like an arrant sleepy head,
Had stayed at home behind me and was fast asleep in bed.

* * *

Count that day lost whose low descending sun
Views from thy hand no worthy action done.
(From Stamford's Art of Reading, 1803)

619

LOVE'S OLD SWEET SONG

G. Clifton Bingham

Once in the dear dead days beyond recall,
When on the world the mists began to fall,
Out of the dreams that rose in happy throng,
Low to our hearts love sang an old sweet song,
And in the dusk where fell the fire-light gleam,
Softly wove itself into our dream.

Chorus:

Just a song at twilight, when the lights are low,
And the flick'ring shadows softly come and go—
Tho' the heart be weary, sad the day and long,
Still to us at twilight comes love's old sweet song.

Even today we hear love's song of yore,
Deep in our hearts it dwells forever more;
Footsteps may falter, weary grow the way,
Still we can hear it at the close of day.
So to the end, when life's dim shadows fall,
Love will be found the sweetest song of all. (*Chorus.*)

FATHER, DEAR FATHER, COME HOME WITH ME NOW

Henry Clay Work

Father, dear father, come home with me now!
The clock in the steeple strikes one;
You said you were coming right home from the shop,
As soon as your day's work was done.
Our fire has gone out, our house is all dark,
And mother's been watching since tea,
With poor brother Benny so sick in her arms,
And no one to help her but me.
Come home! Come home! Come home!
Please, father, dear father, come home.

Chorus:

Hear the sweet voice of the child
Which the night winds repeat as they roam!
Oh, who could resist this most plaintive of prayers?
Please, father, dear father, come home!

Father, dear father, come home with me now,
The clock in the steeple strikes two;
The night has grown colder, and Benny is worse,—
But he has been calling for you.
Indeed, he is worse—Ma says he will die,
Perhaps before morning shall dawn;
And this is the message she sent me to bring—
"Come quickly, or he will be gone."
Come home! Come home! Come home!
Please, father, dear father, come home. (*Chorus.*)

Father, dear father, come home with me now!
The clock in the steeple strikes three;
The house is so lonely—the hours are so long
For poor weeping mother and me.
Yes, we are alone—poor Benny is dead,
And gone with the angels of light;
And these were the very last words he said:—
"I want to kiss papa good night."
Come home! Come home! Come home!
Please, father, dear father, come home! (*Chorus.*)

AULD LANG SYNE

Robert Burns

Should auld acquaintance be forgot,
　　And never brought to min'?
Should auld acquaintance be forgot,
　　And auld lang syne?

Chorus:—For auld lang syne, my dear,
　　　　For auld lang syne,
　　　　We'll tak a cup o' kindness yet
　　　　For auld lang syne.

And surely ye'll be your pint-stowp,
　　And surely I'll be mine
And we'll tak a cup o' kindness yet
　　For auld lang syne. (*Chorus.*)

We twa hae run about the braes,
   And pu'd the gowans fine;
But we've wandered monie a weary fit
   Sin' auld lang syne. (*Chorus.*)

We twa hae paidled i' the burn,
   From mornin' sun till dine;
But seas between us braid hae roared
   Sin' auld lang syne. (*Chorus.*)

And there's a hand, my trusty fiere,
   And gie's a hand o' thine;
And we'll tak a right guid-willie waught
   For auld lang syne. (*Chorus.*)

AT BUNKER HILL

Daniel Webster

This uncounted multitude before me and around me proves the feeling which the occasion has excited. These thousands of human faces, glowing with sympathy and joy, and from the impulses of a common gratitude turned reverently to heaven in this spacious temple of the firmament, proclaim that the day, the place, and the purpose of our assembling have made a deep impression on our hearts.

If indeed, there be anything in local association fit to affect the mind of man, we need not strive to repress the emotions which agitate us here. We are among the sepulchres of our fathers. We are on ground distinguished by their valor, their constancy, and the shedding of their blood. We are here, not to fix an uncertain date in our annals, nor to draw into notice an obscure and unknown spot. If our humble purpose had never been conceived, if we ourselves had never been born, the 17th of June, 1775, would have been a day on which all subsequent history would have poured its light, and the eminence where we stand a point of attraction to the eyes of successive generations. But we are Americans. We live in what may be called the early age of this great continent; and we know that our posterity, through all time, are here to enjoy and suffer the allotments of humanity. We see before us a probable train of great events; we know that our own fortunes have been happily cast; and it is natural, therefore, that we should be moved by the contemplation of occurrences which have guided our destiny before many of us were born, and settled the condition in which we should pass that portion of our existence which God allows to men on earth.

We do not read even of the discovery of this continent, without feeling something of a personal interest in the event; without being reminded how much it has affected our own fortunes and our own existence. It would be still more unnatural for us, therefore, than for others, to contemplate with unaffected minds that interesting, I may say that most touching and pathetic scene, when the great discoverer of America stood on the deck of his shattered bark, the shades of night falling on the sea, yet no man sleeping; tossed on the billows of an unknown ocean, yet the stronger billows of alternate hope and despair tossing his own troubled thoughts; extending forward his harassed frame, straining westward his anxious and eager eyes, till Heaven at last granted him a moment of rapture and ecstasy, in blessing his vision with the sight of the unknown world.

Nearer to our times, more closely connected with our fates, and therefore still more interesting to our feelings and affections, is the settlement of our own country by colonists from England. We cherish every memorial of these worthy ancestors; we celebrate their patience and fortitude; we admire their daring enterprise; we teach our children to venerate their piety; and we are justly proud of being descended from men who have set the world an example of founding civil institutions on the great and united principles of human freedom and human knowledge. To us, their children, the story of their labors and sufferings can never be without interest. We shall not stand unmoved on the shore of Plymouth, while the sea continues to wash it, nor will our brethren in another early and ancient Colony forget the place of its first establishment, till their river shall cease to flow by it. No vigor of youth, no maturity of manhood, will lead the nation to forget the spots where its infancy was cradled and defended.

But the great event in the history of the continent which we are now met here to commemorate, that prodigy of modern times, at once the wonder and the blessing of the world, is the American Revolution. In a day of extraordinary prosperity and happiness, of high national honor, distinction, and power, we are brought together, in this place, by our love of country, by our admiration of exalted character, by our gratitude for signal services and patriotic devotion. . . .

We rear a memorial of our conviction of that unmeasured benefit which has been conferred on our own land, and of the happy influence which has been produced, by the same events, on the general interests of mankind. We come, as Americans, to mark a spot which must for ever be dear to us and our posterity. We wish that whosoever, in all coming time, shall turn his eye hither, may behold that the place is not undistinguished where the first great battle of the Revolution was fought. We wish that this structure may proclaim the magnitude and importance of that event to every class and every age. We wish that infancy may learn the purpose of its erection from maternal lips, and that weary and withered age may behold it, and be solaced by the recollection which it suggests. We wish that labor may look up here, and be proud, in the midst of its toil. We wish that, in those days of disaster, which, as they come upon all nations, must be expected to come upon us also, desponding patriotism may turn its eyes hitherward, and be assured that the foundations of our national power are still strong. We wish that this column, rising towards heaven among the pointed spires of so many temples dedicated to God, may contribute also to produce, in all minds, a pious feeling of dependence and gratitude. We wish, finally, that the last object to the sight of him who leaves his native shore, and the first to gladden him who revisits it, may be something which shall remind him of the liberty and the glory of his country. Let it rise! let it rise, till it meet the sun in his coming; let the earliest light of the morning gild it, and the parting day linger and play on its summit.

We live in a most extraordinary age. Events so various and so important that they might crowd and distinguish centuries, are, in our times, compressed within the compass of a single life. When has it happened that history has had so much to record, in the same term of years, as since the 17th of June, 1775? Our own Revolution, which, under other circumstances, might itself have been expected to occasion a war of half a century, has been achieved; twenty-four sovereign and independent States erected; and a general government established over them, so safe, so wise, so free, so practical, that we might well wonder its establishment should have been accomplished so soon, were it not for the greater wonder that it should have been established at all. Two or three millions of people have been augmented to twelve, the great forests of the West prostrated beneath the arm of successful industry, and the dwellers on the banks of the Ohio and the Mississippi become the fellow-citizens and neighbors of those who cultivate the hills of New England. We have a commerce that leaves no sea unexplored; navies, which take no law from superior force; revenues, adequate to all the exigencies of government, almost without taxation; and peace with all nations, founded on equal rights and mutual respect. . . .

Yet, notwithstanding that this is but a faint abstract of the things which have happened since the day of the battle of Bunker Hill, we are but fifty years removed from it; and we now stand here to enjoy all the blessings of our own condition, and to look abroad on the brightened prospects of the world, while we still have among us some of those who were active agents in the scenes of 1775, and who are now here, from every quarter of New England, to visit once more, and under circumstances so affecting, I had almost said so overwhelming, this renowned theatre of their courage and patriotism.

VENERABLE MEN! you have come down to us from a former generation. Heaven has bounteously lengthened out your lives, that you might behold this joyous day. You are now where you stood fifty years ago, this very hour, with your brothers and your neighbors, shoulder to shoulder, in the strife for your country. Behold, how altered! The same heavens are indeed over your heads; the same ocean rolls at your feet; but all else how changed! You hear now no roar of hostile cannon, you see no mixed volumes of smoke and flame rising from burning Charlestown. The ground strewed with the dead and the dying; the impetuous charge; the steady and successful repulse; the loud call to repeated assault; the summoning of all that is manly to repeated resistance; a thousand bosoms freely and fearlessly bared in an instant to whatever of terror there may be in war and death;—all these you have witnessed, but you witness them no more. All is peace. The heights of yonder metropolis, its towers and roofs, which you then saw filled with wives and children and countrymen in distress and terror, and looking with unutterable emotions for the issue of the combat, have presented you to-day with the sight of its whole happy population, come out to welcome and greet you with a universal jubilee. Yonder proud ships, by a felicity of position appropriately lying at the foot of this mount, and seeming fondly to cling around it, are not means of annoyance to you, but your country's own means of distinction and defence. All is peace; and God has granted you this sight of your country's happiness, ere you slumber in the grave. He has allowed you to behold and to partake the reward of your patriotic toils; and he has allowed us, your sons and countrymen, to meet you here, and in the name of the present generation, in the name of your country, in the name of liberty, to thank you!

But, alas! you are not all here! Time and the sword have thinned your ranks. Prescott, Putnam, Stark, Brooks, Reed, Pomeroy, Bridge! our eyes seek for you in vain amid this broken band. You are gathered to your fathers, and live only to your country in her grateful remembrance and your own bright example. But let us not too much grieve, that you have met the common fate of men. You lived at least long enough to know that your work had been nobly and successfully accomplished. You lived to see your country's independence established, and to sheathe your swords from war. On the light of Liberty you saw arise the light of Peace, like

> "another morn,
> Risen on mid-noon";

and the sky on which you closed your eyes was cloudless.

But, ah! Him! the first great martyr in this great cause! Him! the premature victim of his own self-devoting heart! Him! the head of our civil councils, and the destined leader of our military bands, whom nothing brought hither but the unquenchable fire of his own spirit! Him! cut off by Providence in the hour of overwhelming anxiety and thick gloom; falling ere he saw the star of his country rise; pouring out his generous blood like water, before he knew whether it would fertilize a land of freedom or of bondage!—how shall I struggle with the emotions that stifle the utterance of thy name! Our poor work may perish; but thine shall endure! This monument may moulder away; the solid ground it rests upon may sink down to a level with the sea; but thy memory shall not fail! Wheresoever among men a heart shall be found that beats to the transports of patriotism and liberty, its aspirations shall be to claim kindred with thy spirit.

But the scene amidst which we stand does not permit us to confine our thoughts or our sympathies to those fearless spirits who hazarded or lost their lives on this consecrated spot. We have the happiness to rejoice here in the presence of a most worthy representation of the survivors of the whole Revolutionary army.

VETERANS! you are the remnant of many a well-fought field. You bring with you marks of honor; from Trenton and Monmouth, from Yorktown, Camden, Bennington, and Saratoga. VETERANS

OF HALF A CENTURY! when in your youthful days you put every thing at hazard in your country's cause, good as that cause was, and sanguine as youth is, still your fondest hopes did not stretch onward to an hour like this! At a period to which you could not reasonably have expected to arrive, at a moment of national prosperity such as you could never have foreseen, you are now met here to enjoy the fellowship of old soldiers, and to receive the overflowings of a universal gratitude.

But your agitated countenances and your heaving breasts inform me that even this is not an unmixed joy. I perceive that a tumult of contending feelings rushes upon you. The images of the dead, as well as the persons of the living, present themselves before you. The scene overwhelms you, and I turn from it. May the Father of all mercies smile upon your declining years, and bless them! And when you shall here have exchanged your embraces, when you shall once more have pressed the hands which have been so often extended to give succor in adversity, or grasped in the exultation of victory, then look abroad upon this lovely land which your young valor defended, and mark the happiness with which it is filled; yea, look abroad upon the whole earth, and see what a name you have contributed to give to your country, and what a praise you have added to freedom, and then rejoice in the sympathy and gratitude which beam upon your last days from the improved condition of mankind! . . .

A new spirit of enterprise and industry begins to prevail; all the great interests of society receive a salutary impulse; and the progress of information not only testifies to an improved condition, but itself constitutes the highest and most essential improvement.

When the battle of Bunker Hill was fought, the existence of South America was scarcely felt in the civilized world. The thirteen little colonies of North America habitually called themselves the "continent." Borne down by colonial subjugation, monopoly, and bigotry, these vast regions of the South were hardly visible above the horizon. But in our day there has been, as it were, a new creation. The southern hemisphere emerges from the sea. Its lofty mountains begin to lift themselves into the light of heaven; its broad and fertile plains stretch out, in beauty, to the eye of civilized man, and at the mighty bidding of the voice of political liberty the waters of darkness retire. . . .

We are not propagandists. Wherever other systems are preferred, either as being thought better in themselves, or as better suited to existing conditions, we leave the preference to be enjoyed. Our history hitherto proves, however, that the popular form is practicable, and that with wisdom and knowledge men may govern themselves; and the duty incumbent on us is to preserve the consistency of this cheering example, and take care that nothing may weaken its authority with the world. If, in our case, the representative system ultimately fail, popular governments must be pronounced impossible. No combination of circumstances more favorable to the experiment can ever be expected to occur. The last hopes of mankind, therefore, rest with us; and if it should be proclaimed, that our example had become an argument against the experiment, the knell of popular liberty would be sounded throughout the earth.

These are excitements to duty; but they are not suggestions of doubt. Our history and our condition, all that is gone before us, and all that surrounds us, authorize the belief, that popular governments though subject to occasional variations, in form perhaps not always for the better, may yet, in their general character, be as durable and permanent as other systems. We know, indeed, that in our country any other is impossible. The principle of free governments adheres to the American soil. It is bedded in it, immovable as its mountains.

And let the sacred obligations which have devolved on this generation, and on us, sink deep into our hearts. Those who established our liberty and our government are daily dropping from among us. The great trust now descends to new hands. Let us apply ourselves to that which is presented to us, as our appropriate object. We can win no laurels in a war for independence. Earlier and worthier hands have gathered them all. Nor are there places for us by the side of Solon, and Alfred, and other founders of states. Our fathers have filled them. But there remains to us a great duty of defence and preservation; and there is opened to us, also, a noble pursuit, to which the spirit of the times strongly invites us. Our proper business is improvement. Let our age be the age of improvement. In a day of peace, let us advance the arts of peace and the works of peace. Let us develop the resources of our land, call forth its powers, build up its institutions, promote all its great interests, and see whether we also, in our day and generation, may not perform something worthy to be remembered. Let us cultivate a true spirit of union and harmony. In pursuing the great objects which our condition points out to us, let us act under a settled conviction, and an habitual feeling, that these twenty-four States are one country. Let our conceptions be enlarged to the circle of our duties. Let us extend our ideas over the whole of the vast field in which we are called to act. Let our object be, OUR COUNTRY, OUR WHOLE COUNTRY, AND NOTHING BUT OUR COUNTRY. And by the blessing of God, may that country itself become a vast and splendid monument, not of oppression and terror, but of Wisdom, of Peace, and of Liberty, upon which the world may gaze with admiration for ever.

(From "The First Bunker Hill Oration")

THE DOG IN THE MANGER

A Dog was lying upon a manger full of hay. An Ox, being hungry, came near, and offered to eat of the hay; but the envious, ill-natured cur, getting up and snarling at him, would not suffer him to touch it. Upon which the Ox, in the bitterness of his heart, said, "A curse light on thee, for a malicious wretch, who wilt neither eat hay thyself, nor suffer others to do it."

(From Aesop's Fables)

JUST A WEARYIN' FOR YOU

Frank L. Stanton

Just a wearyin' for you,
All the time a-feelin' blue,
Wishin' for you, wonderin' when
You'll be comin' home again,
Restless, don't know what to do,
Just a wearyin' for you.

Mornin' comes, the birds awake,
Used to sing so for your sake,
But there's sadness in the notes
That come thrillin' from their throats.
Seem to feel your absence, too,
Just a wearyin' for you.

* * *

It is magnificent, but it is not war.

(From François Canrobert, on seeing the charge of the Light Brigade at Balaklava)

629

ABRAHAM LINCOLN WALKS AT MIDNIGHT

Vachel Lindsay

It is portentous, and a thing of state
    That here at midnight, in our little town
A mourning figure walks, and will not rest
    Near the old court-house pacing up and down.

Or by his homestead, or in shadowed yards
    He lingers where his children used to play,
Or through the market, on the well-worn stones
    He stalks until the dawn-stars burn away.

A bronzed, lank man! His suit of ancient black,
    A famous high-top-hat and plain worn shawl
Make him the quaint great figure that men love,
    The prairie-lawyer, master of us all.

He cannot sleep upon his hillside now.
    He is among us, as in times before!
And we who toss and lie awake for long
    Breathe deep, and start, to see him pass the door.

His head is bowed. He thinks on men and kings.
    Yea, when the sick world cries, how can he sleep?
Too many peasants fight, they know not why,
    Too many homesteads in black terror weep.

The sins of all the war-lords burn his heart.
    He sees the dreadnaughts scouring every main.
He carries on his shawl-wrapt shoulders now
    The bitterness, the folly and the pain.

He cannot rest until a spirit-dawn
    Shall come;—the shining hope of Europe free;
The league of sober folk, the Workers' Earth
    Bringing long peace to Cornland, Alp and Sea.

It breaks his heart that kings must murder still,
    That all his hours of travail here for men
Seem yet in vain. And who will bring white peace
    That he may sleep upon his hill again?

THE SUGAR-PLUM TREE

Eugene Field

Have you ever heard of the Sugar-Plum Tree?
'Tis a marvel of great renown!
It blooms on the shore of the Lollypop Sea
In the garden of Shut-Eye Town;
The fruit that it bears is so wondrously sweet
(As those who have tasted it say)
That good little children have only to eat
Of that fruit to be happy next day.

When you've got to the tree, you would have a hard time
To capture the fruit which I sing;
The tree is so tall that no person could climb
To the boughs where the sugar-plums swing!
But up in that tree sits a chocolate cat,
And a gingerbread dog prowls below—
And this is the way you contrive to get at
Those sugar-plums tempting you so:

You say but the word to that gingerbread dog
And he barks with such a terrible zest
That the chocolate cat is at once all agog,
As her swelling proportions attest.
And the chocolate cat goes cavorting around
From this leafy limb unto that,
And the sugar-plums tumble, of course, to the ground—
Hurrah for that chocolate cat!

There are marshmallows, gumdrops, and peppermint canes
With stripings of scarlet and gold,
And you carry away of the treasure that rains,
As much as your apron can hold!
So come, little child, cuddle closer to me
In your dainty white nightcap and gown,
And I'll rock you away to that Sugar-Plum Tree
In the garden of Shut-Eye Town.

* * *

Knowledge comes but wisdom lingers.
—Tennyson

OFT HAVE I SEEN AT SOME CATHEDRAL DOOR

Oft have I seen at some cathedral door,
A laborer, pausing in the dust and heat,
Lay down his burden, and with reverent feet
Enter, and cross himself, and on the floor
Kneel to repeat his paternoster o'er;
Far off the noises of the world retreat;
The loud vociferations of the street
Become an indistinguishable roar.
So, as I enter here from day to day,
And leave my burden at this minster gate,
Kneeling in prayer, and not ashamed to pray,
The tumult of the time disconsolate
To inarticulate murmurs dies away,
While the eternal ages watch and wait.

(From Divina Commedia, transl. Longfellow)

MY MARYLAND

J. R. Randall

The despot's heel is on thy shore,
    Maryland! My Maryland!
His torch is at thy temple door,
    Maryland! My Maryland!
Avenge the patriotic gore
That fleck'd the streets of Baltimore,
And be the Battle-Queen of yore,
    Maryland! My Maryland!

Hark to a wand'ring son's appeal!
    Maryland! My Maryland!
My Mother State, to thee I kneel,
    Maryland! My Maryland!
For life and death, for woe and weal,
Thy peerless chivalry reveal,
And gird thy beauteous limbs with steel,
    Maryland! My Maryland!

Thou wilt not cower in the dust,
    Maryland! My Maryland!
Thy beaming sword shall never rust,
    Maryland! My Maryland!
Remember Carroll's sacred trust,
Remember Howard's warlike thrust—
And all thy slumberers, with the just,
    Maryland! My Maryland!

Come, for thy shield is bright and strong,
    Maryland! My Maryland!
Come, for thy dalliance does thee wrong,
    Maryland! My Maryland!
Come! to thine own heroic throng,
That stalks with Liberty along.
And give a new Key to thy song.
    Maryland! My Maryland!

Dear Mother! burst the tyrant's chain,
    Maryland! My Maryland!
Virginia should not call in vain!
    Maryland! My Maryland!
She meets her sisters on the plain—
"Sic semper" is the proud refrain,
That baffles minions back amain,
    Maryland! My Maryland!

I see the blush upon thy cheek,
    Maryland! My Maryland!
But thou wast ever bravely meek,
    Maryland! My Maryland!
But lo! there surges forth a shriek
From hill to hill, from creek to creek,
Potomac calls to Chesapeake
    Maryland! My Maryland!

Thou wilt not yield the vandal toll,
    Maryland! My Maryland!
Thou wilt not crook to his control,
    Maryland! My Maryland!

Better the fire upon the roll,
Better the blade, the shot, the bowl,
Than crucifixion of the soul,
            Maryland! My Maryland!

I hear the distant thunder hum,
            Maryland! My Maryland!
The Old Line's bugle, fife and drum,
            Maryland! My Maryland!
She is not dead, nor deaf, nor dumb—
Huzza! she spurns the Northern scum!
She breathes—she burns! she'll come! she'll come!
            Maryland! My Maryland!

THIS ENGLAND

William Shakespeare

This royal throne of kings, this scepter'd isle,
This earth of majesty, this seat of Mars,
This other Eden, demi-paradise,
This fortress built by Nature for herself
Against infection and the hand of war,
This happy breed of men, this little world,
This precious stone set in the silver sea,
Which serves it in the office of a wall
Or as a moat defensive to a house,
Against the envy of less happier lands,
This blessed plot, this earth, this realm, this England,
This nurse, this teeming womb of royal kings,
Fear'd by their breed and famous by their birth,
Renowned for their deeds as far from home,
For Christian service and true chivalry,
As is the sepulchre in stubborn Jewry
Of the world's ransom, blessed Mary's Son,
This land of such dear souls, this dear dear land,
Dear for her reputation through the world,
Is now leased out, I die pronouncing it,
Like to a tenement or pelting farm:
England, bound in with the triumphant sea,
Whose rocky shore beats back the envious siege
Of watery Neptune, is now bound in with shame,

With inky blots and rotten parchment bonds:
That England, that was wont to conquer others,
Hath made a shameful conquest of itself.
Ah, would the scandal vanish with my life,
How happy then were my ensuing death!

(From King Richard II)

NOBODY'S CHILD

Phila H. Case

Alone in the dreary, pitiless street,
With my torn old dress, and bare, cold feet,
All day I have wandered to and fro,
Hungry and shivering, and nowhere to go;
The night's coming on in darkness and dread,
And the chill sleet beating upon my bare head.
Oh! why does the wind blow upon me so wild?
Is it because I am nobody's child?

Just over the way there's a flood of light,
And warmth and beauty, and all things bright;
Beautiful children, in robes so fair,
Are caroling songs in their rapture there.
I wonder if they, in their blissful glee,
Would pity a poor little beggar like me,
Wandering alone in the merciless street,
Naked and shivering, and nothing to eat?

Oh! what shall I do when the night comes down,
In its terrible blackness all over the town?
Shall I lay me down 'neath the angry sky,
On the cold, hard pavement, alone to die,
When the beautiful children their prayers have said,
And their mammas have tucked them up snugly in bed?
For no dear mother on me ever smiled,—
Why is it, I wonder, I'm nobody's child?

No father, no mother, no sister, not one
In all the world loves me, e'en the little dogs run
When I wander too near them; 'tis wondrous to see,
How everything shrinks from a beggar like me!

Perhaps 'tis a dream; but sometimes, when I lie
Gazing far up in the dark blue sky,
Watching for hours, some large, bright star,
I fancy the beautiful gates are ajar,

And a host of white-robed, nameless things,
Come fluttering o'er me on gilded wings;
A hand that is strangely soft and fair
Caresses gently my tangled hair,
And a voice like the carol of some wild bird—
The sweetest voice that ever was heard—
Calls me many a dear, pet name,
Till my heart and my spirit are all aflame.
They tell me of such unbounded love,
And bid me come up to their home above;
And then with such pitiful, sad surprise,
They look at me with their sweet, tender eyes,
And it seems to me, out of the dreary night,
I am going up to that world of light;
And away from the hunger and storm so wild,
I am sure I shall then be somebody's child.

AFTER THE BALL

Charles K. Harris

A little maiden climbed an old man's knee,
Begged for a story, "Do, Uncle, please;
Why are you single, why live alone?
Have you no babies, have you no home?"
"I had a sweetheart, years, years ago,
Where she is now, pet, you will soon know.
List to the story, I'll tell it all,
I believed her faithless, after the ball.

Chorus:
"After the ball is over, after the break of morn,
After the dancers leaving, after the stars are gone;
Many a heart is aching, if you could read them all;
Many's the hopes that have vanished, after the ball.

"Bright lights were flashing in the grand ball-room,
Softly the music, playing sweet tunes,
There came my sweetheart, my love, my own,
'I wish some water; leave me alone!'
When I returned, dear, there stood a man,
Kissing my sweetheart as lover can.
Down fell the glass, pet, broken, that's all,
Just as my heart was, after the ball. (*Chorus.*)

"Long years have passed, child, I've never wed,
True to my lost love, though she is dead,
She tried to tell me, tried to explain,
I would not listen, pleadings were vain;
One day a letter came, from that man,
He was her brother, the letter ran.
That's why I'm lonely, no home at all,
I broke her heart, pet, after the ball." (*Chorus.*)

WHEN THE FROST IS ON THE PUNKIN

James Whitcomb Riley

When the frost is on the punkin and the fodder's in the shock,
And you hear the kyouck and gobble of the struttin' turkey-cock,
And the clackin' of the guineys, and the cluckin' of the hens,
And the rooster's hallylooyer as he tiptoes on the fence;
Oh, it's then's the times a feller is a-feelin' at his best,
With the risin' sun to greet him from a night of peaceful rest,
As he leaves the house, bareheaded, and goes out to feed the stock,
When the frost is on the punkin and the fodder's in the shock.

They's something kind o' harty-like about the atmusfere
When the heat of summer's over and the coolin' fall is here.—
Of course we miss the flowers, and the blossoms on the trees,
And the mumble of the hummin'-birds and buzzin' of the bees;
But the air's so appetizin', and the landscape through the haze
Of a crisp and sunny morning of the airly autumn days
Is a pictur' that no painter has the colorin' to mock,—
When the frost is on the punkin and the fodder's in the shock.

The husky, rusty russel of the tossels of the corn,
And the raspin' of the tangled leaves, as golden as the morn;

The stubble in the furries—kind o' lonesome-like, but still
A-preachin' sermuns to us of the barns they growed to fill;
The straw-stack in the medder, and the reaper in the shed;
The hosses in theyr stalls below, the clover overhead,—
Oh, it sets my hart a-clickin' like the tickin' of a clock,
When the frost is on the punkin and the fodder's in the shock!

Then your apples all is gethered, and the ones a feller keeps
Is poured around the cellar-floor in red and yaller heaps;
And your cider-makin' 's over, and your wimmern-folks is through
With their mince and apple butter, and theyr souse and sausage,
     too!—
I don't know how to tell it—but ef sich a thing could be
As the Angels wantin' boardin', and they'd call around on *me*—
I'd want to 'commodate 'em—all the whole-indurin' flock—
When the frost is on the punkin and the fodder's in the shock!

BRAHMA

Ralph Waldo Emerson

If the red slayer think he slays,
  Or if the slain think he is slain,
They know not well the subtle ways
  I keep, and pass, and turn again.

Far or forgot to me is near;
  Shadow and sunlight are the same;
The vanished gods to me appear;
  And one to me are shame and fame.

They reckon ill who leave me out;
  When me they fly, I am the wings;
I am the doubter and the doubt,
  And I the hymn the Brahmin sings.

The strong gods pine for my abode,
  And pine in vain the sacred Seven;
But thou, meek lover of the good!
  Find me, and turn thy back on heaven.

* * *

It is better to have no ideas than false ones.
                              —Thomas Jefferson

UPON JULIA'S CLOTHES

Robert Herrick

Whenas in silks my Julia goes,
Then, then, methinks, how sweetly flows
The liquefaction of her clothes.

Next, when I cast mine eyes, and see
That brave vibration, each way free,
O, how that glittering taketh me!

A PERFECT DAY

Carrie Jacobs-Bond

When you come to the end of a perfect day,
And you sit alone with your thought,
While the chimes ring out with a carol gay,
For the joy that the day has brought,
Do you think what the end of a perfect day
Can mean to a tired heart,
When the sun goes down with a flaming ray
And the dear friends have to part.

Well this is the end of a perfect day,
Near the end of a journey too,
But it leaves a thought that is big and strong,
With a wish that is kind and true,
For mem'ry has painted this perfect day
With colors that never fade,
And we find at the end of a perfect day,
The soul of a friend we've made.

* * *

HAPPINESS

Happy the man, and happy he alone,
He who can call to-day his own;
He who, secure within, can say,
Tomorrow, do thy worst, for I have liv'd today.
(From Dryden's Imitation of Horace)

THE SPIRES OF OXFORD

(SEEN FROM THE TRAIN)

Winifred M. Letts

I saw the spires of Oxford
  As I was passing by,
The gray spires of Oxford
  Against a pearl-gray sky,
My heart was with the Oxford men
  Who went abroad to die.

The years go fast in Oxford
  The golden years and gay,
The hoary Colleges look down
  On careless boys at play.
But when the bugles sounded war
  They put their games away.

They left the peaceful river,
  The cricket field, the quad,
The shaven lawns of Oxford
  To seek a bloody sod—
They gave their merry youth away
  For country and for God.

God rest you, happy gentlemen,
  Who laid your good lives down,
Who took the khaki and the gun
  Instead of cap and gown.
God bring you to a fairer place
  Than even Oxford town.

ST. PAUL ON CHARITY

Holy Bible, I Corinthians 13

1 Though I speak with the tongues of men and of angels, and have not charity, I am become as sounding brass, or a tinkling cymbal.

2 And though I have the gift of prophecy, and understand all mysteries, and all knowledge; and though I have all faith, so that I could remove mountains, and have not charity, I am nothing.

3 And though I bestow all my goods to feed the poor, and though I give my body to be burned, and have not charity, it profiteth me nothing.

4 Charity suffereth long, and is kind; charity envieth not; charity vaunteth not itself, is not puffed up.

5 Doth not behave itself unseemly, seeketh not her own, is not easily provoked, thinketh no evil;

6 Rejoiceth not in iniquity, but rejoiceth in the truth.

7 Beareth all things, believeth all things, hopeth all things, endureth all things.

8 Charity never faileth: but whether there be prophecies, they shall fail; whether there be tongues, they shall cease; whether there be knowledge, it shall vanish away.

9 For we know in part, and we prophesy in part.

10 But when that which is perfect is come, then that which is in part shall be done away.

11 When I was a child, I spake as a child, I understood as a child, I thought as a child; but when I became a man, I put away childish things.

12 For now we see through a glass, darkly; but then face to face: now I know in part; but then shall I know even as also I am known.

13 And now abideth faith, hope, charity, these three; but the greatest of these is charity.

ODE ON A GRECIAN URN

John Keats

Thou still unravish'd bride of quietness,
  Thou foster-child of silence and slow time,
Sylvan historian, who canst thus express
  A flowery tale more sweetly than our rhyme:
What leaf-fring'd legend haunts about thy shape
    Of deities or mortals, or of both,
      In Tempe or the dales of Arcady?
What men or gods are these? What maidens loth?
    What mad pursuit? What struggle to escape?
      What pipes and timbrels? What wild ecstasy?

Heard melodies are sweet, but those unheard
  Are sweeter; therefore, ye soft pipes, play on;

Not to the sensual ear, but, more endear'd,
  Pipe to the spirit ditties of no tone:
Fair youth, beneath the trees, thou canst not leave
  Thy song, nor ever can those trees be bare;
    Bold Lover, never, never canst thou kiss
Though winning near the goal—yet, do not grieve;
  She cannot fade, though thou hast not thy bliss,
    For ever wilt thou love, and she be fair!

Ah, happy, happy boughs! that cannot shed
  Your leaves, nor ever bid the Spring adieu;
And, happy melodist, unwearied,
  For ever piping songs for ever new;
    More happy love! more happy, happy love!
For ever warm and still to be enjoy'd,
  For ever panting, and for ever young;
All breathing human passion far above,
  That leaves a heart high-sorrowful and cloy'd,
    A burning forehead, and a parching tongue.

Who are these coming to the sacrifice?
  To what green altar, O mysterious priest,
Lead'st thou that heifer lowing at the skies,
  And all her silken flanks with garlands dressed?
What little town by river or sea shore,
  Or mountain-built with peaceful citadel,
    Is emptied of this folk, this pious morn?
And, little town, thy streets for evermore
  Will silent be; and not a soul to tell
    Why thou art desolate, can e'er return.

O Attic shape! Fair attitude! with brede
  Of marble men and maidens overwrought,
With forest branches and the trodden weed;
  Thou, silent form, dost tease us out of thought
As doth eternity: Cold Pastoral!
  When old age shall this generation waste,
    Thou shalt remain, in midst of other woe
Than ours, a friend to man, to whom thou say'st,
  "Beauty is truth, truth beauty,"—that is all
    Ye know on earth, and all ye need to know.

* * *

Everyone is as God made him and oftentimes a good deal worse.
                                —Cervantes

THE TIGER

William Blake

Tiger! Tiger! burning bright
In the forests of the night,
What immortal hand or eye
Could frame thy fearful symmetry?

In what distant deeps or skies
Burnt the fire of thine eyes?
On what wings dare he aspire?
What the hand dare seize the fire?

And what shoulder, and what art,
Could twist the sinews of thy heart?
And when thy heart began to beat,
What dread hand? and what dread feet?

What the hammer? what the chain?
In what furnace was thy brain?
What the anvil? what dread grasp
Dare its deadly terrors clasp?

When the stars threw down their spears,
And watered heaven with their tears,
Did he smile his work to see?
Did he who made the Lamb make thee?

Tiger! Tiger! burning bright
In the forests of the night,
What immortal hand or eye
Dare frame thy fearful symmetry?

OTHELLO'S DEFENSE

William Shakespeare

Her father loved me; oft invited me;
Still question'd me the story of my life,
From year to year, the battles, sieges, fortunes,
That I have pass'd.
I ran it through, even from my boyish days,

To the very moment that he bade me tell it;
Wherein I spake of most disastrous chances,
Of moving accidents by flood and field,
Of hair-breadth scapes i' the imminent deadly breach,
Of being taken by the insolent foe
And sold to slavery, of my redemption thence
And portance in my travels' history:
Wherein of antres vast and deserts idle,
Rough quarries, rocks and hills whose heads touch heaven,
It was my hint to speak,—such was the process;
And of the Cannibals that each other eat,
The Anthropophagi and men whose heads
Do grow beneath their shoulders. This to hear
Would Desdemona seriously incline:
But still the house-affairs would draw her thence:
Which ever as she could with haste dispatch,
She'ld come again, and with a greedy ear
Devour up my discourse: which I observing,
Took once a pliant hour, and found good means
To draw from her a prayer of earnest heart
That I would all my pilgrimage dilate,
Whereof by parcels she had something heard,
But not intentively: I did consent,
And often did beguile her of her tears,
When I did speak of some distressful stroke
That my youth suffer'd. My story being done,
She gave me for my pains a world of sighs:
She swore, in faith, 'twas strange, 'twas passing strange,
'Twas pitiful, 'twas wondrous pitiful:
She wish'd she had not heard it, yet she wish'd
That heaven had made her such a man: she thank'd me,
And bade me, if I had a friend that loved her,
I should but teach him how to tell my story,
And that would woo her. Upon this hint I spake:
She loved me for the dangers I had pass'd,
And I loved her that she did pity them.
This only is the witchcraft I have used.

(From Othello)

* * *

Beware the fury of a patient man.
—Dryden

AN ENGLISH PLEA FOR PEACE WITH THE AMERICAN COLONIES

William Pitt

My Lords, this ruinous and ignominious situation, where we cannot act with success nor suffer with honour, calls upon us to remonstrate in the strongest and loudest language of truth, to rescue the ear of Majesty from the delusions which surround it. You cannot, I venture to say, you CANNOT conquer America. What is your present situation there? We do not know the worst; but we know that in three campaigns we have done nothing and suffered much. You may swell every expense, and strain every effort, still more extravagantly; accumulate every assistance you can beg or borrow; traffic and barter with every pitiful German Prince, that sells and sends his subjects to the shambles of a foreign country: your efforts are forever vain and impotent—doubly so from this mercenary aid on which you rely; for it irritates to an incurable resentment the minds of your enemies, to overrun them with the sordid sons of rapine and of plunder, devoting them and their possessions to the rapacity of hireling cruelty! If I were an American, as I am an Englishman, while a foreign troop was landed in my country, I never would lay down my arms!—never! never! never!

November 18, 1777

SWEET AND LOW

Alfred, Lord Tennyson

Sweet and low, sweet and low,
 Wind of the western sea,
Low, low, breathe and blow,
 Wind of the western sea!
Over the rolling waters go,
Come from the dying moon, and blow,
 Blow him again to me;
While my little one, while my pretty one, sleeps.

Sleep and rest, sleep and rest,
 Father will come to thee soon;
Rest, rest, on mother's breast,
 Father will come to thee soon;

Father will come to his babe in the nest,
Silver sails all out of the west
        Under the silver moon:
Sleep, my little one, sleep, my pretty one, sleep.

THE SOLDIER

Rupert Brooke

If I should die, think only this of me:
That there's some corner of a foreign field
That is forever England. There shall be
In that rich earth a richer dust concealed;
A dust whom England bore, shaped, made aware,
Gave, once, her flowers to love, her ways to roam;
A body of England's, breathing English air,
Washed by the rivers, blest by suns of home.
And think, this heart, all evil shed away,
A pulse in the eternal mind, no less
Gives somewhere back the thoughts by England given;
Her sights and sounds; dreams happy as her day;
And laughter, learnt of friends, and gentleness,
In hearts at peace, under an English heaven.

HELPING THE HANDICAPPED

Emily Dickinson

If I can stop one heart from breaking,
I shall not live in vain;
If I can ease one life the aching
Or cool one pain,
Or help one fainting robin
Into its nest again,
I shall not live in vain.

HOME DEFINED

Home is the place where, when you have to go there,
They have to take you in.
        (From Robert Frost's The Death of the Hired Man)

REQUIEM

Robert Louis Stevenson

Under the wide and starry sky
Dig the grave and let me lie.
Glad did I live and gladly die,
And I laid me down with a will.

This be the verse that you grave for me:
Here he lies where he longed to be,
Home is the sailor, home from the sea,
And the hunter home from the hill.

GOOD AND BAD CHILDREN

Robert Louis Stevenson

Children, you are very little,
And your bones are very brittle;
If you would grow great and stately,
You must try to walk sedately.

You must still be bright and quiet,
And content with simple diet;
And remain, through all bewild'ring,
Innocent and honest children.

Happy hearts and happy faces,
Happy play in grassy places—
That was how, in ancient ages,
Children grew to kings and sages.

But the unkind and the unruly,
And the sort who eat unduly,
They must never hope for glory—
Theirs is quite a different story!

Cruel children, crying babies,
All grow up as geese and gabies,
Hated, as their age increases,
By their nephews and their nieces.

647

TROUBLE

David Keppel

Better never trouble Trouble
Until Trouble troubles you;
For you only make your trouble
Double-trouble when you do;
And the trouble—like a bubble—
That you're troubling about,
May be nothing but a cipher
With its rim rubbed out.

SWEET AFTON

Robert Burns

Flow gently, sweet Afton! among thy green braes,
Flow gently, I'll sing thee a song in thy praise;
My Mary's asleep by thy murmuring stream,
Flow gently, sweet Afton, disturb not her dream.

Thou stock-dove whose echo resounds thro' the glen,
Ye wild whistling blackbirds in yon thorny den,
Thou green crested lapwing, thy screaming forbear,
I charge you, disturb not my slumbering Fair.

How lofty, sweet Afton, thy neighbouring hills,
Far mark'd with the courses of clear, winding rills;
There daily I wander as noon rises high,
My flocks and my Mary's sweet cot in my eye.

How pleasant thy banks and green valleys below,
Where, wild in the woodlands, the primroses blow;
There oft, as mild ev'ning weeps over the lea,
The sweet-scented birk shades my Mary and me.

Thy crystal stream, Afton, how lovely it glides,
And winds by the cot where my Mary resides;
How wanton thy waters her snowy feet lave,
As, gathering sweet flowerets, she stems thy clear wave.

Flow gently, sweet Afton, among thy green braes,
Flow gently, sweet river, the theme of my lays;
My Mary's asleep by thy murmuring stream,
Flow gently, sweet Afton, disturb not her dream.

THE BARREL-ORGAN

Alfred Noyes

There's a barrel-organ caroling across a golden street
  In the City as the sun sinks low;
And the music's not immortal; but the world has made it sweet
  And fulfilled it with the sunset glow;
And it pulses through the pleasures of the City and the pain
  That surround the singing organ like a large eternal light;
And they've given it a glory and a part to play again
  In the Symphony that rules the day and night.
And now it's marching onward through the realms of old romance,
  And trolling out a fond familiar tune,
And now it's roaring cannon down to fight the King of France,
  And now it's prattling softly to the moon.
And all around the organ there's a sea without a shore
  Of human joys and wonders and regrets;
To remember and to recompense the music evermore
  For what the cold machinery forgets . . .

    Yes; as the music changes,
      Like a prismatic glass,
    It takes the light and ranges
      Through all the moods that pass:
    Dissects the common carnival
      Of passions and regrets,
    And gives the world a glimpse of all
      The colors it forgets.

    And there *La Traviata* sighs
      Another sadder song;
    And there *Il Trovatore* cries
      A tale of deeper wrong;
    And bolder knights to battle go
      With sword and shield and lance,
    Than ever here on earth below
      Have whirled into—a dance!—

Go down to Kew in lilac-time, in lilac-time, in lilac-time;
  Go down to Kew in lilac-time (it isn't far from London!)
And you shall wander hand in hand with love in summer's wonder
    land;
  Go down to Kew in lilac-time (it isn't far from London!)

The cherry-trees are seas of bloom and soft perfume and sweet
    perfume,
  The cherry-trees are seas of bloom (and oh, so near to London!)
And there they say, when dawn is high and all the world's a blaze
    of sky
  The cuckoo, though he's very shy, will sing a song for London.

The nightingale is rather rare and yet they say you'll hear him there
  At Kew, at Kew in lilac-time (and oh, so near to London!)
The linnet and the throstle, too, and after dark the long halloo
  And golden-eyed *tu-whit, tu-whoo* of owls that ogle London.

For Noah hardly knew a bird of any kind that isn't heard
  At Kew, at Kew in lilac-time (and oh, so near to London!)
And when the rose begins to pout and all the chestnut spires are out
  You'll hear the rest without a doubt, all chorusing for London:—

Come down to Kew in lilac-time, in lilac-time, in lilac-time;
  Come down to Kew in lilac-time (it isn't far from London!)
And you shall wander hand in hand with love in summer's wonder-
    land;
  Come down to Kew in lilac-time (it isn't far from London!)

And then the troubadour begins to thrill the golden street,
  In the City as the sun sinks low;
And in all the gaudy busses there are scores of weary feet
Marking time, sweet time, with a dull mechanic beat,
And a thousand hearts are plunging to a love they'll never meet,
Through the meadows of the sunset, through the poppies and the
    wheat,
  In the land where the dead dreams go.

Verdi, Verdi, when you wrote *Il Trovatore* did you dream
  Of the City when the sun sinks low,
Of the organ and the monkey and the many-colored stream
On the Piccadilly pavement, of the myriad eyes that seem
To be litten for a moment with a wild Italian gleam
As *A che la morte* parodies the world's eternal theme
  And pulses with the sunset-glow?

There's a thief, perhaps, that listens with a face of frozen stone
   In the City as the sun sinks low;
There's a portly man of business with a balance of his own,
There's a clerk and there's a butcher of a soft reposeful tone,
And they're all of them returning to the heavens they have known:
They are crammed and jammed in busses and—they're each of
      them alone
   In the land where the dead dreams go.

There's a laborer that listens to the voices of the dead
   In the City as the sun sinks low;
And his hand begins to tremble and his face is rather red
As he sees a loafer watching him and—there he turns his head
And stares into the sunset where his April love is fled,
For he hears her softly singing and his lonely soul is led
   Through the land where the dead dreams go . . .

There's a barrel-organ caroling across a golden street
   In the City as the sun sinks low;
Though the music's only Verdi there's a world to make it sweet
Just as yonder yellow sunset where the earth and heaven meet
Mellows all the sooty City! Hark, a hundred thousand feet
Are marching on to glory through the poppies and the wheat
   In the land where the dead dreams go.

            So it's Jeremiah, Jeremiah,
               What have you to say
            When you meet the garland girls
               Tripping on their way?
            All around my gala hat
               I wear a wreath of roses
            (A long and lonely year it is
               I've waited for the May!)
            If any one should ask you,
               The reason why I wear it is—
            My own love, my true love, is coming
               home today.

And it's buy a bunch of violets for the lady
   (*It's lilac-time in London; it's lilac-time in London!*)
Buy a bunch of violets for the lady;
   While the sky burns blue above:

651

On the other side the street you'll find it shady
   (It's lilac-time in London; it's lilac-time in London!)
But buy a bunch of violets for the lady,
   And tell her she's your own true love.

There's a barrel-organ caroling across a golden street
   In the City as the sun sinks glittering and slow;
And the music's not immortal; but the world has made it sweet
And enriched it with the harmonies that make a song complete
In the deeper heavens of music where the night and morning meet,
   As it dies into the sunset glow;
And it pulses through the pleasures of the City and the pain
   That surround the singing organ like a large eternal light,
And they've given it a glory and a part to play again
   In the Symphony that rules the day and night.

      And there, as the music changes,
         The song runs round again;
      Once more it turns and ranges
         Through all its joy and pain:
      Dissects the common carnival
         Of passions and regrets;
      And the wheeling world remembers all
         The wheeling song forgets.

      Once more *La Traviata* sighs
         Another sadder song:
      Once more *Il Trovatore* cries
         A tale of deeper wrong;
      Once more the knights to battle go
         With sword and shield and lance
      Till once, once more, the shattered foe
         Has whirled into—a dance!

Come down to Kew in lilac-time, in lilac-time, in lilac-time;
   Come down to Kew in lilac-time (it isn't far from London!)
And you shall wander hand in hand with Love in summer's wonder-
   land,
Come down to Kew in lilac-time (it isn't far from London!)

             *   *   *

   Forty is the old age of youth, fifty is the youth of old age.
                                —Victor Hugo

PERFECT WOMAN

William Wordsworth

She was a Phantom of delight
When first she gleamed upon my sight;
A lovely Apparition sent
To be a moment's ornament;
Her eyes as stars of Twilight fair;
Like Twilight's, too, her dusky hair;
But all things else about her drawn
From May-time and the cheerful Dawn;
A dancing Shape, an Image gay,
To haunt, to startle, and way-lay.

I saw her upon nearer view,
A Spirit, yet a Woman too!
Her household motions light and free,
And steps of virgin-liberty;
A countenance in which did meet
Sweet records, promises as sweet;
A Creature not too bright or good
For human nature's daily food;
For transient sorrows, simple wiles,
Praise, blame, love, kisses, tears and smiles.

And now I see with eye serene
The very pulse of the machine;
A Being breathing thoughtful breath,
A Traveler between life and death;
The reason firm, the temperate will,
Endurance, foresight, strength, and skill;
A perfect Woman, nobly planned,
To warn, to comfort, and command;
And yet a Spirit still, and bright
With something of angelic light.

BENJAMIN FRANKLIN

He snatched the lightning from heaven, and the sceptre from
tyrants.

(Turgot's inscription on Houdon's bust)

FOUR THINGS

Henry Van Dyke

Four things a man must learn to do
If he would make his record true:
To think without confusion clearly;
To love his fellow man sincerely;
To act from honest motives purely;
To trust in God and Heaven securely.

THE NIGHT HAS A THOUSAND EYES

F. W. Bourdillon

The night has a thousand eyes,
And the day but one;
Yet the light of the bright world dies
With the dying sun.

The mind has a thousand eyes,
And the heart but one;
Yet the light of a whole life dies
When love is done.

THE CHILDREN'S HOUR

Henry Wadsworth Longfellow

Between the dark and the daylight,
When the night is beginning to lower,
Comes a pause in the day's occupations,
That is known as the Children's Hour.

I hear in the chamber above me
The patter of little feet,
The sound of a door that is opened,
And voices soft and sweet.

From my study I see in the lamplight,
Descending the broad hall stair,
Grave Alice, and laughing Allegra,
And Edith with golden hair.

A whisper, and then a silence:
  Yet I know by their merry eyes
They are plotting and planning together
  To take me by surprise.

A sudden rush from the stairway,
  A sudden raid from the hall!
By three doors left unguarded
  They enter my castle wall!

They climb up into my turret
  O'er the arms and back of my chair;
If I try to escape, they surround me;
  They seem to be everywhere.

They almost devour me with kisses,
  Their arms about me entwine,
Till I think of the Bishop of Bingen
  In his Mouse-Tower on the Rhine!

Do you think, O blue-eyed banditti,
  Because you have scaled the wall,
Such an old mustache as I am
  Is not a match for you all!

I have you fast in my fortress,
  And will not let you depart,
But put you down into the dungeon
  In the round-tower of my heart.

And there will I keep you forever,
  Yes, forever and a day,
Till the walls shall crumble to ruin,
  And moulder in dust away!

SONG TO CELIA

Ben Jonson

Drink to me only with thine eyes,
  And I will pledge with mine;
Or leave a kiss but in the cup,
  And I'll not look for wine.

The thirst that from the soul doth rise
   Doth ask a drink divine;
But might I of Jove's nectar sup,
   I would not change for thine.

I sent thee late a rosy wreath,
   Not so much honoring thee
As giving it a hope, that there
   It could not withered be.
But thou thereon didst only breathe,
   And sent'st it back to me;
Since when it grows, and smells, I swear,
   Not of itself, but thee.

IF—

Rudyard Kipling

If you can keep your head when all about you
Are losing theirs and blaming it on you;
If you can trust yourself when all men doubt you,
But make allowance for their doubting too;
If you can wait and not be tired by waiting,
Or being lied about, don't deal in lies,
Or, being hated, don't give way to hating,
And yet don't look too good, nor talk too wise;

If you can dream—and not make dreams your master;
If you can think—and not make thoughts your aim;
If you can meet with triumph and disaster
And treat those two impostors just the same;
If you can bear to hear the truth you've spoken
Twisted by knaves to make a trap for fools,
Or watch the things you gave your life to, broken,
And stoop and build 'em up with wornout tools;

If you can make one heap of all your winnings
And risk it on one turn of pitch-and-toss,
And lose, and start again at your beginnings
And never breathe a word about your loss;

If you can force your heart and nerve and sinew
To serve your turn long after they are gone,
And so hold on when there is nothing in you
Except the Will which says to them: "Hold on";

If you can talk with crowds and keep your virtue,
Or walk with kings—nor lose the common touch;
If neither foes nor loving friends can hurt you;
If all men count with you, but none too much;
If you can fill the unforgiving minute
With sixty-seconds' worth of distance run—
Yours is the Earth and everything that's in it,
And—which is more—you'll be a Man, my son!

LIGHT SHINING OUT OF DARKNESS

William Cowper

God moves in a mysterious way
    His wonders to perform;
He plants his footsteps in the sea,
    And rides upon the storm.

Deep in unfathomable mines
    Of never-failing skill
He treasures up his bright designs,
    And works his sovereign will.

Ye fearful saints, fresh courage take!
    The clouds ye so much dread
Are big with mercy, and shall break
    In blessings on your head.

Judge not the Lord by feeble sense,
    But trust him for his grace;
Behind a frowning providence
    He hides a smiling face.

His purposes will ripen fast,
    Unfolding every hour;
The bud may have a bitter taste,
    But sweet will be the flower.

Blind unbelief is sure to err,
And scan his work in vain;
God is his own interpreter,
And he will make it plain.

FIRST IN WAR—FIRST IN PEACE

Henry Lee

First in war—first in peace—and first in the hearts of his countrymen, he was second to none in the humble and endearing scenes of private life; pious, just, humane, temperate and sincere; uniform, dignified and commanding, his example was as edifying to all around him, as were the effects of that example lasting.

To his equals he was condescending, to his inferiors kind, and to the dear object of his affections exemplarily tender; correct throughout, vice shuddered in his presence, and virtue always felt his fostering hand; the purity of his private character gave effulgence to his public virtues.

His last scene comported with the whole tenor of his life—although in extreme pain, not a sigh, not a groan escaped him; and with undisturbed serenity he closed his well-spent life. Such was the man America has lost—such was the man for whom our nation mourns.

Methinks I see his august image, and I hear falling from his venerable lips these deep-sinking words:

"Cease, Sons of America, lamenting our separation; go on, and confirm by your wisdom the fruits of our joint councils, joint efforts, and common dangers; reverence religion, diffuse knowledge throughout your land, patronize the arts and sciences; let Liberty and Order be inseparable companions. Control party spirit, the bane of free governments; observe good faith to, and cultivate peace with all nations, shut up every avenue to foreign influence, contract rather than extend national connection, rely on ourselves only: be Americans in thought, word, and deed;—thus will you give immortality to that union which was the constant object of my terrestrial labors; thus will you preserve undisturbed to the latest posterity the felicity of a people to me most dear, and thus will you supply (if my happiness is now aught to you) the only vacancy in the round of pure bliss high Heaven bestows."

(Funeral oration in honor of George Washington)

A DUTCH LULLABY

Eugene Field

Wynken, Blynken, and Nod one night
  Sailed off in a wooden shoe,—
Sailed on a river of crystal light
  Into a sea of dew.
"Where are you going, and what do you wish?"
  The old moon asked the three.
"We have come to fish for the herring fish
  That live in this beautiful sea;
  Nets of silver and gold have we!"
      Said Wynken,
      Blynken,
      And Nod.

The old moon laughed and sang a song,
  As they rocked in the wooden shoe;
And the wind that sped them all night long
  Ruffled the waves of dew.
The little stars were the herring fish
  That lived in that beautiful sea—
"Now cast your nets wherever you wish,—
  Never afeared are we!"
So cried the stars to the fishermen three,
      Wynken,
      Blynken,
      And Nod.

All night long their nets they threw
  To the stars in the twinkling foam,—
Then down from the skies came the wooden shoe,
  Bringing the fishermen home:
'Twas all so pretty a sail, it seemed
  As if it could not be;
And some folk thought 'twas a dream they'd dreamed
  Of sailing that beautiful sea;
  But I shall name you the fishermen three:
      Wynken,
      Blynken,
      And Nod.

Wynken and Blynken are two little eyes,
  And Nod is a little head,
And the wooden shoe that sailed the skies
  Is a wee one's trundle-bed;
So shut your eyes while Mother sings
  Of wonderful sights that be,
And you shall see the beautiful things
  As you rock in the misty sea
  Where the old shoe rocked the fishermen three:-
    Wynken,
    Blynken,
    And Nod.

IN THE GLOAMING

Meta Orred

In the gloaming, oh, my darling,
When the lights are dim and low,
And the quiet shadows falling,
Softly come, and softly go;
When the winds are sobbing faintly,
With a gentle, unknown woe;
Will you think of me and love me.
As you did once long ago?

In the gloaming, oh, my darling,
Think not bitterly of me.
Tho' I passed away in silence,
Left you lonely, set you free;
For my heart was crushed with longing,
What had been could never be;
It was best to leave you thus, dear,
Best for you and best for me.
It was best to leave you thus,
Best for you and best for me.

* * *

A man always has two reasons for doing anything—a good
reason and the real reason.
                             —J. P. Morgan

THE SONG OF THE SHIRT

Thomas Hood

With fingers weary and worn,
   With eyelids heavy and red,
A woman sat, in unwomanly rags,
   Plying her needle and thread—
Stitch! stitch! stitch!
   In poverty, hunger, and dirt,
And still with a voice of dolorous pitch
   She sang the 'Song of the Shirt.'

'Work! work! work!
   While the cock is crowing aloof!
And work—work—work,
   Till the stars shine through the roof!
It's Oh! to be a slave
   Along with the barbarous Turk,
Where woman has never a soul to save,
   If this is Christian work.

'Work—work—work,
   Till the brain begins to swim;
Work—work—work,
   Till the eyes are heavy and dim!
Seam, and gusset, and band,
   Band, and gusset, and seam,
Till over the buttons I fall asleep,
   And sew them on in a dream!

'Oh, Men, with Sisters dear!
   Oh, Men, with Mothers and Wives!
It is not linen you're wearing out
   But human creatures' lives!
Stitch—stitch—stitch,
   In poverty, hunger, and dirt,
Sewing at once, with a double thread,
   A Shroud as well as a Shirt.

'But why do I talk of Death?
   That Phantom of grisly bone,
I hardly fear its terrible shape,
   It seems so like my own—

It seems so like my own,
    Because of the fasts I keep;
Oh, God, that bread should be so dear,
    And flesh and blood so cheap!

'Work—work—work!
    My labor never flags;
And what are its wages? A bed of straw,
    A crust of bread—and rags.
That shattered roof—this naked floor—
    A table—a broken chair—
And a wall so blank, my shadow I thank
    For sometimes falling there!

'Work—work—work!
    From weary chime to chime,
Work—work—work,
    As prisoners work for crime!
Band, and gusset, and seam,
    Seam, and gusset, and band,
Till the heart is sick, and the brain benumbed,
    As well as the weary hand.

'Work—work—work,
    In the dull December light,
And work—work—work,
    When the weather is warm and bright—
While underneath the eaves
    The brooding swallows cling
As if to show me their sunny backs
    And twit me with the spring.

'Oh! but to breathe the breath
    Of the cowslip and primrose sweet—
With the sky above my head,
    And the grass beneath my feet;
For only one short hour
    To feel as I used to feel,
Before I knew the woes of want
    And the walk that costs a meal.

'Oh! but for one short hour!
    A respite however brief!
No blessèd leisure for Love or Hope,
    But only time for Grief!

A little weeping would ease my heart,
    But in their briny bed
My tears must stop, for every drop
    Hinders needle and thread!'

With fingers weary and worn,
    With eyelids heavy and red,
A woman sat, in unwomanly rags,
    Plying her needle and thread—
Stitch! stitch! stitch!
    In poverty, hunger, and dirt,
And still with a voice of dolorous pitch,—
Would that its tone could reach the Rich!—
She sang this 'Song of the Shirt!'

A CHILD'S PRAYER

John Bannister Tabb

Make me, dear Lord, polite and kind
To every one, I pray.
And may I ask you how you find
Yourself, dear Lord, today?

MERCUTIO'S QUEEN MAB SPEECH

William Shakespeare

O, then, I see Queen Mab hath been with you.
She is the fairies' midwife, and she comes
In shape no bigger than an agate-stone
On the fore-finger of an alderman,
Drawn with a team of little atomies
Athwart men's noses as they lie asleep;
Her waggon-spokes made of long spinners' legs,
The cover of the wings of grasshoppers,
The traces of the smallest spider's web,
The collars of the moonshine's watery beams,
Her whip of cricket's bone, the lash of film,
Her waggoner a small grey-coated gnat,
Not half so big as a round little worm

Prick'd from the lazy finger of a maid;
Her chariot is an empty hazel-nut
Made by the joiner squirrel or old grub,
Time out o' mind the fairies' coachmakers.
And in this state she gallops night by night
Through lovers' brains, and then they dream of love;
O'er courtiers' knees, that dream on court'sies straight,
O'er lawyers' fingers, who straight dream on fees,
O'er ladies' lips, who straight on kisses dream,
Which oft the angry Mab with blisters plagues,
Because their breaths with sweetmeats tainted are:
Sometimes she gallops o'er a courtier's nose,
And then dreams he of smelling out a suit;
And sometimes comes she with a tithe-pig's tail
Tickling a parson's nose as a' lies asleep,
Then dreams he of another benefice:
Sometimes she driveth o'er a soldier's neck,
And then dreams he of cutting foreign throats,
Of breaches, ambuscadoes, Spanish blades,
Of healths five-fathom deep; and then anon
Drums in his ear, at which he starts and wakes,
And being thus frighted swears a prayer or two
And sleeps again. This is that very Mab
That plats the manes of horses in the night,
And bakes the elf-locks in foul sluttish hairs,
Which once untangled much misfortune bodes.

(From Romeo and Juliet)

THE OX AND THE FROG

An Ox, grazing in a meadow, chanced to set his foot among a parcel of young Frogs, and trod one of them to death. The rest informed their mother, when she came home, what had happened; telling her, that the beast which did it was the hugest creature that they ever saw in their lives. "What, was it so big?" says the old Frog, swelling and blowing up her speckled belly to a great degree. "Oh! bigger by a vast deal," say they. "And so big?" says she, straining herself yet more. "Indeed, mama," say they, "if you were to burst yourself, you would never be so big." She strove yet again, and burst herself indeed.

(From Aesop's Fables)

664

A LETTER TO LORD CHESTERFIELD

February 7, 1755.

To the Right Honourable the Earl of Chesterfield.

My Lord,

I have been lately informed, by the proprietor of the World, that two papers, in which my Dictionary is recommended to the publick, were written by your Lordship. To be so distinguished, is an honour, which, being very little accustomed to favours from the great, I know not well how to receive, or in what terms to acknowledge.

When, upon some slight encouragement, I first visited your Lordship, I was overpowered, like the rest of mankind, by the enchantment of your address; and could not forbear to wish that I might boast myself *Le vainqueur du vainqueur de la terre;*—that I might obtain that regard for which I saw the world contending; but I found my attendance so little encouraged, that neither pride nor modesty would suffer me to continue it. When I had once addressed your Lordship in publick, I had exhausted all the art of pleasing which a retired and uncourtly scholar can possess. I had done all that I could; and no man is well pleased to have his all neglected, be it ever so little.

Seven years, my Lord, have now past, since I waited in your outward rooms, or was repulsed from your door; during which time I have been pushing on my work through difficulties, of which it is useless to complain, and have brought it, at last, to the verge of publication, without one act of assistance, one word of encouragement, or one smile of favour. Such treatment I did not expect, for I never had a Patron before.

The shepherd in Virgil grew at last acquainted with Love, and found him a native of the rocks.

Is not a Patron, my Lord, one who looks with unconcern on a man struggling for life in the water, and, when he has reached the ground, encumbers him with help? The notice which you have been pleased to take of my labours, had it been early, had been kind; but it has been delayed till I am indifferent, and cannot enjoy it; till I am solitary, and cannot impart it; till I am known, and do not want it. I hope it is no very cynical asperity not to confess obligations where no benefit has been received, or to be unwilling that the publick should consider me as owing that to a Patron, which Providence has enabled me to do for myself.

Having carried on my work thus far with so little obligation to any favourer of learning, I shall not be disappointed though I should conclude it, if less be possible, with less; for I have been long awakened from that dream of hope, in which I once boasted myself with so much exultation,

My Lord,
Your Lordship's most humble,
Most obedient servant,
S. Johnson.

I HAVE A RENDEZVOUS WITH DEATH

Alan Seeger

I have a rendezvous with Death
At some disputed barricade,
When Spring comes back with rustling shade
And apple-blossoms fill the air—
I have a rendezvous with Death
When Spring brings back blue days and fair.

It may be he shall take my hand
And lead me into his dark land
And close my eyes and quench my breath—
It may be I shall pass him still.
I have a rendezvous with Death
On some scarred slope of battered hill,
When Spring comes round again this year
And the first meadow-flowers appear.

God knows 'twere better to be deep
Pillowed in silk and scented down,
Where love throbs out in blissful sleep,
Pulse nigh to pulse, and breath to breath,
Where hushed awakenings are dear . . .
But I've a rendezvous with Death
At midnight in some flaming town,
When Spring trips north again this year,
And I to my pledged word am true,
I shall not fail that rendezvous.

* * *

All that I am or ever hope to be, I owe to my sainted mother.
—Abraham Lincoln

THE SWING

Robert Louis Stevenson

How do you like to go up in a swing,
    Up in the air so blue?
Oh, I do think it the pleasantest thing
    Ever a child can do!

Up in the air and over the wall,
    Till I can see so wide,
Rivers and trees and cattle and all
    Over the countryside—

Till I look down on the garden green,
    Down on the roof so brown—
Up in the air I go flying again,
    Up in the air and down!

MY HEART LEAPS UP WHEN I BEHOLD

William Wordsworth

My heart leaps up when I behold
A rainbow in the sky:
So was it when my life began;
So is it now I am a man;
So be it when I shall grow old,
Or let me die!
The Child is father of the Man;
And I could wish my days to be
Bound each to each by natural piety.

THE LAST JUDGMENT

Holy Bible, Revelation 20:11–15; 21:1–7

20

11 And I saw a great white throne, and him that sat on it, from whose face the earth and the heaven fled away; and there was found no place for them.

12 And I saw the dead, small and great, stand before God; and

the books were opened: and another book was opened, which is the book of life: and the dead were judged out of those things which were written in the books, according to their works.

13 And the sea gave up the dead which were in it; and death and hell delivered up the dead which were in them: and they were judged every man according to their works.

14 And death and hell were cast into the lake of fire. This is the second death.

15 And whosoever was not found written in the book of life was cast into the lake of fire.

21

1 And I saw a new heaven and a new earth: for the first heaven and the first earth were passed away; and there was no more sea.

2 And I John saw the holy city, new Jerusalem, coming down from God out of heaven, prepared as a bride adorned for her husband.

3 And I heard a great voice out of heaven saying, Behold, the tabernacle of God is with men, and he will dwell with them, and they shall be his people, and God himself shall be with them, and be their God.

4 And God shall wipe away all tears from their eyes; and there shall be no more death, neither sorrow, nor crying, neither shall there be any more pain: for the former things are passed away.

5 And he that sat upon the throne said, Behold, I make all things new. And he said unto me, Write: for these words are true and faithful.

6 And he said unto me, It is done. I am Alpha and Omega, the beginning and the end. I will give unto him that is athirst of the fountain of the water of life freely.

7 He that overcometh shall inherit all things; and I will be his God, and he shall be my son.

* * *

To err is human, to forgive divine.

* * *

The bookful blockhead, ignorantly read,
With loads of learned lumber in his head.

* * *

For fools rush in where angels fear to tread.
(From Pope's Essay on Criticism)

ULALUME

Edgar Allan Poe

The skies they were ashen and sober;
  The leaves they were crispèd and sere,
  The leaves they were withering and sere;
It was night in the lonesome October
  Of my most immemorial year;
It was hard by the dim lake of Auber,
  In the misty mid region of Weir:
It was down by the dank tarn of Auber,
  In the ghoul-haunted woodland of Weir.

Here once, through an alley Titanic
  Of cypress, I roamed with my Soul—
  Of cypress, with Psyche, my Soul.
These were days when my heart was volcanic
  As the scoriac rivers that roll,
  As the lavas that restlessly roll
Their sulphurous currents down Yaanek
  In the ultimate climes of the pole,
That groan as they roll down Mount Yaanek
  In the realms of the boreal pole.

Our talk had been serious and sober,
  But our thoughts they were palsied and sere,
  Our memories were treacherous and sere,
For we knew not the month was October,
  And we marked not the night of the year,
  (Ah, night of all nights in the year!)
We noted not the dim lake of Auber
  (Though once we had journeyed down here),
Remembered not the dank tarn of Auber
  Nor the ghoul-haunted woodland of Weir.

And now, as the night was senescent
  And star-dials pointed to morn,
  As the star-dials hinted of morn,
At the end of our path a liquescent
  And nebulous lustre was born,

Out of which a miraculous crescent
　　Arose with a duplicate horn,
Astarte's bediamonded crescent
　　Distinct with its duplicate horn.

And I said—"She is warmer than Dian:
　　She rolls through an ether of sighs,
　　She revels in a region of sighs:
She has seen that the tears are not dry on
　　These cheeks, where the worm never dies,
And has come past the stars of the Lion
　　To point us the path to the skies,
　　To the Lethean peace of the skies:
Come up, in despite of the Lion,
　　To shine on us with her bright eyes:
Come up through the lair of the Lion,
　　With love in her luminous eyes."

But Psyche, uplifting her finger,
　　Said—"Sadly this star I mistrust,
　　Her pallor I strangely mistrust:
Oh, hasten!—oh, let us not linger!
　　Oh, fly!—let us fly!—for we must."
In terror she spoke, letting sink her
　　Wings until they trailed in the dust;
In agony sobbed, letting sink her
　　Plumes till they trailed in the dust,
　　Till they sorrowfully trailed in the dust.

I replied—"This is nothing but dreaming:
　　Let us on by this tremulous light!
　　Let us bathe in this crystalline light!
Its sibyllic splendor is beaming
　　With hope and in beauty to-night:
　　See, it flickers up the sky through the night!
Ah, we safely may trust to its gleaming,
　　And be sure it will lead us aright:
We safely may trust to a gleaming
　　That cannot but guide us aright,
　　Since it flickers up to Heaven through the night."

Thus I pacified Psyche and kissed her,
　　And tempted her out of her gloom,
　　And conquered her scruples and gloom;

And we passed to the end of the vista,
    But were stopped by the door of a tomb,
    By the door of a legended tomb;
And I said—"What is written, sweet sister,
    On the door of this legended tomb?"
    She replied—"Ulalume—Ulalume—
    'Tis the vault of thy lost Ulalume!"

Then my heart it grew ashen and sober
    As the leaves that were crispèd and sere,
    As the leaves that were withering and sere,
And I cried—"It was surely October
    On this very night of last year
    That I journeyed—I journeyed down here,
    That I brought a dread burden down here:
    On this night of all nights in the year,
    Ah, what demon has tempted me here?
Well I know, now, this dim lake of Auber,
    This misty mid region of Weir:
Well I know, now, this dank tarn of Auber,
    This ghoul-haunted woodland of Weir."

THE KID'S LAST FIGHT

Anonymous

Us two was pals, the Kid and me;
'Twould cut no ice if some gayzee,
As tough as hell jumped either one,
We'd both light in and hand him some.

Both of a size, the Kid and me,
We tipped the scales at thirty-three;
And when we'd spar 'twas give and take,
I wouldn't slug for any stake.

One day we worked out at the gymn,
Some swell guy hangin' round called "Slim,"
Watched us and got stuck on the Kid,
Then signed him up, that's what he did.

This guy called "Slim" he owned a string
Of lightweights, welters, everything;
He took the Kid out on the road,
And where they went none of us knowed.

I guessed the Kid had changed his name,
And fightin' the best ones in the game.
I used to dream of him at night,
No letters came—he couldn't write.

In just about two months or three
I signed up with Bucktooth McGee.
He got me matched with Denver Brown,
I finished him in half a round.

Next month I fought with Brooklyn Mike,
As tough a boy who hit the pike;
Then Frisco Jim and Battlin' Ben,
And knocked them all inside of ten.

I took 'em all and won each bout,
None of them birds could put me out;
The sportin' writers watched me slug,
Then all the papers run my mug.

"He'd rather fight than eat," they said,
"He's got the punch, he'll knock 'em dead."
There's only one I hadn't met,
That guy they called "The Yorkshire Pet."

He'd cleaned 'em all around in France,
No one in England stood a chance;
And I was champ in U. S. A.,
And knocked 'em cuckoo every day.

Now all McGee and me could think
Was how we'd like to cross the drink,
And knock this bucko for a row,
And grab a wagon load of dough.

At last Mac got me matched all right,
Five thousand smackers for the fight;
Then me and him packed up our grip,
And went to grab that championship.

I done some trainin' and the night
Set for the battle sure was right;
The crowd was wild, for this here bout
Was set to last till one was out.

The mob went crazy when the Pet
Came in, I'd never seen him yet;
And then I climbed up through the ropes,
All full of fight and full of hopes.

The crowd gave me an awful yell,
('Twas even money at the bell)
They stamped their feet and shook the place;
The Pet turned 'round, I saw his face!

My guts went sick, that's what they did,
For Holy Gee, it was the Kid!
We just had time for one good shake,
We meant it, too, it wasn't fake.

Whang! went the bell, the fight was on,
I clinched until the round was gone,
A-beggin', that he'd let me take
The fall for him—he wouldn't fake.

Hell, no, the Kid was on the square,
And said we had to fight it fair,
The crowd had bet their dough on us—
We had to fight (the honest cuss).

The referee was yellin' "break,"
The crowd was sore and howlin' "fake."
They'd paid their dough to see a scrap.
And so far we'd not hit a tap.

The second round we both begin.
I caught a fast one on my chin;
And stood like I was in a doze,
Until I got one on the nose.

I started landin' body blows,
He hooked another on my nose,
That riled my fightin' blood like hell,
And we was sluggin' at the bell.

The next round started, from the go
The millin' we did wasn't slow,
I landed hard on him, and then,
He took the count right up to ten.

He took the limit on one knee,
A chance to get his wind and see;
At ten he jumped up like a flash
And on my jaw he hung a smash.

I'm fightin', too, there, toe to toe,
And hittin' harder, blow for blow,
I damn soon knowed he couldn't stay,
He rolled his eyes—you know the way.

The way he staggered made me sick,
I stalled, McGee yelled "cop him quick!"
The crowd was wise and yellin' "fake,"
They'd seen the chance I wouldn't take.

The mob kept tellin' me to land,
And callin' things I couldn't stand;
I stepped in close and smashed his chin,
The Kid fell hard; he was all in.

I carried him into his chair,
And tried to bring him to for fair,
I rubbed his wrists, done everything,
A doctor climbed into the ring.

And I was scared as I could be,
The Kid was starin' and couldn't see;
The doctor turned and shook his head,
I looked again—the Kid was dead!

ON TAKING A WIFE

Thomas Moore

"Come, come," said Tom's father, "at your time of life,
There's no longer excuse for thus playing the rake—
It is time you should think, boy, of taking a wife."—
"Why, so it is, father—whose wife shall I take?"

OH PROMISE ME

Clement Scott

Oh promise me, that some day you and I
Will take our love together to some sky
Where we can be alone and faith renew,
And find the hollows where those flowers grew,
Those first sweet violets of early Spring,
Which come in whispers, thrill us both and sing
Of love unspeakable that is to be;
Oh promise me! Oh promise me!

Oh promise me, that you will take my hand,
The most unworthy in this lonely land,
And let me sit beside you, in your eyes
Seeing the vision of our paradise,
Hearing God's message while the organ rolls
Its mighty music to our very souls;
No love less perfect than a life with thee;
Oh promise me! Oh promise me!

THE BROOK'S SONG

Alfred, Lord Tennyson

I come from haunts of coot and hern,
    I make a sudden sally,
And sparkle out among the fern,
    To bicker down a valley.

By thirty hills I hurry down,
    Or slip between the ridges,
By twenty thorps, a little town,
    And half a hundred bridges.

Till last by Philip's farm I flow
    To join the brimming river,
For men may come and men may go,
    But I go on forever.

I chatter over stony ways,
  In little sharps and trebles,
I bubble into eddying bays,
  I babble on the pebbles.

With many a curve my banks I fret
  By many a field and fallow,
And many a fairy foreland set
  With willow-weed and mallow.

I chatter, chatter, as I flow
  To join the brimming river,
For men may come and men may go,
  But I go on forever.

I wind about, and in and out,
  With here a blossom sailing,
And here and there a lusty trout,
  And here and there a grayling,

And here and there a foamy flake
  Upon me, as I travel
With many a silvery water-break
  Above the golden gravel,

And draw them all along, and flow
  To join the brimming river,
For men may come and men may go,
  But I go on forever.

I steal by lawns and grassy plots,
  I slide by hazel covers;
I move the sweet forget-me-nots
  That grow for happy lovers.

I slip, I slide, I gloom, I glance,
  Among my skimming swallows,
I make the netted sunbeam dance
  Against my sandy shallows.

I murmur under moon and stars
  In brambly wildernesses;
I linger by my shingly bars,
  I loiter round my cresses;

And out again I curve and flow
　　To join the brimming river,
For men may come and men may go,
　　But I go on forever.
　　　　　　　　(From The Brook)

THE LAMPLIGHTER

Robert Louis Stevenson

My tea is nearly ready and the sun has left the sky;
It's time to take the window to see Leerie going by;
For every night at teatime and before you take your seat,
With lantern and with ladder he comes posting up the street.

Now Tom would be a driver and Maria go to sea,
And my papa's a banker and as rich as he can be;
But I, when I am stronger and can choose what I'm to do,
O Leerie, I'll go round at night and light the lamps with you!

For we are very lucky, with a lamp before the door,
And Leerie stops to light it as he lights so many more;
And O, before you hurry by with ladder and with light,
O Leerie, see a little child and nod to him to-night!

MY LOST YOUTH

Henry Wadsworth Longfellow

Often I think of the beautiful town
　　That is seated by the sea;
Often in thought go up and down
The pleasant streets of that dear old town,
　　And my youth comes back to me.
　　　And a verse of a Lapland song
　　　Is haunting my memory still:
　　　"A boy's will is the wind's will,
And the thoughts of youth are long, long thoughts."

I can see the shadowy lines of its trees,
　　And catch, in sudden gleams,
The sheen of the far-surrounding seas,

And islands that were the Hesperides
  Of all my boyish dreams.
    And the burden of that old song,
    It murmurs and whispers still:
    "A boy's will is the wind's will,
And the thoughts of youth are long, long thoughts."

I remember the black wharves and the slips,
  And the sea-tides tossing free;
And Spanish sailors with bearded lips,
And the beauty and mystery of the ships,
  And the magic of the sea.
    And the voice of that wayward song
    Is singing and saying still:
    "A boy's will is the wind's will,
And the thoughts of youth are long, long thoughts."

I remember the bulwarks by the shore,
  And the fort upon the hill;
The sunrise gun with its hollow roar,
The drum-beat repeated o'er and o'er,
  And the bugle wild and shrill.
    And the music of that old song
    Throbs in my memory still:
    "A boy's will is the wind's will,
And the thoughts of youth are long, long thoughts."

I remember the sea-fight far away,
  How it thunder'd o'er the tide!
And the dead captains, as they lay
In their graves, o'erlooking the tranquil bay
  Where they in battle died.
    And the sound of that mournful song
    Goes through me with a thrill:
    "A boy's will is the wind's will,
And the thoughts of youth are long, long thoughts."

I can see the breezy dome of groves,
  The shadows of Deering's Woods;
And the friendships old and the early loves
Come back with a Sabbath sound, as of doves
  In quiet neighborhoods.

And the verse of that sweet old song,
    It flutters and murmurs still:
"A boy's will is the wind's will,
And the thoughts of youth are long, long thoughts."

I remember the gleams and glooms that dart
    Across the school-boy's brain;
The song and the silence in the heart,
That in part are prophecies, and in part
    Are longings wild and vain.
        And the voice of that fitful song
        Sings on, and is never still:
        "A boy's will is the wind's will,
And the thoughts of youth are long, long thoughts."

There are things of which I may not speak;
    There are dreams that cannot die;
There are thoughts that make the strong heart weak,
And bring a pallor into the cheek,
    And a mist before the eye.
        And the words of that fatal song
        Come over me like a chill:
        "A boy's will is the wind's will,
And the thoughts of youth are long, long thoughts."

Strange to me now are the forms I meet
    When I visit the dear old town;
But the native air is pure and sweet,
And the trees that o'ershadow each well-known street,
    As they balance up and down,
        Are singing the beautiful song,
        Are sighing and whispering still:
        "A boy's will is the wind's will,
And the thoughts of youth are long, long thoughts."

And Deering's Woods are fresh and fair,
    And with joy that is almost pain
My heart goes back to wander there,
And among the dreams of the days that were,
    I find my lost youth again.
        And the strange and beautiful song,
        The groves are repeating it still:
        "A boy's will is the wind's will,
And the thoughts of youth are long, long thoughts."

CARDINAL WOLSEY'S FAREWELL

William Shakespeare

Farewell! a long farewell, to all my greatness!
This is the state of man: to-day he puts forth
The tender leaves of hopes; to-morrow blossoms,
And bears his blushing honours thick upon him;
The third day comes a frost, a killing frost,
And, when he thinks, good easy man, full surely
His greatness is a-ripening, nips his root,
And then he falls, as I do. I have ventured,
Like little wanton boys that swim on bladders,
This many summers in a sea of glory,
But far beyond my depth: my high-blown pride
At length broke under me and now has left me,
Weary and old with service, to the mercy
Of a rude stream, that must for ever hide me.
Vain pomp and glory of this world, I hate ye:
I feel my heart new open'd. O, how wretched
Is that poor man that hangs on princes' favours!
There is, betwixt that smile we would aspire to,
That sweet aspect of princes, and their ruin,
More pangs and fears than wars or women have:
And when he falls, he falls like Lucifer,
Never to hope again.

(From King Henry VIII)

SILENT NIGHT

Joseph Mohr

Silent Night! Holy Night!
All is calm, all is bright.
Round yon virgin mother and child!
Holy Infant so tender and mild,
Sleep in heavenly peace, sleep in heavenly peace.

Silent Night! Holy Night!
Shepherds quake at the sight!
Glories stream from heaven afar,
Heav'nly hosts sing Alleluia,
Christ, the Saviour, is born! Christ, the Saviour, is born!

Silent Night! Holy Night!
Son of God, love's pure light;
Radiant beams from Thy holy face,
With the dawn of redeeming grace,
Jesus, Lord, at Thy birth, Jesus, Lord, at Thy birth.

GOODBYE!

G. J. White-Melville

Falling leaf and fading tree,
Lines of white in a sullen sea,
Shadows rising on you and me;
Shadows rising on you and me;
The swallows are making them ready to fly,
Wheeling out on a windy sky.
Goodbye Summer! Goodbye! Goodbye!
Goodbye Summer! Goodbye! Goodbye!

Hush! a voice from the far away!
"Listen and learn", it seems to say,
"All the tomorrows shall be as today."
"All the tomorrows shall be as today."
The cord is frayed the cruse is dry,
The link must break, and the lamp must die—
Goodbye to Hope! Goodbye! Goodbye!
Goodbye to Hope! Goodbye! Goodbye!

What are we waiting for? Oh, my heart!
Kiss me straight on the brows! And part again!
Again! my heart! my heart! What are we wait-
    ing for, you and I?
A pleading look, a stifled cry.
Goodbye, forever! Goodbye, forever!
Goodbye! Goodbye! Goodbye!

* * *

I had rather men should ask why Cato had no statues, than why
he had one.

—Cato

CARRY ME BACK TO OLD VIRGINNY

James Bland

Carry me back to old Virginny,
There's where the cotton and the corn and taters grow,
There's where the birds warble sweet in the spring-time,
There's where the old darkey's heart am long'd to go,
There's where I labored so hard for old Massa,
Day after day in the field of yellow corn,
No place on earth do I love more sincerely
Than old Virginny, the state where I was born.

Carry me back to old Virginny,
There let me live till I wither and decay,
Long by the old Dismal Swamp have I wandered,
There's where this old darkey's life will pass away.
Massa and Missis have long gone before me,
Soon we will meet on that bright and golden shore,
There we'll be happy and free from all sorrow,
There's where we'll meet and we'll never part no more.

THE KILKENNY CATS

Anonymous

There wanst was two cats of Kilkenny,
Each thought there was one cat too many,
So they quarreled and they fit,
They scratch'd and they bit,
Till, barrin' their nails,
And the tips of their tails,
Instead of two cats, there warnt any.

STEALING

James Russell Lowell

In vain we call old notions fudge,
And bend our conscience to our dealing;
The Ten Commandments will not budge,
And stealing will continue stealing.

GIVE ME LIBERTY, OR GIVE ME DEATH!

Patrick Henry

MR. PRESIDENT:

No man thinks more highly than I do of the patriotism, as well as abilities, of the very worthy gentlemen who have just addressed the House. But different men often see the same subjects in different lights; and, therefore, I hope that it will not be thought disrespectful to those gentlemen, if entertaining as I do, opinions of a character very opposite to theirs, I shall speak forth *my* sentiments freely and without reserve. This is no time for ceremony. The question before the House is one of awful moment to this country. For my own part I consider it as nothing less than a question of freedom or slavery. And in proportion to the magnitude of the subject ought to be the freedom of debate. It is only in this way that we can hope to arrive at truth, and fulfil the great responsibility which we hold to God and our country. Should I keep back my opinions at such a time, through fear of giving offense, I should consider myself as guilty of treason toward my country, and of an act of disloyalty toward the majesty of Heaven, which I revere above all earthly kings.

Mr. President, it is natural to man to indulge in the illusions of hope. We are apt to shut our eyes against a painful truth,—and listen to the song of that siren, till she transforms us into beasts. Is this the part of wise men, engaged in a great and arduous struggle for liberty? Are we disposed to be of the number of those who, having eyes, see not, and having ears, hear not, the things which so nearly concern their temporal salvation? For my part, whatever anguish of spirit it may cost, I am willing to know the whole truth; to know the worst and to provide for it. I have but one lamp by which my feet are guided, and that is the lamp of experience. I know of no way of judging of the future but by the past. And judging by the past, I wish to know what there has been in the conduct of the British ministry for the last ten years, to justify those hopes with which gentlemen have been pleased to solace themselves and the House. Is it that insidious smile with which our petition has been lately received? Trust it not, sir; it will prove a snare to your feet. Suffer not yourselves to be betrayed with a kiss. Ask yourselves how this gracious reception of our petition comports with these warlike preparations which cover our waters and darken our land. Are fleets and armies necessary to a work of love and reconciliation? Have we shown ourselves so unwilling to

683

be reconciled, that force must be called in to win back our love? Let us not deceive ourselves, sir. These are the implements of war and subjugation—the last arguments to which kings resort. I ask gentlemen, sir, what means this martial array, if its purpose be not to force us to submission? Can gentlemen assign any other possible motive for it? Has Great Britain any enemy, in this quarter of the world, to call for all this accumulation of navies and armies? No, sir, she has none. They are meant for us; they can be meant for no other. They are sent over to bind and rivet upon us those chains which the British ministry have been so long forging. And what have we to oppose them? Shall we try argument? Sir, we have been trying that for the last ten years. Have we anything new to offer on the subject? Nothing. We have held the subject up in every light of which it is capable; but it has been all in vain. Shall we resort to entreaty and humble supplication? What terms shall we find, which have not been already exhausted? Let us not, I beseech you, sir, deceive ourselves longer. Sir, we have done everything that could be done, to avert the storm which is now coming on. We have petitioned—we have remonstrated—we have supplicated—we have prostrated ourselves before the throne, and have implored its interposition to arrest the tyrannical hands of the ministry and parliament. Our petitions have been slighted; our remonstrances have produced additional violence and insult; our supplications have been disregarded; and we have been spurned with contempt, from the foot of the throne. In vain, after these things, may we indulge the fond hope of peace and reconciliation. There is no longer any room for hope. If we wish to be free—if we mean to preserve inviolate those inestimable privileges for which we have been so long contending—if we mean not basely to abandon the noble struggle in which we have been so long engaged, and which we have pledged ourselves never to abandon until the glorious object of our contest shall be obtained, we must fight! I repeat it, sir, we must fight! An appeal to arms and to the God of Hosts is all that is left us!

They tell us, sir, that we are weak—unable to cope with so formidable an adversary. But when shall we be stronger? Will it be the next week, or the next year? Will it be when we are totally disarmed, and when a British guard shall be stationed in every house? Shall we gather strength by irresolution and inaction? Shall we acquire the means of effectual resistance by lying supinely on our backs, and hugging the delusive phantom of Hope, until our enemies shall have bound us hand and foot? Sir, we are not weak, if we make a proper use of those means which the God of nature

684

hath placed in our power. Three millions of people, armed in the holy cause of liberty, and in such a country as that which we possess, are invincible by any force which our enemy can send against us. Besides, sir, we shall not fight our battles alone. There is a just God who presides over the destinies of nations; and who will raise up friends to fight our battles for us. The battle, sir, is not to the strong alone; it is to the vigilant, the active, the brave. Besides, sir, we have no election. If we, the brave, were base enough to desire it, it is now too late to retire from the contest. There is no retreat, but in submission and slavery! Our chains are forged, their clanking may be heard on the plains of Boston! The war is inevitable,— and let it come! I repeat it, sir, let it come!

It is in vain, sir, to extenuate the matter. Gentlemen may cry, peace, peace—but there is no peace. The war is actually begun! The next gale that sweeps from the north will bring to our ears the clash of resounding arms! Our brethren are already in the field! Why stand we here idle? What is it that gentlemen wish? What would they have? Is life so dear, or peace so sweet, as to be purchased at the price of chains and slavery? Forbid it, Almighty God! I know not what course others may take; but as for me, give me liberty, or give me death!

March 23, 1775

TO LUCASTA, GOING TO THE WARS

Richard Lovelace

Tell me not, Sweet, I am unkind,
    That from the nunnery
Of thy chaste breast and quiet mind
    To war and arms I fly.

True, a new mistress now I chase,
    The first foe in the field;
And with a stronger faith embrace
    A sword, a horse, a shield.

Yet this inconstancy is such
    That thou too shalt adore;
I could not love thee, Dear, so much,
    Loved I not honour more.

LITTLE ORPHANT ANNIE

James Whitcomb Riley

Little Orphant Annie's come to our house to stay,
An' wash the cups and saucers up, and brush the crumbs away,
An' shoo the chickens off the porch, an' dust the hearth, an' sweep,
An' make the fire, an' bake the bread, an' earn her board-an'-keep;
An' all us other children, when the supper things is done,
We set around the kitchen fire an' has the mostest fun
A-list'nin' to the witch-tales 'at Annie tells about,
An' the Gobble-uns 'at gits you
                        Ef you
                            Don't
                                Watch
                                    Out!

Onc't they was a little boy wouldn't say his pray'rs—
An' when he went to bed at night, away up stairs,
His mammy heerd him holler, an' his daddy heerd him bawl,
An' when they turn't the kivvers down, he wasn't there at all!
An' they seeked him in the rafter-room, an' cubby-hole, an' press.
An' seeked him up the chimbly-flue, an' ever'wheres, I guess;
But all they ever found was thist his pants an' roundabout!
An' the Gobble-uns 'll git you
                        Ef you
                            Don't
                                Watch
                                    Out!

An' one time a little girl 'ud allus laugh an' grin,
An' make fun of ever' one, an' all her blood-an'-kin;
An' onc't when they was "company," an' ole folks was there.
She mocked 'em an' shocked 'em, an' said she didn't care!
An' thist as she kicked her heels, an' turn't to run an' hide,
They was two great big Black Things a-standin' by her side,
An' they snatched her through the ceilin' 'fore she knowed what
    she's about!
An' the Gobble-uns 'll git you
                        Ef you
                            Don't
                                Watch
                                    Out!

An' little Orphant Annie says, when the blaze is blue,
An' the lampwick sputters, an' the wind goes woo-oo!
An' you hear the crickets quit, an' the moon is gray,
An' the lightnin' bugs in dew is all squenched away,—
You better mind yer parents, and yer teachers fond and dear,
An' churish them 'at loves you, an' dry the orphant's tear,
An' help the pore an' needy ones 'at clusters all about,
Er the Gobble-uns 'll git you
               Ef you
             Don't
             Watch
             Out!

JESUS, LOVER OF MY SOUL

Charles Wesley

Jesus, lover of my soul,
Let me to Thy bosom fly,
While the nearer waters roll
While the tempest still is high;
Hide me, O my Saviour hide,
Till the storm of life is past:
Safe into the haven guide,
O receive my soul at last.

Other refuge have I none;
Hangs my helpless soul on Thee;
Leave, ah! leave me not alone,
Still support and comfort me.
All my trust on Thee is stayed,
All my help from Thee I bring;
Cover my defenseless head
With the shadow of Thy wing.

Wilt Thou not regard my call?
Wilt Thou not accept my prayer?
Lo, I sink, I faint, I fall!
Lo, on Thee I cast my care;
Reach me out Thy gracious hand!
While I of Thy strength receive,
Hoping against hope I stand,
Dying, and behold I live!

Thou, O Christ, art all I want;
More than all in Thee I find;
Raise the fallen, cheer the faint,
Heal the sick and lead the blind.
Just and holy is Thy name;
I am all unrighteousness;
False and full of sin I am,
Thou art full of truth and grace.

Plenteous grace with Thee is found,
Grace to cover all my sin;
Let the healing streams abound;
Make and keep me pure within.
Thou of life the Fountain art,
Freely let me take of Thee;
Spring Thou up within my heart,
Rise to all eternity.

SUCCESS

Edgar A. Guest

I hold no dream of fortune vast,
Nor seek undying fame.
I do not ask when life is past
That many know my name.

I may not own the skill to rise
To glory's topmost height,
Nor win a place among the wise,
But I can keep the right.

And I can live my life on earth
Contented to the end,
If but a few shall know my worth
And proudly call me friend.

* * *

A politician thinks of the next election; a statesman, of the next generation.

—James Freeman Clarke

DAFFODILS

William Wordsworth

I wandered lonely as a cloud
That floats on high o'er vales and hills,
When all at once I saw a crowd,—
A host, of golden daffodils,
Beside the lake, beneath the trees,
Fluttering and dancing in the breeze.

Continuous as the stars that shine
And twinkle on the Milky Way,
They stretched in never-ending line
Along the margin of a bay:
Ten thousand saw I at a glance,
Tossing their heads in sprightly dance.

The waves beside them danced; but they
Outdid the sparkling waves in glee:
A poet could not but be gay,
In such a jocund company!
I gazed—and gazed—but little thought
What wealth the show to me had brought:

For oft, when on my couch I lie
In vacant or in pensive mood,
They flash upon that inward eye
Which is the bliss of solitude;
And then my heart with pleasure fills,
And dances with the daffodils.

THE BALLAD OF READING GAOL

Oscar Wilde

I

He did not wear his scarlet coat,
  For blood and wine are red,
And blood and wine were on his hands
  When they found him with the dead,
The poor dead woman whom he loved,
  And murdered in her bed.

He walked amongst the Trial Men
  In a suit of shabby gray;
A cricket cap was on his head,
  And his step seemed light and gay;
But I never saw a man who looked
  So wistfully at the day.

I never saw a man who looked
  With such a wistful eye
Upon that little tent of blue
  Which prisoners call the sky,
And at every drifting cloud that went
  With sails of silver by.

I walked, with other souls in pain,
  Within another ring,
And was wondering if the man had done
  A great or little thing,
When a voice behind me whispered low,
  "That fellow's got to swing."

Dear Christ! the very prison walls
  Suddenly seemed to reel,
And the sky above my head became
  Like a casque of scorching steel;
And, though I was a soul in pain,
  My pain I could not feel.

I only knew what hunted thought
  Quickened his step, and why
He looked upon the garish day
  With such a wistful eye;
The man had killed the thing he loved,
  And so he had to die.

Yet each man kills the thing he loves,
  By each let this be heard,
Some do it with a bitter look,
  Some with a flattering word,
The coward does it with a kiss,
  The brave man with a sword!

Some kill their love when they are young,
  And some when they are old;
Some strangle with the hands of Lust,
  Some with the hands of Gold:
The kindest use a knife, because
  The dead so soon grow cold.

Some love too little, some too long,
  Some sell, and others buy;
Some do the deed with many tears,
  And some without a sigh:
For each man kills the thing he loves,
  Yet each man does not die.

He does not die a death of shame
  On a day of dark disgrace,
Nor have a noose about his neck,
  Nor a cloth upon his face,
Nor drop feet foremost through the floor
  Into an empty space.

He does not sit with silent men
  Who watch him night and day;
Who watch him when he tries to weep,
  And when he tries to pray;
Who watch him lest himself should rob
  The prison of its prey.

He does not wake at dawn to see
  Dread figures throng his room,
The shivering Chaplain robed in white,
  The Sheriff stern with gloom,
And the Governor all in shiny black,
  With the yellow face of Doom.

He does not rise in piteous haste
  To put on convict-clothes,
While some coarse-mouthed Doctor gloats, and notes
  Each new and nerve-twitched pose,
Fingering a watch whose little ticks
  Are like horrible hammer-blows.

He does not know that sickening thirst
  That sands one's throat, before
The hangman with his gardener's gloves
  Slips through the padded door,
And binds one with three leathern thongs
  That the throat may thirst no more.

He does not bend his head to hear
  The Burial Office read,
Nor, while the terror of his soul
  Tells him he is not dead,
Cross his own coffin, as he moves
  Into the hideous shed.

He does not stare upon the air
  Through a little roof of glass:
He does not pray with lips of clay
  For his agony to pass;
Nor feel upon his shuddering cheek
  The kiss of Caiaphas.

II

Six weeks our guardsman walked the yard
  In the suit of shabby gray:
His cricket cap was on his head,
  And his step seemed light and gay,
But I never saw a man who looked
  So wistfully at the day.

I never saw a man who looked
  With such a wistful eye
Upon that little tent of blue
  Which prisoners call the sky.
And at every wandering cloud that trailed
  Its ravelled fleeces by.

He did not wring his hands, as do
  Those witless men who dare
To try to rear the changeling Hope
  In the cave of black Despair:
He only looked upon the sun,
  And drank the morning air.

He did not wring his hands nor weep,
    Nor did he peek or pine,
But he drank the air as though it held
    Some healthful anodyne;
With open mouth he drank the sun
    As though it had been wine!

And I and all the souls in pain
    Who tramped the other ring,
Forgot if we ourselves had done
    A great or little thing,
And watched with gaze of dull amaze
    The man who had to swing.

And strange it was to see him pass
    With a step so light and gay,
And strange it was to see him look
    So wistfully at the day,
And strange it was to think that he
    Had such a debt to pay.

For oak and elm have pleasant leaves
    That in the spring-time shoot:
But grim to see is the gallows-tree,
    With its adder-bitten root,
And, green or dry, a man must die
    Before it bears its fruit.

The loftiest place is that seat of grace
    For which all worldlings try:
But who would stand in hempen band
    Upon a scaffold high,
And through a murderer's collar take
    His last look at the sky?

It is sweet to dance to violins
    When Love and Life are fair:
To dance to flutes, to dance to lutes
    Is delicate and rare:
But it is not sweet with nimble feet
    To dance upon the air!

So with curious eyes and sick surmise
    We watched him day by day,
And wondered if each one of us
    Would end the self-same way,
For none can tell to what red Hell
    His sightless soul may stray.

At last the dead man walked no more
    Amongst the Trial Men,
And I knew that he was standing up
    In the black dock's dreadful pen,
And that never would I see his face
    In God's sweet world again.

Like two doomed ships that pass in storm
    We had crossed each other's way:
But we made no sign, we said no word,
    We had no word to say;
For we did not meet in the holy night,
    But in the shameful day.

A prison wall was round us both,
    Two outcast men we were:
The world had thrust us from its heart,
    And God from out His care:
And the iron gin that waits for Sin
    Had caught us in its snare.

III

In Debtors' Yard the stones are hard,
    And the dripping wall is high,
So it was there he took the air
    Beneath the leaden sky.
And by each side a Warder walked,
    For fear the man might die.

Or else he sat with those who watched
    His anguish night and day;
Who watched him when he rose to weep,
    And when he crouched to pray;
Who watched him lest himself should rob
    Their scaffold of its prey.

The Governor was strong upon
    The Regulations Act:
The Doctor said that Death was but
    A scientific fact:
And twice a day the Chaplain called,
    And left a little tract.

And twice a day he smoked his pipe,
    And drank his quart of beer:
His soul was resolute, and held
    No hiding-place for fear;
He often said that he was glad
    The hangman's hands were near.

But why he said so strange a thing
    No Warder dared to ask:
For he to whom a watcher's doom
    Is given as his task,
Must set a lock upon his lips,
    And make his face a mask.

Or else he might be moved, and try
    To comfort or console:
And what should Human Pity do
    Pent up in Murderers' Hole?
What word of grace in such a place
    Could help a brother's soul?

With slouch and swing around the ring
    We trod the Fools' Parade!
We did not care: we knew we were
    The Devil's Own Brigade:
And shaven head and feet of lead
    Make a merry masquerade.

We tore the tarry rope to shreds
    With blunt and bleeding nails;
We rubbed the doors, and scrubbed the floors,
    And cleaned the shining rails:
And, rank by rank, we soaped the plank,
    And clattered with the pails.

We sewed the sacks, we broke the stones.
  We turned the dusty drill:
We banged the tins, and bawled the hymns,
  And sweated on the mill:
But in the heart of every man
  Terror was lying still.

So still it lay that every day
  Crawled like a weed-clogged wave:
And we forgot the bitter lot
  That waits for fool and knave,
Till once, as we tramped in from work,
  We passed an open grave.

With yawning mouth the yellow hole
  Gaped for a living thing;
The very mud cried out for blood
  To the thirsty asphalt ring:
And we knew that ere one dawn grew fair
  Some prisoner had to swing.

Right in we went, with soul intent
  On Death and Dread and Doom:
The hangman, with his little bag,
  Went shuffling through the gloom:
And each man trembled as he crept
  Into his numbered tomb.

That night the empty corridors
  Were full of forms of Fear,
And up and down the iron town
  Stole feet we could not hear,
And through the bars that hide the stars
  White faces seemed to peer.

He lay as one who lies and dreams
  In a pleasant meadow-land,
The watchers watched him as he slept,
  And could not understand
How one could sleep so sweet a sleep
  With a hangman close at hand.

But there is no sleep when men must weep
   Who never yet have wept:
So we—the fool, the fraud, the knave—
   That endless vigil kept,
And through each brain on hands of pain
   Another's terror crept.

Alas! it is a fearful thing
   To feel another's guilt!
For, right within, the sword of Sin
   Pierced to its poisoned hilt,
And as molten lead were the tears we shed
   For the blood we had not spilt.

The Warders with their shoes of felt
   Crept by each padlocked door,
And peeped and saw, with eyes of awe,
   Gray figures on the floor,
And wonder why men knelt to pray
   Who never prayed before.

All through the night we knelt and prayed,
   Mad mourners of a corse!
The troubled plumes of midnight were
   The plumes upon a hearse:
And bitter wine upon a sponge
   Was the savor of Remorse.

The gray cock crew, the red cock crew,
   But never came the day:
And crooked shapes of Terror crouched,
   In the corners where we lay:
And each evil sprite that walks by night
   Before us seemed to play.

They glided past, they glided fast,
   Like travelers through a mist:
They mocked the moon in a rigadoon
   Of delicate turn and twist,
And with formal pace and loathsome grace
   The phantoms kept their tryst.

With mop and mow, we saw them go,
  Slim shadows hand in hand:
About, about, in ghostly rout
  They trod a saraband:
And the damned grotesques made arabesques,
  Like the wind upon the sand!

With the pirouettes of marionettes,
  They tripped on pointed tread:
But with flutes of Fear they filled the ear,
  As their grisly masque they led,
And loud they sang, and long they sang,
  For they sang to wake the dead.

"Oho!" they cried, "The World is wide,
  But fettered limbs go lame!
And once, or twice, to throw the dice
  Is a gentlemanly game;
But he does not win who plays with Sin
  In the secret House of Shame."

No things of air these antics were,
  That frolicked with such glee:
To men whose lives were held in gyves,
  And whose feet might not go free,
Ah! wounds of Christ! they were living things,
  Most terrible to see.

Around, around, they waltzed and wound;
  Some wheeled in smirking pairs;
With the mincing step of a demirep
  Some sidled up the stairs:
And with subtle sneer, and fawning leer,
  Each helped us at our prayers.

The morning wind began to moan,
  But still the night went on:
Through its giant loom the web of gloom
  Crept till each thread was spun:
And, as we prayed, we grew afraid
  Of the Justice of the Sun.

The moaning wind went wandering round
  The weeping prison-wall:
Till like a wheel of turning steel
  We felt the minutes crawl:
O moaning wind! what had we done
  To have such a seneschal?

At last I saw the shadowed bars,
  Like a lattice wrought in lead,
Move right across the whitewashed wall
  That faced my three-plank bed,
And I knew that somewhere in the world
  God's dreadful dawn was red.

At six o'clock we cleaned our cells,
  At seven all was still,
But the sough and swing of a mighty wing
  The prison seemed to fill,
For the Lord of Death with icy breath
  Had entered in to kill.

He did not pass in purple pomp,
  Not ride a moon-white steed.
Three yards of cord and a sliding board
  Are all the gallows' need:
So with rope of shame the Herald came
  To do the secret deed.

We were as men who through a fen
  Of filthy darkness grope:
We did not dare to breathe a prayer,
  Or to give our anguish scope:
Something was dead in each of us,
  And what was dead was Hope.

For Man's grim Justice goes its way,
  And will not swerve aside:
It slays the weak, it slays the strong,
  It has a deadly stride:
With iron heel it slays the strong,
  The monstrous parricide!

We waited for the stroke of eight:
  Each tongue was thick with thirst:
For the stroke of eight is the stroke of Fate
  That makes a man accursed,
And Fate will use a running noose
  For the best man and the worst.

We had no other thing to do,
  Save to wait for the sign to come:
So, like things of stone in a valley lone,
  Quiet we sat and dumb:
But each man's heart beat thick and quick,
  Like a madman on a drum!

With sudden shock the prison clock
  Smote on the shivering air,
And from all the gaol rose up a wail
  Of impotent despair,
Like the sound that frightened marshes hear
  From some leper in his lair.

And as one sees most fearful things
  In the crystal of a dream,
We saw the greasy hempen rope
  Hooked to the blackened beam,
And heard the prayer the hangman's snare
  Strangled into a scream.

And all the woe that moved him so
  That he gave that bitter cry,
And the wild regrets, and the bloody sweats,
  None knew so well as I:
For he who lives more lives than one
  More deaths than one must die.

IV

There is no chapel on the day
  On which they hang a man:
The Chaplain's heart is far too sick,
  Or his face is far too wan,
Or there is that written in his eyes
  Which none should look upon.

So they kept us close till nigh on noon,
   And then they rang the bell,
And the Warders with their jingling keys
   Opened each listening cell,
And down the iron stair we tramped,
   Each from his separate Hell.

Out into God's sweet air we went,
   But not in wonted way,
For this man's face was white with fear,
   And that man's face was gray,
And I never saw sad men who looked
   So wistfully at the day.

I never saw sad men who looked
   With such a wistful eye
Upon that little tent of blue
   We prisoners called the sky,
And at every careless cloud that passed
   In happy freedom by.

But there were those amongst us all
   Who walked with downcast head,
And knew that, had each got his due,
   They should have died instead:
He had but killed a thing that lived,
   Whilst they had killed the dead.

For he who sins a second time
   Wakes a dead soul to pain,
And draws it from its spotted shroud,
   And makes it bleed again,
And makes it bleed great gouts of blood,
   And makes it bleed in vain!

Like ape or clown, in monstrous garb
   With crooked arrows starred,
Silently we went round and round
   The slippery asphalt yard;
Silently we went round and round,
   And no man spoke a word.

Silently we went round and round,
    And through each hollow mind
The Memory of dreadful things
    Rushed like a dreadful wind,
And Horror stalked before each man,
    And Terror crept behind.

The Warders strutted up and down,
    And kept their herd of brutes,
Their uniforms were spick and span,
    And they wore their Sunday suits,
But we knew the work they had been at,
    By the quicklime on their boots.

For where a grave had opened wide,
    There was no grave at all:
Only a stretch of mud and sand
    By the hideous prison-wall,
And a little heap of burning lime,
    That the man should have his pall.

For he has a pall, this wretched man,
    Such as few men can claim:
Deep down below a prison-yard,
    Naked for greater shame,
He lies, with fetters on each foot,
    Wrapt in a sheet of flame!

And all the while the burning lime
    Eats flesh and bone away;
It eats the brittle bone by night,
    And the soft flesh by day,
It eats the flesh and bone by turns,
    But it eats the heart away.

For three long years they will not sow
    Or root or seedling there:
For three long years the unblessed spot
    Will sterile be and bare,
And look upon the wondering sky
    With unreproachful stare.

They think a murderer's heart would taint
    Each simple seed they sow.
It is not true! God's kindly earth
    Is kindlier than men know,
And the red rose would but blow more red,
    The white rose whiter blow.

Out of his mouth a red, red rose!
    Out of his heart a white!
For who can say by what strange way,
    Christ brings His will to light,
Since the barren staff the pilgrim bore
    Bloomed in the great Pope's sight?

But neither milk-white rose nor red
    May bloom in prison air;
The shard, the pebble, and the flint,
    Are what they give us there:
For flowers have been known to heal
    A common man's despair.

So never will wine-red rose or white,
    Petal by petal, fall
On that stretch of mud and sand that lies
    By the hideous prison-wall,
To tell the men who tramp the yard
    That God's Son died for all.

Yet though the hideous prison-wall
    Still hems him round and round,
And a spirit may not walk by night
    That is with fetters bound,
And a spirit may but weep that lies
    In such unholy ground.

He is at peace—this wretched man—
    At peace, or will be soon:
There is no thing to make him mad,
    Nor does Terror walk at noon,
For the lampless Earth in which he lies
    Has neither Sun nor Moon.

They hanged him as a beast is hanged:
    They did not even toll
A requiem that might have brought
    Rest to his startled soul,
But hurriedly they took him out,
    And hid him in a hole.

They stripped him of his canvas clothes,
    And gave him to the flies;
They mocked the swollen purple throat,
    And the stark and staring eyes;
And with laughter loud they heaped the shroud
    In which their convict lies.

The Chaplain would not kneel to pray
    By his dishonored grave:
Nor mark it with that blessed Cross
    That Christ for sinners gave,
Because the man was one of those
    Whom Christ came down to save.

Yet all is well; he has but passed,
    To Life's appointed bourne:
And alien tears will fill for him
    Pity's long-broken urn,
For his mourners will be outcast men,
    And outcasts always mourn.

v

I know not whether Laws be right,
    Or whether Laws be wrong;
All that we know who lie in gaol
    Is that the wall is strong;
And that each day is like a year,
    A year whose days are long.

But this I know, that every Law
    That men have made for Man,
Since first Man took his brother's life,
    And the sad world began,
But straws the wheat and saves the chaff
    With a most evil fan.

This too I know—and wise it were
  If each could know the same—
That every prison that men build
  Is built with bricks of shame,
And bound with bars lest Christ should see
  How men their brothers maim.

With bars they blur the gracious moon,
  And blind the goodly sun:
And they do well to hide their Hell,
  For in it things are done
That Son of God nor Son of Man
  Ever should look upon!

The vilest deeds like poison weeds
  Bloom well in prison-air:
It is only what is good in Man
  That wastes and withers there:
Pale Anguish keeps the heavy gate,
  And the Warder is Despair.

For they starve the little frightened child
  Till it weeps both night and day:
And they scourge the weak, and flog the fool,
  And gibe the old and gray,
And some grow mad, and all grow bad,
  And none a word may say.

Each narrow cell in which we dwell
  Is a foul and dark latrine.
And the fetid breath of living Death
  Chokes up each grated screen,
And all, but Lust, is turned to dust
  In Humanity's machine.

The brackish water that we drink
  Creeps with a loathsome slime,
And the bitter bread they weigh in scales
  Is full of chalk and lime,
And Sleep will not lie down, but walks
  Wild-eyed, and cries to Time.

But though lean Hunger and green Thirst
  Like asp with adder fight,
We have little care of prison fare,
  For what chills and kills outright
Is that every stone one lifts by day
  Becomes one's heart by night.

With midnight always in one's heart,
  And twilight in one's cell,
We turn the crank, or tear the rope,
  Each in his separate Hell,
And the silence is more awful far
  Than the sound of a brazen bell.

And never a human voice comes near
  To speak a gentle word:
And the eye that watches through the door
  Is pitiless and hard:
And by all forgot, we rot and rot,
  With soul and body marred.

And thus we rust Life's iron chain
  Degraded and alone:
And some men curse, and some men weep,
  And some men make no moan:
But God's eternal Laws are kind
  And break the heart of stone.

And every human heart that breaks,
  In prison-cell or yard,
Is as that broken box that gave
  Its treasure to the Lord,
And filled the unclean leper's house
  With the scent of costliest nard.

Ah! happy they whose hearts can break
  And peace of pardon win!
How else may man make straight his plan
  And cleanse his soul from Sin?
How else but through a broken heart
  May Lord Christ enter in?

And he of the swollen purple throat,
  And the stark and staring eyes
Waits for the holy hands that took
  The Thief to Paradise;
And a broken and a contrite heart
  The Lord will not despise.

The man in red who reads the Law
  Gave him three weeks of life,
Three little weeks in which to heal
  His soul of his soul's strife,
And cleanse from every blot of blood
  The hand that held the knife.

And with tears of blood he cleansed the hand,
  The hand that held the steel:
For only blood can wipe out blood,
  And only tears can heal:
And the crimson stain that was of Cain
  Became Christ's snow-white seal.

VI

In Reading gaol by Reading town
  There is a pit of shame,
And in it lies a wretched man
  Eaten by teeth of flame,
In a burning winding-sheet he lies,
  And his grave has got no name.

And there, till Christ call forth the dead,
  In silence let him lie:
No need to waste the foolish tear,
  Or heave the windy sigh:
The man had killed the thing he loved,
  And so he had to die.

And all men kill the thing they love,
  By all let this be heard,
Some do it with a bitter look,
  Some with a flattering word,
The coward does it with a kiss,
  The brave man with a sword!

707

THE END OF THE PLAY

William Makepeace Thackeray

The play is done; the curtain drops,
   Slow falling to the prompter's bell:
A moment yet the actor stops,
   And looks around, to say farewell.
It is an irksome word and task;
   And when he's laughed and said his say,
He shows, as he removes the mask,
   A face that's anything but gay.

One word, ere yet the evening ends,
   Let's close it with a parting rhyme,
And pledge a hand to all young friends,
   As fits the merry Christmas time.
On life's wide scene you, too, have parts,
   That Fate ere long shall bid you play;
Good night! with honest gentle hearts
   A kindly greeting go alway!

Good night!—I'd say, the griefs, the joys,
   Just hinted in this mimic page,
The triumphs and defeats of boys,
   Are but repeated in our age.
I'd say, your woes were not less keen,
   Your hopes more vain than those of men;
Your pangs or pleasures of fifteen
   At forty-five played o'er again.

I'd say, we suffer and we strive,
   Not less nor more as men than boys;
With grizzled beards at forty-five,
   As erst at twelve in corduroys.
And if, in time of sacred youth,
   We learned at home to love and pray,
Pray Heaven that early Love and Truth
   May never wholly pass away.

And in the world, as in the school,
   I'd say, how fate may change and shift;
The prize be sometimes with the fool,
   The race not always to the swift.

The strong may yield, the good may fall,
  The great man be a vulgar clown,
The knave be lifted over all,
  The kind cast pitilessly down.

Who knows the inscrutable design?
  Blessed be He who took and gave!
Why should your mother, Charles, not mine,
  Be weeping at her darling's grave?
We bow to Heaven that will'd it so,
  That darkly rules the fate of all,
That sends the respite or the blow,
  That's free to give, or to recall.

This crowns his feast with wine and wit:
  Who brought him to that mirth and state?
His betters, see, below him sit,
  Or hunger hopeless at the gate.
Who bade the mud from Dives' wheel
  To spurn the rags of Lazarus?
Come, brother, in that dust we'll kneel,
  Confessing Heaven that ruled it thus.

So each shall mourn, in life's advance,
  Dear hopes, dear friends, untimely killed;
Shall grieve for many a forfeit chance,
  And longing passion unfulfilled.
Amen! whatever fate be sent,
  Pray God the heart may kindly glow,
Although the head with cares be bent,
  And whitened with the winter snow.

Come wealth or want, come good or ill,
  Let young and old accept their part,
And bow before the Awful Will,
  And bear it with an honest heart,
Who misses or who wins the prize,
  Go, lose or conquer as you can;
But if you fail, or if you rise,
  Be each, pray God, a gentleman.

A gentleman, or old or young!
  (Bear kindly with my humble lays;)
The sacred chorus first was sung
  Upon the first of Christmas days:

The shepherds heard it overhead—
　　The joyful angels raised it then:
Glory to Heaven on high, it said,
　　And peace on earth to gentle men.

My song, save this, is little worth;
　　I lay the weary pen aside,
And wish you health, and love, and mirth,
　　As fits the solemn Christmas-tide.
As fits the holy Christmas birth,
　　Be this, good friends, our carol still—
Be peace on earth, be peace on earth,
　　To men of gentle will.

ACKNOWLEDGMENTS

The editor and the publishers are grateful to the individuals and publishers named below for their friendly cooperation and generosity in granting permission to reprint the copyrighted selections specified:

MRS. BAMBRIDGE for permission to reprint *Mandalay* and *Gunga Din* from "Barrack Room Ballads" by Rudyard Kipling, *If* from "Rewards and Fairies" by Rudyard Kipling, and *Recessional* from "The Five Nations" by Rudyard Kipling.

A. S. BARNES AND COMPANY for permission to reprint *A History of The U.S.* from "Mother Stoner's Jinglelays for All the World", copyright 1926 by A. S. Barnes and Company.

MARTHA T. BENNETT for permission to reprint *The Flag Goes By* by Henry Holcomb Bennett.

THE BOBBS-MERRILL COMPANY for permission to reprint *Little Orphant Annie* and *The Days Gone By* from "Rhymes of Childhood" by James Whitcomb Riley, Copyright 1890, 1918; *When The Frost Is On The Punkin* from "Neighborly Poems" by James Whitcomb Riley, Copyright 1891, 1919; all used by special permission of the Publishers, The Bobbs-Merrill Company.

CARRIE JACOBS-BOND for permission to reprint the lyrics of *A Perfect Day*.

BRANDT AND BRANDT for permission to reprint *The Thirteen Sisters* from "John Brown's Body", published by Farrar and Rinehart, Copyright 1927, 1928 by Stephen Vincent Benét.

W. B. CONKEY AND COMPANY for permission to reprint the poems by Ella Wheeler Wilcox.

D. L. & W. R. R. for permission to reprint the *Phoebe Snow* jingles.

DODD, MEAD AND COMPANY for permission to reprint *The Soldier, The Dead* and *The Great Lover* from "The Collected Poems of Rupert Brooke", Copyright 1915 by Dodd, Mead and Company; *The Kashmiri Love Song* from "India's Love Lyrics" by Laurence Hope, Copyright 1902 by Dodd, Mead and Company; Robert W. Service's *The Cremation of Sam*

McGee, *The Shooting of Dan McGrew,* and *The Spell of the Yukon;* Thomas Edward Brown's *My Garden; Emmy* by Arthur Symons; *Non Sum Qualis Eram Bonae Sub Regno Cynarae* by Ernest Dowson.

DOUBLEDAY, DORAN AND COMPANY, INC. for permission to reprint *Appointment in Samarra* from "Sheppey" by Somerset Maugham, Copyright 1933; *Mandalay* and *Gunga Din* from "Departmental Ditties and Barrack Room Ballads" by Rudyard Kipling, Copyright 1892, 1893, 1899, 1927, reprinted by permission from Doubleday, Doran and Co., Inc.; *Recessional* from "The Five Nations" by Rudyard Kipling, Copyright 1902, 1931, reprinted by permission from Doubleday, Doran and Co., Inc.; *If* from "Rewards and Fairies" by Rudyard Kipling, Copyright 1910, 1938, reprinted by permission from Doubleday, Doran and Co., Inc.; *O Captain! My Captain!* and *When Lilacs Last in the Dooryard Bloomed* from "Leaves of Grass" by Walt Whitman, Copyright 1924 by Doubleday, Doran and Co., Inc.; *Trees* from "Trees and Other Poems" by Joyce Kilmer, Copyright 1914, 1917, 1918, by Doubleday, Doran and Co., Inc.

E. P. DUTTON AND COMPANY, INC. for permission to reprint *The Spires of Oxford* from "Songs from Leinster" by W. M. Letts; T. W. Arnold translation of *St. Francis' Speech to the Birds* from the "Temple Classics"; *America the Beautiful* by Katharine Lee Bates; *Baby* from "At the Back of the North Wind" by George McDonald; *O Little Town of Bethlehem* by Phillips Brooks; *Strictly Germproof* from "Lyric Laughter" by Arthur Guiterman.

STRICKLAND GILLILAN for permission to reprint *Finnigin to Flannigan* from his book of verse "Gillilan, Finnigin and Company."

HARMS INCORPORATED for permission to reprint the lyrics of *The Bowery.*

HARPER AND BROTHERS for permission to reprint *The Glorious Whitewasher* from "Tom Sawyer", and several briefer selections by Mark Twain; *If I Were King* from "If I Were King" by Justin Huntly McCarthy.

CHARLES K. HARRIS, music publishers, for permission to reprint the lyrics of *After the Ball* and *Heaven Will Protect the Working Girl.*

HENRY HOLT AND COMPANY for permission to reprint A. E. Housman's *When I Was One-and-Twenty, Reveille, To an Athlete*

Dying Young and *Bredon Hill* from "A Shropshire Lad" by A. E. Housman; *The Listeners* from "Collected Poems" by Walter de la Mare and *Silver* from "Peacock Pie" by Walter de la Mare; *Birches* from "Collected Poems of Robert Frost"; *Chicago* from "Chicago Poems" by Carl Sandburg.

HOUGHTON MIFFLIN COMPANY for permission to reprint poems and prose passages by Oliver Wendell Holmes, poems by Henry Wadsworth Longfellow, Ralph Waldo Emerson, James Russell Lowell, John Greenleaf Whittier, Julia Ward Howe's *Battle Hymn of the Republic,* John Godfrey Saxe's *The Blind Men and the Elephant,* Edward Rowland Sill's *The Fool's Prayer,* John Burroughs' *Waiting,* Bret Harte's *Plain Language from Truthful James,* Phoebe Cary's *The Leak in the Dike* and *Nearer Home,* James Thomas Fields' *The Tempest,* Henry Thoreau's *Why I Went to the Woods* from his "Walden," and *Out Where the West Begins* by Arthur Chapman.

D. E. KILGOUR for permission to reprint *In Flanders Fields* by Captain John D. McCrae.

J. B. LIPPINCOTT COMPANY for permission to reprint *Song for a Little House* from "Chimney Smoke" by Christopher Morley.

LITTLE, BROWN AND COMPANY for permission to reprint F. W. Bourdillon's *The Night Has a Thousand Eyes; Chartless* and *Helping the Handicapped* from "The Poems of Emily Dickinson" edited by Martha Dickinson Bianchi and Alfred Leete Hampson; Jean Ingelow's *Seven Times One.*

FRANCIS A. LITZ for permission to reprint *Evolution* and *A Child's Prayer* by John Bannister Tabb.

JOHN A. LOMAX for permission to reprint *Whoopee Ti Yi Yo* from "Cowboy Songs and Other Ballads", published by The Macmillan Company.

LOTHROP, LEE AND SHEPARD COMPANY for permission to reprint *The House by the Side of the Road* from "Dreams in Homespun" by Sam Walter Foss, Copyright 1925, by Carrie Conant Foss. Used by Arrangement.

THE MACMILLAN COMPANY for permission to reprint two-thirds of *The Congo* and *Abraham Lincoln Walks at Midnight* from "Collected Poems" by Vachel Lindsay; *The Man He Killed* and *In Time of the "Breaking of Nations"* from "Collected Poems" by Thomas Hardy; *Time, You Old Gypsy Man* from "Poems" by Ralph Hodgson; *Cargoes, Sea Fever* and

West Wind from "Poems" by John Masefield; the poems of Alfred, Lord Tennyson from "Poetical Works" by Alfred, Lord Tennyson; *Lake Isle of Innisfree* from "Collected Poems" by William Butler Yeats.

VIRGIL MARKHAM for permission to reprint *The Man with the Hoe* by Edwin Markham.

EDWARD B. MARKS MUSIC CORPORATION for permission to reprint the lyrics of *Take Back Your Gold, In the Good Old Summertime, My Mother Was a Lady* and *the Moth and the Flame.*

JUANITA J. MILLER for permission to reprint Joaquin Miller's *Columbus* and *The Bravest Battle.*

CAPTAIN FRANCIS NEWBOLT for permission to reprint *Drake's Drum* and *Vitai Lampada* by Sir Henry Newbolt.

DR. LOUIS I. NEWMAN for permission to reprint his poem *The Voice of God.*

G. P. PUTNAM'S SONS for permission to reprint *Beautiful Hands* by Ellen M. H. Gates.

THE REILLY AND LEE COMPANY for permission to reprint the poems of Edgar A. Guest from his Copyrighted books.

THE ROYCROFTERS AND ELBERT HUBBARD II for permission to reprint Elbert Hubbard's *A Message to Garcia.*

G. SCHIRMER INCORPORATED for permission to reprint the lyrics of *Oh Promise Me;* this company is the copyright owner of the lyrics and of the musical setting by Reginald de Koven.

CHARLES SCRIBNER'S SONS for permission to reprint the poems of Robert Louis Stevenson; Alan Seeger's *I Have a Rendezvous with Death;* Eugene Field's *Little Boy Blue, A Dutch Lullaby, The Duel, Jest 'Fore Christmas, The Sugar-Plum Tree, Seein' Things;* Henry van Dyke's *Four Things;* excerpt from Francis Thompson's *The Hound of Heaven;* Sidney Lanier's *The Song of the Chattahoochee;* William Ernest Henley's *Echoes, England, My England, Invictus* and *Over the Hills and Far Away;* Frank R. Stockton's *The Lady or the Tiger;* Edward Arlington Robinson's *Minniver Cheevy* from "Children of the Night" and Edward Arlington Robinson's *Richard Cory* from "The Town Down the River".

ELIE SIEGMEISTER for permission to reprint the lyrics of *Frankie and Johnny* and *When Johnny Comes Marching Home* as shown in "A Treasury of American Songs", containing words

714

and music, edited by Elie Siegmeister and Olin Downes, published by Alfred A. Knopf.

SIGMUND SPAETH for permission to reprint the lyrics of *The Mermaid* from his "Read 'Em and Weep".

FREDERICK A. STOKES COMPANY for permission to reprint *The Barrel-Organ* from "Collected Poems", Volume I, by Alfred Noyes; Copyright 1913 by Frederick A. Stokes Company.

U.S. MARINE CORPS for permission to reprint the words of *The Marine Corps Hymn*.

VIKING PRESS INCORPORATED for permission to reprint *Unfortunate Coincidence* and *News Item* from "Not So Deep as a Well" by Dorothy Parker, Copyright 1926, 1928, 1931, 1936.

A. P. WATT AND SON, London, England, for permission to reprint *Mandalay* and *Gunga Din* from "Barrack Room Ballads" by Rudyard Kipling, *If* from "Rewards and Fairies" by Rudyard Kipling, and *Recessional* from "The Five Nations" by Rudyard Kipling.

WILLIAM ALLEN WHITE for permission to reprint *Mary White* from "The Emporia Gazette".

M. WITMARK AND SONS for permission to reprint the lyrics of *The Picture That Is Turned toward the Wall*.

A more personal note of appreciation is due the following: the Editors of the "Queries and Answers" department of *The New York Times Book Review* for valuable assistance in locating several selections; Agnes Henahan for meticulous typing; Ann Patricia Fenlon, Richard F. Gibbons, Arthur A. Herrick, Marcella Henahan, Margaret M. Scully, Alfred G. Vanderbilt, and the rather numerous members of the Woods family all made many useful suggestions for this collection. John Tasker Howard of the Music Department of The New York Public Library, Miss A. W. Klingmann of the American Society of Composers, Authors and Publishers, Joseph McLoughlin of Remick Music Corporation, and Max B. Marks, Vice President of Edward B. Marks Music Corporation, went out of their way to guide me through the intricacies of popular song copyrights. Miss Klingmann was exceptionally helpful in this respect. The editors of The Macmillan Company, particularly Lois Dwight Cole and Rollo L. De Wilton, were of immense help, giving generously of their knowledge and time. My wife, Lillias Watt Woods, has helped immeasurably in checking manuscript, library research, preparation of indices and otherwise speeding the work to a conclusion. The experience and wisdom of Harold Matson, my agent, made it possible for me to concentrate wholly on the book and its contents.

RALPH L. WOODS

Queens Village, N.Y.
August 1942

INDEX BY TITLES

INDEX OF FAMILIAR LINES

NOTE: Many of the selections in this book contain more than one familiar line. But this index includes only one familiar line from each selection. Consequently, the choosing of lines has often been arbitrary, representing only the editor's opinion of what is most familiar.

INDEX BY AUTHORS